AIA

Professional 1 Level

TAXATION (UK)

LEARNING & PRACTICE WORKBOOK

In this 2025 edition

- A **user-friendly format** for easy navigation
- **Exam-centred topic coverage**, directly linked to AIA's syllabus
- **Exam focus points** showing you what the examiner will want you to do
- Regular **fast forward** summaries emphasising the key points in each chapter
- **Questions** and **quick quizzes** to test your understanding
- **Practice question bank** containing exam-standard questions with answers
- **Exam question bank** containing recent exam questions with answers
- **Mock exam** for real exam practice
- A full index

FOR EXAMS FROM MAY 2025

Fifth edition revised November 2024

ISBN 9781 0355 2579 9
eISBN 9781 0355 2607 9

British Library Cataloguing-in-Publication Data
A catalogue record for this book is available from the British Library

Published by
BPP Learning Media Ltd
BPP House, Aldine Place
142-144 Uxbridge Road
London W12 8AA

learningmedia.bpp.com

Printed in the United Kingdom

All rights reserved. No part of this publication may be reproduced, stored in a retrieval system or transmitted in any form or by any means, electronic, mechanical, photocopying, recording or otherwise, without the prior written permission of BPP Learning Media.

Contains public sector information licensed under the Open Government Licence v3.0.

The contents of this book are intended as a guide and not professional advice. Although every effort has been made to ensure that the contents of this book are correct at the time of going to press, BPP Learning Media makes no warranty that the information in this book is accurate or complete and accept no liability for any loss or damage suffered by any person acting or refraining from acting as a result of the material in this book.

We are grateful to the Association of International Accountants for permission to reproduce past examination questions. The suggested solutions in the exam answer bank have been prepared by BPP Learning Media Ltd.

©
BPP Learning Media Ltd
2024

A note about copyright

Dear Customer

What does the little © mean and why does it matter?

Your market-leading BPP books, course materials and e-learning materials do not write and update themselves. People write them on their own behalf or as employees of an organisation that invests in this activity. Copyright law protects their livelihoods. It does so by creating rights over the use of the content.

Breach of copyright is a form of theft – as well as being a criminal offence in some jurisdictions, it is potentially a serious breach of professional ethics.

With current technology, things might seem a bit hazy but, basically, without the express permission of BPP Learning Media:

- Photocopying our materials is a breach of copyright

- Printing our digital materials in order to share them with or forward them to a third party or use them in any way other than in connection with your BPP studies is a breach of copyright.

You can, of course, sell your books, in the form in which you have bought them – once you have finished with them. (Is this fair to your fellow students? We update for a reason.) Please note the e-products are sold on a single user licence basis: we do not supply 'unlock' codes to people who have bought them secondhand.

And what about outside the UK? BPP Learning Media strives to make our materials available at prices students can afford by local printing arrangements, pricing policies and partnerships which are clearly listed on our website. A tiny minority ignore this and indulge in criminal activity by illegally photocopying our material or supporting organisations that do. If they act illegally and unethically in one area, can you really trust them?

NO AI TRAINING. Unless otherwise agreed in writing, the use of BPP material for the purpose of AI training is not permitted. Any use of this material to "train" generative artificial intelligence (AI) technologies is prohibited, as is providing archived or cached data sets containing such material to another person or entity.

Contents

Page

Introduction

The introduction pages contain lots of valuable advice and information. They include tips on studying for and passing the exam, also the content of the syllabus and what has been examined.

How the BPP Learning Media Learning & Practice Workbook can help you pass – Help yourself study for your AIA exams – Syllabus – Command words and learning outcomes – The exam paper

Part A Taxation of individuals

1 Principles of income tax 3
2 Pensions 27
3 Property income 41
4 Employment income 53
5 Trade profits 87
6 Capital allowances 111
7 Trading losses 131
8 Partnerships and limited liability partnerships 143
9 Overseas aspects of income tax 151

Part B Capital taxes

10 Chargeable gains: an outline 161
11 Shares and securities 177
12 Chargeable gains: reliefs 185
13 Chargeable gains: additional aspects 203
14 Self assessment for individuals and partnerships 217
15 An introduction to inheritance tax 235
16 Inheritance tax: valuation, reliefs and the death estate 253
17 Inheritance tax: additional aspects 271

Part C Corporation tax

18 Computing taxable total profits 281
19 Chargeable gains for companies 299
20 Computing corporation tax payable 311
21 Losses and deficits on non-trading loan relationships 325
22 Overseas aspects of corporate tax 335

Part D Value Added Tax

23 Value Added Tax 1 345
24 Value Added Tax 2 363
25 Stamp Taxes 375

Part E Ethics

26 Ethics 387

	Page
Practice question bank	405
Practice answer bank	437
Exam question bank	493
Exam answer bank	523
Mock exam	579

How the BPP Learning Media Learning & Practice Workbook can help you pass

> It provides you with the knowledge and understanding, skills and application techniques that you need to be successful in your exams

This Learning & Practice Workbook has been targeted at the **Taxation (UK)** syllabus.

- It is **comprehensive**. It covers the syllabus content. No more, no less.
- It is written at the **right level**. Each chapter is written with AIA's syllabus in mind.
- It is aimed at the **exam**. We have taken account of recent exams, guidance the examiner has given and the assessment methodology.

> It allows you to study in the way that best suits your learning style and the time you have available, by following your personal Study Plan (see page vii)

You may be studying at home on your own or you may be attending a course. You may like to read every word, or you may prefer to do a fast read through and learn through doing practice questions the rest of the time. However you study, you will find the BPP Learning Media Learning & Practice Workbook meets your needs in designing and following your personal Study Plan.

Help yourself study for your AIA exams

Exams for professional bodies such as AIA are very different from those you have taken at college or university. You will be under **greater time pressure before** the exam – as you may be combining your study with work. Here are some hints and tips.

The right approach

1 **Develop the right attitude**

Believe in yourself	Yes, there is a lot to learn. But thousands have succeeded before and you can too.
Remember why you're doing it	You are studying for a good reason: to advance your career.

2 **Focus on the exam**

Read through the Syllabus	This tells you what you are expected to know and is supplemented by **Exam focus points** in the text.
Study the Exam paper section	Past papers are likely to be good guides to what you should expect in the exam.

3 **The right method**

See the whole picture	Keeping in mind how all the detail you need to know fits into the whole picture will help you understand it better. • The **Introduction** of each chapter puts the material in context. • The **Syllabus content** and **Exam focus points** show you what you need to **grasp**.
Use your own words	To absorb the information (and to practise your written communication skills), you need to **put it into your own words**. • Take **notes.** • Answer the **questions** in each chapter. • Draw **mindmaps**. • Try **'teaching'** a **subject** to a colleague or friend.
Give yourself cues to jog your memory	The Learning & Practice Workbook uses **bold** to **highlight key points**. • Try **colour coding** with a highlighter pen. • Write **key points** on cards.

4 **The right recap**

Review, review, review	Regularly reviewing a topic in summary form can **fix it in your memory**. The Learning & Practice Workbook helps you review in many ways. • **Chapter roundups** summarise the 'Fast forward' key points in each chapter. Use them to recap each study session. • The **Quick quiz** actively tests your grasp of the essentials. • Go through the **Examples** in each chapter a second or third time.

Developing your personal Study Plan

BPP recommends that you follow a study plan. Planning and sticking to the plan are key elements of learning successfully.

There are five steps you should work through.

Step 1 **How do you learn?**

What types of intelligence do you display when learning? You might be advised to brush up on certain study skills before launching into this Learning & Practice Workbook, but refer to the 'tackling your studies' section below which will help.

Step 2 **What do you prefer to do first?**

If you prefer to get to grips with a theory before seeing how it is applied, we suggest you concentrate first on the explanations we give in each chapter before looking at the examples and case studies. If you prefer to see first how things work in practice, read through the detail in each chapter, and concentrate on the examples and case studies, before supplementing your understanding by reading the detail.

Step 3 **How much time do you have?**

Work out the time you have available per week, given the following.

- The standard you have set yourself.
- The other exam(s) you are sitting.
- Practical matters such as work, travel, exercise, sleep and social life.

	Hours
Note your time available in box A. A	

Step 4 **Allocate your time**

- Take the time you have available per week for this Learning & Practice Workbook shown in box A, multiply it by the number of weeks available and insert the result in box B.   **B**

- Divide the figure in box B by the number of chapters in this text and insert the result in box C.   **C**

Remember that this is only a rough guide. Some of the chapters in this book are longer and more complicated than others, and you will find some subjects easier to understand than others.

Step 5 **Implement**

Set about studying each chapter in the time shown in box C, following the key study steps in the order suggested by your particular learning style.

This is your personal **Study Plan**. You should try to combine it with the study sequence outlined below. You may want to modify the sequence to adapt it to your **personal style**.

INTRODUCTION

Tackling your studies

The best way to approach this Learning & Practice Workbook is to tackle the chapters in order. Taking into account your individual learning style, you could follow this sequence for each chapter.

Key study steps	Activity
Step 1 **Topic list**	This topic list helps you navigate each chapter; each numbered topic is a numbered section in the chapter.
Step 2 **Introduction**	This sets your objectives for study by giving you the big picture in terms of the context of the chapter. The content is referenced to the syllabus, and Exam guidance shows how the topic is likely to be examined. The Introduction tells you **why** the topics covered in the chapter need to be studied.
Step 3 **Fast forward**	Fast forward boxes give you a quick summary of the content of each of the main chapter sections. They are listed together in the roundup at the end of each chapter to help you review each chapter quickly.
Step 4 **Explanations**	Proceed methodically through each chapter, particularly focusing on areas highlighted as significant in the chapter introduction, or areas that are frequently examined.
Step 5 **Key terms and Exam focus points**	• Key terms are definitions of important concepts that you really need to know and understand before the exam. • Exam focus points highlight areas or topics that may be examined.
Step 6 **Note taking**	Take brief notes, if you wish. Don't copy out too much. Remember that being able to record something yourself is a sign of being able to understand it. Your notes can be in whatever format you find most helpful; lists, diagrams, mindmaps.
Step 7 **Examples**	Work through the examples very carefully as they illustrate key knowledge and techniques.
Step 8 **Case studies**	Study each one and try to add flesh to them from your own experience. They are designed to show how the topics you are studying come alive in the real world.
Step 9 **Questions**	Attempt each one, as they will illustrate how well you've understood what you've read.
Step 10 **Answers**	Check yours against ours, and make sure you understand any discrepancies.
Step 11 **Chapter roundup**	Review it carefully, to make sure you have grasped the significance of all the important points in the chapter.
Step 12 **Quick quiz**	Use the Quick quiz to check how much you have remembered of the topics covered and to practise questions in a variety of formats.
Step 13 **Question practice**	Attempt the quick quiz at the very end of each chapter. These are designed for you to confirm some of the key concepts set out in each chapter. Some of these questions are designed to cover more than one topic area to develop your ability to apply syllabus learning. You can then attempt the questions related to this chapter which are contained in the question bank at the end of this Learning & Practice Workbook.

AIA Achieve

AIA provides an interactive course of study AIA Achieve, which offers candidates the tools, resources and learning environment to study for the exams. The study tools include a course of study e-book, marked practice questions, marked mock exam paper and feedback and technical advice via an e-Tutor. Contact the Study Support team at: Achieve@aiaworldwide.com.

Moving on...

When you are ready to start revising, you should still refer back to this Learning & Practice Workbook.

- As a source of **reference** (you should find the index particularly helpful for this).
- As a way to **review** (the Fast forwards, Exam focus points, Chapter roundups and Quick quizzes help you here).

PQ Qualification Syllabus

The assessment requirements in the AIA exams at the Foundation, Professional 1 and 2 stages reflect a progression of cognitive levels which successful students are expected to demonstrate in satisfying each stage of the qualification. The levels progress from an emphasis on 'knowledge and comprehension' at the Foundation stage, to a predominance of 'application and analysis' at the subsequent Professional 1 and 2 stages and incorporate 'synthesis and evaluation' at the Professional 2 stage.

Indicative weightings for the cognitive levels at each stage of the qualification are defined in the following table.

Stage of qualification	Cognitive levels of learning*			Associated learning outcomes
	Knowledge and comprehension	Application and Analysis	Synthesis and evaluation	
Foundation Level	90%	10%	0%	Outcomes consistent with the International Education Standards Board (IAESB) standards
Professional 1 Level	50%	50%	0%	
Professional 2 Level	10%	70%	20%	

*The cognitive levels of learning are associated with the following:

'Knowledge and comprehension' refer to

The acquisition of concepts, ideas, terms, facts, practices and techniques in accounting and related disciplines and understanding of how they relate to the conduct, management, reporting and assessment of the activities of business and other organisations.

'Application and analysis' refer to

The ability to apply knowledge and comprehension to actual circumstances and situations and to identify constituent components involved (concepts, ideas, terms, facts, practices, and techniques) and the relationship between these elements.

'Synthesis and evaluation' refer to

The ability to bring together a variety of components in order to form a coherent whole, and to form judgements about the application of and value of those components in a particular context or for a particular purpose.

Professional 1 Level Syllabus

Taxation (UK)

The professional accountant frequently encounters issues which require an understanding of taxation, not only in order to provide specific taxation related services but also to evaluate the taxation implications of an alternative course of action. A professional accountant must therefore appreciate the liability of individuals and companies to the main UK taxes and the impact of those taxes on their situations and decisions. This paper provides a grounding in a variety of UK taxes for a newly-qualified accountant, with a focus on practical scenarios.

The paper is structured to meet and exceed the prescribed subject criteria (tax law) within Companies Act for those on the audit route and also to assess learning outcomes consistent with IES 2 Intermediate standard for Taxation and relevant aspects of IES 4.

Candidates sitting in non-UK jurisdictions will sit a different version of the taxation paper.

In designing the syllabus and the related examination papers AIA has employed 'intended learning outcomes' as the means to communicate expectations to potential students and stakeholders and to inform the specification requirements to be tested in the assessment of students.

The use of learning outcomes:

- Is consistent with what is commonly acknowledged as good practice in the higher education sector; and
- Is consistent with the approach embodied in International Accounting Education Standards.

At the Professional 1 Levels students are expected to demonstrate that they are able to achieve the following:

Intended Learning Outcomes[1] – Description of expectations	
Professional 1 level	At the Professional 1 level students are expected to demonstrate that they: • Understand basic principles and concepts underpinning accounting and related practices in organisations and can discuss the conceptual rationale that provides the basis for those practices. • Understand the role of accounting and related practices within the financial and governance context of organisations. • Are able to apply relevant regulations and standards in accounting, auditing, law and taxation. • Know and can execute basic recording and measurement techniques relevant to accounting, management and assurance. • Are able to analyse financial information and interpret it for the purpose of supporting decision making.

---

[1] The description of the levels of proficiency supports the IAESBs use of learning outcomes in its International Education Standards (IESs) 2, 3, and 4.

Relationship to Qualification Structure

Aims

The aim of this paper is to develop and examine the candidate's:

- Understanding of the responsibilities of an accountant working in taxation;
- Knowledge of tax legislation across a breadth of taxation topics;
- Ability to apply their knowledge of various UK taxes in practical situations and their recognition of the cash and other practical implications thereof; and
- Understanding of ethics and professional responsibilities relating to taxation across a range of scenarios, including interactions with clients and with HMRC.

Taxation (UK) Learning outcomes

In order to successfully complete this paper, candidates will demonstrate that they are able to:

1. Use specified tax publications, including selecting the information which applies to a particular entity for given dates;
2. Prepare, or critically assess, direct and indirect tax computations for natural persons, unincorporated entities and artificial legal persons;
3. Advise on the practical aspects of tax, both commercially (tax as a cost and a cash outflow) and regarding dealing with the relevant authorities (reporting, payment, and consequences of non-compliance); and
4. Recognise the ethical and regulatory issues facing an accountant working in taxation and apply the IESBA International Code of Ethics for Professional Accountants.

Taxation (UK) % weighting for each of the taxes

Capital Gains Tax 10-20%

Corporation Tax 10-25%

Income Tax 30-40%

Inheritance Tax 10-15%

National Insurance Contributions 5-10%

VAT and Stamp Taxes 10-15%

Ethics – included within the weightings above 5-10%

INTRODUCTION

Structure of the Paper

Assessment is by a three-hour 15-minute examination consisting of between three and six compulsory questions, some divided into sub-requirements. All questions are compulsory.

Specified externally-published tax tables may be used during the exam. Candidates should take their own hard copy of Whillans Tax Tables into the exam. The book must not be annotated, highlighted or bookmarked in any way. Candidates should ensure that their copy is the relevant edition for that particular exam. Other than this the examination is closed book.

All questions are in an unstructured written format, based on case study/scenarios.

Individual taxes will largely be examined separately from each other but where they appear in the same question they will usually be associated with separate requirements. The allocation of marks to parts of questions will be disclosed in the examination paper.

The emphasis will be on competence, compliance and practical dealings with HMRC, rather than planning or speculation.

Relationship to Qualification Structure

This is a stand-alone tax paper, required because a professional accountant must appreciate the liability of and impact on individuals and companies to the main UK taxes.

Candidates will be required to demonstrate their ability to integrate tax knowledge, technical competence and other skills effectively in responding to the complex situations represented in the Multi-disciplinary case study examination.

Candidates sitting in non-UK jurisdictions can select a different version of the Taxation paper.

Ethics

Ethical and related regulatory issues arising in taxation work will be examined in every paper, making up a minimum of 5% of the examination. The subject of ethics will be examined as part of any one of the tax-technical question scenarios, with its own requirement within this.

Possible scenarios to include the challenges faced when an accountant's duty to a client conflicts with the duty to HMRC and/or the public interest.

Related regulatory issues to include e.g. anti-money laundering, data protection within the context of taxation work.

Candidates will be expected to provide answers in accordance with the IESBA Code and Professional Conduct in Relation to Taxation. For anti-money laundering issues, the CCAB guidance is also relevant.

Recommended Reading

These books are for use for exams in 2025 (up to and including Finance (No 2) Act 2024). You should check the edition of the book you are using is appropriate for the exam date you are sitting, all books should be FA 2024 editions.

AIA International Accountant Magazine
ISSN: 1465 - 5144

AIA Learning and Practice Workbooks
Taxation (UK)
Publisher: BPP Learning Media
ISBN: 9781035525799/ eISBN 9781035526079
Taxation (30th Edition Finance Acts 2024 edition)
Author: Melville, A
Publisher: Pearson Education Limited
ISBN: 9781292730370

Specifically, externally-published tax tables may be used and taken into the exam, as referenced below:

Whillan's Tax Tables 2024-25 (Finance Act edition)
Authors: Walton, K, Veerappa, S
Publisher: Tolley
ISBN: 9781474327886

Command words

The following list contains active command words appropriate for use at the Professional 1 Level of the AIA qualification. Reference to the command words is essential to understanding how the assessment is applied in AIA exams.

Professional Level 1 Command Words

Cognitive Levels of Learning	Command Words	Definitions
Professional 1 Application and Analysis 50% Knowledge and Comprehension 50%	Advise	To inform or notify
	Analyse	Examine in detail in order to interpret its meaning or essential features
	Apply	To use information or a technique in a particular situation
	Calculate Compute	Select the appropriate method and techniques and apply your knowledge and understandings to work out and show how figures were arrived at
	Demonstrate	To show or prove by reasoning or evidence
	Determine	Find out or establish
	Perform	Carry out into effect
	Prepare	To make or get ready for use
	Record	Document the information
	Estimate	Make an approximate judgement/calculation
	Journalise	Produce a double entry of events

Guidance on using Whillans Tax Tables

Whillans Tax Tables (2024/25) is an invaluable source of information during the exam. Many tax rates, allowances, thresholds and deadlines can be accessed direct from Whillans if you know where to look. It is worth getting familiar with the details in the open book to help you in the exam. You can use the contents table on the back cover as a starting point. Throughout this Learning and Practice Workbook you will find references to (Whillans) to indicate information that is available in the book.

INTRODUCTION

Taxation of individuals

Principles of income tax

Topic list
1 The aggregation of income
2 Various types of income
3 Deductible interest
4 Allowances deductible from net income
5 Computing tax liability
6 Computing tax payable
7 Devolved taxes
8 Families

Introduction

We start our study of taxation with a look at income tax, which is a tax on the income individuals make from their jobs, their businesses and their savings and investments. We will study the process of gathering together information relating to an individual's taxable income and performing an income tax computation.

We will also consider some of the basic family aspects of income tax, such as the taxation of joint income of spouses/civil partners.

In later chapters, we will go on to look at particular types of income in more detail.

PART A TAXATION OF INDIVIDUALS

Exam guide

You may be asked to perform a complete income tax computation in the exam and so you need to understand how the computation is put together. You may also be asked to calculate the 'after tax' income that would be derived from a particular source, or the after-tax cost of a course of action (taking into account any income tax savings). This involves understanding the increase or decrease in taxation, rather than performing full liability calculations. Remember to think about the effect of an increase in income on the personal allowance.

1 The aggregation of income

FAST FORWARD

In a personal income tax computation, bring together income from all sources, splitting the sources into non-savings, savings and dividend income.

As a general rule, income tax is charged on receipts which might be expected to recur (such as weekly wages or profits from running a business). **An individual's income from all sources is brought together (aggregated) in a personal tax computation for the tax year**.

Key terms

> The **tax year**, or **fiscal year**, or **year of assessment** runs from 6 April to 5 April. For example, the tax year 2024/25 runs from 6 April 2024 to 5 April 2025.

Three columns are needed in the computation. Here is an example. All items are explained later in this Workbook.

RICHARD: INCOME TAX COMPUTATION 2024/25

	Non-savings income £	Savings income £	Dividend income £	Total £
Income from employment	55,570			
Building society interest		1,360		
ISA interest – exempt				
UK dividends			6,000	
Total income	55,570	1,360	6,000	
Less qualifying interest paid	(2,000)			
Net income	53,570	1,360	6,000	60,930
Less personal allowance	(12,570)			(12,570)
Taxable income	41,000	1,360	6,000	48,360

	£
Income tax on non-savings income	
£37,700 × 20%	7,540
£3,300 × 40%	1,320
Tax on savings income	
£500 × 0% (personal savings allowance)	0
£860 × 40%	344
Tax on dividend income	
£500 × 0% (dividend allowance)	0
£5,500 × 33.75%	1,856
	11,060
Less tax reducer	(3,000)
Tax liability	8,060
Less tax suffered	
PAYE tax on salary (say)	(7,122)
Tax payable	938

1: PRINCIPLES OF INCOME TAX

Key terms

> **Total income** is all income subject to income tax. Each of the amounts which make up total income is called a **component**. **Net income** is total income less deductible interest and trade losses. The **tax liability** is the amount charged on the individual's income. **Tax payable** is the balance of the liability still to be settled in cash.

Income tax is charged on **'taxable income'**. Non-savings income is dealt with first, then savings income and then dividend income.

For non-savings income:

- the first £37,700 (the basic rate band) is taxed at the basic rate (20%);
- income between £37,700 and £125,140 (the higher rate limit) at the higher rate (40%); and
- any remaining income at the additional rate (45%).

Different rates and bands apply to non-savings income received by taxpayers who are resident in Scotland. In the exam, you should assume that a taxpayer is not resident in Scotland unless the question specifically states that they are. We will look at the taxation of the other types of income, later in this chapter.

The remainder of this chapter gives more details of the income tax computation.

2 Various types of income

FAST FORWARD

> Most savings income is received gross. Dividends are also received gross. There are a number of sources of exempt income.

2.1 Classification of income

All income received must be **classified** according to the nature of the income. This is because different computational rules apply to different types of income. The main types of income are:

- Income from employment, pensions and some social security benefits
- Profits of trades, professions and vocations
- Profits of property businesses
- Savings and investment income, including interest and dividends
- Miscellaneous income

The rules for computing employment income, profits from trades, professions and vocations and property letting income will be covered in later chapters. These types of income are **non-savings income**. Pension income is also non-savings income.

2.2 Savings income

Savings income includes interest. Interest is paid on bank and building society accounts, on Government securities, such as Treasury Stock, and on company loan stock.

Interest is usually received gross, but occasionally interest is paid net of 20% tax.

Exam focus point

> For the purpose of the Taxation examination, assume all interest is received gross.

2.3 Dividends on UK shares

Dividends on UK shares are received gross.

2.4 Exempt income

Some income is exempt from income tax. You should familiarise yourself with all of the examples of exemptions that are given in this Workbook and note the following types of exempt income in particular:

(a) **Scholarships** (exempt as income of the scholar; if paid by a parent's employer, a scholarship may be taxable income of the parent)

(b) Betting and gaming winnings, including **premium bond prizes**

(c) Interest or terminal bonus on **National Savings & Investments Certificates**

(d) Certain social security benefits

(e) Income on investments made through **Individual Savings Accounts (ISAs)**

> **Exam focus point**
>
> Learn the different types of exempt income. They frequently appear in the exam. Always state on your exam script that such income is exempt to gain easy marks (do not ignore it).

3 Deductible interest

> **FAST FORWARD**
>
> Deductible interest is deducted from total income to compute net income.

3.1 Interest payments

An individual who pays interest on a loan in a tax year is entitled to relief in that tax year if the loan is for one of the following purposes:

(a) **Loan to buy plant or machinery for partnership use.** Interest is allowed for three years from the end of the tax year in which the loan was taken out. If the plant is used partly for private use, the allowable interest is apportioned.

(b) **Loan to buy plant or machinery for employment use.** Interest is allowed for three years from the end of the tax year in which the loan was taken out. If the plant is used partly for private use, the allowable interest is apportioned.

(c) **Loan to acquire any part of the ordinary share capital of a close company (other than a close investment-holding company) or to lend money to such a company which is used wholly and exclusively for the purpose of its business or that of an associated close company.** A close company is a UK company controlled by its shareholder-directors, or by five or fewer shareholders.

(d) **Loan to buy interest in employee-controlled company.** The company must be an unquoted trading company resident in the UK or another EEA state and not resident outside the EEA, with at least 50% of the voting shares held by employees.

(e) **Loan to invest in a partnership.** The investment may be a share in the partnership or a contribution to the partnership of capital or a loan to the partnership. The individual must be a partner (other than a limited partner in a limited partnership) and relief ceases when he ceases to be a partner.

(f) **Loan to invest in a co-operative.** The investment may be shares or a loan. The individual must spend the greater part of his time working for the co-operative.

(g) **Loan to pay inheritance tax.** The relief in this case is only available in respect of a period ending within 12 months of the loan being made. If such a loan was taken out for a term of three years, only interest in respect of the first 12 months would attract relief.

Tax relief is given by deducting the interest from total income to calculate net income for the tax year in which the interest is paid. It is usually deducted from **non-savings income first, then from savings income and lastly from dividend income**. We deal with situations where it may be beneficial to deduct in a different order later in this chapter.

There is a **limit on the amount of deductions from total income, including deductible interest**, which an individual taxpayer can make in a tax year. This limit is discussed in the chapter on trading losses later in this Learning & Practice Workbook.

3.2 Example

Frederick has taxable trading income for 2024/25 of £53,350, savings income of £1,320 and dividend income of £1,000.

Frederick pays interest of £1,370 in 2024/25 on a loan to invest in a partnership.

Frederick's taxable income is:

	Non-savings Income £	Savings income £	Dividend income £	Total £
Total income	53,350	1,320	1,000	55,670
Less interest paid	(1,370)			(1,370)
Net income	51,980	1,320	1,000	54,300
Less personal allowance	(12,570)			(12,570)
Taxable income	39,410	1,320	1,000	41,730

4 Allowances deductible from net income

4.1 Personal allowance

FAST FORWARD

> The personal allowance is an amount of income that individuals are allowed to receive before income tax starts to apply.

Once income from all sources has been aggregated and any deductible interest deducted, the remainder is the taxpayer's net income. Most individual taxpayers in the UK are entitled to a **personal allowance**, which is deducted from their net income before tax rates are applied to the remainder. It is usually set against **non-savings income first, then savings income and, lastly, dividend income**. We will consider situations where it may be beneficial to deduct in a different order later in this chapter.

Most individuals in the UK (including children) **are entitled to the personal allowance of £12,570** (Whillans p.74. However, if the **individual's adjusted net income exceeds £100,000,** the personal allowance is reduced by £1 for each £2 by which adjusted net income exceeds £100,000 until the personal allowance is nil. In other words, individuals with adjusted net income of £125,140 or more do not benefit from a personal allowance.

Key term

> **Adjusted net income** is net income less the gross amounts of personal pension contributions and gift aid donations.

We will look at personal pension contributions and gift aid donations later in this Workbook and revisit this topic again then. For now, we will look at the situation where net income and adjusted net income are the same amounts.

PART A TAXATION OF INDIVIDUALS

Question — Personal allowance

In 2024/25, Clare receives employment income of £98,300, bank interest of £8,000 and dividends of £7,500.

Calculate Clare's taxable income for 2024/25.

Answer

	Non-savings income £	Savings income £	Dividend income £	Total £
Employment income	98,300			
Bank interest		8,000		
Dividends			7,500	
Net income	98,300	8,000	7,500	113,800
Less personal allowance (W)	(5,670)			(5,670)
Taxable income	92,630	8,000	7,500	108,130

Working

	£
Net income	113,800
Less income limit	(100,000)
Excess	13,800
Personal allowance	12,570
Less half excess £13,800 × ½	(6,900)
	5,670

Where an individual has an adjusted net income between £100,000 and £125,140, the **effective rate of tax on the income between these two amounts will usually be 60%**. This is calculated as 40% (the higher rate on income) plus 40% of half (ie 20%) of the excess adjusted net income over £100,000 used to restrict the personal allowance. The individual should consider **making personal pension contributions (or gift aid donations)** to reduce adjusted net income to below £100,000.

5 Computing tax liability

FAST FORWARD — Income tax is worked out on taxable income. You should first tax non-savings income, then savings income and then dividend income.

5.1 Tax rates

Income tax payable is computed on an individual's taxable income, which comprises net income less the personal allowance. The tax rates are applied to taxable income which is non-savings income first, then to savings income and finally to dividend income. The tax rates, allowances and thresholds can be found in Whillans (p.69).

5.1.1 Savings income starting rate

There is a **tax rate of 0% for savings income between £0 and £5,000 (the savings income starting rate band)** for 2024/25. This rate is called the **savings income starting rate**.

The **savings income starting rate only applies where the savings income falls wholly or partly below the starting rate limit**. Remember that income tax is charged first on non-savings income. So, in most cases, an individual's non-savings income will exceed the starting rate limit and the savings income starting rate will not be available on savings income.

The **savings income starting rate band** counts towards the **basic rate limit of £37,700**.

5.1.2 Personal savings allowance (PSA)

There is a **tax rate of 0%** for **savings income** within the **personal savings allowance (PSA).** The PSA for 2024/25 is **£1,000** if the individual is a **basic rate taxpayer** and **£500** if the individual is a **higher rate taxpayer.** There is **no PSA** for **additional rate taxpayers** (Whillans p.74) Whether the individual is a basic rate taxpayer, higher rate taxpayer or additional rate taxpayer for the purpose of the allowance depends on their highest rate of tax if this allowance is ignored.

The **PSA** counts towards the **basic rate limit of £37,700**.

Question — Savings income starting rate band and PSA

In 2024/25, Joe earned a salary of £12,670 from a part-time job and received bank interest of £7,000.

Calculate Joe's tax liability for 2024/25.

Answer

	Non-savings income £	Savings income £	Total £
Employment income	12,670		
Bank interest		7,000	
Net income	12,670	7,000	19,670
Less personal allowance	(12,570)		(12,570)
Taxable income	100	7,000	7,100

	£
Income tax	
Non-savings income	
£100 × 20%	20
Savings income	
£4,900 (5,000 – 100) × 0% (savings starting rate band)	–
£1,000 × 0% (PSA – basic rate taxpayer)	–
£(7,000 – 1,000 – 4,900) = £1,100 × 20%	220
Tax liability	240

5.1.3 Dividend allowance

There is a **tax rate of 0%** for **dividend income** within the **dividend allowance.** The dividend allowance is **£500** for **all taxpayers** (Whillans p.74).

The **dividend allowance** counts towards the **basic rate limit of £37,700 and the higher rate limit of £125,140**.

PART A TAXATION OF INDIVIDUALS

5.1.4 Basic rate

The basic rate of tax is **20%** for 2024/25 for both non-savings income and savings income.

The basic rate of tax is **8.75%** for 2024/25 for dividend income.

The basic rate band limit for 2024/25 is **£37,700**.

5.1.5 Higher rate

The higher rate of tax is **40%** for 2024/25 for non-savings and saving income.

The higher rate of tax is **33.75%** for 2024/25 for dividend income.

The higher rate band limit for 2024/25 is **£125,140**.

Question — Personal savings allowance, basic rate and higher rate

In 2024/25 Joe had employment income of £43,870 and received bank interest of £7,200.

Calculate Joe's tax liability for 2024/25. Assume the personal allowance is used against non-savings income first.

Answer

	Non-savings income £	Savings income £	Total £
Employment income	43,870		
Bank interest		7,200	
Net income	43,870	7,200	51,070
Less personal allowance	(12,570)		(12,570)
Taxable income	31,300	7,200	38,500

Income tax	£
Non-savings income	
£31,300 × 20%	6,260
Savings income	
£500 × 0% (PSA – higher rate taxpayer)	0
£5,900 (37,700 – 31,300 – 500) × 20%	1,180
£800 (7,200 – 500 – 5,900) × 40%	320
Tax liability	7,760

The question gave an instruction to use the personal allowance against non-savings income first, which is the usual order of offset. However, it would have been beneficial to deduct the personal allowance in a different order, as we shall see later in this chapter.

Question — PSA and dividend allowance, basic rate and higher rate bands

In 2024/25, Margery had employment income of £38,500. She also received building society interest of £2,200 and dividends of £15,000.

Calculate Margery's income tax liability for 2024/25.

Answer

	Non-savings income £	Savings income £	Dividend income £	Total £
Employment income	38,500			
BSI		2,200		
Dividends			15,000	
Net income	38,500	2,200	15,000	55,700
Less personal allowance	(12,570)			(12,570)
Taxable income	25,930	2,200	15,000	43,130

Income tax
Non-savings income
 £25,930 × 20%   5,186
Savings income
 £500 × 0% (PSA – higher rate taxpayer)   –
 £1,700 × 20%   340
Dividend income
 £500 × 0% (dividend allowance)   –
 £(37,700 – 25,930 – 2,200 – 500) = 9,070 × 8.75%   794
 £(15,000 – 500 – 9,070) = 5,430 × 33.75%   1,833
Tax liability   8,153

5.1.6 Additional rate

The additional rate of tax is **45%** for 2024/25 for non-savings and saving income.

The additional rate of tax is **39.35%** for 2024/25 for dividend income.

The additional rate of tax applies to taxable income in excess of £125,140.

Question — Additional rate

In 2024/25, Joao had employment income of £148,000, received bank interest of £6,250 and dividends of £19,500.

Calculate Joao's tax liability for 2024/25.

Answer

	Non-savings income £	Savings income £	Dividend income £	Total £
Employment income	148,000			
Bank interest		6,250		
Dividends			19,500	
Taxable income (no personal allowance)	148,000	6,250	19,500	173,750

Joao is not entitled to the personal allowance as his income exceeds £125,140.

Income tax
Non-savings income

£37,700 × 20%	7,540
£(125,140 – 37,700) = 87,440 × 40%	34,976
£(148,000 – 125,140) = 22,860 × 45%	10,287
Savings income	
£6,250 × 45%	2,813
Dividend income	
£500 × 0% (dividend allowance)	–
£19,000 × 39.35%	7,477
Tax liability	63,093

Joao is not entitled to the PSA as he is an additional rate taxpayer.

5.1.7 Set off of deductible interest and personal allowance

The **usual order** of offset for **deductible interest** (to compute net income) and the **personal allowance** (to compute taxable income) is against **non-savings income first, then savings income and lastly dividend income**.

However, this order may change to make better use of the savings starting rate band and the personal savings allowance. This is not a matter of tax planning or a claim but just the correct way to set off deductible interest and the personal allowance to minimise the individual's tax liability.

For example, they should be **set against dividend income in priority to savings income** where this **preserves the use of the savings starting rate band and the personal savings allowance**.

Question — Set off of personal allowance

In 2024/25 Wayne has trading income from a partnership of £6,150 and receives bank interest of £8,400 and dividends of £19,500.

Calculate Wayne's tax liability for 2024/25.

Answer

	Non-savings income £	Savings income £	Dividend income £	Total £
Trading income	6,150			
Bank interest		8,400		
Dividends			19,500	
Net income	6,150	8,400	19,500	34,050
Less personal allowance (N)	(6,150)	(2,400)	(4,020)	(12,570)
Taxable income	0	6,000	15,480	21,480

Note. Follow these steps to set off the personal allowance correctly.

Step 1 Set off the maximum amount of personal allowance against non-savings income ie £6,150.

Step 2 Work out how much savings income should be taxable in order to use the savings starting rate band and the personal savings allowance ie £5,000 + £1,000 (basic rate taxpayer) = £6,000.

Step 3 Work out difference between net savings income and taxable savings income ie £8,400 – 6,000 = £2,400. This is the amount of the personal allowance to be set off against savings income.

Step 4 Work out the amount of the remaining personal allowance to be set off against dividend income ie £12,570 – 6,150 – 2,400 = £4,020.

	£
Income tax	
Savings income	
£5,000 × 0% (starting rate band)	0
£1,000 × 0% (personal savings allowance – basic rate taxpayer)	0
Dividend income	
£500 × 0% (dividend allowance)	0
£14,980 (15,480 – 500) × 8.75%	1,311
Tax liability	1,311

For a higher rate taxpayer with non-savings and savings income, it may be beneficial to limit the deduction of the personal allowance (or deductible interest) from non-savings income (and so deduct more from savings income) if the personal savings allowance then saves tax at the higher rate rather than the basic rate.

Question — Set off of personal allowance

Consider the earlier question with Joe in Section 5.1.5, but with best use of the personal allowance. In 2024/25 Joe had employment income of £43,870 and received bank interest of £7,200.

Calculate Joe's tax liability for 2024/25.

Answer

	Non-savings income £	Savings income £	Total £
Employment income	43,870		
Bank interest		7,200	
Net income	43,870	7,200	51,070
Less personal allowance (N)	(6,170)	(6,400)	(12,570)
Taxable income	37,700	800	38,500

Set off an amount of the personal allowance against non-savings income only to bring it down to the basic rate limit, ie the maximum here is £6,170 to give £37,700 of taxable non-savings income. Set the remaining personal allowance against the savings income. This ensures that the savings income taxed at 0% within the personal savings allowance now falls in the higher rate band, rather than the basic rate band, so the personal savings allowance saves tax at 40% rather than 20%.

This gives an income tax liability of £7,660, rather than £7,760 as previously calculated.

PART A TAXATION OF INDIVIDUALS

	£
Income tax	
Non-savings income	
£37,700 × 20%	7,540
Savings income	
£500 × 0% (PSA)	0
£300 (800 – 500) × 40%	120
Tax liability	7,660

5.2 Child benefit income tax charge

FAST FORWARD

There is an income tax charge to recover child benefit if the recipient or their partner has adjusted net income over £60,000 in a tax year.

An **income tax charge** applies if a taxpayer receives child benefit (or their partner receives child benefit) and the taxpayer has **adjusted net income over £60,000 in a tax year** (Whillans p.72). **Adjusted net income is defined in the same way as for the restriction of the personal allowance** described earlier in this chapter.

A 'partner' is a **spouse**, a **civil partner**, or an **unmarried partner** where the couple are **living together as though they were married or were civil partners**. A civil partnership is a legal relationship which can be registered by two people who are not related to each other. It affords the same rights as marriage and is available to same-sex and opposite-sex couples. In the UK a same-sex couple may be a married couple.

If the taxpayer has **adjusted net income over £80,000**, the charge is equal to the **full amount of child benefit received**.

If the taxpayer has **adjusted net income between £60,000 and £80,000**, the charge is **1% of the child benefit amount for each £200 of adjusted net income in excess of £60,000**. The calculation, at all stages, is rounded down to the nearest whole number.

If **both partners have adjusted net income in excess of £60,000**, the **partner with the higher adjusted net income** is liable for the charge.

Claimants can **opt not to receive child benefit at all** so that the income tax charge does not apply.

Question — Child benefit income tax charge (1)

Robert and Roslyn are not married but live together as a couple. They have a five-year-old son.

Robert has net income of £64,000 (all non-savings income) in 2024/25. His adjusted net income is also £64,000 since he made no personal pension contributions or gift aid payments in 2024/25. Roslyn has no income. She received child benefit of £1,331 in 2024/25.

Calculate Robert's tax liability for 2024/25.

1: PRINCIPLES OF INCOME TAX

Answer

Robert will be liable to the child benefit income tax charge in 2024/25 since his partner receives child benefit during that year and he has adjusted net income over £64,000.

	£
Net income	64,000
Less personal allowance	(12,570)
Taxable income	51,430
Income tax	
£37,700 @ 20%	7,540
£13,730 @ 40%	5,492
	13,032
Add child benefit income tax charge (W)	266
Tax liability	13,298

Working

	£
Adjusted net income	64,000
Less threshold	(60,000)
Excess	4,000
÷ £200	20
Child benefit income tax charge: 1% × £1,331 × 20	266

Question — Child benefit income tax charge (2)

Samantha is divorced and has two children aged ten and six. She has net income of £72,160 (all non-savings income) in 2024/25. Samantha made personal pension contributions of £4,500 (gross) during 2024/25. She received child benefit of £2,213 in 2024/25.

Calculate Samantha's income tax liability for 2024/25.

Answer

	£
Net income	72,160
Less personal allowance	(12,570)
Taxable income	59,590

	£
Income tax:	
£42,200 @ 20% (W1)	8,440
£17,390 @ 40%	6,956
	15,396
Add child benefit income tax charge (W2)	840
Tax liability	16,236

Workings

1. Basic rate limit (see later in this Workbook)
   £37,700 + £4,500 = £42,200

2. Child benefit income tax charge

	£
Net income	72,160
Less personal pension contributions (gross)	(4,500)
Adjusted net income	67,660
Less threshold	(60,000)
Excess	7,660
÷ £200 (rounded down)	38
Child benefit income tax charge: 1% × £2,213 × 38	840

At all stages of the calculation, round down to the nearest whole number.

5.3 Gift Aid

FAST FORWARD — Gifts to registered charities under the Gift Aid scheme save tax at an individual's highest rate of tax.

The tax calculation may be affected by cash donations to charity made under the Gift Aid scheme.

Exam focus point

In the exam, if an individual makes a gift to a national registered charity, assume that this is made under the Gift Aid scheme. A gift to a local charity may be treated as an allowable trading deduction if certain conditions are met (see later in this Workbook).

Cash donations are treated as being paid net, ie after deduction of income tax at the basic rate (20%). So, a net donation of £800 is worth £1,000 to the charity (£800 × 100/80) as the charity can claim £200 (20% × £1,000) from HMRC.

The donor's basic rate band is also increased by an amount equal to the gross amount of the gift (£1,000 in this example). This only affects higher rate and additional rate taxpayers.

Additional rate relief is available because the increase in the basic rate band also causes the higher rate limit of £125,140 to increase, again by the gross amount of the gift (ie to £126,140 in this example).

As discussed earlier in this chapter, when determining the level of personal allowance available to an individual, net income is reduced by gross donations to give adjusted net income. However, this is only done to determine the level of personal allowance available; taxable income is **not** reduced by charitable donations. Personal pension contributions have the same effect and are discussed further in the next chapter.

1: PRINCIPLES OF INCOME TAX

Question — Gift Aid

The facts about Joao's income are the same as in the question in Section 5.1.6 above, but he had also donated £2,000 to a registered charity during the year under the Gift Aid scheme.

Calculate Joao's tax liability for 2024/25.

Answer

Gross donation = £2,000 × 100/80 = £2,500

Therefore, adjusted net income = £173,750 − £2,500 = £171,250 so there is still no personal allowance as this exceeds £125,140.

Basic rate band is extended to £(37,700 + 2,500) = £40,200

The higher rate limit is increased to £125,140 + £2,500 = £127,640

	Non-savings income £	Savings income £	Dividend income £	Total £
Taxable income (as per previous question)	148,000	6,250	19,500	173,750

	£
Income tax	
Non-savings income	
£40,200 × 20%	8,040
£(127,640 − 40,200) = 87,440 × 40%	34,976
£(148,000 − 127,640) = 20,360 × 45%	9,162
Savings income	
£6,250 × 45%	2,813
Dividend income	
£500 × 0%	–
£19,000 × 39.35%	7,477
Tax liability	62,468

Check:

Tax saving due to donation = £(63,093 − 62,468) = £625

Plus tax relief at source = £(2,500 − 2,000) = £500

Total tax saving = £625 + £500 = £1,125, which is 45% of £2,500, the gross donation.

5.4 Tax reducers

FAST FORWARD — Tax reducers reduce tax on income at a set rate of relief.

5.4.1 Introduction

Tax reducers do not affect income; they reduce tax on income. The examinable tax reducers are:
(a) Transferable personal allowance (marriage allowance)
(b) Relief for non-deductible loan interest on a dwelling for a property business (see property income)

Tax reducers are deducted in computing an individual's income tax liability. The tax liability can only be reduced to zero; a tax reducer cannot create a repayment.

5.4.2 Transferable personal allowance (marriage allowance)

In 2024/25, in limited cases, a spouse or civil partner may elect to transfer £1,260 (Whillans p.74) of their personal allowance to their spouse/civil partner. The transferor spouse must either have no tax liability or be only a basic rate taxpayer after such a reduction in their personal allowance. The recipient spouse must be a basic rate taxpayer (Whillans p.74).

The transferred allowance is given effect by a reduction in the recipient spouse's income tax liability at the basic rate.

Question — Transferable personal allowance

Alec and Bertha are a married couple. In the tax year 2024/25, Alec has net income of £9,000 and Bertha has net income of £26,000. All their income is non-savings income. Alec has made an election to transfer part of his personal allowance to Bertha.

Show Alec and Bertha's taxable income for 2024/25 and compute Bertha's income tax liability.

Answer

Alec

	Non-savings Income £
Net income	9,000
Less personal allowance £(12,570 – 1,260)	(11,310)
Taxable income	0

Bertha

	Non-savings income £
Net income	26,000
Less personal allowance	(12,570)
Taxable income	13,430

Income tax

	£
£13,430 × 20%	2,686
Less transferable personal allowance tax reducer £1,260 × 20%	(252)
Income tax liability	2,434

6 Computing tax payable

FAST FORWARD

From the tax liability, deduct any income tax suffered at source to arrive at tax payable. Tax suffered at source can be repaid.

6.1 Steps in the personal tax computation

Step 1 **The first step in preparing a personal tax computation is to set up three columns**
One column for non-savings income, one for savings income and one for dividend income. Place the income from different sources into the appropriate categories and add them up. The sum of these is known as 'total income'. Deduct deductible interest and trade losses to compute 'net income'. Deduct the personal allowance to compute 'taxable income'.

Step 2 **Deal with non-savings income first**
Any non-savings income up to the basic rate limit of £37,700 is taxed at 20%. Non-savings income between the basic rate limit and the higher rate limit of £125,140 is taxed at 40%. Any further non-savings income is taxed at 45%. Remember that different rates and bands apply to non-savings income for taxpayers resident in Scotland. We will look at this in more detail later in the chapter.

Step 3 **Now deal with savings income**
If non-savings income is below the starting rate limit of £5,000, then tax savings income up to the limit of the savings income starting rate at the savings income starting rate of 0%. Then tax savings income covered by the PSA (for basic rate and higher rate taxpayers) at 0%. Savings income between the starting rate limit and the basic rate limit of £37,700, which is not covered by the PSA, is taxed at 20%. Savings income between the basic rate limit and the higher rate limit of £125,140, which is not covered by the PSA, is taxed at 40%. Any further savings income is taxed at 45%.

Step 4 **Lastly, tax dividend income**
The first £500 is within the dividend allowance and is taxed at 0%. Other dividend income below the basic rate limit of £37,700 is taxed at 8.75%. Other dividend income between the basic rate limit and the higher rate limit of £125,140 is taxed at 33.75%. Any other further dividend income is taxed at 39.35%.

Step 5 **Add the amounts of tax together**

Step 6 Once tax has been computed, **deduct any available tax reducers** (eg marriage allowance).

Step 7 Calculate the amount of any **child benefit income tax charge** and **pension annual allowance charge** (see later in this Workbook) and add to the tax remaining after Step 6. The resulting figure is the **income tax liability.**

Step 8 Finally **deduct the tax deducted at source eg from PAYE**. These amounts can be repaid to the extent that they exceed the income tax liability.

PART A TAXATION OF INDIVIDUALS

Question — Calculation of income tax payable

In 2024/25, Jules had employment income of £56,300, dividends of £7,000 and interest of £4,250. Their PAYE for 2024/25 was £10,000. They paid deductible interest of £3,000.

How much income tax is payable by Jules for 2024/25?

Answer

	Non-savings income £	Savings income £	Dividend income £	Total £
Employment income	56,300			
Dividends			7,000	
Interest		4,250		
Total income	56,300	4,250	7,000	
Less interest paid	(3,000)			
Net income	53,300	4,250	7,000	64,550
Less personal allowance	(12,570)			(12,570)
Taxable income	40,730	4,250	7,000	51,980
Non-savings income				
£37,700 × 20%				7,540
£3,030 × 40%				1,212
Savings income				
£500 × 0% (PSA – higher rate taxpayer)				0
£3,750 × 40%				1,500
Dividend income				
£500 × 0% (dividend allowance)				0
£6,500 × 33.75%				2,194
Tax liability				12,446
Less tax suffered at source – PAYE				(10,000)
Tax payable				2,446

6.2 Calculating additional tax due

FAST FORWARD — Additional income received can have an impact on the availability of the PSA and on the availability of personal allowance.

The above question illustrated a full income tax computation. **Often, a taxpayer is more interested in looking at the after-tax return from a particular investment or transaction.** In each of the following examples, we will **calculate the additional tax due because of the new investment**. Note that it is **not necessary here to use the full income tax proforma**.

6.3 Examples: additional tax due

(a) Katia receives an annual salary of £33,850 and building society interest of £800. Her grandfather died leaving her shares in Axle plc. She received dividends of £25,000 during 2024/25. The additional tax due as a result of receiving the dividend income can be calculated as follows:

Income tax on dividends is at the basic and higher rate as Katia originally had taxable income of £22,080 (£33,850 + £800 − £12,570) and so there is a remaining basic rate band of £15,620.

However, Katia also has a dividend allowance of £500 which uses up some of the remaining basic rate band:

	£
£500 @ 0%	0
£15,120 @ 8.75%	1,323
£9,380 @ 33.75%	3,166
Additional tax due	4,489

You should always check whether an adjustment is needed to the PSA. Here, Katia was originally a basic rate taxpayer and so had a PSA of £1,000. So all £800 of her savings income was taxed at 0%. As she became a higher rate taxpayer the PSA reduced to £500, and so £300 (£800 – £500) of her savings income is now taxed at 20%, ie £60.

So the total additional income tax due as a result of the income from the inheritance is £4,549.

(b) Katia receives an annual salary of £99,000. Her grandfather died leaving her shares in Axle plc. She received dividends of £32,000 during 2024/25. The additional tax due as a result of receiving the dividend income can be calculated as follows:

Katia will no longer be entitled to the personal allowance since her net income is £(99,000 + 32,000) = £131,000.

Income tax on the first £500 will be nil due to the dividend allowance. The next £25,640 of dividend income will be taxed at the higher rate and £5,860 will be taxed as additional rate income. The additional tax due is therefore calculated as follows:

	£
£500 @ 0%	0
£25,640 @ 33.75%	8,654
£5,860 @ 39.35%	2,306
Tax on income previously covered by personal allowance £12,570 @ 40%	5,028
Additional tax due	15,988

6.4 The complete proforma

Here is a complete proforma computation. You can refer back to it as you work through this Workbook. You will also see how losses fit into the proforma later in this Workbook.

	Non-savings income £	Savings income £	Dividend income £	Total £
Trading income	X			
Employment income	X			
Property business income	X			
Bank/building society interest (as many lines as necessary)		X		
Dividends			X	
Total income	X	X	X	
Less interest paid	(X)	(X)	(X)	
Net income	X	X	X	X
Less personal allowance	(X)	(X)	(X)	
Taxable income	X	X	X	X

7 Devolved taxes

FAST FORWARD

The Scottish and Welsh Parliaments have the power to set different income tax rates and bands for non-savings non-dividend income.

PART A TAXATION OF INDIVIDUALS

7.1 Scottish rates and bands applicable to non-savings income

Bands	Band name	Rate
£0 - £2,306	Starter rate	19%
£2,307 - £13,990	Scottish basic rate	20%
£13,991 - £31,092	Intermediate rate	21%
£31,093 - £62,430	Higher rate	42%
£62,431 - £125,140	Advanced rate	45%
Over £125,140	Top rate	48%

These rates are listed in Whillans (p.69).

The personal allowance, including the reduction for those earning over £100,000, works the same as way as seen already for the rest of the UK.

Income tax on savings income and dividends is the same in Scotland as in the rest of the UK.

7.2 Example: Scottish income tax

Rashida is resident in Scotland and earns employment income of £65,000 (PAYE was deducted of £10,000). She also receives dividends of £2,500 and £850 of interest income.

The first £12,570 of her employment income is covered by the personal allowance, so Rashida's taxable non-savings income is £52,430. Her income tax calculation will be as follows:

	Non-savings income £	Savings income £	Dividend income £	Total £
Employment income	65,000			
Dividends			2,500	
Interest		850		
Net income	65,000	850	2,500	68,350
Less personal allowance	(12,570)			(12,570)
Taxable income	52,430	850	2,500	55,780

Non-savings income (Scottish rates)

£2,306 @ 19%	
£11,685 (£13,991 – £2,306) @ 20%	2,337
£17,101 (£31,092 – £13,991) @ 21%	3,591
£21,338 (£52,430 – £31,092) @ 42%	8,962
£52,430	
Savings income (UK rates)	
£500 × 0% (PSA – higher rate taxpayer)	0
£350 × 40%	140
Dividend income (UK rates)	
£500 × 0% (dividend allowance)	0
£2,000 × 33.75%	675
Tax liability	16,143
Less tax suffered at source – PAYE	(10,000)
Tax payable	6,143

7.3 Income tax in Wales

The Welsh Parliament has the power to change income tax rates and bands for taxpayers in Wales. To date they have chosen to keep them the same as for the rest of the UK.

8 Families

FAST FORWARD Spouses, civil partners and children are all separate taxpayers.

8.1 Spouses and civil partners

Spouses and civil partners are taxed as two separate people. Each spouse/civil partner is entitled to a personal allowance depending on their own income.

8.2 Joint property

When spouses/civil partners jointly own income-generating property, it is assumed that they are entitled to equal shares of the income.

If the spouses/civil partners are not entitled to equal shares in the income-generating property (other than shares in close companies), **they may make a joint declaration to HMRC, specifying the proportion to which each is entitled.** These proportions are used to tax each of them separately, in respect of income arising on or after the date of the declaration. For capital gains tax purposes, it is always this underlying beneficial ownership that is taken into account.

PART A TAXATION OF INDIVIDUALS

Chapter roundup

- In a personal income tax computation, bring together income from all sources, splitting the sources into non-savings, savings and dividend income.
- Most savings income is received gross. Dividends are also received gross. There are a number of sources of exempt income.
- Deductible interest is deducted from total income to compute net income.
- All persons are entitled to a personal allowance. It is usually deducted from net income, first against non-savings income, then against savings income and lastly against dividend income. The personal allowance is reduced by £1 for every £2 that adjusted net income exceeds £100,000 and can be reduced to nil.
- Income tax is worked out on the taxable income. First tax non-savings income, then savings income and then dividend income.
- There is an income tax charge to recover child benefit if the recipient or their partner has adjusted net income over £60,000 in a tax year.
- Gifts to registered charities under the Gift Aid scheme save tax at an individual's highest rate of tax.
- Tax reducers reduce tax on income at a set rate of relief.
- From the tax liability, deduct any income tax suffered at source to arrive at tax payable. The tax suffered at source can be repaid.
- Additional income received can have an impact on the availability of the PSA and on the availability of the personal allowance.
- Spouses, civil partners and children are all separate taxpayers.

Quick quiz

1. At what rates is income tax charged on non-savings income?
2. Is UK rental income savings income?
3. What is the amount of the personal savings allowance for an additional rate taxpayer?
4. How is tax relief given on interest payable on a loan to invest in a partnership?
5. How is dividend income taxed?
6. Explain how joint income is treated for married couples and civil partners.

Answers to quick quiz

1. For most of the UK, income tax on non-savings income is charged at 20% in the basic rate band, at 40% in the higher rate band and at 45% above the higher rate limit. In Scotland, income tax on non-savings income is charged at 19% in the starter rate band, 20% in the basic rate band, 21% in the intermediate rate band, 42% in the higher rate band, 45% in the advanced band and 48% above the higher rate limit.

2. No. It is non-savings income.

3. An additional rate taxpayer does not have a personal savings allowance.

4. Interest payable on a loan to invest in a partnership is deductible from total income to compute net income.

5. The first £500 of dividend income is within the dividend allowance and so taxable at 0%. Other dividend income below the basic rate limit is taxed at 8.75%. Other dividend income between the basic rate limit and the higher rate limit is taxed at 33.75% and at 39.35% above the higher rate limit.

6. It is assumed that joint income is shared equally, however a joint election can be made to split the joint income in a different way.

PART A TAXATION OF INDIVIDUALS

Pensions

Topic list
1 Types of pension scheme and membership
2 Contributing to a pension scheme

Introduction

In the previous chapter, we looked at the basic income tax computation. We now look at some of the tax reliefs given to encourage individuals to invest in pensions.

Tax relief is given on contributions to pension schemes and the schemes themselves can grow tax free. There are limits on the amounts that can be invested and a breach of these limits will incur tax charges. Failure to comply with the other rules may also result in tax charges.

In the next chapter, we will look at income from UK property and other investments.

PART A TAXATION OF INDIVIDUALS

Exam guide

In the examination, you may be asked about pension contributions as part of a question.

1 Types of pension scheme and membership

FAST FORWARD

> An employee may be entitled to join their employer's occupational pension scheme. Both employees and the self employed can take out a 'personal pension' with a financial institution such as a bank or building society.

1.1 Types of pension provision

An individual is encouraged by the Government to make financial provision to cover their needs when they reach a certain age. There are state pension arrangements which provide some financial support, but the Government would like an individual not to rely on state provision but to make their own pension provision.

Automatic enrolment has been introduced so that employers must automatically enrol most employees into a workplace pension scheme (although employees can then opt out of the scheme). Under automatic enrolment, **there are minimum contributions to the workplace pension scheme required by law.**

Alternatively, **individuals (employees, self-employed and those who are not working) may make their own pension provision through a personal pension provider such as an insurance company.**

Tax relief is given for such pension provision. This includes relief for contributions to a pension and an exemption from tax on income and gains arising in a pension fund.

1.2 Pension arrangements

An individual may make pension provision in a number of ways.

Key terms

> **Occupational pension schemes** are run by employers for their employees. **Personal pension schemes** are run by financial institutions: anyone may contribute to a personal pension.

Personal pension schemes and the majority of occupational pension schemes are **money purchase schemes**. These are also known as **defined contributions schemes**. The level of pension that the member can draw from such schemes will depend on the investment performance of the money invested.

Some occupational schemes are **final salary schemes**, where the pension depends on the period for which the individual has been a member of the scheme and his salary at the time of retirement. These are also known as **defined benefits schemes**, and are becoming less common due to the high level of contributions required.

An individual may make a number of different pension arrangements depending on their circumstances. For example, they may be a member of an occupational pension scheme and also make pension arrangements independently with a financial provider. If the individual has more than one pension arrangement, the rules we will be looking at in detail later apply to all the pension arrangements they make. For example, **there is a limit on the amount of contributions that the individual can make in a tax year. This limit applies to all the pension arrangements that they make, not EACH of them.**

2 Contributing to a pension scheme

FAST FORWARD

An individual can make tax relievable contributions to their pension arrangements up to the higher of their earnings and £3,600. Contributions to personal pensions are paid net of basic rate tax. Employers normally operate 'net pay' arrangements in respect of contributions to occupational schemes.

2.1 Contributions by a scheme member attracting tax relief

An individual who is **under the age of 75** is entitled to **tax relief on their contributions** to a registered pension scheme in a tax year.

The maximum contributions made by an individual in a tax year attracting tax relief is the higher of:

(a) **The individual's UK relevant earnings chargeable to income tax in the year; and**
(b) **The basic amount (set at £3,600 for 2024/25, Whillans p.100**.

Relevant UK earnings include employment income, trading income, and income from furnished holiday lettings (see later in this Workbook). If the individual does not have any UK earnings in a tax year, the maximum contribution they can obtain tax relief on is £3,600.

Where an individual contributes to more than one pension scheme, the aggregate of their contributions will be used to give the total amount of tax relief.

There is an interaction between this provision and the annual allowance, which will be discussed later.

2.2 Methods of giving tax relief

2.2.1 Relief given at source

This method will be used where an individual makes a contribution to a pension scheme run by a personal pension provider such as an insurance company.

Relief is given at source by the contributions being deemed to be made net of basic rate tax. This applies whether the individual is an employee, self-employed or not employed at all and whether or not they have taxable income. HMRC then pay the basic rate tax to the pension provider.

Further tax relief is given if the individual is a higher rate or additional rate taxpayer. The relief is given by increasing the basic rate limit for the year by the gross amount of contributions for which they are entitled to relief. The higher rate limit of £125,140 is also increased by this amount, giving additional rate relief. This is the same mechanism by which relief is given for charitable donations under the Gift Aid scheme, as discussed earlier in this Workbook.

Question — Higher rate relief

Joe has earnings of £60,000 in 2024/25. He pays a personal pension contribution of £7,200 (net). He has no other taxable income.

Show Joe's tax liability for 2024/25.

PART A TAXATION OF INDIVIDUALS

Answer

	Non-savings Income £
Earnings/Net income	60,000
Less PA	(12,570)
Taxable income	47,430

Tax

	£
£37,700 × 20%	7,540
£9,000 (£7,200 × 100/80) × 20%	1,800
£730 × 40%	292
47,430	9,632

In this question, higher rate relief of 20% has been obtained as non-savings income, ordinarily taxed at 40%, has instead been taxed at 20%. Added to the basic rate relief of 20% given at source due to the pension payment being made net, this gives 40% relief.

The effective rate of relief can be higher where dividend income is also received in the year, as the higher rate relief on dividends shifted from the higher rate band to the basic rate band is 25% (33.75% − 8.75%).

If Joe had taxable (non-savings) income in excess of £125,140, he would have obtained tax relief of 25% (income ordinarily taxed at 45% is instead taxed at 20%), which when added to the tax relief of 20% at source, would have given 45% tax relief.

2.2.2 Example: rate of tax relief

Adam has earnings of £50,300 in 2024/25. He also receives dividends of £12,000. He is thinking of making a contribution of £7,200 (equivalent of £9,000 gross) to his personal pension. Adam's effective rate of tax saved by making the pension contribution can be found as follows:

	Non-savings income £	Dividend Income £
Earnings	50,300	
Dividends		12,000
Net income	50,300	12,000
Less PA	(12,570)	
Taxable income	37,730	12,000

Tax (before contribution)

	£
£37,700 × 20%	7,540
£30 × 40%	12
£500 × 0%	0
£11,500 × 33.75%	3,881
49,730	11,433

Tax (after contribution)

	£
£37,700 × 20%	7,540
£30 × 20%	6
£500 × 0%	0
£8,470 × 8.75%	741
£3,030 × 33.75%	1,023
49,730	9,310

The tax saved by extending the basic rate band is £2,123 (£11,433 – £9,310). If we add to this the basic rate tax saved by making the contribution net (ie £9,000 – £7,200 = £1,800) the total tax saved is £3,923. The effective rate of tax relief on the pension contribution is:

$$\frac{£3,923}{£9,000} \times 100$$

which is 43.59%.

2.2.3 Adjusted net income

Adjusted net income is net income less the gross amounts of personal pension contributions and gift aid donations. The restrictions on the personal allowance are calculated in relation to adjusted net income.

Question — Adjusted net income

Maria earns a salary of £116,000 in 2024/25. In January 2025, she made a personal pension contribution of £5,000 in cash.

Compute Maria's income tax liability for 2024/25.

Answer

		Non-savings Income £
Salary/Net income		116,000
Less personal allowance (W)		(7,695)
Taxable income		108,305

	£	£
Income tax		
Basic rate band	37,700 × 20%	7,540
Basic rate band (extended)	6,250 × 20%	1,250
Higher rate band	64,355 × 40%	25,742
	108,305	34,532

Working	£
Net income	116,000
Less personal pension £5,000 × 100/80	(6,250)
Adjusted net income	109,750
Less income limit	(100,000)
Excess	9,750

Personal allowance	12,570
Less half excess £9,750 × ½	(4,875)
	7,695

Where an individual has an **adjusted net income between £100,000 and £125,140, the rate of tax on the income between these two amounts will usually be 60%.** This is calculated as 40% (the higher rate on income) plus 40% of half (ie 20%) of the excess adjusted net income over £100,000 used to restrict the personal allowance. The individual should **consider making personal pension contributions to reduce adjusted net income to below £100,000.**

2.2.4 Net pay arrangements

An occupational scheme will normally operate net pay arrangements.

In this case, the employer will deduct gross pension contributions from the individual's earnings before operating PAYE. The individual therefore obtains tax relief at his marginal rate of tax without having to make any claim.

Question — Net pay arrangements

Pavithra has taxable earnings of £60,000 in 2024/25. Her employer deducts a pension contribution of £9,000 from these earnings before operating PAYE. She has no other taxable income.

Show Pavithra's tax liability for 2024/25.

Answer

	£
Earnings	60,000
Less pension contribution	(9,000)
Net income	51,000
Less PA	(12,570)
Taxable income	38,430

Tax

	£
£37,700 × 20%	7,540
£730 × 40%	292
£38,430	7,832

This is the same result as Joe in the question above. Joe had received basic rate tax relief of £(9,000 – 7,200) = 1,800 at source, so his overall tax position was £(9,632 – 1,800) = £7,832.

2.3 Contributions not attracting tax relief

An individual can also make contributions to their pension arrangements which do not attract tax relief, for example out of capital. The member must notify the scheme administrator if they make contributions in excess of the higher of their UK relevant earnings and the basic amount.

2.4 Employer pension contributions

FAST FORWARD

Employers must make minimum contributions to their employees' workplace pension scheme and may also contribute further amounts to an employee's pension. In certain circumstances, relief for employers' contributions are spread over a number of years.

Where the active scheme member is an employee, their **employer** is required by law to make at least minimum contributions to a workplace pension scheme under automatic enrolment and **will often make contributions above the minimum required**. Employer contributions are **exempt benefits** for the employee.

There is **no limit** on the amount of the contributions that may be made by an employer but **they always count towards the annual allowance**.

All contributions made by an employer are made gross and the employer will usually obtain tax relief for the contribution by deducting it as an expense in calculating trading profits for the period of account in which the payment is made.

However, HMRC may seek to disallow a contribution which it considers is not a revenue expense or is not made wholly and exclusively for the purposes of the trade.

There are 'spreading provisions' for large contributions, so that part of the contribution is treated as paid in a later period of account.

Note that employer contributions are not treated as earnings or taxable benefits for NIC purposes. Therefore, there is still a slight advantage to the employer making such contributions directly to a pension scheme instead of paying the individual the money for that individual to make contributions.

2.5 Annual allowance

FAST FORWARD

The annual allowance is the limit on the amount that can be paid into a pension scheme each year. If this limit is exceeded there is an income tax charge on the excess contributions. The annual allowance is reduced for 'high-income' individuals. Unused annual allowance can be carried forward for up to three years.

2.5.1 Introduction

The **annual allowance** effectively restricts the amount of tax relievable contributions that can be paid into an individual's pension scheme each year. The amount of the annual allowance for 2024/25 and 2023/24 is **£60,000** (Whillans p.101). Before 2023/24, the annual allowance was £40,000 for many years.

2.5.2 Reduced annual allowance

High-income' individuals have a reduced annual allowance.

In 2024/25, a high-income individual has both:

- **Adjusted income** for the tax year of **more than £260,000 and**
- **Threshold income** for the tax year of **more than £200,000.**

Key term

Adjusted income is net income plus pension contributions to occupational pension schemes.
Threshold income is net income less the individual's gross contributions to their personal pension contributions

PART A TAXATION OF INDIVIDUALS

The annual allowance is reduced by £1 for every £2 that the individual's adjusted income exceeds **£260,000**, subject to a **minimum annual allowance of £10,000** (£4,000 in 2020/21–2022/23). The minimum annual allowance will apply where the individual has adjusted income of £360,000 or more since £(60,000 − [360,000 − 260,000]/2) = £10,000.

The reduction in the annual allowance does not apply unless, in addition to the adjusted income exceeding £260,000, the individual's threshold income exceeds £200,000. Threshold income is usually net income less the individual's gross personal pension contributions. Note that pension contributions by employees to occupational pension schemes under net pay arrangements (see Section 2.2.4) will already have been deducted in computing net income.

	£
Adjusted income	
Net income	
(total income less loss relief against general income and deductible interest)	X
Add Employee's contribution to occupational pension schemes	X
Add Employer's contributions to occupational or personal pension schemes	X
Adjusted income	**X**
Threshold income	
Net income	X
Less individual's contributions to personal pension schemes	(X)
Threshold income	**X**

Question — Reduced annual allowance

In the tax year 2024/25, Atul is an employee earning a salary of £288,000. This is Atul's only income for the tax year. During the tax year 2024/25, Atul has made pension contributions to his occupational pension scheme (OPS) of £10,000 and his employer has made contributions of £20,000, in respect of Atul, to the occupational pension scheme. Atul has also made gross personal pension contributions of £6,000 in 2024/25.

What is Atul's annual allowance for 2024/25?

Answer

We start by working out Atul's net income.

	Non-savings income £
Salary	288,000
Less employee OPS contributions	(10,000)
Employment income/net income	278,000

We now need to compute Atul's adjusted income.

	£
Net income	278,000
Add: employee OPS contributions	10,000
employer pension contributions	20,000
Adjusted income	308,000

We also need to compute Atul's threshold income.

	£
Net income	278,000
Less gross personal pension contributions	(6,000)
Threshold income	272,000

Since Atul's adjusted income exceeds £260,000 and his threshold income exceeds £200,000, his annual allowance will be reduced as follows:

	£
Adjusted income	308,000
Less threshold	(260,000)
Excess	48,000
Annual allowance	60,000
Less half excess £48,000 × ½	(24,000)
Reduced annual allowance	36,000

Exam focus point

Both the adjusted income and threshold income limits need to be exceeded for the taxpayer to be a high-income individual with a reduced annual allowance. Therefore, in the exam, if you calculate that one is not exceeded, you do not also need to calculate the other to know that the annual allowance is not reduced.

There is an **anti-avoidance provision** to prevent individuals reducing their threshold income by sacrificing salary for larger employer pension contributions, but these are outside the scope of this Taxation syllabus.

2.5.3 Carry forward of unused annual allowance

Where **an individual is a member of a registered pension scheme** but **does not make contributions of at least the annual allowance in a tax year**, the individual can **carry forward the unused amount of the annual allowance for up to three years**.

The annual allowance in the current tax year is treated as being used first, then any unused annual allowance from earlier years, using the earliest tax year first. Where the annual allowance has been reduced as described in Section 2.5.2, the reduced amount will be carried forward to later years if it has not been used.

Question — Carry forward of annual allowance

Ted is a sole trader. His gross contributions to his personal pension scheme have been as follows:

Year	£
2020/21	21,000
2021/22	16,000
2022/23	36,000
2023/24	25,000

In 2024/25 Ted has a good trading year making taxable trading profits of £100,000 and wishes to make a large pension contribution in January 2025. He has no other sources of income.

(a) What is the maximum gross pension contribution Ted can make in January 2025 without incurring an annual allowance charge, taking into account any brought forward annual allowance?

(b) If Ted makes a gross personal pension contribution of £63,000 in January 2025, what is the unused annual allowance he can carry forward to 2025/26?

PART A TAXATION OF INDIVIDUALS

Answer

(a)

	£
Annual allowance 2024/25	60,000
Annual allowance unused in 2021/22 £(40,000 – 16,000)	24,000
Annual allowance unused in 2022/23 £(40,000 – 36,000)	4,000
Annual allowance unused in 2023/24 £(60,000 – 25,000)	35,000
Maximum gross pension contribution in 2024/25	123,000

Note. The unused allowance from 2020/21 cannot be used in 2024/25 as it cannot be carried forward for more than three years.

(b)

	£
Annual allowance 2024/25 used in 2024/25	60,000
Annual allowance unused in 2021/22 used in 2024/25	3,000
Contribution in 2024/25	63,000

The remaining £(24,000 – 3,000) = £21,000 of the 2021/22 annual allowance cannot be carried forward to 2025/26 since this is more than three years after 2021/22. The unused annual allowances are therefore £4,000 from 2022/23 and £35,000 from 2023/24 and this is the amount carried forward to 2025/26.

Note. Adjusted income does not exceed £260,000 so the annual allowance for 2024/25 does not need to be restricted.

2.5.4 Contributions in excess of annual allowance

An annual allowance charge arises if tax-relievable contributions exceed the available annual allowance.

If tax-relievable pension contributions exceed the annual allowance, there is a charge to income tax based on the individual's taxable income. This will occur if the taxpayer has relevant earnings in excess of the available annual allowance and makes a contribution in excess of the available annual allowance (including any brought forward annual allowance).

The taxpayer is primarily liable for the tax on the excess contribution but in certain circumstances can give notice to the pension scheme for the charge to be payable from the taxpayer's pension benefits fund.

The annual allowance charge is calculated by treating the excess contribution as an extra amount of income received by the taxpayer. The calculation therefore claws back the tax relief given on the pension contribution.

Question — Annual allowance charge

Jaida had employment income of £370,000 in 2024/25. She made a gross personal pension contribution of £70,000 in 2024/25. She does not have any unused annual allowance brought forward.

What is Jaida's income tax liability for 2024/25?

Answer

	Non-savings income £
Taxable income (no personal allowance available)	370,000
Tax	
£37,700 × 20%	7,540
£70,000 × 20% (increased basic rate limit)	14,000
£87,440 × 40% (N1)	34,976
£195,140	
£174,860 × 45%	78,687
Annual allowance charge	
£60,000 × 45% (N2)	27,000
Tax liability	162,203

Notes

1. The higher rate limit is increased to £(125,140 + 70,000) = £195,140. This preserves the higher rate band of £(195,140 − 37,700 − 70,000) = £87,440.

2. The annual allowance is reduced to the minimum of £10,000 as adjusted income exceeds £360,000. The pension contribution has exceeded the reduced annual allowance by £60,000 (£70,000 − £10,000).

Chapter roundup

- An employee may be entitled to join their employer's occupational pension scheme. Both employees and the self employed can take out a 'personal pension' with a financial institution such as a bank or building society.

- An individual can make tax relievable contributions to their pension arrangements up to the higher of their earnings and £3,600. Contributions to personal pensions are paid net of basic rate tax. Employers normally operate 'net pay' arrangements in respect of contributions to occupational schemes.

- Employers must make minimum contributions to their employees' workplace pension scheme and may also contribute further amounts to an employee's pension. In certain circumstances, employers' contributions are spread over a number of years.

- The annual allowance is the amount that can be paid into a pension scheme each year. If this amount is exceeded, there is an income tax charge on the excess contributions. The annual allowance is reduced for 'high-income' individuals. Unused annual allowance can be carried forward for up to three years.

- An annual allowance charge arises if tax-relievable contributions exceed the available annual allowance.

Quick quiz

1. What are the two types of occupational pension scheme?

2. What is the limit on contributions to a registered pension scheme?

3. What are the consequences of the total of employee and employer contributions exceeding the annual allowance?

4. Eileen is employed by B plc. In the tax year 2024/25, she has employment income of £271,500 after deducting a pension contribution made by her of £8,500 under net pay arrangements. Her employer does not make any contributions to the pension scheme. Eileen has no other income in 2024/25. What is Eileen's annual allowance for 2024/25?

Answers to quick quiz

1. Occupational pension schemes may be final salary schemes or money purchase schemes.

2. Higher of relevant earnings and the basic amount (£3,600).

3. The excess is subject to the annual allowance charge on the employee. Any contributions by the employee which were not eligible for tax relief are ignored.

4. Adjusted income is £(271,500 + 8,500) = £280,000 and so exceeds £260,000.

   Threshold income is £271,500 and so exceeds £200,000, and Eileen is a high-income individual.

   Reduced annual allowance is £(60,000 − [280,000 − 260,000]/2) = £50,000.

PART A TAXATION OF INDIVIDUALS

Property income

Topic list
1 UK property business
2 Furnished holiday lettings
3 Rent a room relief

Introduction

In the previous chapters we have covered the income tax computation, including tax reliefs on pensions.

This chapter looks at the taxation of income arising from the letting of property in the UK. It looks at the basis of assessment of such income and at the computation of assessable profits and losses, and then covers the special rules for furnished holiday lettings and the rent a room relief.

The following chapters will deal with income from employment and self-employment.

PART A TAXATION OF INDIVIDUALS

Exam guide

Make sure you are familiar with the rules for computing income from a UK property business. You also need to look out for the special areas of furnished holiday lettings and rent a room relief when performing calculations.

1 UK property business

1.1 Profits of a UK property business

FAST FORWARD

> Income from a UK property business is computed for tax years on either an accruals basis or a cash basis. Capital allowances are not normally available on plant or machinery used in a dwelling. However, a landlord can instead claim replacement domestic items relief.
>
> Loan interest relief restriction applies in respect of residential properties.
>
> A property allowance of £1,000 is available.

Income from land and buildings in the UK, including caravans and houseboats which are not moved, is taxed as non-savings income.

(a) A taxpayer (or a partnership) with UK rental income is treated as running a business, a 'UK property business'. All the rents and expenses for all properties are pooled, to give a single profit or loss. Profits and losses are computed in one of two ways:

- **Cash basis (default method)**

    A property business with property receipts not exceeding £150,000 in a tax year will use the cash basis as the default method of calculating property income. They will pay tax on rental income received in the tax year less allowable rental expenses paid in the tax year.

    A taxpayer with property receipts of less than £150,000 can elect in their tax return to use the accruals basis.

    In the exam, assume the cash basis applies to taxpayers with property income receipts of less than £150,000 unless told otherwise.

- **Accruals basis**

    Property businesses with property receipts exceeding £150,000 (or those which elect to do so) will use the accruals basis to calculate their property income, using generally accepted accounting practice to calculate rental income receivable in the tax year less rental expenses accrued in the tax year.

    Expenses will sometimes include rent payable where a landlord is a tenant who sub-lets to an occupant. The rules on post-cessation receipts and expenses apply to UK property businesses in the same way that they apply to trades (see later in this Workbook).

    Relief is available for irrecoverable rent

 Question   Accrual vs cash basis

Jack rents out a house at a monthly rental of £1,100 per calendar month, payable on the first day of each month. On 1 November 2024 the rent was increased to £1,200 per calendar month. All rent was received on time except for the April 2025 payment which was not received until 15 April 2025.

Jack paid house insurance of £800 on 1 January 2024 for the year ended 31 December 2024 and £880 on 1 January 2025 for the year ended 31 December 2025.

Other allowable expenses amounted to £5,800 accrued and paid in 2024/25.

Requirement

(a) Calculate Jack's taxable property income for 2024/25 assuming that no election has been made.

(b) Calculate Jack's taxable property income for 2024/25 if he does make an election for the accruals basis.

Answer

(a) **Cash basis**

	£	£
Rent received (6m × £1,100) + (5m × £1,200)		12,600
Less: allowable expenses:		
House insurance paid January 2025	880	
Other expenses	5,800	(6,680)
Taxable property income for 2024/25		5,920

(b) **Accruals basis**

	£	£
Rent accrued (7m × £1,100) + (5m × £1,200)		13,700
Less: allowable expenses:		
House insurance (9/12 × £800) + (3/12 × £880)	820	
Other expenses	5,800	
		(6,620)
Taxable property income for 2024/25		7,080

Note. As Jack's rental receipts are less than £150,000 he will use the cash basis unless he elects for the accruals basis which we can see from the above calculations would not be beneficial to him.

(b) An individual has a **property allowance** of £1,000.

If an individual's property receipts do not exceed £1,000 in a tax year, their property income will not be chargeable to income tax.

If an individual's property receipts do exceed £1,000, they will calculate their property income in the normal way: property receipts less property expenses. However, if an individual's receipts exceed £1,000 but their property expenses are less than £1,000, they can elect to use the alternative method: rental receipts less the £1,000 property allowance.

Note. Where the election is made to deduct the £1,000 property allowance, no tax reducer will be available for any disallowed loan interest amount (see below).

In the exam, if an individual's property receipts are less than £1,000, you will assume that the property allowance applies. In all other circumstances, consider the 'normal' method and the 'alternative' method and use the method which produces the most favourable tax position.

(c) Tax relief for **finance costs** is restricted to 20%. This means that the costs are not deducted from rental income but, instead, relief is available as a basic rate deduction from the tax liability. This applies to mortgage interest, fees incurred on taking out or repaying a mortgage used to buy the property and interest on loans to buy furnishings.

Note. The actual 20% tax reduction is calculated as 20% of the lowest of:

(i) Finance costs for the year plus any finance costs brought forward;

(ii) Property income for the tax year after using any property losses brought forward; and

(iii) Adjusted total income (excluding dividends and savings income) that exceeds the personal allowance for the tax year.

These rules do not apply to furnished holiday lettings (see below).

PART A TAXATION OF INDIVIDUALS

(d) **Capital allowances are given on plant and machinery used in the UK property business, in the same way as they are given for a trading business** with an accounting date of 5 April. Capital allowances are not normally available on plant or machinery used in a dwelling. However, a landlord can instead claim **replacement domestic items relief**.

Domestic items are defined as furniture, furnishings, household appliances and kitchenware. Examples include beds, televisions, fridges, freezers, washing machines, carpets and other floor coverings, curtains, crockery and cutlery. It does not include fixtures which become part of the property including boilers, radiators, baths, washbasins, and other items that are not normally removed if a property is sold. However, replacement of these items would be deductible as a repair to the property itself.

No relief is given for the **initial cost** of providing domestic items. **Relief is given** if a domestic item is **replaced**.

The **amount of the relief** is the **expenditure on the new replacement asset less any proceeds** from selling the old asset which has been replaced, plus any costs of disposal of the old asset. If the **new asset is not the same or substantially the same as the old asset, only the cost of an equivalent asset is given relief ie no relief for improvements unless purely because of advances in technology.**

(e) A landlord who incurs expenditure on the acquisition, lease, hire or use of a car, motorcycle or goods vehicle (such as a van) used in their property business, may make an expense deduction using the **approved mileage allowances** rather than the actual expenditure incurred.

Approved mileage allowances:

Car or goods vehicle: 45p per mile for first 10,000 miles and 25p thereafter

Motorcycle: 24p per mile

Note. The approved mileage allowance cannot be used if the landlord has previously claimed capital allowances in respect of that vehicle or if the landlord made a deduction for the cost of the vehicle under the cash basis in the year of acquisition. No other costs relating to the vehicle may be deducted if this method is chosen.

Once this method has been chosen it must always be used for this vehicle. However, if the landlord acquires an additional/replacement car then this method does not have to be used. It is a choice for each separate vehicle.

Question — UK property income

In 2024/25, Malcolm has employment income of £30,000 and property income of £2,125 (net of allowable expenses but before deduction of mortgage interest of £1,500).

Calculate Malcolm's income tax due for 2024/25.

Answer

	£
Employment income	30,000
Property income	2,125
Total income	32,125
Personal allowance	(12,570)
Taxable income	19,555

	£
Tax	
£19,555 × 20%	3,911
Less finance cost (W2) 20% × £1,500	(300)
Income tax due	3,611

Working

Mortgage interest relief at 20% of lower of:
- Finance costs £1,500
- Property income £2,125
- Adjusted total income £19,555

Question — Definite variables

Carrie lets out a property for £300 per month from 6 October 2024, payable on the 6th of the month. She paid allowable property expenses of £750 and finance costs of £120.

Calculate Carrie's taxable property income for 2024/25.

Answer

Carrie's property income for 2024/25 will be:

	£
Rent received (6 months × £300)	1,800
Less: allowable property expenses	(750)
Taxable property income	1,050

As Carrie's allowable property income expenses are less than £1,000 (750) she should elect to deduct the property allowance instead.

	£
Rent received (as above)	1,800
Less: property allowance	(1,000)
Taxable property income	800

Note. Under this method, Carrie will not be entitled to the income tax reducer of (£120 × 20%) = £24 in this year or future years.

1.2 Losses of UK property business

FAST FORWARD

A loss on a UK property business is carried forward to set against future profits from the UK property business.

A loss from a UK property business is carried forward to set against the first future profits from the UK property business. It may be carried forward until the UK property business ends, but it must be used as soon as possible.

PART A TAXATION OF INDIVIDUALS

Question — UK property income

Over the last few years, Pete has purchased several properties in Manchester as 'buy to let' investments.

5 Whitby Ave is let out furnished at £500 per month. A tenant moved in on 1 March 2024 but left unexpectedly on 1 May 2025 having paid rent only up to 31 December 2024. The tenant left no forwarding address.

17 Bolton Rd has been let furnished to the same tenant for a number of years at £800 per month.

A recent purchase, 27 Turner Close, has been let unfurnished since 1 August 2024 at £750 per month. Before then, it was empty whilst Pete redecorated it after its purchase in March 2023.

Pete's expenses during 2024/25 are:

	No 5 £	No 17 £	No 27 £
Insurance	250	250	200
Letting agency fees	–	–	100
Repairs	300	40	–
Redecoration	–	–	500
Curtains	130	–	–
Washer-dryer	–	600	–
Dining table and chairs	–	350	–

No 27 was in a fit state to let when Pete bought it but he wanted to redecorate the property as he felt this would allow him to achieve a better rental income.

The new curtains for No 5 were replacements for old curtains. Pete sold the old curtains for £15.

The washer-dryer for No 17 was a replacement for a washing machine without a dryer. If Pete had bought a new washing machine without a dryer, similar to the old machine, it would have cost him £475. The old washing machine was scrapped with no proceeds. Pete had not previously provided a dining table and chairs in No 17.

Pete made a UK property business loss in 2023/24 of £300. Pete elects to use the accruals basis to calculate his property income.

What is Pete's taxable property income for 2024/25?

Answer

	No 5 £	No 17 £	No 27 £
Accrued income			
12 × £500	6,000		
12 × £800		9,600	
8 × £750			6,000
Less:			
Insurance	(250)	(250)	(200)
Letting agency fees			(100)
Irrecoverable rent			
3 × £500	(1,500)		
Repairs	(300)	(40)	
Redecoration (note)			(500)
Replacement domestic items relief			
Curtains £(130 – 15)	(115)		

3: PROPERTY INCOME

	No 5	No 17	No 27
	£	£	£
Washer-dryer (limited to cost of washing machine without dryer)		(475)	
Dining table and chairs (no relief for initial expenditure)		(0)	
Property Income	3,835	8,835	5,200

	£
Total property income	17,870
Less loss b/fwd	(300)
Taxable property income for 2024/25	17,570

Note. The redecoration is allowable as the property was already in a usable state. If the redecoration had been needed to put the property into a fit state to be rented, it would not be allowable.

1.3 Real Estate Investment Trusts (REITs)

Property companies may operate as **Real Estate Investment Trusts (REITs)**.

REITs can elect for their property income (and gains) to be exempt from corporation tax and must withhold basic rate (20%) tax from distributions paid to shareholders out of these profits. These distributions are taxed as property income, not as dividends. Therefore, such income must be grossed up by 100/80 for inclusion in the income tax computation and the tax deducted at source reduces the income tax liability when calculating income tax payable.

Distributions by REITs out of other income (ie not property income or gains) are taxed as dividends in the normal way.

2 Furnished holiday lettings

FAST FORWARD

Special rules apply to income from furnished holiday lettings. The income is taxed as property business income but the letting is treated as if it were a trade. Capital allowances are available on the furniture and UK income from a furnished holiday letting is relevant earnings for pension purposes. However, only carry forward trade loss relief is available.

There are special rules for furnished holiday lettings (FHL). The letting is treated as if it were a trade. This means that, although the income is taxed as income from a property business in the computation, the provisions which apply to trades also apply to FHL businesses as follows:

(a) Capital allowances are available on furniture instead of replacement domestic items relief;

(b) The income qualifies as relevant earnings for pension relief (see earlier in this Workbook); and

(c) Capital gains tax rollover relief, business asset disposal relief and relief for gifts of business assets are available (see later in this Workbook).

However, losses from FHLs are generally treated differently to trading losses. If a loss arises on a FHL business, the only similar loss relief available is carry forward loss relief by deduction from the first available future profits of the FHL business. Trading loss reliefs are dealt with later in this Workbook.

Note also that the basis period rules for trades do not apply, and the profits or losses must be computed for tax years.

A FHL must be situated in the UK or within the European Economic Area. Separate computations must be made for a UK furnished holiday lettings business (which may consist of several UK FHL properties) and

an EEA furnished holiday lettings business (which consists of lettings in one or more EEA countries other than the UK).

The letting must be of furnished accommodation made on a **commercial basis with a view to the realisation of profit**. The property must also satisfy the following three conditions:

(a) **The availability condition** – during the **tax year**, the accommodation is available for **commercial let** as **holiday accommodation** to the **public** generally, for **at least 210 days**.

(b) **The letting condition** – during the **tax year**, the accommodation is **commercially let** as holiday accommodation to members of the public **for at least 105 days** (the days let exclude any days that are longer term occupation as defined in condition (c) below).

If the **landlord has more than one FHL**, at least one of which satisfies the 105-day rule ('qualifying holiday accommodation') and at least one of which does not ('the underused accommodation'), they may elect to **average the occupation of the qualifying holiday accommodation and any or all of the underused accommodation**. If the average of occupation is at least 105 days, the underused accommodation will be treated as qualifying holiday accommodation.

Exam focus point

It is possible to make an election so that a rental property continues to qualify as a furnished holiday letting for up to two years after the 105 day test ceases to be met. **This election is not examinable**.

(c) **The pattern of occupation condition** – during the tax year, not more than 155 days fall during periods of longer-term occupation. Longer term occupation is defined as a continuous period of more than 31 days during which the accommodation is in the same occupation unless there are abnormal circumstances.

If someone has furnished holiday lettings and other lettings, **draw up two profit and loss accounts as if they had two separate property businesses**. This is so that the profits and losses treated as trade profits and losses can be identified for the special rules which apply to FHLs. The same rule also applies where someone has an EEA furnished holiday lettings business and other overseas lettings.

Exam focus point

Always check whether property qualifies as furnished holiday lettings – remember the averaging provisions. It does not have to be a seaside cottage but must be in the UK or EEA.

3 Rent a room relief

FAST FORWARD

The first £7,500 of rent received from letting a room or rooms in a main residence is tax free.

If an individual lets a furnished room or rooms in their main residence as living accommodation, a special exemption may apply.

The limit on the exemption is gross rents (before any expenses or capital allowances) of £7,500 a year (Whillans p.98-99) This limit is halved if any other person (including the first person's spouse/civil partner) also received income from renting accommodation in the property while the property was the first person's main residence. Gross rents will be either rents received or rents receivable depending on whether the cash or accruals basis has been used.

If gross rents (plus balancing charges arising because of capital allowances in earlier years) **are not more than the limit, the rents** (and balancing charges) **are wholly exempt from income tax** and expenses and capital allowances are ignored. However, the taxpayer may choose not to use the exemption, for example to generate a loss by taking into account both rent and expenses.

If gross rents exceed the limit, the taxpayer will by default be taxed in the ordinary way, ignoring the rent a room scheme, but can elect to use the 'alternative basis' instead. If such an election is made, tax will apply to: gross receipts plus balancing charges less £7,500 (or £3,750 if the limit is halved) with no deductions for expenses or capital allowances.

An election to ignore the exemption or an election for the alternative basis must be made by the 31 January which is 22 months from the end of the tax year concerned although, in practice, most taxpayers will make the election by completing the relevant box in the tax return.

An election to ignore the exemption applies only for the tax year for which it is made but an election for the alternative basis remains in force until it is withdrawn or until a year in which gross rents do not exceed the limit.

The property allowance will not apply to income eligible for rent a room relief.

Exam focus point

Note the different elections carefully and the relevant time limits.

Question — Rent a Room Relief

Sylvia lives in a house which she owns. She has a spare bedroom and, during 2024/25, this was let to a chef working at a nearby restaurant for £150 per week, including the cost of heating, lighting etc.

Sylvia estimates that, each year, her lodger costs her an extra £160 on gas, £75 on electricity and £50 on buildings insurance.

What is Sylvia's chargeable property income in 2024/25 in respect of this let?

Answer

Sylvia has a choice:

(1) Under the normal method (no election needed), she can be taxed on her actual profit:

	£
Rental income £150 × 52	7,800
Less expenses (160 + 75 + 50)	(285)
	7,515

(2) Under the 'alternative basis' (elect for rent a room relief):

Total rental income of £150 × 52 = £7,800 exceeds £7,500 limit so taxable income is £300 (ie £7,800 – 7,500) if rent a room relief claimed.

Sylvia should be advised to claim the 'alternative basis' (rent a room relief).

PART A TAXATION OF INDIVIDUALS

Chapter roundup

- Income from a UK property business is computed for tax years on either an accruals basis or a cash basis. Capital allowances are not normally available on plant or machinery used in a dwelling. However, a landlord can instead claim replacement domestic items relief.
- Loan interest relief restriction applies in respect of residential properties.
- A property allowance of £1,000 is available.
- A loss on a UK property business is carried forward to set against future profits from the UK property business.
- Special rules apply to income from furnished holiday lettings. The income is categorised as property business income in the tax computation but is treated for some purposes as if it were a trade. Capital allowances are available on the furniture and UK income is relevant earnings for pension purposes. However, only carry forward trade loss relief is available.
- The first £7,500 of rent received from letting a room or rooms in a main residence is tax free.

Quick quiz

1. Describe replacement of domestic items relief.

2. In the tax year 2024/25, Simon lets out a property with annual rent of £2,500. His allowable expenditure is £500 and Simon does not have a mortgage on this property. What is Simon's taxable property income for 2024/25? Assume he makes any beneficial elections.

3. What are the conditions for a letting to be a furnished holiday letting?

4. Ferdinand owns a house which he occupies as his main residence. He wants to let out a furnished room in the house. What is the maximum monthly rent that Ferdinand can charge if the rent is to be wholly exempt from income tax in 2024/25?

5. On 6 May 2024, Gavin bought a house which he immediately let out at a rent of £2,700 a quarter payable on 6 May, 6 August, 6 November and 6 February. The tenant only paid one month out of the three months of the rent due on 6 February 2025 and left the property on 5 April 2025 without giving notice. The remaining two months rent is irrecoverable. Gavin paid an insurance premium of £450 on 6 June 2024 for the 12-month period to 5 June 2025.

    Compute Gavin's property business income for the tax year 2024/25 if:

    (a) the cash basis applies; or
    (b) Gavin elects to use the accruals basis.

Answers to quick quiz

1. No relief for initial expenditure on domestic items. Relief for cost of replacement items, reduced by proceeds of old asset, increased by costs of disposal of old asset. Relief not given for cost of improving asset.

2.
	£
Property income	2,500
Less: property allowance	(1,000)
Taxable property income	1,500

In this case, Simon's property receipts are more than £1,000 but his allowable expenditure is less than £1,000 so he should elect for the property allowance to apply.

3. FHL is:
   - Available for letting at least 210 days per tax year
   - Actually let at least 105 days per tax year
   - Not in longer term occupation (more than 31 days) for not more than 155 days.

4. £7,500/12 = £625 per month

5. (a) Cash basis

	£
Rental income received £(2,700 × 3) + £(2,700 × 1/3)	9,000
Less insurance premium paid 6 June 2024	(450)
Property business income 2024/25	8,550

   (b) Accruals basis

	£
Rental income receivable (6 May to 5 April) £(2,700 × 3) + £(2,700 × 2/3)	9,900
Less: impairment loss (6 March to 5 April) £2,700 × 1/3	(900)
Insurance premium payable (6 June to 5 April) £450×10/12	(375)
Property business income 2024/25	8,625

Note. In the tax year 2025/26, the remaining one month rent receivable for the quarter starting 6 February 2025 will be chargeable but will be matched by an impairment loss.

PART A TAXATION OF INDIVIDUALS

Employment income

Topic list
1 Employment income
2 Taxable benefits
3 Exempt benefits
4 Allowable deductions
5 National Insurance
6 The PAYE system

Introduction

In the previous chapters, we have looked at the basic income tax computation and the taxation of investments.

In this chapter, we look at the tax consequences of benefits and expenses of employment. That is, tax on wages and other benefits received by employees from their employers and the treatment of expenses incurred in relation to employment.

The final parts of this chapter explore National Insurance Contributions, which is a tax on employment and self-employment, and PAYE, which is the system by which tax and National Insurance Contributions are collected for employees.

Exam guide

In the exam, you may be asked to calculate and compare the after-tax income from one benefit package with another. As well as calculating the marginal tax on the benefit provided or foregone, remember to consider other costs. For example, an employee who chooses to receive a higher salary and use a personal car for business will have to bear the running costs of the car themselves personally. Remember also to take national insurance into account. Cases referred to in this chapter are for you to understand their conclusions, you will not be tested on case names.

1 Employment income

1.1 Outline of the charge

Employment income includes income arising from an employment under a contract of service (see below) and the income of office holders, such as directors. The term 'employee' is used in this Workbook to mean anyone who receives employment income (ie both employees and directors).

There are two types of employment income:

- **General earnings**
- **Specific employment income**

General earnings are an employee's earnings (see key term below) plus the 'cash equivalent' of any taxable non-monetary benefits.

> **Key term**
>
> **'Earnings'** means any salary, wage or fee, any gratuity or other profit or incidental benefit obtained by the employee if it is money or money's worth (something of direct monetary value or convertible into direct monetary value) or anything else which constitutes an emolument of the employment.

'Specific employment income' includes payments on termination of employment and share-related income.

'Emolument' is a rather old-fashioned term which is still in use in some areas of tax law. For the purposes of this course, it simply means a form of compensation provided by reason of the employment.

The **taxable earnings from an employment in a tax year are the general earnings received in that tax year**.

1.2 When are earnings received?

> **FAST FORWARD**
>
> General earnings are taxed in the year of receipt. Money earnings are generally treated as received on the earlier of the time payment is made and the time entitlement to payment arises. Non-money earnings are generally treated as received when provided.

General earnings consisting of money are treated as received at the earlier of:

- The time when payment is made; or
- The time when a person becomes entitled to payment of the earnings

If the employee is a director of a company, earnings from the company are received on the earliest of:

- The date identified by applying the general rule (above);
- The date on which the amount is credited in the company's accounting records;
- The end of the company's period of account (if the amount was determined by then); or
- The date on which the amount is determined (if after the end of the company's period of account).

Taxable benefits are generally treated as received when they are provided to the employee.

The **receipts basis does not apply to pension income or taxable social security benefits**. These sources of income are taxed on the amount accruing in the tax year, whether or not it is received in that year.

Question — When are earnings received?

John is a director of X Corp Ltd. His earnings for 2024/25 are:

Salary	£60,000
Taxable benefits	£5,000

For the year ended 31 December 2024, the Board of Directors decide to pay John a bonus of £40,000. This is decided on 1 March 2025 at a board meeting and credited in the company accounts seven days later. However, John only received the bonus in his April pay on 30 April 2025.

What is John's taxable income from employment for 2024/25?

Answer

	£
Salary	60,000
Taxable benefits	5,000
Bonus (1.3.25)	40,000
Taxable employment income	105,000

The salary and benefits were paid during 2024/25 and hence taxed in 2024/25. The bonus was paid on 30 April 2025 (2025/26) **but** was determined after the company's year-end (31 December 2024) by the board meeting on 1 March 2025 (2024/25) – hence taxed in 2024/25.

1.3 Net taxable earnings

Net taxable earnings are calculated by deducting total allowable deductions (see below) **from total taxable earnings. Deductions cannot usually create a loss: they can only reduce the net taxable earnings to nil.**

1.4 Person liable for tax on employment income

The person liable to tax on employment income is generally the **person to whose employment the earnings relate**. However, if the tax relates to general earnings received after the death of the person to whose employment the earnings relate, the person's personal representatives are liable for the tax. The tax is a liability for the deceased's estate.

1.5 Employment and self-employment

FAST FORWARD — Employment involves a contract of service whereas self-employment involves a contract for services.

1.5.1 Introduction

The distinction between employment (receipts taxable as earnings) and self-employment (receipts taxable as trading income) may be difficult to determine. **Employment involves a contract of service, whereas self-employment involves a contract for services**. Taxpayers tend to prefer self-employment because the rules on deductions for expenses are more generous. A worker's status also affects **national insurance**: the self-employed generally pay less than employees.

1.5.2 Factors indicating employment

- The **degree of control** exercised over the person doing the work (a high level of control indicates employment)
- Whether they must **accept further work if offered** (if yes, indicates employment)
- Whether the other party **must provide further work** (if yes, indicates employment)
- Whether the worker is entitled to **employment benefits** such as sick pay, holiday pay and pension facilities (entitlement indicates employment)
- Whether the worker works **for just one person or organisation** (if yes, indicates employment)

1.5.3 Factors indicating self-employment

- Whether the worker **provides their own equipment** (if yes, indicates self-employment)
- Whether the worker **hires their own helpers** (if yes, indicates self-employment)
- What degree of **financial risk** the worker takes (if high risk, indicates self-employment)
- What degree of **responsibility for investment and management** the worker has (if most of responsibility is the worker's, indicates self-employment)
- Whether the worker can profit from **sound management** (if can do so, indicates self-employment)
- Whether the worker can **work when they choose** (if can do so, indicates self-employment)
- Whether the worker works for a **number of different persons or organisations** (if yes, indicates self-employment)

1.5.4 Wording of agreement

The wording used in any agreement between the worker and the person for whom they perform work may also be taken into account. For example, if the contract is described as a contract for services, this would suggest that the worker is self-employed. However, such wording is not conclusive about the actual legal relationship and other factors may show that the contract is, in fact, a contract of service.

1.5.5 Case law

Relevant cases on the distinction between employment and self-employment include (case names are not tested in the exam):

(a) *Edwards v Clinch 1981*

   A civil engineer acted occasionally as an inspector on temporary ad hoc appointments.

   Held: there was no ongoing office which could be vacated by one person and held by another so the fees received were from self-employment not employment.

(b) *Hall v Lorimer 1994*

   A vision mixer was engaged under a series of short-term contracts.

   Held: the vision mixer was self-employed, not because of any one detail of the case but because the overall picture was one of self-employment.

(c) *Carmichael and Anor v National Power plc 1999*

   Individuals were engaged as visitor guides on a casual 'as required' basis.

   Held: that they were not employees. An exchange of correspondence between the company and the individuals was not a contract of employment as there was no provision as to the frequency of work and there was flexibility to accept work or turn it down as it arose. Sickness, holiday and pension arrangements did not apply and neither did grievance and disciplinary procedures.

(d) *Uber 2021*

A private car hire firm lost a case in the Supreme Court which decided that the degree of control exercised over how the drivers performed their job was so high that the relationship between Uber and the drivers was one of employer/employee.

2 Taxable benefits

2.1 Introduction

> **FAST FORWARD** Employees are taxed on benefits under the benefits code.

The Income Tax (Earnings and Pensions) Act 2003 (ITEPA 2003) provides comprehensive legislation covering the taxation of benefits. **The legislation generally applies to all employees.**

2.2 General business expenses

If amounts paid by an employee are reimbursed by an employer, the reimbursed amount is generally a taxable benefit for the employee. An employee may be able to make a claim to deduct the amount as an expense if it meets the rules for allowable deductions set out later in this chapter.

However, to avoid the employer having to record such a benefit on a P11D (see later in this chapter), and then the employee having to make a claim, there are some exemptions. **Such reimbursed expenses are now automatically treated as exempt, provided that the amount of the allowable deduction is at least equal to the amount of the reimbursement**. The exemption applies to actual expenses reimbursed and to flat rate payments such as allowances for travel or meals.

Additionally, when an individual has to spend one or more nights away from home, the employer may reimburse expenses on items incidental to the stay (for example private telephone calls). **Such incidental expenses are exempt** if:

(a) The expenses of travelling to each place where the individual stays overnight, throughout the trip, are incurred necessarily in the performance of the duties of the employment (or would have been, if there had been any expenses); and

(b) The total (for the whole trip) of incidental expenses not deductible under the usual rules is no more than £5 for each night spent wholly in the UK and £10 for each other night. If this limit is exceeded, all of the expenses are taxable, not just the excess. The expenses include any VAT.

This incidental expenses exemption applies to expenses reimbursed and to benefits obtained using credit tokens and non-cash vouchers.

2.3 Vouchers

If an employee receives cash vouchers (vouchers exchangeable for cash), they are taxed on the face value of the vouchers.

If an employee:
(a) Uses a credit token (such as a credit card) to obtain money, goods or services; or
(b) Receives exchangeable vouchers (such as book tokens) – also called non-cash vouchers

they are taxed on the cost to the employer of providing the benefit, less any amount paid by the employee to the employer.

However, childcare vouchers are wholly or partially exempt (see later in this chapter).

2.4 Accommodation

FAST FORWARD

The taxable benefit of accommodation provided by an employer is its 'annual value'. There is an additional benefit if the property cost the employer more than £75,000.

The **taxable value of accommodation provided to an employee is the rent that would have been payable if the premises had been let at an amount equal to their annual value** (taken to be their **rateable value**). **If the premises are rented,** rather than owned by the employer, then **the taxable benefit is the higher of the rent actually paid and the annual value**. If property does not have a rateable value, HMRC estimate a value.

If a property cost the employer more than £75,000, an additional amount is chargeable:

Formula to learn

(Cost of providing the accommodation – £75,000) × the official rate of interest at the start of the tax year

Thus, with an official rate of 2.25%, the total benefit for accommodation costing £95,000 and with an annual value of £2,000 would be £2,000 + £((95,000 – 75,000) × 2.25%) = £2,450.

The **'cost of providing' the living accommodation is the aggregate of the cost of purchase and the cost of any improvements made before the start of the tax year** for which the benefit is being computed. It is therefore not possible to avoid the charge by buying an inexpensive property requiring substantial repairs and improving it.

If the accommodation was acquired more than six years before first being provided to the employee, the market value when first provided plus the cost of subsequent improvements is used as the cost of providing the accommodation. However, unless the actual cost plus improvements to the start of the tax year in question exceeds £75,000, the additional charge cannot be imposed, however high the market value. In addition, the additional charge can only be imposed if the employer owns (rather than rents) the property concerned.

Exam focus point

The 'official rate' of interest is in Whillans tax tables (p85).

There is no taxable benefit in respect of job-related accommodation.

Key term

A person lives in **job-related accommodation** if:

(a) It **is necessary for the proper performance of the employee's duties** (as with a caretaker); or

(b) It is provided **for the better performance of the employee's duties** and the employment is of a kind in which it is **customary for accommodation to be provided** (as with a policeman); or

(c) There is a **special threat to the employee's security** and use of the accommodation is part of security arrangements.

Directors can only claim exemptions (a) or (b) if:

(i) They have no **material interest** ('material' means over 5%) in the company; and
(ii) Either they are **full-time working directors** or the company is **non-profit making or is a charity.**

Any contribution paid by the employee is deducted from the annual value of the property and then from the additional benefit.

If the employee is given a cash alternative to living accommodation, the benefits code still applies in priority to treating the cash alternative as earnings. If the cash alternative is greater than the taxable benefit, the excess is treated as earnings.

2.5 Expenses connected with living accommodation

In addition to the benefit of living accommodation itself, **employees are taxed on related expenses paid by the employer**, such as:

(a) **Heating, lighting or cleaning the premises**
(b) **Repairing, maintaining or decorating the premises**
(c) **The provision of furniture (the annual value is 20% of the cost)**

Unless the accommodation qualifies as 'job-related' (as defined above), **the full cost of ancillary services (excluding structural repairs) is taxable**. If the accommodation is **'job-related'**, however, **taxable ancillary services are restricted to a maximum of 10% of the employee's 'net earnings'**.

For this purpose, net earnings are all earnings from the employment (excluding the ancillary benefits (a)–(c) above) less any allowable expenses, statutory mileage allowances, contributions to registered occupational pension schemes (but not personal pension plans) and capital allowances.

If there are ancillary benefits other than those falling within (a)–(c) above (such as a telephone) they are taxable in full.

Question: Expenses connected with living accommodation

Mr Quinton has a gross salary in 2024/25 of £28,850. He works as a caretaker for a company with a large office in London. He is required to live in a company house adjoining his employer's office, so that he can carry out his duties. The house cost £170,000 three years ago and its annual value is £650. In 2024/25, the company paid an electricity bill of £550, a gas bill of £400, a gardener's bill of £750 and redecoration costs of £1,800. Mr Quinton makes a monthly contribution of £50 for his accommodation. He also pays £1,450 in occupational pension contributions each year.

Calculate Mr Quinton's taxable employment income for 2024/25.

Answer

	£	£
Salary		28,850
Less: occupational pension scheme contributions		(1,450)
Net earnings		27,400
Accommodation benefits		
Annual value: exempt (job-related)		
Ancillary services		
Electricity	550	
Gas	400	
Gardener	750	
Redecoration	1,800	
	3,500	
Restricted to 10% of £27,400	2,740	
Less employee's contribution	(600)	
		2,140
Employment income		29,540

PART A   TAXATION OF INDIVIDUALS

2.6 Cars

FAST FORWARD

> Employees who have a company car are taxed on a % of the car's list price, which depends on the level of the car's CO_2 emissions. The same % multiplied by £27,800 determines the benefit where private fuel is also provided. Authorised mileage allowances can be paid tax free to employees who use their own vehicle for business journeys.

A car provided by reason of the employment to an employee, or member of the employee's family or household, for private use gives rise to a taxable benefit. 'Private use' includes travel from home to work.

(a) A tax charge arises whether the car is provided by the employer or by some other person. The benefit is computed as shown below, even if the car is taken as an alternative to another benefit of a different value.

(b) The starting point for calculating a car benefit is the list price of the car (plus accessories). **The percentage of the list price that is taxable depends on the car's CO_2 emissions**.

(c) The price of the car is the sum of the following items:

  (i) The list price of the car for a single retail sale at the time of first registration, including charges for delivery and standard accessories. The manufacturer's, importer's or distributor's list price must be used, even if the retailer offered a discount. A notional list price is estimated if no list price was published;

  (ii) The price (including fitting) of all optional accessories provided when the car was first provided to the employee, excluding mobile telephones and equipment needed by a disabled employee. The extra cost of adapting or manufacturing a car to run on road fuel gases is not included; and

  (iii) The price (including fitting) of all optional accessories fitted later and costing at least £100 each, excluding mobile telephones and equipment needed by a disabled employee. Such accessories affect the taxable benefit from and including the tax year in which they are fitted. However, accessories which are merely replacing existing accessories and are not superior to the ones replaced are ignored. Replacement accessories which *are* superior are taken into account, but the cost of the old accessory is then deducted.

(d) There is a special rule for classic cars. If the car is at least 15 years old (from the time of first registration) at the end of the tax year, and its market value at the end of the tax year (or, if earlier, when it ceased to be available to the employee) is over £15,000 and greater than the price found under (c), that market value is used instead of the price. The market value takes account of all accessories (except mobile telephones and equipment needed by a disabled employee).

(e) Capital contributions are payments by the employee in respect of the price of the car or accessories. In any tax year, we take account of capital contributions made in that year and previous years (for the same car). The maximum deductible capital contributions is £5,000; contributions beyond that total are ignored.

(f) A company car taxable benefit is calculated as a percentage of its list price. The percentage is based on its CO_2 emissions. For cars that emit **CO_2 of 51-54g/km, the taxable benefit is 15% of the car's list price. This percentage increases by 1% for every 5g/km (rounded down to the nearest multiple of 5) by which CO_2 emissions exceed 50g/km up to a maximum of 37%.** So, for example, for cars with emissions from 55g/km to 59g/km, the relevant percentage is 15 + ((55 − 50)/5) = 16%.

Exam focus point   The relevant percentages for CO_2 emissions will be given to you in the Whillans tax tables (p 76).

(g) For electric cars the percentage is based on the car's range in miles (ie the distance a car can be driven before the battery needs to be recharged). The higher the range, the lower the percentage.

(h) Diesel cars have a supplement of 4% of the car's list price added to the taxable benefit. The maximum percentage, however, remains 37% of the list price. The diesel supplement does not apply to cars registered from 1 September 2017 that either meet or are certified against new standards for nitrogen oxide (NOx) emissions under the 'real driving emissions' (RDE2) regime (known as 'Euro 6d'), or which have a certified NOx emissions figure under RDE2 standards. You will be told in the exam if this is the case.

(i) **The benefit is reduced on a time basis where a car is first made available or ceases to be made available during the tax year** or is incapable of being used for a continuous period of not less than 30 days (for example, because it is being repaired).

(j) **The benefit is reduced by any payment the user must make for the private use of the car** (as distinct from a capital contribution to the cost of the car). Payments for insuring the car do not count. The benefit cannot become negative to create a deduction from the employee's income.

(k) Pool cars are exempt. A car is a pool car if **all** the following conditions are satisfied:
   (i) It is used by more than one employee and is not ordinarily used by any one of them to the exclusion of the others;
   (ii) Any private use is merely incidental to business use; and
   (iii) It is not normally kept overnight at or near the residence of an employee.

There are many ancillary benefits associated with the provision of cars, such as insurance, repairs, vehicle licences and a parking space at or near work. No extra taxable benefit arises as a result of these, with the exception of the cost of providing a driver.

2.7 Fuel for cars

Where fuel is provided there is a further benefit in addition to the car benefit.

No taxable benefit arises where either:

(a) **All the fuel provided was made available only for business travel; or**

(b) **The employee is required to make good, and has made good, the whole of the cost of any fuel provided for private use.**

Unlike most benefits, **a reimbursement of only part of the cost of the fuel available for private use does not reduce the benefit.**

The taxable benefit is a percentage of a base figure. The base figure for 2024/25 is £27,800 (Whillans p.80). **The percentage is the same percentage as is used to calculate the car benefit** (see above).

Exam focus point | The fuel base figure will be given to you in Whillans.

The fuel benefit is reduced in the same way as the car benefit **if the car is not available for 30 days or more**.

The fuel benefit is also reduced if private fuel is not available for part of a tax year. However, if private fuel later becomes available in the same tax year, the reduction is not made. If, for example, fuel is provided from 6 April 2024 to 30 June 2024, then the fuel benefit for 2024/25 will be restricted to just three months. This is because the provision of fuel has permanently ceased. However, if fuel is provided from 6 April 2024 to 30 June 2024, and then again from 1 September 2024 to 5 April 2025, then the fuel benefit will not be reduced since the cessation was only temporary.

PART A TAXATION OF INDIVIDUALS

Question — Car and fuel benefit

An employee was provided with a new car costing £15,000 for the whole of 2024/25. The car emits 104g/km of CO_2. During the year, the employer spent £900 on insurance, repairs and a vehicle licence. The employer paid for all petrol, costing £1,500, without reimbursement.

The employee paid the firm £600 for the private use of the car. Calculate the taxable benefit.

Answer

Taxable percentage = 15% + (100 - 50)/5 = 25%

	£
Car benefit £15,000 × 25%	3,750
Fuel benefit £27,800 × 25%	6,950
	10,700
Less contribution towards use of car	(600)
	10,100

If the contribution of £600 had been towards the petrol, the benefit would have been £10,700. This is because partial reimbursement of private petrol does not reduce the fuel benefit.

2.8 Vans and heavier commercial vehicles

If a van (of normal maximum laden weight up to 3,500 kg) **is made available for an employee's private use, there is an annual scale charge of £3,960** (Whillans p.79). The scale charge covers ancillary benefits such as insurance and servicing. Paragraphs 2.6 (i) and (j) above apply to vans as they do to cars. There is an exception for zero emissions vans, where the taxable benefit is **nil** in 2024/25.

There is **no taxable benefit where an employee takes a van home** (ie uses the van for home to work travel) but is not allowed any other private use.

If the employer provides **fuel for unrestricted private use**, an additional **fuel charge of £757** (Whillans p.79) applies.

If a commercial vehicle of normal maximum laden weight over 3,500 kg is made available for an employee's private use, but the employee's use of the vehicle is not wholly or mainly private, no taxable benefit arises except in respect of the provision to a driver.

2.9 Statutory mileage allowances

A statutory mileage allowance (Whillans p.84) **for business journeys in an employee's own vehicle applies to all cars and vans. There is no income tax on payments up to this allowance and employers do not have to report mileage allowances up to this amount. The allowance for 2024/25 is 45p per mile on the first 10,000 miles in the tax year with each additional mile over 10,000 miles at 25p per mile. The statutory mileage allowance for employees using their own motorcycle is 24p per mile. For employees using their own pedal cycle it is 20p per mile.**

If employers pay less than the statutory allowance, employees can claim tax relief up to that level.

The statutory allowance does not prevent employers from paying higher rates, but any excess will be subject to income tax. There is a similar (but slightly different) system for NICs, covered below.

Employers can make income tax and NIC free payments of up to 5p per mile for each fellow employee making the same business trip who is carried as a passenger. If the employer does not pay the employee for carrying business passengers, the employee cannot claim any tax relief.

Question: Mileage allowance

Sophie uses her own car for business travel. During the tax year, Sophie drove 15,400 miles in the performance of her duties.

How is the mileage allowance received by Sophie treated for tax purposes assuming that the rate paid to Sophie by her employer is:

(a) 40p a mile
(b) 25p a mile

Answer

(a)

	£
Mileage allowance received (15,400 × 40p)	6,160
Less tax free [(10,000 × 45p) + (5,400 × 25p)]	(5,850)
Taxable benefit	310

£5,850 is tax free and the excess amount received of £310 is a taxable benefit.

(b)

	£
Mileage allowance received (15,400 × 25p)	3,850
Less tax-free amount [(10,000 × 45p) + (5,400 × 25p)]	(5,850)
Allowable deduction	(2,000)

There is no taxable benefit and Sophie can claim a deduction from her employment income of £2,000.

2.10 Beneficial loans

FAST FORWARD

Taxable cheap loans are charged to tax on the difference between the official rate of interest and any interest paid by the employee.

2.10.1 Introduction

Employment-related loans to employees and their relatives give rise to a benefit equal to:

(a) **Any amounts written off** (unless the employee has died); and

(b) **The excess of the interest based on an official rate prescribed by the Treasury, over any interest actually charged ('taxable cheap loan')**. Interest payable during the tax year but paid after the end of the tax year is taken into account, but if the benefit is determined before such interest is paid a claim must be made to take it into account.

The following loans are normally not treated as taxable cheap loans for calculation of the interest benefits (but are taxable for the purposes of the charge on loans written off):

(a) A loan on normal commercial terms made in the ordinary course of the employer's money-lending business; and

(b) A loan made by an individual in the ordinary course of the lender's domestic, family or personal arrangements.

2.10.2 Calculating the interest benefit

There are two alternative methods of calculating the taxable benefit. The simpler **'average' method** automatically applies unless the taxpayer or HMRC elect for the alternative **'strict' method**. The taxpayer must elect for the alternative 'strict' method to be applied by 31 January in the next tax year but one (eg an election must be made by 31 January 2027 for the tax year 2024/25). HMRC normally only make the election where it appears that the 'average' method is being deliberately exploited. In both methods, the benefit is the interest at the official rate minus the interest payable.

The 'average' method averages the balances at the beginning and end of the tax year (or the dates on which the loan was made and discharged if it was not in existence throughout the tax year) and applies the official rate of interest to this average. If the loan was not in existence throughout the tax year, only the number of complete tax months (from the 6th of the month) for which it existed are taken into account.

The 'strict' method is to compute interest at the official rate on the actual amount outstanding on a daily basis. However, for exam purposes, it is acceptable to work on a monthly basis. The official rate of interest throughout 2024/25 is 2.25%.

Question
Loan benefit

At 6 April 2024, a taxable cheap loan of £30,000 was outstanding to an employee earning £12,000 a year, who repaid £20,000 on 6 December 2024. The remaining balance of £10,000 was outstanding at 5 April 2025. Interest paid during the year was £250.

What was the benefit under both methods for 2024/25?

Answer

Average method

	£
$2.25\% \times \dfrac{30,000 + 10,000}{2}$	450
Less interest paid	(250)
Benefit	200

Strict method

	£
£30,000 × $\dfrac{8}{12}$ (6 April – 5 December) × 2.25%	450
£10,000 × $\dfrac{4}{12}$ (6 December – 5 April) × 2.25%	75
	525
Less interest paid	(250)
Benefit	275

HMRC might opt for the alternative strict method, although this is unlikely given the difference between the methods is relatively small and it does not appear that the 'average' method is being deliberately exploited.

2.10.3 The de minimis test

The benefit is not taxable if:

(a) The **total of all taxable cheap loans to the employee did not exceed £10,000** at any time in the tax year; or

(b) **The loan is not a qualifying loan and the total of all non-qualifying loans to the employee did not exceed £10,000** at any time in the tax year (Whillans p.85).

A qualifying loan is one on which all or part of any interest paid would qualify as a charge on income.

When the £10,000 threshold is exceeded, a benefit arises on interest on the whole loan, not just on the excess of the loan over £10,000.

When a loan is written off and a benefit arises, there is no £10,000 threshold: writing off a loan of £1 gives rise to a £1 benefit.

2.10.4 Qualifying loans

If the whole of the interest payable on a qualifying loan is eligible for tax relief as deductible interest, then no taxable benefit arises. If the interest is only partly eligible for tax relief, then the employee is treated as receiving earnings because the actual rate of interest is below the official rate. They are also treated as paying interest equal to those earnings. This **deemed interest paid may qualify as a business expense or as deductible interest in addition to any interest actually paid.**

Question — Beneficial loans

Anna has an annual salary of £30,000 and two loans from her employer:

(a) A season ticket loan of £6,300 at no interest.

(b) A loan, 90% of which was used to buy shares in her employee-controlled company, of £71,000 at 0.5% interest.

Anna has no other taxable income.

What is Anna's tax liability for 2024/25?

Answer

	£
Salary	30,000
Season ticket loan: non-qualifying loans not over £10,000	0
Loan to buy shares £71,000 × (2.25 – 0.5 = 1.75%)	1,243
Earnings	31,243
Less deductible interest paid (£71,000 × 2.25% × 90%)	(1,438)
	29,805
Less personal allowance	(12,570)
Taxable income	17,235
Income tax	
£17,235 × 20%	3,447

2.11 Other assets made available for private use

FAST FORWARD — 20% of the value of assets made available for private use is taxable.

When assets are made available to employees or members of their family or household, the **taxable benefit is the higher of 20% of the market value when first provided as a benefit to any employee, or the rent paid by the employer if higher** (Whillans p.89). The 20% charge is time-apportioned when the asset is provided for only part of the year. The charge after any time apportionment is reduced by any contribution made by the employee.

Certain assets, such as bicycles provided for journeys to work, are exempt. These are described later in this chapter.

If an asset made available is subsequently acquired by the employee, **the taxable benefit on the acquisition is the greater of:**

- The **current market value minus the price paid by the employee; and**
- The **market value when first provided minus any amounts already taxed (ignoring contributions by the employee) minus the price paid by the employee.**

This rule prevents tax free benefits arising on rapidly depreciating items through the employee purchasing them at their low second-hand value.

There is an exception to this rule for bicycles which have previously been provided as exempt benefits. The taxable benefit on acquisition is restricted to current market value, minus the price paid by the employee.

2.12 Example: assets made available for private use

A suit costing £400 is purchased by an employer for use by an employee on 6 April 2023. On 6 April 2024, the suit is purchased by the employee for £30, its market value then being £50.

		£
The benefit in 2023/24 is £400 × 20%		80

The benefit in 2024/25 is £290, being the **greater** of:

			£
(a)	Market value at acquisition by employee		50
	Less price paid		(30)
			20
(b)	Original market value		400
	Less already taxed in respect of use		(80)
			320
	Less price paid		(30)
			290

 Question — Bicycles

Rupert is provided with a new bicycle by his employer on 6 April 2024. The bicycle is available for private use as well as commuting to work. It cost the employer £1,500 when new. On 6 October 2024, the employer transfers ownership of the bicycle to Rupert when it is worth £800. Rupert does not pay anything for the bicycle.

What is the total taxable benefit on Rupert for 2024/25 in respect of the bicycle?

Answer

Use benefit	Exempt
Transfer benefit (use MV at acquisition by employee only)	
MV at transfer	£800

2.13 Scholarships

Scholarships that are made to a member of an employee's family will not be taxable unless 75% or more of the total scholarship payments awarded by the fund or scheme in question are made because of the employment of recipients' family members.

2.14 Childcare

FAST FORWARD

> Workplace childcare is an exempt benefit. Employer-supported childcare and childcare vouchers are exempt up to £55 per week (Whillans p.86). Maximum tax relief is limited to £11 per week (the equivalent of £55 × 20%).

The cost of running a **workplace nursery or playscheme is an exempt benefit (without limit)**.

Otherwise, a certain amount of childcare is tax free if the employer contracts with an approved childcare provider or issues childcare vouchers to pay an approved childcare provider. The childcare must usually have been available to all employees and the childcare must either be registered or approved home-childcare.

Exam focus point

> The rules regarding childcare schemes/vouchers changed in October 2018. The scheme was closed to new entrants but employees already registered were permitted to continue to use it. A question in the Taxation exam involving childcare vouchers would involve such an employee. Tax free childcare using an online account has replaced childcare vouchers but the rules for this are outside the scope of the Taxation syllabus.

A **£55 per week limit applies to basic rate employees** who use employer-supported childcare schemes or receive childcare vouchers. The amount of tax relief for a basic rate taxpayer is therefore £55 × 20% = £11 per week.

Higher rate and additional rate employees who use employer-supported childcare schemes or receive childcare vouchers have their tax relief restricted so that it is the equivalent of that received by a basic rate taxpayer. Higher and additional rate employees can therefore only receive vouchers tax-free up to £28 per week and £25 per week respectively, each giving £11 of tax relief which is the same amount a basic rate taxpayer would receive.

Exam focus point

> Whether an employee is considered basic rate, higher rate or additional rate for these purposes, is determined by the level of earnings from employment only (and not other income). However, in a Taxation exam question involving childcare, it will be quite clear at which rate a taxpayer is paying tax.

Question — Childcare

Archie is employed by Marks plc and was paid a salary of £80,000 in 2024/25. He received childcare vouchers from Marks plc, worth £50 per week, for his daughter until she went to school in September 2024 and received them for 22 weeks during 2024/25.

What is Archie's employment income for 2024/25?

Answer

	£
Salary (higher rate employee)	80,000
Childcare vouchers £(50 – 28) × 22	484
Employment income 2024/25	80,484

2.15 Residual charge

FAST FORWARD

There is a residual charge for other benefits, usually equal to the cost of the benefits.

We have seen above how certain specific benefits are taxed. **A 'residual charge' is made on the taxable value of other benefits. In general, the taxable value of a benefit is the cost of the benefit less any part of that cost made good by the employee to the persons providing the benefit.**

The residual charge applies to any benefit provided for an employee or a member of their family or household, by reason of the employment. There is an exception where the employer is an individual and the provision of the benefit is made in the normal course of the employer's domestic, family or personal relationships.

3 Exempt benefits

FAST FORWARD

Some benefits are exempt from income tax. You should learn the examples in this section.

Various benefits are exempt from tax. These include:

(a) **Certain reimbursed expenses** (see earlier in this chapter).

(b) **Entertainment provided to employees by genuine third parties** (eg seats at sporting/cultural events), even if it is provided by giving the employee a voucher.

(c) **Gifts of goods** (or vouchers exchangeable for goods) from third parties (ie not provided by the employer or a person connected to the employer) if the total cost (incl. VAT) of all gifts by the same donor to the same employee in the tax year is £250 or less. If the £250 limit is exceeded, the full amount is taxable, not just the excess.

(d) **Non-cash awards for long service** if the period of service was at least 20 years, no similar award was made to the employee in the past 10 years and the cost is not more than £50 per year of service.

(e) **Awards under staff suggestion schemes if**:

  (i) There is a formal scheme, open to all employees on equal terms.

  (ii) The suggestion is outside the scope of the employee's normal duties.

  (iii) Either the award is not more than £25, or the award is only made after a decision is taken to implement the suggestion.

  (iv) Awards over £25 reflect the financial importance of the suggestion to the business, and either do not exceed 50% of the expected net financial benefit during the first year of implementation or do not exceed 10% of the expected net financial benefit over a period of up to five years.

  (v) Awards of over £25 are shared on a reasonable basis between two or more employees putting forward the same suggestion.

If an award exceeds £5,000, the excess is taxable.

(f) **The first £8,000 of removal expenses if:**
  (1) The employee does not already live within a reasonable daily travelling distance of their new place of employment, but will do so after moving; and
  (2) The expenses are incurred or the benefits provided by the end of the tax year following the tax year of the start of employment at the new location.

(g) **Some childcare** (see earlier in this chapter).

(h) **Sporting or recreational facilities available to employees generally and not to the general public**, unless they are provided on domestic premises or they consist in an interest in or the use of any mechanically propelled vehicle or any overnight accommodation. Vouchers only exchangeable for such facilities are also exempt but membership fees for sports clubs are taxable.

(i) **Assets or services used in performing the duties of employment** provided any private use of the item concerned is insignificant. This exempts, for example, the benefit arising on the private use of employer-provided tools.

(j) **Welfare counselling** and similar minor benefits if the benefit concerned is available to employees generally.

(k) **Bicycles or cycling safety equipment provided to enable employees to get to and from work or to travel between one workplace and another**. The equipment must be available to the employer's employees generally. Also, it must be used mainly for the aforementioned journeys.

(l) **Workplace parking**.

(m) **Up to £15,480 a year paid to an employee who is on a full-time course lasting at least a year**, with average full-time attendance of at least 20 weeks a year. If the £15,480 limit is exceeded, the whole amount is taxable.

(n) **Work related training and related costs. This includes the costs of** training material and assets either made during training or incorporated into something so made.

(o) **Air miles or car fuel coupons** obtained as a result of business expenditure but used for private purposes.

(p) **The cost of work buses and minibuses or subsidies to public bus services**.

A works bus must have a seating capacity of 12 or more and a works minibus a seating capacity of 9 or more but not more than 12 and be available generally to employees of the employer concerned. The bus or minibus must mainly be used by employees for journeys to and from work and for journeys between workplaces.

(q) Transport/overnight costs where public transport is disrupted by industrial action, late night taxis and travel costs incurred where car sharing arrangements unavoidably breakdown.

(r) The private use of one **mobile phone which can be a smartphone**. Top up vouchers for exempt mobile phones are also tax free. If more than one mobile phone is provided to an employee for private use only the second or subsequent phone is a taxable benefit.

(s) **Employer provided uniforms** which employees must wear as part of their duties.

(t) The cost of **staff parties** which are open to staff generally provided that the **cost per staff member per year (including VAT) is £150 or less**. The £150 limit may be split between several parties.

(u) **Private medical insurance premiums paid to cover treatment when the employee is outside the UK in the performance of their duties**. Other medical insurance premiums are taxable as is the cost of medical diagnosis and treatment except for routine check ups. Eye tests and glasses for employees using VDUs are exempt.

(v) Cheap loans **that do not exceed £10,000** at any time in the tax year (see above).

(w) **Job-related accommodation** (see above).

(x) **Employer contributions towards additional household costs incurred by an employee who works wholly or partly at home.** Payments up to £6 pw (or £26 per month for monthly paid employees) may be made without supporting evidence. Payments in excess of that amount require supporting evidence that the payment is wholly in respect of additional household expenses.

(y) Reasonable cost of **providing independent advice** to an individual who is offered an **employee shareholder employment contract under which an employee gives up certain employment rights in exchange for shares in the employer company.**

(z) **Recommended medical treatment** costing up to £500 per tax year paid for by an employer. The treatment must be recommended in writing by a health professional (eg doctor, nurse) and the purpose of the treatment must be to assist the employee to return to work after a period of injury or ill-health of at least 28 days. If the payments exceed £500, they are wholly taxable.

(aa) **Trivial benefits costing up to £50 per employee per tax year** provided these are not in the form of cash or a cash voucher. Examples of exempt trivial benefits include providing an employee with a Christmas or birthday present and sending flowers to an employee on the birth of a baby. There is an annual cap of £300 in respect of such benefits when provided to certain directors.

(ab) Vehicle battery charging provision at or near a workplace, made available to all employees.

Where a voucher is provided for a benefit which is exempt from income tax the provision of the voucher itself is also exempt.

4 Allowable deductions

FAST FORWARD   To be deductible, expenses must fall into a qualifying category.

4.1 General principles

Certain expenditure is specifically deductible in computing net taxable earnings:

(a) **Contributions** (within certain limits) **to registered occupational pension schemes** (see earlier in this Workbook).

(b) **Subscriptions to professional bodies** recognised on the list of bodies issued by HMRC (which includes most UK professional bodies), if relevant to the duties of the employment.

(c) Payments for certain **liabilities relating to the employment** and for insurance against them (see below).

(d) **Payments to charity made under the payroll deduction scheme** operated by an employer.

(e) **Mileage allowance** relief (see above).

Otherwise, **allowable deductions are notoriously hard to obtain. They are limited to:**

- **Qualifying travel expenses** (see below).

- **Other expenses the employee is obliged to incur and pay as holder of the employment which are *incurred wholly, exclusively and necessarily* in the performance of the duties of the employment.**

- **Capital allowances on plant and machinery (other than cars or other vehicles) necessarily provided for use in the performance of those duties.**

4.2 Liabilities and insurance

If a director or employee incurs a liability related to their employment, or pays for insurance against such a liability, the cost is a deductible expense. If the employer pays such amounts, there is no taxable benefit.

A liability relating to employment is one which is imposed in respect of the employee's acts or omissions as employee. Thus, for example, liability for negligence would be covered. Related costs, for example the costs of legal proceedings, are included.

For insurance premiums to qualify, the insurance policy must:

(a) Cover only liabilities relating to employment, vicarious liability in respect of liabilities of another person's employment, related costs and payments to the employee's own employees in respect of their employment liabilities relating to employment and related costs.

(b) Not last for more than two years (although it may be renewed for up to two years at a time), and the insured person must not be required to renew it.

4.3 Travel expenses

Tax relief is not available for an employee's normal commuting costs. This means relief is not available for any costs an employee incurs in getting from home to their normal place of work ('permanent workplace'). However, **employees are entitled to relief for the travel expenses they are obliged to incur in the performance of their duties or when travelling to or from a place which they have to attend in the performance of their duties (other than a permanent workplace).**

4.4 Example: travel in the performance of duties

Judi is an accountant. She often travels to meetings at the firm's offices in the North of England returning to her office in Leeds after the meetings. Relief is available for the full cost of these journeys as the travel is undertaken in the performance of her duties.

Question

Relief for travelling costs

Zoe lives in Wycombe and normally works in Chiswick. Occasionally she visits a client in Wimbledon and travels direct from home. Distances are shown in the diagram below:

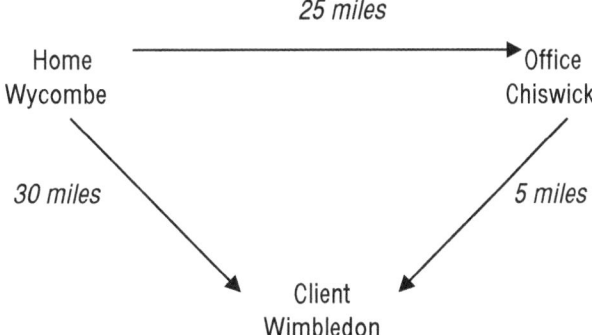

What tax relief is available for Zoe's travel costs?

Answer

Zoe is not entitled to tax relief for the costs incurred in travelling between Wycombe and Chiswick since these are normal commuting costs. However, relief is available for all costs that Zoe incurs when she travels from Wycombe to Wimbledon to visit her client.

To prevent manipulation of the basic rule normal commuting will not become a business journey just because the employee stops enroute to perform a business task (eg make a phone call). Nor will relief be available if the journey is essentially the same as the employee's normal journey to work.

4.5 Example: normal commuting

Judi is based at her office in Leeds City Centre. One day she is required to attend a 9:00 am meeting with a client whose premises are around the corner from her Leeds office. Judi travels from home directly to the meeting. As the journey is substantially the same as her ordinary journey to work relief is not available.

Site-based employees (eg construction workers, management consultants etc) who do not have a permanent workplace are entitled to relief for the costs of all journeys made from home to wherever they are working. This is because these employees do not have an ordinary commuting journey or any normal commuting costs. However, there is a requirement that the employee does not spend more than 24 months of continuous work at any one site.

Tax relief is available for travel, accommodation and subsistence expenses incurred by an employee who is working at a temporary workplace on a secondment expected to last up to 24 months. If a secondment is initially expected not to exceed 24 months, but it is extended, relief ceases to be due from the date the employee becomes aware of the change. When looking at how long a secondment is expected to last, HMRC will consider not only the terms of the written contract but also any verbal agreement by the employer and other factors such as whether the employee buys a house etc.

Question — Temporary workplace

Philip works for Vastbank Plc at its Newcastle City Centre branch. Philip is sent to work full-time at another branch in Morpeth for 20 months at the end of which he will return to the Newcastle branch. Morpeth is about 20 miles north of Newcastle.

What travel costs is Philip entitled to claim as a deduction?

Answer

Although Philip is spending all of his time at the Morpeth branch it will not be treated as his normal work place because his period of attendance will be less than 24 months. Thus, Philip can claim relief in full for the costs of travel from his home to the Morpeth branch.

There is also tax relief for certain travel expenses relating to overseas employment. These are dealt with later in this Workbook.

4.6 Other expenses

The word 'exclusively' strictly implies that the expenditure must give no private benefit at all. If it does, none of it is deductible. In practice, HMRC may ignore a small element of private benefit or make an apportionment between business and private use.

Whether an expense is 'necessary' is not determined by what the employer requires. The test is whether the duties of the employment could not be performed without the expense being incurred.

- *Sanderson v Durbridge 1955*

    The cost of evening meals taken when attending late meetings was not deductible because it was not incurred in the performance of the duties.

- *Blackwell v Mills 1945*

    As a condition of their employment, an employee was required to attend evening classes. The cost of their textbooks and travel was not deductible because it was not incurred in the performance of the duties.

- *Lupton v Potts 1969*

    Examination fees incurred by a solicitor's articled clerk were not deductible because they were incurred neither wholly nor exclusively in the performance of the duties, but in furthering the clerk's ambition to become a solicitor.

- *Brown v Bullock 1961*

    The expense of joining a club that was virtually a requisite of an employment was not deductible because it would have been possible to carry on the employment without the club membership, so the expense was not necessary.

- *Elwood v Utitz 1965*

    A managing director's subscriptions to two residential London clubs were claimed as an expense on the grounds that they were cheaper than hotels.

    The expenditure was deductible as it was necessary in that it would be impossible for the employee to carry out their London duties without being provided with first class accommodation. The residential facilities (which were cheaper than hotel accommodation) were given to club members only.

- *Lucas v Cattell 1972*

    The cost of business telephone calls on a private telephone is deductible, but no part of the line or telephone rental charges is deductible.

- *Fitzpatrick v IRC 1994; Smith v Abbott 1994*

    Journalists cannot claim a deduction for the cost of buying newspapers which they read to keep themselves informed, since they are merely preparing themselves to perform their duties.

The cost of clothes for work is not deductible, except that for certain trades requiring specialist or protective clothing.

An employee required to work at home may be able to claim a deduction for an appropriate proportion of their expenditure on lighting, heating and (if a room is used exclusively for work purposes) **council tax.** Employers can pay up to £6 per week (or £26 per month to monthly paid employees) without the need for supporting evidence of the costs incurred by the employee (see above). Payments above the limit require evidence of the employee's actual costs.

5 National Insurance

5.1 Classes of National Insurance contributions

> **FAST FORWARD**
>
> National Insurance contributions are divided into four classes.

Four classes of National Insurance Contribution (NIC) exist, as set out below.

(a) **Class 1**: This is divided into
  (i) **Primary**, paid by employees
  (ii) **Secondary, Class 1A and Class 1B** paid by employers

(b) **Class 2**: Paid by the self-employed

(c) **Class 3**: Voluntary contributions (paid to maintain rights to certain state benefits)
(d) **Class 4**: Paid by the self-employed

In this section we focus on NIC for employees and their employers.

5.2 General principles

> **FAST FORWARD**
>
> Employees pay Class 1 NICs. Employees pay the main primary rate between the primary earnings threshold and upper earnings limit and the additional rate on earnings above the upper earnings limit. Employers pay Class 1 and Class 1A NICs. For employers, there is no upper earnings limit. There is a different Class 1 threshold where employees are less than 21 years old or apprentices.

5.2.1 Introduction

The National Insurance Contributions Office (NICO), which is part of HMRC, examines employers' records and procedures to ensure that the correct amounts of NICs are collected.

Both employees and employers pay Class 1 NICs related to the employee's earnings. NICs are not deductible from an employee's gross salary for income tax purposes. However, employers' contributions are deductible trade expenses.

5.2.2 What are 'earnings'?

'Earnings' broadly comprise gross pay, excluding benefits which cannot be turned into cash by surrender (eg holidays, cars, accommodation, use of employer's assets – these are subject to Class 1A contributions, see Section 6.3 below). It also includes mileage payments over the approved amount (see below) and readily convertible assets given to employees. No deduction is made for employee pension contributions.

An employer's contribution to a registered personal pension or a registered occupational pension is not 'earnings'. However, NICs are due on employer contributions to non-registered schemes.

In general, income tax and NIC exemptions mirror one another. For example, payment of personal incidental expenses covered by the £5/£10 a night income tax de minimis exemption are excluded from NIC earnings. Relocation expenses of a type exempt from income tax are also excluded from NIC earnings but without the income tax £8,000 upper limit (although expenses exceeding £8,000 are subject to Class 1A NICs as described below). Similarly, the income tax rules for travel expenses are exactly mirrored for NIC treatment.

An expense with a business purpose is not treated as earnings. For example, if an employee is reimbursed for business travel or for staying in a hotel on the employer's business this is not normally 'earnings'. However, if an employee is reimbursed for their own home telephone charges the reimbursed cost of private calls (and all reimbursed rental) is earnings.

Where an employer reimburses an employee using their own car for business mileage, the earnings element is the excess of the mileage rate paid over HMRC's 'up to 10,000 business miles' 'approved mileage allowance payments' (AMAPs). This applies even where business mileage exceeds 10,000 pa.

In general, non-cash vouchers are subject to NICs. However, the following are exempt.

- Childcare vouchers up to the amount exempt for income tax
- Vouchers for the use of sports and recreational facilities (where tax exempt)
- Vouchers for meals on the employer's premises
- Top up vouchers for pay as you go mobile phones where the provision of the phone itself is exempt from income tax
- Vouchers for eye tests and glasses for employees using VDUs
- Any other voucher which is exempt from income tax

5.2.3 Rates

The rates of contribution for 2024/25, and the income bands to which they apply, are set out in Whillans (p.113).

Employees pay main primary contributions of 8% of earnings between the primary threshold and the upper earnings limit (see exam focus point below). They also pay additional primary contributions of 2% on earnings above the upper earnings limit.

In 2024/25 the primary threshold is aligned with the personal allowance for income tax.

Employers pay secondary contributions, for employees aged 21 or over, of 13.8% on earnings above the secondary threshold of £9,100 or the equivalent monthly or weekly limit. There is no upper limit. **The employers' secondary contributions for employees aged under 21 are 13.8% of earnings above the upper secondary threshold of £50,270. The employers' secondary contributions for apprentices aged under 25 are 13.8% of earnings above the apprentice upper secondary threshold of £50,270.**

5.2.4 Earnings period

FAST FORWARD — NICs are based on earnings periods.

NICs are calculated in relation to an earnings period. This is the period to which earnings paid to an employee are deemed to relate. Where earnings are paid at regular intervals, the earnings period will generally be equated with the payment interval, for example a week or a month, and so calculations are usually performed on a weekly or monthly basis. Company directors have an annual earnings period, regardless of how they are paid.

Question — Primary and secondary contributions

Sally, aged 43, works for Red plc. She was paid £54,000 in 2024/25.

Show Sally's primary contributions for 2024/25 and the secondary contributions paid by Red plc, before taking account of the employment allowance (see below 5.2.5).

Answer

Sally

Primary contributions	£
Annual earnings	54,000
Annual primary threshold	12,570
Upper earnings annual limit	50,270
6/4/2024 – 5/4/2025	
£(50,270 – 12,570) = £37,700 × 8% (main) =	3,016
£(54,000 – 50,270) = £3,730 × 2% (additional) =	75
Total primary contributions	3,091

Red plc

	£
Secondary contributions	
£(54,000 – 9,100) = £44,900 × 13.8% =	6,196

PART A TAXATION OF INDIVIDUALS

When an employee is paid monthly or weekly and receives the same amount from their employer each earnings period throughout the tax year, the Class 1 primary contributions for that employee in that tax year can be calculated using the annual primary threshold and upper earnings limit (£12,570 and £50,270). Otherwise, the contributions must be calculated using the thresholds for the earnings period.

Directors' class 1 primary contributions must be calculated using the annual thresholds.

Question — Primary and secondary contributions

Aneeta earns a salary of £42,000 in 2024/25. She receives a bonus of £25,000 from her employer in June 2024.

Calculate Aneeta's class 1 primary contributions assuming:

(a) Aneeta is not a director
(b) Aneeta is a director

Answer

Aneeta is not a director

Primary contributions	£
Monthly earnings (£42,000 ÷ 12)	3,500
Monthly primary threshold (per Whillan's)	1,048
Upper earnings **monthly** limit	4,189

June 2024 primary contributions	
Aneeta receives £(3,500 + 25,000)	28,500
£(4,189-1,048) = £3,141 × 8%	251
£(28,500 – 4,189) = £24,311 × 2%	486
Total primary contributions for June 2024	737
For the other eleven months	
£(3,500 - 1,048) = £2,452 × 8% × 11 months	2,158
Total primary contributions for 2024/25	2,895

Aneeta is a director

Using annual thresholds and total earnings of £(42,000 + 25,000) = £67,000

	£
£(50,270 - 12,570) = £37,700 × 8%	3,016
£(67,000 - 50,270) = £16,730 × 2%	335
	3,351

5.2.5 Employment Allowance

> The Employment Allowance enables an employer to reduce its total Class 1 secondary contributions by up to £5,000 for 2024/25 (Whillans p.113).

An **employer can make a claim** to **reduce its total Class 1 secondary contributions** by an **Employment Allowance of up to £5,000** for 2024/25.

Some employers are **excluded employers** for the purposes of the Employment Allowance. These include **companies** where the **only employed earner for whom the company pays Class 1 secondary contributions is a director of the company.** For the purpose of the Taxation exam, assume all other employers qualify.

5.3 Class 1A NIC

Employers must pay Class 1A NIC at 13.8% on most taxable benefits. However, benefits are exempt if they are either:

- Within Class 1
- Included in a PAYE settlement agreement
- Otherwise not required to be reported on P11Ds

Childcare provision in an **employer-provided nursery or playscheme is wholly exempt** from Class 1A NICs. Provision of **other childcare**, for example where an employer contracts directly for places in a commercial nursery, **is exempt up to the limit allowable for income tax**.

The provision by an employer of fuel for use in an employee's own car does not lead to a Class 1A charge, instead there is a Class 1 charge (see above).

Class 1A contributions are collected annually in arrears. If the payment is made electronically, payment must reach HMRC's bank account no later than 22 July following the end of the tax year. Payment by cheque must reach HMRC no later than 19 July following the end of the tax year.

5.3.1 Example: Class 1A NICs

An employee is provided with benefits totaling £2,755 during 2024/25. The Class 1A contributions due from the employer are (£2,755 @ 13.8%) = £380.

There is no earnings threshold when calculating Class 1A contributions.

Employee contributions are not charged on benefits.

6 The PAYE system

Most tax in respect of employment income is deducted under the PAYE system. The objective of the PAYE system is to collect the correct amount of tax over the year. An employee's PAYE code is designed to ensure that allowances and additional tax costs are spread evenly over the year.

6.1 Introduction

6.1.1 Cash payments

The objective of the PAYE system is to deduct the correct amount of income tax and national insurance over the year. Its scope is very wide. It applies to most cash payments, other than reimbursed business expenses, and to certain non-cash payments.

In addition to wages and salaries, PAYE applies to round sum expense allowances and payments instead of benefits. It also applies to any readily convertible asset.

A readily convertible asset is any asset which can effectively be exchanged for cash. The amount subject to PAYE is the amount that would be taxed as employment income. This is usually the cost to the employer of providing the asset.

Tips paid direct to an employee are normally outside the PAYE system (although still assessable as employment income).

It is the employer's duty to deduct income tax and national insurance contributions from the pay of their employees, whether or not they have been directed to do so by HMRC. **If they fail to do this they** (or sometimes the employee) **must pay over the tax which should have been deducted and the employer may be subject to penalties.**

6.1.2 Benefits

It is not normally compulsory for PAYE to be operated on benefits; instead the employee's PAYE code is restricted (see below). However, employers may now opt to collect and pay to HMRC the tax on all benefits except employer provided living accommodation and interest free/low interest loans, through the PAYE system (this is known as 'voluntary payrolling').

Even without voluntary payrolling, PAYE must be applied to remuneration in the form of a taxable non-cash voucher if at the time it is provided:

(a) The voucher is capable of being exchanged for readily convertible assets; or
(b) The voucher can itself be sold, realised or traded.

PAYE must normally be operated on cash vouchers and on each occasion when a director/employee uses a credit-token (eg a credit card) to obtain money or goods which are readily convertible assets. However, a cash voucher or credit token which is used to defray expenses is not subject to PAYE.

6.2 How PAYE works

6.2.1 Operation of PAYE

Employers must report PAYE information to HMRC under the Real Time Information (RTI) system.

Under RTI, **an employer is required to submit information to HMRC electronically**. This can be done by:

(a) Using commercial payroll software.
(b) Using HMRC's Basic PAYE Tools software (designed for use by an employer who has up to nine employees).
(c) Using a payroll provider (such as an accountant or payroll bureau) to do the reporting on behalf of the employer.

The employer reports payroll information electronically to HMRC, on or before any day when the employer pays someone (ie in 'real time'). This report will normally be carried out by the payroll software (or the payroll provider) at the same time that the payments are calculated and is called **a Full Payment Submission (FPS)**. The FPS includes include details of:

(a) The amounts paid to employees.
(b) The value of benefits under voluntary payrolling (where an employer has opted for this process).
(c) Deductions made under PAYE such as income tax and national insurance contributions.
(d) Details of employees who have started employment or left employment since the last FPS.

The software works out the amount of PAYE tax to deduct on any particular pay day by using the employees' code numbers (see below). Tax is normally worked out on a cumulative basis. This means that with each payment of earnings the running total of tax paid is compared with tax due on total earnings to that date. The difference between the tax due and the tax paid is the tax to be deducted on that particular payday.

National insurance contributions are also calculated by the software in relation to the earnings period (see later in this Workbook).

6.3 Payment under the PAYE system

Under PAYE, income tax and national insurance is normally paid over to HMRC monthly, 17 days after the end of the tax month (if paid electronically) or 14 days after the end of the tax month (if paid by cheque). Large employers (with 250 or more employees) must make electronic payments. **A tax month runs from the 6th of one calendar month to the 5th of the following calendar month.** For example, for the tax month from 6 June 2024 to 5 July 2024, payment must be made by 22 July 2024 (electronically) or 19 July 2024 (cheque).

If an employer's average monthly payments under the PAYE system are less than £1,500, the employer may choose to pay quarterly, within 17 or 14 days (depending on the method of payment) of the end of each tax quarter. Tax quarters end on 5 July, 5 October, 5 January and 5 April. Payments can continue to be made quarterly during a tax year even if the monthly average reaches or exceeds £1,500, but a new estimate must be made and a new decision taken to pay quarterly at the start of each tax year.

6.4 PAYE codes

An employee is normally entitled to various allowances. Under the PAYE system, an amount reflecting the effect of a proportion of these allowances is set against their pay each pay day. To determine the amount to set against their pay the allowances are expressed in the form of a code.

An employee's code will often be L which is the tax code for people entitled to the basic personal allowance.

Other codes are used, for example, where there is a second source of income.

Generally, a tax code number is arrived at by deleting the last digit in the sum representing the employee's tax-free allowances. Every individual is entitled to a personal tax-free allowance of £12,570. The code number for an individual who is entitled to this, but no other allowance is 1257L.

The code number may also reflect other items. For example, **it will be restricted to reflect benefits, small amounts of untaxed income** and **unpaid tax on income from earlier years**. If an amount of tax is in point, it is necessary to gross up the tax in the code using the taxpayer's estimated marginal rate of income tax.

Question — PAYE codes

Adrian is a 40-year-old single man (suffix letter L) who earns £15,000 pa. He has benefits of £1,160 reflected in his PAYE code and his unpaid tax for 2022/23 was £58. Adrian is entitled to a tax-free personal allowance of £12,570 in 2024/25.

Adrian is a basic rate taxpayer.

What is Adrian's PAYE code for 2024/25?

Answer

	£
Personal allowance	12,570
Benefits	(1,160)
Unpaid tax £58 × 100/20	(290)
Available allowances	11,120

Adrian's PAYE code is 1112L.

Codes are determined and amended by HMRC. They are normally notified to the employer on a code list. The employer must act on the code notified until amended instructions are received from HMRC, even if the employee has appealed against the code.

When the payroll is run, an employee is generally given 1/52 or 1/12 of their tax-free allowances against each week's/month's pay. However, because of the cumulative nature of PAYE, if an employee is first paid in, say September, that month they will receive six months' allowances against their gross pay. In cases where the employee's previous PAYE history is not known, this could lead to under-deduction of tax. To avoid this, codes for the employees concerned must be operated on a 'week 1/month 1' basis, so that only 1/52 or 1/12 of the employee's allowances are available each week/month.

PART A TAXATION OF INDIVIDUALS

There are different bands and rates of tax for Scottish taxpayers. There are also Welsh rates of income tax (although in 2024/25 these do not differ from those of other non-Scottish UK taxpayers). Therefore, the tax codes for Scottish and Welsh taxpayers differ from those for other UK taxpayers.

The PAYE code for a **Welsh taxpayer** will be pre-fixed with the letter **C**.

The PAYE code for a **Scottish taxpayer** will be pre-fixed with the letter **S**.

Question

Welsh PAYE codes

Sian is a Welsh taxpayer (suffix letter L) who earns £40,000 pa. She has benefits of £4,950 reflected in her PAYE code. Sian is entitled to a tax-free personal allowance of £12,570 in 2024/25.

What is Sian's PAYE code for 2024/25?

Answer

	£
Personal allowance	12,570
Benefits	(4,950)
Available allowances	7,620

Sian's PAYE code is C762L

6.5 PAYE forms

FAST FORWARD

Employers must complete forms P60, P11D and P45 as appropriate. Form P60 is a year end return. A P45 is needed when an employee leaves. Form P11D records details of benefits.

At the end of each tax year, the employer must provide each employee with a form P60. This shows total taxable earnings for the year, tax deducted, code number, NI number and the employer's name and address. **The P60 must be provided by 31 May following the year of assessment.**

Following the end of each tax year, the employer must submit to HMRC by 6 July:

(a) **Forms P11D** (benefits for employees)
(b) **Forms P11D(b)** (return of Class 1A NICs)

HMRC only accepts original and amended forms P11D and P11D(b) submitted electronically, unless the employer is digitally exempt.

A copy of the form P11D must also be provided to the employee by 6 July. The details shown on the P11D include the full cash equivalent of all benefits, so that the employee may enter the details on their self-assessment tax return. Specific reference numbers for the entries on the P11D are given to assist with the preparation of the employee's self assessment tax return.

When an employee leaves, a form P45 (particulars of Employee Leaving) must be prepared. This form shows the employee's code and details of their income and tax paid to date. One of the parts of the form is the employee's personal copy. If the employee takes up a new employment, they must hand another part of the form P45 to the new employer. The details on the form are used by the new employer to calculate the PAYE due on the next payday.

6.6 Interest and penalties

Daily interest is charged on late payments of income tax and NICs under PAYE by taking the number of days by which a payment is late and applying the relevant late payment interest rate. HMRC make the charge after the end of the tax year.

Exam focus point

For the purposes of the exam, interest rates applied to late payments and overpayments of tax should be the most recent interest rate given in Whillan's tables (page 4 onwards) ie the interest rate from 22 August 2023. The interest rates under the harmonised interest regime is applicable to late payments under PAYE (page 4).

Late payment penalties are charged on PAYE amounts that are not paid in full and on time. Employers are not charged a penalty for the first late PAYE payment in a tax year, unless that payment is over six months late. The amounts of the penalties on subsequent late payments in the tax year depend on how much is late each time and the number of times payments are late in a tax year.

Number of defaults in the tax year	Penalty percentage applied to late payment (ignoring the first default of the tax year)
1 – 3	1%
4 – 6	2%
7 – 9	3%
10 or more	4%

Where a penalty has been imposed and the tax remains unpaid at 6 months, the further penalty is 5% of tax unpaid, with a further 5% if tax remains unpaid at 12 months, even if there is only one late payment in the year.

There are also penalties for making late returns under RTI.

The penalty depends on how many employees the PAYE scheme has:

Number of employees	Monthly penalty
1 to 9	£100
10 to 49	£200
50 to 249	£300
250 or more	£400

If the form is more than three months late, an additional penalty is due of 5% of the tax and NIC that should have been reported.

There are various relaxations for a late full payment submission (FPS). If you submit an FPS after the regular payday, you must provide a valid reason for the delay and select the appropriate "Late reporting reason" code when submitting the FPS.

Penalties for inaccurate returns are subject to the common penalty regime for errors (see later in this Workbook).

HMRC will not charge a penalty if:

- your FPS is late but all reported payments on the FPS are within 3 days of your employees' payday, however employers who regularly file after the payment date but within 3 days may be contacted or considered for a penalty.

- you're a new employer and you sent your first FPS within 30 days of paying an employee.

- it's your first failure in the tax year to send a report on time.

6.7 PAYE settlement agreements

PAYE settlement agreements (PSAs) are arrangements under which employers can make single payments to settle their employees' income tax liabilities on expense payments and benefits which are minor, irregular or where it would be impractical to operate PAYE (Whillans p.113).

6.8 Class 1B NIC

Employers must pay Class 1B NIC at 13.8% when they have entered into a PAYE Settlement Agreement (PSA). The payment date for Class 1B NIC is 19 October following the tax year or 22 October if paid electronically.

Class 1B NIC is charged on the grossed-up value of the benefits included within the PSA. The PSA comprises the benefit plus any income tax that the employer is paying on behalf of its employees.

6.9 Example: Staff party and Class 1B

A company holds a summer party for its 100 employees, at a cost of £180 per head. Of the 100 employees, 64 are basic rate taxpayers and 36 are higher rate taxpayers. As the benefit is not exempt, the company included it in a PSA. The total cost of the benefit is £18,000 and the resulting income tax liability was calculated as £7,200.

	£
Earnings within the PSA	18,000
Income tax payable (W1)	7,200
	25,200

Class 1B NICs	£
£25,200 × 13.8%	3,478

W1

Basic rate employees: 20/80 x £180 = £45 x 64 = £2,880
Higher rate employees: 40/60 x £180 = £120 x 36 = £4,320
£2,880 + £4,320 = £7,200 income tax

Chapter roundup

- General earnings are taxed in the year of receipt. Money earnings are usually treated as received on the earlier of the time payment is made and the time entitlement to payment arises. Non-money earnings are treated as received when provided.
- Employment involves a contract of service whereas self-employment involves a contract for services.
- Employees are taxed on benefits under the benefits code.
- The benefit in respect of employer-provided accommodation is its annual value. There is an additional benefit if the property cost over £75,000.
- Employees who have a company car are taxed on a % of the car's list price which depends on the level of the car's CO_2 emissions. The same % multiplied by £27,800 determines the benefit where private fuel is also provided. Authorised mileage allowances can be paid tax free to employees who use their own vehicle for business journeys.
- Taxable cheap loans are charged to tax on the difference between the official rate of interest and any interest paid by the employee.
- 20% of the value of assets made available for private use is taxable.
- Workplace childcare is an exempt benefit. Employer-supported childcare and childcare vouchers are exempt up to £55 per week. Maximum tax relief is limited to £11 per week (the equivalent of £55 × 20%).
- There is a residual charge for other benefits, usually equal to the cost of the benefits.
- Some benefits are exempt from tax such as removal expenses (subject to certain limits).
- To be deductible, expenses must be for qualifying travel or wholly, exclusively and necessarily incurred.
- National Insurance contributions are divided into four classes.
- Employees pay Class 1 NICs. Employees pay the main primary rate between the primary earnings threshold and upper earnings limit and the additional rate on earnings above the upper earnings limit. Employers pay Class 1 and Class 1A NICs. For employers, there is no upper earnings limit. There is a different employers Class 1 threshold where employees are less than 21 years old and apprentices.
- NICs are based on earnings periods.
- The Employment Allowance enables an employer to reduce its total Class 1 secondary contributions by up to £5,000.
- Most tax in respect of employment income is deducted under the PAYE system. The objective of the PAYE system is to collect the correct amount of tax over the year. An employee's PAYE code is designed to ensure that allowances etc are given evenly over the year.
- Employers must complete forms P60, P11D and P45 as appropriate. Form P60 is a year end return. A P45 is needed when an employee leaves. Form P11D records details of benefits.

PART A   TAXATION OF INDIVIDUALS

Quick quiz

1. Ben is an employee paid £14,000 per annum. For the year ended 31 December 2024, he was paid a £5,000 bonus on 1 May 2025. He was paid a similar bonus of £3,000 on 1 May 2024 based on the year ended 31 December 2023 results. How much is Ben's taxable income for 2024/25? Ben is not a director.

2. Which type of accommodation does not give rise to a taxable benefit?

3. Josh was provided with a brand new company car on 1 August 2025. It cost £25,000 and has a CO_2 emission of 108g/km. Josh used the car 60% for business use as a sales representative. The company paid for Josh's private diesel for use in the car, and the car does not meet the RDE2 standard. What was Josh's benefit(s) in respect of the car in 2024/25?

4. When may an employee who is provided with a fuel by their employer avoid a fuel benefit?

5. To what extent are removal expenses paid for by an employer taxable?

6. When may travel expenses be deducted from the taxable earnings of an employee?

7. Lucy is provided with a mobile phone by her employer costing £350 per annum. What is taxable on Lucy?

8. What is the employment allowance?

9. On which type of income and by whom are Class 1A NICs paid?

Answers to quick quiz

1. £17,000 (£14,000 + £3,000 bonus paid in 2024/25)

2. Job-related accommodation

3. £10,060 (5,000 + 5,060)

    Car: £25,000 × 30%(26 + 4)

    £7,500 for 12m

    £7,500 × 8/12

    Car: £5,000

    Fuel: £27,800 × 30% × 8/12 = £5,560

4. There is no fuel benefit if:
    (a) All the fuel provided was made available only for business travel; or
    (b) The full cost of any fuel provided for private use was completely reimbursed by the employee.

5. The first £8,000 of removal expenses are exempt if:
    (1) The employee does not already live within a reasonable daily travelling distance of their new place of employment, but will do so after moving; and
    (2) The expenses are incurred or the benefits provided by the end of the tax year following the tax year of the start of employment at the new location.

    Any excess is taxable.

6. An employee can deduct travel costs incurred in travelling in the performance of their duties or in travelling to a place which they must attend in the performance of their duties (other than the normal place of work).

7. Nothing. The provision of one mobile phone for private use is an exempt benefit.

8. The employment allowance is a reduction in an employer's Class 1 secondary contributions up to £5,000 per tax year.

9. Class 1A NICs are paid by employers on taxable benefits.

PART A TAXATION OF INDIVIDUALS

Trade profits

Topic list
1 The badges of trade
2 The computation of trade profits
3 Basis periods
4 National Insurance

Introduction

In previous chapters, we have looked at the income tax computation, property and investment income and employment income. We are now going to look at the taxation of income received by unincorporated businesses. We calculate a business's profit as if it were a separate entity (the separate entity concept familiar to you from basic bookkeeping) but, as an unincorporated business has no legal existence separate from its proprietor, we cannot tax it separately. We have to feed its profit into the proprietor's personal tax computation.

In this chapter, we look at the computation and taxation of profits. Standard rules on the computation of profits are used instead of individual traders' accounting policies, so as to ensure fairness. We also need special rules, the basis period rules, to link the profits of periods of account to the personal computations of tax years.

Finally, we see how national insurance contributions apply to the self-employed.

In the next chapters, we study the allowances available for capital expenditure and then we look at losses and partnerships.

Exam guide

In the exam, you may be asked to calculate taxable trading profits. To be able to do this you need a full understanding of the rules for calculating taxable trade profits and allocating them to tax years. Cases referred to in this chapter are for you to understand their conclusions, you will not be tested on case names.

1 The badges of trade

FAST FORWARD

The badges of trade can be used to decide whether or not a trade exists.

1.1 Introduction

Before a tax charge can be imposed, it is necessary to establish the existence of a trade.

Key term

A trade is defined in the legislation only in an unhelpful manner as including every trade, manufacture, adventure or concern in the nature of a trade. It has therefore been left to the courts to provide guidance. This guidance is often summarised in a collection of principles known as the **'badges of trade'**. These are set out below. **Profits from professions and vocations are taxed in the same way as profits from a trade.**

1.2 The subject matter

Whether a person is trading or not may sometimes be decided by examining the subject matter of the transaction. Some assets are commonly held as investments for their intrinsic value: an individual buying some shares or a painting may do so in order to enjoy the income from the shares or to enjoy the work of art. A subsequent disposal may produce a gain of a capital nature rather than a trade profit. But **where the subject matter of a transaction is such as would not be held as an investment** (for example 34m yards of aircraft linen (*Martin v Lowry 1927*) or 1m rolls of toilet paper (*Rutledge v CIR 1929*)), **it is presumed that any profit on resale is a trade profit.**

1.3 The frequency of transactions

Transactions which may, in isolation, be of a capital nature will be interpreted as trading transactions where their **frequency indicates the carrying on of a trade**. It was decided that whereas normally the purchase of a mill-owning company and the subsequent stripping of its assets might be a capital transaction, where the taxpayer was embarking on the same exercise for the fourth time they must be carrying on a trade (*Pickford v Quirke 1927*).

1.4 Existence of similar trading transactions or interests

If there is an **existing trade**, then a **similarity to the transaction which is being considered** may point to that transaction having a trading character. For example, a builder who builds and sells a number of houses may be held to be trading even if they retain one or more houses for longer than usual and claims that they were held as an investment (*Harvey v Caulcott 1952*).

1.5 The length of ownership

The courts may infer 'adventures in the nature of trade' where items purchased are sold soon afterwards.

1.6 The organisation of the activity as a trade

The courts may infer that a trade is being carried on if the transactions are **carried out in the same manner as someone who is unquestionably trading**. For example, an individual who bought a consignment of whiskey and then sold it through an agent, in the same way as others who were carrying on a trade, was also held to be trading (*CIR v Fraser 1942*). On the other hand, if an asset has to be sold in order to raise funds in an emergency, this is less likely to be treated as trading.

1.7 Supplementary work and marketing

When work is done to make an asset more marketable, or steps are taken to find purchasers, the courts will be more ready to ascribe a trading motive. When a group of accountants bought, blended and recasked a quantity of brandy they were held to be taxable on a trade profit when the brandy was later sold (*Cape Brandy Syndicate v CIR 1921*).

1.8 A profit motive

The absence of a profit motive will not necessarily preclude a tax charge as trading income, but its presence is a strong indication that a person is trading. The purchase and resale of £20,000 worth of silver bullion by the comedian Norman Wisdom, as a hedge against devaluation, was held to be a trading transaction (*Wisdom v Chamberlain 1969*).

1.9 The way in which the asset sold was acquired

If goods are acquired deliberately, trading may be indicated. If goods are acquired unintentionally, for example by gift or inheritance, their later sale is unlikely to be trading.

1.10 Method of finance

If the **purchaser has to borrow money to buy an asset such that they have to sell that asset quickly to repay the loan**, it may be inferred that trading was taking place. This was a factor in the *Wisdom v Chamberlain* case as Mr Wisdom financed his purchases by loans at a high rate of interest. It was clear that he had to sell the silver bullion quickly in order to repay the loan and prevent the interest charges becoming too onerous. On the other hand, taking out a long term loan to buy an asset (such as a mortgage on a house) would not usually indicate that trading is being carried on.

1.11 The taxpayer's intentions

Where a transaction is clearly trading on objective criteria, **the taxpayer's intentions are irrelevant**. If, however, a transaction has (objectively) a dual purpose, the taxpayer's intentions may be taken into account. An example of a transaction with a dual purpose is the acquisition of a site partly as premises from which to conduct another trade, and partly with a view to the possible development and resale of the site. This test is not one of the traditional badges of trade but it may be just as important.

Exam focus point

If, on applying the badges of trade, HMRC do not conclude that income is 'trade income' then they can potentially treat it as other income or a capital gain. Remember that capital gains are taxable at a maximum rate of 24% whereas income is taxed at a maximum rate of 45%. HMRC will therefore be looking very carefully to see if a transaction really results in a capital gain or whether it is really a trade receipt.

2 The computation of trade profits

> **FAST FORWARD**
>
> There are two methods of calculating taxable trading profits. The cash basis and the accruals basis. The cash basis is the default method for unincorporated businesses (sole traders and partnerships).

2.1 Two methods of calculating taxable trading profits

There are two bases for calculating taxable trading profits of a sole trader or a partnership:

- The cash basis.
- The accruals basis (section 2.9)

From 2024/25, the cash basis is used as the default method for unincorporated trades (sole traders and partnerships), unless the trader(s) decide to use the accruals basis.

2.2 Cash basis of accounting for small businesses

2.2.1 Introduction

> **FAST FORWARD**
>
> From 2024/25, the default basis for calculating a sole trader's taxable trading profit is the cash basis.

Usually, businesses prepare accounts using generally accepted accounting practice for tax purposes. In particular, this means that **income and expenses are dealt with on an accruals basis**. This is referred to as **'accruals basis'** in this section.

From 2024/25, **the cash basis is the default method for calculating taxable trading profits of unincorporated businesses.**

Exam focus point

In any examination question involving an unincorporated business, it should be assumed that **the cash basis is to be used unless you are told the trader has elected to use the accruals basis.**

2.2.2 Which businesses can use the cash basis?

The cash basis can only be used by unincorporated businesses (sole traders and partnerships). It cannot be used by companies.

The cash basis is **the default method, but an election can be made by the trader to use the accruals accounting basis.** The election is generally effective for the tax year for which it is made and all subsequent tax years. It is made by ticking the opt-out box on the self-assessment return.

2.2.3 Calculation of taxable profits under the cash basis

The taxable trading profits under the cash basis are calculated as:

(a) **Cash receipts;** less
(b) **Deductible business expenses actually paid in the period.**

2.2.4 Cash receipts under the cash basis

Cash receipts include **all amounts received relating to the business** including **cash and card receipts**.

2.2.5 Cash payments

Under the cash basis, **business expenses are deductible when they are paid**. Receipts and payments do not need to be matched with the accounting period.

Question — The cash basis

On 1 January 2024, Kirsty had outstanding trade receivables of £23,000.

In the year ended 31 December 2024, she made sales of £75,000. £3,000 of which were written off as irrecoverable. On 31 December 2024, Kirsty's trade receivables balance was £11,000.

Kirsty did not have any outstanding trade payables at the start or end of the period of account. She had paid expenses of £40,000 relating wholly and exclusively to her trade. This did not include a buildings insurance premium of £6,500, that she paid on 25 November 2024, relating to the 12 months up to 30 November 2025.

Required

Calculate Kirsty's taxable trading profit for the year ended 31 December 2024 using the cash basis.

Answer

	£
Sales receipts (W1)	84,000
Expenses paid (W2)	(46,500)
Taxable trading profit in year ended 31 December 2024	37,500

W1	Sales receipts	£
	Sales invoices raised in the year to December 2024	75,000
	Sales invoices issued in 2024, received in 2025	(11,000)
	Sales invoices issued in 2023, received in 2024	23,000
	less irrecoverable debts	(3,000)
	Sales receipts in 2024	84,000

W2	Expenses paid	£
	Expenses not including insurance	40,000
	Insurance premium paid in 2024	6,500
		46,500

Despite the fact that most of the insurance premium related to the following accounting period, it is deductible from profits in the year ended 31 December 2024 because that is the period in which Kirsty paid it.

2.2.6 Plant and machinery

Although expenditure on plant and machinery is capital expenditure, there are special rules regarding the deductibility of expenditure on plant and machinery when using both the cash basis and the accruals basis.

Plant and machinery includes such items that perform a function within the trade, but not a setting for the trade. So a manufacturing or maintenance equipment would be plant and machinery but a factory, warehouse or office would not. In the cash basis, business expenses for the cash basis of accounting **include capital expenditure on plant and machinery** (except motor cars). **Other capital expenses are not business expenses eg purchase of land, motor cars, and legal fees on such purchases**.

Similarly amounts *received* from the **sale of plant and machinery**, other than on the sale of motor cars would be treated as a trading receipt. We look at the definition of plant and machinery when we look at capital allowances later in this Workbook.

Receipts from the sale of motor cars and capital assets which are not classed as plant and machinery (eg land) are not taxable receipts. We will see how plant and machinery is treated in the accruals basis, as well as further details relevant to the cash basis in chapter 6

2.3 Non-deductible expenditure

Certain expenses are specifically disallowed by the legislation or they are allowed only under certain circumstances. In this section the non-deductible expenditure is discussed in detail. Where different treatment is applied under the accruals basis, that is discussed later in the chapter.

2.3.1 Expenditure not wholly and exclusively for the purposes of the trade

Expenditure is not deductible if it is not for trade purposes (the remoteness test) or if it reflects more than one purpose (the duality test). The private proportion of payments for motoring expenses, rent, heat and light and telephone expenses of a proprietor is not deductible. If an exact apportionment is possible relief is given on the business element. Where the payments are to or on behalf of employees, the full amounts are deductible but the employees are taxed under the benefits code (see earlier in this Workbook).

The remoteness test is illustrated by the following cases:

- *Strong & Co of Romsey Ltd v Woodifield 1906*

    A customer injured by a falling chimney when sleeping in an inn owned by a brewery claimed compensation from the company. The compensation was not deductible: 'the loss sustained by the appellant was not really incidental to their trade as innkeepers and fell upon them in their character not of innkeepers but of householders'.

- *Bamford v ATA Advertising Ltd 1972*

    A director misappropriated £15,000. The loss was not allowable: 'the loss is not, as in the case of a dishonest shop assistant, an incident of the company's trading activities. It arises altogether outside such activities'.

- Expenditure which is wholly and exclusively to benefit the trades of several companies (for example, in a group) but is not wholly and exclusively to benefit the trade of one specific company is not deductible (*Vodafone Cellular Ltd and others v Shaw 1995*).

- *McKnight (HMIT) v Sheppard 1999* concerned expenses incurred by a stockbroker in defending allegations of infringements of Stock Exchange regulations. It was found that the expenditure was incurred to prevent the destruction of the taxpayer's business and that as the expenditure was incurred for business purposes it was deductible. It was also found that although the expenditure had the effect of preserving the taxpayer's reputation, that was not its purpose, so there was no duality of purpose.

The **duality test** is illustrated by the following cases:

- *Caillebotte v Quinn 1975*

    A self-employed carpenter spent an average of 40p per day when obliged to buy lunch away from home but just 10p when he lunched at home. He claimed the excess 30p. It was decided that the payment had a dual purpose and was not deductible: a taxpayer 'must eat to live not eat to work'.

- *Mallalieu v Drummond 1983*

    Expenditure by a barrister on black clothing to be worn in court (and on its cleaning and repair) was not deductible. The expenditure was for the dual purpose of enabling the barrister to be warmly and properly clad as well as meeting her professional requirements.

- *McLaren v Mumford 1996*

    A publican traded from a public house which had residential accommodation above it. He was obliged to live at the public house but he also had another house which he visited regularly. It was held that the private element of the expenditure incurred at the public house on electricity, rent, gas, etc was not incurred for the purpose of earning profits, but for serving the non-business purpose of satisfying the publican's ordinary human needs. The expenditure, therefore had a dual purpose and was disallowed.

However, the cost of overnight accommodation when on a business trip may be deductible and reasonable expenditure on an evening meal and breakfast in conjunction with such accommodation is then also deductible.

2.3.2 Capital expenditure

Under the cash basis, depreciation and amortisation of non-current assets are not deductible. They are not cash expenses.

Although expenditure on plant and machinery is a deductible trading expense under the cash basis, **expenditure on cars and land and buildings is not allowable expenditure so cannot be deducted from profit.**

Sales proceeds for the disposal of cars and buildings are not taxable trading receipts.

Expenditure on the repair and maintenance of capital assets (including cars and land & buildings) is deductible as a trading expense.

The most contentious items of expenditure will often be repairs (revenue expenditure) and improvements (capital expenditure).

- The cost of restoration of an asset by, for instance, replacing a subsidiary part of the asset is revenue expenditure. Expenditure on a new factory chimney replacement was allowable since the chimney was a subsidiary part of the factory (*Samuel Jones & Co (Devondale) Ltd v CIR 1951*). However, in another case a football club demolished a spectators' stand and replaced it with a modern equivalent. This was held not to be repair, since repair is the restoration by renewal or replacement of subsidiary parts of a larger entity, and the stand formed a distinct and *separate* part of the club (*Brown v Burnley Football and Athletic Co Ltd 1980*).

- The cost of initial repairs to improve an asset recently acquired to make it fit to earn profits is disallowable capital expenditure. In *Law Shipping Co Ltd v CIR 1923* the taxpayer failed to obtain relief for expenditure on making a newly bought ship seaworthy prior to using it.

- The cost of initial repairs to remedy normal wear and tear of recently acquired assets is allowable. *Odeon Associated Theatres Ltd v Jones 1971* can be contrasted with the *Law Shipping* judgement. Odeon were allowed to charge expenditure incurred on improving the state of recently acquired cinemas.

Other examples to note include:

- A one-off payment made by a hotel owner to terminate an agreement for the management of a hotel was held to be revenue rather than capital expenditure in *Croydon Hotel & Leisure Co v Bowen 1996*. The payment did not affect the whole structure of the taxpayer's business; it merely enabled it to be run more efficiently.

- A one-off payment to remove a threat to the taxpayer's business was also held to be revenue rather than capital expenditure in *Lawson v Johnson Matthey plc 1992*.

- An initial payment for a franchise (as opposed to regular fees) is capital and not deductible.

2.3.3 Legal and professional charges

Legal and professional charges relating to capital or non-trade items are not deductible. These include charges incurred in acquiring new capital assets or legal rights, issuing shares, drawing up partnership agreements and litigating disputes over the terms of a partnership agreement.

Charges are deductible if they relate directly to trading. Deductible items include:

- Legal and professional charges incurred defending the taxpayer's title to fixed assets;
- Charges connected with an action for breach of contract;
- Expenses of the **renewal** (not the original grant) of a lease for less than 50 years;
- Charges for trade debt collection; and
- Normal charges for preparing accounts/assisting with the self-assessment of tax liabilities.

Accountancy expenses arising out of an enquiry into the accounts information in a particular year's return are not allowed where the enquiry reveals discrepancies and additional liabilities for the year of enquiry, or any earlier year, which arise as a result of negligent or fraudulent conduct.

Where, however, the enquiry results in no addition to profits, or an adjustment to the profits for the year of enquiry only and that assessment does not arise as a result of negligent or fraudulent conduct, the additional accountancy expenses are allowable.

2.3.4 Entertaining and gifts

The general rule is that expenditure on entertaining and gifts is non-deductible. This applies to amounts reimbursed to employees for specific entertaining expenses and gifts, and to round sum allowances which are exclusively for meeting such expenses. There is no distinction between UK and overseas customer entertaining for income tax and corporation tax purposes (a different rule applies for value added tax (VAT)).

There are specific exceptions to the general rule:

- **Entertaining for and gifts to employees are normally deductible** although where gifts are made, or the entertainment is excessive, a charge to tax may arise on the employee under the benefits legislation.

- **Gifts to customers not costing more than £50 per done per year are allowed if they carry a conspicuous advertisement for the business and are not food, drink, tobacco or vouchers exchangeable for goods.**

- Gifts to charities may also be allowed although many will fall foul of the 'wholly and exclusively' rule above. If a gift aid declaration is made in respect of a gift, tax relief will be given under the gift aid scheme, not as a trading expense. If a qualifying charitable donation is made by a company, it will be given tax relief by deduction from total profits (see later in this Workbook).

2.3.5 Subscriptions and donations

The general 'wholly and exclusively' rule determines the deductibility of expenses. Subscriptions and donations are not deductible unless the expenditure is for the benefit of the trade. The following are the main types of subscriptions and donations you may meet and their correct treatments.

(a) Trade subscriptions (such as to a professional or trade association) are generally deductible.

(b) Charitable donations are deductible only if they are small and to local charities. Tax relief may be available for donations under the gift aid scheme. In the latter case they are not a deductible trading expense.

(c) Political subscriptions and donations are generally not deductible.

(d) Where a donation represents the most effective commercial way of disposing of stock (for example, where it would not be commercially effective to sell surplus perishable food), the donation can be treated as for the benefit of the trade and the disposal proceeds taken as £Nil. In other cases, the amount credited to the accounts in respect of a donation of stock should be its market value.

2.3.6 Interest payments

Interest which is allowed as deductible interest (see earlier in this Workbook) is not also allowed as a trading expense.

2.3.7 Appropriations

Salary, interest on capital or drawings paid to the trader are not deductible.

2.3.8 National insurance contributions

No deduction is allowed for any national insurance contributions **except for employer's contributions**. For the purpose of your exam, these are Class 1 secondary contributions and Class 1A and Class 1B contributions. Class 4 National insurance contributions for self-employed individuals are dealt with later in this chapter.

2.3.9 Penalties and interest on tax

Penalties and interest on late paid tax are not allowed as a trading expense. Tax includes income tax, capital gains tax and VAT.

2.3.10 Crime-related payments

A payment is not deductible if making it constitutes an offence by the payer. This covers protection money paid to terrorists, bribes and similar payments made overseas which would be criminal payments if they were made in the UK. Statute also prevents any deduction for payments made in response to blackmail or extortion.

2.4 Deductible expenditure

Most expenses will be deductible under the general rule that expenses incurred wholly and exclusively for the purpose of the trade are not disallowed. Some expenses which might otherwise be disallowed under the 'wholly or exclusively' rule, or under one or other of the specific rules discussed above are, however, specifically allowed by the legislation. These are covered in paragraphs 2.4.1–2.4.10.

2.4.1 Pre-trading expenditure

Expenditure incurred before the commencement of trade is deductible, if it is incurred within seven years of the start of trade and it is of a type that would have been deductible had the trade already started. **It is treated as a trading expense incurred on the first day of trading.**

2.4.2 Incidental costs of obtaining finance

Incidental costs of obtaining loan finance, or of attempting to obtain or redeeming it, are deductible other than a discount on issue or a premium on redemption (which are really alternatives to paying interest). This deduction for incidental costs does not apply to companies because they obtain a deduction for the costs of borrowing in a different way. We will look at companies later in this Workbook.

2.4.3 Restrictive covenants

When an employee leaves an employment, they may accept a limitation on their future activities in return for a payment. **Provided the employee is taxed on the payment as employment income** (see earlier in this Workbook), **the payment is a deductible trading expense.**

2.4.4 Secondments

The **costs of seconding employees to charities or educational establishments are deductible.**

2.4.5 Contributions to agent's expenses

Many employers run payroll giving schemes for their employees. **Any payments made to the agent who administers the scheme towards running expenses are deductible.**

2.4.6 Counselling and retraining expenses

Expenditure on providing counselling and retraining for leaving employees is allowable.

2.4.7 Redundancy

Redundancy payments made when a trade ends are deductible on the earlier of the day of payment and the last day of trading. If the trade does not end, they can be deducted as soon as they are provided for, so long as the redundancy was decided on within the period of account, the provision is accurately calculated and the payments are made within nine months of the end of the period of account. **The deduction extends to additional payments of up to three times the amount of the redundancy pay on cessation of trade.**

2.4.8 Personal security expenses

If there is a particular security threat to the trader because of the nature of the trade, **expenditure on personal security is allowable.**

2.4.9 Patents, trademarks and copyrights

The costs of **registering patents and trademarks** are deductible for trades only (not professions or vocations). Copyright arises automatically and so does not have to be registered. **Patent royalties and copyright royalties paid in connection with a trade are deductible as trading expenses.**

2.4.10 Goods for own use

When a trader purchases goods for use in the business (e.g. goods intended for resale) but then takes goods for their own personal use instead, the trader must not deduct the cost of the goods.

Note. The treatment for this is different if the trader elects to use the accruals basis.

2.4.11 Other items

Here is a list of various other items that you may meet.

Item	Treatment	Comment
Educational courses for staff	Allow	–
Educational courses for trader	Allow	If to update existing knowledge or skills, not if to acquire new knowledge or skills
Removal expenses (to new business premises)	Allow	Only if not an expansionary move
Travelling expenses to the trader's place of business	Disallow	*Ricketts v Colquhoun 1925*: unless an itinerant trader (*Horton v Young 1971*)
Compensation for loss of office and ex gratia payments	Allow	If for benefit of trade: *Mitchell v B W Noble Ltd 1927*
Pension contributions (to schemes for employees and company directors)	Allow	Special contributions may be spread over the year of payment and future years

Item	Treatment	Comment
Parking fines	Allow	For employees using their employer's cars on business
	Disallow	For proprietors/directors
Damages paid	Allow	If not too remote from trade: *Strong and Co v Woodifield 1906*
Preparation and restoration of waste disposal sites	Allow	Spread preparation expenditure over period of use of site. Pre-trading expenditure is treated as incurred on the first day of trading. Allow restoration expenditure in period of expenditure.
Dividends on trade investments	Not taxable as trade income	Taxed as savings income
Rental income from letting part of premises	Not taxable as trade income	Taxed as income of a UK property business unless it is the letting of surplus business accommodation

2.5 Trade income

There are also statutory rules governing whether certain receipts are taxable or not. These are discussed in 2.6.1 to 2.6.5.

2.5.1 Takeover of trade

If a trader takes over a trade from a previous owner, then if they receive any amounts from that trade which related to a period before the takeover they must be brought into account unless the previous owner has already done so.

2.5.2 Insurance receipts

Insurance receipts which are revenue in nature, such as for loss of profits, are trading receipts. Otherwise the receipt must be brought in as trade income if, and to the extent that, any deduction has been claimed for the expense that the receipt is intended to cover.

2.5.3 Gifts of trading stock/equipment to educational establishments or schools

When a business makes a gift of equipment manufactured, sold or used in the course of its trade to an educational establishment or for a charitable purpose, nothing need be brought into account as a trading receipt or (if capital allowances had been obtained on the asset) as disposal proceeds, so full relief is obtained for the cost.

2.6 Excluded income

2.6.1 Income taxed in another way

Although the accounts may include other income, such as interest, such income is not trade income. It will instead be taxed under the specific rules for that type of income, such as the rules for savings income. It is therefore excluded from trade profits.

Certain types of income are specifically exempt from tax, and should be excluded from trade profits.

2.7 Trading allowance

Sole traders with trading receipts that do not exceed £1,000 will have trading profits of nil and there will be no charge to income tax (full relief).

Trading receipts are those calculated using either the accruals or cash basis and can also include miscellaneous income such as income from a one-off project. Both the miscellaneous income and the trading income will need to be added together for the purposes of the £1,000 limit.

A trader can elect for the full relief not to apply, for example if deducting actual expenses under the cash or accruals basis would result in a loss. The election must be made by the first anniversary of the normal self-assessment filing date for the tax year.

Sole traders with receipts that do exceed £1,000 have a choice. In order to work out their taxable trading income, they can either:

- Deduct the £1,000 trading allowance; or
- Deduct actual expenses

Sole traders cannot deduct both the allowance and the actual expenses.

If the trader wants to use the trading allowance they will make an election in their tax return to that effect. This is advantageous if deductible expenses are less than £1,000. The trading allowance does not apply to trading profits from a partnership or a company.

Question
Trading allowance

The following traders have trading receipts and expenses as follows:

	Trading receipts £	Deductible expenses £
Karel	2,500	1,300
The Dennie & Lou partnership	925	875
Frederick	5,000	625
Stellan Limited	10,000	970

Required

State whether each trader can use the cash basis and/or the trading allowance.

If the trading allowance is possible, calculate the taxable trading income for the trader based on the receipts and expenses provided.

Answer

Karel

Karel is a sole trader so will use the cash basis by default unless he elects to use the accruals basis. He can also use the trading allowance. In this period, he will not because he has less taxable trading profit if he deducts the actual expenses.

Karel's trading income is therefore £2,500 - £1,300 = £1,200.

The Dennie & Lou partnership

The Dennie & Lou partnership is an unincorporated business so will use the cash basis as a default. However, the trading allowance is not available to partnerships.

Frederick

Frederick is a sole trader so will use the cash basis as a default unless he elects to use the accruals basis. He can also deduct the trading allowance in full as this gives a lower taxable profit than merely deducting his actual expenses.

Frederick's taxable trading profit is therefore: £5,000 – £1,000 = £4,000.

Stellan Limited

Stellan Limited is a company so cannot use the cash basis. For the same reason, it cannot deduct the trading allowance either.

2.8 Fixed rate expenses

2.8.1 Introduction

FAST FORWARD

Fixed rate expenses can be used in relation to expenditure on motor vehicles, the use of a trader's home for business purposes, and business premises partly used as the trader's home.

Any unincorporated business, including partnerships may, for tax purposes, **deduct certain business expenses at a fixed rate** (prescribed in legislation) rather than on the usual basis of actual expenditure incurred. **Fixed rate deductions can be made both by businesses which use the normal accruals method, and those which use the cash basis of accounting** described above.

The fixed rate deductions are **optional** but are intended to simplify the process for claiming a tax deduction for certain types of expenditure, where the calculation of allowable expenditure can be quite complex eg business use of home premises.

Exam focus point

You will be told in an exam question whether the business makes deductions on a fixed rate basis. Otherwise, you should assume that these do not apply, and you should make the usual deductions for the actual expenditure incurred.

Fixed rate expenses can be deducted in respect of:

(a) Expenditure on **motor vehicles**
(b) Use of **home for business** purposes
(c) **Business premises partly used as the trader's home**

2.8.2 Expenditure on motor vehicles

A sole trader who incurs expenditure on the acquisition, lease, hire or use of a **car, motor cycle or goods vehicle** (such as a van) used in their trade, may make a deduction in respect of the expenditure incurred using **approved mileage allowances**.

The allowable rates per business mile travelled in a period are **45p for the first 10,000 miles and 25p thereafter for a car or goods vehicle** and **24p per mile for a motorcycle**. These are the same rates we saw in relation to employment income for an employee using their own vehicle for business purposes.

Exam focus point

These rates are set out in Whillans tax tables on page 100.

The fixed rate deduction cannot be made if the trader has previously claimed capital allowances in respect of that vehicle. Nor can it be claimed if it is a goods vehicle or motor cycle and the trader made a deduction under the cash basis when acquiring the vehicle.

If such a fixed rate deduction is made, then no other deduction can be made in respect of the expenditure on the vehicle in that period (for example capital allowances or actual running or maintenance costs). In addition, once adopted, the fixed rate method must be used in every future period that that vehicle is used for business purposes. However, a trader does not have to use the same basis for each vehicle used in the business.

2.8.3 Use of home for business purposes

A fixed rate monthly deduction can be claimed where a trader or their employee(s) **use part of the trader's home for business purposes**.

This is **significantly simpler than the normal deduction rules whereby an apportionment of actual household costs** eg heating, lighting, rent, repairs etc between business and private use must be performed. However, the trader still has the **option to use the apportionment method** if it is beneficial.

The fixed rate deduction can only be used if the trader (or their employee(s)) work at least 25 hours per month from the trader's home.

The hours worked must be wholly and exclusively for the purposes of the trade either by the sole trader or their employee(s).

Exam focus point

> These rates are set out in Whillans tax tables on page 100.

2.8.4 Business premises partly used as the trader's home

A fixed rate monthly adjustment can be made where a sole trader uses part of their business premises as their home eg where a sole trader runs a guesthouse and also lives in it. This fixed rate method is different because **the adjustment is deducted from (ie reduces) the actual allowable business premises costs to reflect the private portion of household costs** including food and utilities (eg heat and light). It does not include mortgage interest, rent of the premises, council tax or rates: apportionment of these expenses must be made based on the extent of the private occupation of the premises.

Again, this is a **much simpler method of adjusting for private expenditure** than the usual apportionment of actual costs for business and private use. However, this apportionment method may still be used if beneficial.

The monthly fixed rate adjustment **depends on how many people use the business premises each month as a private home**. Remember that this is the amount by which the allowable costs are reduced, so **if all costs relating to the business premises have been deducted in the accounts, the monthly adjustment must be added back** when calculating the tax adjusted trading profits of the business.

Exam focus point

> These rates are set out in Whillans tax tables on page 100.
> Be careful when using these amounts – they are not the expense itself but the disallowable amount.

2.9 Example of cash basis and fixed rate expenses

Larry started trading as an interior designer on 6 April 2024. The following information is relevant for the year to 5 April 2025.

Revenue was £65,000 of which £8,000 was owed as receivables at 5 April 2025.

A motor car was acquired on 6 April 2024 for £15,000. Larry drove 10,000 miles in the car during the year to 5 April 2025 of which 3,000 miles were for private journeys. The car qualifies for a capital allowance of £1,890, after taking account of private use. The motoring costs were £2,000.

Machinery was acquired on 1 May 2024 for £4,000. The machinery qualifies for a capital allowance of £4,000.

Other allowable expenses were £12,000 of which £1,000 was owed as payables at 5 April 2025.

If Larry uses the cash basis of accounting and fixed rate expenses, his trading profit will be calculated as follows:

	£	£
Revenue (cash received £65,000 – £8,000)		57,000
Less FRM on car 7,000 × 45p	3,150	
cost of machinery	4,000	
other allowable expenses (cash paid £12,000 – £1,000)	11,000	
		(18,150)
Taxable trading profit		38,850

If Larry uses the accruals accounting basis and does not use fixed rate expenses, his trading profit will be calculated as follows:

	£	£
Revenue (accruals)		65,000
Less: capital allowance on motor car	1,890	
business motoring expenses £2,000 × 7/10	1,400	
capital allowance on machinery	4,000	
other allowable expenses (accruals)	12,000	
		(19,290)
Taxable trading profit		45,710

2.10 The accruals basis and the adjustment of profits

Sole traders and partnerships may elect to use the accruals basis rather than the cash basis.

Companies must use the accruals basis.

This means that the statement of profit or loss is the starting point for calculating the taxable trading profit, specifically the net profit or loss figure. Then the net profit or loss is adjusted by adding back disallowable expenditure and deducting profits which have been included in the accounts but which are not taxed as trading income.

Here is an illustrative adjustment of a statement of profit or loss used in the accruals basis:

	£	£
Net profit		140,000
Add: expenditure charged in the accounts which is not deductible from trading profits	50,000	
income taxable as trading profits which has not been included in the accounts	30,000	
		80,000
		220,000
Less: profits included in the accounts but which are not taxable as trading profits	40,000	
expenditure which is deductible for tax purposes but has not been charged in the accounts	20,000	
		(60,000)
Trade profits as adjusted for tax purposes		160,000

You may refer to deductible and non-deductible expenditure as allowable and disallowable expenditure respectively. The two sets of terms are interchangeable.

2.11 Adjustments of relevance to the accruals basis

In addition to the treatment of income and expenditure already covered in the sections on the cash basis, there are a few more items that you should be aware of which are of particular importance to the accruals basis.

2.11.1 Capital expenditure and receipts

Capital expenditure deducted from a trader's profit is generally disallowed when using the accruals basis in the same way as the cash basis. This includes **depreciation** and **amortisation** of non-current assets. If the accounts include a deduction for these items, they must be added back to profit.

Similarly, capital receipts are not included in trade income. The accounting profits may include gains or losses on the sale of a non-current asset, for example. In this case, an accounting gain is not taxable as part of the trading profits and should be *deducted* from profit. Conversely, an accounting loss on disposal is not an allowable deduction for tax purposes and would have to be *added back*.

Illustrative example: Accounting profits and losses on disposal of capital assets.

Grigor is a sole trader. In 2024/25 Grigor's tax-adjusted trading profit was £120,000. This was after all adjustments apart from two disposals which took place in 2024/25:

1   He has sold a workshop which was used in his trade for £60,000. He bought the workshop in 2016 for £45,000. In his accounts at the time of its sale, the workshop had a carrying value of £32,000.

2   In 2024/25 Grigor also sold a machine used in his trade. It was sold for £11,000 when its carrying value in the accounts was £17,000.

Show the adjustments needed to calculate Grigor's taxable trading profit in 2024/25.

	£
Draft tax-adjusted profit	120,000
LESS PROFIT on disposal of the workshop (£60,000 – £32,000)	(28,000)
ADD LOSS on disposal of the machine (£11,000 – £17,000)	6,000
Taxable trading profit	98,000

Note. That the disposal of capital assets normally give rise to a capital gains tax calculation (see later) in addition to the adjustments seen here. The machine is also likely to qualify as plant and machinery so the disposal would be entered into the capital allowance computation too (see later in this workbook).

Compensation received in one lump sum for the loss of income is likely to be treated as income (*Donald Fisher (Ealing) Ltd v Spencer 1989*).

In some trades, (eg petrol stations and public houses), a wholesaler may pay a lump sum to a retailer in return for the retailer only supplying that wholesaler's products for several years (an **exclusivity agreement**). If the payment must be used for a specific capital purpose, it is a capital receipt. If that is not the case, it is an income receipt. If the sum is repayable to the wholesaler but the requirement to repay is waived in tranches over the term of the agreement, each tranche is a separate income receipt when the requirement is waived.

2.11.2 Short leases

A trader may deduct an annual sum in respect of the amount liable to income tax on a lease premium which they paid to their landlord (see earlier in this Workbook). Normally, the amortisation of the lease will have been deducted in the accounts (and must be added back as capital expenditure).

2.11.3 Impaired trade receivables (bad debts)

Only impairment losses where the liability was incurred wholly and exclusively for the purposes of the trade are deductible for taxation purposes. For example, **loans to employees that are written off are not deductible** unless the business is that of making loans or it can be shown that the writing-off of the loan was earnings paid out for the benefit of the trade.

Accounting standards dictate that a review of all trade receivables should be carried out to assess their fair value at the balance sheet date and any impairment losses written off. **The tax treatment follows the accounting treatment so no adjustment is required for tax purposes.** As a result of current accounting standards, it is less likely that any general provisions will now be seen. In the event that they do arise, increases or decreases in a general provision are not allowable/taxable and an adjustment will need to be made.

If an impairment loss which has been deducted for tax purposes is later recovered, the recovery is taxable so no adjustment is required to the amount of the recovery shown in the statement of profit or loss.

2.11.4 Unpaid remuneration

If earnings for employees are charged in the accounts but are not paid within nine months of the end of the period of account, the cost is only deductible for the period of account in which the earnings are paid. When a tax computation is made within the nine month period, it is initially assumed that unpaid earnings will not be paid within that period. The computation is adjusted if they are so paid.

Earnings are treated as paid at the same time as they are treated as received for employment income purposes.

2.11.5 Lease charges for cars with CO2 emissions exceeding 50g/km

The **allowable leasing costs for a car are the loan interest payable and depreciation** of the vehicle (see Chapter 7). However, **where the car has CO_2 emissions exceeding 50g/km, 15% of these leasing costs are disallowed** in the calculation of taxable profits. This only applies to the accruals basis, under the cash basis the full amount of the lease costs paid can be deducted.

2.11.6 Debts released

If the trader incurs a deductible expense but does not settle the amount due to the supplier, then if the creditor releases the debt other than under a statutory arrangement, the amount released must be brought into account as trade income.

2.11.7 Goods for own use

Where a trader is using the accruals basis and takes goods out of the business for their own use, the selling price (not just the cost) of the goods are added back. The trader is treated for tax purposes as having made a sale to themselves. This rule does not apply to supplies of services, which are treated as sold for the amount (if any) actually paid (but the cost of services to the trader or their household is not deductible).

2.12 Capital allowances

Under the Capital Allowances Act 2001 (CAA 2001), **capital allowances are treated as trade expenses and balancing charges are treated as trade receipts** (see later in this Workbook).

PART A TAXATION OF INDIVIDUALS

Exam focus point

In the exam, you could be given a statement of profit or loss and asked to calculate 'taxable trade profits'. You must look at every expense in the accounts to decide if it is (or is not) 'tax deductible'. This means that you must become familiar with the many expenses you may see and the correct tax treatment. Look at the above paragraphs again noting what expenses are (and are not) allowable for tax purposes. Similarly, you must decide whether income included in the accounts should be included in the taxable trade profits, or whether it should be excluded.

Question — Calculation of taxable trade profits

Here is the statement of profit or loss of Andi, a trader who has elected to use the accruals basis.

	£	£
Gross profit		46,000
Other income		
Bank interest received		860
Expenses		
Wages and salaries	7,000	
Rent and rates	2,000	
Depreciation	1,500	
Impairment of trade receivables	150	
Entertainment expenses for customers	750	
Patent royalties paid	1,200	
Loss on disposal of a workshop	16,000	
Legal expenses on acquisition of new factory	250	
		(28,850)
Finance costs		
Bank interest paid		(300)
Net profit		17,710

Salaries include £500 paid to Andi's husband, who works full time in the business.

Compute the adjusted taxable trade profit.

Answer

	£	£
Net profit		17,710
Add wages and salaries	0	
rent and rates	0	
Depreciation	1,500	
impairment of trade receivables	0	
entertainment expenses for customers	750	
patent royalties	0	
loss on disposal of workshop	16,000	
legal expenses (capital)	250	
bank interest paid	0	
		18,500
		36,210
Less bank interest received		(860)
Adjusted taxable trading profit		35,350

2.13 Rounding

Where an individual, a partnership or a single company (not a group of companies) has an annual turnover of at least £5m and prepares its accounts with figures rounded to at least the nearest £1,000, figures in computations of adjusted profits (including, for companies, non-trade profits but excluding capital gains) may generally be rounded to the nearest £1,000.

2.14 The cessation of trades

2.14.1 Post cessation receipts and expenses

Post-cessation receipts (including any releases of debts incurred by the trader) **are chargeable to income tax as miscellaneous income**.

If they are received in the tax year of cessation or the next six tax years, the trader can elect that they be treated as received on the day of cessation. The time limit for electing is the 31 January, which is 22 months after the end of the tax year of receipt.

Certain post cessation expenses paid within seven years of discontinuance may be relieved against other income. The expenses must relate to costs of remedying defective work or goods, or legal expenses of or insurance against defective work claims. Relief is also available for trade receivable that subsequently prove to be impaired.

2.14.2 Valuing trading stock on cessation

When a trade ceases, the closing stock must be valued. The higher the value, the higher the profit for the final period of trading.

If the stock is sold to a UK trader who will deduct its cost in computing their taxable profits, it is valued under the following rules:

(a) If the seller and the buyer are unconnected, take the actual price.

(b) If the seller and the buyer are connected (see below), take what would have been the price in an arm's length sale.

(c) However, if the seller and the buyer are connected, the arm's length price exceeds both the original cost of the stock and the actual transfer price, and both the seller and the buyer make an election, then take the greater of the original cost of the stock and the transfer price. The time limit for election for unincorporated business is the 31 January which is 22 months after the end of the tax year of cessation (for companies, it is two years after the end of the accounting period of cessation).

In all cases covered above, the value used for the seller's computation of profit is also used as the buyer's cost.

Key term

An individual is **connected (connected person)** with their spouse (or civil partner), their own relatives (brothers, sisters, ancestors and lineal descendants) and those of their spouse (or civil partner), and with the spouses (or civil partners) of those relatives. In-laws and step family are included; uncles, aunts, nephews, nieces and cousins are not. They are also connected with their business partners (except in relation to bona fide commercial arrangements for the disposal of partnership assets), and with their spouses (or civil partners) and relatives (see diagram below). An individual is also connected with a company if they have control of that company (or if they, along with connected persons, have control of it). An individual is also connected with the trustees of a trust of which that individual is the settlor.

PART A TAXATION OF INDIVIDUALS

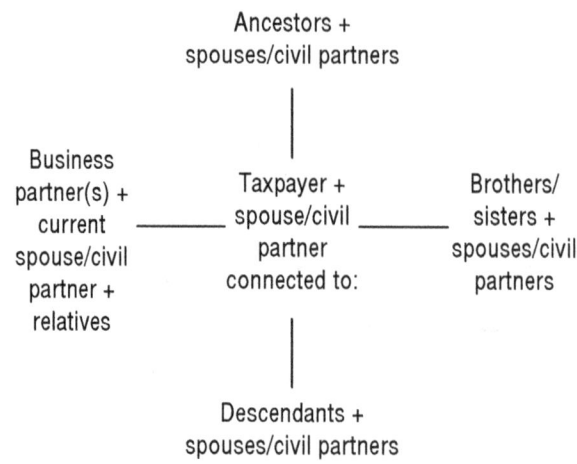

If the stock is not transferred to a UK trader who will be able to deduct its cost in computing their profits, then it is valued at its open market value as at the cessation of trade.

3 Assessable profits

FAST FORWARD

Assessable profits or trading profit assessment refer to the figure included in the income tax computation and income tax return.

3.1 Introduction

Once we have a trading profit for tax purposes for the accounting period, the next step is to calculate the **assessable** trading profits for the tax year, so we know what to include in the individual's income tax computation as trading income. **This is called the tax year basis (TYB).**

A tax year runs from 6 April to 5 April. However, an individual carrying on a trade is not obliged to prepare accounts to 5 April. A trader may, for example, choose to prepare their accounts for the year to 31 December each year (or some other date that suits them and their business). This means that the period used for the tax return is different to that used for the accounts.

The taxable trading profit for a tax year is the profit arising in the tax year. If a business does not have a 5 April or 31 March year end, the trading profits will need to be apportioned to each tax year.

It may, in this case, be necessary to use estimated profits for the second accounting period if it ends later than the submission date for the return. Where this is necessary the return can be corrected after submission (see chapter 14, section 4.2 Amending the self-assessment).

 Question — Calculation of taxable profits

Piotr is a sole trader and his results for the two years to 30 June 2025 are as follows

Period	Profit £
Year ended 30 June 2024	72,000
Year ended 30 June 2025	88,000

Calculate Piotr's assessable profits for 2024/25.

Answer

	£
6 April 2024 - 30 June 2024 (3/12 × £72,000)	18,000
1 July 2024 - 5 April 2025 (9/12 × £88,000)	66,000
Assessable profits for 2024/25	84,000

3.2 Commencement and cessation

FAST FORWARD

If a trader starts a new trade in 2024/25. The profits assessable in 2024/25 are those trading profits arising between the date of commencement up to 5 April 2025.

If a trader starts (commences) a new trade in 2024/25, the profits assessable in 2024/25 are those trading profits for tax purposes arising between the date of commencement up to 5 April 2025.

If a trader stops (ceases) an existing trade in 2024/25. The profits assessable in 2024/25 are those trading profits for tax purposes arising from 5 April 2024.

4 National Insurance

4.1 National Insurance contributions (NICs) for the self-employed

FAST FORWARD

The self-employed pay Class 4 NICs. Class 4 NICs are based on the level of the individual's taxable profits.

The self-employed (sole traders and partners) **pay Class 4 NIC.**

Class 4 NICs are **based on the level of the individual's trade profits**.

Main rate Class 4 NICs are calculated by applying a fixed percentage of 6% to the individual's profits between the lower limit of £12,570 and the upper limit of £50,270.

Additional rate contributions are 2% on profits above that limit (Whillans p.119).

4.2 Example: Class 4 contributions

If a sole trader had trading profits of £17,853 for 2024/25, the Class 4 NIC liability arising from those profits would be as follows:

	£
Profits	17,853
Less lower limit	(12,570)
	5,283

Class 4 NICs = 6% × £5,283 = £317

4.3 Example: additional Class 4 contributions

If an individual's profits were £51,350, additional Class 4 NICs are due on the excess over the upper limit. Thus the amount payable in 2024/25 is as follows:

	£
Profits (upper limit)	50,270
Less lower limit	(12,570)
	37,700

	£
Main rate Class 4 NICs = £37,700 × 6%	2,262
Additional rate class 4 NICs £(51,350 – 50,270) = £1,080 × 2%	22
	2,284

For **Class 4 NIC purposes, profits are the trade profits for income tax purposes less trade losses** (see later in this Workbook).

There is no deduction for personal pension premiums.

Class 4 NICs are collected by HMRC. They are paid **at the same time as the associated income tax liability**. Interest is charged on overdue contributions at 7.75%.

4.4 Comparison of NICs for the employees and the self employed

The NIC burden on the self-employed tends to be lower than that on employees, although the relative burdens vary with the level of income. The following example shows how a comparison may be made.

4.5 Example: employed and self-employed NICs

Two single people, one employed and one self-employed, each have annual gross income of £25,000. Show their national insurance contributions for 2024/25.

Solution

	Employed £	Self-employed £
NICs		
Class 1: £(25,000 − 12,570) × 8%	994	
Class 4: £(25,000 − 12,570) × 6%		746

The self-employed person is better off by £(994 − 746) = £248 a year. However, that person will not be entitled to certain benefits such as job seekers allowance.

5: TRADE PROFITS

Chapter roundup

- The badges of trade can be used to decide whether or not a trade exists.
- The cash basis is used as the default basis for calculating the taxable trading profit of a sole trader. They can elect to use the accruals basis if they wish.
- The trading allowance of £1,000 is available whether the trader uses the cash basis or the accruals basis
- Fixed rate expenses can be used in relation to expenditure on motor vehicles, the use of a trader's home for business purposes, and business premises partly used as the trader's home.
- Assessable profits are profits that are apportioned to tax years.
- The self-employed pay Class 4 NICs. Class 4 NICs are based on the level of the individual's taxable profits.

Quick quiz

1. List the six badges of trade.
2. What are the remoteness test and the duality test?
3. What pre-trading expenditure is deductible?
4. In which period of account are earnings paid 12 months after the end of the period for which they are charged deductible?
5. What is the maximum allowable amount of redundancy pay on the cessation of a trade?
6. Which businesses can use the cash basis of accounting?
7. What is the basis period for the tax year in which a trade commenced?
8. How are Class 4 NICs calculated?

PART A TAXATION OF INDIVIDUALS

Answers to quick quiz

1   (a) The subject matter
    (b) The frequency of transactions
    (c) The length of ownership
    (d) Supplementary work and marketing
    (e) A profit motive
    (f) The way in which goods were acquired

2   Expenditure is not deductible if it is not for trade purposes (the remoteness test) or if it reflects more than one purpose (the duality test).

3   Pre-trading expenditure is deductible if it is incurred within seven years of the start of the trade and is of a type that would have been deductible if the trade had already started.

4   In the period in which they are paid.

5   3 × statutory amount.

6   Unincorporated businesses (sole traders and partnerships) will use the cash basis by default, but can elect to use the accruals basis if they want to.

7   Date of commencement to 5 April in that year.

8   The main rate is a fixed percentage of an individual's profits between the upper limit and lower limit. The additional rate applies above the upper limit.

Capital allowances

Topic list
1 Capital allowances in general
2 Plant and machinery – qualifying expenditure
3 The main pool
4 Special rate pool
5 Private use assets
6 Motor cars
7 Capital allowances, cars and the cash basis
8 Short-life assets
9 Cessation
10 Structures and buildings allowance

Introduction

In the previous chapter, we saw how to adjust the accounting profit to find taxable trade profits and how to allocate those profits to tax years. The adjustments included adding back depreciation as a disallowable expense and deducting capital allowances instead. In this chapter, we look at capital allowances, starting with plant and machinery.

Our study of plant and machinery falls into three parts. Firstly, we look at what qualifies for allowances: many business assets are not eligible. Secondly, we see how to compute the allowances and thirdly, we look at special rules for assets with short lives and in the special rate pool.

Finally, we look at the structures and buildings allowance available on acquisition of some buildings.

PART A TAXATION OF INDIVIDUALS

Exam guide

You may have to calculate capital allowances for either unincorporated businesses or companies in the exam to arrive at the taxable profits. In order to do this you will need to learn the different rules for unincorporated businesses compared to companies. In the exam you may also be calculating capital allowances for short or long accounting periods. Any cases referenced in this chapter are for you to understand their conclusions, you will not be tested on case names.

1 Capital allowances in general

FAST FORWARD

> Capital allowances are available on plant and machinery. The structures and buildings allowance is available for some buildings. There is lots of useful information about capital allowances in Whillans (pp. 37-41).

Capital allowances are a form of relief for expenditure on plant and machinery used in a trade. They are effectively treated as a deductible expense.

Both unincorporated businesses (sole traders and partnerships) and companies are entitled to capital allowances. For completeness, in this chapter we will look at the rules for companies alongside those for unincorporated businesses. We will also look at companies in more detail later in this Workbook.

Remember that sole traders and partners use the cash basis by default to calculate their taxable trade profit. As you saw in chapter 5, when plant and machinery, other than cars, are bought the expenditure is treated as a deduction. The sale proceeds on disposal of plant and machinery is treated as a taxable trade receipt by the sole trader. So, for most plant and machinery bought by a sole trader, there won't be any capital allowances. However, if they use a car in their trade they may claim a capital allowance for the car, assuming they have not claimed a flat-rate expense (also covered in chapter 5). Also, unincorporated business can elect to use the accruals basis to calculate trading profits. If they do so, relief for expenditure on plant and machinery will be in the form of capital allowances.

Companies do not have the option of using the cash basis or flat-rate expenses so companies will have more items in their capital allowance computations.

For unincorporated businesses, capital allowances are calculated for periods of account. These are simply the periods for which the trader chooses to make up accounts. For companies, capital allowances are calculated for accounting periods (see later in this Workbook).

For capital allowances purposes, expenditure is generally deemed to be incurred when the obligation to pay becomes unconditional. This will often be the date of a contract but if, for example, payment is due a month after delivery of a machine, it would be the date of delivery. Amounts due more than four months after the obligation becomes unconditional are deemed to be incurred when they fall due.

Capital allowances give relief for expenditure on **plant and machinery**. In restricted cases, capital expenditure on buildings may qualify for the structures and buildings allowance. This is covered in detail at the end of this chapter. Most of this chapter relates to plant and machinery.

In the tax year 2021/22, a new category of enhanced capital allowances was introduced for use in designated areas, known as freeports, as part of a government project to promote economic development. Freeport-related enhanced capital allowances are not part of the Taxation syllabus for the current year.

2 Plant and machinery – qualifying expenditure

2.1 Introduction

Capital expenditure on plant and machinery qualifies for capital allowances if the plant or machinery is used for a qualifying activity, such as a trade. 'Plant' is not defined by the legislation, although some specific exclusions and inclusions are given. The word 'machinery' may be taken to have its normal everyday meaning.

2.2 The statutory exclusions

FAST FORWARD

Statutory rules generally exclude specified items from treatment as plant, rather than include specified items as plant.

2.2.1 Buildings

Expenditure on a building, and on any asset which is incorporated in a building or is of a kind normally incorporated into buildings, does not qualify as expenditure on plant. There are some exceptions to this rule (see section 2.2.3 below). Also, certain 'integral features' (see 2.2.5 below) are specifically treated as plant.

In addition to complete buildings, **the following assets count as 'buildings', and are therefore not plant (except if they qualify as integral features)**.

- Walls, floors, ceilings, doors, gates, shutters, windows and stairs
- Mains services, and systems, of water, electricity and gas
- Waste disposal, sewerage and drainage systems
- Shafts or other structures for lifts etc

2.2.2 Structures

Expenditure on structures and on works involving the alteration of land **does not qualify as expenditure on plant**, but see below for exceptions.

A 'structure' is a fixed structure of any kind, other than a building. An example is a bridge.

2.2.3 Exceptions

Over the years, a large body of case law has been built up under which plant and machinery allowances have been given on certain types of expenditure which might be thought to be expenditure on a building or structure. Statute therefore gives a list of various assets which *may* still be plant. These include:

- Any machinery not within any other item in this list
- Gas and sewerage systems:
    - Provided mainly to meet the particular requirements of the trade
    - Provided mainly to serve particular machinery or plant used for the purposes of the trade
- Manufacturing or processing equipment, storage equipment, including cold rooms, display equipment, and counters, checkouts and similar equipment
- Cookers, washing machines, refrigeration or cooling equipment, sanitary ware and furniture and furnishings
- Hoists
- Sound insulation provided mainly to meet the particular requirements of the trade
- Computer, telecommunication and surveillance systems
- Sprinkler equipment, fire alarm and burglar alarm systems
- Strong rooms in bank or building society premises, safes
- Partition walls, where movable and intended to be moved
- Decorative assets provided for the enjoyment of the public in the hotel, restaurant or similar trades, advertising hoardings
- Glasshouses which have, as an integral part of their structure, devices which control the plant growing environment automatically

- Swimming pools (including diving boards, slides) and structures for rides at amusement parks
- Caravans provided mainly for holiday lettings
- Movable buildings intended to be moved in the course of the trade
- Expenditure on altering land for the purpose only of installing machinery or plant
- Dry docks and jetties
- Pipelines, and also underground ducts or tunnels with a primary purpose of carrying utility conduits
- Silos provided for temporary storage and storage tanks, slurry pits and silage clamps
- Fish tanks, fish ponds and fixed zoo cages
- A railway or tramway

Items falling within the above list of exclusions will only qualify as plant if they fall within the meaning of plant as established by case law. This is discussed below.

2.2.4 Land

Land or an interest in land does not qualify as plant and machinery. For this purpose 'land' excludes buildings, structures and assets which are installed or fixed to land in such a way as to become part of the land for general legal purposes.

2.2.5 Integral features

The following **integral features of a building or structure** qualify for capital allowances as plant (in the special rate pool, see later in this chapter):

- **Electrical and lighting systems**
- **Cold water systems**
- **Space or water heating systems, a powered system of ventilation, air cooling or air purification, and any floor or ceiling comprised in such a system**
- **External solar shading**
- **Lift, an escalator or a moving walkway**

When a building is sold, the vendor and purchaser can make a joint election to determine how the sale proceeds are apportioned between the building and its integral features.

2.3 The statutory inclusions

Certain expenditure is specifically deemed to be expenditure on plant and machinery.

The following are deemed to be on plant and machinery:

- Expenditure by a trader on thermal insulation of a building used for the trade
- Expenditure by a trader in meeting statutory safety requirements for sports ground (incurred before 1 April 2013)
- Expenditure (by an individual or a partnership, not by a company) on **security assets** provided to meet a special threat to an individual's security that arises wholly or mainly due to the particular trade concerned. Cars, ships, aircraft and dwellings are specifically excluded from the definition of a security asset

On disposal, the sale proceeds for the above are deemed to be zero, so no balancing charge (see below) can arise.

Capital expenditure on computer software (both programs and data) **qualifies as expenditure on plant and machinery**:

(a) Regardless of whether the software is supplied in a tangible form (such as a disk) or transmitted electronically.

(b) Regardless of whether the purchaser acquires the software or only a licence to use it.

Disposal proceeds are brought into account in the normal way, except that if the fee for the grant of a licence is taxed as income of the licensor, no disposal proceeds are taken into account in computing the licensee's capital allowances.

Where someone has incurred expenditure qualifying for capital allowances on computer software (or the right to use software), and receives a capital sum in exchange for allowing someone else to use the software, that sum is brought into account as disposal proceeds. However, the cumulative total of disposal proceeds is not allowed to exceed the original cost of the software, and any proceeds above this limit are ignored for capital allowances purposes (although they may lead to chargeable gains).

If software is expected to have a useful economic life of less than two years, its cost may be treated as revenue expenditure.

For companies the rules for computer software are overridden by the rules for intangible fixed assets unless the company elects otherwise.

2.4 Case law

> **FAST FORWARD**
>
> There are several cases on the definition of plant. To help you to absorb them, try to see the function/setting theme running through them.

The original case law **definition of plant** (applied in this case to a horse) is **'whatever apparatus is used by a [trader] for carrying on their business: not their stock in trade bought or made for sale; but all goods and chattels, fixed or movable, live or dead, kept for permanent employment in the business'** (*Yarmouth v France 1887*).

Subsequent cases have refined the original definition and have largely been concerned with the **distinction between plant actively used in the business (qualifying) and the setting in which the business is carried on (non-qualifying). This is the 'functional' test**. Some of the decisions have now been enacted as part of statute law, but they are still relevant as examples of the principles involved.

The whole cost of excavating and installing a swimming pool was allowed to the owners of a caravan park. *CIR v Barclay Curle & Co 1969* was followed: the pool performed **the function** of giving 'buoyancy and enjoyment' to the persons using the pool (*Cooke v Beach Station Caravans Ltd 1974*) (now covered by statute).

A barrister succeeded in their claim for a law library: 'Plant includes the tools of a trade. It extends to what is used day by day in the course of a profession. It is not confined to physical things like the dentist's chair or the architect's table' (*Munby v Furlong 1977*).

Office partitioning was allowed. Because it was movable it was not regarded as part of the setting in which the business was carried on (*Jarrold v John Good and Sons Ltd 1963*) (now covered by statute).

A ship used as a floating restaurant was regarded as a 'structure in which the business was carried on rather than apparatus employed ... ' (Buckley LJ). No capital allowances could be obtained (*Benson v Yard Arm Club 1978*). The same decision was made in relation to a football club's spectator stand. The stand performed no function in the actual carrying out of the club's trade (*Brown v Burnley Football and Athletic Co Ltd 1980*).

At a motorway service station, false ceilings contained conduits, ducts and lighting apparatus. **They did not qualify because they did not perform a function in the business. They were merely part of the setting in which the business was conducted** (*Hampton v Fortes Autogrill Ltd 1979*).

Light fittings, decor and murals can be plant. A company carried on business as hoteliers and operators of licensed premises. The function of the items was the creation of an atmosphere conducive to the comfort and wellbeing of its customers (*CIR v Scottish and Newcastle Breweries Ltd 1982*) (decorative assets used in hotels etc, now covered by statute).

On the other hand, it has been held that when an attractive floor is provided in a restaurant, the fact that the floor performs the function of making the restaurant attractive to customers is not enough to make it plant. It functions as premises, and the cost therefore does not qualify for capital allowances (*Wimpy International Ltd v Warland 1988*).

General lighting in a department store is not plant, as it is merely setting. Special display lighting, however, can be plant (*Cole Brothers Ltd v Phillips 1982*). Note that changes in legislation mean that it is now possible to claim allowances on lighting as an integral feature (see earlier in this chapter), but the case is still a useful example of the distinction between setting and function.

Free-standing decorative screens installed in the windows of a branch of a building society qualified as plant. Their function was not to act a part of the setting in which the society's business was carried on; it was to attract local custom, and accordingly the screens formed part of the apparatus with which the society carried on its business (*Leeds Permanent Building Society v Proctor 1982*).

In *Bradley v London Electricity plc 1996* an electricity substation was held not to be plant because it functioned as premises in which London Electricity carried on a trading activity rather than apparatus with which the activity was carried out.

3 The main pool

FAST FORWARD

With capital allowances computations, the main thing is to get the layout right. Having done that, you will find that the figures tend to drop into place.

3.1 Main pool expenditure

Most expenditure on plant and machinery, including cars with CO_2 emissions of 50g/km or less, is put into a pool of expenditure (the main pool) on which capital allowances may be claimed. An addition increases the pool whilst a disposal decreases it.

Exceptionally the following items are not put into the main pool:

(a) Assets dealt with in the special rate pool
(b) Assets with private use by the trader
(c) Short-life assets where an election has been made

These exceptions are dealt with later in this chapter.

Expenditure on plant and machinery by a person about to begin a trade is treated as incurred on the first day of trading. Assets previously owned by a trader and then brought into the trade (at the start of trading or later) are treated as bought for their market values at the times when they are brought in.

3.2 Annual investment allowance

FAST FORWARD

Businesses are entitled to an annual investment allowance (AIA) for a 12-month period of account. Related businesses share one allowance between them. The AIA is £1,000,000 for a 12-month accounting period (Whillans p.39).

3.2.1 Amount of annual investment allowance

Businesses can claim an **annual investment allowance (AIA) on qualifying plant or machinery expenditure in the accounting period in which it is incurred**, including assets in the main pool, but not including motor cars. Expenditure on motorcycles does qualify for the AIA.

Where the period of account is more or less than a year, the maximum allowance is proportionately increased or reduced.

After claiming the AIA, the balance of expenditure on main pool assets is transferred to the main pool immediately and is eligible for writing down allowances in the same period.

3.2.2 Allocation of annual investment allowance between related businesses

Related business are entitled to a single annual investment allowance between the businesses. The businesses may **allocate the allowance between them as they think fit.**

Business are related if they are carried on or controlled by the same individual or partnership and either:

- The businesses are **engaged in the same activity**; or
- The businesses **share the same premises**.

A business is controlled by a person in a tax year if it is controlled by the person at the end of the chargeable period for that business ending in that tax year.

The nature of expenditure by one business may be relevant when deciding how to allocate the allowance between the businesses. For example, it is more tax efficient to set the annual investment allowance against special rate pool expenditure because of the lower rate of subsequent writing down allowances on the special rate pool (6% pa) as opposed to the main pool (18% pa).

There are similar (but separate) rules relating to companies under common control and companies in a group.

3.3 First year allowances

FAST FORWARD

A first year allowance (FYA) at the rate of 100% is available on new low emission cars and electric charging points. FYAs are never pro-rated in short periods of account. A special type of first year allowance is available for companies but this is dealt with later in this book.

3.3.1 FYA on low emission cars

Key term

A low emission car is one which has CO_2 emissions of 0g/km.

A 100% first year allowance (FYA) is available for expenditure incurred on new low emission motor cars.

If the FYA is not claimed in full, the balance of expenditure is transferred to the main pool after any writing down allowance has been calculated on the main pool.

Exam focus point

In the exam, you will need to use Whillans tax tables for a car's CO_2 emissions. You will not be told whether it is low emission.

3.3.2 Short periods of account

FYAs are not reduced pro-rata in a short period of account, unlike the AIA and writing down allowances.

PART A TAXATION OF INDIVIDUALS

3.4 Writing down allowances

FAST FORWARD Most expenditure on plant and machinery qualifies for a WDA at 18% every 12 months.

Key term

A **Writing Down Allowance (WDA)** is given on main pool expenditure **at the rate of 18% a year** (on a reducing balance basis) (Whillans p.38). The WDA is calculated on the tax written down value (TWDV) of pooled plant, after adding the current period's additions and taking out the current period's disposals.

When plant is sold, proceeds, **limited to a maximum of the original cost,** are taken out of the pool. Provided that the trade is still being carried on, the pool balance remaining is written down in the future by WDAs, even if there are no assets left.

3.5 Example

Elizabeth has elected to use the accruals basis and has tax written down value on her main pool of plant and machinery of £16,000 on 6 April 2024. In the year to 5 April 2025, she bought a car with CO_2 emissions of 48g/km for £8,000 (no non-business use) and she disposed of plant (which originally cost £4,000) for £6,000.

Calculate the maximum capital allowances claim for the year.

	Main pool £	Allowances £
TWDV b/f	16,000	
Addition (not qualifying for AIA or FYA)	8,000	
Less disposal (proceeds limited to cost)	(4,000)	
	20,000	
WDA @ 18%	(3,600)	3,600
TWDV c/f	16,400	
Maximum capital allowances claim		3,600

Question — Capital allowances – AIA and WDA

Julia has elected to use the accruals basis and makes up accounts to 31 December each year. At 1 January 2024, the tax written down value on her main pool is £12,500.

In the year to 31 December 2024, Julia bought the following assets:

Date	Asset	Cost £
1 June 2024	Van	17,500
12 July 2024	Machine	990,000
10 October 2024	Car for salesman (CO_2 emissions 42g/km)	9,000

Julia disposed of plant on 15 December 2024 for £12,000 (original cost £16,000).

Calculate the maximum capital allowances claim that Julia can make for the year ended 31 December 2024.

Answer

	AIA £	Main pool £	Allowances £
Y/e 31 December 2024			
TWDV b/f		12,500	
Additions qualifying for AIA			
Van	17,500		
Machine	990,000		
AIA (max)	(1,000,000)		1,000,000
	7,500		
Transfer balance to pool	(7,500)	7,500	
Additions not qualifying for AIA			
Car		9,000	
Disposal			
Plant		(12,000)	
		17,000	
WDA @ 18%		(3,060)	3,060
TWDV c/f		13,940	
Maximum capital allowances			1,003,060

3.6 Short and long periods of account

WDAs are 18% × number of months/12:

(a) For unincorporated businesses where the period of account is longer or shorter than 12 months; and

(b) For companies where the accounting period is shorter than 12 months (a company's accounting period for tax purposes is never longer than 12 months), or where the trade concerned started in the accounting period and was therefore carried on for fewer than 12 months. Remember that we will be studying companies in detail later in this Workbook.

Question — Short period of account

Venus is a sole trader and has made up accounts to 30 April each year. She has elected to use the accruals basis.

At 30 April 2024, the tax written down value of her main pool was £66,667. She decides to make up her next set of accounts to 31 December 2024.

In the period to 31 December 2024, the following acquisitions were made:

Date	Acquisition	Expense £
1 May 2024	Plant	680,000
10 July 2024	Car (CO_2 emissions 44g/km)	9,000
3 August 2024	Car (CO_2 emissions 0g/km)	11,000

Venus disposed of plant on 1 November 2024 for £20,000 (original cost £28,000).

Calculate the maximum capital allowances that Venus can claim for the period ending 31 December 2024.

Answer

	AIA £	FYA £	Main pool £	Allowances £
p/e 31 December 2024				
TWDV b/f			66,667	
Additions qualifying for AIA				
1.5.24 Plant	680,000			
AIA £1,000,000 × 8/12	(666,667)			666,667
	13,333			
Transfer balance to pool	(13,333)		13,333	
Additions qualifying for FYA				
3.8.24 Car (low emission)		11,000		
Less: 100% FYA		(11,000)		11,000
Additions not qualifying for AIA nor FYA				
10.7.24 Car			9,000	
Disposals				
1.11.24 Plant			(20,000)	
			69,000	
WDA @ 18% × 8/12			(8,280)	8,280
TWDVs c/f			60,720	
Maximum allowances claim				685,947

Note that the annual investment allowance and the writing down allowance are reduced for the short period of account but the first year allowance is given in full.

Question

Long period of account

Oscar started trading on 1 July 2023 and made up his first set of accounts to 31 December 2024. He elected to use the accruals basis. He bought the following assets:

Date	Asset	Expense £
1 July 2023	Plant	850,000
10 October 2024	Car for business use only (CO_2 emissions 49g/km)	11,000
1 December 2024	Plant	715,000

Calculate the maximum capital allowances claim that Oscar can make for the period ended 31 December 2024.

Answer

	AIA £	Main pool £	Allowances £
p/e 31 December 2024			
Additions qualifying for AIA			
1.7.23 Plant	850,000		
1.12.24 Plant	715,000		
	1,565,000		
AIA £1,000,000 × 18/12	(1,500,000)		1,500,000
	65,000		
Transfer balance to main pool	(65,000)	65,000	
Additions not qualifying for AIA			
10.10.24 Car		11,000	
		76,000	
WDA @ 18% × 18/12		(20,520)	20,520
TWDV c/f		55,480	
Maximum capital allowances			1,520,520

Note that the AIA and the WDA are increased pro rata for the long period of account.

3.7 Small balance on main pool

A writing down allowance equal to unrelieved expenditure in the main pool can be claimed where this is **£1,000 or less** (pro-rated for short or long periods). If the maximum WDA is claimed, the main pool will then have a nil balance carried forward.

Question — Small balance on main pool

Alan has traded for many years, making up accounts to 30 April each year. He does not use the cash basis. At 1 May 2024, the tax written down value of his main pool was £15,000.

On 1 October 2024, he sold some plant and machinery for £14,200 (original cost £16,000).

Calculate the maximum capital allowances claim that Alan can make for the period ending 30 April 2025.

Answer

	Main pool £	Allowances £
Y/e 30 April 2025		
TWDV b/f	15,000	
Disposal	(14,200)	
	800	
WDA (small pool)	(800)	800
TWDV c/f	nil	
Maximum capital allowances		800

3.8 Balancing charges and allowances

Balancing charges occur when the disposal value deducted exceeds the balance remaining in the pool. The charge equals the excess and is effectively a negative capital allowance, increasing profits. Most commonly this happens when the trade ceases and the remaining assets are sold. It may also occur, however, whilst the trade is still in progress.

Balancing allowances on the main and special pools of expenditure arise only when the trade ceases. The balancing allowance is equal to the remaining unrelieved expenditure after deducting the disposal value of all the assets. Balancing allowances may also arise on single pool items (see below) whenever those items are disposed of.

4 Special rate pool

> **FAST FORWARD**
>
> The special rate pool contains expenditure on thermal insulation, long life assets, features integral to a building, solar panels, and cars with CO_2 emissions over 50g/km. The AIA can be used against such expenditure except cars. The WDA is 6%.

4.1 Operation of the special rate pool

Expenditure on thermal insulation, long life assets, features integral to a building, solar panels and cars with CO_2 emissions over 50g/km, is not dealt with in the main pool but in a special rate pool.

The Annual Investment Allowance can apply to expenditure on such assets except on cars. The taxpayer can decide how to allocate the AIA. It will be more tax efficient to set the allowance against special rate pool expenditure in priority to main pool expenditure where there is expenditure on assets in both pools in the period. Expenditure in excess of the AIA is added to the special rate pool and will be eligible for writing down allowance in the same period in which the expenditure is incurred.

The writing down allowance for the special rate pool is 6% for a 12-month period (Whillans p.38). As with the writing down allowance on the main pool, this is adjusted for short and long periods of account. Where the tax written down balance of the special rate pool is £1,000 or less (prorated for short or long periods), a writing down allowance can be claimed of up to £1,000. This is in addition to any similar claim in relation to the main pool.

4.2 Long-life assets

Key term

Long life assets are assets with an expected working life of 25 years or more.

The long-life asset rules only apply to businesses whose total expenditure on assets with an expected working life of 25 years or more in a chargeable period is more than £100,000. If the expenditure exceeds £100,000, the whole of the expenditure enters the special rate pool. For this purpose, all expenditure incurred under a contract is treated as incurred in the first chargeable period to which that contract relates.

The £100,000 limit is reduced or increased proportionately in the case of a chargeable period of less or more than 12 months.

The following are **not** treated as long life assets:

(a) **Plant and machinery in dwelling houses, retail shops, showrooms, hotels and offices**
(b) **Cars**

4.3 Example: integral features

Lucy has been trading for many years. The tax written down value of her main pool at 1 January 2024 was £110,000. In the year to 31 December 2024, Lucy had the following expenditure:

Date	Items	Expense £
10 March 2024	Plant	45,000
12 September 2024	Lighting system in shop	120,000
15 October 2024	Car for business use only (CO_2 emissions 115g/km)	25,000
26 October 2024	Delivery van	15,000
4 December 2024	Lifts	882,500

The maximum capital allowances claim that Lucy can make for the year to 31 December 2024 is:

	AIA £	Main pool £	Special rate pool £	Allowances £
Y/e 31 December 2024				
TWDV b/f		110,000		
Additions for AIA (against SRP first)				
12.09.24 Lighting	120,000			
4.12.24 Lifts	882,500			
	1,002,500			
AIA	(1,000,000)			1,000,000
	2,500			
Transfer balance to special rate pool	(2,500)		2,500	
Additions not given AIA (main pool)				
10.3.24 Plant		45,000		
26.10.24 Van		15,000		
Additions not qualifying for AIA				
15.10.24 Car			25,000	
		170,000	27,500	
WDA @ 18%		(30,600)		30,600
WDA @ 6%			(1,650)	1,650
TWDVs c/f		139,400	25,850	
Allowances				1,032,250

5 Private use assets

An asset which is used privately by a trader is dealt with in a single asset pool and the capital allowances are restricted.

An asset (for example, a car) which is used partly for private purposes by a sole trader or a partner is put into its own pool (single asset pool).

Capital allowances are calculated on the full cost. However, only the business use proportion of the allowances is allowed as a deduction from trading profits. This restriction applies to the AIA, FYAs, WDAs, balancing allowances and balancing charges.

An asset with some private use by an employee (not the owner of the business) suffers no such restriction. The employee may be taxed under the benefits code (see earlier in this Workbook) so the business receives capital allowances on the full cost of the asset.

PART A TAXATION OF INDIVIDUALS

Exam focus point

Capital allowances on assets with some private use is a common exam topic. Check carefully whether the private use is by the owner of the business or by an employee.

Question — Capital allowances on private use car

Jacinth has been in business as a sole trader for many years, making up accounts to 31 March. On 1 November 2024 she bought computer equipment for £2,700 which she uses 75% in her business and 25% privately. She has already used the AIA against other expenditure in the year to 31 March 2025.

Calculate the maximum capital allowance that Jacinth can claim in respect of the computer equipment in the year to 31 March 2025.

Answer

	Computer equipment £	Allowances @ 75% £
Y/e 31 March 2025		
Acquisition	2,700	
WDA @ 18%	(486)	365
TWDV c/f	2,214	
Maximum capital allowance on computer equipment		365

6 Motor cars

FAST FORWARD

Motor cars are generally dealt with in the special rate pool (cars emitting over 50g/km) or the main pool, unless there is private use by the trader.

As we have already seen, motor cars are categorised in accordance with their CO_2 emissions:

(a) **Cars emitting over 50g/km**: expenditure is added to the special rate pool.

(b) **Cars emitting between 1 and 50g/km**: expenditure is added to the main pool.

(c) (New) **cars emitting 0g/km**: expenditure eligible for 100% first year allowance. If allowance not claimed in full, excess added to main pool (Whillans p.38).

Exam focus point

Different rules applied to cars acquired in earlier years but you should assume these rules have always applied in questions involving cars in the Taxation exam.

Cars with an element of private use continue to be kept separate from the main and special pools and are dealt with in single asset pools. They are entitled to a WDA of 18% (car with CO_2 emissions between 1 and 50g/km) or 6% (car with CO_2 emissions over 50g/km).

Question — Capital allowances on private use car

Quodos started to trade on 1 July 2024, making up accounts to 31 December 2024 and each 31 December thereafter. On 1 August 2024, he bought a car for £17,000 with CO_2 emissions of 41g/km. The private use proportion is 10%. The car was sold in July 2027 for £4,000.

Calculate the capital allowances, assuming:

(a) The car was used by an employee; or
(b) The car was used by Quodos and that the capital allowances rates in 2024/25 apply throughout.

Answer

(a)

	Main pool £	Allowances £
Six-month period ending 31.12.24		
Purchase price	17,000	
WDA 18% × 6/12 × £17,000	(1,530)	1,530
	15,470	
Year ending 31.12.25		
WDA 18% × £15,470	(2,785)	2,785
	12,685	
Year ending 31.12.26		
WDA 18% × £12,685	(2,283)	2,283
	10,402	
Year ending 31.12.27		
Proceeds	(4,000)	
	6,402	
WDA 18% × £6,402	(1,152)	1,152
TWDV c/f	5,250	

The private use of the car by the employee has no effect on the capital allowances due to Quodos. The car will be placed in the main pool. No balancing allowance is available on the main pool until trade ceases even though the car has been sold.

(b)

	Car £	Allowances 90% £
Six-month period ending 31.12.24		
Purchase price	17,000	
WDA 18% × 6/12 × £17,000	(1,530)	1,377
	15,470	
Year ending 31.12.25		
WDA 18% × £15,470	(2,785)	2,507
	12,685	
Year ending 31.12.26		
WDA 18% × £12,685	(2,283)	2,055
	10,402	
Year ending 31.12.27		
Proceeds	(4,000)	
Balancing allowance	6,402	5,762

As the private use is by the proprietor, Quodos, only 90% of the WDAs and balancing allowance are available.

7 Capital allowances, cars and fixed rate deductions

Where a sole trader or a partnership purchases a car for use in a trade, the expenditure on the car may be relieved through the capital allowance computation. This is true for both the cash basis and the accruals basis.

However, **under both bases**, traders can choose to relieve expenditure on cars using fixed rate deductions rather than capital allowances.

For each car, the trader must decide between the following two options:

1. Claim capital allowances and the business proportion of relevant expenses
2. Deduct fixed rate expenses

Once the trader has decided on a method for a car, that same method must be used each year for as long as the car is used in the trade. It is not possible to change method from one year to the next.

Question — Capital allowances, fixed rate deductions and cars

Andreas started to trade as a sole trader on 6 April 2024. In the year ended 5 April 2025, he purchased a car for use in his business. The following information is relevant:

- The car had a market value of £15,000 when he started using it for business purposes.
- Its CO_2 emissions rate is 54g/km.
- He drove 18,000 miles in total during 2024/25, 12,000 of those miles were for business.
- The running costs for the car (fuel, maintenance, insurance) was £5,400 in the year.

Required

Calculate Andreas' allowable deductions for the car and motoring expenses in the year ended 5 April 2025 assuming:

(a) He claims capital allowances and expenses
(b) He claims fixed rate expenses

Answer

(a)

	Special rate (PU) asset £	Allowable deduction £
Year ended 5 April 2025		
Cost of the car	15,000	
WDA at 6%	(900)	×12/18 =
	14,100	600
Business proportion of actual expenses (£5,400 ×12/18)		3,600
Allowable deduction		4,200

(b)

	£	Allowable deduction £
10,000 business miles at £0.45	4,500	
2,000 business miles at £0.25	500	
		5,000

8 Short-life assets

FAST FORWARD — Short-life asset elections can bring forward the allowances due on an asset.

A trader can elect that specific items of plant be kept separately from the main pool in a single asset pool. The election is irrevocable. For an unincorporated business, the time limit for electing is the 31 January which is 22 months after the end of the tax year in which the period of account of the expenditure ends. (For a company, it is two years after the end of the accounting period of the expenditure). **Any asset subject to this election is known as a 'short-life asset' and the election is known as a 'de-pooling election'.**

Key term

Provided that the asset is disposed of **within eight years** of the end of the accounting period in which it was bought, it is a **short-life asset** and a balancing charge or allowance arises on its disposal.

If the asset is not disposed of within this time period, its tax written down value is added to the main pool at the beginning of the next period of account (accounting period for companies). This will be after allowances have been claimed nine times on the asset: once in the period of acquisition and then each year for the following eight years. **The election should therefore be made for assets likely to be sold for less than their tax written down values within eight years.** It should not usually be made for assets likely to be sold within eight years for more than their tax written down values. There is no requirement to show from the outset that the asset will actually have a 'short life', so it is a matter of judgement whether the election should be made.

The Annual Investment Allowance can be set against short-life assets. The taxpayer can decide how to allocate the AIA. It will be more tax efficient to set the allowance against main pool expenditure in priority to short-life asset expenditure.

Question — Short life assets

Caithlin bought a machine for business use on 1 May 2024 for £9,000 and elected for de-pooling. She did not claim the AIA in respect of this asset. Her accounting year end is 30 April.

Calculate the capital allowances due if:

(a) The asset is scrapped for £300 in August 2032; and
(b) The asset is scrapped for £200 in August 2033.

And assuming that the capital allowances rates in 2024/25 apply throughout.

Answer

(a) Year to 30.4.25 £
Cost 9,000
WDA 18% (1,620)
7,380

Year to 30.4.26
WDA 18% (1,328)
6,052

Year to 30.4.27
WDA 18% (1,089)
4,963

Year to 30.4.28
WDA 18% (893)
4,070

Year to 30.4.29 £
WDA 18% (733)
3,337

Year to 30.4.30
WDA 18% (601)
2,736

Year to 30.4.31
WDA 18% (492)
2,244

Year to 30.4.32
WDA 18% (404)
1,840

Year to 30.4.33
Disposal proceeds (300)
Balancing allowance 1,540

(b) If the asset is still in use at 30 April 2033, WDAs up to 30.4.32 will be as above. In the year to 30.4.33, a WDA can be claimed of 18% × £1,840 = £331. The tax written down value of £1,840 – £331 = £1,509 will be added to the main pool at the beginning of the next period of account. The disposal proceeds of £200 will be deducted from the main pool in that period's capital allowances computation. No balancing allowance will arise and the main pool will continue.

Short-life asset treatment cannot be claimed for motor cars or plant used partly for non-trade purposes.

9 Cessation

FAST FORWARD Balancing adjustments are calculated when a business ceases.

Balancing adjustments arise on the cessation of a business. No writing down allowances are given, but the final proceeds (limited to cost) on sales of plant are compared with the tax WDV to calculate balancing allowances or charges.

10 Structures and buildings allowance

FAST FORWARD The **structures and buildings allowance** is available on the purchase of certain commercial structures and buildings used in the trade of a business.

The structures and building allowance (SBA) is given on eligible construction costs of various commercial buildings and structures. Residential properties do not qualify.

Eligible construction costs of a structure or building include the construction costs incurred by the business itself or the acquisition cost of a newly-built structure or building when first purchased from the developer. The cost of the land is not included. The construction must have started on or after 29 October 2018.

Exam focus point

> The range of buildings and structures and the exact construction costs that qualify are detailed in the legislation, and have been simplified here. For the Taxation exam, only this level of detail is required. You will not be asked any questions about the enhanced SBA that will be made available for freeports.

The relief is on a straight-line basis as **3% per annum of the eligible construction costs** (Whillans p.41). The allowance can be claimed from when the building is first brought into use. Unlike capital allowances for plant and machinery, **the allowance is pro-rated for the time that the building is in use** in an accounting period, and so will vary in the periods of purchase and sale of the building.

For example, if a new building is purchased and brought into use on 1 July 2024, costing £1,000,000 including £200,000 for the land, the SBA for the year ended 31 December 2024 is £(1,000,000 – 200,000) × 3% × 6/12 = £12,000.

The SBA is also apportioned where the period of account is longer or shorter than 12 months.

Each qualifying building should be treated separately and not pooled.

On the sale of such a building, there are **no balancing adjustments** in respect of the SBA. Instead, the purchaser takes over the remaining allowances. That is, the allowances continue to be based on the original eligible construction costs, and not the price paid by the new owner.

The vendor will calculate a gain, deducting the cost of the building as usual, but also **adding any SBAs that it has claimed since purchase to the proceeds on sale**.

Exam focus point

> When the SBA was first introduced, the rate was 2% per annum, however in the Taxation exam you will only be expected to do calculations involving the 3% rate.

6: CAPITAL ALLOWANCES

Chapter roundup

- Capital allowances are available on plant and machinery. The structures and buildings allowance is available for some buildings.
- Statutory rules generally exclude specified items from treatment as plant, rather than include specified items as plant.
- There are several cases on the definition of plant. To help you to absorb them, try to see the function/setting theme running through them.
- With capital allowances computations, the main thing is to get the layout right. Having done that, you will find that the figures tend to drop into place.
- Businesses are entitled to an annual investment allowance (AIA) of £1,000,000 for a 12-month period of account.
- A first-year allowance (FYA) at the rate of 100% is available on new low emission cars (with emissions of 0g/km) and electric charging points purchased. FYAs are never pro-rated in short periods of account.
- Most expenditure on plant and machinery qualifies for a WDA at 18% every 12 months.
- The special rate pool contains expenditure on thermal insulation, long life assets, features integral to a building, solar panels and cars with CO_2 emissions over 50g/km. The AIA can be used against such expenditure. The WDA is 6%.
- An asset which is used privately by a trader is dealt with in a single asset pool and the capital allowances are restricted.
- Motor cars are generally dealt with in the special rate pool (cars emitting over 50g/km) or the main pool, unless there is private use by the trader.
- Short-life asset elections can bring forward the allowances due on an asset.
- Balancing adjustments are calculated when a business ceases.
- The structures and buildings allowance is available on the purchase of certain commercial structures and buildings used in the trade of a business.

Quick quiz

1. For what periods are capital allowances for unincorporated businesses calculated?
2. Are writing down allowances pro-rated in a six-month period of account?
3. Are first year allowances pro-rated in a six-month period of account?
4. When may balancing allowances arise?
5. Within which period must an asset be disposed of for it to be beneficial for it to be treated as a short-life asset?

Answers to quick quiz

1 Periods of account.

2 Yes. In a six-month period, writing down allowance are pro-rated by multiplying by 6/12.

3 No. First year allowances are given in full in a short period of account.

4 Balancing allowances may arise in respect of pooled expenditure only when the trade ceases. Balancing allowances may arise on non-pooled items whenever those items are disposed of.

5 Within eight years of the end of the period of account (or accounting period) in which it was bought.

Trading losses

Topic list

1 Losses – an overview
2 Carry forward trading loss relief
3 Trading loss relief against general income

Introduction

In earlier chapters, we have seen how to compute taxable trading profits, after capital allowances, and allocate them to tax years.

Traders sometimes make losses rather than profits. In this chapter, we consider the reliefs available for losses. A loss does not in itself lead to receiving tax back from HMRC. Relief is obtained by setting a loss against trading profits, other income or capital gains in order to reduce the amount of income or gains subject to tax. There are restrictions on how much loss relief can be claimed in a tax year.

An important consideration is the choice between different reliefs. The aim is to use a loss to save as much tax as possible, as quickly as possible.

In the next chapter, we will consider how individuals trading in partnership are taxed.

PART A TAXATION OF INDIVIDUALS

Exam guide

There are various ways in which a trader can obtain relief for trading losses. You are likely to have to calculate the most beneficial way of obtaining relief. This will involve considering the rate of tax relief, the potential waste of personal allowances and how soon relief can be obtained. Read the question carefully to establish if the taxpayer has any particular requirements, such as the need to obtain relief as soon as possible.

1 Losses – an overview

FAST FORWARD

Trading losses may be relieved against future profits of the same trade, against general income and against capital gains.

1.1 Trading losses in general

This chapter considers how losses are calculated and how a loss-suffering taxpayer can use a loss to reduce his tax liability. Most of the chapter concerns losses in respect of trades, professions and vocations.

The rules in this chapter apply only to individuals, trading alone or in partnership. Loss reliefs for companies are completely different and are covered later in this Workbook.

When computing taxable trading profits, profits may turn out to be negative, meaning a loss has been made in the basis period. **A loss is computed in exactly the same way as a profit**, making the same adjustments to the accounts profit or loss.

If there is a loss in a period, the taxable trading profits for the tax year based on that period are nil.

Question — Loss relief and the tax year basis

Jonjo is a sole trader. He uses 31 December as his year end. He made the following recent trading profits and losses.

	Profit/(loss) £
Year ended 31 December 2024	(72,000)
Year ended 31 December 2025	24,000

Calculate Jonjo's trading loss attributable to the tax year 2024/25.

Answer

The loss in 2024/25 is calculated using the tax year basis, so profits and losses are time apportioned.

	2024/25 £
6 April 2024 – 31 December 2024 (9/12 x 72,000)	(54,000)
1 January 2025 – 5 April 2025 (3/12 x 24,000)	6,000
Loss attributable to 2024/25	(48,000)

1.2 Other losses

Losses incurred in foreign trades are computed and relieved in a similar manner to those of UK trades and are discussed later in this Workbook.

Losses from a UK property business have been discussed earlier, and losses on an overseas property business are relieved similarly. Losses on furnished holiday lettings can only be relieved using carry forward loss relief against future income from furnished holiday lettings. Losses on UK furnished holiday lettings and EEA furnished holiday lettings must be dealt with separately.

If a loss arises on a transaction which, if profitable, would give rise to taxable miscellaneous income (see earlier in this Workbook), it can be set against any other similar income in the same year, and any excess carried forward for relief against miscellaneous income in future years.

2 Carry forward trading loss relief

> **FAST FORWARD**
> A trading loss carried forward must be set against the first available profits of the same trade.

A trading loss not relieved in any other way must be **carried forward to set against the first available profits of the same trade** in the calculation of net trading income. Losses may be carried forward for any number of years.

2.1 Example: carrying forward losses

B has the following results.

Year ending	£
31 March 2023	(6,000)
31 March 2024	5,000
31 March 2025	11,000

B's net trading income, assuming that he claims carry forward loss relief, are:

	2022/23 £		2023/24 £		2024/25 £
Trading profits	0		5,000		11,000
Less carry forward loss relief	(0)	(i)	(5,000)	(ii)	(1,000)
Profits	0		0		10,000

Loss memorandum		£
Trading loss, 2022/23		6,000
Less use in 2023/24	(i)	(5,000)
use in 2024/25 (balance of loss)	(ii)	(1,000)
		0

3 Trading loss relief against general income

> **FAST FORWARD**
> Where a loss relief claim is made, trading losses can be set against general income (and also gains if a further claim is made) in the current tax year and/or general income (and also gains if a further claim is made) in the preceding tax year.

3.1 Introduction

Instead of carrying a trading loss forward against future trading profits, it may be relieved against general income.

3.2 Relieving the loss

Relief is against the income of the tax year in which the loss arose ("a current year claim"). In addition or instead, relief may be claimed **against the income of the preceding year ("a prior year claim").**

If there are losses in two successive years, and relief is claimed against the first year's income both for the first year's loss and for the second year's loss, relief is given for the first year's loss before the second year's loss.

A claim for a loss must be made by the 31 January which is 22 months after the end of the tax year of the loss: so by 31 January 2027 for a loss in 2024/25.

The taxpayer cannot choose the amount of loss to relieve: so the loss may have to be set against income part of which would have been covered by the personal allowance. However, the taxpayer can choose whether to claim full relief in the current year and then relief in the preceding year for any remaining loss, or the other way round.

When calculating the income tax liability, the loss is usually set against non-savings income, then against savings income and finally against dividend income. However, as with the personal allowance and deductible interest (see Chapter 1), it may be beneficial to deduct in a different order.

Relief is available by carry forward for any loss not relieved against general income.

Question — Loss relief against general income

Janet has a loss in her period of account ending 31 March 2025 of £26,000. Her other income is £20,000 rental income a year, and she wishes to claim loss relief for the year of loss and then for the preceding year. Her trading income in the previous year was £nil.

Show her taxable income for each year, and comment on the effectiveness of the loss relief. Assume that tax rates and allowances for 2024/25 have always applied.

Answer

The year of the loss is 2024/25.

	2023/24 £	2024/25 £
Income	20,000	20,000
Less loss relief against general income - current year claim		(20,000)
Less loss relief against general income - prior year claim	(6,000)	
Net income	14,000	0
Less personal allowance	(12,570)	(12,570)
Taxable income	1,430	0

In 2024/25, £12,570 of the loss has been wasted because that amount of income would have been covered by the personal allowance. If Janet chooses to claim loss relief against general income, there is nothing she can do about this waste of loss relief or the personal allowance.

3.3 Capital allowances

A trader may adjust the size of the total loss relief claim by not claiming all available capital allowances. A reduced claim will increase the balance carried forward to the next year's capital allowances computation. This may be a useful **tax planning point where the effective rate of relief for capital allowances in future periods will be greater than the rate of tax relief for the loss relief.**

3.4 Trading losses relieved against capital gains

Where relief is claimed against general income either as a current year claim or a prior year claim, the taxpayer may include **a further claim in the same tax year to set the loss against their chargeable gains in that year.**

The amount of trading loss that can be offset against capital gains is the lower of:

- The remaining loss after the claim for relief against general income; and
- The capital gains arising in the tax year less capital losses arising in that year less capital losses brought forward into that year. This amount of net gains is computed ignoring the annual exempt amount (see later in this Workbook).

The taxpayer cannot specify the amount to be set against capital gains, so the annual exempt amount may be wasted. We include an example here for completeness. You will study chargeable gains later in this Workbook and we suggest that you come back to this example at that point.

Question — Loss relief against income and gains

Sibyl had the following results for 2024/25:

	£
Trading loss in 2024/25	27,000
Income in 2024/25	19,500
2024/25 capital gains less 2024/25 capital losses	12,500
Annual exempt amount for capital gains tax purposes	3,000
Capital losses brought forward from 2023/24	5,100

Show how the trading loss would be relieved against income and gains.

Answer

	£
Income	19,500
Less current year loss relief against general income	(19,500)
Net income	0
Capital gains	12,500
Less trading loss relief: lower of £(27,000 – 19,500) = £7,500 (note 1) and £(12,500 – 5,100) = £7,400 (note 2)	(7,400)
	5,100
Less annual exempt amount	(3,000)
Capital loss brought forward	(2,100)
	0

Note 1 This equals the loss left after the loss relief against general income claim
Note 2 This equals the gains left after losses b/fwd but ignoring the annual exempt amount

A trading loss of £(7,500 – 7,400) = £100 is carried forward. Sibyl's personal allowance is wasted. Her capital losses brought forward of £(5,100 – 2,100) = 3,000 are carried forward to 2025/26.

3.5 Restrictions on trading loss relief against general income

3.5.1 Commercial basis

FAST FORWARD — Loss relief cannot be claimed against general income unless the loss-making business is conducted on a commercial basis.

PART A TAXATION OF INDIVIDUALS

Relief cannot be claimed against general income unless the loss-making business is conducted on a commercial basis with a view to the realisation of profits throughout the basis period for the tax year.

3.5.2 Relief cap

FAST FORWARD

An individual taxpayer can only deduct the greater of £50,000 and 25% of adjusted total income when making a claim for loss relief against general income.

There is a **restriction on certain deductions which may be made by an individual from total income for a tax year**. For the purposes of the Taxation exam, the restricted deductions concern **trade loss relief against general income (whether claimed for the tax year of the loss or the previous year), early trading losses relief, share loss relief against general income** (these latter two reliefs are both dealt with later in this chapter), and **deduction of interest for qualifying purposes** (see earlier in this Workbook).

The total deductions in a tax year cannot exceed the greater of:

(a) **£50,000**; and
(b) **25% of the taxpayer's adjusted total income for the tax year**.

Key term

Adjusted total income is total income plus payroll giving less the gross amounts of personal pension contributions.

If a claim is made for relief against general income in the previous year, there is no restriction on the amount of loss that can be used against trading income (of the same trade). The restriction only applies to the other income in that year. Any loss which exceeds the maximum deduction can still be carried forward against future profits from the same trade.

The limits apply in each year for which relief is claimed. If a current year and a prior year claim are made, the relief in the current year is restricted to the greater of £50,000 and 25% of the adjusted total income in the current year. The relief in the prior year is restricted to the greater of £50,000 and 25% of the adjusted total income in the prior year.

The restriction only applies to relief against income, not if a claim is extended to capital gains.

Question — Restriction on loss relief

Grace has been trading for many years, preparing accounts to 5 April each year. Her recent results have been as follows:

	Profit/(loss) £
Year to 5 April 2024	20,000
Year to 5 April 2025	(210,000)

Grace also owns a number of investment properties and her property business income is £130,000 in 2023/24 and £220,000 in 2024/25.

Show Grace's taxable income for the tax years 2023/24 and 2024/25 assuming that she claims relief for her trading loss against general income in both of those years. Assume the 2024/25 rates and allowances have always applied.

Answer

	2023/24 £	2024/25 £
Trading income	20,000	0
Property business income	130,000	220,000
Total income	150,000	220,000
Less loss relief against general income	(70,000)	(55,000)
Net income	80,000	165,000
Less personal allowance	(12,570)	(0)
Taxable income	67,430	165,000

Loss relief for 2024/25 is capped at £(220,000 × 25%) = £55,000 since this is greater than £50,000. The personal allowance is not available as adjusted net income exceeds £125,140.

In 2023/24, the loss relief claim against trading income in that year is allowed in full against the trading profit of £20,000 (ie it is not capped). Relief against other income is capped at £50,000 since this is greater than £(150,000 × 25%) = £37,500. The total loss relief claim is therefore £(20,000 + 50,000) = £70,000. The balance of the loss is £(210,000 − 55,000 − 70,000) = £85,000 and is carried forward against future profits of the same trade.

Note that the restriction on loss relief means that the loss has been relieved at the additional rate in 2024/25 and at the additional and higher rates in 2023/24. The personal allowance has also been restored for 2023/24.

3.6 The choice between loss reliefs

FAST FORWARD

It is important for a trader to choose the right loss relief, so as to save tax at the highest possible rate and obtain relief reasonably quickly.

When a trader has a choice between loss reliefs, he should aim to obtain relief both quickly and at the highest possible tax rate. However, do consider that losses relieved against income which would otherwise be covered by the personal allowance are wasted.

Question — The choice between loss reliefs

Felicity's trading results are as follows.

Year ended 5 April	Trading profit/(loss) £
2023	2,500
2024	(21,000)
2025	14,600

Her other income (all non-savings income) is as follows.

	£
2022/23	4,900
2023/24	33,600
2024/25	16,400

Show the most efficient use of Felicity's trading loss. Assume that the personal allowance has been £12,570 throughout and that her income prior to 2022/23 was covered by the personal allowance.

PART A   TAXATION OF INDIVIDUALS

Answer

Relief could be claimed against general income for 2022/23 and/or 2023/24, with any unused loss being carried forward. Relief in 2022/23 would be against general income of £(2,500 + 4,900) = £7,400, all of which would be covered by the personal allowance anyway, so this claim should not be made. A loss relief claim against general income should be made for 2023/24 as this saves tax more quickly than a carry forward loss relief claim in 2024/25 would. The final results will be as follows:

	2022/23 £	2023/24 £	2024/25 £
Trading income	2,500	0	14,600
Less carry forward loss relief	(0)	(0)	(0)
	2,500	0	14,600
Other income	4,900	33,600	16,400
	7,400	33,600	31,000
Less loss relief against general income	(0)	(21,000)	(0)
Net income	7,400	12,600	31,000
Less personal allowance	(12,570)	(12,570)	(12,570)
Taxable income	0	30	18,430

Exam focus point

Before recommending loss relief against general income, consider whether it will result in the waste of the personal allowance, the personal savings allowance, the dividend allowance and any tax reducers. Such waste is to be avoided if at all possible.

Another consideration is that a trading loss cannot be set against the capital gains of a year unless relief is first claimed against general income of the same year. It may be worth making the claim against income and wasting the personal allowance in order to avoid a CGT liability. However, remember that using a loss against capital gains will only result in a maximum 20% tax saving (or 24% for residential property), whereas setting losses against income can give a maximum 45% tax saving.

Finally, it is important to consider how offsetting a loss against income will impact the taxation of any income which remains taxable. For example, setting a loss against non-savings income might mean that savings income becomes taxable at the starting rate, rather than the basic rate, or the personal savings allowance may increase, or higher rate income becomes taxable at the basic rate.

3.7 Example

Luke has been in business as a sole trader for many years. In 2024/25, Luke made a profit of £24,570. He anticipates that he will make a loss of £(12,000) in 2025/26.

In 2024/25, Luke received interest of £7,000. He has no other income in 2025/26, so no claim can be made to set off the loss in that tax year.

Before the loss relief claim, Luke's income tax liability in 2024/25 was as follows:

	Non-savings income £	Savings income £	Total £
Trading income	24,570		
Interest		7,000	
Total/net income	24,570	7,000	31,570
Less personal allowance	(12,570)		
Taxable income	12,000	7,000	19,000

Tax
Non-savings income
£12,000 × 20%   2,400
Savings income
£1,000 × 0%   0
£6,000 × 20%   1,200
Income tax liability   3,600

If loss relief is claimed against general income for 2024/25, Luke's income tax liability will be:

	Non-savings income £	Savings Income £	Total £
Total income	24,570	7,000	31,570
Less carry back loss	(12,000)		
Net income	12,570	7,000	19,570
Less personal allowance	(12,570)		
Taxable income	0	7,000	7,000

Tax
Savings income
£5,000 × 0% (savings starting rate)   0
£1,000 × 0% (personal savings allowance)   0
£(7,000 – 5,000 – 1,000) = £1,000 × 20%   200
Income tax liability   200

The tax saved by making the loss relief claim is therefore £(3,600 – 200) = £3,400, which is just over 28.3% of the loss.

PART A TAXATION OF INDIVIDUALS

Chapter roundup

- Trading losses may be relieved against future profits of the same trade, against general income and against capital gains.
- A trading loss carried forward must be set against the first available profits of the same trade.
- Where a loss relief claim is made, trading losses can be set against general income (and also gains if a further claim is made) in the current tax year and/or general income (and also gains if a further claim is made) in the preceding tax year.
- Loss relief cannot be claimed against general income unless the loss-making business is conducted on a commercial basis.
- An individual taxpayer can only deduct the greater of £50,000 and 25% of adjusted total income when making a claim for loss relief against general income but these limits do not apply to relief claimed against profits of the same trade.
- It is important for a trader to choose the right loss relief, so as to save tax at the highest possible rate and so as to obtain relief reasonably quickly.

Quick quiz

1   Against which types of income can trading losses carried forward be set off?

2   Against which years' total income may a loss be relieved against general income for a continuing business which has traded for many years?

3   Maggie has been in business for many years. In 2023/24, she made trading profits of £11,000. She has property income of £6,000 each year. She makes no capital gains.

    Maggie makes a loss of £(28,000) in 2024/25 and expects to make either a loss or smaller profits in the foreseeable future. How can Maggie obtain loss relief?

4   How much is the relief cap which is imposed on an individual claiming loss relief against general income?

Answers to quick quiz

1. Against profits from the same trade.

2. The year in which the loss arose and/or the preceding year.

3. Maggie could make a claim against her general income of £6,000 in 2024/25, but should not do so, as this amount is covered by her personal allowance. She can claim loss relief against general income of £(11,000 + 6,000) = £17,000 in 2023/24. The remaining loss of £(28,000 − 17,000) = £11,000 will be carried forward and set against the first available trading profits of her trade.

4. The greater of £50,000 and 25% of adjusted total income (which is total income plus payroll giving less gross PPCs).

PART A TAXATION OF INDIVIDUALS

Partnerships and limited liability partnerships

Topic list
1 Partnerships
2 Limited liability partnerships

Introduction

In previous chapters, we dealt with the income tax rules for individuals and sole traders. We now see how those rules are adapted to deal with business partnerships.

On the one hand, a partnership is a single trading entity, making profits as a whole. On the other hand, each partner has a personal tax computation, so the profits must be apportioned to the partners. The general approach is to work out the profits of the partnership, then tax each partner as if they were a sole trader running a business equal to their slice of the partnership (for example, 25% of the partnership).

This concludes our study of the different types of UK income to be included in an income tax computation. In the following chapter, we will turn our attention to the overseas aspects of income tax.

PART A TAXATION OF INDIVIDUALS

Exam guide

A question involving unincorporated businesses may deal with a partnership rather than a sole trader. The principles are the same, whether you are considering trading profits, capital allowances or loss reliefs. Just remember that profits are apportioned to partners in the profit-sharing ratio for the period of account after allocating interest on capital and/or salaries.

1 Partnerships

FAST FORWARD

A partnership is simply treated as a source of profits and losses for trades being carried on by the individual partners. Divide profits or losses between the partners according to the profit-sharing ratio in the period of account concerned. If any of the partners are entitled to a salary or interest on capital, apportion this first, not forgetting to pro-rate in periods of less than 12 months.

1.1 Introduction

A partnership is treated like a sole trader when computing its profits. Partners' salaries and interest on capital are not deductible expenses and must be added back in computing profits, because they are a form of drawings.

Once the partnership's profits for a period of account have been computed, they are shared between the partners according to the profit-sharing arrangements for that period of account.

Question — Allocating profits

Steve and Tanya have been in partnership for many years. For the year ended 31 October 2024, taxable trading profits were £70,000. Steve is allocated an annual salary of £12,000 and Tanya's salary is £28,000. The profit-sharing ratio is 2:1.

Allocate the trade profit to each partner for the year ended 31 October 2024.

Answer

Allocate the profits for the year ended 31 October 2024.

	Total £	Steve £	Tanya £
Profit	70,000		
Salaries	40,000	12,000	28,000
Balance (2:1)	30,000	20,000	10,000
Total	70,000	32,000	38,000

1.2 The tax positions of individual partners

Each partner is taxed like a sole trader who runs a business which:

- Starts trading when they join the partnership
- Ceases trading when they leave the partnership
- Has the same periods of account as the partnership (except that a partner who joins or leaves during a period will have a period which starts or ends part way through the partnership's period)
- Makes profits or losses equal to the partner's share of the partnership's profits or losses

1.3 Changes in profit-sharing ratios

The profits for a period of account are allocated between the partners according to the profit-sharing agreement. If the salaries, interest on capital and profit-sharing ratio change during the period of account the profits are time apportioned to the periods before and after the change and allocated accordingly. The constituent elements are then added together to give each partner's share of profits for the period of account.

Question — Change in profit sharing arrangements

Sue and Tim have been in partnership for many years. For the year ended 31 December 2024, taxable trading profits were £50,000. Sue is allocated an annual salary of £10,000 and Tim's salary is £15,000.

The profit-sharing ratio was 1:1 until 31 August 2024 when it changed to 1:2 with no provision for salaries.

Allocate the trade profit to each partner for the year ended 31 December 2024.

Answer

Allocate the profits for the year ended 31 December 2024.

	Total £	Sue £	Tim £
Profit	50,000		
1 January – 31 August (8 months)	33,333		
Salaries (8/12 × £10,000/£15,000)	16,667	6,667	10,000
Balance (1:1)	16,666	8,333	8,333
	33,333		
1 September – 31 December (4 months)	16,667		
Salaries	Nil	–	–
Balance (1:2)	16,667	5,556	11,111
	16,667		
Total	50,000	20,556	29,444

Note. Since the profit-sharing arrangements changed part way through the period of account, the profits and salaries for the period of account must be pro-rated accordingly.

1.4 Changes in membership

FAST FORWARD — Partners joining or leaving the partnership.

Like individual sole traders, partnerships can choose whichever day of the year as their accounts date. Partners use the tax year basis to calculate their trading profits for tax purposes. Where they do not use 31 March or 5 April as their accounting date, the taxable trading income for a tax year is calculated by time-apportioning profits to arrive at the figure for the tax year.

The same is true for partners joining or leaving part way through the tax year. A new partner includes the profit attributable to them between the date they joined and the 5 April. Partners who are leaving the partnership are assessed on their share of the profit arising from 6 April to the date they leave.

PART A TAXATION OF INDIVIDUALS

Question — Partner joining partnership

Daniel and Ashley have been in partnership for many years preparing accounts to 31 December each year and sharing profits in the ratio 2:1.

On 1 September 2024, Kate joined the partnership. From that date, profits were shared 50% to Daniel and 25% each to Ashley and Kate.

The partnership profits for the years ended 31 December 2024 and 2025 were £72,000 and £260,000 respectively.

Compute the partnership profits taxable on Daniel, Ashley and Kate for 2024/25.

Answer

Allocation of partnership profits

	Total £	Daniel £	Ashley £	Kate £
Y/e 31.12.24				
1.1.24 – 31.8.24				
Profits (8/12) 2:1	48,000	24,000	24,000	n/a
1.9.24 – 31.12.24				
Profits (4/12) 50:25:25	24,000	12,000	6,000	6,000
Profit allocation	72,000	36,000	30,000	6,000
Y/e 31.12.25 (50:25:25)	260,000	130,000	65,000	65,000
2024/25 assessments				
Daniel (9/12 × £36,000 + 3/12 × £130,000		59,500		
Ashley (9/12 × £30,000 + 3/12 × £65,000			18,500	
Kate (£6,000 + 3/12 × £65,000				22,250

For Daniel and Ashley the profits are both apportioned to the tax year (6.4.24-5.4.25), whereas Ashley, a new partner, is taxed on the profits from when she became a partner.

Question — Partner leaving partnership

Maxwell, Laura and Wesley traded in partnership for many years, preparing accounts to 5 April.

Each partner was entitled to 5% interest per annum on capital introduced into the partnership. Each partner had introduced £60,000 of capital on the commencement of the partnership. From that date, profits were shared in the ratio 50% to Maxwell, 30% to Laura and 20% to Wesley.

On 1 November 2024, Wesley left the partnership. From that date profits were shared equally between the two remaining partners and no interest was paid on capital. The partnership taxable trading income for the year to 5 April 2025 was £120,000.

Compute the partnership profits taxable on Maxwell, Laura and Wesley for 2024/25.

Answer

Allocation of partnership profits

	Total £	Maxwell £	Laura £	Wesley £
6.4.24 - 31.10.24				
Interest 7/12 × £60,000 × 5% each	5,250	1,750	1,750	1,750
Profits (7/12) 50:30:20	64,750	32,375	19,425	12,950
	70,000	34,125	21,175	14,700
1.11.24 – 5.4.25				
Profits (5/12) 1:1	50,000	25,000	25,000	n/a
Profits allocated for year	120,000	59,125	46,175	14,700

Note: Wesley's taxable trading profit for 2024/25 is the profit arising from 6 April 2024 to the date he leaves the partnership (31 October 2024).

1.5 Loss reliefs

FAST FORWARD There are restrictions on loss reliefs for non-active partners in the first four years of trading.

Partners are entitled to the same loss reliefs as sole traders. Loss relief against general income and carry forward loss relief is available to partners. Different partners may claim loss reliefs in different ways, for example one partner may choose to carry forward, one may choose to carry back.

In addition to the cap on loss reliefs discussed earlier in this Workbook, **there is a further restriction for loss relief for a partner who does not spend a significant amount of time (less than ten hours a week) in running the trade of the partnership.** Such a partner can only use loss relief against general income or against capital gains and early trade losses relief **up to an amount equal to the amount that they contribute to the partnership** and there is an overall cap on relief of £25,000. These rules apply in any of the first four years in which the partner carries on a trade.

1.6 Example: loss relief restriction

Laura, Mark and Norman form a partnership and each contribute £10,000. Laura and Mark run the trade full time. Norman is employed elsewhere and plays little part in running the trade. Profits and losses are to be shared 45:35:20 to L:M:N. The partnership makes a loss of £60,000 of which £12,000 is allocated to Norman.

Norman may only use £10,000 of loss against general income (plus against capital gains) or early trade loss relief. £2,000 is carried forward, for example to be relieved against future profits.

1.7 Assets owned individually

Where the partners own assets (such as their cars) individually, a capital allowances computation must be prepared in respect of these assets (not forgetting any adjustment for private use). **The capital allowances must go into the partnership's tax computation.**

Exam focus point

> Partners are effectively taxed in the same way as sole traders with just one difference. Before you tax the partner you need to take each set of accounts (as adjusted for tax purposes) and divide the trade profit (or loss) between each partner.
>
> Then carry on as normal for a sole trader – each partner is that sole trader in respect of their trade profits for each period of account.

1.8 Partnership investment income

A partnership may have non-trading income, such as interest on the partnership's bank deposit account or dividends on shares, or non-trading losses. **Such items are kept separate from trading income, but they are shared between the partners in a similar way to trading income.**

2 Limited liability partnerships

FAST FORWARD

> Limited liability partnerships are taxed on virtually the same basis as normal partnerships but loss relief is restricted for all partners.

It is possible to form a limited liability partnership. The difference between a limited liability partnership (LLP) and a normal partnership is that **in a LLP the liability of the partners is limited to the capital they contributed.**

The partners of a LLP are taxed on virtually the same basis as the partners of a normal partnership (see above). However, the amount of loss relief that a partner can claim against general income or by early years trade loss relief when the claim is against non-partnership income is restricted to the capital they contributed and is subject to an overall cap of £25,000. This rule is not restricted to the first four years of trading and the rules apply to all partners whether or not involved in the running of the trade.

8: PARTNERSHIPS AND LIMITED LIABILITY PARTNERSHIPS

Chapter roundup

- A partnership is simply treated as a source of profits and losses for trades being carried on by the individual partners. Divide profits or losses between the partners according to the profit-sharing ratio in the period of account concerned. If any of the partners are entitled to a salary or interest on capital, apportion this first, not forgetting to pro-rate in periods of less than 12 months.
- The commencement and cessation rules apply to partners individually when they join or leave.
- There are restrictions on loss reliefs for non-active partners in the first four years of trading.
- Limited liability partnerships are taxed on virtually the same basis as normal partnerships, but loss relief is restricted for all partners.

Quick quiz

1 How are partnership trading profits divided between the individual partners?

2 What loss reliefs are partners entitled to?

3 Janet and John are partners sharing profits 60:40. For the year ended 30 June 2024 the partnership made profits of £100,000. What is John's share of the trading profits in the year ended 30 June 2024?

4 Yolanda and Yan are in partnership sharing profits 80:20. In 2024/25 the business makes a loss of £40,000. Yan decides to use his share of the loss against general income.

Yolanda must also use her share of the loss against general income. True or False?

5 Is a partnership an unincorporated business or an incorporated business (ie a company)?

6 Pete and Doug have been equal partners for many years. On 1 January 2024, Dave joins the partnership and it is agreed to share profits 40:40:20. For the year ended 30 June 2024, profits are £100,000.

What is Doug's share of these profits?

Answers to quick quiz

1 Profits are divided in accordance with the profit-sharing ratio that existed during the period of account in which the profits arose.

2 Partners are entitled to the same loss reliefs as sole traders. These are loss relief against general income, early years trade loss relief, carry forward loss relief, terminal loss relief, and loss relief on transfer of a trade to a company.

3 £40,000
Year ended 30 June 2024
£100,000 × 40% = £40,000

4 False. Yolanda has a choice of loss reliefs:
Loss relief against general income or carry forward loss relief.
Her loss relief claim is unaffected by Yan's.

5 An unincorporated business.

6 £45,000

	Pete £	Doug £	Dave £
Y/e 30 June 2024			
1.7.23 – 31.12.23			
6m × 100,000			
£50,000 50:50	25,000	25,000	
1.1.24 – 30.6.24			
6m × £100,000			
£50,000 40:40:20	20,000	20,000	10,000
	45,000	45,000	10,000

Overseas aspects of income tax

Topic list
1 Liability to UK income tax: basic principles
2 Double taxation relief (DTR)

Introduction

In the previous chapters, we have studied most aspects of income tax. In this chapter we will look at the overseas aspects of income tax.

We start this chapter by looking at taxpayer residency and its implications. We then look at the tax relief which may be available when income is taxed both overseas and in the UK.

In the next chapter, we turn our attention to capital gains tax (CGT). The overseas aspects of CGT are introduced in Chapter 13. We will consider the administration of income tax when we have finished studying CGT as the personal tax return deals with both income and capital gains.

PART A TAXATION OF INDIVIDUALS

Exam guide

In an exam question, you may have to calculate how an individual will be taxed on income from overseas sources depending on their residence. You may also need to calculate how an individual who has gone overseas will be taxed on their UK income. Where relevant exam questions will give details of a taxpayer's residence status.

1 Liability to UK income tax: basic principles

1.1 Overview

A taxpayer's liability to UK income tax depends largely on their residence status.

Generally, a **UK resident individual is liable to UK income tax on their UK and overseas income as it arises (arising basis)**.

A **non-UK resident is liable to UK income tax only on income arising in the UK**.

1.2 Overseas income

1.2.1 Overseas income: general principles

Individuals who are resident in the UK are generally taxable on their overseas income on an arising basis (ie it is irrelevant whether or not the income is remitted to the UK). Double taxation relief may be available if the income is also taxed in the country in which it arises (see later in this chapter).

Overseas income is identified and taxed in broadly the same way as UK income, but the points set out below should be noted.

1.2.2 Overseas property business

An individual who receives rents and other income from property overseas is treated as carrying on an overseas property business. The income from the overseas property business is liable to income tax in the same way as income from a UK property business and is calculated in the same way. If an individual has both a UK and an overseas property business, the profits must be calculated separately.

If a loss arises in an overseas property business, it may be carried forward and set against future income from the overseas property business, as soon as it arises.

The special treatment of furnished holiday lettings does not apply to overseas properties other than those in the European Economic Area.

1.2.3 Overseas dividends

Overseas dividends are dividends from non-UK companies. The income is taxable in the year it arises as it is taxed in the same way as UK dividend income.

1.2.4 Overseas saving income

Foreign savings income, such as interest, is taxed in the same way as UK savings income, ie at 0% in the savings income starting rate band, 0% for income within the personal savings allowance (PSA), 20% in the basic rate band, at 40% in the higher rate band and at 45% thereafter.

1.3 Individuals not resident in the UK

1.3.1 Personal allowances for non-UK residents

In general, **non-UK residents are not entitled to personal allowances**. However, some individuals are entitled to allowances despite being non-UK resident including:

- Citizens of the European Economic Area
- Individuals resident in the Isle of Man and the Channel Islands

1.3.2 Limit on income tax liability for non-UK residents

There is a **limit on the income tax liability** of an individual who is **not resident in the UK** for a complete tax year. The tax cannot exceed **the tax liability if the individual was taxed on all income, apart from disregarded income, without a personal allowance**.

Disregarded income includes **UK savings and dividend income** but does not include non-savings income such as trading, employment or property income.

1.3.3 Savings income and non-UK residents

Interest that arises on UK government 'Free of Tax to Residents Abroad' (FOTRA) securities (broadly, UK Treasury Stock) **is not taxable** if received by **an individual who is not resident in the UK**.

2 Double taxation relief (DTR)

FAST FORWARD

Double taxation relief may be available to reduce the burden of taxation. It is generally given by reducing the UK tax charged by the overseas tax suffered.

1.4 Introduction

As we have seen, **UK tax applies to the worldwide income of UK residents and the UK income of non-residents.**

When other countries adopt the same approach it is clear that some income may be taxed twice:

- Firstly in the country where it arises
- Secondly in the country where the taxpayer resides

Double taxation relief (DTR) as a result of international agreements may avoid the problem, or at least diminish its impact.

1.5 Double taxation agreements

There are a variety of provisions in double taxation agreements between different countries ('contracting states'). For example, there may be rules which render certain profits taxable in only one rather than both of the contracting states.

Exam focus point

You are not required to know details of double taxation agreements in Taxation, only that they exist to prevent double taxation in two countries. You are more likely to have to calculate unilateral relief as described below.

1.6 Unilateral relief

If no relief is available under a double taxation agreement, UK legislation provides for unilateral relief. However, unilateral relief is not available if relief is specifically excluded under the terms of a double tax agreement.

Overseas income must be included gross (i.e, including overseas tax) in the UK tax computation. The foreign tax is deducted from the UK tax liability (this is credit relief) but the relief cannot exceed the UK tax on the overseas income so the taxpayer bears the higher of:

- The UK tax
- The foreign tax

The UK tax on the foreign income is the difference between:

(a) The UK tax before DTR on all income including the overseas income.
(b) The UK tax on all income except the overseas income.

In both (a) and (b), we take account of the PSA, dividend allowance, and tax reducers.

Question — **Double tax relief**

A UK resident individual has the following income for 2024/25.

Sources of income

	£
UK salary	41,650
Interest on overseas loan stock (net of overseas tax at 5%)	4,750
Overseas rents (net of overseas tax at 60%)	1,500

Assuming that maximum DTR is claimed, show the UK tax liability for 2024/25.

Answer

	Non-savings income	*Savings income*	*Total*
	£	£	£
Salary	41,650		
Overseas interest £4,750 × 100/95		5,000	
Overseas property business £1,500 × 100/40	3,750		
Net income	45,400	5,000	50,400
Less personal allowance	(12,570)		
Taxable income	32,830	5,000	37,830

		£
Non-savings income		
£32,830 × 20%		6,566
Savings income		
£500 × 0% (PSA – higher rate taxpayer)		0
£4,370 × 20%		874
£130 × 40%		52
		7,492
Less double taxation relief (see below)		
Rents	876	
Interest	250	
		(1,126)
UK tax liability		6,366

Since the rents are taxed more highly overseas, these should be regarded as the top slice of UK taxable income. Taxable income excluding the rents is £34,080 and the UK tax on this is:

	£
Non-savings income	
£29,080 × 20%	5,816
Savings income	
£1,000 × 0% (PSA – now basic rate taxpayer)	0
£4,000 × 20%	800
	6,616

The UK tax on the rents is £876 (£7,492 – 6,616). Since foreign tax of £2,250 (60% of £3,750) is greater, the DTR is the smaller figure of £876. Then removing the overseas interest: the DTR is the lower of the UK tax of £800 and the overseas tax of £250, so is £250.

Where there is no point in claiming this credit relief, perhaps because loss relief has eliminated any liability to UK tax, the taxpayer may elect for expense relief instead. No credit is given for overseas tax suffered, but only the income after overseas taxes is brought into the tax computation.

If overseas taxes are not relieved in the year in which the income is taxable in the UK, no relief can be obtained in any earlier or later year.

Taxpayers who have claimed relief against their UK tax bill for taxes paid overseas must notify HMRC in writing of any changes to the overseas liabilities if these changes result in the DTR claimed becoming excessive. This rule applies to all taxes not just income tax.

PART A   TAXATION OF INDIVIDUALS

Chapter roundup

- An individual may be either UK resident or non-UK resident.
- Generally, a UK resident is liable to UK income tax on UK and overseas income as it arises. A non-UK resident is liable to UK income tax only on income arising in the UK.
- Double taxation relief may be available to reduce the burden of taxation. It is generally given by reducing the UK tax charged by the overseas tax suffered.

Quick quiz

1   On what basis is a UK resident taxed on overseas income?
2   What is the maximum amount of credit relief that can be given for overseas tax on overseas income?

Answers to quick quiz

1. On the arising basis.
2. The lower of:
   (a) UK tax on the overseas income; and
   (b) The overseas tax on the overseas income.

PART A TAXATION OF INDIVIDUALS

Capital taxes

Chargeable gains: an outline

Topic list
1 Chargeable and exempt persons, disposals and assets
2 Computing a gain or loss
3 CGT payable by individuals
4 Valuing assets
5 Connected persons
6 Married couples and civil partners
7 Part disposals

Introduction

Now that we have concluded our study of the income tax computation, we will consider the capital gains tax computation. As with income tax, capital gains tax is payable by individuals but different computational principles apply.

Capital gains arise when taxpayers dispose of assets, such as investments or capital assets used in the business. If, for example, you buy a picture for £10,000, hang it on your wall for 20 years and then sell it for £200,000, you will have a capital gain.

In this chapter, we see when a capital gain will be liable to tax and how to work out gains and losses.

We also look at some special cases where the rules are modified because of the relationship between the disposer and the acquirer of an asset; without such rules, people could do deals with their relatives to avoid tax.

In the following chapters, we will look at the special rules for certain types of assets and at what reliefs are available.

PART B CAPITAL TAXES

Exam guide

In the exam, you may be asked to calculate a capital gain on the disposal of an asset, and the relevant capital gains tax. You need to know the rules about the date of disposal and then you need to be able to quantify any tax savings that might result from delaying or advancing a sale.

1 Chargeable and exempt persons, disposals and assets

FAST FORWARD For CGT to apply, there needs to be a chargeable person, a chargeable disposal and a chargeable asset.

Exam focus point

For a chargeable gain to arise there must be:

- A chargeable person
- A chargeable disposal
- A chargeable asset

Otherwise no charge to tax occurs.

1.1 Chargeable persons

The following are chargeable persons:

- **Individuals**
- **Partnerships**
- **Companies**
- **Trustees**

We will look at the taxation of chargeable gains on companies later in this Workbook.

Persons who are not resident in the UK are usually exempt persons, although there are some exceptions. We deal with overseas aspects of CGT later in this Workbook.

1.2 Chargeable disposals

FAST FORWARD A chargeable disposal occurs on the date of the contract or when a conditional contract becomes unconditional.

The following are chargeable disposals:

- Sales of assets or parts of assets
- Gifts of assets or parts of assets
- Receipts of capital sums following the surrender of rights to assets
- The loss or destruction of assets
- The appropriation of assets as trading stock

A chargeable disposal occurs on the date of the contract (where there is one, whether written or oral), or the date of a conditional contract becoming unconditional. This may differ from the date of transfer of the asset. However, when a capital sum is received on a surrender of rights or the loss or destruction of an asset, the disposal takes place on the day the sum is received.

The timing of a disposal should be carefully considered bearing in mind these rules. For example, an individual may wish to accelerate a gain into an earlier tax year to obtain earlier loss relief or to delay a gain until a later tax year when an unused annual exempt amount may be available.

Where a disposal involves an acquisition by someone else, their date of acquisition is the same as the date of disposal.

Transfers of assets on death are exempt disposals. The heirs inherit assets as if they bought them at death for their then market values, but there is no capital gain or allowable loss on death. It is possible to vary or disclaim inherited assets. The CGT effect of such a variation or disclaimer is dealt with later in this Workbook.

1.3 Transfers to and from trading stock

When a taxpayer acquires an asset other than as trading stock and then uses it as trading stock, **the appropriation to trading stock normally leads to an immediate chargeable gain or allowable loss**, based on the asset's market value at the date of appropriation. The asset's cost for income tax purposes is that market value.

Alternatively, the trader can elect to have no chargeable gain or allowable loss. In that case, the cost for income tax purposes is reduced by the gain or increased by the loss.

When an asset which is trading stock is appropriated to other purposes, the trade profits are calculated as if the trader had sold it for its market value, and the base cost for capital gains tax purposes is the same value.

1.4 Chargeable assets

All forms of property, wherever in the world they are situated, are chargeable assets unless they are specifically designated as exempt.

The following are exempt assets (gains not taxable, losses not usually allowable losses; the few exceptions are explained in this Workbook).

- **Motor vehicles** suitable for private use
- **National Savings & Investments certificates and premium bonds**
- Foreign currency for private use
- Decorations awarded for bravery (unless purchased)
- Damages for personal or professional injury
- **Gilt-edged securities** (eg Treasury Stock)
- **Qualifying corporate bonds (QCBs)**
- **Certain chattels**
- Debts (except debts on a security)
- Investments held in new individual savings accounts (ISAs)

PART B CAPITAL TAXES

2 Computing a gain or loss

FAST FORWARD

A gain or loss is computed by taking the proceeds and deducting the cost. Incidental costs of acquisition and disposal are deducted together with any enhancement expenditure reflected in the state and nature of the asset at the date of disposal.

2.1 Basic calculation

A gain (or an allowable loss) is generally calculated as follows:

	£
Disposal consideration	45,000
Less incidental costs of disposal	(400)
Net proceeds	44,600
Less allowable costs	(21,000)
Gain	23,600

Usually the disposal consideration is the proceeds of sale of the asset, but a disposal is deemed to take place at market value:

- Where the disposal is **not a bargain at arm's length**
- Where the disposal is made for a **consideration which cannot be valued**
- Where the disposal is by way of a **gift**

Special valuation rules apply for shares (see later in this Workbook).

Incidental costs of disposal may include:

- Valuation fees
- Estate agency fees
- Advertising costs
- Legal costs

Allowable costs include:

- The original cost of acquisition
- Incidental costs of acquisition
- Capital expenditure incurred in enhancing the asset

Enhancement expenditure is capital expenditure which enhances the value of the asset and is reflected in the state or nature of the asset at the time of disposal, or expenditure incurred in establishing, preserving or defending title to, or a right over, the asset. Excluded from this category are:

- Costs of repairs and maintenance
- Costs of insurance
- Any expenditure deductible from trading profits
- Any expenditure met by public funds (for example council grants)

Question   Calculating the gain

Joanne bought a piece of land as an investment for £20,000. The legal costs of purchase were £250.

Joanne sold the land for £35,000. She incurred estate agency fees of £700 and legal costs of £500 on the sale.

Calculate Joanne's gain on sale.

Answer

	£
Proceeds of sale	35,000
Less costs of disposal £(700 + 500)	(1,200)
Net proceeds of sale	33,800
Less costs of acquisition £(20,000 + 250)	(20,250)
Gain	13,550

3 CGT payable by individuals

FAST FORWARD

CGT is usually payable at the rate of 10% or 20% depending on the individual's taxable income. There are rates of 18% and 24% for residential property. Individuals are entitled to an annual exempt amount.

3.1 Introduction

In general, individuals are liable to CGT on the disposal of assets situated anywhere in the world if they are resident the UK. 'Residence' has the same meaning as for income tax purposes (see earlier in this Workbook). The overseas aspects of CGT are discussed later in this Workbook.

An individual pays CGT on any taxable gains arising in the tax year. **Taxable gains are the net chargeable gains (gains minus losses) of the tax year reduced by the annual exempt amount and then by unrelieved losses brought forward from previous years.**

The annual exempt amount applies each tax year. For 2024/25 it is £3,000 (Whillans p.43). **An individual who has gains taxable at more than one rate of tax may deduct any allowable losses and the annual exempt amount for that year in the way that produces the lowest possible tax charge.** We will look at this topic in detail later in this Workbook when we consider gains on residential property and gains qualifying for business asset disposal relief.

3.2 Calculating CGT

3.2.1 CGT on most taxable gains

Taxable gains (other than those arising from residential property and those qualifying for business asset disposal relief) are chargeable to capital gains tax at the rate of 10% or 20% depending on the individual's taxable income for that tax year (Whillans p.44).

To work out which rate applies, follow these rules:

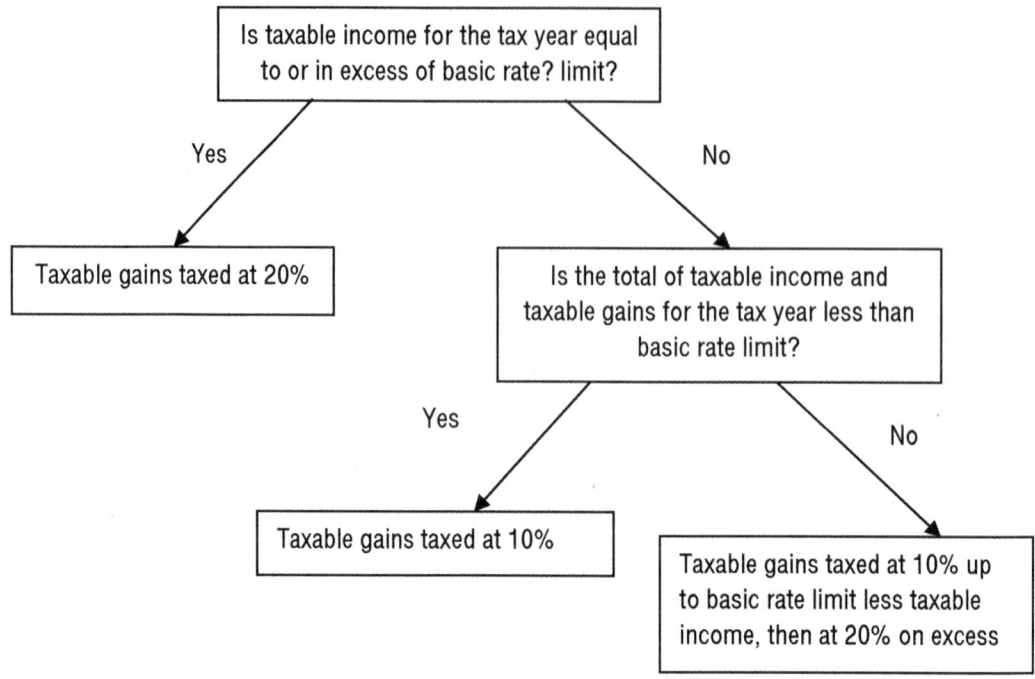

Remember that the basic rate band limit will usually be £37,700 for 2024/25 but the limit will be increased by the gross amount of personal pension contributions and donations made under the Gift Aid scheme.

Question — Rates of CGT on most taxable gains

Mo has taxable income of £26,490 in 2024/25. He made personal pension contributions of £200 (net) per month during 2024/25. In December 2024, he made a chargeable gain of £25,700 on the sale of a painting.

Calculate the CGT payable by Mo for 2024/25.

Answer

	£
Chargeable gain	25,700
Less: annual exempt amount	(3,000)
Taxable gain	22,700
Basic rate band limit	37,700
Add: personal pension contributions £(200 × 12) = £2,400 × 100/80	3,000
Extended basic rate band	40,700
CGT	
£(40,700 – 26,490) = £14,210 (unused basic rate band) @ 10%	1,421
£(22,700 – 14,210) = £8,490 @ 20%	1,698
CGT payable	3,119

3.2.2 CGT on residential property gains

Residential property includes an interest in a dwelling such as a house or flat. It also includes an interest in a contract acquired 'off-plan' where the property has not yet been constructed.

Exam focus point

For the Taxation exam, any gains on land will not be classed as residential property gains.

Taxable gains on residential property which are not fully exempt under private residence relief (see later in this Workbook) **are chargeable to capital gains tax at the rate of 18% or 24%** (Whillans p.44) **depending on the individual's taxable income for the tax year.** Residential property gains within the basic rate band are taxed at 18% and those in excess of the basic rate limit (adjusted as described in the previous section) are taxed at 24%.

If an individual has a mixture of residential property gains and gains on other assets (other than those qualifying for business asset disposal relief – see later in this Workbook), **the annual exempt amount and allowable losses should be deducted first from residential property gains and secondly from gains on other assets.**

Where the individual has unused basic rate band, it should be used on gains other than those on residential property. This will save CGT at 10% rather than 6%.

Question — Rates of CGT on mixture of gains

Rocio has taxable income of £27,500 in 2024/25. In August 2024, she made a chargeable gain of £15,500 on the sale of a painting. In March 2025, she made a chargeable gain of £10,500 on the disposal of a residential property which is not covered by private residence relief.

Calculate the CGT payable by Rocio for 2024/25.

Answer

	Other gain £	Residential property £
Painting	15,500	
Residential property		10,500
Less annual exempt amount (best use)		(3,000)
Taxable gains	15,500	7,500
CGT		
Remaining basic rate band = £10,200 (£37,700 – 27,500)		
If tax residential property gain first		
£7,500 @ 18%		1,350
£2,700 (37,700 – 27,500 – 7,500) @ 10%		270
£12,800 (15,500 – 2,700) @ 20%		2,560
Total CGT		4,180
If tax other gain first		
£10,200 (37,700 – 27,500) @ 10%		1,020
£5,300 (15,500 – 10,200) @ 20%		1,060
£7,500 @ 24%		1,800
Total CGT		3,880

3.2.3 CGT on business asset disposal relief gains

There is also a **special 10% rate of tax** (irrespective of level of income) **for gains for which the taxpayer claims business asset disposal relief.** We will look at this situation later in this Workbook.

3.3 Allowable losses

Deduct allowable capital losses from chargeable gains in the tax year in which they arise. Any loss which cannot be set off is carried forward to set against future chargeable gains. Losses must be used as soon as possible (subject to the rules explained in the following paragraphs). Losses may not normally be set against income.

Allowable losses brought forward are only set off against net chargeable gains (current year chargeable gains less current year allowable losses) **after deduction of the annual exempt amount**. No set-off is made if net chargeable gains for the current year do not exceed the annual exempt amount.

3.4 Example: the use of losses

(a) George has chargeable gains for 2024/25 of £10,000 and allowable losses of £8,000. As the losses are **current year losses** they must be fully relieved against the £10,000 of gains to produce net gains of £2,000, despite the fact that net gains are below the annual exempt amount.

(b) Bob has gains of £15,500 for 2024/25 and allowable losses brought forward of £12,600. The annual exempt amount is deducted from the gain to give £12,500 £(15,500 – 3,000). £12,500 of Bob's brought forward loss is then deducted to bring the taxable gain to nil. The remaining £100 of losses will be carried forward to 2025/26.

(c) Tom has chargeable gains of £2,800 for 2024/25 and losses brought forward of £4,000. His gains of £2,800 are covered by his annual exempt amount for 2024/25 and so the loss of £4,000 is carried forward to 2025/26.

3.5 Losses in the year of death

Losses arising in the tax year in which an individual dies can be carried back to the previous three tax years, later years first, and set against gains of those years after deduction of the appropriate annual exempt amount. Only losses in excess of gains in the year of death can be carried back.

Question — Loss in year of death

Joe dies on 1 January 2025. His chargeable gains and allowable loss have been as follows:

	Gain/(loss) £	Annual exempt amount (AEA) £
2024/25	2,000	3,000
	(33,000)	
2023/24	12,500	6,000
2022/23	9,700	12,300
2021/22	28,700	12,300

How will the loss be set off?

10: CHARGEABLE GAINS: AN OUTLINE

Answer

	Gain/(loss) £
2024/25 net loss to carry back (£33,000 - £2,000)	31,000
2023/24 taxable gain after AEA (£12,500 - £6,000)	(6,500)
2022/23 taxable gain after AEA (£9,700 - £12,300)	-
2021/22 taxable gain after AEA (£28,700 - £12,300)	(16,400)
Unrelieved loss	8,100

The £31,000 net loss which arises in 2024/25 will be carried back. We must set off the current year loss against the 2024/25 gains first, even though the gains are covered by the 2024/25 annual exempt amount.

£6,500 of the loss will be used in 2023/24 against the gain remaining after deducting the annual exempt amount. None of the loss will be used in 2022/23 (because the gains for that year are covered by the annual exempt amount), and so £16,400 of the remaining loss will be used in 2021/22. Repayments of CGT will follow. £8,100 of the loss is wasted because it cannot be carried any further back in time.

4 Valuing assets

FAST FORWARD

Market value must be used in certain capital gains computations. There are special rules for shares and securities.

4.1 General rules

Where market value is used in a chargeable gains computation (see Section 1 above), **the value to be used is the price which the assets in question might reasonably be expected to fetch on a sale in the open market.**

4.2 Shares and securities

Quoted shares and securities are valued using prices in the Stock Exchange Daily Official List.

The valuation method for capital gains tax purposes is as follows:

Lower quoted price + ½ × (higher quoted price – lower quoted price)

In these calculations you should work to the nearest penny.

The valuation for inheritance tax purposes is different (see later in the Workbook).

Question — Calculation of CGT value

Shares in A plc are quoted at 100–110p. The highest and lowest marked bargains were 99p and 110p. What would be the market value for CGT purposes?

Answer

The value will be:

100 + ½ × (110 – 100) = 105

The market value for CGT purposes will therefore be 105p per share.

Note. The marked bargains are not used for CGT valuation.

Unquoted shares are harder to value than quoted shares. HMRC have a special office, Shares and Assets Valuation, to deal with the valuation of unquoted shares.

5 Connected persons

FAST FORWARD

Disposals between connected persons are always deemed to take place for a consideration equal to market value. Any loss arising on a disposal to a connected person can be set only against a gain arising on a disposal to the same connected person.

5.1 Definition and effect

A 'bargain made at arm's length' is a commercial transaction **made under normal circumstances** between two or more **parties. The price and contract terms are influenced by the desire of the parties to each obtain the best possible deal. For CGT purposes, a transaction between 'connected persons' is not considered to be a bargain made at arm's length. This means that, in order to prevent the parties from colluding to create an artificially advantageous tax outcome, the acquisition and disposal are deemed to take place for a consideration equal to the market value of the asset, rather than the actual price paid.** In addition, if a loss results, it can be set only against gains arising in the same or future years from disposals to the same connected person and the loss can only be set off if they are still connected with the person sustaining the loss.

Key term

Connected person. An individual is connected with:

- Their spouse/civil partner
- Their relatives (brothers, sisters, ancestors and lineal descendants)
- The relatives of their spouse/civil partner
- The spouses/civil partners of their relatives and those of their spouse/civil partner
- Their business partners, partners' spouses/civil partners and partners' relatives
- The trustees of a trust of which the individual is the settler

5.2 Assets disposed of in a series of transactions

A taxpayer might attempt to avoid tax by disposing of their property piecemeal to connected persons. For example, a majority holding of shares might be broken up into several minority holdings, each with a much lower value per share, and each of the shareholder's children could be given a minority holding.

To prevent the avoidance of tax in this way, **where a person disposes of assets to one or more persons, with whom they are connected, in a series of linked transactions, the disposal proceeds for each disposal will be a proportion of the value of the assets taken together**. Thus, in the example of the shareholding, the value of the majority holding would be apportioned between the minority holdings. Transactions are linked if they occur within six years of each other.

6 Married couples and civil partners

FAST FORWARD

Spouses/civil partners are treated as separate people. Transfers of assets between spouses/civil partners give rise to neither a gain nor a loss.

Spouses/civil partners are taxed as two separate people. Each has an annual exempt amount and losses of one spouse/civil partner cannot be set against gains of the other.

Disposals between spouses/civil partners who are living together give rise to no gain and no loss, whatever actual price (if any) **was charged by the person transferring the asset** to their spouse/civil partner. This means that there is no chargeable gain or allowance loss and the transferee takes over the transferor's cost.

Since transfers between spouses/civil partners are on a no gain no loss basis, it may be beneficial to transfer the whole or part of an asset to the spouse/civil partner with an unused annual exempt amount or with taxable income below the basic rate limit. The transferee spouse then makes a disposal to a third party, either alone (if the whole asset is transferred) or jointly with the transferor spouse (if only part of the asset is transferred). It is very important that the transferee spouse/civil partner does not have any arrangement to pay back their net proceeds of sale to the transferor spouse/civil partner. If such an arrangement is in place, HMRC may contend that the no gain no loss disposal was not valid and treat the transferor spouse as making the entire disposal.

Question — Inter spouse transfer

Harry has taxable income of £60,000 in 2024/25 and makes chargeable gains of £20,000 in 2024/25 on share disposals. His wife, Margaret, has taxable income of £4,490 in 2024/25 and has no chargeable assets. Harry bought a plot of land for £150,000 in 2016. He gave it to Margaret when it was worth £180,100 on 10 May 2024. Margaret sold it on 27 August 2024 for £185,500. The land does not qualify for business asset disposal relief.

Calculate any chargeable gains arising to Harry and Margaret in respect of the land and show the tax saving arising from the transfer between Harry and Margaret, followed by the disposal by Margaret, compared with Harry directly disposing of the land in August 2024.

Answer

The disposal from Harry to Margaret is a no gain no loss disposal. Harry has no chargeable gain, and the cost for Margaret is Harry's original cost.

The gain on the sale by Margaret is:

	£
Proceeds of sale	185,500
Less cost	(150,000)
Gain	35,500

Margaret's taxable gain after her annual exempt amount is £32,500 (£35,500 − £3,000). Margaret also has £(37,700 − 4,490) = £33,210 of her basic rate band remaining. She will therefore pay CGT at 10% on the taxable gain. By contrast, Harry would have paid CGT on £35,500 at 20%.

The tax saving is therefore:

	£
Tax saved on annual exempt amount £3,000 @ 20%	600
Tax saved at basic rate £32,500 @ (20 − 10)%	3,250
Tax saving on disposal by Margaret instead of Harry	3,850

This tax saving will only be obtained if Margaret does not have an agreement to pay back the net proceeds of sale to Harry.

PART B CAPITAL TAXES

7 Part disposals

FAST FORWARD On a part disposal, the cost must be apportioned between the part disposed of and the part retained.

7.1 Basic rule

The disposal of part of a chargeable asset is a chargeable event. The chargeable gain (or allowable loss) is computed by deducting from the disposal value a fraction of the original cost of the whole asset.

Formula to learn

The fraction is:

$$\frac{A}{A+B} = \frac{\text{value of the part disposed of}}{\text{value of the part disposed of} + \text{market value of the remainder}}$$

In this fraction, A is the proceeds (for arm's length disposals) *before* deducting incidental costs of disposal.

The part disposal fraction should not be applied indiscriminately. Any expenditure incurred wholly in respect of a particular part of an asset should be treated as an allowable deduction in full for that part and not apportioned. An example of this is incidental selling expenses, which are wholly attributable to the part disposed of.

Question
Part disposal

Hannah owns a four-hectare plot of land which originally cost £150,000. Hannah sold one hectare for £60,000. The incidental costs of sale were £3,000. The market value of the three hectares remaining is estimated to be £180,000.

What is the gain on the sale of the one hectare?

Answer

The amount of the indexed cost attributable to the part sold is

$$\frac{60,000}{60,000+180,000} \times £150,000 = £37,500$$

	£
Proceeds	60,000
Less disposal costs	(3,000)
Net proceeds of sale	57,000
Less cost (see above)	(37,500)
Gain	19,500

7.2 Land: small part disposal proceeds

FAST FORWARD On a small part disposal of land, there is no chargeable gain and the net proceeds of disposal are deducted from the cost of the land retained.

Where the **consideration** for a part disposal of land **does not exceed 20% of the market value of the entire holding** of land prior to the part disposal, a chargeable disposal does not take place. The taxpayer must make a **claim** by the first anniversary of 31 January following the end of the tax year. The net disposal proceeds are deducted from allowable expenditure when computing a gain on a later disposal of the remaining land.

Question: Small part disposals of land

Bertha bought 10 acres of land for £20,000. She sold 1½ acres for £5,000 and disposal costs were £50. Market value of the land immediately prior to the disposal was £30,000.

Show Bertha's CGT position.

Answer

The consideration (£5,000) is less than 20% of market value (20% of £30,000 = £6,000). Bertha may therefore claim for the relief to apply. As a result, no chargeable disposal takes place.

Allowable cost of the land retained is:

	£
Cost of 10 acres	20,000
Deduct net proceeds of part disposal (£5,000 – £50)	(4,950)
Allowable expenditure of land retained	15,050

There are two further conditions to meet before this relief can apply:

- Proceeds from the part disposal do not exceed £20,000
- Aggregate proceeds from the part disposal and any other disposals of land (including buildings) in the same tax year do not exceed £20,000

7.3 Example: proceeds exceeding £20,000

If, in the previous example, Bertha had made another disposal of land for £15,750 in the same tax year, the relief could not apply since proceeds for the tax year (ie £15,750 + £5,000 = £20,750) would exceed £20,000. The normal part disposal rules would apply.

PART B   CAPITAL TAXES

Chapter roundup

- For CGT to apply, there needs to be a chargeable person, a chargeable disposal and a chargeable asset.
- A chargeable disposal occurs on the date of the contract or when a conditional contract becomes unconditional.
- A gain or loss is computed by taking the proceeds and deducting the cost. Incidental costs of acquisition and disposal are deducted together with any enhancement expenditure reflected in the state and nature of the asset at the date of disposal.
- CGT is usually payable at the rate of 10% or 20% depending on the individual's taxable income. There are rates of 18% and 24% for residential property. Individuals are entitled to an annual exempt amount.
- Market value must be used in certain capital gains computations. There are special rules for shares and securities.
- Disposals between connected persons are always deemed to take place for a consideration equal to market value. Any loss arising on a disposal to a connected person can be set only against a gain arising on a disposal to the same connected person.
- Spouses/civil partners are treated as separate people. Transfers of assets between spouses/civil partners give rise to neither a gain nor a loss.
- On a part disposal, the cost must be apportioned between the part disposed of and the part retained.
- On a small part disposal of land, there is no chargeable gain and the net proceeds of disposal are deducted from the cost of the land retained.

Quick quiz

1. Give some examples of chargeable disposals.
2. Are the following assets chargeable to CGT or exempt?
   (a) Shares (not held in ISA)
   (b) Car
   (c) Land
   (d) Victoria Cross awarded to owner
   (e) National Savings & Investments Certificates
3. Jed buys a house. He repairs the roof, installs central heating and builds an extension. The extension is blown down in a storm and not replaced. Which of these improvements is allowable as enhancement expenditure on a subsequent sale?
4. At what rate do individuals pay CGT on gains which are not residential property gains and do not qualifying for business asset disposal relief?
5. To what extent must allowable losses be set against chargeable gains?
6. Shares in A plc are quoted at 410 – 414, with bargains at 408, 410 and 416. What is the value for CGT?
7. With whom is an individual connected?
8. 10 acres of land are sold for £15,000, out of a plot of 25 acres. The original cost of the whole plot was £9,000 and costs of sale are £2,000. The rest of the land is valued at £30,000. What is the allowable expenditure?

Answers to quick quiz

1.
   - Sales of assets or parts of assets
   - Gifts of assets or parts of assets
   - Receipts of capital sums following the surrender of rights to assets
   - Loss or destruction of assets
   - Appropriation of assets as trading stock

2.
   (a) Shares – Chargeable
   (b) Car – Exempt as motor vehicle suitable for private use
   (c) Land – Chargeable
   (d) Victoria Cross – Exempt as medal for bravery not acquired by purchase
   (e) National Savings & Investments Certificates – Exempt

3. Repairs to roof – not allowable as enhancement expenditure because not capital in nature
   Central heating – allowable as enhancement expenditure
   Extension – not allowable as not reflected in state of asset at time of disposal

4. 10% and 20%

5. Current year losses must be set off against gains in full, even if this reduces gains below the annual exempt amount. Losses brought forward or carried back from year of death, are set off against gains after deduction of the annual exempt amount.

6. 410 + ½ (414 – 410) = 412

   (Ignore the bargains for CGT purposes)

7. An individual is connected with:
   - Their spouse ('spouse' includes civil partners)
   - Their relatives (brothers, sisters, ancestors and lineal descendants)
   - The relatives of their spouse
   - The spouses of their relatives and their spouse's relatives
   - Their business partners, partners' spouses/civil partners and partners' relatives
   - Trustees of a trust of which the individual is the settlor

8. $\dfrac{15{,}000}{15{,}000 + 30{,}000} \times £9{,}000 = £3{,}000 + £2{,}000$ (costs of disposal) = £5,000

PART B CAPITAL TAXES

Shares and securities

Topic list

1 The matching rules for individuals
2 The share pool
3 Bonus and rights issues

Introduction

In the previous chapter, we have introduced the basic computation of chargeable gains and how to calculate the CGT payable. In this chapter, we look at shares and securities held by individuals.

Shares and securities need special treatment because an investor may hold several shares or securities in the same company, bought at different times for different prices but otherwise identical.

The rules for shares and securities held by companies are different and are dealt with later in this Workbook.

In the next chapter, we will consider CGT deferral reliefs and the CGT implications of varying a will.

Exam guide

Shares and securities are some of the more common assets held by individuals. Knowing how to compute the gain on their disposal is fundamental to an understanding of capital gains.

1 The matching rules for individuals

FAST FORWARD

There are special rules for matching shares sold with shares purchased. Disposals are matched first with shares acquired on the same day, then within the following 30 days and finally with the share pool.

Quoted and unquoted shares and securities present special problems when attempting to compute gains or losses on disposal. For instance, suppose that an individual bought some quoted shares in X plc as follows.

Date	Number of shares	Cost £
5 May 2006	100	150
17 June 2023	50	375

On 15 June 2024, they sold 80 of the shares for £1,450. To determine the chargeable gain, we need to be able to work out which shares out of the two original holdings were actually sold.

We therefore need **matching rules**. These **allow us to decide which shares have been sold and so work out what the allowable cost on disposal should be.**

At any one time, we will only be concerned with shares or securities of the same class in the same company. If an individual owns both ordinary shares and preference shares in X plc, we will deal with the two classes of share entirely separately, because they are distinguishable.

Below 'shares' refers to both shares and securities.

For individuals, share disposals are matched with acquisitions in the following order:

(a) **Same day acquisitions**

(b) **Acquisitions within the following 30 days** (known as the 'bed and breakfast rule') if more than one acquisition on a 'first in, first out' (FIFO) basis

(c) **Any shares in the share pool** (see below)

The 'bed and breakfast' rule stops shares being sold to crystallise a capital gain or loss, usually to use the annual exempt amount and then being repurchased a day or so later. Without the rule a gain or loss would arise on the sale since it would be 'matched' to the original acquisition.

Exam focus point

A crucial first step to getting a shares question right is to correctly match the shares sold to the original shares purchased. You can refer to the matching rules in Whillans (p.45).

2 The share pool

2.1 Composition of pool

We treat any other shares acquired as a 'pool' which grows as new shares are acquired and shrinks as they are disposed.

In making computations which use the share pool, we must keep track of:

(a) The **number** of shares.
(b) The **cost** of the shares.

2.2 Disposals from the share pool

In the case of a disposal, the cost attributable to the shares disposed of is deducted from the amounts within the share pool. **The proportion of the cost to take out of the pool should be computed using the A/(A + B) fraction that is used for any other part disposal**. However, we are not usually given the value of the remaining shares (B in the fraction). We just use numbers of shares.

Question — The share pool

In August 2018, Oliver acquired 4,000 shares in Twist plc at a cost of £10,000. Oliver sold 3,000 shares on 10 July 2024 for £17,000.

Compute the gain and the value of the share pool following the disposal.

Answer

The gain is computed as follows:

	£
Proceeds	17,000
Less cost (working)	(7,500)
Gain	9,500

Working: share pool

	No. of shares	Cost £
Acquisition – August 2018	4,000	10,000
Disposal – July 2024	(3,000)	
Cost $\frac{3,000}{4,000} \times £10,000$		(7,500)
	1,000	2,500

Question — Matching rules

Anita acquired shares in Kent Ltd as follows:

1 July 2001	1,000 shares for £2,000
11 April 2006	2,500 shares for £7,500
17 July 2024	400 shares for £1,680
10 August 2024	500 shares for £2,000

Anita sold 4,000 shares for £16,400 on 17 July 2024.

Calculate Anita's net gain on sale.

PART B CAPITAL TAXES

Answer

First match the disposal with the acquisition on the same day (17/07/2024):

	£
Proceeds $\frac{400}{4,000} \times £16,400$	1,640
Less cost	(1,680)
Loss	(40)

Next match the disposal with the acquisition in the next 30 days (10/08/2024):

	£
Proceeds $\frac{500}{4,000} \times £16,400$	2,050
Less cost	(2,000)
Gain	50

Finally, match the disposal with the shares in the share pool:

	£
Proceeds $\frac{3,100}{4,000} \times £16,400$	12,710
Less cost (W)	(8,414)
Gain	4,296

Net gain £(50 + 4,296 – 40) 4,306

Working

	No. of shares	Cost £
1.7.01 Acquisition	1,000	2,000
11.4.06 Acquisition	2,500	7,500
	3,500	9,500
17.7.24 Disposal	(3,100)	(8,414)
c/f	400	1,086

3 Bonus and rights issues

3.1 Bonus issues (scrip issues)

When a company issues bonus shares all that happens is that the size of the original holding is increased. Since bonus shares are free shares, issued at no cost, there is no need to adjust the original cost. Instead the numbers purchased at particular times are increased by the bonus. The normal matching rules will then be applied.

Question — Bonus issue

Abdi had the following transactions in A Ltd:

1.9.09	Bought 9,000 shares for £16,000
1.3.15	Took up 1 for 3 bonus issue
13.9.24	Sold 3,000 shares for £12,000

Compute the gain arising in September 2024.

Answer

Share pool

	No. of shares	Cost £
1.9.09 Acquisition	9,000	16,000
1.3.15 Bonus issue	3,000	0
	12,000	16,000
13.9.24 Sale	(3,000)	(4,000)
c/f	9,000	12,000

Gain

	£
Proceeds	12,000
Less cost	(4,000)
Gain	8,000

3.2 Rights issues

The difference between a bonus issue and a rights issue is that in a rights issue the new shares are paid for and this results in an adjustment to the original cost.

In an **open offer**, shareholders have a right to subscribe for a minimum number of shares based on their existing holdings and may buy additional shares. Subscriptions up to the minimum entitlement are treated as a rights issue. Additional subscriptions are treated as new purchases of shares.

Question — Rights issue

Simon had the following transactions in S Ltd:

1.10.07	Bought 10,000 shares for £15,000
1.2.13	Took up rights issue 1 for 2 at £2.75 per share
14.10.24	Sold 2,000 shares for £6,000

Compute the gain arising in October 2024.

Answer

Share pool

	No. of shares	Cost £
1.10.07 Acquisition	10,000	15,000
1.2.13 Rights issue	5,000	13,750
	15,000	28,750
14.10.24 Sale	(2,000)	(3,833)
c/f	13,000	24,917

Gain

	£
Proceeds	6,000
Less cost	(3,833)
Gain	2,167

3.3 Sales of rights nil paid

Where the shareholder does not take up rights but sells them to a third party without paying the company for the rights shares, the proceeds are treated as a capital distribution (see above) **and will be dealt with either under the part disposal rules or, if not more than the higher of £3,000 and 5% of the value of the shareholding giving rise to the disposal, as a reduction of original cost** (unless the taxpayer wants the part disposal treatment, for example if the gain would be covered by the annual exempt amount).

Chapter roundup

- There are special rules for matching shares sold with shares purchased. Disposals are matched first with shares acquired on the same day, then within the following 30 days and finally with the share pool.
- Bonus and rights issues involve new shares being allocated to existing shareholders.

Quick quiz

1. In what order are acquisitions of shares matched with disposals for individuals?
2. In July 2007, an individual acquired 1,000 shares. They acquired 1,000 more shares on each of 15 January 2009 and 15 January 2025 in X plc. They sold 1,500 shares on 10 January 2025. How are the shares matched on sale?
3. Sharon acquired 10,000 share in Z plc in 2007. She took up a 1 for 2 rights offer in July 2024. How many shares does Sharon have in her share pool after the rights issue?
4. How are bonus issues dealt with?
5. What is the treatment of the proceeds from the sale of rights nil paid?

PART B   CAPITAL TAXES

Answers to quick quiz

1. The matching of shares sold is in the following order.
   (a) Same day acquisitions
   (b) Acquisitions within the following 30 days
   (c) Shares in the share pool

2. 15 January 2025 1,000 shares (following 30 days)
   Share pool 500 shares

3. 10,000 + 5,000 = 15,000 shares

4. Number of shares increased, no adjustment to cost.

5. The proceeds are treated as a capital distribution and will be dealt with either under the part disposal rules or, if not more than the higher of £3,000 and 5% of the value of the shareholding giving rise to the disposal, as a reduction of original cost (unless the taxpayer wants the part disposal treatment, for example if the gain would be covered by the annual exempt amount).

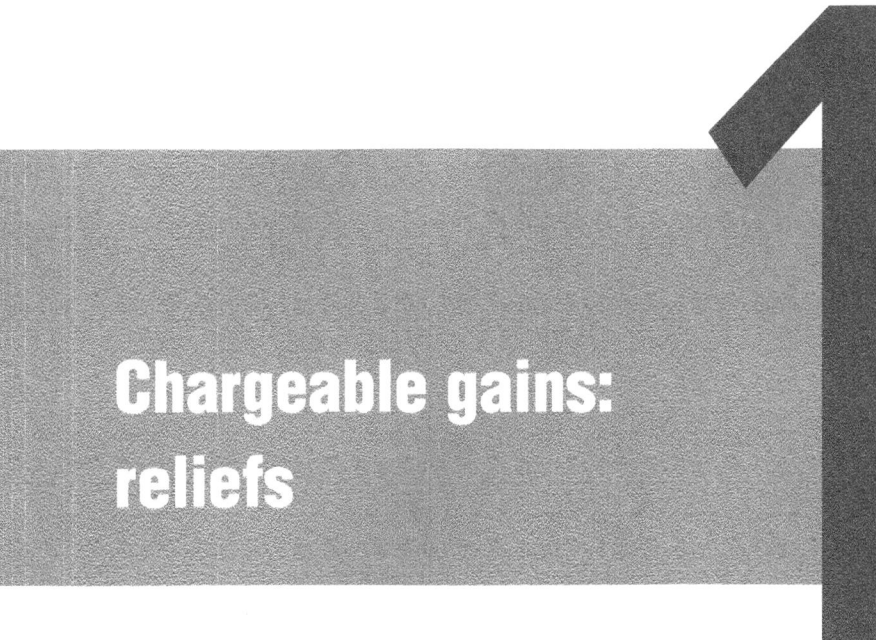

Chargeable gains: reliefs

Topic list
1 Business asset disposal relief
2 Investors' relief
3 Gift relief (holdover relief)
4 The replacement of business assets (rollover relief)

Introduction

In the previous chapters, we have seen how to calculate chargeable gains. We now look at various reliefs relating to gains.

Business asset disposal relief is a very important relief. It applies on the disposal of a business and on the disposal of certain trading company shares. It applies a rate of 10% on all or part of the chargeable gains arising on such disposals, regardless of the level of the individual's taxable income.

Investors' relief also allows a capital gains tax rate of 10% to be applied to qualifying gains. This only applies to share disposals subject to certain conditions relating to those shares.

In certain circumstances, it may be possible to defer a gain – that is, to remove it from an immediate charge to CGT. However, it is important to realise the gain has not been exempted entirely and it may become chargeable in the future.

Deferral reliefs operate in two ways. First, the gain may be deducted from the base cost of an asset (for example, rollover relief for replacement with non-depreciating business assets, gift relief). Second, the gain may be 'frozen' until a certain event occurs (deferral relief for replacement with depreciating business assets).

In the next chapter, we will look at some further rules for gains and losses.

Exam guide

Deferring and minimising tax liabilities are likely to feature at some point in your exam. These reliefs are examined frequently in calculating capital gains tax.

1 Business asset disposal relief

FAST FORWARD

Business asset disposal relief applies on the disposal of a business and certain trading company shares. The rate of tax on gains qualifying for business asset disposal relief is 10%. There is lots of detail in Whillans (p.45).

1.1 Conditions for business asset disposal relief

An individual can claim business asset disposal relief on the following disposals:

- A disposal of the **whole or part of a sole trader business** which has been **owned by the individual** throughout the period of **two years** ending with the date of the disposal.

- A disposal of **one or more assets in use for the purposes of a business at** the time at which the business **ceases to be carried on** provided that:

    - The business was owned by the individual throughout **the period of two years** ending with the date on which the business ceases to be carried on; **and**

    - The date of cessation is within **three years** ending with the date of the disposal.

- Disposal of shares or securities of a company where the company is the individual's personal company; the company is either a trading company or holding company of a trading group; the individual is an officer or employee of the company (or a group company) and these conditions are met either:

    - Throughout the period of **two years** ending with the date of the disposal; **or**

    - Throughout the period of **two years** ending with the date on which the company (or group) **ceases to be a trading company (or trading group)** and that date is within the period of **three years** ending with the date of the disposal.

For the first category to apply, there has be a **disposal of the whole or part of the business as a going concern**, not just a disposal of individual assets. A business includes one carried on as a partnership of which the individual is a partner. The business must be a **trade, profession or vocation** conducted on a **commercial basis with a view to the realisation of profits**.

In relation to the third category, a **personal company** in relation to an individual is one where the individual:

- Holds at least 5% of the ordinary share capital; and

- Can exercise at least 5% of the voting rights in the company by virtue of that holding of shares; and

- Is entitled to either at least 5% of the profits on distribution **and** 5% of the assets on a winding up by virtue of that holding of shares, or at least 5% of the proceeds on a disposal of the whole ordinary share capital.

For both the first and second category, relief is only available on relevant business assets. These are assets used for the purposes of the business and cannot include shares and securities or assets held as investments.

Exam focus point

> A new issue of shares may dilute an individual's shareholding below 5%. Elections are available to help preserve business asset disposal relief in such a scenario but these are outside the scope of the Taxation syllabus.

1.2 The operation of the relief

Where there are disposals of several business assets which result in both gains and losses, the losses are netted off against the gains to give a single chargeable gain on the disposal of the business assets.

The rate of tax on this chargeable gain is 10%, regardless of the level of the individual's taxable income.

An individual may use losses from disposals where business asset disposal relief is not available (or has not been claimed) and the annual exempt amount in the most beneficial way.

This will be achieved if these amounts are **set off in the following order:**

(a) **Residential property gains (18%/ 24%)**
(b) **Other gains not qualifying for business asset disposal relief (10%/ 20%)**
(c) **Business asset disposal relief gains (10%)**

The chargeable gain qualifying for business asset disposal relief is treated as the lowest part of the amount on which an individual is chargeable to capital gains tax. Although this does not affect the tax on the gain qualifying for business asset disposal relief (which is always at 10%), it may have an effect on the rate of tax on other taxable gains.

1.3 Example: Business asset disposal relief

Simon sold his business, all the assets of which qualify for business asset disposal relief, in September 2024. The chargeable gain arising is £13,000.

Simon also made a chargeable gain of £21,600 in December 2024 on an asset which is not residential property and which does not qualify for business asset disposal relief.

Simon has taxable income of £21,000 in 2024/25.

The CGT payable for 2024/25 is calculated as follows:

	Gains £	CGT £
Gains qualifying for business asset disposal relief		
Taxable gains	13,000	
CGT @ 10%		1,300
Gains not qualifying for business asset disposal relief		
Gain	21,600	
Less annual exempt amount (best use)	(3,000)	
Taxable gain	18,600	
CGT on £(37,700 – 21,000 – 13,000) = 3,700 @ 10%		370
CGT on £(18,600 – 3,700) = 14,900 @ 20%		2,980
CGT payable		3,350

Note. The £13,000 gain qualifying for business asset disposal relief is deducted from the basic rate limit for the purposes of computing the rate of tax on the gain not qualifying for business asset disposal relief.

1.4 Lifetime limit

There is a limit of £1 million of gains on which business asset disposal relief can be claimed. This is a lifetime amount applicable to disposals made on or after **6 April 2008**. The amount of the lifetime limit has varied over the years since 2008 (see below) but the £1 million limit applies when computing business asset disposal relief for disposals made on or after 11 March 2020.

There were different lifetime limits in earlier years as follows:

Prior to 6 April 2010	£1 million
From 6 April 2010 to 22 June 2010	£2 million
From 23 June 2010 to 5 April 2011	£5 million
From 6 April 2011 to 10 March 2020	£10 million

These limits are given in the tax rates and allowances table in the exam.

> **Exam focus point**
>
> If a question involving a disposal in the current year gives information about a previous disposal on which business asset disposal relief was claimed, you should check how much of the previous gain would have qualified for business asset disposal relief, using the relevant lifetime limit at the time of that previous disposal. You can then work out how much of the current lifetime limit remains for the disposal in the current year.

Question — Limit on business asset disposal relief

Maureen sold a shareholding in January 2025, realising a gain of £930,000. The conditions for business asset disposal relief are satisfied for this disposal and Maureen makes a claim for the relief to apply. Maureen had already made a claim for business asset disposal relief in respect of a disposal in May 2010, which gave rise to gains totalling £270,000. Maureen also makes an allowable loss of £(23,000) in 2024/25 on an asset not qualifying for business asset disposal relief. Her taxable income for 2024/25 is £200,000.

Calculate the CGT payable by Maureen for 2024/25.

Answer

	Gains £	CGT £
Gains qualifying for business asset disposal relief		
£(1,000,000 – 270,000) (note)	730,000	
CGT @ 10% on £730,000		73,000
Gains not qualifying for business asset disposal relief		
£(930,000 – 730,000)	200,000	
Less: allowable loss (best use)	(23,000)	
Net gain	177,000	
Less: annual exempt amount (best use)	(3,000)	
Taxable gain	174,000	
CGT @ 20% on £174,000		34,800
Total CGT payable		107,800

Note. The disposal in May 2010 fully qualified for business asset disposal relief as it was below the lifetime limit in May 2010 of £2 million.

1.5 Claim

An individual must claim business asset disposal relief; it is not automatic.

The claim deadline is the first anniversary of 31 January following the end of the tax year of disposal. For a 2024/25 disposal, the taxpayer must claim by 31 January 2027.

2 Investors' relief

2.1 The relief

FAST FORWARD

Investors' relief is available to individuals on disposals of shares in unlisted trading companies. Subject to certain conditions, qualifying gains are taxed at 10%.

To qualify for investors' relief, a gain must be on disposal of qualifying shares which satisfy the following conditions:

- The individual taxpayer must have subscribed for them (bought them new);
- The shares are in an unlisted trading company (or unlisted holding company of a trading group); and
- The shares were issued no sooner than 17 March 2016 and were held for a continuous three-year period from 6 April 2016 (or the date of acquisition if later).

There is no minimum shareholding requirement.

Normally, investors' relief is not available to individual taxpayers who are officers or employees of the company in question. There are limited exceptions for unremunerated officers and employees who subsequently join the company.

Investors' relief can be claimed on up to £10 million of qualifying gains throughout the taxpayers' lifetime.

Qualifying gains are taxed at 10%.

Question — Investors' relief

Davina, a higher-rate taxpayer, has disposed of two shareholdings in 2024/25.

1. A 12% shareholding in Danatel plc, generating a gain of £40,000. Danatel plc is the holding company of a trading group and is quoted on a recognised stock exchange. Davina subscribed for the shares in 2018, Davina worked for Danatel plc when she subscribed for the shares but she left in 2020.
2. A 4% shareholding in Seetel Ltd, an unquoted trading company generating a chargeable gain of £12,000. Davina has never been employed by Seetel Ltd. She subscribed for the shares in May 2016.

Davina made no other disposals in 2024/25.

Calculate Davina's capital gains tax liability for 2024/25.

Answer

	Investors' relief £	Other gains £
Gains qualifying for investors' relief - Seetel Ltd shares	12,000	
Other gains		40,000
Annual exempt amount		(3,000)
Taxable gains	12,000	37,000
CGT at 10% and 20%	1,200	7,400
Capital gains tax payable		8,600

Tutorial note

The Danatel plc shares do not qualify for either business asset disposal (BADR) relief or investors' relief (IR). BADR does not apply because she has not been an employee in the two years up to the date of the disposal. IR does not apply because Danatel plc is a quoted company.

Seetel Ltd shares do qualify for investors' relief: unquoted trading company, no employment, shares issued after 17 March 2016 and held for at least three years immediately before disposal.

3 Gift relief (holdover relief)

3.1 The relief

FAST FORWARD

Gift relief is available on both outright gifts and sales at an undervalue of business assets. Gift relief is also available on gifts which are immediately chargeable to inheritance tax.

If an individual gives away a qualifying asset, the donor and the recipient can jointly elect (or, where a trust is the recipient, the donor alone can elect) within four years after the end of the tax year of the transfer (by 5 April 2029 for a disposal in 2024/25), **that the donor's gain be reduced, possibly to nil. The recipient is then deemed to acquire the asset for market value at the date of transfer less the donor's deferred gain.**

If a disposal involves actual consideration rather than being an outright gift, but is still not a bargain made at arm's length, the proceeds are deemed to be the market value of the asset **and any excess of actual consideration over allowable cost is chargeable immediately and only the balance of the gain is deferred.** The amount chargeable immediately is limited to the full gain.

Question
Gift relief

On 6 December 2024, Angelo sold to his son Michael a freehold shop valued at £200,000 for £50,000 and claimed gift relief. Angelo had originally purchased the shop from which he had run his business in July 2008 for £30,000. He continued to run his business from another shop. Michael decided to sell the shop in May 2025 for £195,000.

Compute any chargeable gains arising. Assume the rules of CGT in 2024/25 continue to apply in May 2025.

12: CHARGEABLE GAINS: RELIEFS

Answer

Angelo's CGT position (2024/25)

	£
Proceeds (market value)	200,000
Less cost	(30,000)
Gain	170,000
Less gain deferred	(150,000)
Chargeable gain £(50,000 – 30,000)	20,000

Michael's CGT position (2025/26)

	£
Proceeds	195,000
Less cost £(200,000 – 150,000)	(50,000)
Gain	145,000

You may need to consider whether it would be more beneficial for an individual to claim business asset disposal relief or gift relief or both reliefs. Remember that business asset disposal relief is only available on the disposal of the whole or part of a business and not on individual business assets, so it is possible that only gift relief will apply to the disposal anyway.

An individual might wish to claim business asset disposal relief instead of gift relief if there are only a very small amount of gains (after deduction of losses and annual exempt amount), which are then taxable at the advantageous rate of 10%.

If both reliefs are claimed, gift relief will apply first and then business asset disposal relief will apply to the remaining gain. This may be relevant if there is actual consideration paid so that gift relief covers only part of the gain.

Question

Interaction of reliefs

On 10 January 2025, Zoe sold her business to her son, Darren. The only chargeable assets were goodwill which Zoe had built up from the start of her business and a freehold shop which Zoe had bought in September 2004 for £35,000. The goodwill was valued at £25,000 and the shop at £80,000. Darren paid Zoe £10,000 for the goodwill and £60,000 for the shop.

Zoe made a claim for business asset disposal relief (her first such claim) and Zoe and Darren made a claim for gift relief. Zoe has no other chargeable assets.

Show the CGT positions of Zoe and Darren.

Answer

Zack's CGT position

Goodwill	£	£
Market value	25,000	
Less cost	(nil)	
Gain	25,000	
Less gain deferred	(15,000)	
Chargeable gain £(10,000 – nil)		10,000
Shop		
Market value	80,000	
Less cost	(35,000)	
Gain	45,000	
Less gain deferred (Balancing figure)	(20,000)	
Chargeable gain £(60,000 – 35,000)		25,000
Gains left in charge after gift relief		35,000
Less annual exempt amount		(3,000)
Taxable gains		32,000
CGT @ 10%		3,200

Darren's CGT position

Goodwill	£
Market value	25,000
Less gain deferred	(15,000)
Cost for future disposal	10,000
Shop	£
Market value	80,000
Less gain deferred	(20,000)
Cost for future disposal	60,000

3.2 Qualifying assets

Gift relief can be claimed on gifts or sales at undervalue as follows:

(a) Transfers of **business assets** (Whillans p.47):

    (i) Trade assets
    (ii) Agricultural property
    (iii) Shares and securities (except where the transferee is a company).

(b) Transfers of **any assets** subject to an immediate inheritance tax (IHT) charge. IHT is covered later in this Workbook.

Transfers of business assets are transfers of assets.

(a) **Used in a trade, profession or vocation** carried on:

    (i) By the donor; or
    (ii) If the donor is an individual, by a trading company which is the donor's 'personal company' or a member of a trading group of which the holding company is the donor's 'personal company' (a personal company is one in which the individual can exercise at least 5% of the voting rights); or

(iii) If the donor is a trustee, by the trustee or by a beneficiary who has an interest in possession in the settled property

If the asset was used for the purposes of the trade, profession or vocation for only part of its period of ownership, the gain to be held over is the gain otherwise eligible × period of such use/total period of ownership.

If the asset was a building or structure only partly used for trade, professional or vocational purposes, only the **part of the gain attributable to the part so used is eligible for gift relief.**

(b) **Agricultural property** which would attract inheritance tax agricultural property relief (see later in this Workbook). The restrictions for periods of non-trade use and for partial trade use mentioned above do not apply.

(c) **Shares and securities in trading companies**, or holding companies of trading groups, where:
  (i) The shares or securities are **not listed on a recognised stock exchange** (but they may be on the AIM);
  (ii) If the donor is an individual, the company concerned is their **personal company** (defined as above); or
  (iii) If the donor is a trustee, the trustee can exercise 25% or more of the voting rights.

If relief is claimed on a transfer of business assets, and that transfer is (or later becomes) chargeable to inheritance tax, then when the transferee disposes of the assets their gain is reduced by the IHT finally payable (but not so as to create a loss).

Transfers subject to an immediate IHT charge include most gifts to trusts. A transfer will be regarded as chargeable to IHT even if it falls within the nil rate band of that tax or is covered by the IHT annual exemption. Gifts to settlor interested trusts, however, do not qualify for gift relief.

If a transfer of business assets could also be subject to an immediate charge to inheritance tax, the rules relating to the latter category apply and the restrictions related to period of use and to chargeable business assets therefore do not apply.

Remember that IHT is covered in detail later in this Text. You should return to this section once you have studied the relevant chapters.

3.3 Anti-avoidance rules

Gift relief is not available if the recipient is not resident in the UK at the time of the gift. If the transferee is an individual who becomes non-resident in the UK in any of the six tax years following the year of the transfer and before disposing of the asset transferred, then the gain held over is chargeable on them as if it arose immediately before they become non-resident in the UK.

It is not possible to claim gift relief on transfers to a settlor-interested trust.

Exam focus point

Gift relief is normally used whenever a business or business asset is gifted, but you should look out for the restriction for a non-resident donee.

You should also consider whether retaining the asset until death so as to obtain the tax-free uplift to probate value would be advantageous.

4 The replacement of business assets (rollover relief)

4.1 Conditions

FAST FORWARD

When assets falling within certain classes are sold and other such assets are bought, it is possible to defer gains on the assets sold by claiming rollover relief. See Whillans (p.48).

A gain may be 'rolled over' (deferred) where it arises on the disposal of a business asset which is replaced. This is **rollover relief**. A claim cannot specify that only part of a gain is to be rolled over. A claim for the relief must be made by **the later of** four years from the end of the tax year in which the disposal of the old asset takes place and four years from the end of the tax year in which the new asset is acquired. For example, if the old asset is disposed of in 2022/23 and the new asset is acquired in 2024/25, the time limit for a claim to roll-over relief is 5 April 2029 (four years from the end of the tax year in which the new asset is acquired).

All the following conditions must be met:

(a) **The old asset sold and the new asset bought are both used only in the trade** or trades carried on **by the person claiming rollover relief**. Where part of a building is in non-trade use for all or a substantial part of the period of ownership, the building (and the land on which it stands) can be treated as two separate assets, the trade part (qualifying) and the non-trade part (non-qualifying). This split cannot be made for other assets.

(b) **The old asset and the new asset both fall within one** (but not necessarily the same one) **of the following classes:**
   (i) Land and buildings (including parts of buildings) occupied, as well as used, only for the purpose of the trade
   (ii) Fixed (that is, immovable) plant and machinery
   (iii) Goodwill (not for companies)

(c) **Reinvestment of the proceeds of the old asset takes place in a period beginning one year before and ending three years after the date of the disposal**

(d) **The new asset is brought into use in the trade on its acquisition** (not necessarily immediately, but not after any significant and unnecessary delay)

The new asset can be for use in a different trade from the old asset.

A rollover claim is not allowed when a taxpayer buys premises, sells part of the premises at a profit and then claims to roll over the gain into the part retained. However, a rollover claim is allowed (by concession) when the proceeds of the old asset are spent on improving a qualifying asset which the taxpayer already owns. The improved asset must already be in use for a trade, or be brought into trade use immediately the improvement work is finished.

4.2 Operation of relief

FAST FORWARD

If an amount less than the proceeds of the old asset is invested in the new assets, a gain equal to the difference will be chargeable up to a maximum of the actual gain.

Deferral is obtained by deducting the chargeable gain from the cost of the new asset. For full relief, the whole of the consideration for the disposal must be reinvested. Where only part is reinvested, a part of the gain equal to the lower of the full gain and the amount not reinvested will be liable to tax immediately.

The new asset will have a base cost for chargeable gains purposes, of its purchase price less the gain rolled over into its acquisition.

Question — Rollover relief

A freehold factory was purchased by Zoë for business use in August 2006. It was sold in December 2024 for £70,000, giving rise to a gain of £17,950. A replacement factory was purchased in June 2025 for £60,000.

Compute the base cost of the replacement factory, taking into account any possible rollover of the gain from the disposal in December 2024.

Answer

	£
Total gain	17,950
Less gain rolled over	(7,950)
Chargeable immediately (ie amount not reinvested: £(70,000 – 60,000))	10,000
Cost of new factory	60,000
Less rolled over gain	(7,950)
Base cost of new factory	52,050

You may need to consider whether an individual should claim rollover relief or business asset disposal relief or both reliefs. It will be relatively unusual for both reliefs to be available. This is because business asset disposal relief only applies on the disposal of a business or part of a business and rollover relief is typically relevant where there is the sale of an individual business asset and the individual continues to carry on the business.

However, if both reliefs can be claimed, consider whether it would better for the individual to claim business asset disposal relief instead of rollover relief, if only a very small amount of gain (after deduction of losses and the annual exempt amount) are left in charge and are taxable at the advantageous rate of 10%.

If both reliefs are claimed, business asset disposal relief will apply to the gain left in charge after rollover relief has been applied. This will be relevant when there is an amount not reinvested so that rollover relief does not cover the whole of the gain.

4.3 Depreciating assets

Where the replacement asset is a depreciating asset, the gain is not rolled over by reducing the cost of the replacement asset. Rather it is 'frozen', ie deferred, until it crystallises (ie becomes chargeable) on the earliest of:

(a) The disposal of the replacement asset

(b) The date the replacement asset ceases to be used in the trade (but the gain does not crystallise on the taxpayer's death)

(c) Ten years after the acquisition of the replacement asset

Key term

An asset is a **depreciating asset** if it is, or within the next ten years will become, a wasting asset. So, any asset with an expected life of 60 years or less is covered by this definition. Plant and machinery is always treated as depreciating.

PART B CAPITAL TAXES

> **Question** — Deferred gain on investment into depreciating asset

Norma bought a freehold shop for use in her business in June 2016 for £125,000. She sold it for £140,000 on 1 August 2023. On 10 July 2023, Norma bought some fixed plant and machinery to use in her business, costing £150,000. She then sold the plant and machinery for £167,000 on 19 November 2024.

Show Norma's chargeable gains.

> **Answer**

Gain deferred

	£
Proceeds of shop	140,000
Less cost	(125,000)
Gain	15,000

Sale of plant and machinery

	£
Proceeds	167,000
Less cost	(150,000)
Gain	17,000

Total gain chargeable on sale (gain on plant and machinery plus crystallised gain)
£(15,000 + 17,000) — **£32,000**

Where a gain on disposal is deferred on the purchase of a replacement depreciating asset, it is possible to transfer the deferred, or 'frozen', gain to a non-depreciating asset provided the non-depreciating asset is bought before the deferred gain has crystallised.

4.4 Identifying availability of reliefs

It can be confusing to identify the availability of replacement of business assets (rollover) relief and/or gift relief and/or business asset disposal relief on a disposal because the conditions are similar. The following examples show whether these reliefs are available in a variety of circumstances. Remember that **all of these reliefs require a claim** so it is possible to choose which relief to claim and that **it may be possible to claim more than one relief** on a disposal.

4.5 Example: rollover relief, gift relief and business asset disposal relief

(a) Gary sold 10,000 ordinary shares in N Ltd for their market value of £20,000 in May 2024. Gary had subscribed for the shares four years previously when he also became an employee of N Ltd. N Ltd has always been a trading company. The shares represent 10% of the ordinary shares in N Ltd and carry the same percentage of voting rights, entitlement to profits and entitlement to assets in the company. Two months later, Gary acquired a 5% shareholding in Q plc, another unquoted trading company, for £20,000.

Relief	Available	Comments
Rollover relief	No	Shares are not qualifying assets for replacement of business assets relief (neither as the old assets nor the new asset).
Gift relief	No	Sale at market value does not have an element of gift (must be either outright gift or sale at less than market value).
Business asset disposal relief	Yes	(a) N Ltd is Gary's personal company (at least 5% ordinary share capital, voting rights etc) (b) N Ltd is a trading company (c) Gary is an employee of N Ltd And these conditions are satisfied throughout the period of two years ending with the date of the disposal.
Investors' relief	No	Gary is an employee.

(b) Marial sold a freehold warehouse for £150,000 (market value) which she had occupied and used for five years in her sole trader business. The gain arising was £45,000. She had bought a freehold shop which she immediately occupied and started using in her trade for £130,000 eight months previously.

Relief	Available	Comments
Rollover relief	Yes – partially	(a) The old asset sold and the new asset bought are both used only in the trade or trades carried on by the person claiming rollover relief. (b) The old asset and the new asset both fall within one of the classes of assets (here both are land and buildings). (c) Reinvestment of the proceeds of the old asset takes place in a period beginning one year before and ending three years after the date of the disposal. (d) The new asset is brought into use in the trade on its acquisition. The excess proceeds not reinvested £(150,000 – 130,000) = £20,000 are chargeable immediately. The remainder of the gain £(45,000 – 20,000) = £25,000 is rolled over into the base cost of the new asset.
Gift relief	No	Sale at market value does not have an element of gift (must be either outright gift or sale at less than market value).
Business asset disposal relief	No	The disposal of individual assets in a continuing business does not qualify for business asset disposal relief.
Investors' relief	No	Only available on shares (not buildings)

(c) Lynne had been in business as a sole trader for five years. She closed her business which had two assets, a freehold shop she had owned for three years and a freehold warehouse she had owned for six months. Immediately after cessation, she sold the warehouse to her son Steven at less than market value. The price paid by Steven was £9,000 more than Lynne had paid for the warehouse. Four months after cessation, she sold the shop to Joss at market value. The gain on the warehouse based on market value would be £15,000.

PART B CAPITAL TAXES

Relief	Available	Comments
Rollover relief	No	There is no acquisition of replacement assets.
Gift relief	No – on shop Yes – partial on warehouse	Sale at market value. Sale at undervalue of asset used in business by donor (there is no qualifying period). £9,000 of the gain is chargeable immediately. The remaining £(15,000 – 9,000) = £6,000 is eligible for gift relief.
Business asset disposal relief	Yes on both shop and warehouse	Disposal of one or more assets in use for the purposes of a business at the time at which the business ceases to be carried on since: (a) The business was owned by Lynne throughout the period of two years ending with the date on which the business ceased to be carried on; and (b) The date of cessation is within three years before the date of the disposal. The qualifying period applies to the **business**, not to individual assets and so business asset disposal relief is still available on the warehouse.
Investors' relief	No	Only available on disposals of qualifying shares.

4.6 Example: gift relief and business asset disposal relief

Here we consider the availability of gift relief and business asset disposal relief on the gift of shares in a company. When considering reliefs in relation to shares, it is particularly important to look at the percentage shareholding represented by the shares, whether the company is quoted or not, and whether the individual is an employee or officer of the company.

These conditions are illustrated in the examples below. We have assumed that the shares have been owned for two years prior to the disposal and other circumstances relevant for business asset disposal relief (eg whether the company is a trading company, whether the shareholder is an office or employee of the company) have existed throughout the period of ownership.

Trading company or holding company of trading group	Unquoted company	Percentage shareholding and voting rights	Officer or employee of company or group company	Gift relief available?	Business asset disposal relief available?
Yes	Yes	3%	No	Yes – any % of unquoted trading co. shares, no employment condition	No – because the transferor must be an officer or employee in the company of which they are disposing of the shares
No	Yes	8%	Yes	No – relief only available for disposals of trading company shares	No – relief only available for disposals of trading company shares

12: CHARGEABLE GAINS: RELIEFS

Trading company or holding company of trading group	Unquoted company	Percentage shareholding and voting rights	Officer or employee of company or group company	Gift relief available?	Business asset disposal relief available?
Yes	Yes	4%	Yes	Yes – if unquoted trading co. shares then % holding is irrelevant	No – must be personal company (at least 5% ordinary share capital, voting rights etc)
Yes	No	8%	No	Yes – quoted company but personal company (at least 5% of the voting rights), no employment condition	No – because the transferor must be an officer or employee in the company of which they are disposing of the shares
Yes	No	15%	Yes	Yes – personal company (at least 5% of the voting rights)	Yes – personal company (at least 5% ordinary share capital, voting rights etc) and officer or employee

PART B   CAPITAL TAXES

Chapter roundup

- Business asset disposal relief applies on the disposal of a business and certain trading company shares. The rate of tax on gains qualifying for business asset disposal relief is 10%.
- Investors' relief applies on the disposal of qualifying shares: shares in unquoted trading companies, subscribed for and held by the taxpayer for three years up to disposal where the individual is not an employee.
- Gift relief is available on both outright gifts and sales at an undervalue of business assets. Gift relief is also available on gifts which are immediately chargeable to inheritance tax.
- When assets falling within certain classes are sold and other such assets are bought, it is possible to defer gains on the assets sold by claiming rollover relief.
- If an amount less than the proceeds of the old asset is invested in the new assets, a gain equal to the difference will be chargeable up to a maximum of the actual gain.

Quick quiz

1. Petra sold her business as a going concern in August 2024, realising gains of £500,000. She has not made any previous disposals. Calculate Petra's CGT on the disposal.

2. Which disposals of shares qualify for gift relief?

3. What assets are eligible for rollover relief on the replacement of business assets by an individual?

4. What deferral of a gain is available when a business asset is replaced with a depreciating business asset?

5. Alice sells a factory for £500,000 realising a gain of £100,000. She acquires a factory two months later for £480,000. How much rollover relief is available?

6. Patrick has been running a trading business for five years. In 2024/25, he sold the business to Andrew realising gains of £75,000. Patrick has already used his annual exempt amount for 2024/25 against other gains. He has not made any previous claims for business asset disposal relief. What is Patrick's CGT liability?

7. What shares may qualify for business asset disposal relief but not investors' relief?

Answers to quick quiz

1.

	£
Gains	500,000
Less annual exempt amount	(3,000)
Taxable gain	497,000
CGT @ 10%	49,700

2. Shares which qualify for gift relief are those in trading companies which:

   - Are not listed on a recognised stock exchange; or
   - Where the donor is an individual, which are in that individual's personal company; or
   - Where the donor is a trustee, where the trustee can exercise 25% or more of the voting rights in the company.

3. Assets eligible for rollover relief by an individual are:

   - Land and buildings
   - Fixed plant and machinery
   - Goodwill

4. Where a depreciating asset is acquired, the gain is 'frozen', or deferred until it crystallises on the earliest of the disposal of the replacement asset, the date the replacement asset ceases to be used in the trade and ten years after the acquisition of the replacement asset.

5. Amount not invested £(500,000 – 480,000) = £20,000. Rollover relief £(100,000 – 20,000) = £80,000.

6. CGT @ 10% on £75,000 = £7,500.

7. Shares in a company which employs the taxpayer making the disposal or shares in quoted trading companies as long as the taxpayer held at least 5% of the share capital/voting rights etc.

PART B CAPITAL TAXES

Chargeable gains: additional aspects

Topic list
1 Chattels
2 Wasting assets
3 Private residences
4 Overseas aspects of CGT

Introduction

In the previous chapters, we have learnt how to calculate capital gains and we have looked at some of the reliefs available. We now look at some more of the rules for particular assets and particular situations.

This chapter looks at wasting assets. Unless capital allowances have been claimed, there are special rules to ensure that the cost of the asset is restricted to reflect the fall in value of the asset over time.

The next section looks at the gains people make on their homes, which are usually exempt. This means there is no capital gains tax charge when people move home but also that there is no relief if their house is sold at a loss.

Finally, this chapter looks at the overseas aspects of capital gains tax.

In the next chapter, we will study the administration of income tax and capital gains tax.

PART B CAPITAL TAXES

Exam guide

Watch out for Private Residence Relief (PRR) and the circumstances in which the relief is restricted.

Do not be caught out by the overseas aspects. For CGT purposes, the most useful exclusion is the fact that individuals who are not resident in the UK are not usually taxable on their UK gains, even on assets situated in the UK. An exception is that gains on UK property are taxable, even where the vendor is non-resident.

1 Chattels

1.1 What is a chattel?

Key terms

A **chattel** is tangible moveable property.

A **wasting asset** is an asset with an estimated remaining useful life of 50 years or less.

Plant and machinery, whose predictable useful life is always deemed to be less than 50 years, is an example of a wasting chattel (unless it is immoveable, in which case it will be wasting but not a chattel). Machinery includes, in addition to its ordinary meaning, motor vehicles (unless exempt as cars), railway and traction engines, engine-powered boats and clocks.

1.2 Wasting chattels

FAST FORWARD

Gains on most wasting chattels are exempt and losses are not allowable.

Wasting chattels are exempt (so that there are no chargeable gains and no allowable losses).

There is one exception to this: assets used for the purpose of a trade, profession or vocation in respect of which capital allowances have been or could have been claimed. This means that items of plant and machinery used in a trade are not exempt merely on the ground that they are wasting. (However, cars are always exempt.)

1.3 Gains on non-wasting chattels

FAST FORWARD

When a non-wasting chattel is sold for less than £6,000, any gain is exempt. There is marginal relief for gains where sale proceeds exceed £6,000.

If a chattel is not exempt under the wasting chattels rule, any gain arising on its disposal will still be exempt if the asset is sold for gross proceeds of £6,000 or less, even if capital allowances were claimed on it.

If sale proceeds exceed £6,000, any gain is limited to a maximum of 5/3 × (gross proceeds − £6,000) (Whillans p.43).

Question
Chattels: gains

Adam purchased a Chippendale chair for £1,800. On 10 October he sold the chair at auction for £6,300 (which was net of the auctioneer's 10% commission).

What is the gain?

Answer

	£
Proceeds (£6,300 × 100/90)	7,000
Less incidental costs of sale	(700)
Net proceeds	6,300
Less cost	(1,800)
Gain	4,500

The maximum gain is 5/3 × £(7,000 – 6,000) = £1,667

The chargeable gain is the lower of £4,500 and £1,667, so it is £1,667.

1.4 Losses on non-wasting chattels

FAST FORWARD   A loss on the sale of a non-wasting chattel is restricted where proceeds are less than £6,000.

Where a chattel which is not exempt under the wasting chattels rule is sold for less than £6,000 and a loss arises, the allowable loss is restricted by assuming that the chattel was sold for £6,000. This rule cannot turn a loss into a gain, only reduce the loss, perhaps to zero.

Question
Chattels: losses

Eve purchased a rare first edition for £8,000 which she sold in October at auction for £2,700 (which was net of 10% commission).

Compute the gain or loss.

Answer

	£
Proceeds (assumed)	6,000
Less incidental costs of disposal (£2,700 × 10/90)	(300)
	5,700
Less cost	(8,000)
Allowable loss	(2,300)

1.5 Chattels and capital allowances

FAST FORWARD   The CGT rules are modified for assets eligible for capital allowances.

The wasting chattels exemption does not apply to chattels on which capital allowances have been claimed or could have been claimed. The chattels rules based on £6,000 do apply.

Where a chattel on which capital allowances have been obtained is sold at a loss, the allowable cost for chargeable gains purposes is reduced by the lower of the loss and the net amount of allowances given (taking into account any balancing allowances or charges). The result is no gain and no loss. This is because relief for the loss has already been given through the capital allowances computation.

If the chattel is sold at a gain the cost is not adjusted for capital allowances. This is because the capital allowances will have been repaid through the balancing charge.

2 Wasting assets

FAST FORWARD Other wasting assets generally have their cost written down over time.

2.1 Introduction

A wasting asset is one which has an estimated remaining useful life of 50 years or less and whose original value will depreciate over time. **Freehold land is never a wasting asset**, and there are special rules for leases of land (see below).

Wasting chattels are exempt except for those on which capital allowances have been (or could have been) **claimed**.

2.2 Options

An option (for example an option to buy shares) is a right to buy or sell something at a specified price within a specified time. **An option is usually a wasting asset** because after a certain time it can no longer be exercised.

2.2.1 The grant of an option

The grant of an option is the disposal of an asset, namely the option itself, rather than a part disposal of the asset over which the option has been granted. The only allowable expenditure will be the incidental costs of the grant, such as legal fees. If the option is exercised, the CGT treatment changes.

2.2.2 The exercise of an option

Where an option is exercised, the granting of the option and the subsequent disposal of the asset under the option are treated as a single transaction taking place when the option is exercised. Proceeds from the grant of the option plus the disposal of the asset are combined and become the disposal proceeds of the grantor and the allowable base cost of the grantee.

Where tax was paid on the original grant of the option, it will usually be treated as a payment on account of the tax on the exercise.

2.2.3 Example: exercise of an option

Tom owned a plot of investment land which he bought for £10,000 in May 2016. He granted an option to Penelope for £1,000 in July 2016 whereby he would sell the land for £25,000 at any time nominated by Penelope before 30 June 2025. Penelope exercised her option in July 2024.

Tom's gain in 2024/25 will be:

	£
Proceeds (£1,000 + £25,000)	26,000
Less cost	(10,000)
Gain	16,000
Penelope's base cost will be: £1,000 + £25,000 =	26,000

The date of disposal is July 2024 (ie when the option is exercised).

2.2.4 Abandoned options

Where an option is abandoned, the position of the grantor and grantee are different. The grantor makes a chargeable disposal at the time when the option is granted. The grantee acquires a chargeable asset at the same time, but the abandonment of the option amounts to a disposal only where the option is:

(a) A quoted option to subscribe for shares in a company
(b) A traded option or financial option
(c) An option to acquire assets for the purposes of a trade

2.2.5 Disposal of an option

The disposal (eg by sale to a third party) of an option (other than a quoted, traded or financial option) to buy or sell quoted shares or securities gives rise to a chargeable gain or allowable loss computed in accordance with the normal rules for wasting assets (see below). These options are assets which waste on a straight-line basis.

2.3 Other wasting assets

The cost is written down on a straight-line basis. So, if a taxpayer acquires such an asset with a remaining life of 40 years and disposes of it after 15 years (with 25 years remaining) only 25/40 of the cost is deducted from the disposal consideration.

Examples of such assets are **copyrights** (with 50 years or less to run) and **registered designs**.

Where the asset has an estimated residual value at the end of its predictable life, it is the cost less residual value which is written off on a straight-line basis over the asset's life. Where additional expenditure is incurred on a wasting asset the additional cost is written off over the life remaining when it was incurred.

Assets eligible for capital allowances and used throughout the period of ownership in a trade, profession or vocation do not have their allowable expenditure written down.

3 Private residences

3.1 General principles

FAST FORWARD

> There is an exemption for gains on principal private residences, but the exemption may be restricted because of periods of non-occupation or because of business use. See Whillans (p.48).

A gain arising on the sale of an individual's only or main private residence (sometimes referred to as the Private Residence Relief, or PRR) is exempt from CGT. The exemption covers total grounds, including the house, of up to half a hectare. The total grounds can exceed half a hectare if the house is large enough to warrant it, but if not, the gain on the excess grounds is taxable. If the grounds do not adjoin the house (for example when a road separates the two), they **may** still qualify but they may not; each case must be argued on its merits.

For the exemption to be available, the taxpayer must have occupied the property as a residence rather than just as temporary accommodation.

3.2 Occupation

The gain is wholly exempt where the owner has occupied the whole of the residence throughout his period of ownership. Where occupation has been for only part of the period, a proportion of the gain is exempted.

Formula to learn

> The exempt proportion is:
>
> $$\text{Gain before relief} \times \frac{\text{Periods of occupation}}{\text{Total period of ownership}}$$

The **last nine months of ownership are always** treated as **a period of occupation**, if at some time the residence has been the taxpayer's main residence, even if within those last nine months the taxpayer also has another house which is his principal private residence.

3.3 Deemed occupation

The **period of occupation is also deemed to include certain periods of absence, provided the individual had no other exempt residence at the time and the period of absence was at some time both preceded by and followed by a period of actual occupation.** Deemed but non-actual occupation during the last nine months of ownership does not count for this purpose.

These periods of **deemed occupation** are:

(a) Any period (or periods taken together) of absence, for any reason, **up to three years**

(b) **Any periods** during which the owner was **required by his employment (ie employed taxpayer) to live abroad**

(c) Any period (or periods taken together) **up to four years** during which the owner was **required to live elsewhere due to his work** (ie both employed and self-employed taxpayer) so that he could not occupy his private residence

It does not matter if the residence is let during the absence.

Exempt periods of absence must normally be preceded and followed by periods of **actual occupation**. An extra-statutory concession relaxes this where an individual who has been required to work abroad or elsewhere (ie the latter two categories mentioned above) is unable to resume residence in his home because the terms of his employment require him to work elsewhere.

Question — Private residence relief

Mr A purchased a house on 1 April 1999 for £88,200. He lived in the house until 31 December 2000. He then worked abroad for two years before returning to the UK to live in the house again on 1 January 2003. He stayed in the house until 30 June 2019 before retiring and moving out to live with friends until the house was sold on 31 December 2024 for £150,000.

Calculate the gain arising.

Answer

	£
Proceeds	150,000
Less cost	(88,200)
Gain before PRR	61,800
Less PRR (working) $\frac{252}{309} \times £61,800$	(50,400)
Gain	11,400

Working: Exempt and chargeable periods

Period		Total months	Exempt months	Chargeable months
(i)	April 1999 – December 2000 (occupied)	21	21	0
(ii)	January 2001 – December 2002 (working abroad)	24	24	0
(iii)	January 2003 – June 2019 (occupied)	198	198	0
(iv)	July 2019 – March 2024 (see below)	57	0	57
(v)	April 2024 – December 2024 (last nine months)	9	9	0
		309	252	57

No part of the period from July 2019 to March 2024 can be covered by the exemption for three years of absence for any reason because it is not followed at any time by actual occupation.

13: CHARGEABLE GAINS: ADDITIONAL ASPECTS

Exam focus point

To help you to answer questions such as the one above, it is useful to draw up a table showing period of ownership, exempt months (real/deemed occupation) and chargeable months (non-occupation). You should also provide an explanation for any periods of deemed occupation.

3.4 Business use

Where part of a residence is used exclusively for business purposes (eg the owner runs their business from the property or part of the property is let out to a lodger) throughout the period of ownership, the gain attributable to use of that part is taxable.

The 'last nine months always exempt' rule does not apply to that part.

Question — Business use of PRR

Mr Smail purchased a property for £35,000 on 31 May 2018 and began operating a dental practice from that date in one quarter of the house. He closed the dental practice on 31 December 2024, selling the house on that date for £130,000.

Compute the gain, if any, arising.

Answer

	£
Proceeds	130,000
Less cost	(35,000)
Gain before PRR	95,000
Less PRR 0.75 × £95,000	(71,250)
Gain	23,750

Exemption is lost on one quarter throughout the period of ownership (including the last nine months) because of the use of that fraction for business purposes for the whole period of ownership.

If part of a house was used for business purposes for part of the period of ownership, the gain is apportioned between chargeable and exempt parts in a just and reasonable manner. If the business part was **at some time** used as part of the only or main residence, the gain apportioned to that part **will** qualify for the last nine months exemption.

3.5 More than one residence

3.5.1 The election for a residence to be treated as the main residence

Where a person has more than one residence (owned or rented), he may elect for one to be regarded as his main residence by giving notice to HMRC within two years of commencing occupation of the second residence. An election can have effect for any period beginning not more than two years prior to the date of election until it is varied by giving further notice. The further notice may itself be backdated by up to two years.

In order for the election to be made, the individual must actually reside in both residences.

Any period of ownership of a residence not nominated as the main residence will be a chargeable period for that residence.

3.5.2 Job-related accommodation

The rule limiting people to only one main residence is relaxed for individuals living in job-related accommodation.

Such individuals will be treated as occupying any second dwelling house which they own if they intend in due course to occupy the dwelling house as their only or main residence. Thus, it is not necessary to establish any actual residence in such cases. This rule extends to self-employed persons required to live in job-related accommodation (eg tenants of public houses).

Key term

> A person lives in **job-related accommodation** where:
>
> (a) It is necessary for the **proper performance of their duties**; or
>
> (b) It is provided for the **better performance of their duties** and theirs is one of the kinds of employment in which it is **customary** for employers to provide accommodation; or
>
> (c) There is a **special threat to the employee's security** and use of the accommodation is part of security arrangements.

3.6 Spouses/civil partners

Where a married couple/civil partners live together, only one residence may qualify as the main residence for relief. If each owned one property before marriage/registration of the civil partnership, a new two-year period for making an election in respect of the main residence will begin on the date of marriage/registration.

Where a marriage/civil partnership has broken down and one spouse/civil partner owning or having an interest in the matrimonial home has ceased to occupy the house, by concession the departing spouse/civil partner will continue to be treated as resident for capital gains tax purposes provided that the other has continued to reside in the home and the departing spouse/civil partner has not elected that some other house should be treated as their main residence for this period. This only applies where one spouse disposes of their interest to the other spouse.

Where a house passes from one spouse/civil partner to the other (eg on death), the new owner also inherits the old owner's periods of ownership and occupation for PRR purposes.

3.7 Letting relief

FAST FORWARD

> If PRR is restricted due to an owner letting out part of the property as a residential let, letting relief may apply to the part of the gain not covered by PRR.

When the owner lets part of the property, the absence from the let part cannot be a deemed period of occupation because the owner has another residence (the rest of the property). However, as long as the owner shares occupation of the property with the tenant, then letting relief will apply.

The letting must be for residential use.

The extra exemption (ie letting relief) is restricted to the lowest of:

(a) The amount of the total **gain** which is already **exempt under the PRR provisions** (including the last nine months exemption); or

(b) The gain attributable to the letting; or

(c) **£40,000**.

If a lodger lives as a member of the owner's family, sharing their living accommodation and eating with them, the whole property is regarded as the owner's main residence, and therefore the whole of any gain will be relieved.

Question: Letting relief

Miss Coe purchased a house in July 2004 for £200,000. She sold it in July 2024 for £350,000. Throughout the 20 years she lived in the house as her only residence and let out two spare rooms, which amounted to 25% of the property, to tenants who had exclusive use of their rooms (and their rooms only). What is Miss Coe's chargeable gain?

Answer

	£
Proceeds	350,000
Less cost	(200,000)
Gain before PRR	150,000
Less PRR (working)	
£150,000 × 75%	(112,500)
	37,500
Less letting relief, lowest of:	
(a) gain exempt under PRR rules: £112,500	
(b) gain attributable to letting: £150,000 × 25% = £37,500	
(c) £40,000 (maximum)	(37,500)
Gain	Nil

4 Overseas aspects of CGT

FAST FORWARD

CGT applies primarily to individuals resident in the UK. Non-UK resident individuals only pay CGT on disposals of assets used in the trade of their UK branch or agency and on UK property gains.

4.1 Liability to CGT

4.1.1 UK resident individuals

In general, individuals are subject to CGT on the disposal of assets situated anywhere in the world if they are resident in the UK in the tax year of the disposal.

4.1.2 Non-UK resident individuals

In general, an individual who is not UK resident in a tax year is not subject to CGT on the disposal of any assets, wherever situated, in that tax year. There are exceptions where the non-UK resident individual either operates a business through a branch or agency or disposes of a UK property. These are discussed later in this section.

Exam focus point

It is important to note that a non-UK resident is not liable to CGT on investment assets, even if those assets are situated in the UK. However, there is an exception to this rule: non-UK resident taxpayers are liable to CGT on UK land and buildings.

4.2 Situation of assets

Some of the rules about where assets are situated are contained in legislation. Some of them are a **matter of general law**. Most of the rules are obvious, for example, land is situated where it actually is, chattels are situated where they are physically present. There are special rules relating to intangible assets, the most important of which are shares and securities in a company. **All shares and securities of a UK incorporated company are treated as situated in the UK, regardless of where the share certificate is kept.**

4.3 Double taxation relief

If a gain made on the disposal of an overseas asset suffers overseas taxation, relief will be available in the UK against any CGT on the same disposal.

4.4 Calculation of non-UK gains

If an asset is bought and/or sold for amounts in a foreign currency, each such amount is first translated into sterling (using the rate at the time of purchase or sale), and the gain is computed using these sterling amounts.

Exam focus point
> Note that losses on non-UK assets have specific rules associated with them but are not included in the Taxation exam.

Question — Overseas gain

Farrah is resident in the UK. In 2024/25, she had taxable income of £22,700. She also made the following capital gains and losses on the disposal of UK assets.

	Gains/(losses) £
Shares in a UK investment company	25,000
UK residential property (no PRR)	50,000
Shop premises held as an investment (no BADR)	(30,000)

In addition, Farrah sold a residential property located in Utopia for $118,000, when the exchange rate was £1 = $1.18. Farrah purchased the property for $97,920 when the exchange rate was £1 = $1.36. Farrah paid overseas tax on this disposal of £8,400.

Calculate Farrah's UK capital gains tax liability for 2024/25.

Answer

The overseas gain is calculated using the exchange rates on the days of sale and purchase:

	$	Exch rate	£
Proceeds	118,000	1.18	100,000
Cost	(97,920)	1.36	(72,000)
Gain			28,000

Capital gains tax computation

Tax rate	Note	Other gains (UK) £	Residential property (UK) £	Residential property (Overseas) $	$
UK gains on shares	1	25,000			
UK gains on land			50,000		
OS gains on land				28,000	
Losses	2		(30,000)		
Annual exempt amount	2		(3,000)		
Taxable gains		25,000	17,000	28,000	
15,000 × 10%					1,500
10,000 × 20%					2,000
17,000 × 24%					4,080
28,000 × 24%					6,720
					14,300
DTR	3				(6,720)
Tax due					7,580

Note.

1. Allocate the remaining basic rate band to the UK gains which are taxed at 10%/20% (the BRB gives the biggest saving in this case).

2. Allocate losses and AEA to gains which will be taxed most highly but giving priority to gains which have not been taxed overseas. The double taxation relief will be maximised this way. But remember, we must allocate all of the loss, even if that means allocating it against gains that are taxed at 10% or have already been taxed overseas.

3. The DTR is the lower of the UK tax on the overseas gain (£6,720) and the overseas tax on that gain (£8,400), ie £6,720.

PART B CAPITAL TAXES

Chapter roundup

- Gains on most wasting chattels are exempt and losses on them are not allowable.
- When a non-wasting chattel is sold for less than £6,000, any gain is exempt. There is marginal relief for gains where sale proceeds exceed £6,000.
- A loss on the sale of a non-wasting chattel is restricted where proceeds are less than £6,000.
- The CGT rules are modified for assets eligible for capital allowances.
- Other wasting assets generally have their cost written down over time.
- There is an exemption for gains on principal private residences, but the exemption may be restricted because of periods of non-occupation or because of business use.
- There is also a relief for letting out part of a main private residence.
- CGT applies primarily to individuals resident in the UK. Non-UK resident individuals only pay CGT on disposals of assets used in the trade of their UK branch or agency and on UK property gains.

Quick quiz

1   What is the general treatment of intangible wasting assets (eg a copyright)?
2   For what periods may an individual be deemed to occupy their principal private residence?
3   What is the maximum letting exemption?

Answers to quick quiz

1. The cost is written down on a straight-line basis.
2. Periods of deemed occupation are:
   - Last nine months of ownership;
   - Any period of absence up to three years;
   - Any period during which the owner was required by their employment to work abroad; and
   - Any period up to four years during which the owner was required to live elsewhere due to their work (employed or self-employed) so that they could not occupy their private residence.
3. £40,000 but can be restricted further to the PRR claimed and the gain relating to the letting period if smaller.

PART B CAPITAL TAXES

Self assessment for individuals and partnerships

Topic list
1 The administration of taxation
2 Notification of liability to income tax and CGT
3 Tax returns and keeping records
4 Self-assessment and claims
5 Payment of income tax and capital gains tax
6 HMRC powers
7 Penalties

Introduction

In the previous chapters, we have studied the computation of income tax and capital gains tax liabilities.

In this chapter, we look at the overall system for the administration of tax. We then see how individuals and partnerships must 'self assess' their liability to income tax and capital gains tax. We deal with self assessment for companies later in this Workbook.

In the next chapter, we will commence our study of inheritance tax.

PART B   CAPITAL TAXES

Exam guide

In any tax advice question, you must consider the administrative requirements and time limits that apply. You must know the taxpayer's responsibilities for making returns and paying tax and the rules that HMRC can use to enforce compliance.

1 The administration of taxation

> **FAST FORWARD**
>
> Taxes are administered by HM Revenue and Customs.

The **Treasury** is the UK government department which formally imposes and collects taxation. The management of the Treasury is the responsibility of the Chancellor of the Exchequer. **The administrative function for the collection of tax is undertaken by HM Revenue and Customs (HMRC).** Rules on these administrative matters are contained in the **Taxes Management Act 1970 (TMA 1970)**.

HMRC consists of the Commissioners for HM Revenue and Customs and staff known as **Officers of Revenue and Customs,** who are responsible for supervising the self assessment system and agreeing tax liabilities.

Tax appeals are heard by the **Tax Tribunal** which is made up of **two tiers:**

(a) **First-tier Tribunal**
(b) **Upper Tribunal**

The **First-tier Tribunal deals with most cases** other than complex cases. The **Upper Tribunal deals with complex cases** which either involve an important issue of tax law or a large financial sum. The Upper Tribunal **also hears appeals** against decisions of the First-tier Tribunal. We look at the appeals system in more detail later in this chapter.

Many taxpayers arrange for their accountants to prepare and submit their tax returns. The taxpayer remains responsible for submitting the return and for paying the tax; the accountant acts as the taxpayer's agent.

There are two additional government departments involved in the administration of tax in the UK. Revenue Scotland is responsible for the collection of Land and Buildings Transaction Tax, and the Welsh Revenue Authority is responsible for the collection of Land Transaction Tax in Wales. These taxes are discussed in more detail later in this Workbook.

2 Notification of liability to income tax and CGT

> **FAST FORWARD**
>
> Individuals who do not receive a tax return or who have a new source of income or gains must notify their chargeability to income tax or CGT.

Individuals who have not received a notice to file a return, or who have a new source of income or gains in the tax year, are required to give notice of chargeability to HMRC within six months from the end of the year, ie by 5 October 2025 for 2024/25.

A person who has no chargeable gains and who is not liable to higher rate tax does not have to give notice of chargeability if all the income:

(a) Is taken into account under PAYE;
(b) Is from a source of income not subject to tax under self assessment;
(c) Has had (or is treated as having had) income tax deducted at source.

A penalty is charged for late notification (see later in this chapter).

3 Tax returns and keeping records

Tax returns must usually be filed by 31 October (paper) or 31 January (electronic) following the end of the tax year.

3.1 Tax returns

The tax return comprises a basic eight-page return form, together with supplementary pages for particular sources of income. Taxpayers are sent a return and a number of supplementary pages depending on their known sources of income, together with a Tax Return Guide and various notes relating to the supplementary pages. Taxpayers with simple tax returns may be asked to complete a short four-page tax return. If a return for the previous year was filed electronically the taxpayer may be sent a notice to file a return, rather than the official HMRC form.

HMRC also has the power to make an assessment (known as a simple assessment) of an individual's income tax or capital gains tax liability without the individual completing a tax return. Such a simple assessment is possible where HMRC has sufficient information regarding the individual's income or gains, where the information may be received from the individual or a third party.

Exam focus point

For the purpose of the Taxation exam, you should assume a simple assessment has not been issued, and that the taxpayer has the usual self assessment obligations, unless you are told otherwise.

Partnerships must file a separate return which includes a 'Partnership Statement' showing the firm's profits, losses, proceeds from the sale of assets, tax suffered, tax credits and the division of all these amounts between partners.

A partnership return must include a declaration of the name and tax reference of each partner, as well as the usual declaration that the return is correct and complete to the best of the signatory's knowledge.

Each partner must then include their share of partnership profits on their personal tax return.

3.2 Time limit for submission of tax returns

Key term

The latest **filing date for a personal tax return** for a tax year (Year 1) is:

- 31 October in the next tax year (Year 2), for a non-electronic return (eg a paper return).
- 31 January in Year 2, for an electronic return (eg made via the internet) (Whillans p.11).

There are **two exceptions to this general rule**.

The **first exception applies if the notice to file a tax return is issued by HMRC to the taxpayer after 31 July in Year 2, but on or before 31 October in Year 2**. In this case, the **latest filing date is**:

- **The end of three months following the notice, for a non-electronic return.**
- **31 January in Year 2, for an electronic return.**

The second exception applies **if the notice to file the tax return is issued to the taxpayer after 31 October in Year 2**. In this case, **the latest filing date is the end of three months following the notice**.

PART B CAPITAL TAXES

Question: Submission of tax returns

Advise each of the following clients of the latest filing date for her personal tax return for 2024/25 if the return is:

(a) Paper
(b) Electronic

Norma   Notice to file tax return issued by HMRC on 6 April 2025
Melanie Notice to file tax return issued by HMRC on 10 August 2025
Olga   Notice to file tax return issued by HMRC on 12 December 2025

Answer

	Non-electronic	Electronic
Norma	31 October 2025	31 January 2026
Melanie	9 November 2025	31 January 2026
Olga	11 March 2026	11 March 2026

A partnership return may be filed as a non-electronic return or an electronic return. **The general rule and the exceptions to the general rule for personal returns apply also to partnership returns.**

3.3 Standard accounting information

The tax return requires trading results to be presented in a standard format. Although there is no requirement to submit accounts with the return, accounts may be filed. If accounts accompany the return, HMRC's power to raise a discovery assessment (see below) is restricted.

Only 'three line' accounts (ie income less expenses equals profit) need be included on the tax return of businesses with a turnover (or gross rents from property) of less than the threshold for VAT registration (£85,000). This is not as helpful as it might appear, as underlying records must still be kept for tax purposes (disallowable items etc) when producing three line accounts.

Large businesses with a turnover of at least £5 million which have used figures rounded to the nearest £1,000 in producing their published accounts can compute their profits to the nearest £1,000 for tax purposes.

3.4 Keeping of records

All taxpayers must retain all records required to enable them to make and deliver a correct tax return.

Records must be retained until the later of:

(a) (i) **Five years after the 31 January following the tax year where the taxpayer is in business** (as a sole trader or partner or letting property). Note that this applies to all of the records, not only the business records; or

(ii) **One year after the 31 January following the tax year otherwise;** or

(b) Provided notice to deliver a return is given before the date in (a):

(i) **The time after which a compliance check enquiry by HMRC into the return can no longer be commenced**; or

(ii) **The date any such a compliance check enquiry has been completed.**

HMRC can specify a shorter time limit for keeping records where the records are bulky and the information they contain can be provided in another way.

Where a person receives a notice to deliver a tax return after the normal record-keeping period has expired, they must keep all records in their possession at that time until no compliance check enquiry can be raised in respect of the return or until such compliance check enquiries have been completed.

Taxpayers can keep 'information', rather than 'records', but must show that they have prepared a complete and correct tax return. The information must also be able to be provided in a legible form on request. Records can be kept in electronic format.

HMRC can inspect 'in-year' records, ie before a return is submitted, if they believe it is reasonably required to check a tax position.

4 Self assessment and claims

> **FAST FORWARD**
>
> If a paper return is filed the taxpayer can ask HMRC to compute the tax due. Electronic returns have tax calculated automatically.

4.1 Self assessment

Key term

> A **self assessment** is a calculation of the amount of taxable income and gains after deducting reliefs and allowances, and a calculation of income tax and CGT payable after taking into account tax deducted at source and tax credits on dividends.

If the taxpayer is filing a **paper return (other than a Short Tax Return), they may make the tax calculation on their return or ask HMRC to do so on their behalf.**

If the taxpayer wishes HMRC to make the calculation for Year 1, a paper return must be filed:

- **On or before 31 October in Year 2;** or
- **Within two months of the notice, if the notice to file the tax return is issued after 31 August in Year 2.**

If the taxpayer is filing an **electronic return, the calculation of tax liability is made automatically when the return is made online.**

4.2 Amending the self assessment

The taxpayer may amend the return (including the tax calculation) for Year 1 within 12 months after the filing date. For this purpose the filing date means:

- **31 January of Year 2;** or
- **Where the notice to file a return was issued after 31 October in Year 2, the last day of the three month period starting with the issue.**

A return may be amended by the taxpayer at a time when a compliance check enquiry is in progress into the return. The amendment does not restrict the scope of a compliance check enquiry into the return but may be taken into account in that enquiry. If the amendment made during a compliance check enquiry is the amount of tax payable, the amendment does not take effect while the compliance check enquiry is in progress.

A return may be amended by HMRC to correct any obvious error or omission in the return (such as errors of principle and arithmetical mistakes) or anything else that an officer has reason to believe is incorrect in the light of information available. The correction must usually be made within nine months after the day on which the return was actually filed. The taxpayer can object to the correction but must do so within 30 days of receiving notice of it.

Similar rules apply to the amendment and correction of partnership returns.

4.3 Claims

All claims and elections which can be made in a tax return must be made in this manner if a return has been issued. A claim for any relief, allowance or repayment of tax must be quantified at the time it is made.

In general, the time limit for making a claim is four years from the end of tax year. Where different time limits apply these have been mentioned throughout this Workbook.

4.4 Recovery of overpaid tax

If a taxpayer discovers that tax has been overpaid, for example because they have made an error in their tax return, they can make a claim to have the overpaid tax repaid. The claim must be made within four years of the end of the tax year to which the overpayment relates.

5 Payment of income tax and capital gains tax

FAST FORWARD | Two payments on account and a final balancing payment of income tax and Class 4 NICs are due.

5.1 Payments on account and final payment

5.1.1 Introduction

The self assessment system may result in the taxpayer making three payments of income tax and Class 4 NICs.

Date	Payment
31 January in the tax year	1st payment on account
31 July after the tax year	2nd payment on account
31 January after the tax year	Final payment to settle the remaining liability

See Whillans p.2. HMRC issues 'Statements of Account', which include payslips, but there is no statutory obligation for it to do so and **the onus is on the taxpayer to pay the correct amount of tax by the due date.**

5.1.2 Payments on account

Key terms

Payments on account are usually required where the income tax and Class 4 NICs due in the previous year exceeded the amount of income tax deducted at source; this excess is known as **'the relevant amount'**. Income tax deducted at source includes tax suffered, PAYE deductions and tax credits on dividends.

The payments on account are each equal to 50% of the relevant amount for the previous year.

Question — Payments on account

Sue is a self-employed writer who paid tax for 2023/24 as follows:

	£
Total amount of income tax charged	9,200
This included: Tax deducted on employment income	3,200
She also paid: Class 4 NIC	2,046

How much are the payments on account for 2024/25 and by what dates are they due?

Answer

	£
Income tax:	
Total income tax charged for 2023/24	9,200
Less tax deducted for 2023/24	(3,200)
	6,000
Class 4 NIC	2,046
'Relevant amount'	8,046
Payments on account for 2024/25:	
31 January 2025 £8,046 × 50%	4,023
31 July 2025 As before	4,023

Payments on account are not required if the relevant amount falls below a de minimis limit of £1,000. Also, payments on account are not required from taxpayers who paid 80% or more of their tax liability for the previous year through PAYE or other deduction at source arrangements.

If the previous year's liability increases following an amendment to a self assessment, or the raising of a discovery assessment, an adjustment is made to the payments on account due.

5.1.3 Reducing payments on account

Payments on account are normally fixed by reference to the previous year's tax liability but if a taxpayer expects the actual liability to be lower than this **a claim can be made to reduce the payments on account to:**

(a) A stated amount; or
(b) Nil.

The claim must state the reason why the taxpayer believes the tax liability will be lower or nil.

If the taxpayer's eventual liability is higher than estimated, the payments on account will have been reduced too far. Although the payments on account will not be adjusted, the taxpayer will suffer an interest charge on late payment of the difference.

A penalty of the difference between the reduced payment on account and the correct payment on account may be levied if the reduction was claimed fraudulently or negligently.

5.1.4 Balancing payment

The balance of any income tax and Class 4 NICs, together with all CGT due for a year, is normally payable on or before the 31 January following the tax year.

Question
Payment of tax

Giles made payments on account for 2024/25 of £6,500 each on 31 January 2025 and 31 July 2025, based on his 2023/24 liability. He then calculates his total income tax and Class 4 NIC liability for 2024/25 at £18,000 of which £2,750 was deducted at source. In addition, his CGT liability for disposals in 2024/25 is £5,120.

How much is the final payment due for 2024/25?

Answer

Income tax and NIC: £18,000 − £2,750 − £6,500 − £6,500 = £2,250

Final payment due on 31 January 2026 for 2024/25 = £2,250 + £5,120 = £7,370

There is an exception to the balancing payment being due by 31 January following the tax year. **If a taxpayer has notified chargeability by 5 October but the notice to file a tax return is not issued before 31 October, then the due date for the payment is three months after the issue of the notice.**

Tax charged on an amended self assessment return is usually payable on the later of:

(a) The normal due date, generally 31 January following the end of the tax year; and
(b) The day following 30 days after the making of the revised self assessment.

Tax charged on a discovery assessment (see below) is due thirty days after the issue of the assessment.

5.2 Penalty for late payment of tax

FAST FORWARD — A penalty is chargeable where tax is paid after the due date based on the amount of unpaid tax. Up to 15% of that amount is payable where the tax is more than 12 months late.

A penalty is chargeable where tax is paid after the penalty date. The penalty date is 30 days after the due date for the tax. Therefore no penalty arises if the tax is paid within 30 days of the due date.

The penalty chargeable is (Whillans p.18):

Date of payment	Penalty
Not more than five months after the penalty date	5% of tax which is unpaid at the penalty date.
More than five months after the penalty date but not more than 11 months after the penalty date	5% of tax which is unpaid at the end of the 5 month period. This is in addition to the 5% penalty above.
More than 11 months after the penalty date	5% of tax which is unpaid at the end of the 11 month period. This is in addition to the two 5% penalties above.

Penalties for late payment of tax apply to:

(a) **Balancing payments of income tax and NICs and any CGT** under self assessment or a determination
(b) Tax due on the amendment of a self assessment return
(c) Tax due on a discovery assessment

Penalties for late payment do not apply to late payments on account.

5.3 Interest on late paid tax

Interest is chargeable on late payment of both payments on account and balancing payments.

Exam focus point

> The interest rate charged is 7.75% and is in Whillans tax tables on page 4 under the heading harmonised interest regime. Although different interest rates apply to different periods where tax was outstanding, in your exam use the most recent interest rate given in the Whillan's tables as a simplification.

Interest is charged from 31 January following the tax year (or the normal due date for the balancing payment, in the rare event that this is later) even if this is before the due date for payment on:

(a) Tax payable following an amendment to a self assessment return
(b) Tax payable in a discovery assessment
(c) Tax postponed under an appeal which becomes payable

Since a determination (see below) is treated as if it were a self assessment, interest runs from 31 January following the tax year.

If a taxpayer makes a claim to reduce payments on account and there is still a final payment to be made, interest is normally charged on the payments on account as if each of those payments had been the lower of:

(a) The reduced amount, plus 50% of the final income tax liability; and
(b) The amount which would have been payable had no claim for reduction been made.

Question — Interest

Herbert's payments on account for 2024/25 based on his income tax liability for 2023/24 were £4,500 each. However, when he submitted his 2023/24 income tax return in January 2025 he made a claim to reduce the payments on account for 2024/25 to £3,500 each. The first payment on account was made on 31 January 2025, and the second on 1 November 2025.

Herbert filed his 2024/25 tax return in December 2025. The return showed that his tax liabilities for 2024/25 (before deducting payments on account) were income tax and Class 4 NIC: £10,000, capital gains tax: £2,500. Herbert paid the balance of tax due of £5,500 on 1 April 2026.

For which periods (to the nearest month) and in respect of what amounts will Herbert be charged interest?

Answer

Herbert made an excessive claim to reduce his payments on account and will therefore be charged interest on the reduction. The payments on account should have been £4,500 each based on the original 2023/24 liability (not £5,000 each based on the 2024/25 liability). Interest will be charged as follows:

(a) First payment on account
  (i) On £3,500 – nil – paid on time
  (ii) On £1,000 from due date of 31 January 2025 to payment date, 1 April 2026 (14 months)

(b) Second payment on account
  (i) On £3,500 from due date of 31 July 2025 to payment date, 1 November 2025 (3 months)
  (ii) On £1,000 from due date of 31 July 2025 to payment date, 1 April 2026 (8 months)

(c) Balancing payment
  (i) On £3,500 from due date of 31 January 2026 to payment date, 1 April 2026 (2 months)

Where interest has been charged on late payments on account but the final balancing settlement for the year produces a repayment, all or part of the original interest is repaid.

5.4 Repayment of tax and repayment supplement

Tax is repaid when claimed unless a greater payment of tax is due in the following 30 days, in which case it is set-off against that payment.

Interest is paid on overpayments of:

(a) Payments on account
(b) Final payments of income tax and Class 4 NICs and CGT, including tax deducted at source or tax credits on dividends
(c) Penalties

Repayment supplement runs from the original date of payment (even if this was prior to the due date), until the day before the date the repayment is made. Income tax deducted at source and tax credits are treated as if they were paid on the 31 January following the tax year concerned.

Repayment supplement paid to individuals is tax free.

5.5 Payment of CGT

> **FAST FORWARD**
>
> Capital gains tax is usually due on 31 January following the end of the tax year. However, the capital gains tax due on residential property gains is due within 30 days of the completion date.

5.5.1 General rule

Capital gains tax is usually payable in one payment on 31 January following the end of the tax year.

5.5.2 Residential capital gains

For disposals of residential properties which are completed from 27 October 2021, a return and the capital gains tax is due within 60 days of the completion of that disposal (Whillans p.1). The capital gains tax is an estimate of the tax taking into account the following:

- other gains on residential property up to the date of completion;
- any losses (brought forward and current year) up to the date of completion;
- remaining basic rate band using estimated taxable income for the year; and
- the annual exempt amount.

Remember the tax will be calculated at 18/24%.

6 HMRC powers

6.1 Compliance check enquiries

> **FAST FORWARD**
>
> A compliance check enquiry into a return, claim or election can be started by an officer of HMRC within a limited period.

6.1.1 Starting a compliance check enquiry

HM Revenue and Customs (HMRC) has powers to make compliance check enquiries into returns, claims or elections which have already been submitted.

Some returns, claims or elections are **selected for a compliance check enquiry at random, others for a particular reason**, for example, if HMRC believes that there has been an **underpayment of tax** due to the taxpayer's failure to comply with tax legislation.

An officer of the Revenue and Customs has a limited period within which to commence a compliance check enquiry into a return or amendment. **The officer must give written notice of their intention by:**

(a) **The first anniversary of the actual filing date** (if the return was delivered on or before the due filing date); or

(b) **If the return is filed after the due filing date, the quarter day following the first anniversary of the actual filing date.** The quarter days are 31 January, 30 April, 31 July and 31 October.

If the taxpayer amended the return after the due filing date, the compliance check enquiry 'window' extends to the quarter day following the first anniversary of the date the amendment was filed. Where the compliance check enquiry was not raised within the limit which would have applied had no amendment been filed, the enquiry is restricted to matters contained in the amendment.

The officer does not have to have, or give, any reason for starting a compliance check enquiry. In particular, the taxpayer will not be advised whether they have been selected at random for an audit. Compliance check enquiries may be full enquiries or may be limited to 'aspect' enquiries, which focus on a particular part of the tax return.

6.1.2 During the compliance check enquiry

In the course of the compliance check enquiry, **the officer may require the taxpayer to produce documents, accounts or any other information required. The taxpayer can appeal to the Tax Tribunal against such a requirement.**

6.1.3 Completing a compliance check enquiry

An officer must issue a notice that the compliance check enquiry is complete, state their conclusions and amend the self assessment, partnership statement or claim accordingly.

If the taxpayer is not satisfied with the officer's amendment they may, within 30 days, appeal to the Tribunal.

Once a compliance check enquiry is complete, the officer cannot make a further compliance check enquiry into that return. HMRC may, in limited circumstances, raise a discovery assessment if they believe that there has been a loss of tax (see below).

6.2 Determinations

If notice has been served on a taxpayer to submit a return but the return is not submitted by the due filing date, an officer of HMRC may make a determination of the amounts liable to income tax and CGT tax and of the tax due. Such a determination must be made to the best of the officer's information and belief, and is then treated as if it were a self assessment. This enables the officer to seek payment of tax, including payments on account for the following year and to charge interest.

A determination must be made within four years following the end of the relevant tax year.

6.3 Discovery assessments

If an officer of HMRC discovers that profits have been omitted from assessment, that any assessment has become insufficient, or that any relief given is, or has become excessive, an assessment may be raised to recover the tax lost.

If the tax lost results from an error in the taxpayer's return but the return was made in accordance with prevailing practice at the time, no discovery assessment may be made.

A discovery assessment may only be raised where a return has been made if:

(a) There has been **careless or deliberate understatement** by the taxpayer or their agent; or

(b) At the time that compliance check enquiries into the return were completed, or could no longer be made, the officer **did not have information** to make them aware of the loss of tax.

Information is treated as available to an officer if it is contained in the taxpayer's return or claim for the year or either of the two preceding years, or it has been provided because of a compliance check covering those years, or it has been specifically provided.

The time limit for raising a discovery assessment is four years from the end of the tax year but this is extended to 6 years if there has been careless understatement and 20 years if there has been deliberate understatement. The taxpayer may appeal against a discovery assessment within 30 days of issue.

6.4 Dishonest conduct of tax agents

> HMRC can investigate dishonest conduct by a tax agent and issue a civil penalty of up to £50,000 where there has been dishonest conduct.

HMRC can investigate whether there has been dishonest conduct by a tax agent (ie an individual who, during business, assists clients with their tax affairs). Dishonest conduct occurs when a tax agent does something dishonest with a view to bringing about a loss of tax.

HMRC can issue a civil penalty of up to £50,000 where there has been **dishonest conduct, and the tax agent fails to supply the information or documents that HMRC has requested.**

7 Penalties

7.1 Penalties for errors

> There is a common penalty regime for errors in tax returns, including income tax, NICs, corporation tax and VAT. Penalties range from 30% to 100% of the Potential Lost Revenue. Penalties may be reduced if the taxpayer takes certain steps to co-operate with HMRC.

A common penalty regime for errors in tax returns for income tax, national insurance contributions, corporation tax and value added tax. A penalty may be imposed where **a taxpayer makes an inaccurate return** if they have:

- Been **careless** because they have not taken reasonable care in making the return or discovers the error later but does not take reasonable steps to inform HMRC; or
- Made a **deliberate error** but **does not make arrangements to conceal it**; or
- Made a **deliberate error** and **has attempted to conceal it** eg by submitting false evidence in support of an inaccurate figure.

Note that **an error which is made where the taxpayer has taken reasonable care** in making the return and which they **do not discover later, does not result in a penalty**.

In order for a penalty to be charged, the **inaccurate return must result in**:

- **An understatement of the taxpayer's tax liability**; or
- **A false or increased loss for the taxpayer**; or
- **A false or increased repayment of tax to the taxpayer**.

If a return contains more than one error, a penalty can be charged for each error.

The rules also extend to **errors in claims for allowances and reliefs** and in **accounts submitted in relation to a tax liability**.

Penalties for error also apply where **HMRC has issued an assessment estimating a person's liability** where:

- **A return has been issued to that person and has not been returned**; or
- The taxpayer was **required to deliver a return to HMRC but has not delivered it**.

The taxpayer will be charged a penalty where:

- The **assessment understates the taxpayer's liability** to income tax, capital gains tax, corporation tax or VAT; and
- **The taxpayer fails to take reasonable steps within 30 days of the date of the assessment** to tell HMRC that there is an under-assessment.

The amount of **the penalty for error is based on the Potential Lost Revenue (PLR)** to HMRC as a result of the error. For example, if there is an understatement of tax, this understatement will be the PLR.

The maximum amount of the penalty for error depends on the type of error (Whillans p.13):

Type of error	Maximum penalty payable
Careless	30% of PLR
Deliberate not concealed	70% of PLR
Deliberate and concealed	100% of PLR

Question — Penalty for error

Alex is a sole trader. He files his tax return for 2024/25 on 10 January 2026. The return shows his trading income (his only income) to be £60,000. In fact, due to carelessness, his trading income should have been stated to be £68,000.

State the maximum penalty that could be charged by HMRC on Alex for his error.

Answer

The Potential Lost Revenue because of Alex's error is:

£(68,000 – 60,000) = £8,000 × [40% (income tax) + 2% (NICs)]   £3,360

Alex's error is careless so the maximum penalty for error is:

£3,360 × 30%   £1,008

A **penalty for error may be reduced if the taxpayer tells HMRC about the error – this is called a disclosure**. The reduction depends on the **circumstances of** the disclosure and the **help that the taxpayer gives to HMRC in relation to the disclosure**.

An **unprompted disclosure is one made at a time when the taxpayer has no reason to believe HMRC has discovered, or is about to discover, the error**. Otherwise, the disclosure will be a **prompted disclosure**.

The **minimum penalties** that can be imposed are as follows:

Type of error	Unprompted	Prompted
Careless	0% of PLR	15% of PLR
Deliberate not concealed	20% of PLR	35% of PLR
Deliberate and concealed	30% of PLR	50% of PLR

Question — Reduction of penalty

Sue is a sole trader. She files her tax return on time. The return shows a trading loss for the year of £(18,000). In fact, Sue has deliberately increased this loss by £(12,000) and has submitted false figures in support of her claim. HMRC initiate a review into Sue's return and, in reply, Sue makes a disclosure of the error. Sue is a higher rate taxpayer due to her substantial property income and she has made a claim to set the loss against general income in the current tax year.

State the maximum and minimum penalties that could be charged by HMRC on Sue for her error.

> **Answer**
>
> The potential lost revenue as a result of Sue's error is:
>
> £12,000 × 40%   £4,800
>
> Sue's error is deliberate and concealed so the maximum penalty for error is:
>
> £4,800 × 100%   £4,800
>
> Sue has made a prompted disclosure so the minimum penalty for error is:
>
> £4,800 × 50%   £2,400

The help that the taxpayer gives to HMRC relates to when, how and to what extent the taxpayer:

- **Tells HMRC about the error,** making full disclosure and explaining how the error was made;
- **Gives reasonable help** to HMRC to enable it **to quantify the error**;
- **Allows access to business and other records** and other relevant documents.

A taxpayer can appeal to the First-tier Tribunal against:

- The **penalty being charged; and**
- The **amount of the penalty.**

7.2 Penalties for late notification of chargeability

FAST FORWARD A common penalty regime also applies to late notification of chargeability.

A common penalty regime also applies to certain taxes for failures to notify chargeability to, or liability to register for, tax that result in a loss of tax. The taxes affected include income tax, NICs, PAYE, CGT, corporation tax and VAT. Penalties are behaviour related, increasing for more serious failures, and are based on the 'potential lost revenue'.

The minimum and maximum penalties as percentages of PLR are as follows (Whillans p.14):

Behaviour	Maximum penalty	Minimum penalty with unprompted disclosure		Minimum penalty with prompted disclosure	
Deliberate and concealed	100%	30%		50%	
Deliberate but not concealed	70%	20%		35%	
		>12m	<12m	>12m	<12m
Careless	30%	10%	0%	20%	10%

Note that there is no zero penalty where a taxpayer can show that they have taken reasonable care (as there is for penalties for errors on returns – see above) but the penalty may be reduced to 0% if the failure is rectified within 12 months through unprompted disclosure. The penalties may also be reduced at HMRC's discretion in 'special circumstances'. However, inability to pay the penalty is not a 'special circumstance'.

The same penalties apply for failure to notify HMRC of a new taxable activity.

Where the taxpayer's failure is not classed as deliberate, there is no penalty if they can show they have a 'reasonable excuse'. Reasonable excuse does not include having insufficient money to pay the penalty. Taxpayers have a right of appeal against penalty decisions to the First-tier Tribunal, which may confirm, substitute or cancel the penalty.

7.3 Penalties for late filing of tax return

FAST FORWARD A penalty can be charged for late filing of a tax return based on how late the return is and how much tax is payable (Whillans p.16).

An individual is liable to a penalty where a tax return is filed after the due filing date. The penalty date is the date on which the return will be overdue (ie the date after the due filing date).

The initial penalty for late filing of the return is £100.

If the failure continues after the end of the period of three months starting with the penalty date, HMRC may give the individual notice specifying that a daily penalty of £10 is payable for a maximum of 90 days. The daily penalty runs from a date specified in the notice which may be earlier than the date of the notice but cannot be earlier than the end of the three-month period.

If the failure continues after the end of the period of six months starting with the penalty date, a further penalty is payable. This penalty is the greater of:

- **5% of the tax liability** which would have been shown in the return; and
- £300

If the failure continues after the end of the period of 12 months starting with the penalty date, a further penalty is payable. This penalty is determined in accordance with the taxpayer's conduct in withholding information which would enable or assist HMRC in assessing the taxpayer's liability to tax.

The penalty is computed as follows:

Type of conduct	Penalty
Deliberate and concealed	Greater of: • 100% of tax liability which would have been shown on return; and • £300
Deliberate not concealed	Greater of: • 70% of tax liability which would have been shown on return; and • £300
Any other case (eg careless)	Greater of: • 5% of tax liability which would have been shown on return; and • £300

7.4 Penalty for late payment of tax

This penalty was dealt with in Section 5.2 earlier in this chapter.

7.5 Penalties for failure to keep records

The maximum (mitigable) penalty for each failure to keep and retain records is £3,000 per tax year/accounting period (Whillans p.21).

PART B   CAPITAL TAXES

Chapter roundup

- UK taxes are administered by His Majesty's Revenue and Customs (HMRC).
- Individuals who do not receive a tax return or who have a new source of income or gains must notify their chargeability to income tax or CGT.
- Tax returns must usually be filed by 31 October (paper) or 31 January (electronic) following the end of the tax year.
- If a paper return is filed the taxpayer can ask HMRC to compute the tax due. Electronic returns have tax calculated automatically.
- Two payments on account and a final balancing payment of income tax and Class 4 NICs are due.
- A penalty is chargeable where tax is paid after the due date based on the amount of unpaid tax. Up to 15% of that amount is payable where the tax is more than 12 months late.
- Capital gains tax is usually due on 31 January following the end of the tax year. However, we have only 60 days to pay CGT in respect of disposals of UK residential property interests.
- A compliance check enquiry into a return, claim or election can be started by an officer of HMRC within a limited period.
- HMRC can investigate dishonest conduct by a tax agent and issue a civil penalty of up to £50,000 where there has been dishonest conduct.
- There is a common penalty regime for errors in tax returns, including income tax, NICs, corporation tax and VAT. Penalties range from 30% to 100% of the Potential Lost Revenue. Penalties may be reduced.
- A common penalty regime also applies to late notification of chargeability.
- A penalty can be charged for late filing of a tax return based on how late the return is and how much tax is payable.

Quick quiz

1. By which date must a taxpayer who has a new source of income in 2024/25 give notice of their chargeability to income tax?
2. What is the deadline for a taxpayer to file a paper tax return for 2024/25?
3. What are the normal payment dates for income tax?
4. What penalties are due in respect of income tax payments on account that are paid two months late?
5. Mark sells an investment residential property on 1 June 2024, making a gain of £83,070. He has already made a gain in 2024/25 of £15,000 on the disposal of some shares. He has capital losses brought forward of £2,500 and realised a loss of £14,700 on the disposal of a painting on 15 April 2024. Mark expects his taxable income for 2024/25 to be in the region of £55,000. Calculate Mark's CGT due on the disposal of the residential property and state the due date.

Answers to quick quiz

1. Within six months of the end of the year, ie by 5 October 2025.

2. By 31 October 2025 or, if the return is issued after 31 July 2025, by the end of three months following the issue of the notice to file the return.

3. Two payments on account of income tax are due on 31 January in the tax year and on the 31 July following. A final balancing payment is due on 31 January following the tax year.

4. None. Penalties do not apply to late payment of payments on account.

5. Capital gains tax due:

	£
Gain	83,070
Less 2024/25 capital loss realised by 1/6/24	(14,700)
Less capital loss brought forward	(2,500)
Less AEA	(3,000)
	62,870
Tax @ 24% (higher rate taxpayer)	15,089

Due date: 60 days after completion = 31 July 2024

PART B CAPITAL TAXES

An introduction to inheritance tax

Topic list
1 Basic principles
2 Computing transfers of value
3 Exemptions
4 Calculation of tax on lifetime transfers

Introduction

In this chapter, we introduce a new tax: inheritance tax (IHT). IHT is primarily a tax on wealth left on death but it also applies to gifts made within seven years of death and to lifetime transfers of wealth into trusts.

The tax is different from income tax and CGT, where the basic question is: how much has the taxpayer made? With IHT, the basic question is: how much have they given away? We tax the amount which the taxpayer has transferred – the amount by which they are worse off. If the taxpayer pays IHT on a lifetime gift, they are worse off by the amount of the gift plus the tax due, and we have to take that into account. Some transfers are, however, exempt from IHT.

We will see that the first £325,000 of transfers is taxed at 0% (the 'nil rate band'), and is therefore effectively tax-free. To stop people from avoiding IHT by, for example, giving away £1.625m in five lots of £325,000, we need to look back seven years every time a transfer is made to decide how much of the nil rate band is available to set against the current transfer.

In the next chapter, we will look at IHT reliefs and transfers on death.

PART B CAPITAL TAXES

Exam guide

Inheritance tax (IHT) will be examined in all sittings of the Taxation exam. The concepts of potentially exempt transfers (PETs), chargeable lifetime transfers (CLTs) and the seven-year cumulation principle are all fundamental to an understanding of IHT and you must learn how to calculate lifetime tax and any additional tax arising on death. Making full use of any available exemptions is a straightforward but very important part of any IHT calculation.

1 Basic principles

IHT is a tax on gifts or **'transfers of value'** made by **chargeable persons**. This generally involves a transaction as a result of which wealth is transferred by one person to another, either directly or via a trust.

1.1 Chargeable persons

Chargeable persons for IHT purposes are:

(a) Individuals
(b) Trustees of settled property

Companies are not chargeable persons, although if companies are used to transfer wealth, an IHT liability can be charged on the shareholders (the details are outside the scope of your syllabus).

Spouses and civil partners are taxed separately, although there is an exemption for transfers between the couple. There are also special valuation rules, which are dealt with later.

1.2 The scope of the charge

All transfers of assets (worldwide) made by persons domiciled, or deemed to be domiciled, in the UK (see section 1.3 below), **whether during lifetime or on death, are within the charge to IHT.**

For individuals not domiciled in the UK, only transfers of UK assets are within the charge to IHT.

1.3 Domicile

1.3.1 UK domicile

FAST FORWARD A UK domiciled, or deemed UK domiciled, individual is subject to inheritance tax on transfers of all assets, wherever situated.

If an individual is **UK domiciled**, or deemed UK domiciled (see below), **transfers of all assets, wherever situated, are subject to IHT.**

Domicile for IHT has the same meaning as in general law, namely **the country of one's permanent home**.

Also, an individual is **deemed to be domiciled in the UK for IHT purposes**:

(a) If the individual has been **resident in the UK for at least 15 out of the previous 20 tax years**, including at least one of the four tax years ending with the current tax year. The term 'residence' has the same meaning as for income tax (see earlier in this Workbook).

(b) **For 36 months after ceasing to be domiciled in the UK** under general law.

(c) If the individual is a 'formerly domiciled resident' for the tax year. This is someone who:

• was born in the UK with a UK domicile of origin;
• is resident in the current tax year; and
• was resident in the UK in at least one of the two tax years prior to the current tax year.

2 Computing transfers of value

2.1 Introduction

There are two main chargeable occasions for individuals:

(a) Gifts made in the lifetime of the donor (**lifetime transfers**).
(b) Gifts made on death, for example when property is left in a will (**death estate**).

We will look in detail at lifetime transfers later in this chapter and at the death estate in the next chapter.

First, however, we start our study of IHT by looking at some general principles which apply to both chargeable occasions.

2.2 Transfers of value and chargeable transfers

> **FAST FORWARD**
>
> IHT applies to transfers to trusts, transfers on death and to transfers within the seven years before death.

IHT cannot arise unless there is a transfer of value. This is any gratuitous disposition (eg gift) made by a person which results in that person being worse off, that is, the disposition causes a diminution (ie reduction) in the value of the estate.

The measure of a gift is always the loss to the transferor (the diminution in value of their estate), not the amount gained by the transferee.

2.3 Chargeable transfers

Inheritance tax arises on any **chargeable transfer. This is any transfer of value not covered by an exemption**.

Chargeable transfers made during the individual's lifetime are called **chargeable lifetime transfers (CLTs)**.

On death, an individual is treated as if they have made a transfer of value of the property comprised in their estate. This will be a chargeable transfer to the extent that it is not exempt.

2.4 Potentially exempt transfers

Key term

> A **potentially exempt transfer (PET)** is a **lifetime transfer made by an individual to another individual**. Any other lifetime transfer by an individual (eg gift to a trust) not covered by an exemption is a CLT.

A PET is exempt from IHT when made, and will remain so if the transferor survives for at least seven years from making the gift. If the transferor dies within seven years of making the gift, it will become chargeable to IHT.

2.5 Diminution in value

In many cases, the diminution in value of the transferor's estate will be the same as the increase in the value of the transferee's estate. However, sometimes the two will not be the same.

2.6 Example: diminution in value

A holds 5,100 of the shares in an unquoted company which has an issued share capital of 10,000 shares. Currently A's majority holding is valued at £15 per share.

A wishes to give 200 shares to her son, B. However, to B the shares are worth only £2.50 each, since B will have only a small minority holding in the company. After the gift A will hold 4,900 shares and these will be worth £10 each. The value per share to A will fall from £15 to £10 per share since she will lose control of the company.

The diminution in value of A's estate is £27,500, as follows.

	£
Before the gift: 5,100 shares × £15	76,500
After the gift: 4,900 shares × £10	(49,000)
Diminution in value	27,500

B has only been given shares with a market value of 200 × £2.50 = £500. Remember, a gift is also a deemed disposal at market value for CGT purposes, and it is this value that will be used in any CGT computation. IHT, however, uses the principle of diminution in value which can, as in this case, give a much greater value than the value of the asset transferred.

2.7 Exceptions to the IHT charge

The following are not chargeable to IHT:

(a) **Transfers where there is no gratuitous intent**: for example selling a painting for £1,000 which later turns out to be worth £100,000. The transaction must have been made at arm's length between unconnected persons.

(b) **Transfers made in the course of a trade**: for example Christmas gifts to employees.

(c) **Expenditure on family maintenance**: for example school fees paid for a child.

(d) Waivers of remuneration.

(e) Waivers of dividends provided the waiver is made within the 12 months before the dividend is declared.

(f) Any transfer covered by a specific exemption (see further below).

(g) **Transfers of excluded property** (see below).

3 Exemptions

FAST FORWARD

Exemptions may apply to make transfers or parts of transfers non chargeable. Some exemptions only apply on lifetime transfers (annual, normal expenditure out of income, marriage/civil partnership), whilst some apply on both life and death transfers (eg spouses, charities, political parties).

3.1 Introduction

There are various exemptions available to eliminate or reduce the chargeable amount of a lifetime transfer or property passing on an individual's death. Some exemptions apply to both lifetime transfers and property passing on death, whilst others apply only to lifetime transfers.

The lifetime exemptions apply to PETs as well as to CLTs. Only the balance of such gifts after the lifetime exemptions have been taken into account is then potentially exempt.

Exam focus point

Where CLTs and PETS are made in the same year, the CLTs should be made first to use any available exemptions. If used up against the PETs an exemption will be wasted if the PET never becomes chargeable.

3.2 Exemptions applying to lifetime transfers only

3.2.1 The small gifts exemptions

Outright gifts to individuals totalling £250 or less per donee in any one tax year are exempt. If gifts total more than £250, the whole amount is chargeable. A donor can give up to £250 each year to each of as many donees as they wish. The small gifts exemption cannot apply to gifts into trusts.

3.2.2 The annual exemption (AE)

The first £3,000 of value transferred in a tax year is exempt from IHT. (Whillans p.110). The annual exemption is used only after all other exemptions (such as for transfers to spouses/civil partners or charities (see below)).

If several gifts are made in a year, the £3,000 exemption is applied to earlier gifts before later gifts. The annual exemption is used up by PETs as well as CLTs, even though the PETs might never become chargeable.

Any unused portion of the annual exemption is carried forward for one year only. Only use it the following year **after** that year's own annual exemption has been used.

Question — Annual exemptions

F had no unused annual exemption brought forward at 6 April 2022.

On 1 August 2022, she made a transfer of £600 to P.
On 1 September 2022, she made a transfer of £2,000 to Q.
On 1 July 2023, she made a transfer of £3,300 to a trust for her grandchildren.
On 1 June 2024 she made a transfer of £5,000 to R.

Show the application of the annual exemptions.

Answer

	£
2022/23	
1.8.22 Gift to P	600
Less AE 2022/23	(600)
	0

	£
1.9.22 Gift to Q	2,000
Less AE 2022/23	(2,000)
	0

The unused 2022/23 annual exemption carried forward is £3,000 − £600 − £2,000 = £400.

	£	£
2023/24		
1.7.23 Gift to trust		3,300
Less: AE 2023/24	3,000	
AE 2022/23 b/f	300	
		(3,300)
		0

The unused annual exemption carried forward is zero because the current year (2023/24) exemption must be used before the exemption brought forward. The balance of £100 of the 2022/23 exemption is lost, because it cannot be carried forward for more than one year.

2024/25

	£
1.6.24 Gift to R	5,000
Less AE 2024/25	(3,000)
	2,000

3.2.3 Normal expenditure out of income

Inheritance tax is a tax on transfers of capital, not income. A transfer of value is exempt if:

(a) It is made as part of the normal expenditure of the transfer; or
(b) Taking one year with another, it was made out of income; and
(c) It leaves the transferor with sufficient income to maintain their usual standard of living.

As well as covering such things as regular presents, **this exemption can cover regular payments out of income such as a grandchild's school fees or the payment of life assurance premiums on a policy for someone else**.

3.2.4 Gifts in consideration of marriage/civil partnership

Gifts in consideration of marriage/civil partnership are exempt up to:

(a) **£5,000 if from a parent of a party to the marriage/civil partnership;**
(b) **£2,500 if from a remoter ancestor or from one of the parties to the marriage/civil partnership;**
(c) **£1,000 if from any other person.**

The limits apply to gifts from any one donor for any one marriage/civil partnership. The exemption is available only if the marriage/civil partnership actually takes place.

3.3 Exemptions applying to both lifetime transfers and transfers on death

3.3.1 Gifts between spouses/civil partners

Any transfers of value between spouses/civil partners are exempt provided the transferee is domiciled (see later in this Workbook) in the UK at the time of transfer. The exemption covers lifetime gifts between them and property passing under a will or on intestacy.

If the transferor spouse/civil partner is domiciled in the UK but the transferee spouse/civil partner is not domiciled in the UK, the exemption is limited to a cumulative total equal to the amount of the nil rate band at the date of transfer ie £325,000 for 2024/25. Any gift in excess of the £325,000 cumulative total will be a PET. If neither spouse/civil partner is domiciled in the UK there is no limit on the exemption.

An election may be made for a non-UK domiciled individual who is, or was, the spouse or civil partner of a UK domiciled individual, to be treated as UK domiciled for IHT purposes. We look at this election later in this Workbook when we deal with overseas aspects of IHT.

A simple planning point follows from this general spousal exemption. Spouses/civil partners may avoid IHT, at least in the short term, if each makes a will leaving his property to the other.

A claim can also be made to transfer any unused nil rate band from one spouse/civil partner to the surviving spouse/civil partner (see later in this Workbook).

Question — Exemptions

D made a gift of £153,000 to her son on 17 October 2022 on the son's marriage. D gave £400,000 to her spouse on 1 January 2025. D gave £70,000 to her daughter on 11 May 2025. The only other gifts D made were birthday and Christmas presents of £100 each to her grandchildren.

Show what exemptions are available assuming:

(a) D's spouse is domiciled in the UK
(b) D's spouse is not domiciled in the UK

Answer

(a) **17 October 2022**

	£
Gift to D's son	153,000
Less: ME	(5,000)
AE 2022/23	(3,000)
AE 2021/22 b/f	(3,000)
PET	142,000

1 January 2025

	£
Gift to D's spouse	400,000
Less spouse exemption	(400,000)
	0

11 May 2025

	£
Gift to D's daughter	70,000
Less: AE 2025/26	(3,000)
AE 2024/25 b/f	(3,000)
PET	64,000

The gifts to the grandchildren are covered by the small gifts exemption.

(b) **17 October 2022**

As in part (a)

1 January 2025

	£
Gift to D's spouse	400,000
Less spouse exemption (restricted)	(325,000)
Less: AE 2024/25	(3,000)
AE 2023/24 b/f	(3,000)
PET	69,000

Note. The annual exemption is available to set against the gift remaining after deducting the spouse exemption.

11 May 2025

	£
Gift to D's daughter	70,000
Less AE 2025/26	(3,000)
PET	67,000

3.3.2 Other exempt transfers

Transfers (whether outright or by settlement) **to UK charities are exempt** from inheritance tax.

Gifts to a qualifying political party are exempt. A political party qualifies if, at the general election preceding the transfer of value, either:

(a) At least two members were elected to the House of Commons; or
(b) One member was elected and the party polled at least 150,000 votes.

Gifts for national purposes are exempt. Eligible recipients include museums and art galleries.

4 Calculation of tax on lifetime transfers

4.1 Basic principles

FAST FORWARD

Transfers are cumulated for seven years so that the nil rate band is not available in full on each of a series of transfers in rapid succession.

There are two aspects of the calculation of tax on lifetime transfers:

(a) Lifetime tax on CLTs;
(b) Additional death tax on CLTs and on PETs where the transferor dies within seven years of making the transfer.

Exam focus point

You should always calculate the lifetime tax on any CLTs first, then move on to calculate the death tax on all CLTs and PETs made within seven years of death.

4.2 Lifetime tax

FAST FORWARD

IHT is charged on what a donor loses. If the donor pays the IHT on a lifetime gift, they lose both the asset given away and the money with which they paid the tax due. Grossing up is required.

4.2.1 Transferee pays tax

When a CLT is made and the transferee (ie the trustees) pays the lifetime tax, follow these steps to work out the lifetime IHT on it:

Step 1 Look back seven years from the date of the transfer to see if any other CLTs have been made. If so, these transfers use up the nil rate band available for the current transfer. Work out the value of any nil rate band still available.

Step 2 Compute the gross value of the CLT. You may be given this in the question or you may have to work out the diminution of value, deduct reliefs (such as business property relief as described later in the Workbook) or exemptions (such as the annual exemption described earlier in this chapter).

Step 3 Any part of the CLT covered by the nil rate band is taxed at 0%. Any part of the CLT not covered by the nil rate band is charged at 20%.

Exam focus point

The nil rate band since 2009/10 (ie £325,000) will be given to you in Whillans (p.107).

Question — Transferee pays the lifetime tax

Eric makes a gift of £336,000 to a trust on 10 July 2024. He has not used his annual exemption in 2024/25 nor in 2023/24. The trustees agree to pay the tax due.

Calculate the lifetime tax payable by the trustees if Eric has made:

(a) A lifetime chargeable transfer of value of £100,000 in August 2016
(b) A lifetime chargeable transfer of value of £100,000 in August 2017
(c) A lifetime chargeable transfer of value of £350,000 in August 2017

Answer

(a) **Step 1** No lifetime transfers in seven years before 10 July 2024. Nil rate band for 2024/25 (at the date of the gift) of £325,000 available.

Step 2

	£
Gift	336,000
AE 2024/25	(3,000)
AE 2023/24 b/f	(3,000)
Chargeable lifetime transfer	330,000

Step 3

	IHT £
£325,000 × 0%	0
£5,000 × 20%	1,000
£330,000	1,000

(b) **Step 1** Lifetime transfer of value of £100,000 in seven years before 10 July 2024 (transfers after 10 July 2017). Nil rate band of £(325,000 − 100,000) = £225,000 available.

Step 2 Value of CLT is £330,000 (as before).

Step 3

	IHT £
£225,000 × 0%	0
£105,000 × 20%	21,000
£330,000	21,000

(c) **Step 1** Lifetime transfer of value of £350,000 in seven years before 10 July 2024 (transfers after 10 July 2017). No nil rate band available as all used by previous transfer.

Step 2 Value of CLT is £330,000 (as before).

Step 3

	IHT £
£330,000 @ 20%	66,000

4.2.2 Transferor pays tax

Where IHT is payable on a CLT, the **primary liability to pay tax is on the transferor,** although the transferor may agree with the transferee, ie the trustee (as in the above example), that the transferee is to pay the tax instead.

If the transferor pays the lifetime IHT due on a CLT, the total reduction in value of their estate is the transfer of value plus the IHT due on it. The transfer is therefore a net transfer and must be grossed up in order to find the gross value of the transfer. **We do this by working out the tax as follows.**

Formula to learn

> Chargeable amount (ie not covered by nil band) × $\dfrac{20 \text{ (rate of tax)}}{80 \text{ (100 minus the rate of tax)}}$

When a CLT is made and the transferor pays the lifetime tax, follow these steps to work out the lifetime IHT on it:

Step 1 Look back seven years from the date of the transfer to see if any other CLTs have been made. If so, these transfers use up the nil rate band available for the current transfer. Work out the value of any nil rate band still available.

Step 2 Compute the net value of the CLT. You may be given this in the question or may have to work out the diminution of value, deduct reliefs (such as business property relief as described later in the Workbook) or exemptions (such as the annual exemption discussed earlier in this chapter).

Step 3 Any part of the CLT covered by the nil rate band is taxed at 0%. Any part of the CLT not covered by the nil rate band is taxed at 20/80.

Step 4 Work out the gross transfer by adding the net transfer and the tax together. You can check your figure by working out the tax on the gross transfer.

Question — Transferor pays the lifetime tax

James makes a gift of £336,000 to a trust on 10 July 2024. He has not used his annual exemption in 2024/25 nor in 2023/24. James will pay the tax due.

Calculate the lifetime tax payable, if James has made:

(a) A lifetime chargeable transfer of value of £100,000 in August 2016
(b) A lifetime chargeable transfer of value of £100,000 in August 2017
(c) A lifetime chargeable transfer of value of £350,000 in August 2017

Answer

(a) **Step 1** No lifetime transfers in seven years before 10 July 2024. Nil rate band for 2024/25 (at the date of the gift) of £325,000 available.

Step 2

	£
Gift	336,000
AE 2024/25	(3,000)
AE 2023/24 b/f	(3,000)
Net CLT	330,000

Step 3

	IHT £
£325,000 × 0%	0
£5,000 × 20/80	1,250
£330,000	1,250

Step 4 Gross transfer is £(330,000 + 1,250) = £331,250. **Check:** Tax on the gross transfer would be:

	IHT £
£325,000 × 0%	0
£6,250 × 20%	1,250
£331,250	1,250

(b) **Step 1** Lifetime transfer of value of £100,000 in seven years before 10 July 2024 (transfers after 10 July 2017). Nil rate band of £(325,000 – 100,000) = £225,000 available.

Step 2 Net value of CLT is £330,000 (as before).

Step 3

	IHT £
£225,000 × 0%	0
£105,000 × 20/80	26,250
£330,000	26,250

Step 4 Gross transfer is £(330,000 + 26,250) = £356,250. **Check:** Tax on the gross transfer would be:

	IHT £
£225,000 × 0%	0
£131,250 × 20%	26,250
£356,250	26,250

(c) **Step 1** Lifetime transfer of value of £350,000 in seven years before 10 July 2024 (transfers after 10 July 2017). No nil rate band available as all used by previous transfer.

Step 2 Net value of CLT is £330,000 (as before).

Step 3

	IHT £
£330,000 × 20/80	82,500

Step 4 Gross transfer is £(330,000 + 82,500) = £412,500. **Check:** Tax on the gross transfer would be:

	IHT £
£412,500 × 20%	82,500

4.3 Death tax

The longer the transferor survives after making a gift, the lower the death tax. This is because taper relief (Whillans p.111) applies to lower the amount of death tax payable as follows:

Years between transfer and death	% reduction in death tax
Three years or less	0
More than three but less than four	20
More than four but less than five	40
More than five but less than six	60
More than six but less than seven	80

PART B CAPITAL TAXES

Death tax on a lifetime transfer is **always** payable by the transferee, so grossing up is not relevant.

Follow these steps to work out the death tax on a CLT:

Step 1 Look back seven years from the **date of the transfer** to see if any other chargeable transfers were made. If so, these transfers use up the nil rate band available for the current transfer (ie the nil rate band at the date of death). Work out the value of any nil rate band remaining.

Step 2 Compute the value of the CLT. This is the gross value of the transfer that you worked out for computing lifetime tax.

Step 3 Any part of the CLT covered by the nil rate band is taxed at 0%. Any part of the CLT not covered by the nil rate band is charged at 40%.

Step 4 Reduce the death tax by taper relief (if applicable).

Step 5 Deduct any lifetime tax paid. The death tax may be reduced to nil, but there is no repayment of lifetime tax.

Exam focus point

The nil rate band since 2009/10 (ie £325,000) and previous years will be given in Whillans (p.107). However, take care when deciding whether you need to use these because when calculating death tax the nil rate band **at death** is required, not that at the date of the gift.

Question — Lifetime tax and death tax on CLTs

Trevor makes a gross chargeable transfer of value of £220,000 in December 2015. He then makes a gift to a trust of shares worth £206,000 on 15 November 2020. The trustees pay the lifetime tax due.

Trevor dies in August 2024.

Compute:

(a) The lifetime tax payable by the trustees on the lifetime transfer in November 2020
(b) The death tax (if any) payable on the lifetime transfer in November 2020

Answer

Lifetime tax

Step 1 Lifetime transfer of value of £220,000 in seven years before 15 November 2020 (transfers after 15 November 2013). Nil rate band of £(325,000 [nil rate band in 2020/21] – 220,000) = £105,000 available.

Step 2

		£
Gift		206,000
Less	AE 2020/21	(3,000)
	AE 2019/20 b/f	(3,000)
		200,000

Step 3

	IHT
	£
£105,000 × 0%	0
£ 95,000 × 20%	19,000
£200,000	19,000

246

Death tax

Step 1 Lifetime transfer of value of £220,000 in seven years before 15 November 2020 (transfers after 15 November 2013). Nil rate band of:
£(325,000 [nil rate band in 2024/25] – 220,000) = £105,000 available.

Step 2 Value of CLT is £200,000.

Step 3

	IHT £
£105,000 × 0%	0
£95,000 × 40%	38,000
£200,000	38,000

Step 4 Death more than three years but less than four years after transfer:

	£
Death tax	38,000
Less taper relief @ 20%	(7,600)
Death tax left in charge	30,400

Step 5 Tax due £(30,400 – 19,000)   11,400

4.4 Death tax on potentially exempt transfers

If the transferor dies within seven years of making a PET, it will become chargeable to death tax in the same way as a CLT. There will be no lifetime tax paid, so Step 5 above does not apply.

Remember that the exemptions which apply to lifetime transfers only, such as the annual exemption and the marriage/civil partner exemption, are available to set against PETs. **You must apply them in chronological order**, so that if a PET is made before a CLT in the same tax year, the exemption is set against the PET. This may waste the exemption (unless the donor dies within seven years), and is disadvantageous in cash flow terms since lifetime tax is paid on CLTs but not on PETs.

We will now work through an example where there is both a PET and a CLT.

Exam focus point

Calculate lifetime tax on CLTs first. Then move on to death tax, working through all CLTs and PETs in chronological order. Remember: on death PETs become chargeable so must be taken into account when calculating the death tax on later CLTs.

Question   Lifetime tax and death tax on CLTs and PETs

Louise gave £346,000 to her son on 1 February 2021. This was the first transfer that Louise had made.

On 10 October 2024, Louise gave £376,000 to a trust. The trustees paid the lifetime IHT due.

On 11 January 2025, Louise died.

Compute:

(a) The lifetime tax payable by the trustees on the lifetime transfer made in 2024
(b) The death tax payable on the lifetime transfer made in 2021
(c) The death tax payable on the lifetime transfer made in 2024

PART B CAPITAL TAXES

Answer

(a) **Lifetime tax – 2024 CLT**

Step 1 There are no chargeable lifetime transfers in the seven years before 10 October 2024 because the 2021 transfer is a PET and therefore exempt during Louise's lifetime. Nil rate band of £325,000 available.

Step 2

	£
Gift	376,000
Less AE 2024/25	(3,000)
AE 2023/24 b/f	(3,000)
CLT	370,000

Step 3

	IHT £
£325,000 × 0%	0
£45,000 × 20%	9,000
£370,000	9,000

(b) **Death tax – 2021 PET becomes chargeable**

Step 1 No lifetime transfers of value in seven years before 1 February 2021 (transfers after 1 February 2014). Nil rate band of £325,000 available.

Step 2

	£
Gift	346,000
Less AE 2020/21	(3,000)
AE 2019/20 b/f	(3,000)
PET now chargeable	340,000

Step 3

	IHT £
£325,000 × 0%	0
£15,000 × 40%	6,000
£340,000	6,000

Step 4 Death more than three years but less than four years after transfer.

	£
Death tax	6,000
Taper relief @ 20%	(1,200)
Death tax due	4,800

(c) **Death tax – 2024 CLT additional tax**

Step 1 Lifetime transfer of value of £340,000 in seven years before 10 October 2024 (transfers after 10 October 2017). Note that as the PET becomes chargeable on death, its value is now included in calculating the death tax on the CLT. No nil rate band available.

Step 2 Value of CLT is £370,000 (as before).

Step 3

		IHT £
	£370,000 @ 40%	148,000

Step 4 Death within three years of transfer so no taper relief.

Step 5 Tax due £(148,000 – 9,000) — 139,000

Chapter roundup

- IHT applies to transfers to trusts, transfers on death and to transfers within the seven years before death.
- Exemptions may apply to make transfers or parts of transfers non chargeable. Some exemptions only apply on lifetime transfers (annual, normal expenditure out of income, marriage/civil partnership), whilst some apply on both life and death transfers (eg spouses, charities, political parties).
- Transfers are cumulated for seven years so that the nil rate band is not available in full on each of a series of transfers in rapid succession.
- IHT is charged on what a donor loses. If the donor pays the IHT on a lifetime gift they lose both the asset given away and the money with which they paid the tax due on it. Grossing up is required.

Quick quiz

1 What is a transfer of value?
2 Who is chargeable to inheritance tax?
3 What types of transfer by an individual are potentially exempt transfers?
4 To what extent may unused annual exemption be carried forward?
5 Don gives some money to his daughter on her marriage. What marriage exemption is applicable?
6 Which lifetime transfers may lead to tax being charged on death of the transferor?
7 Why must some lifetime transfers be grossed up?
8 What is taper relief?

Answers to quick quiz

1 A transfer of value is any gratuitous disposition by a person resulting in a diminution of the value of their estate.

2 Individuals and trustees.

3 A potentially exempt transfer is a lifetime transfer made by an individual to another individual.

4 An unused annual exemption can be carried forward one tax year.

5 The marriage exemption for a gift to the transferor's child is £5,000.

6 An IHT charge on death arises on PETs and CLTs made within seven years of the transferor's death.

7 Where the donor pays the lifetime tax due it must be grossed up to calculate the total reduction in value of the estate.

8 Taper relief reduces death tax where a transfer is made between three and seven years before death.

PART B CAPITAL TAXES

Inheritance tax: valuation, reliefs and the death estate

Topic list

1 The valuation of assets for IHT purposes
2 Business property relief (BPR)
3 Agricultural property relief (APR)
4 The death estate

Introduction

We started our study of IHT in the previous chapter with a look at which transfers are exempt from IHT and the charge to IHT on lifetime transfers which are, or become, chargeable.

This chapter opens with a section on how assets are valued. Pay particular attention to the related property rules, which prevent one way of avoiding IHT.

Two of the reliefs described in this chapter, business property relief and agricultural property relief, are very generous. If the conditions are satisfied, assets can be exempted from IHT without any limit on the value of the assets. These reliefs are meant to ensure that a family business or farm does not have to be sold when an owner dies, but they also extend to non-family businesses and farms.

Finally, we will see how to bring together all of a deceased person's assets at death, and compute the tax on the estate.

In the next chapter, we turn our attention to some additional aspects of IHT including the overseas aspects and administration rules.

PART B CAPITAL TAXES

Exam guide

Business and agricultural property reliefs are extremely valuable reliefs as they enable assets to be passed on tax free. You should note the withdrawal of the relief on lifetime transfers if the donee sells the property or ceases to use if for business or agricultural purposes. There is no such limitation for gifts on death. The residence nil rate band may be available when calculating IHT on a death estate.

1 The valuation of assets for IHT purposes

FAST FORWARD

There are special rules for valuing particular kinds of assets, such as quoted shares and securities. The related property rules prevent artificial reductions in value.

1.1 The general principle

The value of any property for the purposes of IHT is the price which the property might reasonably be expected to fetch if sold in the open market at the time of the transfer.

Two or more assets can be valued jointly if disposal as one unit is the course that a prudent hypothetical vendor would have adopted in order to obtain the most favourable price: *Gray v IRC 1994*.

1.2 Quoted shares and securities

The valuation of quoted shares and securities is easy: the Stock Exchange daily official list gives the closing bid and offer prices of all quoted securities. **Inheritance tax valuations differ from those for CGT** (see earlier in the Workbook). **For IHT the value is calculated by taking the lower of:**

(a) Lower quoted price + ¼ × (higher quoted price − lower quoted price) ('quarter up' rule).
(b) The average of the highest and lowest marked bargains (ignoring bargains marked at special prices).

Question

Calculation of IHT value

Shares in A plc are quoted at 100–110p. The highest and lowest marked bargains were 99p and 110p. What would be the market value for IHT purposes?

Answer

The value will be the lower of:

(a) $100 + ¼ \times (110 - 100) = 102.5$

(b) $\dfrac{110 + 99}{2} = 104.5$

The market value for IHT purposes will therefore be 102.5p per share.

The transfer may take place on a day on which the Stock Exchange is closed, in which case the valuation is done on the basis of the prices or bargains marked on the last previous day of business or the first following day of business. The lowest of, in this case, the four alternatives will be taken.

Valuations for transfers on death must be cum-dividend or cum-interest, including the value of the right to the next dividend or interest payment. However, if the question gives an **ex-dividend** or an ex-interest price and the transfer is on death then the valuation is done on the basis of **adding the whole of the impending dividend**, or the whole of the impending interest payment.

> **Exam focus point**
>
> If a question just gives a closing price, you may assume that it is the cum-dividend or cum-interest price.

For lifetime transfers, the Stock Exchange list prices are used without adjustment, whether they are cum or ex dividend or interest.

1.3 Example: securities quoted ex interest

If someone owned £10,000 12% Government stock (interest payable half yearly) quoted at 94–95 ex interest, the valuation on death would be as follows:

	£
£10,000 at 94.25 (quarter up rule)	9,425
Add ½ × 12% × £10,000	600
	10,025

1.4 Unquoted shares and securities

There is no easily identifiable open market value for shares in an unquoted company. Shares and Assets Valuation at HMRC is the body with which the taxpayer must negotiate. If agreement cannot be reached, an appeal can be made to the Tax Tribunal.

1.5 Unit trusts

Units in authorised unit trusts are valued at the managers' bid price (**the lower of the two published prices**).

1.6 Life assurance policies

Where a person's estate includes a life policy which matures on their death, the proceeds payable to their personal representatives must be included in their estate for IHT purposes. But, where a person's estate includes a life policy which matures on the death of someone else, the open market value must be included in their estate.

If an individual writes a policy in trust, or assigns a policy, or makes a subsequent declaration of trust, the policy proceeds will not be paid to their estate but to the assignee or to the trustees for the trust beneficiaries. The proceeds will, therefore, not be included as part of their free estate at death. It is common to write policies in trust for the benefit of dependants to avoid IHT. In many cases these transfers will be exempted as normal expenditure out of income.

1.7 Overseas property

The basis of valuation is the same as for UK property. The value is converted into sterling at the exchange rate (the 'buy' or 'sell' rate) which will give the lower sterling equivalent. Overseas debts are deductible.

If the property passes on death, the costs of administering and realising overseas property are deductible up to a maximum of 5% of the gross value of the property, so far as those expenses are attributable to the property's location overseas. **Capital taxes paid overseas which are the foreign equivalent of IHT may give rise to double taxation relief** (see later in this Workbook). Such taxes are given as a credit against the IHT payable; they do not reduce the value of the asset.

1.7.1 Example: Overseas property

Sam died with a foreign asset included in her estate which was valued at €105,600. Sam's personal representatives incurred administration costs in dealing with the overseas asset of £6,100.

The exchange rate on the date of Sam's death was quoted at €1.07 - €1.10/£.

The value of the overseas asset to be included in the death estate is as follows:

	£
Overseas asset (€105,600/€1.10) =	96,000
Less admin costs: (max 5% x £96,000) =	(4,800)
Value of the overseas asset in the death estate	91,200

Using the quoted price of €1.10 gives the lowest sterling equivalent.

1.8 Related property

FAST FORWARD

Related property must be valued as a proportion of the value of the whole of the related property if this produces a higher value than the stand-alone value.

Key term

Property is related to that in a person's estate (**related property**) if:

(a) It is included in the estate of his spouse/civil partner; or

(b) It has been given to a charity, political party, national public body or housing association as an exempt transfer by either spouse or civil partner and still is, or within the preceding five years has been, the property of the body it was given to.

To reduce the value transferred individuals might fragment an asset into several parts which are collectively worth less than the whole. This way of reducing the value of an asset or set of assets is normally prevented using the diminution in value principle. However, this application of the principle could be thwarted by use of exempt inter-spouse/civil partner transfers. To deter this method of avoiding IHT, there are provisions under which related property is taken into account.

Property which is related to other property must be valued as a proportion of the value of the whole of the related property but only if, by so doing, a higher value is produced. For example, where a husband and wife each hold 40% of the issued shares of a company, the husband's holding will normally be valued as a proportion (one half) of the price which an 80% shareholding would fetch, as an 80% interest would normally be more valuable than two 40% interests.

1.9 Example: related property

Lofty has a leasehold interest in a property. The value of his interest is £25,000. His wife Michelle holds the freehold reversion of the property, which has a market value of £40,000. The value of the freehold not subject to the lease (that is the value of the freehold reversion plus the lease) is £80,000. If Lofty wishes to transfer his interest to their daughter Vicky the value transferred will be the greater of:

(a) The value of the interest by itself, £25,000

(b) The value of his part of the total related property, which is:

$$\frac{\text{The value of the property transferred at its \textbf{unrelated} value}}{\text{The value of the property transferred at its \textbf{unrelated} value} + \text{The value of any related property at its \textbf{unrelated} value}} \times \text{The value of the whole property}$$

$$\frac{25,000}{25,000 + 40,000} \times £80,000 = £30,769.$$

16: INHERITANCE TAX: VALUATION, RELIEFS AND THE DEATH ESTATE

The higher value is £30,769. This is therefore the value transferred by Lofty.

Exam focus point

If the property in question is shares, then in arriving at the fraction set out above, the numbers of shares held are used instead of unrelated values.

Question — Valuation of shares

Shares in an unquoted company are held as follows:

	Number of shares
Husband (H)	4,000
Wife (W)	2,000
Son (S)	750
Shares given by H to a charity by an exempt transfer eight years ago (and still owned by the charity)	3,250
	10,000

Estimated values for different sizes of shareholding are as follows:

Number of shares	Pence per share	£
750	60	450
2,000	90	1,800
4,000	130	5,200
7,250	200	14,500
9,250	250	23,125

What is the value of H's holding, taking into account related property?

Answer

There are three related holdings.

	Shares
H	4,000
W	2,000
Charity	3,250
	9,250

The value of H's 4,000 shares is $\frac{4,000}{9,250} \times £23,125 = £10,000$ (ie 250 pence × 4,000 shares).

If in the above exercise H gives away half of his holding to his son, the transfer of value is as follows:

	£
Holding before transfer (as above)	10,000
Less holding after transfer	
$\frac{2,000}{7,250} \times £14,500$	(4,000)
Transfer of value	6,000

If H transferred all his shares the value transferred would be £10,000 (no holding after, so no value in the calculation performed above).

2 Business property relief (BPR)

FAST FORWARD
> BPR can reduce the values of assets by 100% or 50%. However, there are strict conditions, which are largely intended to prevent people near death from obtaining the reliefs by investing substantial sums in businesses.

2.1 Business property

BPR is applied to the value of relevant business property transferred, to prevent large tax liabilities arising on transfers of businesses.

Relevant business property is:

(a) Property consisting of a business or an interest (such as a partnership share) in a business.
(b) Securities of a company which are unquoted and which (alone or with other securities or unquoted shares) gave the transferor control of the company immediately before the transfer (control may be achieved by taking into account related property).
(c) Any unquoted shares (not securities) in a company.
(d) Shares in or securities of a company which are quoted and which (alone or with other such shares or securities) gave the transferor control of the company immediately before the transfer (control may be achieved by taking into account related property).
(e) Any land or building, machinery or plant which, immediately before the transfer, was used wholly or mainly for the purposes of a business carried on by a company of which the transferor then had control, or by a partnership of which they were then a partner.

Shares or securities on the AIM count as unquoted.

The reliefs available are percentage reductions in the value transferred: 100% for assets within Paragraph (a), (b) or (c) above, and 50% for assets within Paragraph (d) or (e) above (Whillans p.110).

2.2 Conditions for BPR

BPR is only available if the relevant business property was owned by the transferor for at least the two years preceding the transfer; or

If, as a result of the donor's death within seven years of a gift, a PET becomes chargeable or additional tax is due on a CLT, two further conditions must be fulfilled for BPR to be available.

(a) The donee must still own the original property at the date of the donor's death, or the donee's death if earlier.
(b) The original property must still qualify as relevant business property at the date of the donor's death, or the donee's death if earlier.

These conditions are fulfilled if the donee disposed of the original property but reinvested **all** of the disposal proceeds in replacement property within three years of the disposal.

2.3 Non-qualifying businesses

BPR is not available if the business consists wholly or mainly of:

(a) Dealing in securities, stocks and shares (except for discount houses and market makers on the Stock Exchange or on LIFFE).
(b) Dealing in land or buildings.
(c) Making or holding investments (including land which is let).

Shares in holding companies, where the subsidiaries have activities which would qualify shares in them for BPR, are eligible for relief.

16: INHERITANCE TAX: VALUATION, RELIEFS AND THE DEATH ESTATE

Question — BPR

On 31 July 2024, relevant business property valued at £16,800 is transferred to a trust.

Assuming that the 2023/24 and 2024/25 annual exemptions have not been used what will the chargeable transfer be if:

(a) The property consists of unquoted shares?
(b) The property consists of land used by a company in which the transferor has a controlling interest?
(c) The property consists of quoted shares which formed part of a 20% interest before the transfer?

Answer

	(a) £	(b) £	(c) £
Value transferred	16,800	16,800	16,800
Less BPR	(16,800)	(8,400)	0
	0	8,400	16,800
Less AE 2024/25		(3,000)	(3,000)
AE 2023/24 b/f		(3,000)	(3,000)
Chargeable transfer	0	2,400	10,800

Question — BPR and related property

J had shares in a quoted trading company, J plc. The shares in the company were held as follows:

	%
J	40
J's husband	30
Other unconnected persons	30
	100

The shareholdings have been unchanged since 2001. On 1 May 2024, J gave a 30% holding to her son. The values of the shares in May 2024 were agreed as follows:

	£
70% holding	1,600,000
40% holding	900,000
30% holding	840,000
10% holding	200,000

J, who had made a previous chargeable lifetime transfer of £350,000 in 2019, died in January 2025.

Calculate the IHT arising on the gift of the shares, if:

(a) J's son still holds the shares in January 2025
(b) J's son sells the shares in June 2024 and retains the cash proceeds

PART B CAPITAL TAXES

Answer

No IHT arises when the gift was made because it was a PET. It becomes chargeable as a result of J's death within seven years as follows:

PET – May 2024

(a) If J's son still holds the shares, BPR at 50% is available to reduce the chargeable transfer:

	£
Before: $\dfrac{40\%}{40\%+30\%} \times £1,600,000$	914,286
After: $\dfrac{10\%}{10\%+30\%} \times £900,000$	(225,000)
	689,286
Less BPR at 50% (control of quoted company – with related property)	(344,643)
	344,643
Less AE 2024/25	(3,000)
AE 2023/24 b/f	(3,000)
Chargeable transfer	338,643

Gross chargeable transfers in the seven years before May 2024 amount to £350,000. This means none of the nil band remains and IHT payable on death amounts to:

IHT at 40% = £135,457

(b) If J's son does not hold the shares on J's death, BPR is not available to reduce the value of the chargeable transfer:

	£
Transfer (see above)	689,286
Less AE 2024/25	(3,000)
AE 2023/24 b/f	(3,000)
Chargeable transfer	683,286

IHT @ 40% = £273,314

3 Agricultural property relief (APR)

> **FAST FORWARD**
>
> APR usually reduces a transfer of agricultural property by 100% of agricultural value.

3.1 Agricultural property

APR is available on the agricultural value of agricultural property.

Agricultural property is agricultural land or pasture (including short rotation coppice) situated in the UK. It includes woodland and any building used in connection with the intensive rearing of livestock or fish where the occupation of the woodland or building is ancillary to that of the land or pasture. It also includes cottages, farm buildings and farmhouses of a character appropriate to the property.

> **Exam focus point**
>
> The agricultural value will be given to you in the exam.

APR works like BPR in reducing the value being transferred by a certain percentage before any exemptions. APR is given before BPR and double relief cannot be obtained on the agricultural value. The non-agricultural part of the value of the property meets the relevant business property conditions, however, BPR will be available on that value. **The percentage reduction in agricultural value is, in general, 100%** (it is 50% on some land held under pre-September 1995 tenancies) (Whillans p.110).

3.2 Conditions for relief

For relief to apply the transferor must either:

(a) Own the property and have occupied it themselves for the purpose of agriculture for the two years before the transfer (ie they farm the land themselves); or

(b) Own the property for at least the seven years before the transfer, during which it must have been occupied for the purposes of agriculture by either the transferor or a tenant (ie the property is or has been let out).

If a company controlled by the transferor occupies the property the transferor is treated as occupying it. A farmhouse which is being redecorated, renovated or altered is not treated as though it is occupied for agricultural purposes.

3.3 Additional conditions for lifetime transfers

If, as a result of the donor's death within seven years of a gift, a PET becomes chargeable or additional tax is due on a CLT, two further conditions must be fulfilled for APR to be available.

(a) The donee must still own the original property at the date of the donor's death, or the donee's death if earlier; and

(b) The original property must still qualify as agricultural property immediately prior to the date of the donor's death, or the donee's death if earlier, and must have been occupied as such since the original transfer.

These conditions are fulfilled if the donee disposed of the original property but reinvested **all** of the disposal proceeds in replacement property within three years of the disposal.

4 The death estate

FAST FORWARD — When someone dies, we must bring together all their assets to find the value of their death estate.

4.1 Composition of death estate

An individual's death estate consists of all the property they owned immediately before death. The estate also includes anything acquired as a result of death, for example the proceeds of a life assurance policy.

Tax on the free estate is payable by the personal representatives (PRs) (executors or administrators).

The whole of the death estate will be chargeable to tax, subject to reliefs (such as BPR and APR) and any exemptions which may be available on death. In particular, if property passes to the deceased person's spouse this will be an exempt transfer. A transfer to any other person eg children, will be chargeable to IHT, whether this is made outright or to any type of trust.

In order to calculate the tax on the death estate, use the following steps:

Step 1 Look back seven years from the date of death to see if any CLTs or PETs which have become chargeable have been made. If so, these transfers use up the nil rate band available for the death estate. Work out the value of any nil rate band still available.

Step 2 Compute the gross value of the death estate (see further below).

Step 3 Any part of the death estate covered by the nil rate band or residence nil rate band (see later) is taxed at 0%. Any part of the death estate not covered by the nil rate bands is charged at 40%.

PART B CAPITAL TAXES

Question — Tax on death estate

Laura dies on 1 August 2024, leaving a free estate valued at £400,000 to a discretionary trust for her children.

Laura had made a transfer of value of £163,000 to her sister on 11 September 2023. The amount stated is after all exemptions and reliefs.

Compute the tax payable by Laura's personal representatives.

Answer

Death tax

Note. There is no death tax on the September 2023 PET which becomes chargeable as a result of Laura's death, as it is within the nil rate band at her death. However, it will use up part of the nil rate band, as shown below.

Step 1   Lifetime transfer of value of £163,000 in seven years before 1 August 2024 (transfers after 1 August 2017). Nil rate band of £(325,000 – 163,000) = £162,000 available.

Step 2   Value of death estate is £400,000.

Step 3

	IHT £
£162,000 × 0%	0
£238,000 × 40%	95,200
£400,000	95,200
Tax payable by personal representatives	£95,200

The computation of an individual's chargeable estate at death should be set out as follows:

Death estate	£	£
Freehold property (keep UK and foreign property separate)	X	
Less repayment mortgages	(X)	
		X
Stocks and shares		X
Insurance policy proceeds		X
Personal chattels		X
Cash		X
		X
Less debts due by deceased	X	
funeral expenses	X	
		(X)
Chargeable estate		X

4.2 Debts and funeral expenses

The rules on debts are as follows:

(a) Only debts incurred by the deceased *bona fide* and for full consideration may be deducted.

(b) The debts must be such as an executor could pay without making themselves personally liable for a misuse of the assets of the estate. So gaming debts are not deductible but statute barred debts are, provided the executor pays them.

(c) **Debts incurred by the deceased but payable after the death may be deducted.**

(d) Rent and similar amounts which accrue day by day should be accrued up to the date of death.

(e) **Taxes to the date of death may be deducted** as they are a liability imposed by law.

(f) **Debts incurred by the executor are not allowed.**

(g) **If a debt is charged on a specific property it is deductible primarily from that property**; a mortgage on freehold property is therefore deductible from that freehold.

(h) Debts contracted abroad must first be deducted from non-UK property (whether or not the value of that property is chargeable to inheritance tax). If the foreign debts exceed the value of the foreign property the excess is allowed as a deduction from UK property provided it represents debts recoverable in the UK.

Reasonable funeral expenses may be deducted:

(a) What is reasonable depends on the deceased's condition in life.
(b) Reasonable costs of mourning for the family (and servants) are allowed.
(c) **The cost of a tombstone is deductible.**

Question — The death estate

Z died on 19 June 2024. His estate consisted of the following.

(i) 10,000 shares in A plc, quoted at 84p – 89p with bargains marked at 85p, 87p and 90p.

(ii) 8,000 shares in B plc, quoted ex div at 111p – 115p; a dividend of 4p per share was paid on 21 July 2023.

(iii) Freehold property valued at £150,000 subject to a mortgage of £45,040.

Liabilities and funeral expenses amounted to £2,450.

Z had made a chargeable lifetime transfer of £340,000 in July 2019.

None of the assets were passed to direct descendants.

Required

Calculate the IHT liability on the death estate.

Answer

Death estate

	£	£
Freehold property	150,000	
Less mortgage	(45,040)	
		104,960
A plc shares		
10,000 at lower of 85.25p and 87.5p (N1)		
10,000 × 85.25p		8,525
B plc shares, ex dividend		
8,000 × 112p (N2)	8,960	
Dividend 8,000 × 4p	320	
		9,280
		122,765
Less debts and funeral expenses		(2,450)
Chargeable estate		120,315

Chargeable transfers in the seven years prior to death exceeded the nil band, so IHT on the death estate is £120,315 at 40% = £48,126.

N1:

For IHT the value is calculated by taking the lower of:

(a) Lower quoted price + ¼ × (higher quoted price – lower quoted price) ('quarter up' rule).

= 84p + ¼ × (89p-84p)   =   85.25p

(b) The average of the highest and lowest marked bargains (ignoring bargains marked at special prices).

= (90p + 85p)/2   =   87.5p

N2:

Valuations for transfers on death must be cum-dividend or cum interest, including the value of the right to the next dividend or interest payment. However, if the question gives an **ex-dividend** or an ex-interest price and the transfer is on death then the valuation is done on the basis of **adding the whole of the impending dividend**, or the whole of the impending interest payment.

No. shares at quarter up rule = 8,000 @ 111p + ¼ × (115p-111p) = 8,000 @ 112p
Add whole value of right to dividend = 8,000 @ 4p.

4.3 Residence nil rate band (RNRB)

The residence nil rate band is available if an individual dies on or after 6 April 2017, owns a home that is included in their death estate and that home is inherited by direct descendants of the deceased, such as their children (and spouse/civil partner) or grandchildren (and spouse/civil partner).

The RNRB available is the lower of the value of the home (net of outstanding mortgages) or £175,000 (Whillans p.107).

The RNRB only applies to residential property in the death estate and not to life gifts of residential property. The residential property must have been lived in by the deceased at some point in their lifetime.

The RNRB is in addition to, but offset before, the nil rate band of £325,000.

If an individual's death estate is valued at more than £2 million, the RNRB is reduced by £1 for every £2 over £2 million. Once the estate reaches £2.35 million the RNRB is tapered to nil. The value of the estate used in deciding whether tapering applies is the value of all assets less debts or liabilities but before deducting any exemptions such as spouse or charity exemptions or any reliefs such as BPR or APR.

If a spouse/civil partner dies without utilising their full RNRB, the unused percentage of their RNRB is transferred to the surviving spouse. This applies even if the first death was before 6 April 2017 – in this case 100% of the RNRB is available.

Note. The value of the RNRB is offset against the whole of the taxable death estate, not just the value of the home.

Question — Transfer of nil rate band

Jimmy died on 24 April 2024. His estate consisted of:

	£
House in Liverpool (left to his son James)	475,000
Shares (not qualifying for BPR)	100,000
Cash	80,000
Chattels	70,000
Debts	10,000
Funeral expenses	3,000

Calculate the inheritance tax due as a result of Jimmy's death. Jimmy did not make any lifetime gifts.

> **Answer**

Death estate

	£
House in Liverpool (left to his son James)	475,000
Shares (not qualifying for BPR)	100,000
Cash	80,000
Chattels	70,000
Debts	(10,000)
Funeral expenses	(3,000)
Chargeable estate	712,000
Less RNRB	(175,000)
Less NRB	(325,000)
Taxable estate	212,000
Tax due £212,000 × 40%	£84,800

4.4 Transfer of unused nil rate band

4.4.1 How the transfer of unused nil rate band works

If:

- **An individual ('A') dies;** and
- **A had a spouse or civil partner ('B') and A and B were married or in a civil partnership immediately before B's death;** and
- **B had unused nil rate band (wholly or in part) on death;**

then **a claim may be made to increase the nil rate band maximum at the date of A's death by B's unused nil-rate band** in order to calculate the IHT on A's death. The revised nil band will apply to the calculation of additional death tax on CLTs made by A, PETs made by A and death tax on A's death estate.

4.4.2 Example

Robert and Claudia were married for many years until the death of Robert on 10 April 2024 leaving an estate of £500,000.

In his will, Robert left £100,000 to his sister and the remainder of his estate to Claudia. He had made no lifetime transfers.

Claudia died on 12 January 2025, leaving an estate (including the assets passed to her by Robert) of £850,000 to her brother. Claudia had made a chargeable lifetime transfer of £50,000 in 2021.

The inheritance tax payable on the death of Claudia, assuming that a claim is made to transfer Robert's unused nil rate band, is calculated as follows:

Step 1 (a) Lifetime transfer of value of £50,000 in seven years before 12 January 2025 (transfers after 12 January 2018).

(b) Nil rate band at death is £325,000. Nil rate band is increased by claim to transfer Robert's unused nil rate band at death £(325,000 − 100,000) = £225,000. The maximum nil rate band at Claudia's death is therefore £(325,000 + 225,000) = £550,000 and the available nil rate band is £(550,000 − 50,000) = £500,000.

Step 2 Value of death estate is £850,000.

Step 3

	IHT
	£
£500,000 × 0%	0
£350,000 × 40%	140,000
£850,000	140,000

Step 4 Tax payable by personal representatives £140,000

Note that the legacy to Robert's sister was a chargeable death transfer but that the gift of the rest of the estate to Claudia was exempt under the spouse exemption.

4.4.3 Changes in nil rate band between deaths of spouses/civil partners

If the nil rate band increases between the death of B and the death of A, the amount of B's unused nil rate band must be scaled up so that it represents the same proportion of the nil rate band at A's death as it did at B's death.

For example, if the nil rate band at B's death was £300,000 and B had an unused nil rate band of £90,000, the unused proportion in percentage terms is therefore 90,000/300,000 × 100 = 30%. If A dies when the nil rate band has increased to £325,000, B's unused nil rate band is £325,000 × 30% = £97,500 and this amount is transferred to increase the nil rate band maximum available on A's death.

The increase in the nil rate band maximum cannot exceed the nil rate band maximum at the date of A's death eg if the nil rate band is £325,000, the increase cannot exceed £325,000, giving a total of £650,000.

Question — Transfer of nil rate band

Jenna and Rachida were civil partners until the death of Jenna on 19 August 2007.

Jenna made no lifetime transfers. Her death estate was £440,000 and she left £200,000 to Rachida and the remainder to her mother.

The nil rate band in 2007/08 was £300,000.

Rachida died on 24 February 2025. Her death estate was £550,000 (including the assets passed to her by Jenna) and she left her entire estate to her nephews and nieces. She had made no lifetime transfers.

You are required to calculate the inheritance tax payable on the death of Rachida, assuming that any beneficial claims are made.

Answer

Step 1 (a) No lifetime transfers of value in seven years before 24 February 2025.

(b) Nil rate band at death is £325,000. Nil rate band is increased by claim to transfer Jenna's unused nil rate band at death. The nil rate band at Jenna's death in August 2007 was £300,000. Unused proportion was £(300,000 – 240,000) = 60,000/300,000 × 100 = 20%. The adjusted unused proportion is therefore £325,000 × 20% = £65,000. The maximum nil rate band at Rachida's death is therefore £(325,000 + 65,000) = £390,000 and this is also the available nil band.

Step 2 Value of death estate is £550,000.

Step 3		*IHT*
		£
	£390,000 × 0%	0
	£160,000 × 40%	64,000
	£550,000	64,000
Step 4	Tax payable by personal representatives	£64,000

4.4.4 Claim

The claim to transfer the unused nil rate band is usually made by the personal representatives of A. The time limit for the claim is two years from the end of the month of A's death (or the period of three months after the personal representatives start to act, if later) or such longer period as an officer of HMRC may allow in a particular case.

If the personal representatives do not make a claim, a claim can be made by any other person liable to tax chargeable on A's death within such later period as an officer of HMRC may allow in a particular case.

PART B CAPITAL TAXES

Chapter roundup

- There are special rules for valuing particular kinds of assets, such as quoted shares and securities. The related property rules prevent artificial reductions in value.
- Related property must be valued as a proportion of the value of the whole of the related property if this produces a higher value than the stand-alone value.
- BPR can reduce the values of assets by 100% or 50%. However, there are strict conditions, which are largely intended to prevent people near death from obtaining the reliefs by investing substantial sums in businesses.
- APR usually reduces a transfer of agricultural property by 100% of agricultural value.
- When someone dies, we must bring together all their assets to find the value of their death estate.

Quick quiz

1. How are quoted securities valued?
2. What is related property?
3. What rate of BPR is given on a controlling shareholding in:
   (a) A quoted trading company
   (b) An unquoted trading company
4. What periods of ownership or occupation are required to obtain agricultural property relief?
5. Sonia dies leaving the following debts:
   (a) Grocery bill
   (b) HM Revenue and Customs – income tax to death
   (c) Mortgage on house
   (d) Gambling debt

   Which are deductible against her death estate and why?

6. Mark and Hitesh had been married for many years. Mark died on 11 May 2024, leaving his estate, including the family home, to Hitesh. He had made a gross chargeable transfer of £160,000 in July 2020. If Hitesh dies in February 2025 and leaves the family home to their daughter Sandy, what is the total value of the nil rate bands available on Hitesh's death?

Answers to quick quiz

1. The value is the lower of:
   - The value on the quarter up basis (bid price plus 1/4 of the difference between the bid and offer prices).
   - The average of highest and lowest marked bargains for the day (ignoring special price bargains).

2. Related property is property:
   - Comprised in the estate of the transferor's spouse; or
   - Which has been given to a charity, political party, national public body or housing association as an exempt transfer by either spouse and still is, or has been within the past five years, been the property of the body it was given to.

3. (a) 50%
   (b) 100%

4. For APR the transferor must have either:
   - Owned and farmed the land themselves for two years before the transfer; or
   - Owned the property for at least seven years before the transfer during which time it was farmed either by the transferor or a tenant.

5. (a) Grocery bill – deductible as incurred for full consideration
   (b) Income tax to death – deductible as imposed by law
   (c) Mortgage – deductible, will be set against value of house primarily
   (d) Gambling debt – not allowable as executor be liable for misuse of estate assets if paid

6. Hitesh's residence nil rate band is £175,000 and his nil rate band is £325,000. Mark's residence nil rate band (RNRB) is £175,000 and his unused nil rate band is £(325,000 – 160,000) = £165,000. The total value of the nil rate bands available on Hitesh's death is therefore £840,000.

   The total RNRB of £350,000 will only be deducted in full if the home is worth at least this amount, and the full £350,000 is also only available if each estate is not worth more than £2 million (in which case the RNRB is tapered).

PART B CAPITAL TAXES

Inheritance tax: additional aspects

Topic list
1 Overseas aspects
2 The administration of IHT

Introduction

In the previous two chapters, we have studied the charge to IHT both on lifetime transfers and on death, and looked at some exemptions and reliefs.

In this chapter, we look at overseas aspects, including relief where property is subject both to IHT and to a similar tax abroad.

We also look at the administration and payment of IHT.

PART B CAPITAL TAXES

Exam guide

The rules for assets outside of the UK are beneficial to non-domiciled individuals. Note, however, that you must take positive action to change your domicile and that the deemed domicile rules mean that it takes at least three years to escape the UK IHT net. In the exam the aspects of this chapter may feature in an IHT calculation or in explaining the IHT due dates for transfers in life or on death.

1 Overseas aspects

1.1 Domicile

1.1.1 UK domicile

FAST FORWARD

> A UK domiciled, or deemed UK domiciled, individual is subject to inheritance tax on transfers of all assets, wherever situated.

As mentioned earlier in chapter 15, if an individual is **UK domiciled**, or deemed UK domiciled (see below), **transfers of all assets, wherever situated, are subject to IHT**.

Domicile for IHT has the same meaning as in general law, namely **the country of one's permanent home**.

Also, an individual is **deemed to be domiciled in the UK for IHT purposes**:

(a) If the individual has been **resident in the UK for at least 15 out of the previous 20 tax years** including at least one of the four tax years ending with the current tax year. The term 'residence' has the same meaning as for income tax (see earlier in this Workbook).

(b) **For 36 months after ceasing to be domiciled in the UK** under general law.

(c) If the individual is a 'formerly domiciled resident' for the tax year. This is someone who:

- was born in the UK with a UK domicile of origin;
- is resident in the current tax year; and
- was resident in the UK in at least one of the two tax years prior to the current tax year.

FAST FORWARD

> An election may be made for a non-UK domiciled individual who is, or was, the spouse or civil partner of a UK domiciled individual, to be treated as UK domiciled for IHT purposes.

An individual who is:

(a) **Not UK domiciled, nor deemed UK domiciled and**
(b) **Is the spouse or civil partner of a UK domiciled individual,**

may make an irrevocable election to be treated as UK domiciled for IHT purposes only.

The **effect of the election** is that **transfers by the UK domiciled spouse/civil partner to the non-UK domiciled individual are wholly exempt** and not subject to the restriction for transfers to a non-domiciled spouse/civil partner detailed earlier in this Workbook. However, the election also has the effect of **bringing the non-UK domiciled individual's assets situated outside the UK within the charge to IHT**. It is therefore important to consider both these aspects before the election is made.

| Exam focus point | Further details of the timing and operation of the election are not required in the Taxation exam. |

17: INHERITANCE TAX: ADDITIONAL ASPECTS

1.1.2 Non-UK domicile

FAST FORWARD Non-UK assets of individuals not domiciled in the UK are not subject to IHT.

For individuals **not domiciled in the UK, only transfers of UK assets are within the charge to IHT**, and even some assets within the UK are excluded property.

1.2 Excluded property

As we saw earlier, foreign property of a non-UK domiciled individual is excluded property so is ignored for IHT purposes. The following are also excluded property:

(a) Foreign assets in a trust established when the settlor was non-UK domiciled for IHT purposes. No IHT is due on the trust assets even if the settlor later becomes UK domiciled at a later date.

(b) Certain UK Government securities whose terms of issue provide that they shall be exempt from taxation so long as they are owned by non-UK domiciled or not ordinarily resident individuals (the extended IHT definition of deemed domicile above does not apply).

(c) The following savings if held by persons domiciled in the Channel Islands or the Isle of Man (the extended IHT definition of deemed domicile above does not apply):

　(i)　War savings certificates
　(ii)　National Savings & Investments certificates
　(iii)　Premium savings bonds
　(iv)　Deposits in National Savings & Investments accounts or with a trustee savings bank
　(v)　SAYE savings schemes (see earlier in this Workbook)

(d) Unit trust units or shares in open ended investment companies (OEICs) held by non-UK domiciliaries.

In addition, if someone dies when neither domiciled nor resident in the UK, a foreign currency account held at a UK bank is ignored in computing their death estate.

1.3 Double taxation relief (DTR)

FAST FORWARD Double taxation relief may reduce the IHT on assets also taxed overseas.

DTR applies to transfers (during lifetime and on death) of assets situated overseas which suffer tax overseas as well as IHT in the UK. Relief may be given under a treaty, but if not then the default DTR rules apply.

DTR is given as a tax credit against the IHT payable on the overseas asset. The amount available as a tax credit is the lower of the foreign tax liability and the IHT (at the average rate) on the asset.

Question
DTR

Pau died leaving a chargeable estate of £282,000. Included in this total is a foreign asset valued at £80,000 in respect of which foreign taxes of £20,000 were paid.

Calculate the IHT payable on the estate, assuming that Pau made a gross chargeable lifetime transfer of £187,000 one year before his death. Pau was domiciled in the UK and his chargeable estate did not include a residential property.

Answer

	£
IHT on chargeable estate of £282,000	
(available nil rate band £(325,000 – 187,000) = £138,000 @ 0%, £144,000 @ 40%	57,600
(Average rate: 57,600/282,000 = 20.42553%)	
Less DTR lower of:	
(a) £20,000	
(b) £80,000 × 20.42553% = £16,340	(16,340)
IHT payable on the estate	41,260

2 The administration of IHT

FAST FORWARD

IHT is administered by HMRC's Inheritance Tax department. The due date for payment depends on the type of event giving rise to the charge to tax. Make sure you use Whillans p.3

2.1 Accounts

IHT is administrated by HMRC's Inheritance Tax department.

There is no system of regular returns as there is for income tax, corporation tax and capital gains tax. Instead, any person who is liable for IHT on a transfer is required to deliver an account giving details of the relevant assets and their value. An account delivered by the personal representatives (PRs) of a deceased person must provide full details of the assets in the death estate. The PRs must also include in their account details of any chargeable transfers made by the deceased person in the seven years before their death.

PRs must deliver an account within 12 months following the end of the month in which death occurred or, if later, three months following the date when they become PRs. Where no tax is due, and certain other conditions are satisfied, it is not necessary to submit an account. Estates where no account needs to be submitted are called excepted estates.

A person responsible for the delivery of an account in relation to a PET that has become chargeable by reason of death, must do so within 12 months following the end of the month in which death occurred unless already reported by the PRs.

Any other account (such as for a chargeable lifetime transfer) must be delivered within 12 months of the end of the month in which the transfer was made or, if later, within three months from the date liability to tax arose.

If a person has delivered an account and then discovers a material defect in it, they must deliver a corrective account within six months.

2.2 Power to call for documents

HMRC may require any person to provide any information, documents, etc needed for the purposes of IHT. There is a right of appeal against such an information notice.

17: INHERITANCE TAX: ADDITIONAL ASPECTS

2.3 Determinations and appeals

HMRC issue a written notice of determination where, for example, they do not agree a value of transfer or where payment of tax has not been made. It may be made on the basis of a submitted account or to the best of the inspector's judgement.

An appeal against a notice of determination may be made to the Tax Chamber of the Tribunal within 30 days of its being served. Questions of land valuation are dealt with by the Lands Tribunal.

HMRC cannot take legal proceedings to recover tax charged by a notice of determination while an appeal is pending.

2.4 Liability for IHT

FAST FORWARD — The liability to pay IHT depends on the type of transfer and whether it was made on death.

On death, liability for payment is as follows:

(a) **Tax on the free estate is paid by the PRs** out of estate assets, with the burden generally falling on the residuary legatee (ie the recipient of the assets in the residue).

(b) **Tax on PETs that have become chargeable is paid and borne by donees**.

(c) **Additional liabilities on CLTs must be paid and borne by the donees**.

HMRC can look beyond the person primarily responsible. Most significantly a PR may become liable where the tax remains unpaid. This overall liability is limited to the value of estate assets in their possession. HMRC will not pursue the PR for tax if lifetime transfers are later discovered and the PR has made the fullest reasonably practicable enquiries to discover lifetime transfers and has obtained a certificate of discharge before distributing the estate.

If the PRs do not pay IHT due on an estate, HMRC may collect the tax from beneficiaries under the will to the extent they receive assets under the will.

The donor is primarily liable for the tax due on chargeable lifetime transfers.

2.5 Due dates

(a) For chargeable lifetime transfers the due date is the later of:

  (i) 30 April just after the end of the tax year of the transfer
  (ii) Six months after the end of the month of the transfer

  Interest (not tax deductible) is payable from the due date to the day before the day on which payment is made (inclusive).

(b) **Tax arising on the free estate at death (and on gifts with reservation if the reservation still existed at death) is payable by the PRs on delivery of their account**. The time limit for this is 12 months from the end of the month in which the death occurred or, if earlier, when probate is obtained. Interest, however, runs from six months after the end of the month when death occurred.

(c) **Tax arising on death in respect of PETs and CLTs with additional tax is payable within six months from the end of the month of death, and interest runs from this due date.**

Interest (not taxable) is paid on repayments of tax from the date of payment to the date of repayment.

Exam focus point

> The interest rate charged is 7.75% and is in Whillans tax tables on page 7. Although different interest rates apply to different periods where tax was outstanding, in your exam you should use the most recent interest rate given in the Whillan's tables as a simplification.

Question: Interest on IHT

Peter died on 10 March 2025. IHT of £375,000 on his estate was paid on 1 November 2025.

Calculate the interest payable on the late paid IHT, assuming an interest rate of 7.75%.

Answer

Interest runs from 30 September 2025 to 31 October 2025 (inclusive).

Interest = £375,000 × 7.75% × 1/12 = £2,422

Chapter roundup

- A UK domiciled, or deemed UK domiciled, individual is subject to inheritance tax on transfers of all assets wherever situated.
- An election may be made for a non-UK domiciled individual who is, or was, the spouse or civil partner of a UK domiciled individual, to be treated as UK domiciled for IHT purposes.
- Non-UK assets of individuals not domiciled in the UK are not subject to IHT.
- Double taxation relief may reduce the IHT on assets also taxed overseas.
- IHT is administered by HMRC Inheritance Tax. The due date for payment depends on the type of event giving rise to the charge to tax.
- The liability to pay IHT depends on the type of transfer and whether it was made on death.

Quick quiz

1. How is domicile defined for IHT purposes?
2. How is double taxation relief given?
3. Susan died leaving a chargeable estate of £360,000. This included a villa in Spain worth £40,000 in respect of which Spanish death duties of £10,000 were paid. Susan made no gifts during her lifetime. She is UK domiciled and left her estate to her niece. Calculate the IHT payable as a result of Susan's death.
4. When is lifetime inheritance tax on a chargeable lifetime transfer due for payment?
5. Who is liable for payment of IHT as a result of death on:
   - Death estate
   - PETs
   - CLTs

PART B CAPITAL TAXES

Answers to quick quiz

1 Domicile for IHT is:

- Domicile under the general law (permanent home)
- Deemed domicile in the UK if resident for at least 15 out of the previous 20 tax years, including at least one of the four tax years ending with the current tax year.
- Deemed domicile in the UK if ceased to be domiciled under general law in last 36 months
- Deemed domicile If the individual is a 'formerly domiciled resident' for the tax year. This is someone who:
    - was born in the UK with a UK domicile of origin;
    - is resident in the current tax year; and
    - was resident in the UK in at least one of the two tax years prior to the current tax year.

2 DTR is given as a tax credit against IHT payable on the overseas asset to the extent of the lower of foreign tax and the IHT (at average rate) on it.

3 The correct answer is:

	£	£
Chargeable estate		360,000
IHT payable		14,000
£(360,000 – 325,000) × 40%		
Less: DTR lower of		
Overseas tax	10,000	
UK IHT	1,556	
14,000/360,000 × 40,000		(1,556)
		12,444

4 The due date for lifetime tax on a chargeable lifetime transfer is the later of:

(a) 30 April just after the end of the tax year of the transfer; and
(b) Six months after the end of the month of transfer.

5
- PRs out of estate assets ie suffered by residuary legatee(s)
- Donee
- Donee

Corporation tax

Computing taxable total profits

Topic list

1 The scope of corporation tax
2 Taxable total profits
3 Loan relationships
4 Research and development

Introduction

At this point in our studies, we turn to corporation tax, covering the basic corporation tax rules in this chapter.

We start by looking at accounting periods, which are the periods for which companies pay corporation tax. We then see how to bring together all of a company's profits in a corporation tax computation and discuss the special rules for certain types of income and gains that apply to companies.

In the next chapter, we will deal with the rules on chargeable gains for companies.

PART C   CORPORATION TAX

Exam guide

Exam questions involving corporation tax will require you to know how taxable total profits are calculated. You may be required to consider how certain types of income and expenditure should be included in the computation where special rules apply, such as for loan relationships and research and development expenditure. You may also be examined in detail on adjustments to profits or the rules for capital allowances. You must therefore have a thorough understanding of these rules and be able to apply them, even when a complete corporation tax computation is not required.

1 The scope of corporation tax

1.1 Introduction

FAST FORWARD

Companies pay corporation tax on their taxable total profits for each accounting period.

Corporation tax is paid by companies. It is charged on the taxable total profits (which includes chargeable gains) of each accounting period. Corporation tax is not charged on dividends received from UK resident or non-resident companies.

Key term

A **'company'** is any corporate body (limited or unlimited) or unincorporated association eg sports clubs.

1.2 The residence of companies

A company incorporated in the UK is resident in the UK. A company incorporated abroad is also resident in the UK if its central management and control are exercised here.

1.3 Accounting periods

FAST FORWARD

An accounting period cannot exceed 12 months in length. A long period of account must be split into two accounting periods, the first of which is 12 months long.

Corporation tax is chargeable in respect of accounting periods. It is important to understand the difference between an accounting period and a period of account. A period of account is any period for which a company prepares accounts; usually this will be 12 months in length but it may be longer or shorter than this.

An accounting period starts when a company starts to trade, or otherwise becomes liable to corporation tax, or immediately after the previous accounting period finishes.

An accounting period finishes on the earliest of:

- 12 months after its start
- The end of the company's period of account
- The company starting or ceasing to trade
- On the company entering/ceasing to be in administration (see later in this Workbook)
- The company ceasing to be resident in the UK
- The company ceasing to be liable to corporation tax
- On commencement of a company's winding up

In many cases, the company will have a period of account of 12 months and an accounting period of 12 months. We will deal with long periods of account (exceeding 12 months) later in this chapter.

282

2 Taxable total profits

Taxable total profits are the total profits (income and gains) less some losses and qualifying charitable donations.

2.1 Introduction

The corporation tax computation draws together all of the company's income and gains from various sources. The income from each different type of source must be computed separately because different computational rules apply.

The taxable total profits for an accounting period are derived as follows:

	£
Trading income	X
Interest income from non-trading loan relationships	X
Miscellaneous income	X
Property business income	X
Chargeable gains	X
Total profits	X
Less losses relieved by deduction from total profits	(X)
Less qualifying charitable donations	(X)
Taxable total profits for an accounting period	X

Each of the above items is dealt with in further detail later in this Workbook.

The tax rate used to determine the corporation tax liability depends on the level of profits. This rate can be between 19% and 25% and this is dealt with in chapter 20 of this workbook.

Exam focus point

You must learn this pro forma. The calculation of taxable total profits may be required in an exam, so you must understand how different types of income and gains are dealt with. You will then be able to advise on the marginal tax effects of suggested courses of action.

Dividends received from both UK and non-UK resident companies are usually exempt and so not included in taxable total profits.

Exam focus point

Dividends which are taxable in the hands of the recipient company are not examinable.

2.2 Trading income

The trading income of companies is derived from the profit before taxation figure in the accounts. The adjustments that need to be made to the accounts are broadly the same for companies as they are for income tax purposes (companies cannot use the cash basis) (see Chapter 5). Where shares in UK companies are held as trading assets, and not as investments, any dividends on those shares will be treated for tax purposes as trading profits.

Qualifying charitable donations are added back into calculation of adjusted profit. They are instead deducted from total profits (see below).

Interest received on a trading loan relationship (see later in this chapter) is included within trading profits on an accruals basis. Similarly, interest paid on a trading loan relationship is deducted at arriving at trading profits.

Pre-trading expenditure incurred by the company within the seven years before trade commences is treated as an allowable expense incurred on the first day of trading provided it would have been allowable had the company been trading when the expense was actually incurred.

Trading income also includes post cessation receipts arising from a trade which would not otherwise be chargeable to tax.

The calculation of capital allowances follows income tax principles although, for companies, there is never any restriction of allowances to take account of any private use of an asset. The director or employee suffers a taxable benefit instead.

Another key difference is that, from 1 April 2023, **companies** have been able to claim two additional first-year allowances (FYAs). These allowances are:

- A **100%** first-year allowance for **main pool** expenditure, known as **full expensing**; and
- A **50%** first-year allowance for **special rate pool** expenditure

These allowances are available to companies subject to UK corporation tax and they result in a deduction of all or 50% of qualifying expenditure from the companies trading profits in the year qualifying plant and machinery is bought.

They are available in addition to the annual investment allowance (AIA) of £1 million per 12-month accounting period.

To qualify for the 100% and 50% FYAs, the expenditure must be incurred:

- Since 1 April 2023;
- On new and unused plant and machinery;
- On plant and machinery other than cars.

Interaction with the AIA

In the Taxation exam, apply the AIA to relieve qualifying capital expenditure in preference to full expensing or the FYA at 50%. There are two reasons for this:

1   Firstly, when an asset which was relieved using a 100% FYA when it was acquired will generate a **balancing charge when it is disposed of**. The balancing charge will increase the company's trading income and therefore increase its tax charge. This balancing charge on disposal of a main pool asset is 100% of the disposal value depending on which FYA was given.

    If the asset was a special rate asset and it was given a 50% FYA on acquisition, its disposal will result in **a balancing charge equal to 50% of its disposal value**. The remainder of the disposal value will be deducted from the special rate pool before the writing down allowance is calculated.

    If only part of the expenditure was relieved using the 50% or 100% FYA the balancing charge is proportionately reduced with the remainder of the disposal value deducted from the relevant pool (see example later).

2   Secondly, the AIA relieves 100% of the expenditure so using it to relieve special rate expenditure gives a larger capital allowance.

    If an asset is disposed of, having been relieved using the AIA, the disposal proceeds are deducted from the relevant pool. The use of the AIA therefore avoids or reduces the balancing charge.

2.3 Example

Biscuits Ltd has tax written down value on its main pool of plant and machinery of £20,000 on 1 April 2024. In the year to 31 March 2025, the company purchased the following plant and machinery:

		£
May 2024	Second-hand construction equipment	750,000
July 2024	Integral features for use in its factories	500,000
August 2024	Fleet of cars for employees, all with CO_2 emissions greater than 50g/km	150,000
December 2024	New office equipment	225,000

Calculate the capital allowance claim for the year ended 31 March 2025,

(i) assuming full expensing and 50% FYAs are used wherever possible; and
(ii) assuming the best use of the AIA.

(i) **use of FYAs in priority**

	FYA £	AIA £	Main pool £	Special rate pool £	Allowances £
TWDV b/f			20,000		
Construction equipment (not new so no FYA)		750,000			
AIA		(750,000)			750,000
Integral features (50% FYA)	500,000				
FYA at 50%	(250,000)				250,000
Fleet of cars (no FYA or AIA)				150,000	
Office equipment	225,000				
FYA at 100%	(225,000)				225,000
	250,000		20,000	150,000	
Writing down allowance at 18%			(3,600)		3,600
Writing down allowance at 6%				(9,000)	9,000
Transfer to special rate pool	(250,000)			250,000	
			16,400	391,000	1,237,600

Where a 50% FYA is applied to special rate expenditure in one accounting period, the remaining 50% of the expenditure cannot be relieved using writing down allowances or AIA in that same period. For this reason the balance on the FYA column is transferred to the special rate pool *after* the calculation of the writing down allowances. Conversely, it is possible to apply the available AIA first and any expenditure not covered by that AIA can then qualify for a 50% FYA.

(ii) **Best use of the AIA**

If we look at the acquisitions in the period and consider how we can relieve the expenditure **most quickly**, we can summarise the options as follows:

	Note	AIA	FYA	WDA
Fleet of cars	1	0%	0%	6%
Construction equipment (second-hand asset main pool)	2	100%	0%	18%
Office equipment (new asset, main pool)	3	100%	100%	18%
Integral features (new asset, special rate pool)	4	100%	50%	6%

Notes

To determine the use of the AIA, we should then consider what the next best alternative treatment would be for each of the assets acquired.

1. The **fleet of cars** can only be relieved in the special rate pool, with neither the 50% FYA nor the AIA available for cars.
2. If we do not use the AIA on the **construction equipment** the next best alternative for that expenditure is to claim a writing-down allowance of 18%. This is because the construction equipment is second-hand rather than new so the FYA is not available.
3. The **office equipment** is new, so it qualifies for both the AIA and the FYA (both 100% relief immediately).
4. If not relieved using the AIA the **integral features** would qualify for a 50% FYA.

So the AIA should be used to relieve the expenditure on the construction equipment first (it has the worst of the next-best alternatives), then the integral features and then the office equipment because even if this expenditure does not get a share of the AIA it still has an unlimited FYA at 100%

(ii) best use of AIA	FYA £	AIA £	Main pool £	Special rate pool £	Allowances £
TWDV b/f			20,000		
Construction equipment		750,000			
AIA		(750,000)			750,000
Integral features	250,000	250,000			
AIA		(250,000)			250,000
FYA at 50%	(125,000)				125,000
Office equipment	225,000				
FYA at 100%	(225,000)				225,000
Fleet of cars (no FYA or AIA)				150,000	
	125,000		20,000	150,000	
Writing down allowance at 18%			(3,600)		3,600
Writing down allowance at 6%				(9,000)	9,000
Transfer to special rate pool	(125,000)			125,000	
			16,400	266,000	1,362,600

2.4 Example

Continuing from Example 2.3, Biscuits Ltd disposes of all of the integral features bought in July 2024. They were sold for £260,000 on 28 February 2026. No other acquisitions or disposal of plant and machinery took place in that accounting period.

Calculate the capital allowance claim for the year ended 31 March 2026,

(i) **assuming 50% FYAs were used to relieve the expenditure on integral features in July 2024; and**
(ii) **assuming the AIA was used to best effect.**

In either case the disposal value of the integral features is the lower of the original cost (£500,000) and its disposal proceeds (£260,000) ie £260,000.

(i) use of FYA in y/e 31.3.2025

	Main pool £	Special rate pool £	Allowances £
TWDV b/f	16,400	391,000	
Disposal of integral features			
Balancing charge at 50% of disposal value			(130,000)
Deduct remainder from SRP		(130,000)	
	16,400	261,000	
Writing down allowances 18%/6%	(2,952)	(15,660)	18,612
TWDV c/f and total allowances/(charge)	13,448	245,340	(111,388)

(ii) use of AIA in y/e 31.3.2025

	Main pool £	Special rate pool £	Allowances £
TWDV b/f	16,400	266,000	
Disposal of integral features			
Bal charge:			
250/500 × 50% × £260,000			(65,000)
Balance of disposal value (£260k-£65k)		(195,000)	
	16,400	71,000	
Writing down allowances 18%/6%	(2,952)	(4,260)	7,212
TWDV c/f and total		66,740	
allowances/(charge)	13,448		(57,788)

The use of the AIA on acquisition of the integral features has reduced the balancing charge. This is because more of the disposal value has been removed from the pool rather than automatically triggering a balancing charge equal to 50% of the disposal value.

Unincorporated businesses (sole traders and partnerships) are not able to claim the 100% or 50% first-year allowances. However, these businesses do still have access to a £1 million annual investment allowance (AIA).

Prior to 1 April 2023

Between 1 April 2021 and 31 March 2023, companies were able to claim enhanced capital allowances, known as a 'super-deduction' for main pool items, and a first year allowance (FYA) for special rate pool items.

- An unlimited 130% FYA super-deduction on qualifying expenditure on new plant and machinery (excluding cars) that would normally fall within the main rate pool; and

- An unlimited 50% FYA on expenditure on new plant and machinery (excluding cars) that would normally fall within the special rate pool.

On disposal of an asset acquired before 1 April 2023 and on which enhanced capital allowances have been claimed, an immediate balancing charge will arise. The amount of the balancing charge depends on the disposal date and whether the asset qualified for the super-deduction, or the special rate first year allowance.

PART C CORPORATION TAX

Exam focus point

> For 2025 exams candidates will only be tested on disposals which take place in accounting periods starting after 1 April 2023.

Key term

> Disposal value is the lower of the sale proceeds and the original cost of the asset.

Therefore, for assets on which the 130% super-deduction was claimed, the balancing charge is calculated based on 100% of the disposal value. No disposal value will be deducted from the main pool.

For assets on which the 50% special rate FYA was claimed, the balancing charge is based on 50% of the disposal value. The balance of the disposal value will be deducted from the special rate pool.

The balancing charge arising for both the super-deduction and the special rate pool FYA assets is proportionately reduced if not all of the expenditure qualified for the relevant enhanced capital allowances, eg if the AIA was used against some of the expenditure. In this case the proceeds not treated as giving rise to a balancing charge will be deducted from either the main or special rate pools, depending on the type of asset being disposed of.

2.5 Example

On 1 April 2024, Cookies Ltd has a tax written down value on its main pool of £95,000 and a balance on its special rate pool of £100,000.

In the year ended 31 March 2025, Cookies Ltd had the following transactions in plant and machinery:

Acquisitions		Cost £
April 2024	Computer equipment	60,000
June 2024	Integral features	55,000

Disposals		Proceeds £
November 2024	Office equipment bought in January 2022 for £200,000 (super deduction claimed in the year ended 31 March 2022)	78,000
December 2024	Integral features bought in May 2022 for £140,000 (first year allowance claimed in the year ended 31 March 2023)	55,000
March 2025	Integral features bought in May 2023 for £110,000 (first year allowance claimed in the year ended 31 March 2024)	35,000
March 2025	Computer equipment bought in April 2022 for £27,000 (AIA claimed in the year ended 31 March 2023)	10,000

Calculate the maximum capital allowances claim for the year.

	FYA £	AIA £	Main pool £	Special rate pool £	Allowances £
TWDV b/f			95,000	100,000	
Acquisitions - qualifying for AIA					
Computer equipment		60,000			
Integral features		55,000			
AIA		(115,000)			115,000
Disposals					
Office equipment (100% x £78,000)					(78,000)
Integral features (acquired 2022)				(27,500)	(27,500)
Integral features (acquired 2023)				(17,500)	(17,500)
Computer equipment			(10,000)		
			85,000	55,000	
Writing down allowances at 18%/6%			(15,300)	(3,300)	18,600
			69,700	51,700	10,600

2.6 Property business income

The taxation of UK property business income follows similar rules to those for income tax (see earlier in this Workbook), but only the accruals basis is used. In summary:

(a) All UK rental activities are treated as a single source of income calculated in the same way as trading profits.

(b) Capital allowances on plant and machinery (but not furniture in residential properties) are taken into account when computing property income or losses.

Interest paid by a company on a loan to buy or improve property is not a property income expense, and is not treated as a tax reducer. The loan relationship rules apply instead (see later in this chapter).

2.7 Interest income

UK companies normally receive interest gross. Interest relating to non-trading loan relationships is taxed separately as interest income on an accruals basis (see later in this chapter for the loan relationship rules).

2.8 Miscellaneous income

Income and expenditure relating to intellectual property, which is not used in the trade nor in a property business, are dealt with as miscellaneous income.

2.9 Chargeable gains

Companies do not pay capital gains tax. Instead their chargeable gains are included in the taxable total profits. We look at companies' chargeable gains in the next chapter.

2.10 Qualifying charitable donations

Having arrived at a company's total profits, qualifying charitable donations are deducted to arrive at the taxable total profits.

PART C CORPORATION TAX

They are deducted from total profits **after all current year reliefs**, such as relief for trading losses (but before group relief). The interaction with relief for trading losses is explained later in this Workbook.

Qualifying charitable donations include **donations of money to registered charities**. Gifts of quoted shares and securities and UK land to charities, are also qualifying charitable donations.

Relief is generally given in the period in which the donations are **paid (rather than on an accruals basis)**.

Small donations to local charities where a benefit to the business (eg publicity) can be demonstrated (and so which are incurred wholly and exclusively for the purpose of the trade) are **allowable trading deductions** from trading income, rather than qualifying charitable donations.

> **Exam focus point**
>
> For the purposes of the exam, charitable donations paid during the accounting period to national registered charities should be assumed to be qualifying charitable donations.
>
> To get relief for them in the current year, make sure they have been paid before the end of the accounting period.

Question — The calculation of taxable total profits

The following is a summary of the income statement of A Ltd for the year to 31 March 2025.

	£	£
Gross profit		180,000
Other income		
Treasury stock interest (non-trading investment)		700
Dividends from UK companies (net)		3,600
Loan interest from UK company (non-trading investment)		4,000
Building society interest received (non-trading investment)		292
Expenses		
Trade expenses (all allowable)	62,000	
Qualifying charitable donation paid	1,100	
		(63,100)
Profit before taxation		125,492

The capital allowances for the period total £5,500. There was also a chargeable gain of £13,867.

Calculate the taxable total profits.

Answer

	£	£
Profit before taxation		125,492
Less: treasury stock interest	700	
dividends received	3,600	
building society interest	292	
loan interest received	4,000	
		(8,592)
		116,900
Add qualifying charitable donation		1,100
		118,000
Less capital allowances		(5,500)
Trading income		112,500
Interest income £(700 + 292 + 4,000)		4,992
Chargeable gain		13,867
Total profits		131,359
Less qualifying charitable donation		(1,100)
Taxable total profits		130,259

2.11 Long periods of account

If a company has a long period of account, exceeding 12 months, it is split into two accounting periods: the first 12 months and the remainder.

Where the period of account differs from the corporation tax accounting periods, profits are **allocated to the relevant periods** as follows:

- **Trading income** before capital allowances and property income are apportioned on a **time basis**.
- **Capital allowances** and balancing charges are **calculated for each accounting period.**
- **Other income is allocated to the period to which it relates** (eg rents to the period when accrued). Miscellaneous income, however, is apportioned on a time basis.
- **Chargeable gains and losses** are allocated to the **period in which they are realised.**
- **Qualifying charitable donations** are deducted in the accounting **period in which they are paid**.

Question — Long period of account

Xenon Ltd makes up an 18 month set of accounts to 31 March 2025 with the following results.

	£
Trading profits	180,000
Interest income	
18 months @ £500 accruing per month	9,000
Capital gain (1 February 2025 disposal)	250,000
Less qualifying charitable donation (paid 30 September 2024)	(50,000)
	389,000

What are the taxable total profits for each of the accounting periods?

Answer

The 18 month period of account is divided into:

Year ending 30 September 2024
Six months to 31 March 2025

Results are allocated:

	Y/e 30.9.24 £	6m to 31.3.25 £
Trading profits 12:6	120,000	60,000
Interest income		
12 × £500	6,000	
6 × £500		3,000
Capital gain (1.2.25)		250,000
Total profits		
Less qualifying charitable donation (30.9.24)	(50,000)	
Taxable total profits	76,000	313,000

3 Loan relationships

FAST FORWARD A loan relationship arises when a company lends or borrows money. Trading loan relationships are dealt with as trading income. Non-trading loan relationships are dealt with as interest income.

3.1 Introduction

If a company borrows or lends money, including issuing or investing in debentures or buying gilts, it has a loan relationship. This can be a creditor relationship (where the company lends or invests money) or a debtor relationship (where the company borrows money or issues securities). The loan relationship rules apply to both revenue and capital items.

3.2 Trading loan relationships

If the company is a party to a **loan relationship for trade purposes, any debits, ie interest payable or other debt costs, charged through its accounts are allowed as a trading expense** and are therefore deductible in computing trading profits. For example, a company paying interest on a loan taken out to purchase plant and machinery, or a factory or office premises for use in the trade will be able to deduct the interest payable for tax purposes.

Similarly **if any credits, ie interest income or other debt returns, arise on a trading loan, these are treated as a trading receipt and are taxable as part of trading profit.** This is not likely to arise unless the trade is one of money lending so will usually fall within the rules for non-trading loan relationships (below).

3.3 Non-trading loan relationships

If the company is a party to a **loan relationship for non-trade purposes, any debits and credits must be pooled.** For example, a company paying interest on a loan taken out to purchase an investment property will not be able to deduct the interest from trading profits for tax purposes. Instead this 'non-trade debit' must be netted off against 'non trade credits' such as bank interest.

A net credit (ie income) on the pool is chargeable as interest income. Relief is available if there is a net 'deficit' (ie loss) (see later in this Text).

3.4 Example: loan relationships

Jello Ltd received bank interest of £13,500 and loan stock interest from Wobble Ltd of £45,400. It also paid loan stock interest of £40,000 to Shaker Ltd on a loan of £1m. The loan stock was issued to Shaker Ltd in May 2021 to raise £700,000 for the purchase of a factory to use in the trade and £250,000 for the purchase of an investment property. The balance was used as working capital. All figures are stated gross and are the amounts shown in the accounts.

The loan stock interest payable to Shaker Ltd was used partly for trade purposes, and partly for non trade purposes and must be apportioned:

	£
Non-trade purposes 250,000 × £40,000/1,000,000	10,000
Trade purposes (700,000 + 50,000 (bal)) = 750,000 × £40,000/1,000,000	30,000
Total interest payable	40,000

The £30,000 of interest paid for trade purposes is deducted in the computation of trading profits.

The £10,000 of interest paid for non-trade purposes is deducted from non-trading interest received. The amount taxable as a non-trading loan relationship credit is:

	£
Bank interest (received gross)	13,500
Loan stock interest receivable from Wobble Ltd	45,400
	58,900
Non-trade loan stock interest paid to Shaker Ltd	(10,000)
Non-trading loan relationship credit	48,900

3.5 Incidental costs of loan finance

Under the loan relationship rules, expenses ('debits') are allowed if incurred directly when:

(a) Bringing a loan relationship into existence;
(b) Entering into or giving effect to any related transactions;
(c) Making payment under a loan relationship or related transactions; or
(d) Taking steps to ensure the receipt of payments under the loan relationship or related transaction.

A related transaction means 'any disposal or acquisition (in whole or in part) of rights or liabilities under the relationship, including any arising from a security issue in relation to the money debt in question'.

The above categories of incidental costs are also allowable even if the company does not enter into the loan relationship (ie abortive costs). Cost directly incurred in varying the terms of a loan relationship are also allowed.

3.6 Other matters

It is not only the interest costs of borrowing that are allowable or taxable. The capital costs are treated similarly. Thus, if a company issues a loan at a discount and repays it eventually at par, the capital cost is allowed over the life of the loan.

Relief for pre-trading expenditure extends to expenses incurred on trading loan relationships in accounting periods ending within seven years of the company starting to trade. An expense that would have been a trading debit if it was incurred after the trade had commenced, is treated as a trading debit of the first trading period. An election has to be made within two years of the end of the first trading period.

Interest charged on underpaid tax is deductible and interest received on overpaid tax is assessable under the loan relationship rules as interest income.

4 Research and development (R&D)

> **FAST FORWARD**
>
> Companies can claim an R&D expenditure credit (RDEC) for its qualifying research and development costs which can give companies more beneficial tax relief than a simple deduction from profit. The expenditure credit is 20% of the R&D spend and operates as an "above-the-line" (ATL) relief.

4.1 General rules

'Research and development' covers any activities that would be described as such under generally accepted accounting practice. It is related to the trade if it will lead to an extension of the trade or is directed towards the medical welfare of workers employed in the trade. The definition does not cover expenditure incurred on acquiring rights arising from research and development.

Revenue expenditure on research and development is an allowable deduction against a company's trading income if it is related to the company's trade and the activity is undertaken by the company or on its behalf. For companies, qualifying revenue expenditure includes the following expenses.

(a) **Staff costs**, ie salaries (but not benefits), pension contributions and employer's Class 1 NICs

(b) **Software, data licences and cloud computing**

(c) **Consumable items**, including fuel, power and water

(d) Payments for contracted out R&D activities

(e) 65% of expenditure on externally provided workers

Relief for consumable materials is restricted if the consumable is incorporated into an item which becomes part of normal production.

Expenditure on **R&D work contracted out to overseas** third parties or for payments **for externally provided workers (EPWs) overseas** do not qualify for the RDEC. The relief is available only for work taking place in the UK unless all three of the following applies:

1 The conditions necessary for the R&D are not present in the UK;

2 The necessary conditions are present where the R&D is undertaken; and

3 It would be wholly unreasonable to replicate the conditions in the UK.

Expenditure of a capital nature on research and development related to the company's trade is also wholly allowable as a first year allowance of 100% allowance is available. This covers capital expenditure on the provision of laboratories and research equipment. Note, however, that no allowance is available for expenditure on land. If any proceeds are received from the disposal of the capital assets, that receipt is taxable as trading income.

4.2 R&D relief: Research and development expenditure credits (RDEC)

Large companies may claim an R&D expenditure credit (RDEC).

The company must elect for the tax credit within two years of the end of the accounting period.

The credit is 20% of qualifying revenue R&D expenditure. It is treated as both a taxable receipt and a credit against the company's corporation tax liability.

For **companies with no corporation tax liability**:

(a) The tax credit is **paid net of corporation tax** (19% or 25%, depending on the size of the company's profits).

(b) A PAYE cap potentially limits the amount of credit repayable to the company claiming it. The cap is based on the company's PAYE costs. The maximum repayment £20,000 plus 300% of the company's total PAYE and Class 1 NIC liabilities for the accounting period.

Exam focus point

The use of the RDEC is more complex than described here, but you only need to know these simplified rules for the purpose of the Taxation exam.

Question — R&D expenditure for large companies

Innovative plc spends £100,000 on qualifying R&D expenditure during the year to 31 March 2025. The company has taxable total profits of £2,135,000 before any deduction is taken for the R&D expenditure.

Calculate the company's corporation tax liability for the year to 31 March 2025.

> **Answer**
>
> | | £ |
> |---|---:|
> | Taxable total profit before R&D expenditure | 2,135,000 |
> | Add ATL credit £100,000 × 20% | 20,000 |
> | Less R&D expenditure | (100,000) |
> | Taxable total profit | 2,055,000 |
> | Corporation tax £2,055,000 × 25% | 513,750 |
> | Less ATL credit £100,000 × 20% | (20,000) |
> | Corporation tax payable | 493,750 |
>
> **Note.** The tax saving using the ATL credit is as follows:
>
> | | £ |
> |---|---:|
> | Corporation tax on additional income £20,000 × 25% | 5,000 |
> | Less ATL credit deducted from CT liability £100,000 × 20% | (20,000) |
> | Corporation tax saving (15% of R&D expenditure) | 15,000 |

4.3 R&D: Claim notification

The claim for R&D relief is done in the company tax return which is generally submitted 12 months after the period of account to which it relates. For accounting periods starting on or after 1 April 2023, companies planning to make a claim for R&D relief must notify HMRC in advance of making the claim.

A claim notification form must be submitted if:

- The company is making a claim for the first time; or
- The last claim made by the company was made more than three years before the last date of the claim notification period

The company must submit the claim notification during the notification period, unless it actually submits a claim before the end of the notification period. This runs from the first day of the period of account to six months after the end of the period of account.

4.4 Example

If a company has a 12-month accounting period ending on 31 March 2025 and in that period there is qualifying R&D expenditure:

- The claim can be made up to two years from the end of the period of account ie by 31 March 2027, but assume it is made in the company tax return on 31 March 2026.

- The company must normally notify HMRC of the forthcoming claim at any point from 1 April 2024 (first day of the period) to 30 September 2025 (6 months after the end of the period of account)

- It is possible that the company can take advantage of a three-year exemption if it has made a previous claim for R&D relief in the three years up to the end of the notification period. ie the three years from 1 October 2022 to 30 September 2025. If the company has made a claim for R&D relief in those 3 years, there is no need to notify HMRC of the forthcoming claim.

The notification sent to HMRC will include:

- particulars (the unique taxpayer reference)
- The main internal R&D contact responsible for the claim
- Accounting period and period of account start and end dates
- Summary of the planned activities demonstrating that it meets the standard definition of R&D

4.5 Additional information

Since 8 August 2023, companies must submit an additional information form to support all R&D claims **before the relevant company tax return is filed**. The additional information is submitted online and includes much more detailed information relating to the company's R&D activities than that contained in the claim notification.

If an R&D claim is made in the company tax return and it is not supported with an additional information submission, HMRC will remove the claim from the return as it will be invalid.

The information to be provided includes the following:

(a) **The company's particulars**, eg Registered name, unique taxpayer reference, VAT registration number;

(b) **Company officer responsible for the claim**, eg name, role, contact details

(c) **Agent/tax adviser** eg name, reference number, contact details

(d) Details of the **R&D claim:**

   (i) Start and end dates of the accounting period and periods of account.

   (ii) Amount of the expenditure credit

   (iii) Whether it relates to activities in the UK

   (iv) The number and nature of the R&D projects, including a description of how existing scientific or technological knowledge was to be improved by the projects.

   (v) Categories of qualifying expenditures

More detail of the information to be provided is specified in Schedule 2 of SI2023/813.

18: COMPUTING TAXABLE TOTAL PROFITS

Chapter roundup

- Companies pay corporation tax on their taxable total profits of each accounting period.
- An accounting period cannot exceed 12 months in length. A long period of account must be split into two accounting periods, the first of which is 12 months long.
- Taxable total profits are the total profits (income and gains) less some losses and qualifying charitable donations.
- A loan relationship arises when a company lends or borrows money. Trading loan relationships are dealt with as trading income. Non-trading loan relationships are dealt with as interest income.
- Companies can claim relief for revenue and capital expenditure on research and development.

Quick quiz

1. When does an accounting period end?
2. How are trading profits (before capital allowances) of a long period of account divided between accounting periods?
3. Does a company pay loan stock interest to another UK company gross or net of tax?
4. How is interest arising on a non-trading loan relationship taxed?
5. Companies can claim an above the line _____ for its qualifying revenue expenditure on R&D projects. It can claim a _____ on capital expenditure related to its R&D expenditure.

PART C CORPORATION TAX

Answers to quick quiz

1   An accounting period ends on the earliest of:
    (a) 12 months after its start
    (b) The end of the company's period of account
    (c) The company starting or ceasing to trade
    (d) On the company entering/ceasing to be in administration
    (e) The company ceasing to be resident in the UK
    (f) The company ceasing to be liable to corporation tax
    (g) On commencement of a company's winding up

2   Trading income (before capital allowances) is apportioned on a time basis.

3   Gross

4   Interest on a non-trading loan relationship is aggregated with all other income and gains from non-trading loans. From this is deducted interest paid on and losses on non-trading loans. The resulting net amount is taxed as interest income.

5   R&D expenditure credit (RDEC), 100% first year allowance (FYA)

Chargeable gains for companies

Topic list
1 Corporation tax on chargeable gains
2 Indexation allowance
3 Disposal of shares by companies
4 Disposal of substantial shareholdings
5 Relief for replacement of business assets (rollover relief)

Introduction

We studied chargeable gains for individuals earlier in this Workbook. In this chapter, we will consider the treatment of chargeable gains for companies.

Companies pay corporation tax on their chargeable gains, rather than capital gains tax. The computation of gains for companies is slightly more complicated than for individuals because companies are entitled to indexation allowance.

We also consider the matching rules for companies which dispose of shares in other companies. Again, these rules are slightly more complicated than for individuals. We also consider the relief for substantial shareholdings.

Next, we look at how the relief for replacement of business assets applies to companies.

In the next chapter, we look at computation of corporation tax.

PART C CORPORATION TAX

Exam guide

You may be asked questions involving the gains of a company. Unlike individuals, companies receive what is known as an 'indexation allowance' (see later in this chapter). Ensure you remember to deduct an indexation allowance if appropriate and that, more generally, you do not confuse reliefs available to companies with those available to individuals.

1 Corporation tax on chargeable gains

FAST FORWARD

Chargeable gains for companies are computed in broadly the same way as for individuals. Two key differences are that indexation allowance applies and there is no annual exempt amount.

Companies do not pay capital gains tax. Instead their chargeable gains are included in taxable total profits. A company's capital gains or allowable losses are computed in a similar way to individuals but with a few major differences:

- There is relief for inflation up to December 2017 called the indexation allowance
- No annual exempt amount is available
- Different matching rules for shares apply if the shareholder is a company

2 Indexation allowance

FAST FORWARD

The indexation allowance gives relief for the inflation element of a gain up to December 2017. See Whillans p.50.

The purpose of having an indexation allowance is to remove the inflation element of a gain from taxation.

Companies are entitled to indexation allowance from the date of acquisition until the earlier of the date of disposal of an asset or December 2017. It is based on the movement in the retail price index (RPI) between those two dates.

For example, if J Ltd bought a painting on 2 January 2003 and sold it on 19 November 2024 the indexation allowance is available from January 2003 until December 2017.

Exam formula

The indexation factor is:

$$\frac{\text{RPI for month of disposal / Dec 17} - \text{RPI for month of acquisition}}{\text{RPI for month of acquisition}}$$

The calculation is expressed as a decimal and is rounded to three decimal places.

Indexation allowance is available on the allowable cost of the asset from the date of acquisition (including incidental costs of acquisition). It is also available on enhancement expenditure from the month in which such expenditure becomes due and payable. Indexation allowance is not available on the costs of disposal.

Exam focus point

The retail price indices (RPIs) will be given in Whillans (p.52 to 53). Therefore you must remember to use them to calculate the indexation allowance in a question involving disposals by **companies** but **not** if disposals are made by individuals.

19: CHARGEABLE GAINS FOR COMPANIES

Question — The indexation allowance

An asset is acquired by a company on 15 February 2003 at a cost of £5,000. Enhancement expenditure of £2,000 is incurred on 10 April 2004. The asset is sold for £25,500 on 20 July 2024. Incidental costs of sale are £500.

Calculate the chargeable gain arising.

Answer

The indexation allowance is only available until December 2017 (NOT until the date of disposal as this was after December 2017) and is computed as follows.

	£
$\dfrac{278.1 - 179.3}{179.3} = 0.551 \times £5,000$	2,755
$\dfrac{278.1 - 185.7}{185.7} = 0.498 \times £2,000$	996
	3,751

The computation of the chargeable gain is as follows.

	£
Proceeds	25,500
Less incidental costs of sale	(500)
Net proceeds	25,000
Less allowable costs £(5,000 + 2,000)	(7,000)
Unindexed gain	18,000
Less indexation allowance (see above)	(3,751)
Indexed gain	14,249

Indexation allowance cannot create or increase an allowable loss. If there is a gain before the indexation allowance, the allowance can reduce that gain to zero but no further. If there is a loss before the indexation allowance, there is no indexation allowance.

If the indexation allowance calculation gives a negative figure, treat the indexation as nil: do not add to the indexed gain.

3 Disposal of shares by companies

There are special rules for matching shares sold by a company with shares purchased. Disposals are matched with acquisitions on the same day, the previous nine days and the FA 1985 share pool.

3.1 The matching rules

We have discussed the share matching rules for individuals earlier in this Workbook. We also need special rules for companies.

For companies, the matching of shares sold is in the following order (Whillans p.45):

(a) Shares acquired on the **same day**
(b) Shares acquired in the **previous nine days**, if more than one acquisition on a 'first in, first out' (FIFO) basis
(c) Shares from the **FA 1985 pool**

The composition of the FA 1985 pool in relation to companies which are shareholders is explained below.

> **Exam focus point**
>
> Learn the 'matching rules' because a crucial first step to getting a shares question right is to correctly match the shares sold to the original shares purchased.

3.2 Example: share matching rules for companies

Nor Ltd acquired the following shares in Last plc:

Date of acquisition	No. of shares
9.11.02	15,000
15.12.04	15,000
11.7.24	5,000
15.7.24	5,000

Nor Ltd disposed of 20,000 of the shares on 15 July 2024.

We match the shares as follows:

(a) Acquisition on same day: 5,000 shares acquired 15 July 2024

(b) Acquisitions in previous nine days: 5,000 shares acquired 11 July 2024

(c) FA 1985 share pool: 10,000 shares out of 30,000 shares in FA 1985 share pool (9.11.02 and 15.12.04)

3.3 The FA 1985 share pool

The FA 1985 pool comprises the following shares of the same class in the same company.

- **Shares held by a company on 1 April 1985 and acquired by that company on or after 1 April 1982.**
- **Shares acquired by that company on or after 1 April 1985.**

We must keep track of:

(a) The **number** of shares
(b) The **cost** of the shares ignoring indexation
(c) The **indexed cost** of the shares

The first step in constructing the FA 1985 share pool is to calculate the value of the pool at 1 April 1985 by indexing the cost of each acquisition before that date up to April 1985.

3.4 Example: the FA 1985 share pool

Oliver Ltd bought 1,000 shares in Judith plc for £2,750 in August 1984 and another 1,000 for £3,250 in December 1984. The FA 1985 pool at 1 April 1985 is as follows:

	No. of shares	Cost £	Indexed cost £
August 1984 (a)	1,000	2,750	2,750
December 1984 (b)	1,000	3,250	3,250
	2,000	6,000	6,000

Indexation allowance

$\dfrac{94.8 - 89.9}{89.9} = 0.055 \times £2,750$ 151

$\dfrac{94.8 - 90.9}{90.9} = 0.043 \times £3,250$ 140

Indexed cost of the pool at 1 April 1985   6,291

19: CHARGEABLE GAINS FOR COMPANIES

Disposals and acquisitions of shares which affect the indexed value of the FA 1985 pool are termed **'operative events'. Prior to reflecting each such operative event within the FA 1985 share pool, a further indexation allowance (an 'indexed rise') must be computed up to the date of the operative event concerned from the date of the last such operative event** (or from the later of the first acquisition and April 1985 if the operative event in question is the first one).

Indexation calculations within the FA 1985 pool (after its April 1985 value has been calculated) **are not rounded to three decimal places**. This is because rounding errors would accumulate and have a serious effect after several operative events. If there are several operative events between 1 April 1985 and the date of a disposal, the indexation procedure described above will have to be performed several times over.

Question — Value of FA 1985 pool

Following on from the above example, assume that Oliver Ltd acquired 2,000 more shares on 10 July 1986 at a cost of £4,000. Recalculate the value of the FA 1985 pool on 10 July 1986 following the acquisition.

Answer

	No. of shares	Cost £	Indexed cost £
Value at 1.4.85 b/f	2,000	6,000	6,291
Indexed rise $\frac{97.5 - 94.8}{94.8} \times £6,291$			179
	2,000	6,000	6,470
Acquisition	2,000	4,000	4,000
Value at 10.7.86	4,000	10,000	10,470

In the case of a disposal, following the calculation of the indexed rise to the date of disposal (or December 2017), the cost and the indexed cost attributable to the shares disposed of are deducted from the amounts within the FA 1985 pool. The proportions of the cost and indexed cost to take out of the pool should be computed by using the proportion of cost that the shares disposed of bear to the total number of shares held.

The indexation allowance is the indexed cost taken out of the pool minus the cost taken out. As usual, the indexation allowance cannot create or increase a loss.

Question: Disposals from the FA 1985 pool

Continuing the above exercise, suppose that Oliver Ltd sold 3,000 shares on 10 July 2024 for £23,000. Compute the gain, and the value of the FA 1985 pool following the disposal.

Answer

	No of shares	Cost £	Indexed cost £
Value at 10.7.86	4,000	10,000	10,470
Indexed rise to December 2017			
$\frac{278.1 - 97.5}{97.5} \times £10,470$			19,394
	4,000	10,000	29,864
Disposal	(3,000)		
Cost and indexed cost $\frac{3,000}{4,000} \times £10,000$ and £29,864		(7,500)	(22,398)
Value at 10.7.24	1,000	2,500	7,466

The gain is computed as follows:

	£
Proceeds	23,000
Less cost	(7,500)
Unindexed gain	15,500
Less indexation allowance £(22,398 – 7,500)	(14,898)
Indexed gain	602

3.5 Bonus and rights issues

When **bonus issue shares are issued**, all that happens is that **the size of the original holding is increased**. Since bonus issue shares are issued at no cost there is **no need to adjust the original cost** and there is **no operative event for the FA 1985 pool** (so no indexation allowance needs to be calculated).

When **rights issue shares are issued**, the **size of the original holding is increased** in the same way as for a bonus issue. So if the original shareholding was part of the FA 1985 pool, the rights issue shares are added to that pool. This might be important for the matching rules if a shareholding containing the rights issue shares is sold shortly after the rights issue.

However, in the case of a rights issue, the **new shares are paid for and this results in an adjustment to the original cost**. For the purpose of **calculating the indexation allowance, expenditure on a rights issue is taken as being incurred on the date of the issue** and not the date of the original holding.

3.6 Example: bonus and rights issue

S Ltd bought 10,000 shares in T plc in May 2000 at a cost of £45,000.

There was a 2 for 1 bonus issue in October 2002.

There was a 1 for 3 rights issue in June 2006 at a cost of £4 per share. S Ltd took up all of its rights entitlement.

S Ltd sold 20,000 shares in T plc for £120,000 in January 2025.

FA 1985 share pool

		No of shares	Cost £	Indexed cost £
May 2000	Acquisition	10,000	45,000	45,000
Oct 2002	Bonus 2:1	20,000		
		30,000		
June 2006	Indexed rise			
	$\frac{198.5-170.7}{170.7} \times £45,000$			7,329
	Rights 1:3	10,000	40,000	40,000
		40,000	85,000	92,329
Jan 2025	Index rise to Dec 2017			
	$\frac{278.1-198.5}{198.5} \times 92,329$			37,025
				129,354
	Disposal	(20,000)	(42,500)	(64,677)
c/f		20,000	42,500	64,677

The gain is:

	£
Proceeds	120,000
Less cost	(42,500)
Unindexed gain	77,500
Less indexation allowance (£64,677 – 42,500)	(22,177)
Indexed gain	55,323

4 Disposal of substantial shareholdings

4.1 Principles

FAST FORWARD

Where a company owns shares in a trading company, there is an exemption on disposal if 10% or more of the shares are held for a 12-month period.

There is an exemption from corporation tax for any gain arising when a **company disposes of the whole or any part of a substantial shareholding in a trading company** (or in the holding company of a trading group or sub-group).

Key term

A **substantial shareholding** is one where the investing company holds 10% of ordinary share capital and is beneficially entitled to at least 10% of:

(a) The profits available for distribution to equity holders.
(b) The assets of the company available for distribution to equity holders on a winding up.

To meet the 10% test, shares owned by members of a chargeable gains group (see later in this Workbook) may be amalgamated. **The 10% test must have been met for a continuous 12-month period during the six years preceding the disposal.**

The 12-month period condition can also be satisfied by including a period during which assets, which are being used in its trade by the company whose shares are being disposed of (Company A), were being used in the trade of another group company (Company B) and then transferred to Company A before the sale of the Company A shares. This enables the exemption to apply in the situation where an existing trade carried on by one group company is transferred to a new group company before that new company is sold outside the group. This may be preferred to selling the original company carrying on the trade, for example if it also has contingent liabilities.

The exemption is given automatically and cannot be disclaimed. This means that as well as exempting gains, it denies relief for losses.

The exemption applies to the disposal of part of a substantial holding. This means that if A Ltd owns 10% of the ordinary share capital in B Ltd, and disposes of 1% of that share capital, any gain will be exempt. In addition, the disposal of the remaining 9% may result in an exempt gain.

4.2 Example: disposal of substantial shareholding

On 1 December 2010, SD Ltd bought 20% of the shares in AM Ltd. The shareholding qualifies for the substantial shareholding exemption. During its accounting period to 31 March 2025, SD Ltd made the following disposals:

(a) On 30 June 2024, it disposed of a 15% holding in AM Ltd.
(b) On 30 December 2024, it disposed of the remaining 5% holding in AM Ltd.

Both disposals qualify for the substantial shareholding exemption.

1 The first disposal is out of a shareholding of at least 10% which had been held for 12 months prior to disposal.

2 The second disposal also qualifies despite being only a 5% holding, because SD Ltd owned a 10% holding throughout a 12-month period beginning in the six years prior to this second disposal.

5 Relief for replacement of business assets (rollover relief)

FAST FORWARD — Rollover relief for replacement of business assets is available to companies to defer gains arising on the disposal of business assets. See Whillans p.48.

5.1 Conditions for relief

As for individuals, a gain may be rolled over by a company where the proceeds on the disposal of a business asset are spent on a replacement business asset. This is known as rollover relief.

A claim for the relief must be made by the later of four years of the end of the accounting period in which the disposal of the old asset takes place and four years of the end of the accounting period in which the new assets is acquired. For example, if a disposal is made by a company in its accounting period to 30 June 2025 and a claim to roll-over relief is made in respect of a new asset acquired in the accounting period to 30 June 2024, the time limit for a claim is 30 June 2029 (four years after the end of the accounting period in which the disposal of the old asset was made).

The conditions for the relief to apply to company disposals are:

(a) The old assets sold and the new asset bought are both used only in the trade of the company (apportionment into business and non-business parts available for buildings).

(b) The old asset and the new asset both fall within one (but not necessarily the same one) of the following classes.

    (i) **Land and buildings** (including parts of buildings) occupied as well as used only for the purposes of the trade

    (ii) **Fixed plant and machinery**

(c) Reinvestment of the proceeds received on the disposal of the old asset takes place in a period beginning one year before and ending three years after the date of the disposal.

(d) The new asset is brought into use in the trade on its acquisition.

Note. Goodwill is **not** a qualifying asset for the purposes of corporation tax.

5.2 Operation of relief

Deferral is obtained by deducting the indexed gain from the cost of the new asset. For full relief, the whole of the proceeds must be reinvested. If only part is reinvested, a gain equal to the amount not invested, or the full gain, if lower, will be chargeable to tax immediately.

The new asset will have a base cost for chargeable gains purposes of its purchase price less the gain rollover over.

Question
Rollover relief

D Ltd acquired a factory in April 2000 at a cost of £120,000. It used the factory in its trade throughout the period of its ownership.

In August 2024, D Ltd sold the factory for £250,000. In November 2023, it acquired another factory at a cost of 220,000.

Calculate the gain chargeable on the sale of the first factory and the base cost of the second factory.

Answer

Chargeable gain on sale of first factory

	£
Proceeds	250,000
Less cost	(120,000)
Unindexed gain	130,000
$\dfrac{278.1-170.1}{170.1} = 0.635 \times £120,000$	(76,200)
Indexed gain	53,800
Less rollover relief (balancing figure)	(23,800)
Chargeable gain: amount not reinvested £(250,000 – 220,000)	30,000

Base cost of second factory

	£
Cost of second factory	220,000
Less rolled over gain	(23,800)
Base cost	196,200

5.3 Depreciating assets

The relief for investment into depreciating assets works in the same way for companies as it does for individuals.

The indexed gain is calculated on the old asset and is deferred until the gain crystallises on the earliest of:

(a) The disposal of the replacement asset
(b) The date the replacement asset ceases to be used in the trade
(c) Ten years after the acquisition of the replacement asset

PART C CORPORATION TAX

Chapter roundup

- Chargeable gains for companies are computed in broadly the same way as for individuals. Two important differences are that indexation allowance applies and there is no annual exempt amount.
- The indexation allowance gives relief for the inflation element of a gain up to December 2017.
- There are special rules for matching shares sold by a company with shares purchased. Disposals are matched with acquisitions on the same day, the previous nine days and the FA 1985 share pool.
- Where a company owns shares in another trading company, there is an exemption on disposal if 10% or more of the shares are held for a 12-month period.
- Rollover relief for replacement of business assets is available to companies to defer gains arising on the disposal of business assets.

Quick quiz

1   A company is entitled to an annual exempt amount against its chargeable gains. TRUE/FALSE?

2   For disposals by companies in financial year 2024, indexation allowance runs from the date of ___ to date of ___ to ___. Fill in the blanks.

3   What are the share matching rules for company shareholders?

4   A Ltd has a long standing 15% shareholding in B Ltd, an investment company. Does the substantial shareholding exemption apply on a disposal of an 8% holding by A Ltd?

5   H Ltd sells a warehouse for £400,000. The warehouse cost £220,000 and the indexation allowance available is £40,000. The company acquires another warehouse ten months later for £375,000. What is the amount of rollover relief?

Answers to quick quiz

1 FALSE. A company is not entitled to an annual exempt amount against its chargeable gains.

2 For disposals by companies in financial year 2024, indexation allowance runs from the date of acquisition to December 2017.

3 The matching rules for shares disposed of by a company shareholder are:

   (a) Shares acquired on the same day
   (b) Shares acquired in the previous nine days
   (c) Shares from the FA 1985 pool

4 No. B Ltd is an investment company, not a trading company.

5 The gain on the sale of first warehouse is:

	£
Proceeds	400,000
Less cost	(220,000)
Unindexed gain	180,000
Less indexation allowance	(40,000)
Indexed gain	140,000
Less rollover relief (balancing figure)	(115,000)
Chargeable gain: amount not reinvested £(400,000 – 375,000)	25,000

PART C CORPORATION TAX

Computing corporation tax payable

Topic list

1 Charge to corporation tax
2 Returns, records, compliance checks, assessments and claims
3 Payment of corporation tax and interest

Introduction

In this chapter, we look at how to calculate the corporation tax payable on taxable total profits.

Then we look at the administration of corporation tax, including the payment of corporation tax.

In the next chapter, we will look at the rules for corporate losses.

PART C CORPORATION TAX

Exam guide

You may have to calculate the corporation tax payable for an accounting period and you may have to use this knowledge to work out tax savings. You must also know the rules regarding administration as the company's obligations could form a part of a question.

1 Charge to corporation tax

1.1 Financial years

FAST FORWARD Tax rates are set for financial years.

The rates of corporation tax are fixed for financial years.

A financial year runs from 1 April to the following 31 March and is identified by the calendar year in which it begins. For example, the year ended 31 March 2025 is the Financial Year 2024 (FY 2024). This should not be confused with a tax year, which runs from 6 April to the following 5 April.

1.2 The rates of corporation tax

FAST FORWARD Companies are taxed on their taxable total profits (TTP) for the accounting period.

The rate of tax used to calculate the corporation tax liability depends on the company's **augmented profits** for the period and the length of the period.

Augmented profits means taxable total profits plus exempt dividends received from UK and non-UK companies (known as exempt ABGH distributions). There is an **exception for dividends which are received from a 51% subsidiary of the recipient company** or from a company where both the paying company and the recipient company are 51% subsidiaries of a third company (sometimes referred to as 'group dividends' or 'group income') – **such dividends are ignored.**

Augmented profits are therefore calculated as follows:

Taxable total profit	X
Add exempt dividends received from non-group companies from minority shareholdings	X
Augmented profits	X

Dividends from non-group companies refer to dividends received.

Exam focus point Although augmented profits are used to determine the tax rate, the rate is never actually applied to the augmented profit. The tax liability is calculated by applying the tax rate to the TTP.

For a 12-month accounting period the following rates of corporation tax apply (Whillans p.55):

Augmented profits		%
Greater than £250,000 (the upper limit)	Main rate	25
Less than £50,000 (the lower limit)	Small profits rate	19

Where augmented profits for the accounting period fall between £50,000 and £250,000, the TTP is taxed at 25% but the liability is then reduced for **marginal relief**. Marginal relief is calculated using the following formula and it allows for a gradual increase in the average tax rate between 19% and 25% as profits rise from £50,000 to £250,000.

3/200 × (Upper limit − Augmented profits) × (TTP/Augmented profits)

20: COMPUTING CORPORATION TAX PAYABLE

Question — Calculation of corporation tax

B Ltd makes up accounts to 31 March 2025. The company has TTP of £650,000 and dividend income of £50,000. The dividends are from non-group companies.

Calculate the corporation tax liability of B Ltd.

Answer

	£
Augmented profits £(650,000 + 50,000)	700,000
With this level of augmented profits B Ltd will pay corporation tax at the main rate.	
Corporation tax liability £650,000 × 25%	162,500

Question — Calculation of corporation tax

K Ltd makes up accounts to 31 March 2025. The company has TTP of £72,000 and dividend income of £10,000. The dividends are from non-group companies.

Calculate the corporation tax liability of K Ltd.

Answer

	£
Augmented profits £(72,000 + 10,000)	82,000
With this level of augmented profits K Ltd will pay corporation tax at the main rate reduced by marginal relief.	
Corporation tax liability £72,000 × 25%	18,000
Less marginal relief: 3/200 × (250,000 – 82,000) × (72,000/82,000)	(2,213)
Corporation tax liability	15,787

The upper and lower limits of £250,000 and £50,000 are reduced if the company has a short accounting period (ie less than 12 months). In this case the limits are both multiplied by $^n/_{12}$, 'n' being the number of months in the accounting period.

The limits are also reduced if the company has associated companies, in other words, if it is in a 51% group with other companies in the accounting period. However, Taxation exams in 2025 will not examine the impact of associated companies on the corporation tax rate.

These rates apply to TTP arising in FY2023 onwards. Exams in 2025 will not test any knowledge of corporation tax rates before 1 April 2023.

Question — Calculation of corporation tax

P Ltd makes up accounts for the nine months to 28 February 2025. The company has TTP of £66,000 and dividend income of £12,000. The dividends are from non-group companies.

Calculate the corporation tax liability of P Ltd.

Answer

	£
Augmented profits £(66,000 + 12,000)	78,000
Upper limit (9/12 × £250,000)	187,500
Lower limit (9/12 × £50,000)	37,500
Corporation tax liability £66,000 × 25%	16,500
Less marginal relief: 3/200 × (187,500 – 78,000) × (66,000/78,000)	(1,390)
Corporation tax liability	15,110

2 Returns, records, compliance checks, assessments and claims

2.1 Notification to HMRC

FAST FORWARD — A company must notify HMRC within three months of starting to trade.

A company must **notify HMRC of the beginning of its first accounting period** (ie usually when it starts to trade) and the beginning of any subsequent period that does not immediately follow the end of a previous accounting period. The notice must be in the prescribed form and **submitted within three months of the relevant date**.

A company which is chargeable to tax for an accounting period and has not received a notice to file a tax return must give **notice of chargeability within 12 months of the end of the accounting period**. The common penalty regime for failing to notify applies (see earlier in this Workbook).

2.2 Returns

FAST FORWARD — Corporation tax returns must usually be filed within 12 months of the end of an accounting period.

A company's tax return must be filed electronically and must include a self assessment of any tax payable. Limited companies are also required to file electronically a copy of their accounts. The filing of accounts must be done in InLine eXtensible Business Reporting Language (iXBRL).

iXBRL is a standard for reporting business information in an electronic form which uses tags which can be read by computers. HMRC supplies software which can be used by small companies with simple accounts. This software automatically produces accounts and tax computations in the correct format. Other companies can use:

(a) Other software that automatically produces iXBRL accounts and computations;
(b) A tagging services which will apply the appropriate tags to accounts and computations; or
(c) Software that enables the appropriate tags to be added to accounts and computations.

The tags used are contained in dictionaries known as taxonomies, with different taxonomies for different purposes. The tagging of tax computations is based on the corporation tax computational taxonomy which includes over 1,200 relevant tags.

An obligation to file a return arises only when the company receives a notice requiring a return. A return is required for each accounting period ending during or at the end of the period specified in the notice requiring a return. A company also has to file a return for certain other periods which are not accounting periods (eg for a period when the company is dormant).

A notice to file a return may also require other information, accounts and reports. For a UK resident company the requirement to deliver accounts normally extends only to the accounts required under the Companies Act.

A return is due on or before the filing date. This is the later of (Whillans p.11):

(a) **12 months after the end of the period to which the return relates;**

(b) **If the relevant period of account is not more than 18 months long, 12 months from the end of the period of account;**

(c) **If relevant the period of account is more than 18 months long, 30 months from the start of the period of account; or**

(d) **Three months from the date on which the notice requiring the return was made.**

The relevant period of account is that in which the accounting period to which the return relates ends.

The company has the right to amend its tax return for any reason within 12 months of the normal due submission date (not the actual submission date).

Question — Filing date

A Ltd prepares accounts for the eighteen months to 30 June 2025. A notice requiring a return for the period ended 30 June 2025 was issued to A Ltd on 1 September 2025.

State the periods for which A Ltd must file a tax return and the filing dates.

Answer

The company must file a return for the two accounting periods ending in the period specified in the notice requiring a return. The first accounting period is the 12 months to 31 December 2024 and the second is the six months to 30 June 2025. The filing date is 12 months after the end of the relevant period of account, 30 June 2026.

There is a £100 penalty for a failure to submit a return on time, rising to £200 if the delay exceeds three months. These penalties become £500 and £1,000 respectively when a return was late (or never submitted) for each of the preceding two accounting periods.

An additional tax geared penalty is applied if a return is more than six months late. The penalty is 10% of the tax unpaid six months after the return was due if the total delay is up to 12 months, and 20% of that tax if the return is over 12 months late.

The common penalty regime for making errors in tax returns discussed earlier in this Workbook also applies for corporation tax.

HMRC may amend a return to correct obvious errors, or anything else that an officer has reason to believe is incorrect in the light of information available, within nine months of the day the return was filed, or if the correction is to an amended return, within nine months of the filing of an amendment. The company may amend its return so as to reject the correction. If the time limit for amendments has expired, the company may reject the correction by giving notice within three months.

2.3 Records

Companies must keep records until the latest of:

(a) Six years from the end of the accounting period;
(b) The date any compliance checks are completed; or
(c) The date after which compliance checks may not be commenced.

All business records and accounts, including contracts and receipts, must be kept, or information showing that the company has prepared a complete and correct tax return.

If a return is demanded more than six years after the end of the accounting period, any records which the company still has must be kept until the later of the end of any compliance check and the expiry of the right to start a compliance check.

Failure to keep records can lead to a penalty of up to £3,000 for each accounting period affected. However, this penalty does not apply when the only records which have not been kept are ones which could only have been needed for the purposes of claims, elections or notices not included in the return.

2.4 Compliance checks

> **FAST FORWARD** A compliance check enquiry into a return, claim or election can be started by an officer of HMRC within a limited period.

2.4.1 Starting a compliance check enquiry

HMRC may decide to conduct a compliance check enquiry on a return, claim or election that has been submitted by a company, in the same way as for individuals.

The officer of HMRC must give written notice of his intention to conduct a compliance check enquiry. At the latest, the notice must be given by **a year after**:

(a) **The due filing date** (most group companies) or the actual filing date (other companies), if the return is filed on or before the due filing date;

(b) **The 31 January, 30 April, 31 July or 31 October** (quarter days) next following the actual date of delivery of the return, if the return is filed after the due filing date.

If the company amends the return after the due filing date, the compliance check enquiry 'window' extends to the quarter day following the first anniversary of the date the amendment was filed. Where the compliance check enquiry was not started within the limit which would have applied had no amendment been filed, the enquiry is restricted to matters contained in the amendment.

2.4.2 Conduct of compliance check enquiry

The procedure for the conduct of compliance check enquiries relating to individuals, discussed earlier in this Workbook, also applies to companies.

2.5 Determinations and discovery assessments

The rules about determinations and discovery assessments relating to individuals, discussed earlier in this Workbook, also apply to companies.

2.6 Appeals

The procedure for HMRC internal reviews and appeals relating to individuals, discussed earlier in this Workbook, also applies to companies.

2.7 Personal accountability of senior accounting officer of large company

The senior accounting officer of a qualifying company has personal accountability for ensuring that financial systems are maintained by the company to enable it to accurately report taxable profits and gains. A qualifying company is one which, in the previous financial year, had a relevant turnover of £200 million and/or a balance sheet total of more than £2 billion.

The senior accounting officer (probably the finance director of the company) **must take reasonable steps to establish and monitor accounting systems within the company that are adequate for the purposes of accurate tax reporting.** The senior accounting officer must also certify annually that the accounting systems are in operation or specify any inadequacies.

The company must notify HMRC of the identity of the senior accounting officer of the company. The company and/or the senior accounting officer personally may be liable to a financial penalty for a careless or deliberate failure to comply with these requirements. The penalty applicable to the senior accounting officer is likely to be £5,000.

3 Payment of corporation tax and interest

FAST FORWARD

Large and very large companies pay their corporation tax in four quarterly instalments. Other companies pay their tax nine months and one day after the end of an accounting period (Whillans p.1-2).

3.1 Normal due date

FAST FORWARD

The due date for payment of corporation tax is dependent upon the level of the augmented profits. Augmented profits are taxable total profits plus exempt ABGH distributions.

Corporation tax is due for payment by companies which have augmented profits below £1.5m **nine months and one day after the end of the accounting period**. This is the limit for a single company with a 12-month accounting period. So, if an accounting period ends on 31 December 2024, the corporation tax for that period is due on 1 October 2025.

3.2 Large companies

FAST FORWARD

The limits which are used to determine payment dates are pro-rated on a time basis if an accounting period lasts for less than 12 months.

Large companies and very large companies must pay their corporation tax in instalments. **Broadly, a large company is a company that is a single company with augmented profits that exceed £1.5m but do not exceed £20m in a 12-month period. A very large company has augmented profits that exceed £20m in a 12-month period.** Very large companies are considered in sections 3.5 and 3.6.

Instalments are due on the 14th day of the month. For a large company, these **start in the seventh month.** Provided that the accounting period is 12 months long **subsequent instalments are due in the tenth month during the accounting period and in the first and fourth months after the end of the accounting period.**

If an accounting period is less than 12 months long the augmented profits limit is reduced pro rata, so a company with an eight-month accounting period pays in instalments if augmented profits are at least £1m (£1.5m × 8/12).

Subsequent instalments are due at three monthly intervals but with the final payment being due in the fourth month of the next accounting period.

The limits are also reduced if the company has any associated companies in the accounting period. This impact will not be tested in exams in 2025.

3.3 Example: quarterly instalments for large company

X Ltd is a large company with a 31 December accounting year end. Instalments of corporation tax will be due to be paid by X Ltd on:

- 14 July and 14 October in the accounting period
- 14 January and 14 April after the accounting period ends

So for the year ended 31 December 2024 instalment payments are due on 14 July 2024, 14 October 2024, 14 January 2025 and 14 April 2025.

Instalments are **based on the estimated corporation tax liability for the current period** (not the previous period). It is extremely important for companies to forecast their tax liabilities accurately. Large companies whose directors are poor at estimating may find their company's incurring significant interest charges.

The amount of each instalment is computed by:

(a) Working out **3 × CT/n** where CT is the amount of the estimated corporation tax liability payable in instalments for the period and n is the number of months in the period.

(b) Allocating the smaller of that amount and the total estimated corporation tax liability to the first instalment.

(c) Repeating the process for later instalments until the amount allocated is equal to the corporation tax liability. This gives **four equal instalments for 12-month accounting periods** and also caters for periods which end earlier than expected.

The company is therefore required to estimate its corporation tax liability before the end of the accounting period, and usually revises its estimate each quarter.

Question — Short accounting period

A large company has a CT liability of £880,000 for the eight-month period to 31 March 2025. Accounts had previously always been prepared to 31 July.

Show when the CT liability is due for payment.

Answer

£880,000 must be paid in instalments.

The amount of each instalment is $3 \times \dfrac{£880,000}{8} = £330,000$

The due dates are:

	£
14 February 2025	330,000
14 May 2025	330,000
14 July 2025	220,000 (balance)

3.4 Exceptions for paying by instalments

A company is not required to pay instalments in the first year that it is 'large', unless its profits exceed £10m.

Any company whose liability does not exceed £10,000 need not pay by instalments.

3.5 Very large companies

A very large company has augmented profits that exceed £20m in a 12-month period. Again, the limit is scaled down for a short accounting period. The limit is reduced if the company has any associated companies in the accounting period. This impact will not be tested in exams in 2025.

Instalments are also due on the 14th day of the month but begin earlier than for a large company. The **first instalment is in the third month of the accounting period.** Provided that the accounting period is 12 months long, **subsequent instalments are due in the sixth, ninth and twelfth months during the accounting period.**

For a **shorter accounting period**, subsequent instalments are due at three monthly intervals but with the **final payment usually being due in the last month of the accounting period**.

3.6 Example: quarterly instalments for very large company

Z Ltd is a very large company. Instalments of corporation tax are due for the year ended 31 December 2024 on 14 March 2024, 14 June 2024, 14 September 2024 and 14 December 2024.

A very large company must still pay instalments on these dates even if the company was not very large in the previous year (although a new company cannot be considered very large in its first 12-month accounting period). However, if the tax liability is less than £10,000, instalments are not required.

3.7 Interest on late or overpaid tax

3.7.1 Late paid tax and overpayments where no instalments are due

FAST FORWARD

> The normal due date for payments of corporation tax is nine months and one day after the end of the accounting period.
>
> Companies which do not pay by instalments are charged interest if they pay their corporation tax after the normal due date and will receive interest if they overpay their tax or pay it early.

For late payments, the interest payable by the taxpayer runs from the due date to the date of payment.

For overpayments (paying more than is due), the interest payable by HMRC runs from the normal due date to the date of the repayment.

Exam focus point

The interest rate applicable depends on the Bank of England base rate ("the base rate"), which changes from time to time, so you will find the applicable interest rates in Whillans pages 5 and 7. The applicable rates had been in force since August 2023 and were as follows.

Tax paid after the normal due date	7.75%
Overpaid tax at the normal due date	4.25%

Exam focus point

In the exam, use the most recent interest rate in the relevant table in Whillans. Not only are you expected to be able to work out the interest arising on payments of corporation tax, you should be able to identify the dates between which interest will run.

Question — Interest on late paid and overpaid tax

In the year ended 31 December 2023, Floren Ltd has taxable total profit of £72,000. The correct amount of tax is paid on 31 October 2024.

In its year ended 31 December 2024, Floren Ltd has taxable total profit of £300,000. It paid corporation tax of £90,000 to HMRC in respect of this period on 1 October 2025. The overpayment was refunded by HMRC on 31 January 2026.

Calculate and explain the interest payable by or repayable to Floren Ltd. Use FY2024 rates throughout.

Answer

Floren Ltd does not need to pay instalments in either period, so payments of corporation tax were due on the normal due date (NDD), nine months and one day after the end of the accounting period the tax relates to.

The correct corporation tax payments and NDDs are:

		£	Normal due date
Year ended 31 December 2023	£72,000 × 25%	18,000	
	Marginal relief		
	3/200 × (£250,000 − £72,000)	(2,670)	
		15,330	1.10.2024
Year ended 31 December 2024	£300,000 × 25%	75,000	1.10.2025

In respect of the year ended 31 December 2023, the payment is late by 1 month. The interest payable by Foren Ltd is 1/12 × 7.75% × £15,330 = £99.01.

In respect of the year ended 31 December 2024, the payment is overpaid for a period of four months (1 October 2025 to 31 January 2026). Interest receivable by Floren Ltd is 4/12 × 4.25% × (£90,000 − £75,000) = £212.50.

3.7.2 Early payments where no instalments are due

Where a company does not have to pay corporation tax in quarterly instalments and it pays its corporation tax early, a special rate of overpayment interest is paid by HMRC.

Again, this interest rate varies with the base rate so can change. Use the most recent interest rate in the "Special rates" tables on page 8 of Whillans. Use the most recent interest rates given in the tables, which had been put in place in August 2023. That was 5%.

The interest runs from the day the excess arose i.e. when the early payment was made to the earlier of the repayment by HMRC and the normal due date (NDD). If it is repaid after the NDD the normal interest rates in 3.7.1 apply until the repayment is made.

Question
Interest on early payments of tax

In its year ended 31 December 2024, Floren Ltd has taxable total profit of £300,000. It paid corporation tax of £90,000 to HMRC in respect of this period on 30 June 2025. The overpayment was refunded by HMRC on 31 January 2026.

Calculate and explain the interest payable to Floren Ltd.

Answer

As in the previous question the payment of corporation tax should be £75,000, due on 1 October 2025.

Early payment interest runs from the early payment (30 June 2025) to the earlier of the normal due date (1 October 2025) and the repayment (31 January 2026).

30 June 2025 to 1 October 2025 is three months, after which the excess becomes an overpayment.

		£
Early payment of £90,000		
30.06.2025 – 01.10.2025	3/12 × 5% × £90,000	1,125.00
Overpayment of £15,000		
01.10.2025 – 31.01.2026	4/12 × 4.25% × £15,000	212.50
Interest payable to Floren Ltd		1,337.50

3.7.3 Underpayments and overpayments of instalments

Where companies must pay corporation tax in instalments, they are calculated based on estimates of the companies' profit for that accounting period. It is important that companies are able to make reliable estimates of their profit so their instalments are as accurate as possible.

If a company underestimates its instalment, this delays the payment of corporation tax and HMRC will charge interest on that underpayment. Conversely, if profits, and therefore instalments are overestimated, this leads to an overpayment of tax so HMRC pays interest to the taxpayer to compensate for that.

Use the most recent of the rates given in the tables (ie. since August 2023), they were 6.25% and 5.00% for underpayments and overpayments respectively (but remember from section 3.7.1, 7.75% and 4.25% from the NDD).

Question — Interest on underpaid or overpaid instalments

In its year ending 31 March 2025, Stuboz Ltd has taxable total profits of £1.75 million and a final corporation tax liability of £437,500. Stuboz Ltd was also large in the year ended 31 March 2024.

Due to trading difficulties in the year ended 31 March 2025, Stuboz Ltd found it difficult to estimate its corporation tax liability. Its quarterly instalments were paid on the due dates as follows.

Instalment paid	Estimated TTP
	£
14 October 2024	1.62m
14 January 2025	1.85m
14 April 2025	1.55m
14 July 2025	1.75m

Calculate the instalments and interest receivable or payable by Stuboz Ltd in the year ended 31 March 2025.

Answer

Instalments

Instalment paid	Estimated TTP		Instalment
	£		£
14 October 2024	1.62m	0.25 × 25% × £1.62m =	101,250
14 January 2025	1.85m	Total due (0.50 × 25% × £1.85m)	231,250
		Less paid to date	(101,250)
		Instalment to pay	130,000
14 April 2025	1.55m	Total due (0.75 × 25% × £1.55m)	290,625
		Less paid to date	(231,250)
		Instalment to pay	59,375

14 July 2025	1.75m	Total due (25% × £1,750,000)		437,500
		Less paid to date		(290,625)
		Instalment to pay		146,875

Each instalment brings Stuboz Ltd up to date based on their most recent estimate of its taxable profit for the accounting period. But because that estimate has changed as time progresses the instalments paid are not the same each quarter.

To calculate the interest payable or receivable on underpaid or overpaid instalments we should compare the cumulative amount paid with what the cumulative payments should have been based on the final liability.

Instalment paid	Cumulative paid based on estimated profits £	Cumulative paid based on final liability £	(Underpaid) or overpaid £
14 October 2024	101,250	109,375	(8,125)
14 January 2025	231,250	218,750	12,500
14 April 2025	290,625	328,125	(37,500)
14 July 2025	437,500	437,500	–

Using the most recent interest rate applicable to under- and overpaid instalments the interest payable and repayable would be:

		Interest (payable)/receivable £
14 Oct 2024 – 13 Jan 2025	£8,125 × 3/12 × 6.25%	(126.95)
14 Jan 2025 – 13 April 2025	£12,500 × 3/12 × 5.00%	156.25
14 April 2025 – 13 July 2025	£37,500 × 3/12 × 6.25%	(585.94)
		(556.64)

If a company pays instalments but there are instalments still outstanding or underpaid by the normal due date (nine months and one day after the accounting period), the interest rate that applies reverts to the interest rates used in section 3.7.1 as it is late paid tax, rather than an underpaid instalment.

3.7.3 Tax treatment of interest payments and receipts

Interest paid/received on late payments or overpayments of corporation tax is dealt with as investment income as interest paid/received on a non-trading loan relationship.

Chapter roundup

- Tax rates are set for financial years.
- Companies are taxed on their taxable total profits for the accounting period.
- The rate applied to the TTP depends on the company's augmented profits for the period.
- A company must notify HMRC within three months of starting to trade.
- Corporation tax returns must usually be filed within 12 months of the end of an accounting period.
- A compliance check enquiry into a return, claim or election can be started by an officer of HMRC within a limited period.
- Large and very companies pay their corporation tax in four quarterly instalments. Other companies pay their tax nine months and one day after the end of an accounting period.
- The due date for payment of corporation tax is dependent upon the level of the augmented profits. Augmented profits are taxable total profits plus exempt ABGH distributions.
- The limits which are used to determine payment dates are pro-rated on a time basis if an accounting period lasts for less than 12 months.
- Interest is charged by HMRC for late paid corporation tax and underpaid instalments. HMRC pays interest to the taxpayer if they pay early or make overpayments on their instalments.

Quick quiz

1. Youngs Ltd will make up a 12-month set of accounts to 31 December 2025. When must the company file its CT return based on these accounts?

2. What are the fixed penalties for failure to deliver a corporation tax return on time?

3. When must HMRC give notice that they are going to start a compliance check enquiry if a return was filed on time by a company not in a group?

4. Which companies must pay quarterly instalments of their corporation tax liability?

5. State the due dates for the payment of quarterly instalments of corporation tax for a 12 month accounting period for both a large company and a very large company.

6. Freeman Ltd changes its accounting date and makes up accounts for the eight months to 31 December 2025. The company is large and is due to pay tax by instalments. Outline when the tax is due.

7. In question 7, if the CT liability is £1m for the 8-month period what amount is due at each date?

PART C CORPORATION TAX

Answers to quick quiz

1   By 31 December 2026.

2   There is a £100 penalty for failure to submit a return on time rising to £200 if the delay exceeds three months. These penalties increased to £500 and £1,000 respectively when a return was late for each of the preceding two accounting periods.

3   Notice must be given by one year after the actual filing date.

4   'Large' and 'very large' companies ie companies that have augmented profits of at least £1.5 million (single company for a 12 month period).

5   Large company due dates are on 14th day of:

    (a)   7th month in AP
    (b)   10th month in AP
    (c)   1st month after AP ends
    (d)   4th month after AP ends

    Very large company due dates are on 14th day of:

    (a)   3rd month in AP
    (b)   6th month in AP
    (c)   9th month in AP
    (d)   12th month in AP

6   Due dates are:

    14 November 2025
    14 February 2026
    14 April 2026

7   £375,000, £375,000 and finally £250,000

Losses and deficits on non-trading loan relationships

Topic list
1 Reliefs for losses – overview
2 Trading losses
3 Reliefs for deficits on non-trading loan relationships
4 Restrictions on loss relief

Introduction

We have studied the computation of taxable total profits and the corporation tax payable.

We now consider how a company may obtain relief for trading losses and also for deficits on non-trading loan relationships.

In the next chapter, we will turn to the overseas aspects of corporation tax.

PART C CORPORATION TAX

Exam guide

You are likely to come across company losses at some point in the exam. Always look to see if any requirements are specified in the question, such as the need to claim relief as early as possible, and then consider how to optimise the relief.

1 Reliefs for losses – overview

1.1 Trading losses

FAST FORWARD

Trading losses may be relieved against current total profits, against total profits of earlier periods or against future total profits.

In summary, the following reliefs are available for trading losses incurred by a company:

(a) Claim to deduct from current total profits
(b) Claim to carry back and deduct from the previous twelve months' total profits
(c) Carry forward and claim to deduct from future total profits

These reliefs may be used in combination. The options open to the company are:

(a) Carry forward and claim to deduct from future total profits.
(b) Claim to deduct from current period total profits, and carry any remaining unrelieved loss forward and claim to deduct from future total profits.
(c) Claim to deduct from current period total profits, then claim to carry any unused loss back and deduct from the previous twelve months' total profits, and then carry any remaining unrelieved loss forward and claim to deduct from future total profits.
(d) Claim to deduct from current and previous period total profits and apply the temporary extension to any excess remaining to carry back against total profits for up to three years before the year in which the loss was incurred.

The reliefs are explained in further detail below.

1.2 Non-trading deficits

Non-trading deficits on loan relationships can be relieved in similar ways to trading losses but with some differences (see below).

1.3 Capital losses

Capital losses can only be set against chargeable gains in the same or future accounting periods, never against income. Capital losses must be set against the first available gains.

1.4 Property income losses

FAST FORWARD

Property business losses are set off first against total profits of the current period and can then be carried forward against future total profits. Any amount of the carried forward loss can be used in future accounting periods.

Property business losses are first deducted from the company's total profits of the current accounting period. Any excess is then **carried forward to the next accounting period** and can be treated as a loss made by the company in that period (ie set against total profits); or

Relief for a carried forward loss must be claimed within two years of the end of the accounting period in which the loss is relieved.

2 Trading losses

2.1 Carry forward trade loss relief

FAST FORWARD

Trading losses can be carried forward and set against future total profits.

Exam focus point

Different rules apply when carrying forward trading losses that originated pre-1 April 2017. The Taxation paper only tests the rules for carry forward of post-1 April 2017 losses, as detailed here. In a question, assume a carried forward loss arose post-1 April 2017.

If a company does not make a current year/carry back relief claim for its trading losses, or if there is any loss remaining after such a claim, the loss is carried forward and the company can make a claim to set the loss against its total profits in the following accounting period.

This carried forward relief is not automatic and a claim must be made within two years of the end of the accounting period in which it is relieved. The amount relieved may be subject to certain restrictions if the loss carried forward is large (see Section 4.1 below).

Tax planning – the company can choose the amount of brought forward loss to use in the year and therefore can elect to only use as much of the loss as it needs to reduce total profits to the amount of any qualifying charitable donations.

Carrying forward losses may not be the best option if future profits are uncertain.

Question — Carrying forward losses

A Ltd has the following results for the three years to 31 March 2025:

	Year ended 31.3.23 £	Year ended 31.3.24 £	Year ended 31.3.25 £
Trading profit/(loss)	(8,550)	3,000	6,000
Property income	0	1,000	1,000
Qualifying charitable donation	300	1,000	1,700

Calculate the taxable total profits for all three years showing any losses available to carry forward at 1 April 2025.

Answer

	Year ended 31 March 2023 £	Year ended 31 March 2024 £	Year ended 31 March 2025 £
Trading income	0	3,000	6,000
Property income	0	1,000	1,000
Total profits	0	4,000	7,000
Less carried forward trade loss relief		(3,000)	(5,300)
Less qualifying charitable donation (QCD)	0	(1,000)	(1,700)
Taxable total profits	0	0	0
Unrelieved qualifying charitable donation	300	0	0

Note. The carried forward loss relief is not an 'all or nothing' claim. Instead, a specific amount can be claimed so that the charitable donations are not wasted.

Any qualifying charitable donations that become unrelieved are wasted as they cannot be carried forward.

Loss memorandum

	£
Loss for y/e 31.3.23	8,550
Less used y/e 31.3.24 (claim restricted to save the QCD)	(3,000)
Loss carried forward at 1.4.24	5,550
Less used 31.3.25 (claim restricted to save the QCD)	(5,300)
Loss carried forward at 1.4.25	250

2.2 Trade loss relief against total profits

> **FAST FORWARD**
>
> Loss relief against total profits may be given against current period profits and against profits of the previous 12 months. A claim for current period loss relief can be made without a claim for carry back. However, if a loss is to be carried back a claim for current period relief must be made first.

2.2.1 Current year claim

A company may claim to set a trading loss (arising in a UK trade) **incurred in an accounting period against total profits of the same accounting period** *before* **deducting qualifying charitable donations.**

2.2.2 Carry back claim

Such a loss may then be carried back and set against total profits before deducting qualifying charitable donations of an accounting period falling wholly or partly within the 12 months prior to the start of the period in which the loss was incurred.

Any possible loss relief claim for the period of the loss must be made before any excess loss can be carried back to a previous period.

Any carry back is to more recent periods before earlier periods. Relief for earlier losses is given before relief for later losses.

Any loss remaining unrelieved after any loss relief claims against total profits is carried forward and may be set against future profits.

2.2.3 The claim

A claim for relief against current or prior period profits must be made within two years of the end of the accounting period in which the loss arose.

Any claim must be for the **whole** loss (to the extent that profits are available to relieve it). The loss can however be reduced by not claiming full capital allowances, so that higher capital allowances are given (on higher tax written down values) in future years.

Question — Loss relief against total profits

Helix Ltd has the following results:

	Y/e 31.01.24 £	Y/e 31.01.25 £
Trading profit/(loss)	22,500	(39,500)
Bank interest	500	500
Chargeable gains	0	4,000
Qualifying charitable donation	250	250

Show the taxable total profits for each year affected, assuming that loss relief against total profits is claimed as early as possible.

Answer

The loss of the year to 31 January 2024 is relieved against current year total profits and then those of the previous 12 months.

	Y/e 31.01.24 £	Y/e 31.01.25 £
Trading profit	22,500	0
Investment income	500	500
Chargeable gains	0	4,000
Total profits	23,000	4,500
Less current period loss relief	0	(4,500)
	23,000	0
Less carry back loss relief	(23,000)	(0)
	0	0
Less qualifying charitable donation	0	0
Taxable total profits	0	0
Unrelieved qualifying charitable donation	250	250

Loss memorandum

	£
Loss incurred in y/e 31.01.25	39,500
Less used: y/e 31.01.25	(4,500)
y/e 31.01.24	(23,000)
Loss available to carry forward	(12,000)

2.2.4 Periods of account which are not 12 months in length

If an accounting period falls only partly into the 12 months prior to a loss-making period, the profits of the period are apportioned so that carry back relief is only given in relation to the amount relating to that 12-month period.

PART C CORPORATION TAX

Question — Short accounting period and loss relief

Tallis Ltd had the following results for the three accounting periods to 31 December 2025:

	Y/e 30.9.24 £	Three months to 31.12.24 £	Y/e 31.12.25 £
Trading profit (loss)	20,000	12,000	(39,000)
Building society interest	1,000	400	1,800
Qualifying charitable donations	600	500	0

Show the taxable total profits for all accounting periods. Assume loss relief is claimed against total profits where possible.

Answer

	Y/e 30.9.24 £	Three months to 31.12.24 £	Y/e 31.12.25 £
Trading profit	20,000	12,000	0
Interest income	1,000	400	1,800
Total profits	21,000	12,400	1,800
Less current period loss relief			(1,800)
	21,000	12,400	0
Less carry back loss relief	(15,750)	(12,400)	
	5,250	0	0
Less qualifying charitable donations	(600)		0
Taxable total profits	4,650	0	0
Unrelieved qualifying charitable donations	0	500	0

Loss memorandum

	£
Loss incurred in y/e 31.12.25	39,000
Less used y/e 31.12.25	(1,800)
Less used p/e 31.12.24	(12,400)
Less used y/e 30.9.24 £21,000 × 9/12 (max)	(15,750)
C/f	9,050

Notes

1 The loss can be carried back to set against profits of the previous 12 months. This means profits in the y/e 30.9.24 must be time apportioned by multiplying by 9/12.

3 Reliefs for deficits on non-trading loan relationships

FAST FORWARD Deficits on non-trading loan relationships can be used in a similar way to trading losses.

Exam focus point Different rules apply for deficits that originated pre-1 April 2017. The Taxation paper only tests the rules for post-1 April 2017 deficits, as detailed here. In a question, assume a deficit arose post-1 April 2017.

A deficit on a non-trading loan relationship may be set, in whole or part, against any profit of the same accounting period. Maximum relief is calculated as total profits before:

- relief for any NTLR deficit carried back from a later accounting period;
- relief is given for a trading loss of the same or later periods; and
- relief for trading losses carried forward

Question — Relief for deficit on non-trading loan relationship

Witherspoon Ltd has the following results for the two years ended 31 December 2025:

	2024 £	2025 £
Trading profit/(loss)	70,000	(42,000)
Trading losses brought forward	(20,000)	–
Bank interest receivable	2,000	
Interest payable on a loan for non-trading purposes	(11,000)	

Show how relief may be given for the deficit on the non-trading loan relationship in the year ended 31 December 2024.

Answer

Y/e 31.12.24	£
Trading income/Total profits	70,000
Less non-trading deficit £(11,000 – 2,000)	(9,000)
Less losses brought forward	(20,000)
Losses carried back	(41,000)
Taxable total profits	Nil

Loss memorandum	
Incurred in y/e 31.12.25	42,000
Less used y/e 31.12.24	(41,000)
Available to carry forward	1,000

A deficit may be set against non-trading income arising from loan relationships in the previous 12 months. In this case, relief is given after any trading loss of the same or future period. A claim can be made for any amount and must be made within two years of the deficit period.

Any deficits unrelieved after claiming the above reliefs are carried forward and a claim can be made to offset them, wholly or partly, against total profits of future periods.

A company can choose how much deficit to relieve in the current period, how much to carry back and how much to carry forward; unlike trading loss relief, these are not all or nothing claims, and the company can choose to carry back a deficit even if it does not claim current period relief.

PART C CORPORATION TAX

4 Restrictions on loss relief

FAST FORWARD From 1 April 2017, there is a restriction on the amount of profits (arising on or after that date) that can be relieved by carrying forward losses.

4.1 Restrictions on carried forward loss relief

From 1 April 2017, there is a restriction on the amount of profits (arising on or after that date) that can be relieved by carried forward losses for companies with losses of more than £5 million. The losses included in this restriction are:

- trading losses
- deficits on non-trading loan relationships
- property business losses
- capital losses – although the restriction only applies to capital losses incurred after 1 April 2020

For a single company, the profits that can be relieved are limited to a 'deductions allowance' of £5 million per 12-month period, plus 50% of the excess profits over this amount. The total is referred to as the 'relevant maximum'.

Question
Definite variables

Purple plc, a single company, has trading losses brought forward at 1 April 2024 of £12 million.

The results for the two years ending 31 March 2026 were as follows:

	y/e 31.3.25 £m	y/e 31.3.26 £m
Trading profits	4	13
Profit on non-trading loan relationships	2	2

Explain how the brought forward losses can be relieved.

Answer

Purple plc is a single company with losses brought forward of more than £5 million, so the restriction applies.

Purple plc can make a claim to offset the loss carried forward against total profits of the year ended 31 March 2025. The profits that can be relieved are restricted to:

£5m + 50% of £1m (£4m + £2m – £5m) = £5.5 million (the 'relevant maximum')

Purple plc can then claim to offset the remaining losses of £6.5 million (£12m – £5.5m) against total profits of 31 March 2026 without restriction as the 'relevant maximum' in this year will be £10 million (£5m + (50% × (£13m + £2m – £5m))).

21: LOSSES AND DEFICITS ON NON-TRADING LOAN RELATIONSHIPS

Chapter roundup

- Trading losses may be relieved against current total profits, against total profits of earlier periods or against future total profits.
- Property business losses are set off first against total profits of the current period and can then be carried forward against future total profits. Any amount of the carried forward loss can be used in future accounting periods.
- Trading losses can be carried forward and set against future total profits.
- Loss relief against total profits may be given against current period profits and against profits of the previous 12 months. A claim for current period loss relief can be made without a claim for carry back. However, if a loss is to be carried back a claim for current period relief must be made first.
- Deficits on non-trading loan relationships can be used in a similar way to trading losses.
- From 1 April 2017 there is a restriction on the amount of profits (arising on or after that date) that can be relieved by carrying forward losses.

Quick quiz

1. Against what profits may trading losses carried forward be set?
2. To what extent may losses in a continuing trade be carried back?
3. What relief is available in the current AP for a non-trading deficit?
4. What are the two key factors in choosing which loss relief claim to make?
5. Why might a company make a reduced capital allowances claim?
6. From 1 April 2017, what is the restriction on the amount of profits (arising on or after that date) that can be relieved by carried forward losses for companies with losses of more than £5 million?

Answers to quick quiz

1. Total profits of the future accounting periods.

2. A loss may usually be carried back and set against total profits (before deducting qualifying charitable donations) of the prior 12 months. The loss carried back is the trading loss left unrelieved after a claim against total profits (before deducting qualifying charitable donations) of the loss-making AP has been made.

3. A deficit on a non-trading loan relationship may be set against profits of the same AP.

    Relief is given before:

    - relief for any NTLR deficit carried back from a later accounting period;
    - relief is given for a trading loss of the same or later periods; and
    - relief for trading losses carried forward.

4. - How quickly relief will be obtained.
   - The extent to which relief for qualifying charitable donations might be lost.

5. Reducing capital allowances in the current accounting period reduces the loss available for relief against total profits. This relief demands that all of the available loss is utilised. Reducing capital allowances reduces the size of the available loss.

6. £5m + 50% × (profits − £5m)

Overseas aspects of corporate tax

Topic list
1 Company residence
2 Double taxation relief (DTR)

Introduction

We have nearly completed our study of corporation tax, except for the consideration of overseas aspects.

This chapter starts by considering which country a company is resident in. We then see how relief may be given in the UK for overseas taxes suffered and, finally, we look briefly at overseas companies trading in the UK.

In the next chapter, we will turn our attention to VAT.

Exam guide

A question on the overseas aspects of corporation tax could require you to calculate double tax relief. Double tax relief allows a company to avoid paying tax twice on the same overseas income.

1 Company residence

> **FAST FORWARD**
> Company residence is important in determining whether its profits are subject to UK tax.

1.1 Introduction

A company is resident in the UK if it is incorporated in the UK or if its central management and control are exercised in the UK. Central management and control are usually treated as exercised where the board of directors meets.

A UK resident company is subject to corporation tax on its worldwide profits.

1.2 UK resident companies with overseas income

If a UK resident company makes investments overseas, it will be liable to corporation tax on the profits made. The taxable amount is computed before the deduction of any overseas taxes. The profits may be any of the following:

(a) Trading income: profits of an overseas permanent establishment (a fixed place of business) controlled from the UK

(b) Interest income: income from foreign securities, for example, debentures in overseas companies

(c) Overseas income: income from other overseas possessions including:

  (i) Dividends from overseas subsidiaries
  (ii) Profits of an overseas branch or agency controlled abroad

(d) Chargeable gains on disposals of foreign assets

A UK resident company may receive dividends from an overseas subsidiary. Most dividends received by a UK resident company from a non-UK resident company are exempt from corporation tax.

> **Exam focus point**
> Taxable overseas dividends will not be examined in this paper.

A company may be subject to overseas tax as well as to UK corporation tax on the same profits usually if it has a PE in that overseas country. Double taxation relief (see below) is available in respect of the overseas tax suffered.

2 Double taxation relief (DTR)

> **FAST FORWARD**
> A company may obtain DTR for overseas withholding tax. The allocation of qualifying charitable donations and losses can affect the relief.

2.1 General principles

In the UK relief for foreign tax suffered by a company may be currently available in one of three ways.

(a) **Treaty relief**
Under a treaty entered into between the UK and the overseas country, a treaty may exempt certain profits from taxation in one of the countries involved, thus completely avoiding double taxation. More usually treaties provide for credit to be given for tax suffered in one of the countries against the tax liability in the other.

(b) **Unilateral credit relief**
Where no treaty relief is available, unilateral relief may be available in the UK giving credit for the foreign tax against the UK tax.

(c) **Unilateral expense relief**
Not examined in your syllabus.

2.2 Treaty relief

A tax treaty based on the OECD model treaty may use either the exemption method or the credit method to give relief for tax suffered on income from a business in country B by a resident of country R.

(a) Under the **exemption method**, the income is not taxed at all in country R, or if it is dividends or interest (which the treaty allows to be taxed in country R) credit is given for any country B tax against the country R tax.

(b) Under the **credit method**, the income is taxed in country R, but credit is given for any country B tax against the country R tax.

Under either method, any credit given is limited to the country B tax attributable to the income.

2.3 Unilateral credit relief

> **FAST FORWARD**
>
> Double tax relief (DTR) is the lower of the UK tax on overseas profits and the overseas tax on overseas profits.

Relief is available for overseas tax suffered on PE profits, interest and royalties, up to the amount of the UK corporation tax (at the company's average rate) attributable to that income. The tax that is deducted overseas is usually called withholding tax. The gross income including the withholding tax is included within the taxable total profits. It is not relevant whether those profits are remitted back to the UK or not.

The amount of double tax relief (DTR) is the lower of:

(a) **The UK tax on overseas profits**
(b) **The overseas tax on overseas profits**

Question   Unilateral credit relief

AS plc has UK trading income of £2m in the year to 31 March 2025. In that year, AS plc also operated an overseas branch. The profits of the branch were £82,000, after deduction of 18% withholding tax. Compute the corporation tax payable.

Answer

	Total £	UK £	Overseas £
Trading income	2,000,000	2,000,000	
Overseas trading income (W)	100,000		100,000
Taxable total profits	2,100,000	2,000,000	100,000
Corporation tax at 25%	525,000	500,000	25,000
Less DTR (W2)	(18,000)		(18,000)
	507,000	500,000	7,000

Workings

1 £82,000 × 100/(100 – 18) = £100,000.
2 DTR is lower of

    (i)   UK tax on overseas profit £100,000 × 25% = £25,000
    (i)   Overseas tax on overseas profit £100,000 × 18% = £18,000

A company may allocate its qualifying charitable donations and losses relieved against total profits in whatever manner it likes for the purpose of computing double taxation relief. It should set the maximum amount against any UK profits, thereby maximising the corporation tax attributable to the overseas profits and hence maximising the double taxation relief available.

If a company has several sources of overseas profits, then deficits, qualifying charitable donations and losses should be allocated first to UK profits, and then to overseas sources which have suffered the **lowest** rates of overseas taxation.

A company with a choice of loss reliefs should consider the effect of its choice on double taxation relief. For example, a loss relief claim might lead to there being no UK tax liability, or a very small liability, so that foreign tax would go unrelieved.

Companies that have claimed DTR must notify HMRC if the amount of foreign tax they have paid is adjusted and this has resulted in the DTR claim becoming excessive. The notification must be in writing within one year of any adjustment to the foreign tax.

Question — Allocation of qualifying charitable donations

Kairo plc is a UK resident company with two overseas branches, one in Atlantis and one in Utopia. The company produced the following results for the year to 31 March 2025:

	£
UK trading profits	10,000
Profits from overseas branch in Atlantis (before overseas tax of £6,800)	40,000
Profits from overseas branch in Utopia (before overseas tax of £66,000)	150,000
Qualifying charitable donations	(15,000)

Kairo plc received no dividends in the period.

Compute the UK corporation tax liability, assuming an election has not been made to exempt the profits of overseas PEs.

22: OVERSEAS ASPECTS OF CORPORATE TAX

Answer

Kairo plc – corporation tax year to 31 March 2025

	Total £	UK £	Atlantis £	Utopia £
Total profits	200,000	10,000	40,000	150,000
Less qualifying charitable donations (W)	(15,000)	(10,000)	(5,000)	–
Taxable total profits	185,000	Nil	35,000	150,000
Corporation tax @ 25% (N)	46,250	–	8,750	37,500
$3/200 \times (250,000 - 185,000)$	(975)			
$(45,275/185,000) = 24.473\%$	45,275		8,566	36,709
Less DTR (W)	(43,509)	–	(6,800)	(36,709)
Corporation tax	2,741	–	1,950	791

Working

The DTR is the lower of:

Atlantis: UK tax 24.473% (N) × £35,000 = £8,566;
Overseas tax £6,800 (Rate of overseas tax = 17%)

Utopia: UK tax 24.473% (N) × £150,000 = £36,709;
Overseas tax £66,000 (Rate of overseas tax = 44%)

Note. The Atlantis branch profits suffer the lower rate of overseas tax so the qualifying charitable donations remaining after offset against the UK income are allocated against the Atlantis branch income in preference to the Utopia branch income.

Exam focus point

If there are several sources of overseas income, it is important to keep them separate and to calculate double tax relief on each source of income separately. Get into the habit of setting out a working with a separate column for UK income and for each source of overseas income. You should then find arriving at the right answer straightforward.

PART C CORPORATION TAX

Chapter roundup

- Company residence is important in determining whether its profits are subject to UK tax.
- A company may obtain double tax relief (DTR) for overseas withholding tax. The allocation of qualifying charitable donations and losses can affect the relief.
- DTR is the lower of the UK tax on overseas profits and the overseas tax on overseas profits.

Quick quiz

1. When is a company UK resident?
2. How do you calculate double tax relief?
3. How best should qualifying charitable donations be allocated in computing credit relief for overseas tax?

Answers to quick quiz

1. A company is resident in the UK if it is incorporated in the UK or if its central management and control are exercised in the UK.

2. The lower of :

   (a) **The UK tax on overseas profits**
   (b) **The overseas tax on overseas profits**

3. Qualifying charitable donations should be set-off firstly from any UK profits, then from overseas income sources suffering the lowest rates of overseas taxation before those suffering at the higher rates.

PART C CORPORATION TAX

Value added tax

Value Added Tax 1

Topic list
1 Basic principles
2 The scope of VAT
3 Registration
4 Accounting for VAT
5 The tax point
6 The valuation of supplies
7 Administration
8 Penalties

Introduction

In this and the next chapter, we will study Value Added Tax (VAT). VAT is a tax on turnover rather than on profits.

As the name of the tax suggests, it is charged on the value added to a product or service. If someone in a chain of manufacture or distribution buys goods for £1,000 and sells them for £1,200, they have increased their value by £200. They may have painted them, packed them or distributed them to shops to justify the mark-up, or they may simply be good at making deals to buy cheaply and sell at a profit. Because they have added value of £200, they collect VAT of £200 × 20% = £40 (the standard rate being 20%) and pay this over to HMRC. The VAT is collected bit by bit along the chain and finally hits the consumer, who does not add value but uses up the goods.

VAT is a tax with simple computations but many detailed rules to ensure its enforcement. You may find it easier to absorb the detail if you ask yourself, in relation to each rule, exactly how it helps to enforce the tax.

In the next chapter, we will look at the rules for zero-rated and exempt supplies and the rules for imports and exports.

PART D VALUE ADDED TAX

Exam guide

VAT will be examined in all sittings of Taxation. VAT is a very important tax for businesses as many are required to account for it. You may be required to advise on almost any aspect, including the rules around registration and deregistration, and to carry out VAT calculations.

1 Basic principles

FAST FORWARD

VAT is charged on turnover at each stage in a production process but in such a way that the burden is borne by the final consumer.

1.1 Introduction

The legal basis of Value Added Tax (VAT) is to be found in the Value Added Tax Act 1994 (VATA 1994), supplemented by regulations made by statutory instrument and amended by subsequent Finance Acts. VAT is administered by HM Revenue and Customs (HMRC). When the UK was a member of the EU, VAT rules had to comply with requirements set by the European Union (EU). Some changes to the applicable rules have taken place since the UK left the EU. We will consider these changes in this and later chapters.

VAT is a tax on turnover, not on profits. The basic principle is that the VAT should be collected by VAT registered traders, who will account for it to HMRC, but the actual cost of paying the tax is borne by the final consumer. For this reason, VAT is sometimes referred to as an 'indirect tax'. The other taxes we have looked at so far have been examples of 'direct taxes', which taxpayers calculate and pay directly to HMRC.

Registered traders may deduct the VAT costs which they incur on supplies they receive in their supply chain (these VAT costs are known as input tax) from the tax which they charge on the supplies they make to their customers (known as output tax). When the trader completes a VAT return, the VAT payable to HMRC is calculated by deducting input tax from output tax. In other words, the net VAT paid by each trader in a supply chain is on the value added at that stage.

1.2 Example: the VAT charge

A forester sells wood to a furniture maker for £100 plus VAT of 20%. The furniture maker uses this wood to make a table and sells the table to a shop for £150 plus VAT. The shop then sells the table to the final consumer for £300 plus VAT. VAT will be accounted for to HMRC as follows:

	Cost £	Input tax 20% £	Net sale price £	Output tax 20% £	Payable to HMRC £
Forester	0	0	100	20	20
Furniture maker	100	20	150	30	10
Shop	150	30	300	60	30
					60

Because the traders involved account to HMRC for VAT charged less VAT suffered, their profits for income tax or corporation tax purposes are based on sales and purchases net of VAT.

If input tax exceeds output tax, a trader will receive a repayment from HMRC of the difference. So, for example, if the forester in this example incurred £30 of input tax, they would receive a £10 repayment from HMRC.

2 The scope of VAT

VAT is charged on taxable supplies of goods and services made by a taxable person in their business.

2.1 General principles

VAT is charged on taxable supplies of goods and services made in the UK by a taxable person in the course or furtherance of any business carried on by him. It is also chargeable on the import of goods into the UK (whether they are imported for business purposes or not, and whether the importer is a taxable person or not), and on certain services received from abroad if a taxable person receives them for business purposes. Special rules for trade between Northern Ireland and the EU are covered later.

Key term

A **taxable supply** is a supply of goods or services made in the UK, other than an exempt supply or a supply outside the scope of VAT (see later in this Workbook).

A taxable supply is either standard-rated, reduced-rated or zero-rated. The standard rate is 20%.

On certain supplies, for example the supply of domestic fuel and power, a reduced rate is charged of 5%. Zero-rated supplies are taxed at 0%. An exempt supply is not chargeable to VAT. The categories of zero-rated, reduced-rated and exempt supplies are listed in the next chapter.

2.2 Supplies of goods

Goods are supplied if exclusive ownership of the goods passes to another person.

The following are treated as supplies of goods:

- The supply of any form of power, heat, refrigeration or ventilation, or of water
- The grant, assignment or surrender of a major interest (the freehold or a lease for over 21 years) in land
- Taking goods permanently out of the business for the non-business use of a taxable person or for other private purposes including the supply of goods by an employer to an employee for his private use
- Transfers under an agreement contemplating a transfer of ownership, such as a hire purchase agreement

Gifts of goods are normally treated as sales at cost (so VAT is due). **However, business gifts are not supplies of goods if:**

(a) **The total cost of gifts made to the same person does not exceed £50 in any 12 month period.** If the £50 limit is exceeded, output tax will be due in full on the total of gifts made. Once the limit has been exceeded a new £50 limit and new 12 month period begins;

(b) **The gift is a sample** (unlimited number of different samples allowed).

2.3 Supplies of services

Apart from a few specific exceptions, **any supply which is not a supply of goods and which is done for a consideration is a supply of services**. Consideration is any form of payment in money or in kind, including anything which is itself a supply.

A supply of services also takes place if:

- Goods are lent to someone for use outside the business
- Goods are hired to someone
- Services bought for business purposes are used for private purposes

The European Court of Justice (ECJ) has ruled that restaurants supply services rather than goods. Although the UK has left the EU, decisions made by the ECJ are still used to help interpret the application of VAT law in the UK.

2.4 Taxable persons

The term 'person' includes **individuals, partnerships** (which are treated as single entities, ignoring the individual partners), **companies, clubs, associations and charities. If a person is in business making taxable supplies, the value of these supplies is called the taxable turnover. If a person's taxable turnover exceeds certain limits, they are a taxable person and should be registered for VAT.**

3 Registration

FAST FORWARD

A trader becomes liable to register for VAT if the value of taxable supplies in any period up to 12 months exceeds £85,000 or if there are reasonable grounds for believing that the value of the taxable supplies will exceed £85,000 in the next 30 days. A trader may also register voluntarily.

3.1 Compulsory registration

At the end of every month a trader must calculate the cumulative turnover of taxable supplies made in the 12 months running up to that date. **The trader becomes liable to register for VAT if the value of cumulative taxable supplies in that 12-month period** (excluding VAT) **exceeds £90,000** (Whillans p.149). The person is required to notify HMRC within 30 days of the end of the month in which the £90,000 limit is exceeded. HMRC will then register the person with effect from the end of the month following the month in which the £90,000 was exceeded, or from an earlier date if they and the trader agree. For example, if a trader exceeds the £90,000 limit in September 2024, notification must be made by 30 October 2024 and the registration will take effect from 1 November 2024, unless an earlier date is agreed.

Registration under this rule is not required if HMRC are satisfied that the value of the trader's taxable supplies (excluding VAT) in the year then starting will not exceed £88,000.

A person is also liable to register at any time if there are reasonable grounds for believing that taxable supplies (excluding VAT) in the following 30 days will exceed £90,000. For this test, only the anticipated taxable turnover of that 30-day period is considered, **not** cumulative past turnover. HMRC must be notified by the end of the 30-day period and registration will be with effect from the beginning of that period.

When determining the value of a person's taxable supplies for the purposes of registration, supplies of goods and services that are *capital assets* of the business are to be disregarded, except for non zero-rated taxable supplies of interests in land.

If a business makes taxable supplies in the UK but has no establishment here, it has to register for VAT, whatever the value of its taxable supplies, ie even if this is below the VAT registration threshold.

Exam focus point

Unless factors in the question indicate otherwise, assume the business does have an establishment in the UK when determining whether to register for VAT.

Question

VAT registration

Fred started to trade in cutlery on 1 January 2024. Sales (excluding VAT) were £8,000 a month for the first nine months and £10,500 a month thereafter.

From what date should Fred be registered for VAT?

Answer

	£
Sales to 31 October 2024 (9 × £8,000 + £10,500)	82,500
Sales to 30 November 2024 (9 × £8,000 + 2 × £10,500)	93,000 (exceeds £90,000)

Fred must notify his liability to register by 30 December 2024 (not 31 December) and will be registered from 1 January 2025 or from an agreed earlier date.

When a person is liable to register in respect of a past period, it is that person's responsibility to pay VAT. Even if the VAT cannot be collected from those to whom the taxable supplies were made, the supplier is legally responsible for paying the appropriate amount of VAT to HMRC. A person must start keeping VAT records and charging VAT to customers as soon as they become a taxable person. However, VAT should not be shown separately on any invoices until the registration number is notified by HMRC. The invoice should show the VAT inclusive price and customers should be informed that VAT invoices will be forwarded once the registration number is known. Formal VAT invoices should then be sent to such customers within 30 days of receiving the registration number.

Notification of liability to register must be made on form VAT 1. This can be downloaded from the HMRC website, can be requested by telephone, or an application to register can be made online through the website. Simply writing to, or telephoning, a local VAT office is not enough. On registration, the VAT office will send the trader a certificate of registration. This shows the VAT registration number, the date of registration, the end of the first VAT period and the length of later VAT periods.

If a trader makes a supply before becoming **liable** to register, but receives payment after registration, VAT is not due on that supply.

3.2 Voluntary registration

A person may decide to become registered even if taxable turnover falls below the registration limit. Registration is necessary in order for a trader to recover input tax (see above in this chapter).

Voluntary registration is advantageous where a person wishes to recover input tax on purchases. For example, consider a trader who has one input during the year, which cost £1,000 plus £200 VAT. The trader works on the input, which becomes their sole output for the year, and decides to sell it at a price that will make a profit of £1,000.

(a) If the trader is not registered for VAT, they will charge £2,200 and the customer will obtain no relief for any VAT.
(b) If the trader is registered for VAT, they will charge £2,000 plus VAT of £400. The customer will have input tax of £400 which they will be able to recover if they, too, are registered.

If the customer is a non-taxable person (ie not capable of recovering input tax), they would prefer (a) as the cost to them is £2,200. If they are taxable, they would prefer (b) as the net cost is £2,000. Thus, a decision about whether or not to register voluntarily may depend upon the status of customers. It may also depend on the status of the outputs and the business image the trader wishes to project (registration may give the impression of a substantial business). The administrative burden of registration, as well as the risk of incurring penalties for late payment and filing (see later in this chapter), should also be considered.

3.3 Intending trader registration

If a trader satisfies HMRC that they are carrying on a business, and intend to make taxable supplies, they are entitled to be registered if they choose. But, once registered, they are obliged to notify HMRC within 30 days if they no longer intend to make taxable supplies.

3.4 Exemption from registration

If a person makes only zero-rated supplies, they may request exemption from registration. The trader is obliged to notify HMRC of any material change in the nature of their supplies after exemption is agreed.

HMRC may also allow exemption from registration if only a small proportion of supplies are standard-rated, provided that the trader would normally receive repayments of VAT if registered.

3.5 Deregistration

3.5.1 Voluntary deregistration

A person is eligible for voluntary deregistration if HMRC are satisfied that the value of their taxable supplies (net of VAT and excluding supplies of capital assets) **in the following one year period will not exceed £88,000** (Whillans p.150). However, voluntary deregistration will not be allowed if the reason for the expected fall in value of taxable supplies is the cessation of taxable supplies or the suspension of taxable supplies for a period of 30 days or more in that following year.

HMRC will cancel a person's registration from the date the request is made or from an agreed later date.

3.5.2 Compulsory deregistration

Traders may be compulsorily deregistered. Failure to notify a requirement to deregister within 30 days may lead to a penalty. Compulsory deregistration may also lead to HMRC reclaiming input tax which has been wrongly recovered by the trader since the date on which he should have deregistered.

Other points to note are:

- If HMRC are misled into granting registration then the registration is treated as void from the start.
- A person may be compulsorily deregistered if HMRC are satisfied that he is no longer making nor intending to make taxable supplies.
- Changes in legal status also require cancellation of registration. For example:
    - A sole trader becoming a partnership
    - A partnership reverting to a sole trader
    - A business being incorporated
    - A company being replaced by an unincorporated business

3.5.3 The consequences of deregistration

On deregistration, VAT is chargeable on all stocks and capital assets in a business on which input tax was claimed, since the registered trader is in effect making a taxable supply to themselves as a newly unregistered trader. If the VAT chargeable does not exceed £1,000, it need not be paid.

This special VAT charge does not apply if the business (or a separately viable part of it) **is sold as a going concern to another taxable person** (or a person who immediately becomes a taxable person as a result of the transfer). **Such transfers are outside the scope of VAT** (except for certain buildings being transferred which are 'new' or opted buildings and the transferee does not make an election to waive exemption – refer to the section on land in the next chapter).

If the original owner ceases to be taxable, the new owner of the business may take over the existing VAT number. If they do so, they take over the rights and liabilities of the transferor as at the date of transfer.

3.6 Pre-registration input tax

VAT on expenses incurred before registration can be treated as input tax and recovered from HMRC subject to certain conditions.

If the claim is for input tax suffered on **goods** purchased prior to registration then the following conditions must be satisfied:

(a) The goods were acquired for the purpose of the business which either was carried on or was to be carried on by him at the time of supply;

(b) The goods have not been supplied onwards or consumed before the date of registration (although they may have been used to make other goods which are still held); and

(c) The VAT must have been incurred in the four years prior to the effective date of registration.

If the claim is for input tax suffered on the supply of **services** prior to registration then the following conditions must be satisfied:

(a) The services were supplied for the purposes of a business which either was carried on or was to be carried on by him at the time of supply; and

(b) The services were supplied within the six months prior to the date of registration.

Input tax attributable to supplies made by the business before registration is not deductible even if the input tax concerned is treated as having been incurred after registration.

3.7 Disaggregation

A person's registration covers all his business activities together. **The turnover of all business activities carried on by a 'person' must be aggregated to find taxable turnover.** However, if the same individual both carries on trade A alone and is a member of a partnership carrying on trade B, the turnover of the two trades will not normally be aggregated: the individual will have their taxable turnover in respect of trade A only, and the partnership will have its taxable turnover in respect of trade B only.

For example, a brother and sister might operate a pub with catering and bed and breakfast facilities. The catering could be operated by the brother, the pub could be operated by a partnership of the two people and the bed and breakfast business could be operated by the sister. This could avoid the need to register and account for output tax if the turnover of each business was below the threshold for registration.

There are anti-avoidance provisions to prevent VAT advantages from being obtained by operating a business through multiple entities in this way. These provisions enable HMRC to direct that any connected businesses which have avoided VAT by artificially separating should be treated as one, whatever the reason for the separation. When deciding whether businesses are artificially separated, HMRC consider the extent to which those persons are bound by financial, economic or organisational links.

4 Accounting for VAT

4.1 VAT periods

FAST FORWARD

VAT is accounted for on regular returns which are usually filed online within one month plus seven days of the end of the VAT period. Extensive records must be kept.

The VAT period (also known as the tax period) is the period covered by a VAT return. It is usually three calendar months. The return shows the total input and output tax for the tax period.

HMRC allocate VAT periods according to the class of trade carried on (ending in June, September, December and March; July, October, January and April; or August, November, February and May), to spread the flow of VAT returns evenly over the year. When applying for registration, a trader can ask for VAT periods which fit in with their own accounting year. It is also possible to have VAT periods to cover accounting systems not based on calendar months.

A registered person whose input tax will regularly exceed output tax can elect for a one month VAT period but will have to balance the inconvenience of making 12 returns a year against the advantage of obtaining more rapid repayments of VAT. The election can be made either by updating the trader's registration details online or by submitting a form 748 by mail to HMRC.

4.2 The VAT return

The regular VAT return to HMRC is made on form VAT 100. The UK VAT return changed following the UK's exit from the EU on 31 December 2020. For VAT returns relating to periods after 1 January 2021, the required information is:

(a) Box 1: VAT due on sales and other outputs

(b) Box 2: VAT due in the period on acquisitions of goods made in Northern Ireland from EU Member States

(c) Box 3: The total of boxes 1 and 2

(d) Box 4: VAT reclaimed in the period on purchases and other inputs (including acquisitions from the EU in NI)

(e) Box 5: Net VAT to be paid or reclaimed: the difference between boxes 3 and 4

(f) Box 6: Total value (before cash discounts) of sales and all other outputs, excluding VAT but including the total in box 8

(g) Box 7: Total value (before cash discounts) of purchases and all other inputs, excluding VAT but including the total in box 9

(h) Box 8: Total value of all sales and related services to other EU member states from Northern Ireland

(i) Box 9: Total value of all purchases and related services from other EU member states to Northern Ireland

Exam focus point

> For the Taxation exam, you do not need to learn what goes in the specific boxes of the VAT return, although you may be required to calculate the net VAT payable, ie the figure that would go in box 5.

Input and output tax figures must be supported by the original or copy tax invoices and records must be maintained for six years.

4.3 Electronic filing

Nearly all VAT registered businesses must file their VAT returns online and make payments electronically.

The time limit for submission and payment is one month plus seven days after the end of the VAT period. For example, a business which has a VAT quarter ending 31 March 2025 must file its VAT return and pay the VAT due by 7 May 2025.

4.4 Refunds of VAT

There is a four-year time limit on the right to reclaim overpaid VAT. This time limit does not apply to input tax which a business could not have reclaimed earlier because the supplier only recently invoiced the VAT, even though it related to a purchase made some time ago. Nor does it apply to overpaid VAT penalties.

If a taxpayer has overpaid VAT and has overclaimed input tax by reason of the same mistake, HMRC can set off any tax, penalty, interest or surcharge due to them against any repayment due to the taxpayer and repay only the net amount. In such cases, the normal four-year time limit for recovering VAT, penalties, interest, etc by assessment does not apply.

HMRC can refuse to make any repayment which would unjustly enrich the claimant. They can also refuse a repayment of VAT where all or part of the tax has, for practical purposes, been borne by a person other than the taxpayer (eg by a customer of the taxpayer) except to the extent that the taxpayer can show loss or damage to any of his businesses as a result of mistaken assumptions about VAT.

4.5 Records

Every VAT registered trader must keep records for six years, although HMRC may sometimes grant permission for their earlier destruction. They may be kept on paper, on microfilm or microfiche or on computer. Whichever format the trader uses, there must be adequate facilities for HMRC to inspect the records.

All records must be kept up to date and in a way which allows:

- The calculation of VAT due
- Officers of HMRC to check the figures on VAT returns

The following records are needed:

- Copies of VAT invoices, credit notes and debit notes issued
- A summary of supplies made
- VAT invoices, credit notes and debit notes received
- A summary of supplies received
- Records of goods received from and sent to EU member states
- Documents relating to imports from and exports to countries outside the EU
- A VAT account
- Order and delivery notes, correspondence, appointment books, job books, purchases and sales books, cash books, account books, records of takings (such as till rolls), bank paying-in slips, bank statements and annual accounts
- Records of zero-rated and exempt supplies, gifts or loans of goods, taxable self-supplies and any goods taken for non-business use

4.6 VAT invoices

Only a VAT registered person may issue a VAT invoice. If someone issues a VAT invoice despite not being authorised to do so, HMRC may issue them with a 'VAT wrongdoing' penalty. This is calculated as a percentage of the VAT purported to be charged by the false invoice, ranging between 30% and 100%. This measure is intended to deter the fraudulent use of VAT invoices.

A VAT invoice must contain a number of details, including:

- Invoice number
- The business name, address and VAT number
- The customer's name and address
- The invoice date and tax point of supply
- A description of the goods or service and its price, quantity and VAT rate
- The total amount of the invoice exclusive of VAT, and the total amount of VAT

The level of detail can be relaxed in some circumstances:

- A 'simplified' invoice can be issued for supplies under £250. This contains an invoice number, the business details as above, a description of the goods or service and a total payable amount including the VAT.
- Retailers can issue a 'modified' invoice for supplies over £250 and this is similar to a full invoice plus the VAT inclusive price of products, with a VAT inclusive total.

PART D VALUE ADDED TAX

5 The tax point

FAST FORWARD

The tax point is the deemed date of supply. The basic tax point is the date on which goods are removed or made available to the customer or the date on which services are completed. If a VAT invoice is issued or payment is received before the basic tax point, the earlier of these dates becomes the actual tax point. If the earlier date rule does not apply, and the VAT invoice is issued within 14 days after the basic tax point, the invoice date becomes the actual tax point.

5.1 The basic tax point

The tax point of each supply is the deemed date of supply. The basic tax point is the date on which the goods are removed or made available to the customer, or the date on which services are completed.

The tax point determines the VAT period in which output tax must be accounted for and credit for input tax will be allowed. The tax point also determines which rate applies if the rate of VAT or a VAT category changes (for example, when a supply ceases to be zero-rated and becomes standard-rated).

5.2 The actual tax point

If a VAT invoice is issued or payment is received before the basic tax point, the earlier of these dates automatically becomes the tax point. If the earlier date rule does not apply and if the VAT invoice is issued within 14 days after the basic tax point, the invoice date becomes the tax point (although the trader can elect to use the basic tax point for all his supplies if he wishes). This 14-day period may be extended to accommodate, for example, monthly invoicing; the tax point is then the VAT invoice date or the end of the month, whichever is applied consistently.

Question
Tax point

Julia sold a sculpture to the value of £1,000 net of VAT. She received a payment on account of £250 plus VAT on 25 April. The sculpture was delivered on 28 May. Julia's VAT return period is to 30 April. She issued an invoice on 4 June.

Outline the tax point(s) and amount(s) due.

Answer

A separate tax point arises in respect of the £250 deposit and the £750 balance payable.

Julia should account for VAT as follows:

(a) **Deposit**

25 April: tax at 20% × £250 = £50. This is accounted for in her VAT return to 30 April. The charge arises on 25 April because payment is received before the basic tax point (which is 28 May – date of delivery).

(b) **Balance**

4 June: tax at 20% × £750 = £150. This is accounted for on the VAT return to 31 July. The charge arises on 4 June because the invoice was issued within 14 days of the basic tax point of 28 May (delivery date).

5.3 Miscellaneous points

Goods supplied on a 'sale or return' basis are treated as supplied on the earlier of adoption by the customer or 12 months after despatch.

Continuous supplies of services paid for periodically normally have tax points on the earlier of the receipt of each payment and the issue of each VAT invoice, unless one invoice covering several payments is issued in advance for up to a year. The tax point is then the earlier of each due date or date of actual payment. However, for connected businesses the tax point will be created periodically, in most cases based on 12-month periods.

6 The valuation of supplies

FAST FORWARD

VAT is charged on the VAT exclusive price. If a discount is offered for prompt payment, there are two possible treatments.

6.1 General principles

The value of a supply is the VAT exclusive price on which VAT is charged. The consideration for a supply is the amount paid in money or money's worth. Thus, with a standard rate of 20%:

Value + VAT = consideration
£100 + £20 = £120

The VAT fraction is:

$$\frac{\text{Rate of tax}}{100 + \text{Rate of tax}} = \frac{20}{100 + 20} = \frac{1}{6}$$

Provided the consideration for a bargain made at arm's length is paid in money, the value for VAT purposes is the VAT exclusive price charged by the trader. If it is paid in something other than money, as in a barter of some goods or services for others, it must be valued and VAT will be due on the value.

If the price of goods is effectively reduced with money off coupons, the value of the supply is the amount actually received by the taxpayer.

6.2 Prompt Payment Discounts

Where a discount is offered for prompt payment, it is often not known at the time when the invoice is issued, whether the customer will take up the discount. The supplier has two choices:

- The supplier can **charge the full amount of VAT** on the undiscounted amount, **then issue a separate credit note** if the customer takes up the discount; or

- The supplier invoice must contain the **full terms of the discount showing the discounted amount, the VAT on this and the total amount due if paid within the time period**. The invoice must also include a **statement that the customer can only recover as input tax the VAT actually paid to the supplier.**

Question
Settlement discounts

Eliza makes a standard rated taxable supply of goods. She issues an invoice for £2,000 (exclusive of VAT) to Angela on 30 June.

A 5% discount is offered for payment within 15 days of the invoice date.

What is the value of the supply and how much output VAT is charged overall, assuming that Angela pays the invoice within 15 days?

PART D VALUE ADDED TAX

Answer

	£
Value before discount	2,000
Less discount (5% × £2,000)	(100)
Value of supply	1,900
VAT charged (£1,900 × 20%)	£380

Note that if the payment had not been made within the prompt payment period, the full VAT of £400 (£2,000 × 20%) would have been payable.

6.3 Miscellaneous

For goods supplied under a hire purchase agreement, VAT is chargeable on the cash selling price at the start of the contract.

If a trader charges different prices to customers paying with credit cards and those paying by other means, the VAT due in respect of each standard-rated sale is the full amount paid by the customer × the VAT fraction.

When goods are permanently taken from a business for non-business purposes VAT must be accounted for on their market value. Where business goods are put to a private or non-business use, the value of the resulting supply of services is the cost to the taxable person of providing the services. If services bought for business purposes are used for non-business purposes (without charge), then VAT must be accounted for on their cost, but the VAT to be accounted for is not allowed to exceed the input tax deductible on the purchase of the services.

7 Administration

> **FAST FORWARD**
>
> VAT is administered by HMRC and the Tax Tribunal hears appeals against HMRC decisions.

7.1 Introduction

The administration of VAT is dealt with by HM Revenue and Customs (HMRC).

7.2 Local offices

Local offices are responsible for the local administration of VAT and for providing advice to registered persons whose principal place of business is in their area. They are controlled by regional collectors.

From time to time, a registered person will be visited by staff from a local office (a control visit) to ensure that the law is understood and is being applied properly. If a trader disagrees with any decision as to the application of VAT given by HMRC they can ask their local office to reconsider the decision. It is not necessary to appeal formally while a case is being reviewed in this way. Where an appeal can be settled by agreement, a written settlement has the same force as a decision decided through the normal appeals process (see below). A trader can ask for a reconsideration even if they have already appealed to a VAT Tribunal.

HMRC may issue assessments of VAT due, determined to the best of their judgement, if they believe that a trader has failed to make returns or if they believe those returns to be incorrect or incomplete. The time limit for making assessments is normally four years after the end of a VAT period, but this is

extended to 20 years in the case of fraud, dishonest conduct, certain registration irregularities and the unauthorised issue of VAT invoices.

HMRC sometimes write to traders, setting out their calculations, before issuing assessments. The traders can then query the calculations.

7.3 Appeals

A trader may appeal to the Tax Tribunal in the same way as an appeal may be made for income tax and corporation tax (see earlier in this Workbook). VAT returns and payments shown thereon must have been made before an appeal can be heard.

The Tribunal can waive the requirement to pay all VAT shown on returns before an appeal is heard in cases of hardship. It cannot allow an appeal against a purely administrative matter such as HMRC's refusal to apply an extra statutory concession.

7.4 Tax avoidance and evasion

Significant resources are deployed to tackle fraud, tax evasion and avoidance.

Avoidance is also countered by the requirement for traders to disclose to HMRC any use of a notifiable VAT avoidance scheme (see later in this Workbook).

8 Penalties

8.1 VAT penalty regime

> **FAST FORWARD** A new VAT penalty system applies to VAT returns for periods starting from 1 January 2023, with separate penalties for late submissions and late payment of VAT.

8.1.1 New penalty system for late submission

For each VAT return submitted late, a business will receive one late submission penalty point. This applies to any VAT return including a nil or repayment return. Once a penalty threshold is reached, the business will receive a £200 penalty for that late submission, and a further £200 penalty for each subsequent late submission (Whillans p163). The points total will not increase.

The threshold will vary according to the submission frequency:

Submission frequency	Penalty points threshold	Period of compliance
Annually	2	24 months
Quarterly	4	12 months
Monthly	5	6 months

Provided the business remains below the penalty threshold, points will have a lifetime of 2 years after which they will automatically expire. The 2 years start from the 1st of the month after the month in which the failure to submit occurred. For example, a quarterly or monthly return for the period ending 30 June 2024 would be due for submission on 7 August 2024, therefore a point for late submission would expire on 1 September 2026.

However, once a business has hit the penalty points threshold, the points do not expire and it will only be able to reset its points to zero if it has satisfied both of the following conditions:

- the business has submitted all its returns on or before the due date for the relevant period of compliance (based on their submission frequency, as above); and
- all outstanding returns due for the previous 24 months have been received by HMRC.

8.1.2 Penalty system for late payment

The new late payment penalty applies to late payments of VAT due on a monthly, quarterly or annual return, and to payments on account, unless the taxpayer has agreed a Time-to-Pay (TTP) arrangement with HMRC. This arrangement would stop any penalties accruing, and allow the taxpayer time to agree a manageable schedule of payments.

The new late payment penalty consists of two separate charges.

The **first charge** will become payable 30 days after the payment due date and will be a set percentage of the amount outstanding. The amount of that charge will depend on any payments made or TTP arrangements made during the first 30 days after the due date (Whillans p163).

Days late	Payment	Penalty
0-15	Payment made or taxpayer proposes a TTP that is eventually agreed	No penalty
16-30	Payment made or taxpayer proposes a TTP that is eventually agreed	2% x amount outstanding
Day 30	No payment made, no TTP agreed	4% x amount outstanding

The **second charge** is calculated at a rate of 4% per annum, calculated on a daily basis on the total unpaid tax on day 31. The penalty will stop accruing from the date payment is made, or a TTP is proposed, which is eventually agreed.

In line with other penalty regimes the taxpayer will not be liable to a point or a penalty if they have a reasonable excuse for not making the relevant submission or payment on time and will have the right to appeal against points and penalties.

Question   New VAT penalties

Peter Popper is having trouble submitting his returns and paying his VAT on time. His VAT return for the quarter to 31.3.24 is late, although he pays the VAT on time. He then submits returns for the quarters to 30.9.24 and 31.12.24 late as well as making late payment of the tax due of £12,000 (on 10.11.24) and £5,000 (on 20.3.25) respectively. Peter has not yet tried to reach a TTP arrangement.

All other VAT returns and VAT payments are made on time.

Outline the result of Peter Popper's submissions and payments, calculating any penalties due.

Answer

Late submission

Peter will accumulate 3 late submission penalty points for his 3 late returns since 1 January 2024. As he is making quarterly returns he has a threshold of 4 points before suffering any late submission penalty.

He will get a 4th point and suffer a £200 penalty if he submits another return late before the earliest point expires on 1.6.26 (2 years from the 1st of the month after the due date of the return for the quarter ended 31.3.24).

Late payment

The VAT for the quarter ended 30.9.24 was due on 7.11.24. As it was paid within 15 days on 10.11.24 this was early enough to avoid a penalty.

The VAT for the quarter ended 31.12.24 was due 7.2.25 and no payment has been made by Day 30 (8.3.25) therefore Peter will suffer a first charge of 4% × £5,000 = £200. Payment is eventually made on Day 42 so Peter will suffer a second charge of 4% × £5,000 × 12/366 = £7.

8.2 Penalties for errors

FAST FORWARD

There is a common penalty regime for errors in tax returns, including VAT. Errors in a VAT return up to certain amounts may be corrected in the next return.

8.2.1 Common penalty regime

The common penalty regime for making errors in tax returns discussed earlier in this Text applies for value added tax.

8.2.2 Errors corrected in next return

Errors on previous VAT returns not exceeding the greater of:

- £10,000 (net under-declaration minus over-declaration); or
- 1% × **net VAT turnover for return period** (maximum £50,000)

may be **corrected in the next return**.

Other errors should be notified to HMRC on form VAT652 or by letter.

In both cases, a penalty for error may be imposed. Correction of an error on a later return is not, of itself, an unprompted disclosure of the error and fuller disclosure is required for the penalty to be reduced. Default interest (see below) on the unpaid VAT as a result of the error is only charged where the limit is exceeded for the error to be corrected on the next VAT return.

8.3 Interest on unpaid VAT

FAST FORWARD

Default interest is charged on unpaid VAT if HMRC raise an assessment for VAT or the trader makes a voluntary payment before an assessment is raised. It runs from the date the VAT should have been paid to the actual date of payment but cannot run for more than three years before the assessment or voluntary payment.

Interest (not deductible in computing taxable profits) **is charged on VAT which is the subject of an assessment** (where returns were not made or were incorrect), **or which could have been the subject of an assessment but was paid before the assessment was raised. It runs from the reckonable date until the date of payment.** This interest is sometimes called 'default interest'.

The reckonable date is when the VAT should have been paid (one month from the end of the return period), or in the case of VAT repayments, seven days from the issue of the repayment order. However, where VAT is charged by an assessment, interest does not run from more than three years before the date of the assessment. Where the VAT was paid before an assessment was raised, interest does not run for more than three years before the date of payment.

In practice, interest is only charged when there would otherwise be a loss to the Exchequer. It is not, for example, charged when a company failed to charge VAT but if it had done so another company would have been able to recover the VAT.

8.4 Reasonable excuse

A penalty may not be due if the trader can show that there is reasonable excuse for the failure, or the penalty may be mitigated by HMRC or by the Tribunal. There is no definition of 'reasonable excuse'. However, the legislation states that the following are not reasonable excuses:

- An insufficiency of funds to pay any VAT due
- Reliance upon a third party (such as an accountant) to perform the task in question

Many cases have considered **what constitutes a reasonable excuse** but decisions often conflict with one another. Each case depends on its own facts. Here are some examples:

(a) Whilst **'Ignorance of basic VAT law'** is not an excuse, ignorance of more complex matters can constitute a reasonable excuse.

(b) There have been a number of cases where it has been accepted that **misunderstandings as to the facts** give rise to a reasonable excuse.

(c) Although the law expressly excludes an insufficiency of funds from providing a reasonable excuse, the Tribunal will, in exceptional circumstances, look behind the shortage of funds itself and examine the case of it – this is generally restricted to cases where an unexpected event (eg bank error) has led to the shortage of funds.

Chapter roundup

- VAT is charged on turnover at each stage in a production process, but in such a way that the burden is borne by the final consumer.
- VAT is charged on taxable supplies of goods and services made by a taxable person in their business.
- A trader becomes liable to register for VAT if the value of taxable supplies in any period up to 12 months exceeds £90,000 or if there are reasonable grounds for believing that the value of the taxable supplies will exceed £90,000 in the next 30 days. A trader may also register voluntarily.
- No VAT is charged on the transfer of a business as a going concern.
- VAT is accounted for on regular returns which are usually filed online within one month plus seven days of the end of the VAT period. Extensive records must be kept.
- The tax point is the deemed date of supply. The basic tax point is the date on which goods are removed or made available to the customer, or the date on which services are completed. If a VAT invoice is issued or payment is received before the basic tax point, the earlier of these dates becomes the actual tax point. If the earlier date rule does not apply, and the VAT invoice is issued within 14 days of the basic tax point, the invoice date becomes the actual tax point.
- VAT is charged on the VAT exclusive price. Where a discount is offered for prompt payment, there are two possible treatments.
- VAT is administered by HMRC and the Tax Tribunal hears appeals.
- Penalty points are awarded for late filing of VAT returns. Once the number of late filings reaches a threshold the taxpayer must pay a financial penalty.
- There is a late payment penalty which grows as the payment of the VAT liability is delayed.
- There is a common penalty regime for errors in tax returns, including VAT. Errors in a VAT return up to certain amounts may be corrected in the next return.
- Default interest is charged on unpaid VAT if HMRC raise an assessment of VAT or the trader makes a voluntary payment before the assessment is raised. It runs from the date the VAT should have been paid to the actual date of payment but cannot run for more than three years before the assessment or voluntary payment.

Quick quiz

1. On what transactions will VAT be charged?
2. What is a taxable person?
3. When may a taxable person be exempt from registration?
4. When may a person choose to be deregistered?
5. What is the time limit in respect of claiming pre-registration input tax on goods?

PART D VALUE ADDED TAX

Answers to quick quiz

1. VAT is charged on taxable supplies of goods and services made in the UK by a taxable person in the course or furtherance of any business carried on by him.

2. Any 'person' whose taxable turnover exceeds the registration limit, or a person with no UK establishment, making taxable supplies in the UK. The term 'person' includes individuals, partnerships, companies, clubs, associations and charities.

3. If a taxable person makes only zero-rated supplies, he may request exemption from registration.

4. A person is eligible for voluntary deregistration if HMRC are satisfied that the value of his taxable supplies in the following year will not exceed £88,000.

5. The VAT must have been incurred in the four years prior to the effective date of registration.

Value Added Tax 2

Topic list
1 Zero-rated and exempt supplies
2 Land and buildings
3 The deduction of input tax
4 Imports, exports, acquisitions and dispatches

Introduction

In this chapter, we continue our VAT studies by looking at zero-rated and exempt supplies and we see how making exempt supplies can affect the deduction of input tax.

VAT needs to be applied to imports, so that people do not have a tax incentive to buy abroad, and VAT is taken off many exports in order to encourage sales abroad. The UK left the European Union on 31 December 2020 and we will consider the rules that apply since that date on imports and exports.

In the next chapter, we will look at stamp duties.

PART D VALUE ADDED TAX

Exam guide

In the exam you may be required to calculate VAT, including VAT relating to overseas transactions. When the UK was a member of the European Union (EU), different VAT rules applied to transactions depending on whether they took place between the UK and EU, or the UK and a non-EU country. Since the UK has left the EU, this distinction has largely been removed, although there are some exceptions, which we will consider in this chapter.

1 Zero-rated and exempt supplies

FAST FORWARD Some supplies are taxable (either standard-rated, reduced-rated or zero-rated). Others are exempt.

1.1 Types of supply

Zero-rated supplies are taxable at 0%. A taxable supplier whose outputs are zero-rated, but whose inputs are standard-rated, will obtain repayments of the VAT paid on purchases.

A **person making exempt supplies is unable to recover VAT on inputs that relate to those exempt supplies** (in exactly the same way as for a non-registered person). An exempt supplier therefore has to bear the cost of VAT on purchases in the same way as a consumer does in a typical supply chain. A supplier in this position may increase prices to pass on the charge but will be unable to issue a VAT invoice, which would enable a taxable customer to obtain a credit for VAT, since no VAT is chargeable on his supplies.

1.2 Example: standard-rated, zero-rated and exempt supplies

Here are figures for three traders, the first with standard-rated outputs, the second with zero-rated outputs and the third with exempt outputs. All their inputs are standard-rated at 20%.

	Standard-rated £	Zero-rated £	Exempt £
Inputs	20,000	20,000	20,000
VAT	4,000	4,000	4,000
	24,000	24,000	24,000
Outputs	30,000	30,000	30,000
VAT	6,000	0	0
	36,000	30,000	30,000
Pay/(reclaim)	2,000	(4,000)	0
Net profit	10,000	10,000	6,000

VAT legislation lists zero-rated, reduced-rate and exempt supplies. There is no list of standard-rated supplies.

If a trader makes a supply you need to categorise that supply for VAT as follows:

Step 1 Consider if it is a zero-rated supply. If not;

Step 2 Consider if it is exempt. If not;

Step 3 Consider if it is reduced-rated supply. If not;

Step 4 The supply is standard-rated.

1.3 Zero-rated supplies

The following are some common items on the **zero-rated list**:

(a) Human and animal food
(b) Printed matter used for reading (eg books, newspapers) and e-books
(c) Construction work on new homes or the sale of the freehold, or a lease over 21 years (at least 20 years in Scotland), of new homes by builders
(d) Exports of goods
(e) Clothing and footwear for young children and certain protective clothing, eg motor cyclists' crash helmets

1.4 Exempt supplies

The following are some common items on the **exempt** list:

(a) Sales of freeholds of buildings (other than commercial buildings within three years from completion) and leaseholds of land and buildings of any age including a surrender of a lease
(b) Financial services
(c) Insurance

1.5 Reduced rate of VAT

Certain supplies are charged at **5%**. **As with the zero rate, these reduced rate supplies are still taxable supplies.**

The main supplies are:

(a) Supplies of fuel for domestic use
(b) Supplies of the services of installing energy saving materials to homes

1.6 Exceptions to the general rule

Although a general rule may apply to a particular category (eg that the supply of food is zero-rated), there are many exceptions to these general rules.

For example, the zero-rated list states human food is zero-rated. However, the legislation then states that food supplied in the course of catering (eg restaurant meals, hot takeaways) is standard-rated. Luxury items of food (eg crisps, peanuts, chocolate covered biscuits) are also standard-rated.

In the exempt list, we are told that financial services are exempt. However, the legislation then goes on to state that credit management and processing services are standard-rated. Investment advice is also standard-rated.

Great care must be taken when categorising goods or services as zero-rated, exempt or standard-rated. It is not as straightforward as it may first appear.

1.7 Standard-rated supplies

There is no list of standard-rated supplies. If a supply is not zero-rated, not reduced-rated and is not exempt then it is treated as standard-rated. The standard rate of VAT is 20%.

2 Land and buildings

> **FAST FORWARD** Transactions in land may be zero-rated, standard-rated or exempt.

2.1 Transactions in land

Transactions in land may be zero-rated, standard-rated or exempt.

(a) **The construction of new dwellings or buildings to be used for residential or charitable purposes is zero-rated. The definition of 'new' is the first grant of a major interest,** ie freehold or leasehold over 21 years.

(b) **The sale of the freehold of a 'new' commercial building is standard-rated. The definition of 'new' is less than three years old**. The construction of commercial buildings is also standard-rated.

(c) Other sales and most leases of land and buildings are exempt.

2.2 Option to tax

Owners may elect to treat sales and leases of land and commercial buildings as taxable instead of exempt. This is known as 'waiving the exemption' or making an option to tax.

The owner must become registered for VAT (if not already so registered) in order to make the election. The election replaces an exempt supply with a standard-rated one, usually to enable the recovery of input VAT.

A taxpayer may make a 'real estate election' (REE) instead of making separate elections for each property he owns. **If a taxpayer makes a REE, he will be treated as having made the election for each property he acquires after making the REE**, although he may revoke the option on a particular property under the 'cooling-off' provisions described below.

The election may be revoked:

(a) **During the 'cooling off' period**: within six months of the election taking effect, provided that no use (including own use) has been made of the land, no tax has been charged on a supply of the land as a result of the option, no TOGC has occurred and HMRC has been notified of the revocation on the appropriate form

(b) **Where no interest has been held in the property for over six years**

(c) **Where more than 20 years have elapsed since the election first had effect**, provided certain conditions are met or with the prior consent of HMRC

3 The deduction of input tax

> **FAST FORWARD** Not all input VAT is deductible, eg VAT on most motor cars.

3.1 Introduction

Input tax is deductible for supplies to a taxable person in the course of his business provided that (a) it relates to a taxable supply and (b) it does not relate to a specifically non-deductible item (see below).

3.2 Capital items

There is no distinction between capital and revenue expenditure for VAT. So, a manufacturer paying VAT on the purchase of plant to make taxable supplies will be able to obtain a credit for all the VAT immediately (but see below for the capital goods scheme).

3.3 Non-deductible input tax

The following input tax is not deductible:

(a) **VAT on motor cars** not used wholly for business purposes. VAT on cars is never reclaimable unless the car is acquired new for resale or is acquired for use in or leasing to a taxi business, a self-drive car hire business or a driving school (see below for treatment of motor expenses). **If VAT is not recoverable on a car because it is not used wholly for business purposes then VAT is not charged if the car is subsequently sold.**

(b) **VAT on business entertaining** where the cost of the entertaining is not a tax deductible trading expense unless the entertainment is of overseas customers in which case the input tax is deductible.

(c) **VAT on expenses incurred on domestic accommodation for directors or proprietors of a business.**

(d) **VAT on non-business items passed through the business accounts.** If goods are bought partly for business use the purchaser may:

   (i) Deduct all the input tax, and account for output tax in respect of the private use; or
   (ii) Deduct only the business proportion of the input tax.

3.4 Irrecoverable VAT

Where input tax on a purchase is not deductible for VAT purposes, the irrecoverable amount **is included in the cost of the associated expenditure for the purposes of income tax, corporation tax, capital allowance or capital gains computations.**

Deductible VAT, however, is not included in the cost of expenditure for these computations; the net amount should be used. Similarly, sales (and proceeds in chargeable gains computations) **are shown net of VAT**, because the VAT is paid over to HMRC.

3.5 Motoring expenses

3.5.1 Accessories and maintenance costs

Input VAT can be reclaimed if accessories for business use are fitted after the original purchase of a car and a separate invoice is raised. If a car is used for business purposes then any VAT charged on repair and maintenance costs can be treated as input tax.

3.5.2 Fuel

FAST FORWARD

If fuel is supplied for private purposes, all input VAT incurred on the fuel is allowed and the business will normally account for output VAT using a set of scale charges.

If a business pays for fuel which is only used for business purposes, it can claim all the input tax paid on that fuel. However, many businesses will pay for fuel which is used for private motoring by employees.

PART D VALUE ADDED TAX

If a business does provide fuel for private and business use to an employee but the employee reimburses the business the full cost of the private fuel, there is an actual taxable supply by the business valued at the amount received from that employee. The business can claim its input tax on all fuel, but then must account for output tax on the amount paid by the employee. HMRC will accept that the full cost of all private fuel has been reimbursed where a log is kept recording private miles and the employee pays a fuel-only mileage rate that covers the average fuel cost (on its website, HMRC publish a set of such rates for different sizes of engine).

If a business provides fuel to its employees for private use without charge or at a charge below the full cost, there is a deemed taxable supply. The business then has the following options for how to account for VAT on fuel:

(i) **Not to claim any input tax in respect of fuel** purchased by the business. **No output tax is charged.** In effect, the fuel is not brought into the VAT system at all.

(ii) **Claim input VAT only on the fuel purchased for business journeys.** This requires the business to keep detailed mileage records of business and private use. **No output tax is charged in respect of private use.** In effect, the private fuel is not brought into the VAT system.

(iii) **Claim input tax on all fuel purchased and charge output tax based either on the full cost of the private fuel supplied** (again, this requires detailed mileage records to be kept) **or the fuel scale charge which reflects the deemed output in respect of private use. The fuel scale charge is based on the CO_2 emissions of the car.**

Exam focus point

> In the Taxation exam, questions on the treatment of private use fuel will normally involve the use of the fuel scale charge.

The above rules apply **even where employees pay for the fuel themselves and the business reimburses them**: as long as the business obtains VAT invoices for the fuel, it can treat the fuel as its own purchase/input.

Exam focus point

> The scale figures can be found in Whillans tax tables on page 158

The output tax is the VAT inclusive scale charge × 1/6 or the VAT exclusive scale charge × 20% as appropriate.

Question — VAT and private use fuel

Iain is an employee of ABC Ltd. He has the use of a car with CO_2 emissions of 176g/km for one month and a car with CO_2 emissions of 208g/km for two months during the quarter ended 31 August.

ABC Ltd pay all the petrol costs in respect of both cars without requiring Iain to make any reimbursement in respect of private fuel. Total petrol costs for the quarter amount to £300 (including VAT). ABC Ltd wishes to use the fuel scale charge as detailed records of private mileage have not been kept.

What is the VAT effect of the above on ABC Ltd?

VAT Scale rates (VAT inclusive) for three month periods (assumed)

CO_2 emissions	£
175	437
205	544

Answer

Value for the quarter:

	£
Car 1	
£437 × 1/3 =	146
Car 2	
£544 × 2/3 =	363
	509
Output tax:	
1/6 × £509	85
Input tax:	
1/6 × £300	50

3.6 Relief for impairment losses (bad debts)

FAST FORWARD

Relief for VAT on impairment losses (bad debts) is available if the VAT has been accounted for, the debt is over six months old (measured from when the payment is due) and has been written off in the trader's accounts.

A trader may claim a refund of VAT on amounts unpaid by debtors if:

(a) The VAT has been accounted for to HMRC;
(b) The debt is over six months old; and
(c) The debt has been written off in the creditor's accounts.

If the debtor later pays all (or part) of the amount owed, the corresponding amount of VAT repaid must be paid back to HMRC.

Claims for relief must be made within four years of the time the debt became eligible for relief (in other words, within four years and six months from when the payment was due).

4 Imports, exports, acquisitions and dispatches

FAST FORWARD

In general, imports to the UK are subject to VAT at the rate applicable to the goods being imported and exports to outside the UK are zero-rated. However, there is an important exception that applies where a trader imports or exports goods between Northern Ireland and an EU country. This exception is considered in more detail below.

4.1 Introduction

Exam focus point

The UK left the EU on 31 December 2020, which resulted in changes to the VAT treatment of imports and exports between the UK and EU countries. Taxation exams in 2025 will require you to apply the rules that came into effect on 1 January 2021.

The terms **import and export** refer to purchases and sales of goods with countries **outside the UK**.

The terms **acquisition and dispatch** refer to purchases and sales of goods between countries **in the EU** and traders in Northern Ireland. These will not be tested in Taxation UK exams in 2025.

4.2 Place of supply

The place of supply of goods and services is important because it determines how the supply is treated for VAT. For example, if a supply is made in the UK, it is subject to the rules and rates of UK VAT.

If the supply is a **supply of goods**, it will be treated as **made in the UK if the goods are in the UK at the time they are supplied**. Similarly, a supply of goods which are not in the UK when they are supplied will not be treated as made in the UK and so will not be subject to UK output tax.

If the supply is a **supply of services**, the basic rule for services made to a **VAT registered business** (B2B supplies) is that the **supply is made where the customer has established his business**.

The basic rule for **supplies of services to other consumers** (B2C supplies) **is that the supply is made where the supplier has established his business**. There are some exceptions to this rule. For example, certain services relating to land are treated as made where the land is located.

4.3 Trade in goods outside the UK

4.3.1 Imports

The rules explained in this section apply to imports to Great Britain from outside the UK and to imports to Northern Ireland from outside the EU. We will look in a later section at the rules applicable to goods imported to Northern Ireland from EU countries.

As we saw in an earlier part of this Workbook, the rate of UK VAT that applies to goods is determined by the nature of the goods. If goods are imported into Great Britain from outside the UK, VAT will apply at the same rate as if the goods were being supplied domestically. For example, an import of food products would be zero-rated for VAT.

Special rules apply to imports where the value of the consignment of goods is no more than £135. These rules shift the requirement to account for VAT from the point of import to the point of sale:

- **If the goods are sold to a UK consumer** (ie a buyer who is not VAT registered in the UK) by an overseas seller, the seller must register for VAT in the UK and account for the applicable VAT to HMRC.

- **If the goods are sold to a UK consumer through an Online Marketplace (OMP)**, the OMP must register and account for the VAT on the price.

- **If the goods are sold to a UK VAT registered customer by an overseas seller**, the purchaser will account for the applicable VAT using the reverse charge mechanism.

If the value of a consignment exceeds £135:

- **If the goods are sold to a UK consumer**, import VAT is payable by the importer (for the purposes of the Taxation exam, we will assume that the importer is the seller) at the point of entry to the UK or when the goods are delivered to the customer.

- **If the goods are sold to a UK VAT registered business** (and the purchasing business provides the overseas seller with its VAT registration number), the UK purchaser is responsible for accounting for the import VAT in its tax return under the reverse charge mechanism. This is sometimes referred to as 'postponed accounting' because the VAT does not have to be paid until the VAT payment date for the relevant return period, which is likely to be a considerable time after the date of import.

4.3.2 Exports

The export of goods from Great Britain to a destination outside the UK are zero-rated. The export of goods from Northern Ireland to a destination outside the EU are also zero-rated. We will look in the next section at the treatment of goods exported from Northern Ireland to the EU.

In order to apply the zero-rating, the trader must provide evidence of the export, such as copy invoices and consignment notes.

4.4 Trade in goods between Northern Ireland and the European Union

4.4.1 Purchases (acquisitions)

The Northern Ireland Protocol means that the following basic rules continue to apply to UK purchasers receiving goods in Northern Ireland (which is treated as an EU country for this purpose only):

(a) When a VAT registered business in one EU country supplies goods to a VAT registered business in another EU country, the supply is zero-rated in the country of origin and the customer accounts for VAT on the 'acquisition' in the destination country. The transaction is entered on the relevant VAT return as an output *and* an input so, assuming the trader meets the normal requirements for being able to recover input tax in full, the effect is neutral. Thus the trader is in the same position as they would have been if they had acquired the goods from a UK supplier.

(b) If the customer cannot provide a VAT number (for example, because it is not VAT registered), the supplier must charge VAT in the country of origin.

Supplies between Great Britain and Northern Ireland should, in general, be treated in the same way as any other domestic supply in the UK. However, special rules apply to goods which are sold from Great Britain to Northern Ireland for onward supply into the EU. You do not need to know the special rules about GB to NI supplies for the Taxation exam.

The Taxation exams in 2025 assume the EU comprises Austria, Belgium, Bulgaria, Croatia, the Czech Republic, Republic of Cyprus, Denmark, Estonia, Finland, France, Germany, Greece, Hungary, Ireland, Italy, Latvia, Lithuania, Luxembourg, Malta, the Netherlands, Poland, Portugal, Romania, Slovakia, Slovenia, Spain and Sweden.

4.4.2 Sales (dispatches)

Where goods are sold from Northern Ireland to a customer in an EU member state, the supply is described as a 'dispatch' rather than an export. The supply is zero-rated if the following conditions are satisfied:

- **The goods are sent out of the UK from Northern Ireland to an EU country**
- **The supply is made to a VAT registered trader**
- **The supplier quotes his customer's VAT number on the invoice**
- **The supplier holds evidence that the goods were delivered to another member state**

If these conditions are not satisfied, the trader must charge VAT in the same way as for a supply to a customer within the same member state as the trader.

4.5 International services

FAST FORWARD

International services between VAT registered businesses require the customer to account for both output and input tax under the reverse charge rules. Output tax on other international services is usually accounted for by the supplier in the usual way.

As we have seen, **B2B services are treated as supplied in the place where the customer has established their business. Where the supply is treated as made in the UK under these rules, the UK business customer must apply the 'reverse charge'. This means that the UK business charges itself output tax which it recovers as input tax in the normal way.** This means that the foreign supplier has no obligation to register for VAT in the UK or to charge UK VAT on such supplies. Instead, the customer is required to account for VAT.

If the customer is not registered for VAT, the purchase of the services counts as a deemed supply in measuring the registerable turnover for the customer. This might lead to the customer becoming liable to register for VAT.

If the business customer only makes taxable supplies, the overall effect of the reverse charge will normally be tax-neutral as the output tax and input tax will cancel each other out. However, if the business customer is partially exempt, not all of the input tax may be recoverable and so the reverse charge will lead to a net payment of output tax.

The tax point for a single supply to which the reverse charge applies is the earlier of:

- **The time the service is completed**
- **The time the service is paid for**

If the supply is continuous, the tax point will be the end of each billing or payment period, Where the service is not subject to billing or payment periods, the tax point will be 31 December each year unless a payment has already been made, in which case the tax point will be the date of the payment.

For B2C services, the supply will be made by the supplier where he has established his business and the supplier will charge output tax in the normal way. No input tax is recoverable on B2C supplies since, by definition, the consumer is not a VAT registered business.

Chapter roundup

- Some supplies are taxable (either standard-rated, reduced-rated or zero-rated). Others are exempt.
- Transactions in land may be zero-rated, standard-rated or exempt.
- Not all input VAT is deductible, eg VAT on most motor cars.
- If fuel is supplied for private purposes, all input VAT incurred on the fuel is allowed and the business will normally account for output VAT using a set of scale charges.
- Relief for VAT on impairment losses (bad debts) is available if the VAT has been accounted for, the debt is over six months old (measured from when the payment is due) and has been written off in the trader's accounts.
- Imports from outside the UK are subject to UK VAT and exports to outside the UK are zero-rated. An exception applies where the trader is in Northern Ireland, in which case purchases from EU states are treated as taxable acquisitions from other EU states and are also subject to VAT, and sales to registered traders in other EU states are zero-rated.
- International services between VAT registered businesses require the customer to account for both output and input tax under the reverse charge rules. Output tax on other international services is usually accounted for by the supplier in the usual way.

Quick quiz

1. What input tax is never deductible?
2. What relief is available for bad debts?
3. Are goods exported from the UK standard-rated or zero-rated?
4. Mr Higgins is registered for VAT in the UK. He only makes taxable supplies. Mr Higgins is supplied with services by a French business on 1 December 2024. The value of the supply is £50,000. What are the VAT consequences of the supply?

PART D VALUE ADDED TAX

Answers to quick quiz

1. VAT on:
    - Motor cars (where there is an element of private use)
    - Business entertaining (UK customers)
    - Expenses incurred on domestic accommodation for directors
    - Non-business items passed through the accounts

2. Where a supplier has accounted for VAT on a supply and the customer fails to pay, then the supplier may, after six months, write it off in the accounts and claim a refund of the VAT.

3. In general, exports from the UK are zero-rated.

    If a VAT-registered trader is supplying goods from Northern Ireland to an EU country (referred to as a dispatch) then:

    - The supply will be zero-rated in the UK if the purchaser is VAT registered in the destination country and provides the seller with its VAT registration number. The purchaser will account for VAT in the destination country.

    - If the purchaser is not VAT registered, the seller must account for VAT at the appropriate rate in the country of origin.

4. Mr Higgins will have to account for output tax of £50,000 × 20% = £10,000 on the supply and also £10,000 of input tax. The reverse charge is therefore tax neutral for him.

Stamp Taxes

Topic list
1 Stamp duty
2 Stamp duty reserve tax
3 Stamp taxes on land and buildings
4 Exemptions relating to stamp taxes

Introduction

In this chapter we look at stamp taxes, which are payable by a purchaser when they buy shares or land.

The next chapter is the last one and we will have a look at Ethics.

PART D VALUE ADDED TAX

Exam guide

Stamp taxes will make up a minor part of a question but still present an opportunity to earn valuable marks and, in practice, must not be overlooked as they can constitute a significant cost in many transactions.

1 Stamp duty

> Stamp duty applies to the transfers of shares and securities effected by a paper stock transfer form. See Whillans p.143.

Stamp duty applies to **transfers of shares and securities** which are effected by a paper **stock transfer form**. It is payable by the **purchaser**.

Stamp duty applies at a **rate of 0.5% of the consideration** unless the consideration is ≤ £1,000, or the transfer falls within one of the specific exemptions (see later in this chapter). The duty is rounded up to the nearest £5.

Stamp duty is administered by HMRC Stamp Taxes.

Stamp duty is payable on presentation of the stock transfer form to HMRC which must be **within 30 days of the transaction**.

Interest may be charged if stamp duty is paid late (unless the interest is less than £25). The interest period runs from the end of the 30-day period above to the day before payment.

Penalties may also be payable. The baseline penalties are as set out below rounded down to the nearest £5 (and not charged if less than £20). Additional penalties may be due where there is evidence of a deliberate failure to present documents for stamping and the delay is over 12 months.

Length of delay	Penalty
Up to 12 months	10% of duty capped at £300
12 to 24 months	20% of the duty
Over 24 months	30% of the duty

2 Stamp duty reserve tax (SDRT)

> Stamp duty reserve tax applies to the transfers of shares and securities effected by an electronic paperless transaction. See Whillans p.144.

Stamp duty reserve tax (SDRT) is applicable to **transfers of shares and securities** which are effected by an **electronic paperless transaction**. It is payable by the **purchaser**.

Most of these transactions are made through an **electronic system** called **CREST**. Some shares are held outside CREST ('Off Market') but may still be transferred electronically, for example if they are held by a nominee such as a bank.

SDRT applies at a **rate of 0.5% of the consideration** unless the transfer falls within one of the specific exemptions (see later in this chapter). The duty is rounded up to the nearest penny.

SDRT is administered by HMRC Stamp Taxes but is collected automatically by the stockbrokers and is payable on the 7th day of the month following the month the sale is agreed.

Penalties for not filing returns or late payment of SDRT are under the common penalty regime. Interest is also charged on unpaid SDRT.

3 Stamp taxes on land and buildings

FAST FORWARD Stamp duty land tax (SDLT) applies to land transactions in England and Northern Ireland. Similar taxes are called Land and Buildings Transaction Tax (LBTT) in Scotland, and Land Transaction Tax (LTT) in Wales. See Whillans pp.137–142.

Exams in 2025 will be based on the relevant thresholds and rates in operation from the autumn 2022. Earlier rates will not be tested.

3.1 England and Northern Ireland

A land transaction is a transfer of land or an interest in, or right over, land. SDLT is generally payable based on the consideration of the land transaction. It is payable by the purchaser. The amount of the SDLT depends on whether the land is residential (eg house, flats) or non-residential (eg shops, warehouse, factories).

The rate is applied to the VAT inclusive purchase price where appropriate.

Both the duty and the relevant forms are due within 14 days of the transaction.

SDLT: residential property rates

Portion of value £	Rate %	Additional property rate %
0–250,000	0	3*
250,001–925,000	5	8
925,001–1,500,000	10	13
1,500,001 and over	12	15

* The additional residential property rate supplement only applies to transactions in residential property with a value of £40,000 or more.

The **additional property** rate applies to individuals who already own a residential property and to companies.

An additional 2% surcharge applies to the above rates for residential properties purchased by **non-residents**.

Where all buyers in the transaction are **first-time buyers** and the purchase price is no more than £625,000, the nil rate threshold is £425,000.

SDLT: non-residential or mixed property rates

Portion of value £	Rate %
0–150,000	0
150,001–250,000	2
250,001 and over	5

Exam focus point You will find all the rates of stamp taxes in Whillans tax tables.

PART D VALUE ADDED TAX

Question — Non-residential property

James buys an investment residential property for £725,000 in January 2025. He already owns a number of other properties.

Charlotte buys a flat to live in for £450,000 in November 2024. Charlotte is a first-time buyer.

Raymond buys a freehold shop in England in November 2024 for £145,000.

Klear plc buys a freehold factory in Northern Ireland in August 2024 for £350,000.

How much stamp duty land tax is payable in each case?

Answer

James:

	£
£250,000 × 3%	7,500
£475,000 (£725,000 – 250,000) × 8%	38,000
	45,500

Charlotte:

£25,000 (£450,000 – 425,000) × 5% = £1,250

Raymond:

£145,000 × 0% = £0

Klear plc:

	£
£150,000 × 0%	0
£100,000 (£250,000 – 150,000) × 2%	2,000
£100,000 (£350,000 – 250,000) × 5%	5,000
	7,000

3.2 Scotland and Wales

The devolved governments of Scotland and Wales have the power to set their own rates of tax. The calculation of stamp duty on transfers of land and buildings is very similar to those in England and Northern Ireland but with different rates and thresholds. These are set out below and can be found in Whillans (pp.141–143).

Residential property rates

LBTT (Scotland) Portion of value	Rate	Additional Dwelling Supplement
£	%	%
0–145,000*	0	6 **
145,001*–250,000	2	8
250,001–325,000	5	11
325,001–750,000	10	16
750,001 and over	12	18

* £175,000/£175,001 for first-time buyers

** The additional dwelling supplement only applies to transactions in residential property where the purchaser's interest in the property is £40,000 or more.

The Additional Dwelling Supplement apply in a similar way to the Additional Property Rate for SDLT ie on additional properties or those purchased by companies.

The LTT (Wales) rates for residential property operate in a similar way to LBTT (Scotland) and SDLT (England and NI) except that there are different thresholds in Wales for the main rate and the higher rate. The higher rate with its own thresholds are used where the purchaser of residential property already owns a residential property.

LTT (Wales) Portion of value	Main Rate	LTT (Wales) Portion of value	Higher residential rate)
£	%	£	%
0–225,000	0	0–180,000	4%*
225,001–400,000	6	180,001–250,000	7.5%
400,001–750,000	7.5	250,001–400,000	9%
750,001–1,500,000	10	400,001–750,000	11.5%
1,500,001 and over	12	750,001–1,500,000	14%
		Over 1,500,000	16%

* The higher residential rate only applies to transactions in residential property with a value of £40,000 or more.

Non-residential or mixed property rates

LBTT (Scotland) Portion of value £	Rate %	LTT (Wales) Portion of value £	Rate %
0–150,000	0	0–225,000	0
150,001–250,000	1	225,001–250,000	1
250,001 and over	5	250,001–1,000,000	5
		1,000,001 and over	6

3.3 Administration

3.3.1 England and Northern Ireland

SDLT is administered by HMRC Stamp Taxes. An SDLT return must be submitted to **HMRC** by the purchaser who must also pay any tax due within **14 days** after the effective date of the transaction. An SDLT return must be submitted even if there is no SDLT payable.

Interest is charged on late payments from the end of the 14-day period to the day before SDLT is paid. A penalty may also be imposed if the SDLT return is submitted late (Whillans p.147):

- £100 if up to three months late
- £200 if over three months late
- Tax geared based on SDLT due if over twelve months late.

3.3.2 Wales and Scotland

LBTT returns must be submitted to **Revenue Scotland** by the purchaser who must also pay any tax due within **30 days** of the day after the transaction date. Penalties are due for late submission of returns and late payment.

If the return is late, the following penalties apply (Whillans p.16):

- £100 on the day after the date on which the tax return was due
- After three months, daily penalties of £10 per day for 90 additional days
- After six months, a further penalty of £300 or 5% of the tax liability (whichever is greater)
- After 12 months, a second further penalty of the greater of £300 or 5% of the tax liability or £300 or 100% of the tax liability if the taxpayer has deliberately withheld information

If tax is paid late, the following penalties apply (Whillans p.18):

- An initial penalty of 5% of the unpaid tax
- A second penalty of 5% of the unpaid tax after five months
- A third penalty of 5% of the unpaid tax after 11 months

LTT returns must be submitted to the **Welsh Revenue Authority** by the purchaser who must also pay any tax due within a **30 days period starting on the day after the transaction date**. Penalties are due for late submission of returns and late payment.

If the return is late, the following penalties apply (Whillans p.148 and p.16):

- Up to six months overdue, a penalty of £100
- Between six and 12 months overdue, an additional penalty of £300 or 5% of the unpaid tax, whichever is greater
- Over 12 months, a further penalty of £300 or 5% of the unpaid tax, whichever is greater
- If the taxpayer has deliberately withheld information to prevent tax from being assessed, a penalty of £300 or 95% of the tax liability may be applied

If the tax is paid late, the following penalties apply (Whillans p.148):

- An initial penalty of 5% of the unpaid tax
- More than six months overdue (starting 30 days before the date stated on the taxpayer's penalty notice), 5% of the unpaid tax
- More than 12 months overdue, an additional 5% of the unpaid tax

4 Exemptions relating to stamp taxes

> **FAST FORWARD** Transfers with no consideration are exempt from stamp taxes.

4.1 Transfers with no consideration

Stamp taxes are charged on the consideration passing under the document or transaction. If there is no consideration, there is an exemption from stamp taxes. Examples include:

(a) **Gifts** (except a gift of land to a connected company)
(b) A **transfer on divorce**, annulment of marriage or judicial separation
(c) **Variations of a will or intestacy** made within two years of death for no consideration
(d) Transfers to **charities** if the shares or land is to be used for charitable purposes

Question — Stamp duty relief

James gifts 200 shares in DHC Ltd to each of his three children on 5 April 2025. The shares are worth £20 each.

Explain the stamp duty implications.

Answer

There is no stamp duty payable as these are gifts with no consideration.

PART D   VALUE ADDED TAX

Chapter roundup

- Stamp duty applies to transfers of shares and securities transferred by a stock transfer form. It is 0.5% of the consideration (rounded up to the nearest £5) and is paid by the purchaser.
- Stamp duty reserve tax applies to electronic transfers of shares and securities. It is 0.5% of the consideration and is paid by the purchaser.
- Stamp duty land tax applies to the sale of land, or of rights over land, in England and Northern Ireland. Equivalent but separate taxes apply in Scotland (Land and Buildings Transaction Tax) and Wales (Land Transaction Tax). It is calculated based on the consideration using the rates and thresholds in the tax tables and is paid by the purchaser.
- There are exemptions for stamp taxes when the transfer does not involve consideration, such as a gift.

Quick quiz

1   Shona sells her shares in X Ltd to Helen for £49,650. A stock transfer form is used to effect the transfer. Calculate the stamp duty and state by whom it is payable.

2   Tom sells his house located in England to Edward for £380,000. Calculate the SDLT payable by Edward if he owns no other property.

3   Charlotte buys a house in Northern Ireland from Zelda for £780,000. She already owns her own home and Charlotte intends to use this new one as a holiday house. Calculate the SDLT payable by Charlotte.

4   Z Ltd buys a small industrial unit located in Wales from Y Ltd for £260,000. Calculate the LTT due and state by whom it is payable.

5   Howard buys some shares on 22 April 2024. When is the stamp duty due?

6   List four examples of transactions which are exempt from stamp duty.

Answers to quick quiz

1. £49,650 × 0.5% = £248 rounded up to £250, payable by Helen.

2.
	£
£250,000 × 0%	0
£130,000 (£380,000 – 250,000) × 5%	6,500
£380,000	6,500

3.
	£
£250,000 × 3%	7,500
£530,000 (£780,000 – 250,000) × 8%	42,400
£780,000	49,900

4.
	£
£225,000 × 0%	0
£25,000 (£250,000 – 225,000) × 1%	250
£10,000 (£260,000 – 250,000) × 5%	500
£260,000	750

   Payable by Z Ltd

5. Within 30 days of 22 April 2024.

6. Gifts (except a gift of land to a connected company)

   A transfer on divorce, annulment of marriage or judicial separation

   Variations of a will or intestacy made within two years of death for no consideration

   Transfers to charities if the shares or land is to be used for charitable purposes

PART D VALUE ADDED TAX

Ethics

Ethics

Topic list
1 Introduction
2 The fundamental principals, threats and resolutions
3 Tax planning, avoidance and evasion
4 Tax planning standards
5 Client take-on procedures
6 HMRC/client/adviser relationships
7 Conflicts of interest
8 Fees
9 Confidentiality
10 Data protection
11 Money laundering issues

Introduction

You have now completed your studies of the individual taxes covered in the syllabus so we will now consider the rules that apply when you use your tax knowledge. In this chapter, we look at the ethical rules which should be applied to every situation that you are required to consider.

PART E ETHICS

Exam guide

You may be asked to discuss relevant ethical issues as part of any question.

1 Introduction

In common with most professional organisations, the AIA require members and students to observe the highest professional standards in all aspects of their work. This section discusses how these standards can be maintained, with particular reference to taxation work. The requirements apply equally to members and students and, in this section, the term 'members' should be taken to include students.

In addition to the AIA's own requirements, there are many instances where **members are required to comply with statutory and regulatory requirements imposed by the Government**. If a member is in doubt as to the course of action they should take, they should approach the AIA for guidance. **Failure to observe the AIA's standards may result in disciplinary action**.

The AIA publish a **Code of Ethics and Conduct** covering the standards and ethical requirements which they expect. It details the **fundamental principles and sets out a framework for applying those principles**. Members must apply this framework to particular situations to identify instances where compliance with the ethical standards may be compromised so that safeguards may be put in place to avoid threats, or to reduce them to below the minimum level that can be regarded as acceptable.

Normally, a member's responsibility will be to a client, or to an employer, but there may be instances where a member may need to act in the public interest.

2 The fundamental principles, threats and resolutions

2.1 The fundamental principles

FAST FORWARD The fundamental principles of ethics should underlie all of a member's professional behaviour.

The fundamental principles are:

(a) **Integrity**: Requires all members to be straightforward and honest in professional and business relationships.

A member should not be associated with information if they believe that the information contains a materially false or misleading statement, statements or information furnished recklessly, or omits or obscures information required to be included where such omission or obscurity would be misleading.

(b) **Objectivity**: Imposes an obligation on members not to compromise their professional or business judgement because of bias, conflict of interest or the undue influence of others.

Relationships that bias or unduly influence the professional judgement of the member should be avoided.

(c) **Professional competence and due care**: Requires members to

(i) Maintain professional knowledge and skill at the level required to ensure that clients or employers receive competent professional service based on current developments in practice, legislation and techniques

(ii) Act diligently in accordance with applicable technical and professional standards when providing professional services

Any limitations relating to the service being provided must be made clear to clients and other users to ensure that misinterpretation of facts or opinions does not take place.

(d) **Confidentiality**: Imposes an obligation on members to refrain from

   (i) Disclosing outside the firm confidential information acquired as a result of professional and business relationships without proper and specific authority or unless there is a legal or professional right or duty to disclose

   (ii) Using confidential information acquired as a result of professional and business relationships to their personal advantage or the advantage of third parties

   A member should consider the need to maintain confidentiality of information within the firm. A member should also maintain confidentiality of information disclosed by a prospective client or employer.

   The need to maintain confidentiality continues even after the end of relationships between a member and a client or employer. When a member changes employment or acquires a new client, the member is entitled to use prior experience, but not confidential information obtained from the previous relationship.

(e) **Professional behaviour**. Imposes an obligation on a member to comply with relevant laws and regulations and avoid any action that may bring discredit to the profession.

   This includes actions which a reasonable and informed third party, having knowledge of all relevant information, would conclude negatively affects the good reputation of the profession.

   Members should be honest and truthful and should not:

   (i) Make exaggerated claims for the services they are able to offer, the qualifications they possess, or experience they have gained

   (ii) Make disparaging references or unsubstantiated comparisons to the work of others

2.2 The conceptual framework

2.2.1 Introduction

A member may find himself in a situation where there is a **specific threat to compliance with the fundamental principles**. There are many possible scenarios, and rather than trying to specify how each situation should be dealt with, the AIA provide a conceptual framework that requires members to identify, evaluate and address such threats. Unless an identified threat is clearly insignificant, members should apply safeguards to eliminate the threat or reduce it to an acceptable level so that compliance with the fundamental principles is not compromised.

2.2.2 Threats

The member is obliged to evaluate any threat as soon as they know, or should be expected to know, of its existence. Both qualitative and quantitative factors should be taken into account.

Most threats to compliance with the fundamental principles fall into the following categories:

(a) **Self-interest threat**, which may occur as a result of the financial or other interests of a member or of an immediate or close family member

(b) **Self-review threat**, which may occur when a previous judgment needs to be re-evaluated by the member responsible for that judgment

(c) **Advocacy threat**, which may occur when a member promotes a position or opinion to the point that subsequent objectivity may be compromised

(d) **Familiarity threats**, which may occur when, because of a close relationship, a member becomes too sympathetic to the interests of others

(e) **Intimidation threats**, which may occur when a member may be deterred from acting objectively by threats, actual or perceived

2.2.3 Safeguards to offset the threats

If a member cannot implement appropriate safeguards, they should decline or discontinue the specific professional service involved, or where necessary resign from the client.

Safeguards that may eliminate or reduce threats to an acceptable level fall into two broad categories:

(a) **Safeguards created by the profession, legislation or regulation**, such as education and training, continuing professional development, professional or regulatory monitoring and disciplinary procedures

(b) **Safeguards in the work environment**, such as effective, well publicised complaints systems operated by the employing organisation

The nature of the safeguards to be applied will vary depending on the circumstances. In exercising professional judgment, a member should consider what a reasonable and informed third party, having knowledge of all relevant information, including the significance of the threat and the safeguards applied, would conclude to be unacceptable.

2.3 Ethical conflict resolution

There may be instances where a particular situation leads to a **conflict in the application of the fundamental principles**.

When initiating either a formal or informal conflict resolution process, a member should consider five factors:

(a) **Relevant facts**
(b) **Ethical issues**
(c) **Fundamental principles related to the matter**
(d) **Established internal procedures**
(e) **Alternative courses of action**

Having considered these issues, the appropriate course of action can be determined which resolves the conflict with all or some of the five fundamental principles. If the matter remains unresolved, the member should consult with other appropriate persons within the firm for help in obtaining resolution.

Where a matter involves a conflict with, or within, an organisation, a member should also consider consulting with those charged with governance of the organisation.

It is advisable for the member to **document the issue and details of any discussions held or decisions taken, concerning that issue**.

If a significant conflict cannot be resolved, a member may wish to obtain **professional advice from the AIA or legal advisors**, to obtain guidance on ethical and legal issues without breaching confidentiality.

If, after exhausting all relevant possibilities, **the ethical conflict remains unresolved, a member should, where possible, refuse to remain associated with the matter creating the conflict.**

The member may determine that, in the circumstances, it is appropriate to withdraw from the engagement team or specific assignment, or to resign altogether from the engagement or the firm.

3 Tax planning, avoidance and evasion

FAST FORWARD

Tax planning is legal and is used by taxpayers to minimise their tax.
Tax avoidance is also legal, but may nevertheless be unacceptable to HMRC.
Tax evasion is illegal and could lead to prosecution for both taxpayer and accountant.

3.1 Tax planning

Taxpayers may try to minimise their tax liabilities by the use of legislation. For example setting off an annual exemption against gains in the most beneficial way, or minimising the tax paid on savings by using an ISA.

3.2 Tax avoidance

In the past, the terms tax planning and tax avoidance have been used interchangeably. However, over recent years tax avoidance has been taken to imply a bending of the rules in a way not intended by the legislation. If a tax relief is used excessively or aggressively by those not intended to use it, then it is likely to be challenged by HMRC.

In general, the more complex and artificial a transaction appears to be, the more aggressive the avoidance becomes, and the less likely it is to succeed.

3.3 Tax evasion

Tax evasion is illegal. It consists of **seeking to mislead HMRC** by either:

- suppressing information to which HMRC is entitled, or
- providing HMRC with deliberately false information.

3.3.1 Discovery of errors

A member may discover that a client has committed a taxation offence. Tax legislation prescribes monetary penalties for a number of offences. There is also the possibility of criminal proceedings being brought against the client.

The evasion or attempted evasion of tax may be the subject of criminal charges under both tax law and money laundering legislation. This applies not only to direct taxes such as income tax or corporation tax, but also to indirect taxes such as VAT.

The member has the following responsibilities:

(a) If the information obtained concerns computations or returns that the member is currently preparing, the member must ensure that the information is accurately reflected therein. **If the client fails to provide any information requested by the member, or objects to way in which the member has presented the information, the member needs to consider whether they can continue to act for that client.**

(b) If the information obtained concerns computations or returns that the member has already prepared and submitted to HMRC, the member cannot allow HMRC to continue to rely on them. They **should advise their client to make full disclosure to HMRC, or to authorise them to do so, without delay. If the client refuses, then the member can no longer act for the client.** The client should be advised of this, and also that the member must inform HMRC that they have ceased to act for the client. If the documents submitted to HMRC contain any accountant's report, the member must also advise HMRC that the report should no longer be relied on. The member should not, however, advise HMRC in what way the accounts are defective unless the client has consented to such disclosure.

(c) If the information relates to a new client and concerns computations or returns that have been prepared by the client or a third party and submitted to HMRC, the member should advise the client to make full and prompt disclosure. If the error affects the current computations or returns then the member must inform the client that an appropriate adjustment must be made in the current accounts, and **if the client refuses the member should consider whether they should act for that client**. Indeed, even if the error does not affect current returns and computations the member should consider whether they should act for the client if the client refuses to disclose the error to HMRC.

Whether or not the member feels able to act for a client, they are still under a **professional duty to ensure that the client understands the seriousness of offences against HMRC**. They should also warn the client that notification that they are no longer acting for a client may alert HMRC, and urge the desirability of making a full disclosure, subject to any legal advice obtained. Any accounts, returns, computations or reports submitted on behalf of taxpayers are deemed to be submitted by the taxpayer and/or with their consent unless they prove otherwise.

This emphasises the need for members to ensure that clients have approved computations and returns, and signified their approval by signing them. There should always be a letter of engagement in place setting out the precise responsibilities of both the member and the client.

3.3.2 Example

You are preparing the tax return for Mrs Y and amongst her papers you find a bank statement for a new account which was opened with the transfer of a significant amount from her own account. Mrs Y says that this new account belongs to her young son, and that the interest should not be put on her tax return. What should you do?

First you should explain that income from funds provided by a parent are taxed as the parent's income, unless the income is less that £100, so that the interest must be shown. If Mrs Y still refuses to enter the interest on her return you should advise her that you can no longer act for her, and you must also advise HMRC that you no longer act. You are not obliged to disclose the reason to HMRC.

At this stage you have a suspicion that a tax offence may be committed, and you should discuss this with your firm's money laundering reporting officer.

4 Tax planning standards

Professional Conduct in Relation to Taxation (PCRT) has developed an additional five standards which professional accountants must observe when advising on tax planning. These supplement the Fundamental Principles, they are not a substitute for them.

The five standards are:

4.1 Client specific

Tax planning must be specific to the particular client's facts and circumstance. Clients must be alerted to the wider risks and the implications of any courses of action.

4.2 Lawful

At all times members must act lawfully and with integrity and expect the same from their clients. Tax planning should be based on a realistic assessment of the facts and on a credible view of the law. Members should draw their clients' attention to where the law is materially uncertain, for example because HMRC is known to take a different view of the law. Members should consider taking further advice appropriate to the risks and circumstances of the particular case, for example where litigation is likely.

4.3 Disclosure and transparency

Tax advice must not rely for its effectiveness on HMRC having less than the relevant facts. Any disclosure must fairly represent all relevant facts.

4.4 Tax planning arrangement

Members must not create, encourage, or promote tax planning arrangements or structures that:

(i) set out to achieve results that are contrary to the clear intention of Parliament in enacting relevant legislation; and/or

(ii) are highly artificial or highly contrived and seek to exploit shortcomings within the relevant legislation.

4.5 Professional judgement and appropriate documentation

Applying these requirements to particular client advisory situations requires members to exercise professional judgement on a number of matters. Members should keep notes on a timely basis of the rationale for the judgments exercised in seeking to adhere to these requirements.

5 Client take-on procedures

Members invited to act as tax advisers by clients must **contact the existing tax advisers** to ascertain if there are any matters they should be aware of when deciding whether to accept the appointment.

5.1 Acceptance

Before accepting a new client, members should consider whether acceptance of the client or the particular engagement would create any threats to compliance with the fundamental principles.

Potential threats to integrity or professional behaviour may be created from, for example, questionable issues associated with the client, or a threat to professional competence and due care may be created if the engagement team does not possess the necessary skills to carry out the engagement. Where it is not possible to implement safeguards to reduce the threats to an acceptable level, members should decline to enter into the relationship.

There are also client identification procedures to be followed (see later in this chapter).

5.2 Changes in professional appointment

Members who are asked to replace another accountant should ascertain whether there are any professional or other reasons for not accepting the engagement. This may require direct communication with the existing accountant to establish the facts and circumstances behind the proposed change so that members can decide whether it is appropriate to accept the engagement.

Communication with the existing accountant is not just a matter of professional courtesy. Its main purpose is to enable members to ensure that there has been no action by the client which would on ethical grounds, preclude members from accepting the appointment and that, after considering all the facts, the client is someone for whom members would wish to act. Thus, members must always communicate with the existing accountant on being asked to accept appointment for any recurring work.

The existing accountant is bound by confidentiality. This means the extent to which a client's affairs may be discussed with a prospective accountant will depend on the nature of the engagement and on whether the client's permission has been obtained. **If the client refuses permission, the existing accountant should inform the prospective accountant, who should then inform the client that they are unable to accept the appointment.**

If the existing accountant fails to communicate with the prospective accountant despite the client's permission, the prospective accountant will need to make other enquiries to ensure there are no reasons not to accept the appointment. This could be through communications with third parties, such as banks.

Where the member is the existing accountant then, subject to obtaining the client's permission, they should disclose all information requested without delay.

5.3 Example

You have acted for Mr X. but have discovered a serious tax irregularity which Mr X has refused to correct and you have advised Mr X that you can no longer act for him. You receive a letter from another AIA member advising you that he has been asked to act for Mr X. Mr X has forbidden you to divulge any information to him. What should you do?

You should advise the new accountant that Mr X has not given you permission to divulge any information. The new accountant should then refuse to act for Mr X.

5.4 Responsibility for tax returns

Where you are performing tax compliance work, eg preparing and submitting tax returns, you will be acting as agent to the client. This means that the client remains responsible under tax legislation for all of the information provided in the return. The client may be able to take civil legal action for harm caused by a negligent tax advisor but this will not change the underlying tax liability to HMRC.

5.5 Tax planning concerns

At the very least: **anything you recommend must be legal**. There is a difference between tax avoidance (seeking to reduce tax liabilities in ways that are legal) and tax evasion (illegal, such as fraud). Apart from the specific rules regarding disclosure of avoidance schemes (see below), you must understand that the taxpayer has the responsibility of preparing a tax return that is complete and correct (see above), and this will include an accurate disclosure of the facts.

That is not to say that you may not suggest a course of action where HMRC might disagree with your conclusion as to the tax consequences. You need to explain to the client that full details must be given to enable HMRC to consider the matter, and you should warn them that any negotiations with HMRC will take time and incur expense.

Make sure that you **know the time limits for any claims** that need to be made. If you miss the limit, the relief will be denied. Late returns incur penalties, and late payment of tax leads to an interest charge.

6 HMRC/client/adviser relationships

6.1 HMRC powers

HMRC have certain statutory powers to compel disclosure in particular instances. Where information is sought under such powers, members must check that the statutory power being invoked actually covers the information sought and, if in any doubt, should take legal advice.

In some cases HMRC will ask for information to be provided voluntarily, rather than resorting to the use of their statutory powers. In this case the member must consider carefully whether it is in the client's interest to make voluntary disclosure, rather than await a statutory demand, and again may wish to take legal advice.

6.2 Errors by HMRC in the taxpayers' favour

Problems may arise if HMRC erroneously makes an excessive repayment of tax to taxpayers, even though they have received full disclosure of the facts.

If the repayment is made directly to the client, the member should urge them to refund the excess sum to HMRC as soon as possible. Failure to correct the error may be a civil and/or criminal offence by the client. **If the client refuses the member must consider whether they should continue to act for the client.** If they cease to act, they must notify HMRC that they no longer act for the client but is under no duty to give HMRC any further details, although it may be necessary to consider whether a report should be made under the money laundering rules.

If the repayment is made to the member on the client's behalf, the member must notify the tax authorities. Failure to do so could involve both the member and client in a civil and/or criminal offence.

It should be noted that if HMRC make the repayment because they have adopted a different treatment of a transaction to that taken by the member and client, this is not an excessive repayment, it merely arises from a different interpretation of the legislation. This is subject to the proviso that full details of the transaction has been returned, so that HMRC have reached their decision on an informed basis.

7 Conflicts of interest

> **FAST FORWARD** A conflict of interest is a commonly met threat to compliance with the fundamental principles.

7.1 The threat of a conflict of interest

A member should take reasonable steps to identify circumstances that could pose a conflict of interest. These may give rise to threats to compliance with the fundamental principles.

A conflict may arise between the firm and the client or between two conflicting clients being managed by the same firm. For example, where a firm acts for both a husband and wife in a divorce settlement or acts for a company and for its directors in their personal capacity.

Evaluation of threats includes consideration as to whether the member has any business interests or relationships with the client or a third party that could give rise to threats. Safeguards should be considered and applied as necessary.

7.2 Safeguards

Depending upon the circumstances giving rise to the conflict, safeguards should ordinarily include the member in public practice:

(a) **Notifying the client** of the firm's business interest or activities that may represent a conflict of interest.

(b) **Notifying all known relevant parties** that the member is acting for two or more parties in respect of a matter where their respective interests are in conflict.

(c) **Notifying the client that the member does not act exclusively for any one client** in the provision of proposed services (for example, in a particular market sector or with respect to a specific service).

In each case the member should obtain the consent of the relevant parties to act.

Where a member has requested consent from a client to act for another party (which may or may not be an existing client) and that consent has been refused, then they must not continue to act for one of the parties in the matter giving rise to the conflict of interest.

The following additional safeguards should also be considered:

(a) The use of separate engagement teams

(b) Procedures to prevent access to information (eg strict physical separation of such teams, confidential and secure data filing)

(c) Clear guidelines for members of the engagement team on issues of security and confidentiality

(d) The use of confidentiality agreements signed by employees and partners of the firm

(e) Regular review of the application of safeguards by a senior individual not involved with relevant client engagements

Where a conflict of interest poses a threat to one or more of the fundamental principles that cannot be eliminated or reduced to an acceptable level through the application of safeguards, the member should conclude that it is not appropriate to accept a specific engagement or that resignation from one or more conflicting engagements is required.

7.3 Example

You have acted for Robenick Ltd for several years, and also for the three director shareholders, Rob, Ben and Nick. During the year Rob has a disagreement with Ben and Nick over the direction of the company. What should you do?

When you started acting for both the company and Rob, Ben and Nick you should have advised each that you were acting for the others, and asked their permission to act. Providing there were no areas where the interests of the clients conflicted, there is no reason why you should not have acted for all the clients, although it may be advisable to have ensured that, for example, a different tax manager was responsible for each client.

However, now that there has been a disagreement between Rob and the other clients the situation has changed and there is a conflict of interest. It is most likely that it would be inappropriate to continue to act for all the clients, and you will need to cease to act, either for Rob, or for Ben, Nick, and the company.

8 Fees

Fees are arranged by commercial negotiation and should be agreed in writing.

Possible arrangements include:

- Time and expenses
- Fixed fees
- Contingent or success fees
- Fees that may be wholly or partly covered by professional fee insurance.

Fees should be set out in the engagement letter.

9 Confidentiality

The fundamental principle of confidentiality means that, in relation to information acquired as a result of professional and business relationships, an accountant should not:

- Disclose such information acquired; nor
- Use it for their own advantage or that of third parties.

9.1 Disclosure of information

9.1.1 When to disclose

A member may disclose confidential information if:

(a) Disclosure is permitted by law and is authorised by the client or the employer
(b) Disclosure is required by law, such as under anti-money laundering legislation
(c) There is a professional duty or right to disclose, when not prohibited by law, such as under a quality review

9.1.2 Factors to consider regarding disclosure

In deciding whether to disclose confidential information, members should consider:

(a) Whether the interests of all parties, including third parties, could be harmed if the client or employer consents to the disclosure of information

(b) Whether all the relevant information is known and substantiated, to the extent it is practicable to do so. When the situation involves unsubstantiated facts, incomplete information or unsubstantiated conclusions, professional judgment should be used in determining the type of disclosure to be made, if any

(c) The type of communication that is expected and to whom it is addressed; in particular, members should be satisfied that the parties to whom the communication is addressed are appropriate recipients

10 Data protection

> **FAST FORWARD**
>
> Under the Data Protection Act 2018, anybody who handles personal information has a number of legal obligations and must comply with the General Data Protection Regulation (GDPR).

Since the EU exit, there are now two sets of rules that UK data handlers must consider: UK GDPR and EU GDPR. Every organisation that holds data on EU citizens must comply with EU GDPR.

10.1 GDPR requirements

The GDPR requires that personal data shall be:

- Processed lawfully, fairly and in a transparent manner
- Collected for specified, explicit and legitimate purposes, and not processed further
- Adequate, relevant and limited to what is necessary
- Accurate and up to date
- Kept in a form which permits identification of individuals for no longer than is necessary, and
- Processed in a manner that ensures appropriate security of personal data.

10.2 GDPR compliance

Compliance with GDPR is monitored by the Information Commissioner's Office (ICO), and many organisations have to appoint a Data Protection Officer (DPO).

Where there is a breach of data likely to result in a risk to rights and freedoms of individuals the breach needs to be reported within 72 hours of it being uncovered. Tiered fines apply to organisations in breach of GDPR which can be very severe.

11 Money laundering issues

Money laundering is the process by which criminals attempt to conceal the true origin and ownership of the proceeds of their criminal activity, often with the unwitting assistance of professionals such as accountants and lawyers.

11.1 Members' responsibilities

Members are bound by legislation to implement preventative measures and to report suspicions to the appropriate authority. Failure to follow these legislative requirements will often be a criminal offence, leading to a fine and/or imprisonment. The legal position and its application to any given set of facts may not be straightforward and members are advised to take legal advice whenever they are uncertain as to their conduct.

Members should have appropriate procedures to ensure that client identification procedures are carried out correctly and that knowledge and suspicions of money laundering are reported to the firm's money laundering reporting officer.

11.2 Client identification procedures

Where a new client is taken on a member should verify their identity by reliable and independent means. This could comprise the following:

(a) Where the client is an individual: by obtaining independent evidence, such as a passport, driving licence, HMRC document such as a notice of coding, and proof of address

(b) Where the client is a company: by obtaining proof of incorporation; by establishing the primary business address; by identifying the members and directors of the company; and by establishing the identities of those persons instructing the member on behalf of the company and verifying that those persons are authorised to do so

If satisfactory evidence cannot be obtained, no work should be undertaken.

Members should **retain all client identification records for at least five years after the end of the client relationship**, together with records of all work carried out for the client.

11.3 Suspicions of money laundering

During the course of the engagement, members should regularly review the client's actions to satisfy themselves that they are consistent with the client's usual activities. Anything which appears to be out of the ordinary should be closely examined and a written record made of the member's conclusions. **If members' suspicions are aroused, a money laundering report should be made**.

Suspicion is more than mere speculation but falls short of proof based on firm evidence. Something that is suspicious in relation to one client may not be suspicious in relation to another client. Therefore, the key to recognising a suspicious transaction or situation is for members to have a full understanding of the client and their activities.

Transactions which appear to have no apparent economic or visible lawful purpose should be looked at carefully to establish their purpose and any findings recorded in writing. If no purpose for the transaction can be established, this may be a ground for suspicion.

Where members know or suspect that funds are directly or indirectly the proceeds of crime, they should report their suspicions first to their firm's money laundering reporting officer (MLRO). The MLRO (or the member himself if a sole practitioner) will decide whether to report to the National Crime Agency (NCA) in the form of a suspicious activity report (SAR). Where tax evasion is involved members will also need to examine their responsibilities to the tax authorities, taking into account the balancing consideration of client confidentiality.

Where the work done by members for their clients is covered by legal professional privilege, members are not required to report their suspicions. Whether or not legal professional privilege applies to members and in what circumstances will depend on local law and members are strongly advised to seek legal advice as and when the issue arises.

11.4 Tipping off

Members should not 'tip off' a client that a report has been made. This may cause a member difficulties if a client refuses to disclose tax irregularities to HMRC as ceasing to act for the client might tip off the client that a report has been made. Any attempts to persuade a client not to proceed with an intended crime will not constitute tipping off.

11.5 Economic crime (Anti-money laundering) Levy

From 1 April 2023, a new levy became payable called the anti-money laundering (AML) levy. It applies to AML regulated entities such as accountants, solicitors and financial institutions like banks and insurance companies. The levy payable by a particular entity is a fixed fee based on their UK revenue bands. The following table shows those bands and the relevant levy for each band:

Size	Revenue range	Levy
Small	Up to £10.2 million	Exempt
Medium	£10.2m to £36m	£10,000
Large	£36m to £1bn	£36,000
Very large	More than £1 billion	£500,000

The levy payable in the financial year 2024 (1 April 2024 to 31 March 2025) is based on each entity's revenue in their accounting periods ending in financial year 2023. It will be payable on 30 September 2025 and it is not deductible for corporation tax purposes.

PART E ETHICS

Chapter roundup

- The fundamental principles of ethics should underlie all of a member's professional behaviour.
- A conflict of interest is a commonly met threat to compliance with the fundamental principles.
- If a member discovers that a client has misled them in order to obtain a tax advantage, the member has to consider their position in relation to both the client and the tax authorities.
- There are disclosure requirements for promoters of direct tax avoidance schemes. Businesses may be required to disclose use of VAT avoidance schemes.
- There is a general anti-abuse rule to enable HMRC to counteract tax advantages gained from abusive tax arrangements.

Quick quiz

1 Can an AIA member act for both a husband and wife?

2 What should you do if, when preparing a client's tax return, you suspect they may have been involved in money laundering?

3 What is the maximum initial penalty for failure to notify a tax avoidance scheme relating to income tax?

4 Tax evasion is legal. True or false?

5 Which of the following actions by a taxpayer would not constitute tax evasion?

   (a) Obtaining tax-free interest by investing in an ISA
   (b) Claiming capital allowances on a fictitious item of plant
   (c) Choosing not to declare rental income received
   (d) Failing to notify HMRC of a profitable trade commenced two years ago

Answers to quick quiz

1. It depends on whether there are any relationships between the two that could give rise to a conflict of interest. For example, they may be business partners or one may employ the other. In some cases, it may be sufficient to ensure that each is aware that you act for both, provided you keep the position under review. In other cases, the potential conflict of interest might be such that you should not. For example, it would not be appropriate to act for both if they were in the course of a divorce.

2. You should report your suspicions to the firm's money laundering reporting officer. You should not 'tip off' a client that a report has been made.

3. £5,000

4. False. Tax evasion is illegal.

5. A

PART E ETHICS

Practice Question Bank

PRACTICE QUESTION BANK

The front page of the Taxation exam will give you an instruction similar to the following:

Unless instructed otherwise, assume that tax rates and rules for 2024/25 and Financial Year 2024 continue to apply in future years.

You should apply the same approach when completing this Practice Question Bank.

1 Alf

You work in the personal tax department of a firm of accountants. You have been asked to help three long-standing clients with their income tax.

One of your clients, Alf, is one of the directors of Bell plc. He is paid a salary of £20,000 a year and is given the following benefits throughout the tax year 2024/25:

- Private use of hi-fi equipment which cost Bell plc £800.
- Private use of a company van. Bell plc pays for all fuel.
- Mobile phone for business and private use which cost Bell plc £250.
- Medical insurance which cost Bell plc £700. Similar insurance would have cost Alf £900 had he taken it out personally.
- A non-cash long-service award for 30 years of employment £300. He has never previously received a long-service award from this employer.

Required

(a) Calculate Alf's employment income for the tax year 2024/25. **(5 marks)**

Another client, Shirley needs help with her income tax return. She has employment income of £109,000 for the tax year 2024/25 (PAYE £31,100). She also receives building society interest of £5,250 and dividends of £5,000 in the tax year. She makes a contribution of £7,600 cash into her personal pension scheme in December 2024.

Required

(b) Calculate Shirley's income tax payable for the tax year 2024/25. **(8 marks)**

Janine is an employee with a salary of £45,000 in the tax year 2024/25. Income tax deducted via PAYE was £6,486 in 2024/25. She also owns a residential investment property, with a net profit (before interest is taken into account) of £12,500 in 2024/25. During 2024/25, she paid bank interest of £2,500 on a loan to improve this property.

Required

(c) Calculate Janine's income tax payable for 2024/25. **(4 marks)**

(d) Calculate Janine's payments on account in respect of her income tax payable for 2025/26 and state the dates they fall due. **(3 marks)**

(Total 20 marks)

2 Ken

You work in the Owner Managed Businesses department of a small firm of accountants and you have been asked to help out with three unconnected clients, Ken, Simon and Desmond.

Ken is a sole trader and has made no election in relation to the cash basis. He calculated the taxable trading profit of £19,000 for the year ended 31 December 2024. Included in this profit were the following items.

PRACTICE QUESTION BANK

Salary for Ken	£3,000
Salary for Sameer (an employee)	£4,000
Legal expenses in connection with the purchase of new freehold premises	£400
Personal tax advice unrelated to business	£550
Leasing cost for car used in business (CO_2 emission rate of 128g/km)	£2,200
An unpaid sales invoice issued to a customer on 31 December 2024	£6,000

Required

(a) Compute Ken's taxable trading profit for the year ended 31 December 2024. **(5 marks)**

Desmond ceased trading on 30 November 2024, having made up his accounts to 31 December each year. He had never used the cash basis. The main pool tax written down value at 1 January 2024 was £17,212. Plant was acquired on 1 November 2024 for £15,000. The only disposal occurred at cessation when all the plant was sold for £14,000 (no proceeds exceeded cost).

Required

(b) Calculate the capital allowances for the final period from 1 January 2024 to 30 November 2024.

(3 marks)
(Total 8 marks)

3 Vipul

You work at a firm of accountants whose clients are entrepreneurs.

One of the firm's clients, Vipul, is UK resident and lives in England. Vipul started a new business on 1 July 2024 making standard-rated supplies and voluntarily registered for VAT from that date and elected to use the accruals basis to calculate his taxable trading profit.

He has no employees.

Your firm is engaged to act for Vipul on all tax compliance matters, including his quarterly digital VAT returns. Vipul's VAT year ends on 30 June.

Vipul's monthly sales (exclusive of VAT) in the first year were:

	£/month
July – December 2024	10,000
January – March 2025	16,000
April – June 2025	18,000

Vipul expects his sales to continue to be £18,000 per month for the foreseeable future.

Vipul is concerned that his products are expensive compared with a competitor who does not charge VAT. He has asked you whether it is compulsory that he is VAT-registered.

Required

(a) Applying the rules of compulsory registration, determine the date by which Vipul was required to notify HMRC of his need to register, and the date from which he would then have been registered.

(4 marks)

You are reviewing the information regarding Vipul's capital purchases before preparing his self-assessment income tax return for 2024/25:

Vipul purchased a newly-constructed commercial building in England on 1 July 2024 for a cost of £400,000 (stated exclusive of VAT) for use in his business.

Required

(b) Calculate the stamp duty land tax payable on the purchase of the building. **(3 marks)**

Also on 1 July 2024, Vipul purchased a car with CO_2 emissions of 150g/km for £32,000. He used the car 75% for private use. He also purchased equipment for £50,000 for sole use in the business.

Both these amounts are stated inclusive of VAT.

Required

(c) (i) Calculate the input VAT recoverable on the purchases of the car and equipment. **(2 marks)**
    (ii) Calculate Vipul's capital allowances for the year ended 30 June 2025. **(4 marks)**

Your colleague has completed the accounts for Vipul's trade for the year ended 30 June 2025:

	£	£
Gross profit		132,000
Expenses:		
Depreciation	9,800	
Entertaining potential customers	2,000	
Legal advice regarding sales contracts	1,000	
Insurance for Vipul's car purchased on 1 July 2024	600	
Advertising in local paper	500	
Subscription to trade association	300	
		(14,200)
Net profit		117,800

Required

(d) (i) Calculate Vipul's tax-adjusted trading profit for the year ended 30 June 2025, recording your treatment of each expense. **(7 marks)**

   (ii) Calculate Vipul's assessable trading profit for 2024/25. **(1 mark)**

Vipul has told you that he rents out a property in Parpadone, an overseas country. During 2024/25, he received rental income of £9,000, after deduction of 10% withholding tax in Parpadone. This was Vipul's only income aside from his trading income.

Required

(e) (i) Calculate Vipul's income tax liability for 2024/25. **(5 marks)**
    (ii) Calculate Vipul's national insurance contributions for 2024/25. **(3 marks)**

Vipul has said that he is very busy in the business during the first few months of 2026 and he will not have time to deal with his self-assessment tax return. He has told you in a telephone call:

'I doubt it will matter if I don't submit my return yet – I am new to running a business so have a good excuse if this is late as I do not yet understand the tax rules. HMRC should just be grateful that I will submit a tax return at all.'

Required

(f) Advise Vipul of the due date for submission of his self-assessment income tax return online, and whether he has a 'reasonable excuse' for late delivery of the return. **(2 marks)**

Vipul says:

'My friend is always complaining that her accountants suddenly tell her she has to pay tax, and she is not expecting it. I will not tolerate that. I want a schedule covering the whole of the year ended December 2026, showing when I will have to pay which taxes because of the business.'

PRACTICE QUESTION BANK

Required

(g) Prepare the schedule requested by Vipul. Calculations of the amounts due are not required.

(5 marks)

(Total 36 marks)
Note – this question is from the AIA sample paper

4 Alessia

You work as a trainee in a firm of accountants. You have been asked to work on the file of a personal tax client, Alessia.

On 31 May 2024, Alessia left her job as a personnel manager as she had decided to set up her own interior design business.

Alessia had an annual salary of £34,000. She was also provided with a petrol car with CO_2 emissions of 123g/km. The car had a list price of £18,500. Prior to that she had used her own car but had done minimal business miles. During 2024/25, PAYE of £967 was deducted from Alessia's earnings.

Required

(a) Calculate Alessia's employment income for 2024/25. **(3 marks)**

In order to fund the set-up of her new business, Alessia borrowed £50,000 from the bank on 1 August 2024 at an interest rate of 8% per annum.

In preparation for running her business, Alessia went on an interior design course in June 2024 at a cost of £600. She also attended a series of bookkeeping update seminars at a further cost of £150.

Alessia leased a car for use in her business. The lease payments were £220 per month. The car had CO_2 emissions of 62g/km and Alessia uses it 80% for business purposes.

She decided to lease a workshop. The lease is for five years and the annual rental is £2,700. The lease was taken out on 1 October 2024. Additionally she incurred further capital expenditure as follows in September 2024:

	£
Computer and design software	4,800
Machinery including sewing machine	5,300
Fixtures and fittings including cutting table	2,000

The adjusted trading profits calculated using the cash basis and before accounting for any of the items mentioned above are:

	£
1 October 2024 to 31 March 2025	32,718
Year ended 31 March 2026 (estimated)	13,558

On 31 March 2025, sales invoices totalling £2,000 and supplier invoices of £500 were outstanding.

Alessia expects to make a sizeable profit in the year ended 31 March 2027.

Required

(b) Calculate Alessia's trading income for her first two accounting periods. **(7 marks)**

Alessia receives gross dividends each year of £9,500 from shares she inherited from her father. This is her only other income.

Required

(c) Prepare Alessia's income tax computation for 2024/25. **(5 marks)**

(d) Prepare a list for Alessia showing the deadlines for:
- notifying HMRC that she has started trading
- filing her 2024/25 income tax return
- payment of income tax

Assume that the tax rates and rules in 2024/25 apply in all relevant years. **(3 marks)**

(Total 18 marks)

5 Nexis Ltd

You work as a junior in a firm of accountants and have been asked to work on the file of a client, Ibrahim. Ibrahim left Exus plc to work for a competitor, Nexis Ltd, from 6 April 2024.

Nexis Ltd paid Ibrahim £15,000 on 6 April 2024 as an inducement to persuade him to leave Exus plc in order to join their smaller firm as a director.

Ibrahim receives an annual salary of £45,000 from Nexis Ltd and a number of additional benefits as follows:

He has use of a company car from 6 April 2024 onwards with a list price of £75,000 and CO_2 emissions of 233g/km. Ibrahim requested a number of extras to be added to the basic model at an additional cost of £8,000. Nexis Ltd pays for all the diesel for Ibrahim's business and private mileage.

Ibrahim is provided with a company flat, which he can use whenever he chooses. The flat was purchased in October 2019 at a cost of £189,000. A number of improvements were subsequently made in January 2020 at a cost of £16,000. Its market value on 6 June 2024, when it was first made available to Ibrahim, was £430,000. The flat was fully refurnished prior to being used by Ibrahim at a cost of £42,000 in April 2024. Nexis Ltd pays for all cleaning costs and electricity and other bills at an annual cost of £6,800. The annual value of the flat is £9,200.

Ibrahim made a contribution to his personal pension scheme on 5 April 2025 of £48,000. In 2023/24, the first year in which he made a pension contribution, he paid £12,000.

Required

(a) Calculate the taxable income of Ibrahim for 2024/25. You are not required to calculate any tax liabilities **(10 marks)**

(b) State the deadlines for Nexis Ltd to issue Ibrahim's P60 to him and the submission of his P11D to HMRC for the tax year 2024/25

The official rate of interest is 2.25%. **(2 marks)**

(Total 12 marks)

6 Marcia

You are a newly qualified accountant who has recently started work in a medium-sized accountancy firm. Marcia is one of the firm's long-standing clients.

Marcia has operated a business for many years. The taxable trading profits for the year ended 31 December 2024 are £30,000.

In 2024/25, Marcia also received £1,100 interest from a National Savings and Investments Certificate and a distribution of £2,000 from a Real Estate Investment Trust (REIT). The distribution was paid out of the REIT's tax exempt property income.

Marcia rents out a small flat in the UK at an annual rent of £4,500. Expenses in the year amounted to £800 plus finance costs of £150.

Marcia expects similar levels of income from the same sources in future years.

Required

(a) (i) Calculate Marcia's property income on the flat under (i) the normal basis and (ii) if she elects for the property allowance for 2024/25. **(5 marks)**

(ii) Calculate Marcia's income tax payable (ignoring the property income from part a(i)) for 2024/25 **(4 marks)**

Capital investment

On 1 January 2025, Marcia intends to buy a new car (with CO_2 emissions of 176g/km), which costs £18,000 plus VAT. Marcia will use the car 70% of the time in her business. Total mileage will be 17,500 miles per year and running costs are estimated at £4,000 per year.

Required

(b) Calculate the allowable deduction from Marcia's trading profits in in the year ending 31 December 2025 for the cost of the car and its running costs assuming:

(i) She claims fixed rate deductions for the car;
(ii) She claims capital allowances for the car.

(5 marks)

(Total 14 marks)

7 Kelly

You work in the personal taxes department of a medium-sized accountancy firm and are assisting with some calculations for four unconnected clients.

Kelly is intending to sell a 10% shareholding in Bumble Ltd, a trading company, for £800,000 in the tax year 2024/25. She had acquired these shares on 1 October 2022 for £250,000 when she also became an employee of the company. Kelly is a higher rate taxpayer and will make no other disposals in the tax year 2024/25.

Required

(a) Calculate Kelly's net proceeds of sale after tax having sold the shares on:
(i) 1 September 2024; or
(ii) 1 November 2024. **(4 marks)**

On 23 May 2024, Del sold a freehold retail property for £150,000 which had cost £60,000 on 31 March 2011. On 2 February 2024, Del acquired another retail property for £140,000. The old and new property are both used in Del's trade.

Required

(b) Calculate the chargeable gain after any available reliefs have been claimed, and the base cost of the replacement property. **(3 marks)**

On 19 June 2024, Gretel sold a residential property, realising a gain of £16,300. The property did not qualify for private residence relief. On 23 December 2024, Gretel sold some shares in Cress plc, realising a gain of £25,000. Business asset disposal relief will not apply to this disposal. Gretel is a higher rate taxpayer.

PRACTICE QUESTION BANK

Required

(c) Calculate Gretel's capital gains tax liability for 2024/25. **(3 marks)**

Tula, a sole trader with no other income, paid the following amounts of tax for the tax year 2023/24:
Income tax £16,000
Class 4 national insurance contributions £3,000

For the tax year 2024/25, Tula's final tax assessments are expected to be as follows:
Income tax £19,300
Class 4 national insurance contributions £3,500

Required

(d) State the due dates of payment of income tax and Class 4 national insurance contributions in respect of Tula's 2024/25 tax liabilities, together with the amounts payable on each date.

Note. You should ignore any payments on account for the tax year 2025/26. **(4 marks)**

Callum's payments on account for 2024/25 based on his income tax liability for 2023/24 were £7,500 each. However, when he submitted his 2023/24 income tax return in January 2025 he made a claim to reduce the payments on account for 2024/25 to £5,000 each. The first payment on account was made on 31 January 2025, and the second on 31 July 2025.

Callum filed his 2024/25 tax return in on 31 January 2026. The return showed that his total liability to income tax and Class 4 NIC for 2024/25 (before deducting payments on account) was £12,000. Callum paid the balance of tax due on 31 January 2026.

Required

(e) Calculate the interest payable (to the nearest day) by Callum in respect of his payments on account for 2024/25? **(4 marks)**
(Total 18 marks)

8 Isabella

You work as a trainee at a firm of accountants. One of your clients, Isabella, sold a number of investments in 2024/25.

On 1 June 2024, she sold a residential property for £280,000. Isabella had never lived in the property. She had bought the property in 2018 for £190,000.

She sold the following on 31 January 2025:

- 700 shares in OBD plc for £1,650. These had been purchased in May 2007 for £4 per share.

- 2,500 shares in BSR plc for £22,856. Isabella had originally purchased 1,000 shares in September 2002 for £1,050. In February 2007 she had bought another 3,000 shares for £2.50 each.

- 400 shares in Upsy Ltd for £61 per share. Isabella acquired these shares (a 6% holding) at par value of £1 in January 2005 and worked for Upsy Ltd until leaving to travel overseas in February 2025.

Isabella's taxable income for 2024/25 is £55,000 and she is UK-resident for tax purposes.

Required

(a) Calculate Isabella's capital gains tax liability for 2024/25. **(10 marks)**
(b) State the payment dates for Isabella's capital gains tax for 2024/25. **(5 marks)**
(Total 15 marks)

9 Armani

You work in the personal tax department of a medium-sized firm of accountants. You are working on the file of one of the firm's clients, Armani. Armani has decided he is going to leave the UK permanently to relocate and settle in USA in May 2025 which will be in the 2025/26 tax year. He prepared for the move by making gifts and disposals of his assets, and completing a disposal of his company, AMI Ltd, all in 2024/25.

AMI Ltd

AMI Ltd is a trading company incorporated 20 years ago with Armani subscribing £5,000 for 1,000 ordinary shares, representing 100% of the company's issued share capital. Armani was the managing director and worked full-time for the company.

On 31 March 2025, Armani completed a sale of the entire share capital of AMI Ltd to Majestel plc for £85,500.

Armani's house and possessions

1. Armani sold his house on 31 March 2025 for £285,000. He had bought the house 20 years earlier for £180,000, and had lived in it throughout. During the period of ownership, Armani used the basement as an office for his business, representing 10% of the house.

2. Armani gave one of a pair of matching antique bookcases to his daughter Priya on 1 October 2024. He gave the other bookcase to his son Kahid on 1 March 2025. The market values at both these dates were £50,000 for the pair, and £20,000 for one bookcase. Armani had bought the pair for £30,000 five years ago.

3. The remaining items of furniture were sold for £20,000, and had cost Armani £30,000 in total. None of the individual items had been bought or were sold for more than £6,000.

4. In the tax year 2024/25, Armani has available £6,200 of capital losses brought forward from a previous year.

Required

(a) Calculate Armani's capital gains tax liability for 2024/25. **(11 marks)**

10 Michael

You are a tax assistant in a large firm of accountants. You have been asked to help with some capital gains calculations. A client, Michael, has disposed of two assets during the tax year 2024/25.

Firstly, on 19 May 2024, Michael sold a freehold warehouse for £522,000. The warehouse was purchased on 6 August 2004 for £258,000, and was extended at a cost of £99,000 during April 2006. In January 2010, the floor of the warehouse was damaged by flooding and had to be replaced at a cost of £63,000. The warehouse was sold because it was surplus to the business's requirements as a result of Michael purchasing a replacement warehouse for £509,000 during October 2023. Both warehouses have always been used for business purposes in a wholesale business run by Michael as a sole trader.

Required

(a) Calculate the chargeable gain arising from the disposal of the warehouse assuming Michael claims rollover relief.

Note. You are not required to calculate the taxable gains or the amount of tax payable. **(4 marks)**

Secondly, on 24 September 2024, Michael sold 700,000 shares in Rolling Ltd, an unquoted trading company, for £3,675,000. He had originally purchased 500,000 shares in Rolling Ltd on 2 June 2008 for £960,000. On 1 December 2013, Rolling Ltd made a 3 for 2 bonus issue. Michael has been a director of

Rolling Ltd since 1 January 2008, and he has not made any claims for business asset disposal relief before.

Required

(b) Calculate the capital gains tax arising from the disposal of the shares assuming Michael claims business asset disposal relief and the annual exempt amount is used against the warehouse disposal. **(6 marks)**

(c) State Michael's deadlines for making the claims for rollover relief in respect of his warehouses and business asset disposal relief in respect of his shares in Rolling Ltd. **(2 marks)**

(Total 12 marks)

11 Churchill

You are a capital gains tax specialist in a firm of accountants. You are asked to prepare some calculations for two clients.

On 19 May 2024, Churchill disposed of a painting, and this resulted in a chargeable gain of £38,260. For the tax year 2024/25, Churchill has taxable income of £24,900 after the deduction of the personal allowance.

Required

(a) Assuming the painting was Churchill's only disposal in 2024/25, calculate his capital gains tax liability for the tax year. **(3 marks)**

Churchill is considering the sale of a business that he has run as a sole trader since 1 July 2011. The business will be sold for £260,000 and this figure, along with the respective cost of each asset, is made up as follows:

	Sale proceeds £	Cost £
Freehold shop	140,000	80,000
Freehold warehouse	88,000	102,000
Net current assets	32,000	32,000
	260,000	

The freehold warehouse has never been used by Churchill for business purposes.

Required

(b) Calculate Churchill's capital gains tax liability for the tax year 2024/25 if he sold his sole trader business on 25 March 2025 as well as the painting in May 2024. **(4 marks)**

On 3 December 2024, Ronald sold two hectares of land at auction for gross proceeds of £92,000. The auctioneers' commission was 5% of the sale price.

Ronald's wife's father had originally purchased three hectares of land on 4 August 2003 for £19,500. He died on 17 June 2010, and the land was inherited by Ronald's wife. On that date the three hectares of land were valued at £28,600.

Ronald's wife transferred the land to Ronald on 14 November 2013. On that date the three hectares of land were valued at £39,000. The market value of the unsold hectare of land as at 3 December 2024 was £38,000.

Required

(c) Compute Ronald's chargeable gain in respect of the disposal on 3 December 2024. **(3 marks)**

(Total 10 marks)

PRACTICE QUESTION BANK

12 Star Ltd

You work in a small accountancy partnership and have been asked to work on two unconnected clients.

Star Ltd commenced trading on 1 April 2024 and its results for the 15-month period of account ended 30 June 2025 were as follows:

1. The trading profit as adjusted for tax purposes is £525,000. This figure is before taking account of capital allowances.

2. Star Ltd bought a new car with zero CO_2 emissions for £8,000 on 15 December 2024 and machinery for £49,500 on 15 June 2025.

3. Star Ltd opened a deposit account with Nateast Bank on 1 April 2025. Interest of £800 was accrued to 30 June 2025.

4. On 31 December 2024, Star Ltd disposed of a piece of land and this resulted in a chargeable gain of £2,500.

5. Star Ltd paid a qualifying charitable donation of £2,500 on 16 June 2025.

Required

(a) (i) Calculate Star Ltd's taxable total profits for the accounting periods relating to the 15-month period of account ended 30 June 2025. **(6 marks)**

(ii) Calculate Star Ltd's corporation tax liability for these periods. **(4 marks)**

(iii) State when corporation tax returns and payments are due in respect of the accounting periods and liabilities you have calculated in (a)(i) and (ii). **(4 marks)**

Arnold died on 3 August 2024, leaving his estate to his son, George. The assets in the estate consisted of a main residence valued at £215,000 and other assets valued at £210,000. Arnold's wife survived him.

The only lifetime transfers Arnold had ever made were on 12 March 2020 when he gave £274,000 (cash) to his son, George, and on 24 July 2020 when he gave £150,000 to his daughter, Clarissa.

Required

(b) (i) Calculate the inheritance tax payable on the lifetime gifts as a result of Arnold's death **(6 marks)**

(ii) Calculate the inheritance tax payable on Arnold's death estate. State the date by which the tax should be paid, assuming the personal representatives delivered the account on 1 November 2024. **(5 marks)**

(Total 25 marks)

13 Stephen

You are a tax assistant at a small firm of accountants. One client, Stephen, died on 2 January 2025.

Stephen had made one lifetime gift of £400,000 cash to his son, Matt, in March 2021, on the occasion of Matt's marriage.

Required

(a) Calculate the inheritance tax arising as a result of his death in 2024/25 on Stephen's gift to Matt in March 2021. **(5 marks)**

Stephen left his entire estate to Matt. It comprised the following assets and liabilities.

Business interests and investments:

- An interest in a trading partnership, where Stephen had been a partner for eighteen months. Stephen's share has a probate value of £350,000.
- A farm in the UK which Stephen had owned since January 2008 and had rented to a tenant who has farmed it since then. The total value of the farm was £375,000 at 2 January 2025, and the agricultural value of the land was £200,000.
- £28,000 worth of shares in Salsat Ltd, an unquoted trading company. Stephen had inherited the shares on the death of his father on 20 December 2019.

Other assets and liabilities:

- A house which he bought in 2004 valued at £300,000 at the date of death.
- A painting which was one of a set of three. His wife owned the other two paintings in the set. At the date of Stephen's death, each painting was valued at £20,000 when valued separately, two taken together as a pair were valued at £50,000 and the set of all three together was valued at £90,000.
- A vintage car (Rolls Royce) which was valued at £80,000 at the date of his death.
- Cash and chattels worth £50,000.
- Stephen owed income tax of £11,000 at the date of his death.

Required

(b) Calculate the inheritance tax arising on Stephen's death estate. **(11 marks)**
(Total 16 marks)

14 Sally

You work in the capital taxes department of a firm of accountants and you have been asked to look at the files of a client, Sally who died on 31 May 2024.

Sally had made two gifts during her lifetime.

On 4 August 2017, Sally gave a painting worth £487,000 to a discretionary trust. Sally paid any inheritance tax due on the gift.

Required

(a) Calculate the inheritance tax arising on this gift into a discretionary as a result of Sally's death.
(7 marks)

On 18 December 2022, Sally gifted her 60,000 shares in Collinste plc, a quoted trading company, to her nephew. There were 100,000 shares in issue and Sally had owned her shares since April 2013.

On 18 December 2022, the shares in Collinste plc were quoted at 118p – 122p, and there were bargains at 116p, 119p and 124p.

On 31 May 2024, the shares were quoted at 220p – 260p, and there were no bargains. Sally's nephew still owned the 60,000 shares he had received from Sally.

Required

(b) Calculate the inheritance tax arising on this gift of shares as a result of Sally's death. **(6 marks)**

On her death, Sally left her entire chargeable estate worth £1,200,000 including a residential property (worth £500,000) to her son.

Sally's husband died in 2022 utilising 100% of his nil rate band but none of his residence nil rate band.

Required

(c) Calculate the inheritance tax due on Sally's death estate. **(4 marks)**

(Total 17 marks)

15 Pauline

You have just joined an accountancy partnership and have been asked to help out with some calculations regarding Pauline, who died on 31 March 2025.

Pauline had been married. In October 2011, Pauline's husband Barry had died, leaving £100,000 cash to their son, Roger, and the remainder of his estate (£80,000) to Pauline. Barry had made no lifetime gifts.

Pauline had made the following lifetime gifts:

On 1 February 2013, she gave £400,000 to a discretionary trust and agreed to pay the inheritance tax herself.

Required

(a) Calculate the value of the gross chargeable transfer arising from this gift. **(4 marks)**

On 1 January 2020, Pauline gave away 1,000 shares in an investment company, Facia Ltd to her sister. Pauline had subscribed for 6,000 shares in Facia Ltd when the company was incorporated in January 2018. The remaining 4,000 shares in the company were owned by Pauline's son, Roger.

The shares were valued on 1 January 2020 at:

% shareholding	£ per share
75% and above	130
51% – 74%	85
25% – 50%	30
Less than 25%	10

Required

(b) Calculate the value of the PET and the inheritance tax on this PET which becomes due as a result of Pauline's death. **(12 marks)**

Death estate

Pauline had chargeable assets at the date of her death worth £920,000, including her remaining Facia Ltd shares and a residential property worth £305,000 which she left to her son. She also had an outstanding income tax liability of £20,000. She left £15,000 to a UK national registered charity and the remainder to her son Roger.

Required

(c) Calculate the inheritance tax arising on Pauline's death estate. **(4 marks)**

(Total 20 marks)

16 Arthur and Mary

You work in the private client department of a small firm of accountants. You represent Arthur and Mary, who live together but are not married nor are in a civil partnership. They have a son, Peter. You have just been informed that Arthur died on 31 December 2024.

Arthur had made one lifetime gift in February 2018, of £375,000 cash into trust. Arthur agreed to pay any inheritance tax due on this gift.

Required

(a) (i) Calculate the value of the gross chargeable transfer arising from this gift. **(4 marks)**

(ii) Calculate the inheritance tax on this lifetime gift which becomes due as a result of Arthur's death. **(4 marks)**

Arthur died owning the following assets and liabilities:

- House of value £350,000. Arthur and Mary have lived in the house for several decades, but the house is owned solely by Arthur.

- Cottage in the UK countryside of value £500,000. Arthur and Mary lived there when they were first married before moving to their current home and now spend most of their weekends there.

- 800 shares in Deck plc, a quoted trading company. This represents a very small shareholding. The shares are quoted at 1278p – 1284p, with bargains of 1279p, 1280p and 1291p. Arthur had bought the shares in January 2005 for £7,000.

- 2,500 shares in Acril Ltd. Acril Ltd is a company which owns and rents out residential properties. It has 10,000 issued shares. Mary owns 4,500 shares in Acril Ltd, and the remaining 3,000 shares are owned by Peter. Each shareholder subscribed for their shares at par value on 2 January 2002.

The values of Acril Ltd shares are as follows:

	Value per share £
Less than 25%	10
25% – 50%	15
Greater than 50%, less than 75%	60
75% – 100%	100

- Cash and chattels of £250,000.

- Life assurance policy on Arthur's life, which is written into trust for the benefit of his son. The amount receivable on Arthur's death is £80,000.

In his will, Arthur leaves the cottage to his son, and the remainder of his estate to Mary.

Required

(b) Calculate the inheritance tax payable on Arthur's death estate. **(10 marks)**

(Total 18 marks)

17 Claire and William

You work in the capital taxes department of a firm of accountants.

On 23 August 2018, Claire made a gift of a house valued at £420,000 to her son, William. This was a wedding gift when William got married. The nil rate band for the tax year 2018/19 is £325,000.

Claire

Claire died on 20 March 2025 at which time her estate was valued at £880,000. Under the terms of her will, Claire divided her estate equally, before inheritance tax, between her husband and her son, William. Claire had not made any gifts during her lifetime except for the gift of the house to William. Claire did not own a main residence.

Required

(a) Calculate the inheritance tax that will be payable as a result of Claire's death. **(7 marks)**

William

William sold the house which he received as a wedding gift from Claire, on 5 April 2025. The following information relates to the property:

	£
Net sale proceeds after costs of disposal	490,100
Cost of new boundary wall around the property (there was previously no boundary wall)	(5,200)
Cost of replacing the property's chimney	(2,800)

William has taxable income (after deduction of the personal allowance) of £13,950 in 2024/25. The house was never occupied by William.

Required

(b) Calculate William's capital gains tax liability for the tax year 2024/25. **(6 marks)**

(Total 13 marks)

18 Annie

You work in the capital taxes department of a firm of accountants and have been asked to take a look at the file of Annie, one of the firm's long-standing clients. Annie died on 29 November 2024. She had made two gifts during her lifetime.

Firstly, on 14 September 2023, Annie made a gift of 6,500 £1 ordinary shares in Cassava Ltd, an unquoted investment company, to her daughter.

Before the transfer Annie owned 8,000 shares out of Cassava Ltd's issued share capital of 10,000 £1 ordinary shares. On 14 September 2023, Cassava Ltd's shares were worth £3 each for a holding of 15%, £7 each for a holding of 65%, and £8 each for a holding of 80%.

Required

(a) Calculate the value of the PET arising from Annie's gift of shares. **(2 marks)**

Secondly, on 27 January 2024, Annie made a cash gift of £400,000 to a trust. Annie paid the inheritance tax arising from this gift.

Required

(b) (i) Calculate the gross chargeable transfer arising from Annie's gift into the trust. **(2 marks)**
    (ii) Calculate the inheritance tax arising on these lifetime gifts as a result of Annie's death.
    (3 marks)

On 29 November 2024, Annie's estate was valued at £623,000 including her main residence which was valued at £90,000. Her executors paid funeral expenses of £3,000 on 12 January 2025. Under the terms of her will Annie left £150,000 cash to her husband, a specific legacy of £40,000 to her sister, and the residue of the estate to her children.

The nil rate band for the tax year 2023/24 is £325,000.

PRACTICE QUESTION BANK

Required

(c) (i) Calculate the inheritance tax which will be payable on Annie's death estate. **(4 marks)**
    (ii) Calculate the amount of the inheritance which will be received by Annie's children.
    (2 marks)
    (Total 13 marks)

19 Elland plc

You work in the Business department of a firm of accountants and have been asked to work on two unconnected clients.

Elland plc commenced trading on 1 July 2022. The company's results for its first five periods of trading are as follows:

	Period ended 31 December 2022 £	Year ended 31 December 2023 £	Year ended 31 December 2024 £	Period ended 30 September 2025 £	Year ended 30 September 2026 £
Trading profits/(loss)	(63,800)	44,000	86,500	78,700	(186,800)
Property business profit	6,600	9,400	6,500		
Chargeable gains		5,100		9,700	
Qualifying charitable donations	(1,000)	(800)	(1,200)		

Required

(a) Assuming that Elland plc claims relief for its trading losses as early as possible, calculate the company's taxable total profits for the six-month period ended 31 December 2022, each of the years ended 31 December 2023 and 2024 and the nine-month period ended 30 September 2025. Your answer should also clearly identify any qualifying charitable donations that become unrelieved and the amount of any unrelieved trading losses as at 30 September 2026.
(8 marks)

Victor is registered for VAT and is in the process of completing his VAT return for the quarter ended 31 March 2025. The following information is available:

1. Sales invoices totalling £18,000 were issued in respect of standard rated sales.

2. During the quarter ended 31 March 2025, Victor spent £600 on mobile telephone calls of which 40% related to private calls.

3. On 6 January 2025 Victor purchased a car for £12,000. On 18 March 2025, £987 was spent on repairs to the car. The car is used in Victor's business although 10% of the mileage is for private journeys. Both figures are inclusive of VAT.

4. On 29 March 2025, equipment was purchased for £1,760. Victor paid for the equipment on this date but did not take delivery of the equipment or receive an invoice until 3 April 2025.

5. In addition, Victor also had other standard rated expenses amounting to £2,200 in the quarter ended 31 March 2025. This figure includes £400 for entertaining UK customers.

Unless stated otherwise all of the figures above are exclusive of VAT.

Required

(b) Calculate the VAT payable by Victor for the quarter ended 31 March 2025. **(6 marks)**
(Total 14 marks)

419

PRACTICE QUESTION BANK

20 Spanner Ltd

You are a newly-qualified accountant who has recently started work in the Accounts Department of Spanner Ltd, a small engineering company.

In an attempt to cut costs last year, Spanner Ltd stopped using an external accountancy firm to complete its corporation tax compliance work. Instead, the finance director Jeff purchased software to use to prepare the corporation tax returns.

Jeff has found this more difficult than he expected and he has not yet submitted the corporation tax return for the year ended 30 September 2024. Jeff has now put you in charge of the company's corporation tax compliance and wants you to advise the Board of Directors on such matters.

Required

(a) Prepare a schedule for the directors of Spanner Ltd in relation to the corporation tax return for the year ended 30 September 2024, which records:

- the due date for submission of the return
- how the return should be submitted and with what information
- the penalties for late filing if the correct return is submitted by 10 January 2026.

(4 marks)

Jeff has used the software and prepared a draft computation, but has now given this to you to complete, saying:

'Don't find too many mistakes here. I need the other directors to think that I was right to stop paying high fees to an external firm to do this, and they will not be happy if the liability is higher than this. And I don't want to regret employing you.'

Required

(b) Applying ethical guidelines, state the threats to the fundamental principles you face from this instruction, and which fundamental principles are threatened. **(3 marks)**

Jeff's draft corporation tax computation for the year ended 30 September 2024

	£	£
Tax-adjusted trading profits		620,000
Profit on commercial property (note)		
Proceeds	1,200,000	
Less net book value	(1,000,000)	
		200,000
Dividends received from UK quoted shares		50,000
Non-trading loan relationships income:		
Bank interest receivable		12,000
Property income:		
Rent receivable	24,000	
Costs for agent to manage property	(1,000)	
Mortgage interest payable on let property	(5,000)	
		18,000
Taxable total profits		900,000
Corporation tax liability @ 19%		£171,000

Note. The commercial property sold was purchased for £700,000 in January 2006. The net book value of £1,000,000 is the market value in January 2016 when the property was revalued.

You have determined that the amounts shown above for each receipt and expense are correct, although they have not always been treated correctly in the tax computation.

Required

(c) Prepare a correct corporation tax computation for the year ended 30 September 2024, demonstrating your treatment of the various income and gains for corporation tax purposes.

Ignore VAT and stamp taxes.

(8 marks)
(Total 15 marks)
Note – this question is from the AIA sample paper

21 Og Ltd

You are a newly-qualified accountant who has recently started work in the Accounts Department of Og Ltd, a UK resident company that manufactures bags and other accessories for the fashion industry. You have been asked to assist in the preparation of Og Ltd's corporation tax computations for the year ended 31 March 2025.

The tax written down values at 1 April 2024 were as follows:

	£
Main pool	42,817
Special rate pool	50,000

The only addition during the year was the purchase of a new machine in July 2024 at a cost of £364,000. Due to the weight of the machine, a section of the factory floor had to be reinforced and resurfaced at a cost of £3,380 prior to its installation.

Required

(a) Calculate the capital allowances for Og Ltd for the year ended 31 March 2025. **(4 marks)**

Og Ltd received £40,000 in July 2024 for the sale of shares in Abacos Ltd, an unquoted trading company. This represents Og Ltd's entire holding of shares in Abacos Ltd (a 16% holding), which the company had purchased for £10,000 in May 2019. The profit on the shares of £30,000 has not been reflected in the profit of £1,844,232 below.

Required

(b) Explain why Og Ltd's gain on disposal of its shares in Abacos Ltd is exempt from corporation tax.
(3 marks)

Og Ltd's results for the year ended 31 March 2025 were as follows:

	Notes	£	£
Gross trading profit			2,057,062
Add			
Bank interest receivable		1,500	
UK dividend income	1	28,820	
			30,320
Less			
Depreciation		35,920	
Debenture interest payable	2	12,000	
Donation to charity	3	2,150	
Repairs	4	6,760	
Other allowable costs		186,320	
			(243,150)
Profit			1,844,232

Notes

1 The dividends were received as follows:

		£
19 May 2024	Dividend from Finley Ltd a company in which Og Ltd has a 20% holding (purchased in June 2014)	22,400
23 September 2024	Dividend from Aspen Ltd, a company in which Og Ltd has a 5% holding	6,420
		28,820

2 Og Ltd has in issue £150,000 8% debentures issued in January 2019. Interest is paid half-yearly on 1 April and 1 October each year. The debentures were used to raise funds to purchase a new factory.

3 £2,150 was paid to a national registered charity during the year.

4 The repairs expenditure was incurred for the replacement of a section of roof of the factory that was damaged in storms in November 2024.

Required

(c) Calculate the tax adjusted trading profit made by Og Ltd for the year ended 31 March 2025.

(4 marks)

Og Ltd had taxable total profits of £1,700,000 in the year ended 31 March 2024.

Required

(d) Calculate the corporation tax payable by Og Ltd for the year ended 31 March 2025 and state the corporation tax due dates. **(6 marks)**

In April 2025, Og Ltd is planning to purchase extra warehousing facilities in Wales for £325,000.

Required

(e) Calculate the land transaction tax payable by Og Ltd on the purchase of the new warehouse and advise when it should be paid. **(3 marks)**

(Total 20 marks)

22 Histlip plc

Histlip plc, a UK trading company, prepares its accounts to 31 March each year.

Research and development (R&D)

The company has undertaken qualifying research and development (R&D) activities for the first time during the year ended 31 March 2025. The following expenditure was incurred by the R&D department during the year ended 31 March 2025:

	£
Research staff salaries (5 employees earning £37,000 per annum each)	185,000
R&D Laboratory machinery	156,000
R&D Laboratory consumables (not incorporated in normal production)	40,000
Legal costs of rights issue to raise finance for R&D project	10,000
Interest on loan to finance machinery purchase	6,000
	397,000

In these figures, no account has yet been taken of the company's national insurance liabilities on the salaries.

Required

(a) Calculate the total amount deductible from Histlip plc's trading profits and the research and development expenditure credit in respect of the expenditure incurred by the R&D department in the year ended 31 March 2025.

Clearly show your treatment of each item and use a zero for any expenditure which is not revenue expenditure. **(7 marks)**

(b) Explain why and when Histlip plc must submit a claim notification in respect of its R&D expenditure in the year ended 31 March 2025. **(3 marks)**

Trading profit

In the year ended 31 March 2025, Histlip plc's trading profit before any deduction for R&D expenditure was £1,200,000. It had no other sources of income in the period.

Required

(c) Calculate Histlip plc's corporation tax payable for the year ended 31 March 2025 after taking account of relief for research and development expenditure. **(4 marks)**

Compliance check enquiry

The finance director received notice on 20 April 2025 from HM Revenue & Customs (HMRC) of a compliance check enquiry into the corporation tax return for the year ended 31 March 2023.

The finance director had submitted that corporation tax return on 8 April 2024, and believes that it is too late for HMRC to begin such an enquiry.

Required

(d) Advise the finance director of whether the notice from HMRC is within the time limit for starting a compliance check enquiry into the corporation tax return for the year ended 31 March 2023.

(3 marks)
(Total 17 marks)

23 Beam Ltd

Beam Ltd prepared accounts for the 18 months ended 31 March 2026.

Required

(a) State the accounting period(s) and date(s) by which any corporation tax returns should be submitted in relation to the 18 months to 31 March 2026. **(3 marks)**

On 1 August 2025, Beam Ltd sold a small shareholding (less than 1%) in a quoted company Percile plc for £300,000. The shares had been purchased in December 2009 for £180,000. No dividends were received in the 18 months ended 31 March 2026.

Required

(b) Calculate Beam Ltd's capital gain on disposal of the shares in Percile plc. **(2 marks)**

The company undertook the following transactions during the period:

Date	Transaction
1 March 2025	Sale of loan stock for £20,000. The loan stock had cost £12,000 on 1 March 2012.
1 May 2025	Purchase of car for £80,000 with CO_2 emissions of 186g/km for use by the managing director with 20% private use.
1 July 2025	Purchase of a new car with CO_2 emissions of 0g/km for £12,500.

The company had a tax written down value on its main pool of £61,978 on 1 October 2024 and a trade loss brought forward at 1 October 2024 of £27,000.

Required

(c) Calculate Beam Ltd's capital allowances for the 18 months ended 31 March 2026. **(5 marks)**

The tax-adjusted trading profits before capital allowances for the 18 months ended 31 March 2026 were £130,200. This does not include an annual qualifying charitable donation to a UK registerd charity of £4,000 each year on 1 January.

Required

(d) Calculate Beam Ltd's corporation tax payable for the 18 months ended 31 March 2026 and state the due date(s). **(10 marks)**

(Total 20 marks)

24 Fraser

You work in the Direct Taxes department of a medium-sized accountancy firm. You have a new client, Fraser, who started a new business on 1 November 2024.

In the first year of trade, his monthly sales (exclusive of VAT) were:

	Sales per month £
November 2024	2,000
December 2024	3,000
January – March 2025	5,000
April – June 2025	11,000
July – September 2025	20,000
October 2025	60,000

Fraser sold only standard rated goods, and future monthly sales are expected to be similar to those in October 2025.

Required

(a) Advise Fraser of the date by which he should notify HMRC that he should register for VAT, and the date from which he should have started to charge VAT. **(3 marks)**

Fraser did not know when he had to register for VAT and so to be prudent he registered voluntarily from 1 August 2025.

Fraser's expenditure from 1 November 2024 to 31 October 2025 was as follows:

Date	Expenditure	£
Each month	Materials purchased (standard rated) (note)	1,500
Each month	Bookkeeping services	100
1 September 2025	Workshop for use in the trade, purchased when the workshop was two years old.	84,000
30 September 2025	Bad debt, payment due 30 August 2025 and not yet received	800
1 October 2025	Purchase of a car with 75% business use	18,000
30 October 2025	Entertaining UK customers	1,200

All purchases are shown inclusive of VAT where appropriate.

Note. The material purchased each month was used to make items which were sold by the end of that month.

Required

(b) (i) On the basis that Fraser actually registered for VAT on 1 August 2025, calculate the VAT payable for the quarter ended 31 October 2025. **(4 marks)**

(ii) Advise how and when Fraser should submit his VAT return and pay the VAT for the quarter ended 31 October 2025. **(2 marks)**

Purchase of shares

Fraser is considering an investment of £2,020 in shares and has heard he may have to pay stamp duty, but doesn't know much about it.

Required

(c) Calculate the stamp duty Fraser would need to pay on his share purchase and advise him when it would be due. **(3 marks)**

(Total 12 marks)

25 Barnacle Ltd

Barnacle Ltd, one of your clients, is a profitable company which achieves small growth in sales each year.

The new financial accountant of Barnacle Ltd has asked for help when preparing the company's VAT return for the quarter ended 30 April 2025, which was a typical quarter for the current year.

The accountant has specifically asked you about a new customer of Barnacle Ltd, Patchy Ltd. Patchy Ltd placed an order with Barnacle Ltd on 23 March 2025 for standard rated goods priced at £50,000 (excluding VAT). The sales director of Barnacle Ltd was concerned that the customer may not pay for the goods, and so demanded a 30% deposit, paid on 3 April 2025. The goods were delivered on 14 May 2025, the invoice was issued on 16 May 2025 and the remaining payment was made on 20 May 2025.

Required

(a) Determine the tax point or points for the Patchy Ltd order. **(3 marks)**

Barnacle Ltd made the following sales (exclusive of VAT) during the quarter, before taking account of discounts and the samples (see below).

	£
Standard rated supplies	300,000
Zero rated supplies	5,000

The accountant has discovered that Barnacle Ltd offered a prompt payment discount of 2% to its regular customers. These regular customers accounted for 75% of the sales above, and the discount was applied if invoices were settled within 30 days of being issued. 50% of those customers who were offered a discount, paid within this period.

Barnacle Ltd gave two free samples of a new product to each of ten customers on 30 March 2025. The market value of these samples totalled £1,200 (excluding VAT).

Required

(b) Calculate Patchy Ltd's output VAT for the quarter ended 30 April 2025

The company incurred the following expenditure, inclusive of VAT where appropriate, during the quarter ended 30 April 2025.

	£
Standard rated costs of production and distribution	180,000
Entertaining of Chinese customers	2,820
Entertaining of British customers	6,000
Purchase of machinery	25,500
Purchase of car used by sales director, with 50% private use	36,000

Required

(c) Calculate the VAT payable or repayable for the quarter ended 30 April 2025, showing clearly your treatment of each item. **(9 marks)**

(Total 12 marks)

26 Astia Ltd

You are a member of the finance team at Astia Ltd, a UK resident company with shareholdings in a number of other trading companies. Astia Ltd owns a 4% holding in Oryx Ltd and a 25% shareholding in Dopx Ltd.

On 1 April 2024 the tax written down value on the main pool was £146,000 and there was a short life asset with a tax written down value of £18,000.

During the year ended 31 March 2025, the following acquisitions and disposals were made by Astia Ltd:

Date		£
10.07.24	Audi car (CO_2 emissions 182g/km)	53,000
15.07.24	The short life asset was sold for £13,700	(13,700)
01.09.24	New Toyota Car (CO_2 emissions 0g/km)	15,000
10.01.25	Electrical systems and solar shading (designated as integral features)	25,000

For the year ended 31 March 2025 Astia Ltd has an adjusted profit of £958,820 after deducting the following items, but before capital allowances:

	Note	£
Research and development		
Staff costs and consumables	1	54,000
Machinery for R&D laboratory	1	45,500
Charitable donations	2	1,650
Advertising	3	10,000

Notes

1 Astia Ltd has deducted the costs above in calculating trading profits. Included in the staff costs are PAYE/NIC liabilities relating to R&D staff totalling £4,624.

2 The £1,650 was payable to the NSPCC, a national registered charity. The figure includes a year end accrual of £250.

3 The advertising expenditure includes expenditure of £2,100 on bottles of fine wine (cost £35 each) labelled with the Astia Ltd's corporate logo for clients; advertising in trade magazines at a cost of £4,300 and the remaining £3,600 was incurred on an employee party.

Required

(a) (i) Calculate the capital allowances for the year ended 31 March 2025 for Astia Ltd. **(6 marks)**

(ii) Calculate the adjusted trading profits for the year ended 31 March 2025 for Astia Ltd.

(4 marks)

Other information

Astia Ltd sold its shareholding (4,000 shares) in Oryx Ltd on 31 January 2025 for £58,000 before selling costs of £1,460. Astia Ltd had acquired 3,000 shares on 18 March 2009 for £15,000 and had paid £3.50 per share in a rights issue on 7 May 2010 acquiring one share for every three held.

Required

(b) Calculate the chargeable gain on disposal of the Oryx shares. **(6 marks)**

Astia Ltd received a dividend of £40,000 during the year from Dopx Ltd, which is not included in the adjusted profit figure of £958,820.

Required

(c) Calculate the corporation tax liability for the year ended 31 March 2025 for Astia Ltd. **(4 marks)**

Entertaining

The managing director of Astia Ltd is planning to take several potential clients on a weekend holiday to Paris in August 2025, at a cost of £10,000. He is aware that client entertaining is not an allowable deduction against taxable trading profits, but has told the finance assistant to record this as 'Advertising expenditure' in order to claim a deduction in the corporation tax computation for the year ended 31 March 2026.

The finance assistant is unhappy about this and is seeking your advice as to whether this is acceptable.

Required

(d) Advise the finance assistant on the acceptability of the proposed treatment of the entertaining expenditure by the managing director. **(4 marks)**

(Total 24 marks)

27 Mitesh

Mitesh is a director and shareholder of Track Ltd. He earns an annual basic salary of £50,000 from the company. In the tax year 2024/25, he receives dividends from the company of £10,000 and a bonus of £25,000.

He has no other sources of income in 2024/25.

In 2023/24, Mitesh joined a pension scheme for the first time, with a contribution to a personal scheme amounting to £30,000 (gross). Mitesh was not a high-income individual in 2023/24 for pension purposes.

Mitesh wants further contributions to be made to his pension scheme in 2024/25. However, he is unsure whether he should make the contributions personally, or whether the contributions should be made by Track Ltd. He requires advice on which arrangement would give the lower after-tax cost.

The amount of salary, bonus and dividend received by Mitesh would remain the same, whichever way the pension contribution is made.

Required

(a) Assuming Mitesh alone contributes to his pension scheme in 2024/25, calculate the maximum gross contribution which would qualify for income tax relief and which would not incur additional charges. **(4 marks)**

Mitesh decides that a gross contribution in 2024/25 of £25,000 would be sufficient and that this can either be made by him personally or by Track Ltd. Track Ltd has augmented profits in excess of £2 million.

Required

(b) Calculate the after-tax cost of a £25,000 gross contribution if it were made by:

    (i) Track Ltd; or
    (ii) Mitesh. **(6 marks)**

(Total 10 marks)

28 Lucy

You work in the private clients department of a firm of accountants and you have been asked to do some calculations requested by Lucy, a client. Assume that it is 1 March 2024.

Lucy is considering two work arrangements. She will start her chosen arrangement on 6 April 2024 and will continue with that arrangement for the whole of the tax year 2024/25.

Employment with Red plc

Lucy has been offered employment with Red plc. She would be paid a salary of £36,000 and would be required to work at Red plc's offices.

Lucy would travel from home to Red plc's offices by train and would buy an annual season ticket costing £1,500.

Required

(a) (i) Calculate the income tax which would be payable if Lucy was employed by Red plc. **(2 marks)**

   (ii) Calculate the NIC payable if Lucy was employed by Red plc. **(2 marks)**

   (iii) Calculate Lucy's post-tax income if she was employed by Red plc. **(2 marks)**

Self-employment

Lucy would work for a number of clients at their offices. She would receive fees of £36,000 from her clients in the year to 5 April 2025.

Lucy would travel from home to client offices in her own car. Her business mileage would be 4,600 miles during the year and she estimates this would actually cost 40p per mile.

Lucy would prepare accounts to 5 April 2025 using the cash basis and approved mileage allowances.

Required

(b) (i) Calculate the income tax which would be payable if Lucy was self-employed. **(2 marks)**

   (ii) Calculate the NIC payable if Lucy was self-employed. **(2 marks)**

   (iii) Calculate Lucy's post-tax income if she was self-employed. **(2 marks)**

Lucy has never been registered for self-assessment before. She decided to become self-employed and work as a sole trader from 6 April 2024. She was informed by a friend that she needs to notify HMRC of her chargeability to income tax. She did so immediately on 1 December 2025. Lucy filed her first self-assessment return online on 31 January 2026 and paid the income tax and class 4 (as per part (b)) on the same day.

Required

(c) Calculate and explain the likely penalty for late notification that Lucy is liable to. **(3 marks)**

(Total 15 marks)

29 Nima

Nima began to trade on 1 July 2024. She prepared her first set of accounts for the 9 months ended 5 April 2025.

Her tax adjusted trading profits for the 9 months ended 5 April 2025 were £63,000.

Nima also rented out a furnished house during 2024/25 with receipts and payments as follows:

	£
Rental income receipts	12,000
Payments	
Building a new wall in the garden	800
Letting agent fees	500
Replacement of sofa with similar model	1,200
Interest on loan to buy sofa	200

During 2024/25, Nima made payments to her personal pension scheme totalling £240.

Nima's total income tax liability for 2023/24 was £15,000. Of this liability, £4,000 was paid by deduction at source.

Required

(a) Calculate Nima's income tax liability for 2024/25. **(12 marks)**

(b) Calculate Nima's Class 4 national insurance contributions for 2024/25. **(3 marks)**

(c) State the due dates, and calculate the corresponding amounts, for payment of Nima's 2024/25 income tax and Class 4 national insurance liabilities. **(5 marks)**

(Total 20 marks)

30 Kristina

Kristina is employed by Salsa plc, receiving an annual salary of £85,000, paid monthly. During 2024/25, she also received the following benefits from Salsa plc:

- Car with list price of £30,000 and CO_2 emissions of 61 g/km.

- Diesel for all Kristina's car journeys, including private journeys. The cost to the company of diesel for private journeys was £1,500 and that for business journeys was £2,500.

- Accommodation in an apartment rented by Salsa plc. The rent paid by Salsa plc was £18,000 per annum and the annual value of the property was £17,000.

- Use of the company's private gym situated at Salsa plc's head office. The cost for Salsa plc of running the gym was £1,000 per employee.

- £6,000 contributed by Salsa plc to an occupational pension scheme. Kristina also contributed a further £3,000 to the scheme, which was deducted under a net pay arrangement.

Required

(a) Calculate Kristina's income tax liability for 2024/25, showing clearly your treatment of each benefit. **(10 marks)**

(b) Calculate the Class 1 secondary and Class 1A national insurance contributions payable by Salsa plc in respect of Kristina for the year 2024/25. **(2 marks)**

(c) Explain the dates by which Salsa plc must pay the Class 1 secondary national insurance and state the date by which Salsa plc must pay the Class 1A national insurance. **(3 marks)**

Kristina's brother is self-employed and makes payments on account under self-assessment each year. He does not understand why Kristina does not have to make such payments.

Required

(d) Explain why Kristina does not make payments on account in respect of her income tax liability. **(2 marks)**

(Total 17 marks)

PRACTICE QUESTION BANK

31 Jamie

Jamie has a baking business, which he has run as a sole trader for six years. He uses the cash basis to calculate his taxable trading profit. Jamie lives in Dundee, Scotland.

On 6 April 2024, Jamie had a car with a CO2 emissions of 42g/km. The car's private usage was agreed as 30%. The tax-written down value of the car on 6 April 2024 was £2,500. Jamie had paid £5,500 for it in 2020.

On 15 June 2024, Jamie sold his car for £1,000. He replaced the car with a new van which cost £25,000. His private usage of the van was agreed as 30%.

Required

(a) Calculate Jamie's capital allowances for the year ended 6 April 2025. **(4 marks)**

Jamie runs his baking business from rented premises. His recent rent payments have been as follows.

Date paid	Rental period	£
01 February 2024	3 months to 30 April 2024	10,000
01 May 2024	3 months to 30 July 2024	10,000
01 August 2024	3 months to 31 October 2024	10,000
01 November 2024	3 months to 31 January 2025	10,000
01 February 2025	3 months to 30 April 2025	12,000

In the year ended 5 April 2025, Jamie paid insurance and bills relating to the premises of £20,000. The premises has three floors including one floor which is entirely living accommodation, occupied by Jamie alone.

Required

(a) Calculate the allowable deduction from Jamie's trading profits in relation to his premises, based on:

    (i) a fixed rate adjustment; or
    (ii) actual expenditure and usage. **(4 marks)**

In the year ended 5 April 2025, Jamie's receipts from customers were £225,000, total motoring expenses paid in relation to his car and van were £7,000 and other deductible payments (not including the items in parts (a) and (b), were £73,000. Assume Jamie makes a claim for a fixed rate adjustment for the expenses relating to his business premises.

(b) Calculate Jamie's taxable trading profit for 2024/25. **(2 marks)**

In 2024/25, Jamie had taxable property income of £42,000 and received bank interest of £1,200.

Because of plans to replace a lot of his kitchen equipment in 2025/26, Jamie expects to make a trading loss in the year ending 5 April 2026 of £100,000. He would like to have loss relief as early as possible.

Required

(c) Calculate Jamie's income tax liability for 2024/25. **(6 marks)**
(Total 16 marks)

32 Jennifer

Jennifer made the following disposals during 2024/25.

Sale of 5,000 ordinary shares in Architravepe plc for £13,000 on 1 March 2025. Architravepe plc has one million shares in issue. Jennifer had purchased shares in Architravepe plc over several years as follows:

	Number of shares	Cost £
1 March 2020	1,000	2,000
1 March 2021	2,000	4,500
24 February 2025	4,000	9,000
10 March 2025	3,000	7,500

Sale of a painting on 1 April 2025 for £20,100, which had cost Jennifer £7,000 in January 2012.

Sale of Jennifer's home in London on 1 January 2025 for £600,000. Jennifer purchased the house for £440,000 on 1 January 2015 and began living in it immediately. Between 1 January 2016 and 1 January 2021, Jennifer lived elsewhere in London with her partner, during which time she rented out her house. After separating from her partner, she moved back into the house on 1 January 2021, living there until she sold it.

Jennifer had taxable income in 2024/25 of £60,000 and capital losses brought forward at 6 April 2024 of £26,000.

Required

(a) Identify which of Jennifer's purchased shares are matched with the disposal on 1 March 2025.

(2 marks)

(b) Calculate Jennifer's capital gains tax liability for the year 2024/25. **(13 marks)**

(c) State the date(s) and amount(s) to be paid in respect of Jennifer's capital gains tax liability for 2024/25. **(2 marks)**

(Total 17 marks)

33 Flavia

Flavia made the following disposals during 2024/25:

1. Sale of 3,000 shares in Scroll plc, a quoted company, on 1 May 2024 for £21,000.

   Flavia had purchased 5,000 shares at a cost of £2 per share on 1 May 2016. On 1 January 2018, there was a rights issue of 1 share for every 5 held. Flavia took up her full rights at a cost of £5 per share.

   On 20 May 2024, Flavia purchased 1,000 shares for £6,750.

   Flavia's shareholding was always less than 1% of the share capital of the company.

2. Sale of a vintage car for £8,000 on 5 July 2024. The car had cost £10,000 in October 2008.

3. Sale of a commercial property for £180,000 on 7 August 2024. Flavia paid legal fees of £5,000 in respect of the sale. The property had cost £70,000 in May 2004. Flavia had paid £3,000 for redecoration in May 2009 and £16,000 for an extension of the property in January 2011.

4. Sale of a business on 14 September 2024. Flavia had started the business in April 2015. The only chargeable asset of the business was internally-generated goodwill, sold for £60,000 on 14 September 2024. Flavia has made no previous business disposals.

   Flavia had taxable income in 2024/25 of £80,000 and had a capital loss of £9,700 brought forward at 6 April 2024.

Required

(a) Calculate Flavia's capital gains tax liability for the year 2024/25. **(15 marks)**

34 Sandley Ltd

Sandley Ltd prepared accounts for the year ended 31 March 2025.

Required

(a) State the due date for submission of Sandley Ltd's corporation tax return for the year ended 31 March 2025. **(1 mark)**

(b) State the time period for which Sandley Ltd must keep records in respect of the year ended 31 March 2025. **(1 mark)**

Sandley Ltd's accounts showed an accounting profit before taxation of £2,560,400. This was after deduction of the following expenditure:

	£
Legal fees in respect of an issue of shares in Sandley Ltd	13,000
Legal fees incurred in collecting bad debts from customers	4,500
Depreciation	54,000
Staff entertaining (summer party)	1,700
Operating lease costs of car with CO_2 emissions of 192 g/km used by managing director 40% for private use	10,000
Redecorating office building	20,000
Donation to a UK political party	8,600

During the year ended 31 March 2025, Sandley Ltd received bank interest of £10,000 and dividends from unrelated companies of £9,000.

Sandley Ltd had a tax written down value on its main pool brought forward at 1 April 2024 of £182,900. On 30 June 2024, the company sold office furniture for £2,000 (original cost on 5 February 2023 was £4,200 and a superdeduction was claimed on this expenditure). On 1 August 2024, the company purchased a new printing machine for £28,240.

Required

(c) Calculate the corporation tax liability for Sandley Ltd for the year ended 31 March 2025. **(14 marks)**

Sandley Ltd had taxable total profits of £1,839,200 for the year ended 31 March 2024.

Required

(d) Calculate Sandley Ltd's augmented profits for the year ended 31 March 2025 and state the due dates, and amounts due, for payment of corporation tax for that year. **(3 marks)**

(Total 19 marks)

35 Raidet Ltd

Raidet Ltd prepared accounts for the year ended 31 March 2025.

The tax-adjusted trading profits for the year were £358,900 before capital allowances.

Interest

On 31 December 2024, Raidet Ltd received interest on loan stock of £600 which had accrued evenly throughout the year ended 31 December 2024. On 31 March 2025, Raidet Ltd had further interest accrued on this loan stock of £150.

During the year ended 31 March 2025, Raidet Ltd had to pay interest of £95 on overdue corporation tax.

Capital disposals

On 1 August 2024, Raidet Ltd disposed of its entire shareholding (1%) in Medalle plc for £25,000. Raidet Ltd had bought the shares in June 2003 for £8,500.

On 1 September 2024, Raidet Ltd sold a car for £9,000. The car had CO_2 emissions of 45g/km and had originally cost £15,200 two years ago.

Charitable donation

On 1 January 2025, the company made a qualifying charitable donation of £800 to a UK registered charity.

Amounts brought forward

At 1 April 2024, the tax written down value of the main pool was £36,150 and that of the special rate pool was £67,467.

At 1 April 2024, Raidet Ltd had brought forward trading losses of £13,800 and brought forward capital losses of £3,836 arising in the year ended 31 March 2024.

Required

(a) Calculate the corporation tax liability for Raidet Ltd for the year ended 31 March 2025. **(15 marks)**

36 Osney Ltd, Cherwell Ltd & Thames Ltd

Three unconnected clients have asked for your advice on VAT matters.

Osney Ltd

Osney Ltd makes both standard rated and zero-rated supplies and has a VAT year end of 31 March. On 1 April 2024, Osney Ltd sold a factory in England for £1,500,000. Osney Ltd used the property for a number of years to manufacture shoes but, following a supply chain restructuring, it is now surplus to requirements. Osney Ltd incurred £10,000 in professional fees in relation to the sale.

Amounts are stated exclusive of VAT. The option to tax has not been exercised.

Required

(a) Advise Osney Ltd of the VAT treatment of the sale of the building and the associated professional fees. **(4 marks)**

Cherwell Ltd

Cherwell Ltd makes standard rated supplies and has a VAT year end of 31 July. The company has a factory in Northern Ireland and sometimes supplies customers from that location. Maeve, the financial controller of Cherwell Ltd, is responsible for completing the company's quarterly VAT return.

Maeve is confused by the changes that have taken place since the UK left the EU. In particular, she is unsure how to treat the following transactions:

- Sale of goods from the Northern Ireland factory worth £300,000 to a VAT registered business in Spain.

- Purchase of goods worth £10,000 from a VAT registered business in Belgium, supplied to Cherwell's head office in Oxford, England.

- Purchase of IT services (which are standard rated in the UK) from a company based in the USA.

Required

(b) Explain how Maeve should treat the specified items in Cherwell Limited's VAT return. **(8 marks)**

PRACTICE QUESTION BANK

Thames Ltd

Thames Ltd makes standard rated supplies and is classed as a substantial trader so is required to make payments on account of VAT. For the year ended 31 March 2025, the payments on account were each determined as £300,000.

Thames Ltd's VAT liability for the quarter ended 31 December 2024 was £960,000. The company's financial controller was on sick leave from 2 December 2024 and any VAT payments due after this date were not made until 6 February 2025 when the financial controller returned to work.

The company had made one previous late payment default in respect of the quarter ended 30 June 2024.

Required

(c) Assess when Thames Ltd's VAT liability for the quarter ended 31 December 2024 should have been paid and state Thames Ltd's penalty for late payment. **(8 marks)**

(Total 20 marks)

Practice Answer Bank

PRACTICE ANSWER BANK

1 Alf

(a)

	£
Salary	20,000
Hi-fi equipment – annual value 800 × 20%	160
Van	3,960
Van fuel	757
Mobile phone – one phone exempt	0
Medical insurance – cost to employer	700
Long service award – non-cash less than £50 per year exempt	0
Employment income	25,577

> **Tutorial note**
>
> The van benefit and van fuel benefit are in Whillans tax tables available in the exam.

(b)

	Non-savings £	Savings £	Dividend £
Employment income	109,000		
Building Society Interest		5,250	
Dividend Income			5,000
Net income	109,000	5,250	5,000
Less PA (W)	(7,695)		
Taxable income	101,305	5,250	5,000

BR band (37,700 + 9,500) = 47,200

Income tax

	£
47,200 × 20%	9,440
54,105 (101,305 – 47,200) × 40%	21,642
500 × 0%	0
4,750 (5,250 – 500) × 40%	1,900
500 × 0%	0
4,500 (5,000 – 500) × 33.75%	1,519
	34,501
Less PAYE	(31,100)
Tax payable	3,401

Working

	£
Total income (109,000 + 5,250 + 5,000)	119,250
Less pension contribution (7,600 × 100/80)	(9,500)
	109,750
Less limit	(100,000)
	9,750
PA 12,570 – (½ × 9,750) =	7,695

(c)

	Non-savings £
Employment income	45,000
Property business income	12,500
Net income	57,500
Less PA	(12,570)
Taxable income	44,930

Income tax

	£
37,700 × 20%	7,540
7,230 (44,930 – 37,700) × 40%	2,892
Less finance costs tax reducer £2,500 × 20%	(500)
Tax liability	9,932
PAYE paid	
Income tax payable	

(d) Payments on account

Based on the income tax payable in 2024/25 of £3,446, Janine must make payments on account of £1,723 (50% of £3,446) in respect of her liability in 2025/26.

The first payment on account for 2025/26 of £1,723 is due on 31 January 2026.

The second payment is due on 31 July 2026.

Marking scheme

	Marks
Employment income	5
Shirley's taxable income	3½
Shirley's tax payable	4½
Janine's taxable income	1½
Janine's tax liability	2½
Janine's payments on account	3
	20

2 Ken

(a) Ken

	£
Net profit	19,000
Add: Salary for Ken (appropriation of profit)	3,000
Salary for Sameer (correctly treated)	0
Legal expenses (capital item)	400
Tax advice (personal expense)	550
Car lease payments (No disallowance when using the cash basis)	0
Unpaid sales invoice	(6,000)
	16,950

(b)

	Main pool £	Allowance £
P/e 30.11.24		
B/f	17,212	
Addition	15,000	
Disposal	(14,000)	
Balancing allowance	18,212	18,212

> **Tutorial note**
>
> There is no AIA and no WDAs in the final period.

Marking scheme

	Marks
Ken's trading profit	5
Desmond's capital allowances	3
	8

3 Vipul

(a) On 28 February 2025, taxable supplies since commencement of trade (eight months) = (6 × £10,000) + (2 × £16,000) = £92,000 which exceeds the VAT registration threshold of £90,000.

If Vipul wasn't already VAT registered he would have been required to notify HMRC by 30 March 2025 and he would have had to register from 1 April 2025. This registration is compulsory.

(b) SDLT on VAT inclusive price of £400,000 × 1.2 = £480,000

	£
£(250,000 – 150,000) @ 2%	2,000
£(480,000 – 250,000) @ 5%	11,500
SDLT	13,500

(c) (i) Input VAT recoverable:

	£
Car	0
Equipment (£60,000 × 1/6)	10,000
Input VAT recoverable	10,000

(ii) Capital allowances:

	Main pool £	Private use car £		PU
AIA addition	50,000			
AIA	(50,000)			50,000
Car addition		32,000		
WDA @ 6%		(1,920)	× 25%	480
		30,080		50,480

Structures and Buildings Allowance = 3% × £400,000 = £12,000
Total capital allowances = £50,480 + £12,000 = £62,480

(d) (i) Tax-adjusted trading profit for the year ended 30 June 2025

	£
Net profit	117,800
Add:	
Depreciation	9,800
Entertaining potential customers	2,000
Legal advice regarding sales contracts	–
Car insurance private use element 75% × £600	450
Advertising in local paper	–
Subscription to trade association	–
Less capital allowances	(62,480)
	67,570

(ii) 2024/25 assessment based on the profits arising 1 July 2024 – 5 April 2025 (his first tax year as a trader).

9/12 × £67,570 = £50,678

(e) (i) Income tax computation:

	£
Trading income	50,678
Overseas rental income £9,000 × 100/90	10,000
	60,678
Personal allowance	(12,570)
	48,108
Income tax liability:	
£37,700 @ 20%	7,540
£10,408 @ 40%	4,163
	11,703
Less DTR, lower of £1,000 and UK tax at 40%	(1,000)
	10,703

(ii) National insurance contributions:

	£
Class 4	
£(50,270 – 12,570) = £37,700 @ 8%	3,016
£(50,678 – 50,270) @ 2%	8
	3,024

(f) 31 January 2026
Ignorance of the tax rules is not deemed a reasonable excuse by HMRC.

(g) VAT payments:
7 February 2026
7 May 2026
7 August 2026
7 November 2026

Income tax and NIC:
31 January 2026 – payment of income tax and class 4 NIC for 2024/25
31 January 2026 – payment on account for 2025/26 of income tax and class 4 NIC
31 July 2026 – payment on account for 2025/26 of income tax and class 4 NIC

Marking scheme

	Marks
Registration dates	4
SDLT	3
Input VAT recoverable	2
P&M capital allowances	3
SBAs	1
	4
Trading profit	8
Taxable income	2½
Income tax liability	2½
	5
Class 4 NICs	3
	3
Due date	2
VAT due dates	1½
Income tax and NIC due dates	3½
	5
	36

4 Alessia

(a) Employment income

	2024/25 £
Salary (£34,000 × 2/12)	5,667
Car benefit	
£18,500 × 29% × 2/12	894
	6,561

Car benefit percentage
16% + (120 − 55)/5 = 29%

(b) Trading income

	1.10.24–31.3.25 £	Y/e 31.3.26 £
Adjusted trading profit per question	32,718	13,558
Outstanding receivables (profit already calculated using the cash basis)	–	
Outstanding payables (profit already calculated using the cash basis)	–	
Interior design course (deemed to be capital as imparting new knowledge)	–	
Bookkeeping seminars	(150)	
Bank interest		
(£50,000 × 8% × 8/12)	(2,667)	(4,000)
Rental		
£2,700 × 6/12	(1,350)	(2,700)

	1.10.24–31.3.25 £	Y/e 31.3.26 £
Plant and machinery (excluding car) (4,800 + 5,300 + 2,000)	(12,100)	
Leased car (6 months and 12 months × £220 × 80%)	(1,056)	(2,112)
	15,395	4,746

(c) Income Tax Computation 2024/25

	Non-savings £	Dividends £	Total £
Employment income (W1)	6,561		6,561
Trading income (W2)	15,395		15,395
Dividends		9,500	9,500
Total income	21,956	9,500	31,456
PA	(12,570)	–	(12,570)
Taxable income	9,386	9,500	18,886

Income Tax:	
£9,386 × 20%	1,877
£500 × 0% (dividend allowance)	0
£9,000 × 8.75%	788
Income tax liability	2,665
PAYE	(967)
Income tax payable	1,698

(d)
Notify HMRC of starting to trade – 5 October 2025
Filing 2024/25 income tax return – 31 January 2026
Paying income tax payable – (first year of trading) 31 January 2026

Marking scheme

	Marks
Employment income	3
Computation of trading income	7
Income tax computation	5
Deadlines	3
	18

5 Nexis Ltd

Ibrahim

(a) **Income Tax Computation 2024/25**

	£	£
Employment income		
Inducement to work for Nexis Ltd		15,000
Salary		45,000
Car benefit (230g/km)		
Max = 37%		
List price = £75,000 + £8,000 = £83,000		
37% × £83,000		30,710
Fuel benefit		
£27,800 × 37%		10,286
Flat		
Annual value £9,200 × 10/12	7,667	
Additional charge		
[(£189,000 + £16,000) − £75,000] × 2.25% × 10/12	2,438	
Furnishing £42,000 × 20% × 10/12	7,000	
Cleaning £6,800 × 10/12	5,667	
		22,772
Net income		123,768
Personal allowance		(12,570)
Adjusted net income = £123,768 − (£48,000 × 100/80) = £63,768,		
ie less than £100,000, therefore full personal allowance available		
Taxable income		111,198

(b) Deadline for P60 – 31 May 2025

Deadline for P11D – 6 July 2025

Marking scheme

			Marks
(a)	Salary and inducements	1	
	Car and fuel	3	
	Accommodation	5	
	Personal allowance	2	
		11	
	Max		10
(b)	P60	1	
	P11D	1	
			2
			12

6 Marcia

(a) (i) Property income (normal basis)

	£
Rental income	4,500
Allowable expenses	(800)
Taxable property income	3,700

She will also get relief for the finance costs of £150 × 20% = £30

(ii) Property income (property allowance)

	£
Rental income	4,500
Property allowance	(1,000)
Taxable property income	3,500

(iii)

	£
Trading profits	30,000
Interest from NS&I Certificate	–
REIT distribution – taxed as property income £2,000 × 100/80	2,500
	32,500
Less personal allowance	(12,570)
	19,930
£19,930 @ 20%	3,986
Less tax deducted on REIT distribution	(500)
	3,486

(b) *Costs of car purchase*

Fixed rate deductions
Business mileage is 70% × 17,500 = 12,250

	£
10,000 miles at £0.45	4,500
2,250 miles at £0.25	563
	5,063

Fixed rate deduction includes relief for running costs

Capital allowances and running costs

	£
Capital allowance (6% × £18,000 × 70%)	756
Running costs (70% × £4,000)	2,800
	3,556

Marking scheme

		Marks
Rental income under each method		5
Income tax payable		4
Fixed rate deductions and capital allowances		5
		14

7 Kelly

(a)

		£
For both (i) and (ii)		
Proceeds		800,000
Cost		(250,000)
		550,000
Less AEA		(3,000)
		547,000

(i) CGT payable @ 20% (no business asset disposal relief applies as conditions not satisfied for at least two years) — 108,800

Net proceeds of sale 800,000 – 108,800 — 691,200

(ii) CGT payable @ 10% (business asset disposal relief applies as conditions satisfied for at least two years) — 54,700

Net proceeds of sale 800,000 – 54,700 — 745,300

(b)

	£
Proceeds	150,000
Cost	(60,000)
Gain	90,000
Rollover relief (balance)	80,000
Taxable now (150,000 – 140,000)	10,000

Base cost of new property

	£
Cost	140,000
Less gain rolled over	(80,000)
	60,000

(c)

	Residential property gain £	Other gain £
Gains	16,300	25,000
Less annual exempt amount	(3,000)	–
Taxable gains	13,300	25,000
Tax at 24%/20%	3,192	5,000
CGT liability £(3,192 + 5,000)		8,192

Tutorial note

The annual exempt amount is set against the residential property gain in priority to the other gain as it saves tax at 24% instead of 20%.

(d)

	£
First payment on account – 31 January 2025	
50% of 2023/24 income tax and Class 4 contributions	
£(16,000 + 3,000) × 50%	9,500
Second payment on account – 31 July 2025	
Calculated as above	9,500
Balancing payment – 31 January 2026	
£(19,300 + 3,500) – (£9,500 × 2)	3,800

(e) The payments on account are made on time but Callum claimed to reduce them so much that they were insufficient to cover his income tax and Class 4 NIC liabilities. The final liability was £12,000 but the reduced payments on account totalled only £10,000, leaving £2,000 outstanding.

Interest is charged on the lower of:

- the original payment on account (£7,500)
- the reduced amount plus 50% of the outstanding balance on the final liability (£5,000 + £2,000 × 50% = £6,000)

ie £6,000

Payment on account 1

£5,000 paid on time
£1,000 excessive reduction, interest runs from 31 January 2025 to 31 January 2026 =
7.75% × £1,000 × 365/365 = £77.50

Payment on account 2

Same as payment on account 1 but interest runs from 31 July 2025 to 31 January 2026 (184 days)
Interest = 7.75% × 184/365 × £1,000 = £39.07.

Marking scheme

	Marks
Kelly's gain	1
Net proceeds after tax	3
	4
Del's Gain	2
Base cost	1
	3
Gretel's CGT liability	3
Tula's due dates	1½
Amounts payable	2½
	4
Callum's excessive reduction of £1,000	1
Payment on account 1	1
Payment on account 2	2
	4
	18

8 Isabella

(a)

	£
Gains chargeable at 24%	
Investment residential property (£280,000 - £190,000)	90,000
Less current year loss (OBD shares)	(1,150)
Less annual exempt amount (best use)	(3,000)
	85,850
Capital gains tax @ 24%	20,604
Gains chargeable at 20%	
Shares in OBD plc (W1)	–
Shares in BSR plc (W2)	17,512
	17,512
Capital gains tax @ 20%	3,502
Gains chargeable at 10% (Business asset disposal relief)	
Shares in Upsy Ltd (W3)	24,000
Capital gains tax @ 10%	2,400
Total capital gains tax 20,604 + 3,502 + £2,400	26,506

Workings

1   Shares in OBD plc

	£
Proceeds	1,650
Cost (700 × £4)	(2,800)
Loss	(1,150)

2   Shares in BSR plc

	£
Proceeds	22,856
Cost (W4)	(5,344)
	17,512

3   Shares in Upsy Ltd

	£
Proceeds (400 × £61)	24,400
Cost (400 × £1)	(400)
Gain	24,000

4   BSR plc share pool

	Number of shares at takeover	Cost
	£	£
Sept 2002	1,000	1,050
Feb 2007 (3,000 × £2.50)	3,000	7,500
	4,000	8,550
Disposal	(2,500)	(5,344)
	1,500	3,206

(b) Capital gains tax for 2024/25 payable as follows

			£
31 July 2024	Re investment residential property (£90,000 - £3,000) × 24%		
	NB the loss had not arisen by the date of completion		20,880
31 January 2026	Balance		5,626
	Capital gains tax liability 2024/25		26,506

Marking scheme

	Marks
Residential property gain	1
OBD loss	1
BSR gain	3
Upsy gain	1
Loss and annual exempt amount use	2
CGT	2
Payment date for residential property	1
Payment on account for the property	2
Balancing payment and date	2
	15

9 Armani

	Qualifying for Business Asset Disposal relief £	Other gains £	Residential property gains £
AMI Ltd (W1)	80,500		
House (W2)			10,500
Bookcases (W3)		20,000	
Furniture	–	–	–
	80,500	20,000	10,500
Less annual exempt amount			(3,000)
Less capital losses brought forward			(6,200)
			1,300
CGT @ 10%/20%/24%	8,050	4,000	312
Total			12,362

Workings

1. **AMI Ltd**

	£
Proceeds	85,500
Cost	(5,000)
	80,500

2. **House**

	£
Proceeds	285,000
Cost	(180,000)
	105,000
PRR – 90%	(94,500)
Chargeable gain	10,500

3. **Bookcases**

    Each disposal

	£
Market value = ½ × £50,000	25,000
Cost = ½ × £30,000	(15,000)
Gain	10,000

    Total gain of the pair = 2 × £10,000 = £20,000

4. The items of furniture were each bought and sold for <£6,000 and are exempt under chattels rules.

Marking scheme

	Marks
Gains calculation	3
AMI Ltd (W1)	2
House (W2)	4
Bookcases (W3)	2
	11

10 Michael

(a) **Freehold warehouse**

	£	£
Disposal proceeds		522,000
Less: cost	258,000	
enhancement expenditure: extension	99,000	
enhancement expenditure: floor	0	
		(357,000)
		165,000
Rollover relief (balancing figure)		(152,000)
Chargeable gain (£522,000 – £509,000)		13,000

> **Tutorial note**
>
> The cost of replacing the warehouse's floor is revenue expenditure as the floor is a subsidiary part of the property.
>
> The proceeds not reinvested form the chargeable gain taxed on disposal.

(b) **Shares in Rolling Ltd**

	£
Disposal proceeds	3,675,000
Less cost (W)	(537,600)
Chargeable gain	3,137,400

Capital gains tax payable

	£
£1,000,000 × 10%	100,000
£2,137,400 × 20%	427,480
£3,137,400	527,480

Working: Share pool

	Number	Cost £
Purchase June 2008	500,000	960,000
Bonus issue December 2013		
500,000 × 3/2	750,000	0
Disposal September 2024	1,250,000	960,000
960,000 × 700,000/1,250,000	(700,000)	(537,600)
Balance carried forward	550,000	422,400

(c) Claims for relief

- Michael may make a claim for rollover relief on his warehouse gain by 5 April 2029.
- He may make a claim for BADR in respect of his shares in Rolling Ltd up to 31 January 2027.

PRACTICE ANSWER BANK

Marking scheme

	Marks
Warehouse gain	2
Rollover relief	2
Shares gain	4
Shares CGT payable	2
Claims	2
	12

11 Churchill

(a) **Churchill – CGT liability 2024/25**

	£
Chargeable gain on painting	38,260
Less annual exempt amount	(3,000)
Taxable gain	35,260
CGT liability: £(37,700 – 24,900) = 12,800 @ 10%	1,280
£(35,260 – 12,800) = 22,460 @ 20%	4,492
	5,772

(b) **Churchill – Revised CGT liability 2024/25**

	£
Gain qualifying for business asset disposal relief	
Gain on freehold shop £(140,000 – 80,000)	60,000
Gain not qualifying for business asset disposal relief	
Painting	38,260
Less allowable loss on warehouse £(102,000 – 88,000)	(14,000)
Net gain	24,260
Less annual exempt amount	(3,000)
Taxable gain	21,260

	£
CGT liability: £60,000 @ 10%	6,000
£21,260 @ 20%	4,252
	10,252

Tutorial note

1 The capital loss on the sale of the freehold warehouse and the annual exempt amount are set against the chargeable gain from the sale of the painting as this saves CGT at the higher rate of 20%. Although the warehouse is being sold with the business, it was never actually used in the business, and so this aspect of the sale does not qualify for business asset disposal relief. If it had been used in the business, the loss of £14,000 would have been deducted from the gain on the shop to give a net gain on sale of the business of £46,000. CGT would then be charged on £46,000 at 10%.

2 The unused basic rate tax band of £12,800 is effectively used by the gain qualifying for business asset disposal relief of £60,000 even though this has no effect on the 10% tax rate.

(c) **Ronald – Chargeable gain 3 December 2024**

	£
Gross proceeds	92,000
Less auctioneers' commission (cost of disposal) £92,000 × 5%	(4,600)
Net proceeds	87,400
Less cost £28,600 × $\dfrac{92,000}{92,000 + 38,000}$	(20,240)
Chargeable gain	67,160

> **Tutorial note**
>
> 1 The cost of the land is £28,600, which is the value when Ronald's father-in-law died. Ronald would have taken over this cost when his wife transferred the land to him.
>
> 2 The gross proceeds of sale are used in the part disposal fraction.

Marking scheme

	Marks
CGT on painting	3
CGT with disposal of business	4
Ronald's gain	3
	10

12 Star Ltd

(a) (i) **Star Ltd taxable total profits for the 15-month period of account ended 30 June 2025**

	Year ended 31 March 2025 £	Period ended 30 June 2025 £
Trading profit (12:3)	420,000	105,000
Capital allowances: FYA on low emission car	(8,000)	
Capital allowances: AIA		(49,500)
	412,000	55,500
Interest income (accruals basis)	–	800
Chargeable gain	2,500	–
Total profits	414,500	56,300
Less qualifying charitable donation	–	(2,500)
Taxable total profits	414,500	53,800

(ii)

	Year ended 31 March 2025 £	Period ended 30 June 2025 £
Upper limit	250,000	62,500
Lower limit	50,000	12,500
Corporation tax at 25%	103,625	13,450
Less 3/200 × (£62,500 - £53,800)		(131)
Corporation tax payable	103,625	13,319

(iii)

	Year ended 31 March 2025	Period ended 30 June 2025
Filing date	30 June 2026	30 June 2026
Payment date	1 January 2026	1 April 2026

(b) (i) No life tax as all gifts PETs.

Death tax

		£
(1)	12.3.20 PET	274,000
	AE – 2019/20	(3,000)
	2018/19 b/f	(3,000)
		268,000

No death tax as covered by nil rate band.

		£	£
(2)	24.7.20 PET		150,000
	AE – 2020/21		(3,000)
			147,000
	Nil band @ death	325,000	
	Less GCT < seven years	(268,000)	(57,000)
			90,000 × 40% = 36,000
	Less taper relief (four to five years) 40%		(14,400)
			21,600

(ii)

	£
Estate £(215,000 + 210,000)	425,000
Residence nil rate band (lower of £175,000 and £215,000)	
£175,000 @ 0%	0
£250,000 @ 40%	100,000
£425,000	100,000

(Nil rate band used up by lifetime gifts becoming chargeable)

Inheritance tax in relation to the July 2020 PET due 28 February 2025 (6 months after the end of month in which death occurs)

Inheritance tax in relation to Arnold's estate is due when the account is delivered by the personal representatives or 6 months from the end of the month of death if that is earlier. Therefore 1 November 2024.

Marking scheme

	Marks
TTP	6
CT liability	4
Filing and payment dates for CT	4
IHT on son's PET	3
IHT on daughter's PET	3
	6
IHT on death estate	3
Payment dates for IHT	2
	25

13 Stephen

(a) **Inheritance tax payable on lifetime gift**

	£	£
PET in March 2021		
Gift of cash		400,000
ME		(5,000)
AE current year		(3,000)
AE brought forward		(3,000)
		389,000
NRB at death		(325,000)
		64,000
IHT @ 40%		25,600
Taper relief @ 20% (three to four years)		(5,120)
		20,480

(b) **Death estate**

	£	£
Partnership interest		350,000
Farm less APR (part a) (£375,000 – £200,000)		175,000
Salsat Ltd shares less 100% BPR		–
House		300,000
Painting (W1)		25,714
Vintage car		80,000
Cash and chattels		50,000
Less income tax liability		(11,000)
		969,714
RNRB at death		(175,000)
NRB at death	325,000	
Less transfers in previous seven years (W2)	(389,000)	
		–
Chargeable estate		794,714
IHT @ 40%		317,886

Working 1

Value of painting

Valued as related property with his wife (as greater than single valuation) = £20,000/(£20,000 + £50,000) × £90,000 = £25,714.

Working 2

Lifetime transfers in the prior 7 years:

	£
Gift of cash to son	400,000
Less marriage exemption	(5,000)
Less A/E 2020/21 and 2019/20	(6,000)
PET	389,000

PRACTICE ANSWER BANK

> **Tutorial note**
>
> No BPR on the partnership share as Stephen has not owned the business property for two years at the time of his death.

Marking scheme

		Marks
(a)	Tax on PET	5
(b)	Death estate	9
	Valuation of painting	2
		11
		16

14 Sally

Inheritance tax payable on death

(a)
	£	£
CLT on 4 August 2017		
Gift of painting (W1)		520,000
NRB at death		(325,000)
		195,000
IHT @ 40%		78,000
Taper relief @ 80% (six to seven years)		(62,400)
		15,600
Less lifetime tax (restricted, cannot generate a repayment)		(15,600)
		Nil

(b)
	£	£
PET on 18 December 2022		
Gift of shares in Collinste plc (W2)		71,400
Less AE current year		(3,000)
Less AE brought forward		(3,000)
		65,400
NRB at death	325,000	
Less transfers in previous seven years	(520,000)	
		–
		65,400
IHT @ 40%		26,160

(c)
Death estate		
Chargeable estate		1,200,000
RNRB (Sally's RNRB + unused spouse RNRB)		(350,000)
NRB at death	325,000	
Less transfers in last seven years (£520,000 + £65,400)	(585,400)	
		–
		850,000
IHT @ 40%		340,000

Workings

1 CLT – lifetime tax paid

	£
Gift of painting	487,000
Less AE current year	(3,000)
Less AE brought forward	(3,000)
	481,000
Less NRB 2017/18	(325,000)
	156,000
IHT @ 20/80	39,000
Gross chargeable transfer (£481,000 + £39,000)	520,000

2 Value of shares in Collinste plc
Value at the date of gift
Lower of:
¼ up value 118p + ¼ (122 – 118) = £1.19
Mid bargain (116p + 124p)/2 = £1.20
The value of 60,000 shares = 60,000 × £1.19 = £71,400

Marking scheme

			Marks
(a)	Painting – lifetime	4	
	Painting – on death	3	
			7
(b)	Shares		6
(c)	Death estate		4
			17

15 Pauline

(a) Lifetime tax on gift 1 February 2013

	£
Gift into discretionary trust	400,000
AE current year	(3,000)
AE brought forward	(3,000)
	394,000
NRB 2012/13	(325,000)
	69,000
IHT @ 20/80	17,250
Gross chargeable transfer = £394,000 + £17,250	411,250

Tutorial note

1 February 2013 – this was more than seven years before death, so no further IHT due.

(b) *PET of Facia Ltd shares – 1 January 2020*

	£
Value of shares before the gift 6,000 × £85	510,000
Value of shares after the gift 5,000 × £30	(150,000)
	360,000
No BPR – investment company	–
AE current year	(3,000)
AE brought forward	(3,000)
	354,000

Death tax due on PET of 1 January 2020	£	£
Gift of shares (see above)		354,000
NRB at death (W1)	550,000	
Less GCTs in seven years before 1.1.20 (see part a above)	(411,250)	
		(138,750)
		215,250
IHT @ 40%		86,100
Taper relief @ 60% (five to six years)		(51,660)
		34,440

(c) **Death estate**

		£
Value of death estate £(920,000 – income tax owed of 20,000)		900,000
Less charitable donation		(15,000)
RNRB (£175,000 × 2 = £350,000) capped at value of property		(305,000)
NRB at death (W1)	550,000	
Less transfers in last seven years (PET 1.1.20)	(354,000)	
		(196,000)
		384,000
IHT @ 40%		153,600

Workings

1 *Transfer of nil rate band*

NRB at Barry's death in 2011/12 = £325,000 of which £100,000 used on gift to son. The gift to Pauline was exempt (as spouse), so £225,000 unused.

Total NRB for Pauline = £325,000 + £225,000 = £550,000.

Unused residential nil rate band of £175,000 also transferred to Pauline.

Marking scheme

			Marks
(a)	Lifetime tax/gross transfer on CLT		4
(b)	Valuation of shares	4	
	Death tax on CLT	3	
	NRB/RNRB at death – spouse transfer (W1)	5	
			12
(c)	Death estate		4
			20

16 Arthur and Mary

(a) (i) IHT during lifetime on gifts

	£
CLT	375,000
AE current year	(3,000)
AE brought forward	(3,000)
	369,000
NRB 2017/18	(325,000)
	44,000
IHT @ 20/80	11,000
Gross chargeable transfer = £(369,000 + 11,000)	380,000

(ii) IHT on lifetime gift due to death

	£
Gross chargeable transfer	380,000
NRB	(325,000)
	55,000
IHT @ 40%	22,000
Taper relief @ 80% (six to seven years)	(17,600)
	4,400
Less lifetime tax (restricted, cannot generate a repayment)	(4,400)
IHT due on lifetime gift	–

(b) *Death estate*

	£
House	350,000
Cottage	500,000
Shares in Deck plc (W1)	10,236
BPR – none as not a controlling shareholding	
Shares in Acril Ltd (W2)	37,500
BPR – none as holds investments	
Cash and chattels	250,000
Life assurance policy (W3)	–
Death estate	1,147,736
RNRB at death	(175,000)
NRB at death (used on lifetime gift)	(0)
	972,736
IHT @ 40%	389,094

The cottage was once Arthur's residence and is left to his son. The cottage therefore qualifies for the residence nil rate band. There is no spouse exemption as Arthur and Mary are not married.

Workings

1 *Shares in Deck plc*

The shares are valued at the lower of:

Quarter up:
£12.78 + ¼ (12.84 – 12.78) = £12.795.

Mid-bargain:
½ £(12.79 + 12.91) = £12.85.

Therefore, value of shares = 800 × £12.795 = £10,236.

2 *Shares in Acril Ltd*

As not married, there is no related property.

Arthur owns 25% of the shares which are valued at £15 per share.

Total value = 2,500 × £15 = £37,500.

3 *Life Assurance Policy*

The life assurance policy is written into trust and therefore does not form part of the death estate. Trusts have their own separate IHT trust calculations.

Marking scheme

		Marks
(a)	Lifetime tax on CLT	4
(b)	Death tax on CLT	4
(c)	Death estate	10
		18

17 Claire and William

(a) **Claire – Inheritance tax (IHT) arising on death**

Lifetime transfer 23 August 2018

	£
Gift	420,000
Less: marriage exemption	(5,000)
annual exemption cy	(3,000)
annual exemption b/f	(3,000)
Potentially exempt transfer	409,000
IHT	
£325,000 @ 0%	0
£84,000 @ 40%	33,600
£409,000	
Less taper relief (six to seven years @ 80%)	(26,880)
IHT payable	6,720

Tutorial note

The potentially exempt transfer becomes chargeable as a result of Claire dying within seven years of making it.

Death estate

	£
Value of estate	880,000
Less spouse exemption £880,000/2	(440,000)
Chargeable estate	440,000
IHT on £440,000 @ 40%	176,000

(b) **William – Capital gains tax computation 2024/25**

	£
Net disposal proceeds	490,100
Less: cost	(420,000)
enhancement expenditure	(5,200)
Gain	64,900
Less annual exempt amount	(6,000)
Taxable gain	58,900

	£
CGT on £23,750 (37,700 – 13,950) @ 18%	4,275
CGT on £35,150 (58,900 – 23,750) @ 24%	8,436
	12,711

> **Tutorial note**
>
> 1 The cost of replacing the property's chimney is revenue expenditure because the chimney is a part of the house and so this is a repair to the house. The cost of the new boundary wall is capital expenditure because the wall is a separate structure which is not part of the house.
>
> 2 Because the house is residential property, the gain is taxed at 18% and 24% rather than 10% and 20%.

Marking scheme

			Marks
(a)	Lifetime gift	5	
	Death estate	2	
(b)	Gain	4	
	CGT	2	
			13

18 Annie

(a) PET – 14 September 2023 (2023/24)

	£
Value of shares held before transfer 8,000 × £8	64,000
Less value of shares held after transfer 1,500 × £3	(4,500)
Transfer of value	59,500
Less: annual exemption cy (2023/24)	(3,000)
annual exemption b/f (2022/23)	(3,000)
Potentially exempt transfer	53,500

(b) (i) CLT – 27 January 2024 (2023/24)

	£
Net chargeable transfer	400,000
IHT	
325,000 × 0%	0
75,000 × 20/80 (donor pays tax)	18,750
400,000	18,750
Gross chargeable transfer £(400,000 + 18,750)	418,750

(ii) Additional tax on lifetime transfer on death of donor

14 September 2023

Potentially exempt transfer of £53,500 becomes chargeable as donor dies within seven years.

Within nil rate band at death, no tax to pay.

27 January 2024

Nil rate band available £(325,000 − 53,500) = £271,500.

	£
Gross chargeable transfer	418,750
IHT	
271,500 × 0%	0
147,250 × 40%	58,900
418,750	58,900
No taper relief (death within three years of transfer)	
Less lifetime tax paid	(18,750)
Additional tax payable on death	40,150

(c) (i) Death estate

	£
Assets at death	623,000
Less funeral expenses	(3,000)
Value of estate for IHT purposes	620,000
Less exempt legacy to spouse	(150,000)
Chargeable estate	470,000
Less residence nil rate band (lower of £90,000 and £175,000)	(90,000)
Taxable estate	380,000
IHT liability £380,000 × 40%	152,000

The nil rate band was used by lifetime transfers.

(ii) Annie's children will inherit the residue of £(620,000 − 150,000 − 40,000 − 152,000) = £278,000.

Marking scheme

		Marks
Lifetime transfer – PET		2
Lifetime transfer – CLT		2
Death tax on lifetime transfers – PET	2	
– CLT	1	
		3
Death tax on estate		4
Residue of estate		2
		13

19 Elland plc

(a)

	Period ended 31 December 2022 £	Year ended 31 December 2023 £	Year ended 31 December 2024 £	Period ended 30 September 2025 £
Trading income	0	44,000	86,500	78,700
Property business income	6,600	9,400	6,500	0
Chargeable gains	0	5,100	0	9,700
Total profits	6,600	58,500	93,000	88,400
Less current year loss relief	(6,600)			
Less carry back loss relief			(23,250)	(88,400)
Less carry forward loss relief		(57,200)		
Less qualifying charitable donations		(800)	(1,200)	
Taxable total profits	0	500	68,550	0
Unrelieved qualifying charitable donations	1,000			

	£
Loss memorandum	
Loss in p/e 31.12.22	63,800
Less used p/e 31.12.22	(6,600)
Less used y/e 31.12.23	(57,200)
	0
Loss in y/e 30.09.26	186,800
Less used p/e 30.09.25	(88,400)
Less used in y/e 31.12.24 max 3/12 × 93,000	(23,250)
Loss remained unrelieved	75,150

(b)

	£
Output tax	
Sales £18,000 × 20%	3,600
Input tax	
Telephone £600 × 20% × 60% (Note 1)	(72)
Car purchase (Note 2)	0
Car repairs (note 3) £987 × 1/6	(165)
Equipment £1,760 × 20% (Note 4)	(352)
Other expenses (£2,200 − 400) × 20% (Note 5)	(360)
VAT payable	2,651

Tutorial note

1. Only the business element of the telephone is recoverable.
2. No input tax can be recovered on a car not exclusively used for business purposes.
3. The whole of the input tax on the car repairs is recoverable because there is some business use of the car.
4. The input tax on the equipment is recoverable in this VAT period because the tax point is 29 March 2025, when payment was made.
5. No input tax is recoverable on UK customer entertaining.

Marking scheme

	Marks
TTPs	8
VAT payable	6
	14

20 Spanner Ltd

This question tests the submission of corporation tax returns including penalties for late filing. It also requires the preparation of a corporation tax computation, correcting mistakes of a colleague and the ethical issues for an accountant in this scenario.

(a) Corporation Tax Compliance Schedule for the year ended 30 September 2024

Due date: 30 September 2025
How the return should be submitted: Online
Computations and accounts must be submitted in iXBRL format.

Penalty:
£200 penalty for over three months late

(b) Threats:
Self-interest
Intimidation
And no other threat stated

Fundamental principles:
Objectivity
Integrity
And no other principle stated

(c) Corporation tax computation for the year ended 30 September 2024

	£	£
Tax-adjusted trading profits		620,000
Gain on commercial property:		
Proceeds	1,200,000	
Less cost	(700,000)	
	500,000	
Less indexation allowance		
(278.10 – 193.40)/193.40 (0.438) × £700,000	(306,600)	
		193,400
Dividends received from UK quoted shares		0
Non-trading loan relationships income:		
Bank interest receivable	12,000	
Less mortgage interest	(5,000)	
		7,000
Property income:		
Rent receivable	24,000	
Costs for agent to manage property	(1,000)	
		23,000
Taxable total profits		843,400
Corporation tax liability @ 25%		210,850

Marking scheme

		Marks
Schedule		4
Threats	1½	
Fundamental principles	1½	
		3
Gain on property	3	
Other adjustments	5	
		8
		15

21 Og Ltd

(a)

	AIA £	Main pool £	Special rate pool £	Total £
TWDV b/f		42,817	50,000	
Additions qualifying for AIA (£364,000 + £3,380)	367,380			
AIA	(367,380)			367,380
WDA @ 18%		(7,707)		7,707
WDA @ 6%			(3,000)	3,000
TWDV c/f	–	35,110	47,000	378,087

(b) There is no chargeable gain on the disposal of these shares as Og Ltd has owned **more than 10% of the shares** in this unquoted **trading** company for more than **12 months in the last six year**s, so the **substantial shareholding exemption** applies.

(c) *Tax adjusted trading profit*

	£
Profit for the year	1,844,232
Less:	
Bank interest receivable	(1,500)
UK dividend income	(28,820)
Add:	
Depreciation	35,920
Debenture interest payable (allowable as relating to the trade)	–
Charitable donation	2,150
Repairs (allowable as replacement expenditure)	–
Less capital allowances	
– Plant and machinery (part (a) above)	(378,087)
Trading income	1,473,895

(d) **Corporation Tax computation**

Year ended 31 March 2025

	£
Trading income (part (b) above)	1,473,895
Non-trading loan relationships	1,500
Gain on shares (Substantial shareholding exemption)	–
Less qualifying charitable donation	(2,150)
Taxable total profits	1,473,245
ABGH dividends	28,820
Augmented profits	1,502,065

	£
Corporation tax liability:	
£1,473,245 × 25%	368,311

Corporation tax payable

Due dates and amounts for the year ended 31 March 2025:

14 October 2024	£92,078
14 January 2025	£92,078
14 April 2025	£92,078
14 July 2025	£92,078

> **Tutorial note**
>
> Og Ltd has augmented profits in excess of £1,500,000 for the year ended 31 March 2025 and also for the previous year, the year ended 31 March 2024. Therefore, corporation tax is due by quarterly instalments.

(e) **Land transaction tax**

	£
£225,000 × 0%	0
£25,000 (£250,000 – 225,000) × 1%	250
£75,000 (£325,000 – 250,000) × 5%	3,750
	4,000

This is payable within 30 days of the transaction.

Marking scheme

			Marks
(a)	Plant and machinery allowances		4
(b)	Substantial shareholding exemption		3
(c)	Tax adjusted trading profit		4
(d)	Calculation of augmented profits	3	
	Calculation of corporation tax liability	1	
	Quarterly instalment payments	2	
			6
(e)	LTT calculation	2	
	LTT due date	1	
			3
			20

22 Histlip plc

(a)

	Qualifying R&D	Trading deduction
	£	
Research staff salaries	185,000	
Class 1 secondary NIC on staff salaries (W)	19,251	
Laboratory machinery FYA @100%		156,000
Laboratory consumables	40,000	
Legal fees	0	0
Interest on loan to finance machinery purchase		6,000
	244,251	162,000
R&D expenditure credit at 20%	48,850	

Total relief against trading profits = £244,251 + £162,000 = £406,251

Working

Class 1 secondary NIC

5 × (37,000 − 9,100) × 13.8% = £19,251

> **Tutorial note**
>
> The R&D expenditure credit is available against expenditure on qualifying R&D (see calculation).
>
> The purchase of capital machinery does not qualify for enhanced R&D relief, but qualifies for 100% first year allowance. A 100% research and development FYA is available as a trading deduction on laboratories constructed for research and development (not applicable to this question).
>
> The legal fees are capital in nature and so there is no deduction.
>
> The interest on the loan is for trading purposes, so is deductible but does not qualify for enhanced relief.
>
> The employment allowance is not deducted as it would have been used against the Class 1 secondary NIC of other employees that the company is assumed to have.

(b) Histlip plc must notify HMRC of its claim for R&D relief in the year ended 31 March 2025 because this is the first time it has made a claim. The notification period, within which the notification form must be submitted is 1 April 2024 to 30 September 2025.

> **Tutorial note**
>
> The notification period runs from the first day of the accounting period to six months from its end.

(c) Corporation tax payable

	£
Trading income before R&D deduction	1,200,000
LESS Deduction for R&D (part (a))	(406,251)
ADD Research and development expenditure credit (part (a))	48,850
TTP	842,599
Corporation tax at 25%	210,650
LESS Research and development expenditure credit	(48,850)
Corporation tax payable	161,800

(d) The corporation tax return for the year ended 31 March 2023 was due by 31 March 2024 and so was submitted late. HMRC usually has one year from the actual filing date to give notice of a compliance check enquiry.

However, as the return was submitted late, HMRC has one year from the quarter date after the actual filing date, ie until 30 April 2025.

The notice is therefore within the time limit.

Marking scheme

	Marks	
Allocation of expenditure (R&D and trading deduction)	2	
100% FYA	1	
Legal fees capital	1	
Calculation of R&D credit	1	
Total deduction against trade profits	1	
NIC	1	
		7
First R&D claim	1	
Notification period	2	
		3
Taxable total profit	2	
Corporation tax	2	
		4
Enquiry deadline		3
		17

23 Beam Ltd

(a) Accounting period 1: 1 October 2024 – 30 September 2025

Accounting period 2: 1 October 2025 – 31 March 2026

The corporation tax returns for both accounting periods (one separate return for each accounting period) to be submitted by 31 March 2027.

(b) Chargeable gains

	£
Proceeds	300,000
Cost	(180,000)
	120,000
IA £180,000 × (278.1 – 212.9)/212.9 (not rounded in share pool)	(55,124)
	64,876

(c) Capital allowances

Y/e 30 September 2025	Main pool £	Special rate pool £	Allowances £
TWDV b/f	61,978		
Car (no restriction on private use in a company)		80,000	
Low emission new car	12,500		
FYA	(12,500)		12,500
	61,978		
WDA @ 18%/6%	(11,156)	(4,800)	15,956
	50,822	75,200	28,456
6 m/e 31 March 2026			
WDA @ 18%/6% × 6/12	(4,574)	(2,256)	6,830
	46,248	72,944	

(d) Corporation tax computations for the year ended 30 September 2025 and the six months ended 31 March 2026

	Y/e 30 September 2025 £	6 m/e 31 March 2026 £
Trading profit 12:6	86,800	43,400
Less capital allowances (part (a) above)	(28,456)	(6,830)
	58,344	36,570
Non-trading loan relationships (W1)	8,000	
Gains (part (b) above)	64,876	
Total profits	131,220	36,570
Less trade loss brought forward	(27,000)	
Less qualifying charitable donations	(4,000)	(4,000)
Taxable total profits	100,220	32,570

Corporation tax liability

	Y/e 30 September 2025	6 m/e 31 March 2026
TTP at 25%	25,055	8,143
3/200 × (£250,000 - £100,220)		
3/200 × (£125,000 - £32,570) (W2)	(2,247)	(1,386)
	22,808	6,757
Payable (W2)	1 July 2026	1 January 2027

Workings

1 Non-trading loan relationships

	£
Loan stock – proceeds	20,000
Cost	(12,000)
Non-trading loan relationships	8,000

2 Limits for corporation tax rates and payment in instalments

Year ended 30 September 2025
UL for purpose of the tax rate is £250,000 and for the purpose of determining the payment dates is £1,500,000
6 m/e 31 March 2026
The ULs are multiplied by 6/12 to reflect a six month accounting period so are £125,000 and £750,000.
Corporation tax charged at the marginal relief rate and payable by nine months and one day after the end of each accounting period

Marking scheme

		Marks
(a) Two accounting periods	2	
Filing date	1	
		3
(b) Chargeable gains		2
(c) Capital allowances		5
(d) Corporation tax computations	5	
NTLR	1	
Limits	2	
Payment dates	2	
		10
		20

24 Fraser

(a) **Historic test**

At the end of August, sales exceeded £90,000 (£93,000). Therefore, Fraser was required to notify HMRC by 30 September 2025, and would have charged VAT from 1 October 2025.

(b) (i)

	£	£
Output VAT		
Standard rated sales £(20,000 + 20,000 + 60,000) @ 20%		20,000
Input VAT		
Materials purchased August – October £1,500 × 3 × 1/6	750	
Bookkeeping costs £100 × 9 × 1/6	150	
Workshop £84,000 × 1/6	14,000	
Bad debt	–	
Car	–	
Entertaining UK customers	–	
		(14,900)
VAT payable		5,100

Notes.

1. Material purchased prior to August 2025 had been used to make stock which was sold prior to registration, so the VAT on the pre-registration purchases cannot be recovered.

2. The input VAT on the bookkeeping costs can be recovered for the six months prior to registration, and the three months of the VAT period.

3. The workshop was a new building (less than three years old) when purchased, and so this would have been a standard rated purchase.

4. The VAT in relation to the bad debt cannot yet be recovered as it is not yet overdue by six months.

5. The VAT on the purchase of the car is not recoverable because there is private use of the car.

6. The VAT on UK entertaining is not recoverable.

PRACTICE ANSWER BANK

(ii) The VAT return and payment are due electronically by 7 December 2025.

(c) The stamp duty payable is £2,020 × 0.5% = £10.10 rounded up to £15, payable within 30 days of the transaction.

Marking scheme

	Marks
Register for VAT	3
VAT account	4
Return and payment dates	2
Stamp duty calculation	2
SD due date	1
	12

25 Barnacle Ltd

(a) The basic tax point is when the goods are delivered, ie 14 May 2025.

The deposit is received on 3 April 2025, the tax point for the deposit.

The remainder of the order has a basic tax point of 14 May 2025, but this is replaced by the date when the invoice was raised (16 May 2025) as this was within 14 days of the basic tax point.

> **Tutorial note**
>
> VAT on this remaining element is therefore included on the VAT return for the quarter ended 31 July 2025.

	£	£
(b) Output VAT:		
Standard rated sales (W)		59,550
Zero rated sales		–
Patchy Ltd deposit £50,000 × 30% × 20%		3,000
Samples – not a supply regardless of value/number[1]		–
Output VAT		62,550

(W) Standard rated sales

Standard rated sales taking prompt discount = £300,000 × 75% × 50% = £112,500
VAT on these sales = £112,500 × 98% × 20% = £22,050
VAT on standard rated sales not offered discount = £(300,000 – 112,500) × 20% = £37,500
Total VAT on standard rated sales = £(22,050 + 37,500) = £59,550

(c) VAT payable:
Input VAT:

Costs of production and distribution £180,000 × 1/6	30,000	
Entertaining Chinese customers £2,820 × 1/6	470	
Entertaining British customers	–	
Machinery £25,500 × 1/6	4,250	
Car	–	
		(34,720)
VAT payable		27,830

Tutorial note

1. The free samples of the new product given to customers by Barnacle Ltd meet the HMRC definition of a sample and so are not liable to VAT:

   – 'A specimen of a product which is intended to promote the sales of that product and which allows the characteristics and qualities of that product to be assessed without resulting in final consumption, other than where final consumption is inherent in such promotional transactions.'

Marking scheme

	Marks
Tax point for deposit	1
Tax point for balance	2
VAT account – output tax	5
VAT account – input tax and VAT payable	4
	12

26 Astia Ltd

(a) (i) Capital allowances

	AIA £	FYA £	Main pool £	Special rate pool £	Short life asset £	Allowances £
TWDV b/f			146,000		18,000	
Disposal					(13,700)	
					4,300	
Balancing allowance					(4,300)	4,300
					–	
Audi Car				53,000		
Toyota Car		15,000				
FYA @ 100%		(15,000)				15,000
R&D plant		45,500				
FYA @ 100%		(45,500)				45,500
Electrical systems	25,000					
AIA	(25,000)					25,000
			146,000	53,000	–	
WDA @ 18%			(26,280)			26,280
WDA @ 6%				(3,180)		3,180
TWDV c/f	–	–	119,720	49,820	–	
Total allowances						119,260

(ii) Adjusted profit

	£
Trading profit per question	958,820
R&D Machinery (100% first year allowance so in capital allowances)	45,500
Charitable donation	1,650
Advertising	
Gifts of alcohol disallowed	2,100
Other elements allowable as trade-related	-
Adjusted profit before capital allowances	1,008,070
Capital allowances (part a)	(119,260)
Trading profit	888,810

(b) Chargeable gains

The substantial shareholdings exemption is not available as Astia Ltd has not held a substantial shareholding (4%, less than 10%).

	£
Proceeds	58,000
Less selling costs	(1,460)
	56,540
Less cost (W)	(18,500)
	38,040
Indexation allowance (£24,095 – £18,500) (W)	(5,595)
	32,445

Workings

Shares in Oryx Ltd

Date	Number	Cost £	Indexed cost £
18 March 2009	3,000	15,000	15,000
Index to May 2010 (223.6 – 211.3)/211.3			873
			15,873
7 May 2010	1,000	3,500	3,500
	4,000	18,500	19,373
Index to December 2017 (278.1 – 223.6)/223.6			4,722
			24,095
Disposal	(4,000)	(18,500)	(24,095)
	–	–	–

(c) **Astia Ltd Corporation tax computation for the year ended 31 March 2025**

	£
Trading income (part (b) above)	888,810
RDEC credit (£54,000 × 20%)	10,800
Gain (part (c) above)	32,445
Qualifying charitable donation (£1,650 – £250)	(1,400)
Taxable total profits	930,655
Corporation Tax:	
£930,655 × 25%	232,664
Less RDEC credit (£54,000 × 20%)	(10,800)
Corporation tax liability	221,864

Note. The dividends received are exempt

(d) **Entertaining**

The action of concealing the true nature of the entertaining expense in order to claim a deduction, would constitute tax evasion which is illegal.

This should be made clear to the directors and they should be advised not to record the expenditure in this way, but to disallow it, disclosing it as entertaining. They should be made aware of the consequences, including possible fines and imprisonment, of hiding the amount.

If they follow the proposed action we should consider ceasing to act for Astia Ltd and inform them of this in writing. It would be necessary to inform HMRC that we have ceased to act although there is no need to give reasons.

Tax evasion is a form of money laundering and therefore we should report the activity to the money laundering reporting officer. It is necessary to beware not to tip off the client.

Marking scheme

				Marks
(a)	(i)	Capital allowances		6
	(ii)	Adjustment to profit		4
(b)		Gain		6
(c)		Qualifying charitable donations		1
		CT including RDEC		3
(d)		Tax evasion	1	
		Consequences and actions	2	
		Money laundering	1	
				4
				24

27 Mitesh

(a) Maximum pension contributions by Mitesh on which income tax relief given, are higher of:

- £3,600, and
- Net relevant earnings = salary and bonus = £50,000 + £25,000 = £75,000

ie £75,000.

Annual allowance = £60,000

Check: adjusted income less than £260,000 in 2024/25 (£75,000 + £10,000 = £85,000).

Plus unused annual allowance brought forward from 2023/24 only (since Mitesh had not been a member of a pension scheme prior to 2023/24).

The unused annual allowance from that year of £40,000 – £30,000 = £10,000 can also be used.

Mitesh can therefore make contributions of £60,000 + £10,000 = £70,000 before income tax relief is clawed back.

(b) *Track Ltd*

To make a gross contribution of £25,000, as this is allowable for corporation tax purposes, the net cost = £25,000 × (100 – 25)% = £18,750.

There is no employer's national insurance contribution on pension contributions.

There is no income tax or NIC for Mitesh as an employer's contribution to a pension is an exempt benefit.

Contribution made by Mitesh

Net contribution = 80% × £25,000 (as remainder is recovered from HMRC) = £20,000

Taxable income of Mitesh = £85,000 − £12,570 = £72,430 and so Mitesh is paying income tax at the higher rate.

Mitesh receives further income tax relief by an increase of £25,000 to the basic rate limit – a further £25,000 of earnings is taxed at 20% rather than 40%, saving 20% (£5,000).

Total cost of pension contribution by Mitesh = £20,000 − £5,000 = £15,000.

Tutorial note

If Track Ltd makes the contribution of £25,000, Mitesh's adjusted income will increase to £85,000 + £25,000 = £110,000. This is still less than £260,000 so there is no restriction of the annual allowance in 2024/25.

Marking scheme

	Marks
Pension contribution limits	2
Unused brought forward	2
Contribution by Track Ltd	3
Contribution by Mitesh	3
	10

28 Lucy

(a) **Disposable income if Lucy is employee**

(i) *Income tax*

	£
Employment income/net income	36,000
Less personal allowance	(12,570)
Taxable income	23,430
Income tax @ 20%	4,686

(ii) *Class 1 NIC*

	£
Salary	36,000
Less employee's threshold	(12,570)
	23,430
Class 1 NIC @ 8%	1,874

(iii) *Disposable income*

	£
Salary	36,000
Less: income tax	(4,686)
Class 1 NIC	(1,874)
travel costs	(1,500)
	27,940

(b) **Disposable income if Lucy is self-employed**

(i) *Income tax*

	£
Fees received	36,000
Less fixed rate mileage 4,600 @ 45p per mile	(2,070)
Trading income/net income	33,930
Less personal allowance	(12,570)
Taxable income	21,360
Income tax @ 20%	4,272

(ii) *Class 4 NIC*

	£	£
Trading income	33,930	
Less lower limit	(12,570)	
	21,360	
Class 4 NIC @ 6%		1,282

(iii) *Disposable income*

	£
Fees received	36,000
Less: income tax	(4,272)
Class 4 NIC	(1,282)
travel costs 4,600 @ 40p	(1,840)
	28,606

(c) Notification of chargeability to income tax should have been made no later than 5 October 2025, so her notification is late. It appears to be a careless omission rather than deliberate as she made the notification when she found out that she had to do so.

Because she rectified the late notification unprompted by HMRC within 12 months of the deadline the penalty will be reduced to 0%.

Marking scheme

		Marks
(a)	*Employee*	
	Income tax payable	2
	Class 1 NIC	2
	Income	2
(b)	*Self-employed*	
	Income tax payable	2
	Class 4 NIC	2
	Income	2
(c)	Deadline	1
	Careless	1
	Penalty	1
		15

29 Nima

(a)

	Non-savings £
Tax-adjusted trading income	63,000
Property income (W1)	10,300
Total/net income	73,300
Personal allowance	(12,570)
Taxable income	60,730

Income tax payable

	£
£38,000 @ 20% (W2)	7,600
£(60,730 – 38,000) @ 40%	9,092
	16,692
Less tax reducer re property interest (20% × £200)(W3)	(40)
	16,652

Workings

1. Property income

	£
Rental income	12,000
Less building wall (capital)	–
Less letting agent fees	(500)
Interest	–
Less replacement sofa	(1,200)
	10,300

2. Extension of basic rate band

£37,700 + (£240 × 100/80) = £38,000

3. Tax reducer

Mortgage interest relief at 20% of lowest of:

	£
Finance costs	200
Property income	10,300
Adjusted total income	73,300

(b)

	£
£(50,270 – 12,570) × 9%	3,393
£(63,000 – 50,270) × 2%	255
	3,648

(c)

	£
2023/24	
Income tax	15,000
Less tax deducted at source	(4,000)
Tax payable 2023/24	11,000
POA for 2024/25: 50%	5,500

2024/25

IT liability	16,652
Class 4	3,648
1st POA 31 January 2025	(5,500)
2nd POA 31 July 2025	(5,500)
Balancing payment 31 January 2026	9,300

Marking scheme

			Marks
(a)	Income tax liability		2
	Taxable trading profits	1	
	(W1) Property income	2.5	
	(W2) Extension of basic rate band	1	
	(W3) Tax reducer	4	
	Tax adjusted trade income (part a)	1	
	Personal allowance	0.5	
	Income tax liability	1	
	Deduction of tax reducer	1	
	Total marks part (a)		12
(b)	National insurance		3
(c)	Administration		
	Calculation of POA for 2024/25	2	
	Calculation of balancing payment for 2024/25	1	
	Due dates for POA for 2024/25	1	
	Due date for balancing payment for 2024/25	1	
	Total marks for part (c)		5
Total marks			20

30 Kristina

(a)

	Non-savings £
Employment income (W1)	112,138
Less personal allowance (W2)	(6,501)
Taxable income	105,637

Income tax payable

	£
£37,700 @ 20%	7,540
£(105,637 – 37,700) @ 40%	27,175
	34,715

Workings

1 *Employment income*

	£
Salary	85,000
Car benefit £30,000 × 21% (W)	6,300
Fuel benefit £27,800 × 21%	5,838
No further adjustment for cost of diesel – does not have to be stated	–
Accommodation	18,000
Use of gym – exempt if no public access	–
Pension contribution by Salsa plc – exempt	–

	Less pension contribution by Kristina	(3,000)
	Employment income	112,138

Working: Car benefit value
15% + (60 – 50)/5 + 4% (diesel supplement) = 21%

2 Personal allowance

	£
Personal allowance	12,570
Less ½ (112,138 – 100,000)	(6,069)
	6,501

(b) *Employer's national insurance*

	£
Class 1 Secondary NIC	
£(85,000 – 9,100) × 13.8%	10,474
No deduction for pension	
Class 1A	
£(6,300 + 5,838 + 18,000) × 13.8%	4,159

(c) Class 1 secondary NIC is paid throughout the year (via the PAYE system) within 14 days of the end of each tax month ie by 19th if paid via cheque or 22nd if paid electronically.

Class 1A NIC is paid after the year end, therefore by 22 July 2025 (19 July if paid by cheque).

(d) Payments on account are generally required when the income tax liability exceeds the amounts deducted at source.

Kristina's entire liability is deducted at source under PAYE, and so payments on account are not required.

Marking scheme

			Marks
(a)	*Income tax liability*		
	Salary	0.5	
	Car benefit	2	
	Fuel benefit	1	
	Accommodation	1	
	Use of gym	1	
	ER pension contribution	1	
	EE pension contribution	1	
	Personal allowance	1.5	
	Income tax due	1	
	Total marks part (a)		10
(b)	NIC		2
(c)	Due dates of NIC		3
(d)	Explanation of no POA		2
Total marks			20

31 Jamie

(a) Capital allowances

	£		
Tax written down value	2,500		
Disposal	(1,000)		
	1,500		
Balancing allowance	(1,500)	× 70%	(1,050)
	-		

Using the cash basis, the cost of the van is a trading deduction rather than expenditure which qualifies for capital allowances.

(b) Deduction for business premises

(i) Fixed rate adjustment

Date paid	£
Rent – 01/05/2024	10,000
Rent – 01/08/2024	10,000
Rent – 01/11/2024	10,000
Rent – 01/02/2025	12,000
Total rent using cash basis	42,000
Other bills	20,000
	62,000
Fixed rate adjustment (£350 × 12)	(4,200)
	57,800

(ii) Actual expenditure and usage

	£
Total bills	62,000
less one-third	(20,667)
	41,333

(c) Taxable trading profits

	£
Receipts	225,000
Motoring expenses (70% × £7,000)	(4,900)
Premises	(57,800)
Other expenses paid	(73,000)
	89,300

(d) Income tax liability

	Non-savings £	Savings £
Trading profits	89,300	
Property income	42,000	
Interest		1,200
Loss carried back from 2025/26	(100,000)	
	31,300	1,200
Personal allowance	(12,570)	
Taxable income	18,730	1,200

Scottish starter rate	2,305	×19%	438
Scottish basic rate	11,684	×20%	2,337
Scottish intermediate	4,741	×21%	996
UK savings allowance	1,000	×0%	-
UK basic rate	200	×20%	40
			3,811

Marking scheme

			Marks
(a)	Car only (not van)	1	
	Disposal proceeds	1	
	Balancing adjustment	1	
	Business use %	1	
			4
(b)	Total expenditure re 2024/25 using cash basis	1½	
	Fixed rate add back	1½	
	Disallow one third	1	
			4
(c)	Trading profit		2
(d)	Total income	1½	
	Trading loss	1	
	Personal allowance	½	
	Scottish rate re NSI	1½	
	UK rate re interest	1½	
			6
Total marks			16

32 Jennifer

(a) Match shares with:

Shares purchased in following 30 days, ie 3,000 shares purchased on 10 March 2025.
Match remaining 2,000 shares with the shares in the share pool.

(b)

	Gains/(losses) on other assets £	Gains/(losses) on residential property £
Shares (W2) – Next 30 days	300	
Shares (W3) – share pool	771	
Painting £(20,100 – 7,000)	13,100	
House (W4)		32,000
Less annual exempt amount		(3,000)
Less loss brought forward		(26,000)
	14,171	3,000
CGT @20%/24%	2,834	720
Total CGT		3,554

Workings

1. Share pool

		£
1 March 2020	1,000	2,000
1 March 2021	2,000	4,500
24 February 2025	4,000	9,000
	7,000	15,500
Disposal 1 March 2025	(2,000)	(4,429)
	5,000	11,071

2. Shares in Architravepe plc – 10 March 2025

	£
Proceeds 3,000/5,000 × £13,000	7,800
Cost	(7,500)
Gain	300

3. Shares in Architravepe plc – share pool

	£
Proceeds 2,000/5,000 × £13,000	5,200
Cost (W1)	(4,429)
Gain	771

4. House

	£
Proceeds	600,000
Cost	(440,000)
	160,000
Less PRR £160,000 × 8/10 (W5)	(128,000)
	32,000

5. PPR: exempt and chargeable periods

	Chargeable	Exempt
1 January 2015 – 1 January 2016		1
1 January 2016 – 1 January 2021	2	3*
1 January 2021 – 1 January 2025		4
	2	8

*3 years exempt for any reason if preceded and followed by real occupation

(c) Payments of capital gains tax

Jennifer must pay £720 by 2 March 2025 and £2,834 by 31 January 2026.

Marking scheme

			Marks
(a)	Share matching rules		2
(b)	CGT liability		
	(W1) Share pool	2.5	
	(W2) A plc next 30 days share gain	1.5	
	(W3) A plc share pool gain	1	
	(W4) House	2	
	(W5) PPR periods	2	
	Gain on painting	1	
	Allocation of AEA to residential property	1	
	Allocation of loss b/f to residential property	1	
	CGT on normal gains	0.5	
	CGT on residential gains	0.5	
	Total marks part (b)		13
(c)	Dates and amounts to pay		2
	Total marks		17

33 Flavia

Total gains	Qualifying for BADR £	Not qualifying for BADR £
Scroll plc shares: 20 May 2024 (W1)		250
Scroll plc shares: share pool (W1)		9,000
Car – exempt		0
Commercial property (W3)		89,000
Goodwill of business (W4)	60,000	
Chargeable gains	60,000	98,250
Less annual exempt amount		(3,000)
Less losses brought forward		(9,700)
Taxable gains	60,000	85,550
CGT @ 10%	6,000	
CGT @ 20%		17,110
Total £6,000 + £17,110		23,110

Workings

1   *Scroll plc shares*

Matched first with shares acquired within 30 days of disposal

	£
Shares acquired 20 May 2024	
Proceeds £21,000 × 1,000/3,000	7,000
Cost	(6,750)
Gain	250
Shares from share pool	
Proceeds £21,000 × 2,000/3,000	14,000
Cost (W2)	(5,000)
Gain	9,000

2 Share pool

	Shares	Cost
Purchase 1 May 2016	5,000	10,000
Rights issue January 2018	1,000	5,000
Total	6,000	15,000
Disposal 1 May 2024	(2,000)	(5,000)
	4,000	10,000

3 Commercial property

Gross proceeds	180,000
Costs of sale	(5,000)
	175,000
Cost plus extension (£70,000 + £16,000)	(86,000)
Redecoration	–
Gain	89,000

4 Sale of business

Goodwill proceeds	60,000
Cost	(–)
Gain	60,000

Marking scheme

	Marks
CGT liability	
Next 30 day share gain	1.5
Share pool gain	1.5
Share pool	3
Car	1
Commercial property gain	2.5
Goodwill gain	1.5
Allocation of AEA to non BADR gains	1
Allocation of losses to non BADR gains	1
Calculation of CGT @10%	1
Calculation of CGT @20%	1
Total marks	15

34 Sandley Ltd

(a) Submit corporation tax return by 31 March 2026.
(b) Keep records for six years from 31 March 2025 (31 March 2031).
(c) Corporation tax computation for the year ended 31 March 2025

	£
Trading profits (W1)	2,578,938
Non trade loan relationships	10,000
Taxable total profits	2,588,938

	£
Corporation tax liability:	
£2,588,938 @ 25%	647,235

Workings

1 *Trading profits*

		£	£
Profit before tax			2,560,400
Add:	Legal fees in respect of share issue	13,000	
	Legal fees re debt collection	–	
	Depreciation	54,000	
	Staff entertaining	–	
	Car lease costs (£10,000 × 15%)	1,500	
	Redecorating office building	–	
	Donation to political party	8,600	
			77,100
			2,637,500
Less capital allowances (W2)			(58,562)
Adjusted trading profits			2,578,938

2 *Capital allowances*

	AIA	Main pool £	Allowances £
TWDV at 1 April 2024		182,900	
Addition qualifying for AIA	28,240		
AIA	(28,240)		28,240
		182,900	
Balancing charge			
Disposal (130% × £2,000)			(2,600)
		82,900	
WDA @ 18%		(32,922)	32,922
TWDV at 31 March 2025	0	149,978	58,562

(d) Augmented profits = £2,588,938 + £9,000 = £2,597,938

Quarterly instalments, at 25% of the liability = 25% × £647,235 = £161,809

14 October 2024	£161,809
14 January 2025	£161,809
14 April 2025	£161,809
14 July 2025	£161,809

EXAM ANSWER BANK

Marking scheme

			Marks
(a)	Due date of CT return	1	
(b)	Records	1	
(c)	*Corporation tax*		
	NTLR	1	
	Corporation tax liability	1	
	Trading profits:		
	Legal fees re share issue	1	
	Legal fees re debt collection	1	
	Depreciation	1	
	Staff entertaining	1	
	Car lease	1.5	
	Redecorating	1	
	Donation to political party	1	
	Deduction of capital allowances	1	
	TWDV b/f	0.5	
	AIA	1	
	Disposal	1	
	WDA	1	
	Total marks part (a)		14
(d)	Aug profits and instalments	3	
Total marks			19

35 Raidet Ltd

Corporation tax computation for the year ended 31 March 2025

	£	£
Trading profits		358,900
Less capital allowances (W1)		(8,935)
		349,965
Non trade loan relationships (W2)		505
Gains (W3)	11,584	
Less capital losses brought forward	(3,836)	
		7,748
Total profits		358,218
Less brought forward trading loss		(13,800)
Less qualifying charitable donation		(800)
Taxable total profits		343,618
Corporation tax liability		
£343,618 @ 25%		85,905

Workings

1. Capital allowances

	Main pool	Special rate pool	Allowances
	£	£	£
TWDV at 1 April 2024	36,150	67,467	
Disposal	(9,000)		
	27,150		
WDA @ 18%	(4,887)		4,887
WDA @ 6%		(4,048)	4,048
TWDV at 31 March 2025	22,263	63,419	8,935

2. Non trade loan relationships

	£
Loan stock interest receivable (£600 × 9/12 + £150)	600
Less interest paid on overdue tax	(95)
	505

3. Chargeable gains

	£
Proceeds	25,000
Cost	(8,500)
	16,500
Indexation allowance	
£8,500 × (278.1 − 176.2)/176.2	(4,916)
	11,584

Marking scheme

	Marks
(W1) Capital allowances:	
TWDVs b/f	1
Disposal	1
WDA @ 18%	1
WDA @ 6%	1
(W2) NTLR:	
Interest receivable	2
Interest on overdue tax	1
(W3) Chargeable gains:	
Unindexed gain	1
I/A	1.5
Deduction of capital allowances	1
Deduction of capital losses against capital gains	1
Deduction of trade loss b/f against total profits	1.5
Deduction QCD	1
CT liability	1
Total marks	15

36 Osney Ltd, Cherwell Ltd & Thames Ltd

(a) The company has not opted to tax, therefore the sale will be VAT exempt (a total of £1,500,000 with no VAT will be charged).

Professional fees are standard rated, therefore the company will have to pay a total of £12,000 to the service provider. Since the fees relate to an exempt supply, the £2,000 input tax is not recoverable by Osney.

(b) *Sale to Spain from the Northern Ireland factory*

The Northern Ireland Protocol will require the company to treat the sale as a dispatch rather than an export. Since the purchaser is a VAT registered business, the sale will be zero-rated. The company must retain evidence of the transport of the goods and must quote the purchaser's VAT number on the invoice.

Purchase of goods from Belgium to the London Head Office

Since this transaction does not involve Northern Ireland, the normal rules of importation will apply. Since Cherwell is VAT registered, it will record the applicable import VAT on its VAT return under the reverse charge mechanism (postponed accounting). As Cherwell Ltd makes standard rated supplies, it should be able to recover the import VAT in full at the same time, so the process will be cost neutral for UK VAT purposes.

Purchase of services from the USA

Since Cherwell Ltd is VAT registered, the reverse charge will again apply here. The company should record the relevant amount of VAT in its VAT return and can recover that amount as input tax.

(c) VAT payments due:

	Amount payable £	
Q/e 31 December 2024:		
30 November 2024	300,000	On time
31 December 2024	300,000	Late
31 January 2025	360,000	Late
	960,000	

The payment on account due to be paid on 31 December 2024 was paid on 6 February 2025 and is therefore 37 days late. Penalties are applicable as follows:

- The first penalty is triggered when the payment on account remains unpaid 15 days after it was due (15 January). This penalty is 2% of the amount outstanding at the end of day 15. ie £300,000 x 2% = £6,000.

- This first penalty is repeated when the same £300,000 remains unpaid on day 30 (30 January).

- On the amount outstanding on 31 January (still £300,000) a 4% annual rate will be charged on a daily basis. As the late VAT is paid on 6 February 2025, it is 37 days late so seven days of charge will apply: 7/365 x £300,000 x 4% = £230.

> **Tutorial note**
>
> Candidates will not be asked to 'explain' the tax treatment in the exam and as such explanations here are included for learning purposes.

Marking scheme

		Marks	
(a)	*Osney Ltd*		
	No OTT so exempt sale	1.5	
	Professional fees standard rated	1	
	Fees relate to an exempt supply so input VAT not recoverable	1.5	
	Total marks part (a)		4
(b)	*Cherwell Ltd*		
	Sale to Spain from NI zero rated	1.5	
	Retain transport evidence	1	
	Quote purchasers VAT no.	1	
	Purchase of goods from Belgium normal import	1	
	Reverse charge (PVA)	1	
	Recover the input VAT	1	
	VAT cost neutral	0.5	
	Purchase of IT services from USA – reverse charge	1	
	Total marks part (b)		8
(c)	*Thames Ltd*		
	VAT payments	3	
	December payment: Penalty at 2 % on day 15	1	
	December payment: Penalty at 2% on day 30	1	
	December payment: Second charge at 4%	2	
	January payment: late but less than 15 days	1	
	Total marks part (c)		8
Total marks			20

Exam Question Bank

Past Exams: November 2021

1   You work for a small firm of accountants. One of the partners has met with a potential new client, Fara. The partner tells you:

'Fara heard about us from my good friend, Roger, and I'm sure she will be a good client. Send her an email saying that we accept her as a client. Then you can get on with the work for her.'

Required

(a) Applying ethical guidelines, advise the partner of the steps your firm should take before starting any work for Fara. **(5 marks)**

Once Fara is accepted as a client, you start work on her tax matters. You discover that Fara is married to Darsh and she has annual taxable income of more than £250,000. Fara submits all tax returns online, where possible, including her annual self-assessment tax return.

Fara made several disposals during 2024/25. She has prepared a calculation of her capital gains tax and has made some notes. She has asked your firm to check her calculations:

	£	£
Sale of rental property		
Gross proceeds	250,000	
Less cost	(158,000)	
		92,000
Sale of painting		
Gross proceeds	20,000	
Less cost	(0)	
		20,000
Total gains		112,000
Capital gains tax @ 20%		22,400

Notes provided by Fara:

1   I had bought the rental property for £150,000 in 2010, and I spent £8,000 on redecorating in 2018. I have never lived in the property. I exchanged contracts to sell it on 1 November 2024 and the sale completed on 1 December 2024.

2   The painting has no cost because it was a gift from my husband Darsh in 2010 when it was worth £14,000. Darsh paid £11,000 for the painting in 2007. I sold the painting at auction on 1 April 2025 and I paid auctioneer fees of £200.

(b) Prepare a correct calculation of capital gains tax for Fara for 2024/25. **(5 marks)**

Fara notified HMRC that she made gains in 2024/25 but has not yet provided details of the gains or paid the tax. She will submit any necessary returns and pay the tax by 7 December 2025.

(c) Advise Fara of her obligations to HMRC to report the amount of her taxable gains for 2024/25. **(3 marks)**

(d) Advise Fara, without calculations, of any late filing penalties due if she reports the gains correctly by 7 December 2025. **(4 marks)**

(Total 17 marks)

2   You work in the finance department of a profitable trading company, Feed Ltd. Feed Ltd prepares accounts to 31 March each year.

The financial controller has recently left the company and Bob, the finance director, has asked you to work on corporation tax matters relating to several different periods. The company pays an external firm for all VAT work, so you can ignore VAT throughout your work.

The company is required to make instalment payments of corporation tax as a large company each year. No instalment payments have been made yet for the year ended 31 March 2026. Bob has told you he expects the corporation tax liability for that year to be £380,000. The company expects to receive payment from a customer soon and Bob intends to pay HMRC any instalments of tax already due on 14 December 2025.

Required

(a) Determine the due dates of instalment payments for the year ended 31 March 2026. **(2 marks)**

(b) Calculate the interest payable if instalments are paid up to date on 14 December 2025, assuming the final corporation tax liability will be the amount predicted by Bob. **(2 marks)**

Bob says the financial controller kept several boxes of paper documents which support the amount of capital allowances claimed in past corporation tax returns. He wants to know when the company can scrap these boxes, as the company policy is to use and retain less paper.

(c) Advise Bob of the rule for the date until which a company must retain such documents in respect of its corporation tax returns. **(1 mark)**

Bob asks you to work on the corporation tax computation for the year ended 31 March 2025.

Feed Ltd undertook a qualifying research and development (R&D) project throughout the year ended 31 March 2025. So far, none of the costs related to the project have been deducted from trading profit.

The company employed five research scientists on the project during the year. The company pays each a gross annual salary of £45,000 and contributes 7% of gross salary into the company's occupational pension scheme for each employee.

(d) Calculate the total employer's National Insurance Contributions payable in respect of the research scientists. Ignore the employment allowance. **(2 marks)**

In addition to the costs of employing the research scientists, the company incurred the following costs on the R&D project in the year ended 31 March 2025:

	£
Consumable items for research	66,000
Rent payable on laboratory building	120,000

(e) Calculate the total deduction from trading profits for the R&D expenditure and the research and development expenditure credit (RDEC) for the year ended 31 March 2025. **(6 marks)**

(f) Advise Bob of the date by which the company must (i) make a claim for tax relief for R&D for the year ended 31 March 2025 and (ii) notify HMRC of their intent to make the claim, assuming this is the first time Feed Ltd has made a claim. **(2 marks)**

The company purchased a new car for the sales director on 1 October 2024. The car cost £30,000 and has CO_2 emissions of 150g/km. 30% of the miles travelled in the car by the director are for private journeys.

On the same date, the company purchased a van with CO_2 emissions of 250g/km for use making deliveries only. The van cost £18,500.

At 1 April 2024, the company had a tax written down value on the main pool of £58,000 and on the special rate pool of £16,000.

(g) Calculate Feed Ltd's capital allowances for the year ended 31 March 2025. **(3 marks)**

The company's draft tax-adjusted trading profits before deduction of any costs in respect of the research project, and before capital allowances is £2,560,000. All other necessary tax adjustments to trading profits have been made.

(h) Calculate the tax-adjusted trading profits of Feed Ltd for the year ended 31 March 2025.
(1 mark)

On 1 November 2024, Feed Ltd sold its entire shareholdings in two trading companies as follows:

	Purchased by	Shareholding %	Cost £	Proceeds £
Lama plc	Electronic transfer	0.2	108,600	250,000
Knightli Ltd	Stock transfer form	15	310,400	345,000

Both shareholdings had been purchased on 1 July 2022.

Feed Ltd had received dividends from Lama plc of £20,000 on 30 June 2024.

(i) Identify and calculate the stamp taxes paid on the purchase of the shares by Feed Ltd, assuming the same rules and rates that apply in 2024/25 also applied then. **(3 marks)**

(j) Calculate the company's chargeable gains for the year ended 31 March 2025. **(3 marks)**

(k) Calculate the company's corporation tax liability for the year ended 31 March 2025.
(3 marks)
(Total 28 marks)

3 You work in the Private Client Department of a firm of tax advisers. Anna died on 25 March 2025 and your firm has been engaged by her family to deal with tax matters on Anna's death. Anna's son Jake is already a client of your firm.

Jake confirms that Anna had lived in England. He explains that Anna's only income in 2024/25 was bank interest received of £4,000 and dividend income of £180,000. Anna made a payment of £8,000 to a registered charity in December 2024, making a gift aid declaration.

Anna made her first payment on account of income tax for 2024/25 on 31 January 2025. The amount paid was £23,000. The remaining income tax for 2024/25 has not been paid yet.

Required

(a) Calculate Anna's income tax liability for 2024/25. **(7 marks)**
(b) Calculate Anna's remaining income tax payable for 2024/25. **(1 mark)**

Anna's son Jake has given you a list of assets owned by Anna at the date of her death.

	£
House	600,000
Cash deposits	200,000
Quoted shares in investment companies	700,000

Jake tells you there is a repayment mortgage of £80,000 outstanding in relation to the house. You should assume that the only other amount that Anna owed at the date of her death is her remaining income tax payable for 2024/25.

Anna had made one gift during her lifetime of cash of £157,000 to her sister in September 2021. Anna's husband Stuart had died on 1 April 2017 and left his entire chargeable estate of £500,000 to Anna.

Anna has left her entire estate to Jake.

(c) Calculate the inheritance tax payable on Anna's death. **(10 marks)**

Jake already owns two UK residential investment properties.

Tulip Cottage qualifies as furnished holiday accommodation. The property was let for 30 weeks during 2024/25 at a weekly rent of £1,000. Jake paid £2,000 for cleaning of Tulip Cottage during the year. Holiday properties for large families are in high demand, so in May 2024 Jake paid £800 for an extra children's bed for one of the bedrooms in the cottage.

Maple House was let by Jake to one tenant throughout 2024/25. The tenant paid the monthly rent of £1,200 due on the 1st of each month, but was late paying the amount due on 1 April 2025. The tenant paid this amount on 10 April 2025.

In 2024/25, Jake paid mortgage interest on Maple House of £2,400. He also paid £700 on roof repairs, £500 to replace the washing machine with a better model, and a further £50 to the delivery company to take the old washing machine away. A similar washing machine to the existing model would have cost £400.

(d) Calculate Jake's property income assessable to income tax in 2024/25. **(6 marks)**

Jake has asked for some financial advice in respect of the cash deposits he has inherited from his mother, as he wants these to generate more income. You think you know the answer to Jake's questions based on what other clients have done. However, your firm is not regulated to give such investment advice.

(e) Applying ethical guidelines, analyse which two fundamental principles are threatened in this situation. **(4 marks)**

(Total 28 marks)

4 You are a trainee at a firm of accountants in Edinburgh, Scotland. The firm acts for both the Agsu Partnership and the partners, Agata and Sunil. The partnership is based in Scotland, and both partners are Scottish taxpayers.

The tax-adjusted trading profits for the partnership for the year ended 31 March 2025 are £130,000.

Under the terms of the partnership agreement, Agata is allocated a salary of £30,000 per annum before profits are apportioned between Agata and Sunil in the ratio 1:3. Each partner takes their profit share as drawings each year.

Required

(a) Calculate the assessable trading profit for each partner for 2024/25. **(3 marks)**

Sunil has no other income. He has a trading loss from this partnership of £1,000 brought forward from the year 2023/24.

Sunil's wife Dee received child benefit of £1,331 in 2024/25 which she spent on clothing for their child. She did not receive any other income.

(b) Calculate the 2024/25 income tax liability for Sunil as a Scottish taxpayer. **(5 marks)**

(c) Calculate Sunil's national insurance contributions for 2024/25. **(1 mark)**

Sunil's family living expenses are currently £30,000 per annum, excluding those paid for by Dee using the child benefit receipt. Sunil wants to buy a bigger house which will require higher mortgage repayments. To determine whether this is affordable, he wants to know his net disposable income for 2024/25, after living expenses, income tax and national insurance contributions.

(d) Calculate Sunil's net disposable income for 2024/25. **(2 marks)**

Sunil plans to sell his current house for £260,000 and buy a new house in Scotland for £320,000. He would like to be able to complete the sale and purchase on 7 December 2025.

(e) Calculate the land and buildings transaction tax payable by Sunil as a result of these transactions. You should use rates applying from 1 April 2021. **(2 marks)**

The partners of the Agsu partnership want to employ two assistants from 1 January 2026. These will be the first employees of the partnership. The assistants will be paid £2,000 each on 28th of each month. Agata intends to complete the partnership's payroll herself without spending money on fees to your firm or on expensive software. However, she wants some initial help understanding the partnership's obligations to HMRC.

Your manager has advised Agata to ask for the assistants' forms P45 from their previous employments to help complete the first payroll.

(f) Advise Agata of two pieces of information that she will find on each form P45 which will help her complete the payroll. **(2 marks)**

(g) Advise Agata of the monthly reporting obligations of the partnership in respect of the assistants' salaries. You should not include calculations or details of how any amounts are calculated. **(4 marks)**

The partners are considering the following additional payments in relation to the assistants, but do not know the national insurance contribution (NIC) implications:

(i) Payment of school fees for the children of an assistant where the partnership will contract directly with the school.

(ii) Reimbursement to the assistants of the cost of subscriptions to a golf club.

(iii) Payment to a mobile phone provider for an annual mobile phone contract for each assistant.

(h) For each payment (i), (ii) and (iii) above, record whether the payment is:

- charged to Class 1 secondary NIC
- charged to Class 1A NIC
- not chargeable to national insurance on the partnership. **(3 marks)**

The Agsu Partnership is VAT-registered and makes wholly standard rated supplies of goods. You are completing the VAT return for the quarter ended 31 October 2025. The amounts below relate to that quarter.

The partnership made sales to UK customers totalling £36,000. The partnership made sales to private customers in Australia totalling £5,000. Both sales figures are stated exclusive of VAT.

The partnership incurred business costs of £12,000 inclusive of standard-rated VAT. These costs included £600 for entertaining UK customers.

Agata ensured she collected and retained all necessary records and documentation.

(i) Calculate the VAT payable for the quarter ended 31 October 2025, recording the rate of VAT charged for each amount of output tax. **(4 marks)**

(j) Advise Agata of the due date for submission of the VAT return for the quarter ended 31 October 2025. **(1 mark)**

(Total 27 marks)

Past Exams: May 2022

1. You work in the Employment Taxes department of an accountancy firm. Rebecca is the partner in charge.

   Watsh plc pays your firm for many services, contributing significantly to the firm's income. For many years, your firm has prepared the company's P11D forms. However, the finance director at Watsh plc recently told Rebecca that the fee proposed for the 2024/25 P11D forms is too high.

   Rebecca did not want to reduce the fee for the same level of work as in previous years. Instead, she has agreed to a small reduction in fee in return for a new arrangement, which limits the scope of work by the firm.

   Watsh plc's financial controller now prepares schedules, entering the amounts for many benefits, but omitting those requiring more complicated calculations. The agreement is that your firm reviews these schedules, performing any additional calculations necessary to complete the P11D forms. Your firm is not responsible for checking values or payment amounts provided by Watsh plc.

   Required

   (a) Applying ethical guidelines, identify the threat to fundamental principles faced by Rebecca when negotiating the fee, and one fundamental principle threatened. **(2 marks)**

   You share the review work with colleagues.

   You receive the schedule prepared by Watsh plc for one employee, Sam Jones.

	£
Car benefit	?
Fuel benefit	?
Watsh plc pension contribution for Sam (£2,000 paid)	exempt
Private medical insurance (£870 paid to insurer)	870
Loan benefit £8,000 × 2%	160
Market value of camera given to Sam on 6 April 2024	1,000
Total benefit	To be calculated

   From the financial controller, you discover additional information.

   The company provided Sam with a hybrid (petrol and electric) car for private use throughout 2024/25. The car had a list price of £38,750. The company paid £33,000 for the car but Sam contributed £3,000 to the cost on purchase. The car had CO2 emissions of 41g/km with an electric range of 30 miles.

   Watsh plc spent £4,870 on running and maintaining the car in 2024/25. This included petrol for both business miles (£1,500) and private miles (£500).

   Sam had an interest-free loan from the company £8,000, outstanding throughout 2024/25.

   Sam had been allowed to use the camera privately since 6 April 2023. The value when it was first provided was £2,000. He paid nothing towards its use but paid Watsh plc £250 for the camera on 6 April 2024.

   Watsh plc does not payroll any benefits.

   (b) Calculate Sam's car and fuel benefits for 2024/25. **(3 marks)**

   (c) Prepare a corrected schedule of Sam's benefits for 2024/25, demonstrating your treatment of each item. **(8 marks)**

After you and your colleagues have completed your review work, you collate the information for all 100 employees. The total taxable benefits provided by Watsh plc for 2024/25 are £862,000.

(d) Calculate Watsh plc's Class 1A national insurance (NIC) liability for 2024/25. **(1 mark)**

(e) Advise Watsh plc of how and when the Class 1A NIC should be paid and reported to HMRC.
(3 marks)
(Total 17 marks)

2   You work as an assistant accountant in the internal finance department of a limited liability partnership, Advertz LLP. This is a VAT-registered marketing business based in Wales.

Your manager Leroy prepares the accounts. He has asked you to prepare the computation of tax-adjusted trading profits for the business for the year ended 31 December 2024.

The accounting profit for the year is as follows:

	£
Gross profit	2,450,000
Less expenses:	
Staff costs	(1,780,000)
Depreciation of office equipment	(10,400)
Lunches for clients	(60,700)
Parking fines incurred by partners visiting clients	(500)
Debt collection costs	(12,000)
Allowable office costs	(234,000)
Profit before tax	352,400

The tax written down value on the main pool at 1 January 2024 was £38,600.

Required

(a) Calculate the tax-adjusted trading profit of Advertz LLP for the year ended 31 December 2024 using the accruals basis, starting with the profit before tax, recording with a zero '0' any expense which does not require adjustment. **(6 marks)**

Since January 2025, the partnership has purchased several new assets for long-term use in the marketing business:

- car with CO_2 emissions of 66g/km and 20% private use by an employee
- equipment to provide charging to electric cars of employees
- office building, bought from the developer, to be used from 1 June 2025.

Leroy does not have the cost details available. He is rushing to a meeting with the partners and wants to inform them of the relief available for these purchases.

(b) For each purchase, determine the percentage (%) of the cost that can deducted in calculating the tax-adjusted trading profits of the year ended 31 December 2025. Ignore VAT. **(4 marks)**

You look for further information about the purchase of the office building, which is located in Wales. You discover that the building cost was £1,320,000 inclusive of VAT. The purchase was made on 10 March 2025. Leroy does not know whether the land transaction tax has been paid on the purchase.

(c) Calculate the land transaction tax payable on the purchase of the property in Wales.
(3 marks)

(d) Advise Leroy of the due dates for reporting and paying the land transaction tax and the penalties which have already arisen if neither action has yet been completed as at 27 May 2025. Assume that Advertz LLP will complete these actions by 31 May 2025. **(3 marks)**
(Total 16 marks)

3   You work as a tax trainee in the Corporate Tax department of a large firm of accountants. Your manager is Nayla. You and your colleagues often work from home.

Your firm prepares the corporation tax returns for Greenby Ltd, a profitable trading company. It is a VAT-registered company selling standard-rated goods.

The finance director of Greenby Ltd, Lewis, has contacted you as he has noticed an error in the corporation tax return for the three months ended 30 June 2023. This was submitted on 26 June 2024.

The return showed taxable total profit of £250,000 including a chargeable gain shown as £10,670, when the correct figure should have been £210,670.

To discuss the error, you arranged an online meeting for you, Lewis and Nayla. The meeting was not recorded.

Required

(a) Advise Lewis of the latest date by which an amended corporation tax return could be submitted to HMRC correcting this error. **(1 mark)**

(b) Calculate the maximum penalty for the incorrect return if HMRC discover the error before being notified of it. **(2 marks)**

During the online meeting, Nayla shared her computer screen with you and Lewis so she could show the relevant computation. You realised that information relating to a different client was visible on Nayla's computer screen when she did this.

(c) Record the action which should be taken by your firm due to this data breach. **(2 marks)**

You are completing the corporation tax return for the year ended 30 June 2024. You have already calculated a figure for tax-adjusted trading profits of £680,000. However, this amount does not include any of the following income or expenses.

- Until 31 August 2023, Greenby Ltd rented out unused land next to its UK factory. The tenant used the land as a car park and paid rent of £5,000 monthly in advance. In September 2023, Greenby Ltd repaired the surface of the car park at a cost of £12,000 but has not yet found another tenant.

- Greenby Ltd paid bank interest of £45,000 on a loan taken out to buy the factory. It paid interest of £11,000 on a loan which had been used to buy the land which was rented out.

- The company had interest receivable from bank deposits of £20,000 for the year.

- Greenby Ltd received overseas interest income of £32,000. This was after deduction of £8,000 overseas tax.

(d) Calculate the corporation tax payable for the year ended 30 June 2024. Ignore VAT.
(9 marks)

Greenby Ltd wants assistance in respect of the output VAT relating to two customer orders.

- A customer, Viollit Ltd, placed a large order. Greenby Ltd charged a deposit receiving £60,000 on 15 April 2025. The balance of £240,000 will be due on 1 August 2025, when the goods will be delivered and an invoice raised for the full amount. The amounts are stated inclusive of VAT.

- Greenby Ltd offers another customer, Bluzonne plc, a prompt payment discount of 7% for paying within 14 days of an order. Bluzonne plc placed an order on 1 May 2025, immediately receiving the goods. On that date, Greenby Ltd issued an invoice for the undiscounted amount of £100,000 plus VAT of £20,000. Bluzonne plc settled the invoice on 8 May 2025.

(e) Calculate the output VAT for each of these orders that should be recorded on the VAT return for the quarter ended 30 June 2025. **(3 marks)**

(f) Advise Greenby Ltd of its invoicing obligation after receiving payment from Bluzonne plc. **(1 mark)**

(Total 18 marks)

4 You work for an accountancy firm advising businesses and individuals. Your clients include Martin, and his daughter Emma.

Martin sold two assets during 2024/25 – a painting and his shares in Foodes Ltd. He wants to know his capital gains tax liability and so how much of the proceeds he has left to spend after tax.

He sold the painting for £9,000. The gallery where he sold the painting charged Martin £900 commission. Martin had bought the painting for £3,000 in January 2008.

Required

(a) Calculate the chargeable gain on disposal of the painting. **(3 marks)**

Martin had bought his shares in Foodes Ltd for £50,000 in March 2013 when a stock transfer form was completed.

(b) Calculate the stamp duty paid by Martin on the purchase of the Foodes Ltd shares. **(1 mark)**

Martin sold his shares in Foodes Ltd to his daughter for £180,000, when their market value was £300,000. The shares represented 20% of the ordinary share capital of the company.

Martin had been a director of Foodes Ltd, a trading company, since buying the shares in 2013.

(c) Calculate the chargeable gain on the disposal of the shares, before claiming any reliefs. **(2 marks)**

You inform Martin that both gift relief and business asset disposal relief claims on the disposal of the shares can be made.

(d) Advise Martin of the dates by which the claims for relief should be made and by whom. **(3 marks)**

Martin received employment income of £70,000 from Foodes Ltd in 2024/25.

(e) Calculate Martin's capital gains tax payable for 2024/25, after making the relief claims. **(4 marks)**

(f) Calculate Martin's net proceeds after capital gains tax from the sale of the assets. **(3 marks)**

(Total 16 marks)

5 You are a member of the AIA and work in the Private Client department of a firm of tax advisers.

Your client is Saul. He is in poor health and thinks that he may die within the next few years. He has been taking steps to reduce possible inheritance tax when he dies.

On 1 February 2025 he made a gift of his entire holding of shares in Vilcant Ltd to a discretionary trust for the benefit of his grandchildren. This was his first lifetime gift.

Immediately prior to the gift the shares in Vilcant Ltd, an unquoted investment company, were held as follows:

Shareholder	Number of shares
Saul	2,500
Rita, Saul's wife	5,000
Thomas, Saul's brother	2,500
	10,000

The value of shareholdings in Vilcant Ltd on 1 February 2025 were:

Shareholding	Value of shareholding £
100%	2,000,000
75%	1,350,000
50%	700,000
25%	300,000

Required

(a) Calculate the lifetime inheritance tax payable on Saul's gift to the trust, demonstrating your treatment of the value of the gift. **(6 marks)**

(b) Advise Saul of when the tax must be paid. **(1 mark)**

Saul is unaware that there could be a further inheritance tax charge on this gift when he dies. You need to warn him of the maximum charge, assuming he will die on 31 December 2027.

(c) Calculate the inheritance tax payable on the gift of shares if Saul dies on 31 December 2027. **(4 marks)**

The marketing manager, Fredrick, at your firm wants you to introduce Saul to a private bank, MoneySave. MoneySave sells a product aimed at reducing inheritance tax. Your firm will earn a commission for the introduction.

Fredrick understands that the product involves loans, a trust and several steps which are not made for commercial reasons. The result is that the value of an estate on death can be reduced by a debt even though the debt will never have to be repaid.

Fredrick is not concerned about any ethical issues because a director at MoneySave has given several assurances.

- The bank has sold the product to many clients, whatever their circumstances.

- The tax legislation has been written incorrectly and does not stop the deduction even though Parliament did not intend to allow this.

- Use of the product is always fully disclosed to HMRC and records are kept explaining it.

- The fact that HMRC take a different view on the law involved is fully explained to clients.

(d) Advise Fredrick why you would be breaching the ethical Standards for Tax Planning in PCRT (Professional Conduct in Relation to Taxation) if you were to promote this product to Saul.
(4 marks)
(Total 15 marks)

6 Giovanni

You work for a firm of accountants. Your firm acts for Giovanni and his wife Maria who live in England. Both were born in 1970.

Giovanni usually receives no income but in July 2024 inherited some shares which pay dividends. His only income in 2024/25 is dividend income of £20,000, of which £3,000 relates to shares held in an Individual Savings Account (ISA).

You advise the couple to claim the marriage allowance, with Maria as the recipient.

Required

(a) Advise Giovanni of his obligations to notify HMRC of his dividend income. **(2 marks)**

(b) Calculate Giovanni's income tax liability for 2024/25. **(3 marks)**

Maria is an interior decorator. She is not VAT-registered. You prepare Maria's taxable trading profits using the cash basis of accounting each year.

Maria mostly works at her customers' houses with each job taking one or two weeks. She spends one day per week (8 hours) working at home, planning designs for her customers and doing administration for the business.

Maria has provided you with information about her business for the year ended 31 March 2025.

	£
Cash received from customers for work done during the year	32,340
Deposit received from a customer in March 2025 for work in April 2025	400
Amount owed by a customer for work done in January 2025	800
Payments on materials	6,400
Running costs of Maria's van – total payments made for 10,000 miles	2,000

Maria drove her van 7,500 business miles in the year. The van has CO2 emissions of 45g/km. Maria paid £20,000 for the van in January 2019 and has claimed no deductions in respect of its purchase cost.

When preparing Maria's taxable trading profits, you claim fixed rate expenses where possible. Maria has no other income.

(c) Calculate Maria's trading profits for the year ended 31 March 2025. **(5 marks)**

(d) Calculate Maria's income tax liability for 2024/25. **(3 marks)**

(e) Calculate Maria's total national insurance contributions for 2024/25. **(2 marks)**

You check your firm's files for Maria. You discover that Maria made her first payment on account for 2024/25 on time. The amount paid was £1,230 as correctly advised by your manager.

(f) Advise Maria of when she should pay the remaining income tax liability and national insurance contributions due for 2024/25, stating the amounts payable. **(3 marks)**

(Total 18 marks)

Past Exams: November 2022

1 You work in the Private Client Department of a large accountancy firm.

David is one of your clients. He lives in England and is UK resident. Your firm prepares David's self-assessment tax return each year and advises him on personal tax matters. David invests in quoted company shares, and residential properties which he rents out.

David has already tried to calculate his property income for 2024/25 as follows:

	£
Income:	
Property 1 annual rent payable	60,000
Property 2 annual rent payable	18,000
Property 3 rent received during 2024/25	9,000
Rent received from Vikram	2,500
Less expenses paid:	
Plumbing repair costs for property 1	(800)
Replacement bed for property 2	(1,000)
Insurance costs paid – all properties	(2,700)
Additional utility expenses	(350)
Property income	84,650

Your manager has learned more information from David in a telephone call.

Properties 1 and 2 were rented out throughout 2024/25. The rent was payable at the start of each month. All payments were received on time except for the amounts due for property 2 on 1 March 2025 and 1 April 2025. Both payments were received on 30 April 2025.

Property 3 was sold during the year.

From 1 June 2024 to 31 October 2024, one of David's friends, Vikram, stayed in David's own house. Vikram had moved to take a job near to David's home and lived with David while looking for a house to buy. The 'additional utility expenses' listed above refer to the additional costs of electricity and water incurred by David due to Vikram living in the house with him.

David sold the old bed in property 2 for £100.

Your manager has noticed some errors in David's computation and asks you to calculate the correct property income.

Required

(a) Calculate David's correct property income for 2024/25, identifying any items of income or expenditure which are not taxable or deductible. **(7 marks)**

David's only other income is dividend income from UK quoted companies. David has provided details of his dividend income received in the period from 1 April 2024 to 30 November 2025.

Date received	Dividend amount
	£
2 April 2024	14,000
31 May 2024	28,200
30 September 2024	17,600
28 February 2025	39,000
30 June 2025	15,900

You realise that the dividend received on 2 April 2024 was not included in David's electronic tax return for 2023/24 which was submitted on 28 January 2025.

(b) Advise David of the steps that he and your firm should take to address this error and the possible consequences of the error. Calculations are not required when answering this part.

(4 marks)

(c) Calculate David's income tax liability for 2024/25. **(5 marks)**

You find out that David has also made capital disposals during 2024/25.

David sold 10,000 shares in Kinglly plc for £70,000 on 28 January 2025.

David had bought 20,000 shares in Kinglly plc on 1 May 2010 for £36,000. There was a 1 for 5 rights issue for £3 per share on 8 October 2015. David took up all his rights.

David bought a further 2,000 shares in Kinglly plc on 13 February 2025 for £13,600.

All costs are stated inclusive of all costs of purchase including any stamp taxes.

(d) Calculate the chargeable gain on the disposal of Kinglly plc shares. **(7 marks)**

David made one other disposal during 2024/25. He sold a residential property (property 3) for £260,000 on 15 February 2025.

David had rented out the property and had not lived in it. The property had cost £170,000 on 12 April 2009. The cost is stated inclusive of all costs of purchase including any stamp taxes.

David had a capital loss brought forward from 2023/24 of £12,800.

(e) Calculate David's capital gains tax liability for 2024/25. **(6 marks)**

David wants to invest £100,000 from these disposals. He will choose one of the following options:
- £100,000 invested in shares, transferred by a paper stock transfer form
- £100,000 invested in a residential property in England
- £100,000 invested in a commercial property in England.

He wants you to remind him of the rates he would pay in stamp taxes in each case.

(f) Advise David of the rate (%) of the relevant stamp tax which would be payable for each option. **(3 marks)**

After you tell David this, he discloses that one of the commercial properties he has been looking at is Tania House. David wants specific tax advice on its purchase, including about VAT and any available tax reliefs, as this will help him decide how much he will agree to pay for the property.

You realise that Tania House is owned by Build LLP, another client of your firm. Under the terms of the firm's existing engagement letter with Build LLP, your firm will give tax advice on the sale of Tania House. Therefore, there is a potential conflict of interest. It may not be appropriate to act for David on this matter.

(g) Applying ethical guidelines, determine the circumstances under which your firm may advise David on the purchase, advising two specific safeguards which your firm should adopt.

(4 marks)
(Total 36 marks)

2 You work as an assistant in the finance department of Full Ltd. Full Ltd is a VAT-registered trading company, which makes wholly standard-rated supplies.

The financial controller Lynn has recently started work at the company. She has asked you to work on various tax matters.

The company has expanded its operations over the last few years and has incurred significant costs. As a result, it has a brought forward trading loss of £390,000 from the year ended 31 December 2023.

Lynn has already calculated the draft tax-adjusted trading profits for the year ended 31 December 2024 as £1,990,000. This is before deducting interest payable and capital allowances.

You review the purchases of new plant and machinery made in November 2024. The costs are shown inclusive of VAT at the standard rate.

	£
Processing machine, with a 10-year life	600,000
Zero emissions cars with 70% business use by directors	120,000
Cutting machine, with a 30-year life	300,000

Required

(a) Calculate the VAT recoverable on the purchases of plant and machinery. **(3 marks)**

You check these amounts to the VAT return for the quarter ended 31 December 2024. They have been correctly entered and the VAT return correctly prepared, showing an overall repayment. However, the bank statement shows that the repayment was in fact received twice in error.

You raise this with Lynn who says if HMRC makes a mistake it is not the company's problem and that you can just ignore it.

(b) Applying ethical guidelines, identify one fundamental principle you would breach if you were to do as Lynn says, and the action the company should take instead. **(2 marks)**

As at 1 January 2024, the tax written down value of the main pool was £94,000 and that of the special rate pool was £18,300. The company made no disposals during the year.

(c) Calculate the maximum capital allowances for the year ended 31 December 2024.

(9 marks)

The analysis of interest for the year ended 31 December 2024 is:

	Receivable/(payable)
	£
Interest payable on loan to purchase machines	(31,000)
Interest payable on loan to purchase share investment	(1,800)
Interest received on overpaid corporation tax for previous year	900
Bank interest receivable	2,400

(d) Calculate the tax-adjusted trading profits for the year ended 31 December 2024. **(2 marks)**

(e) Calculate the corporation tax payable for the year ended 31 December 2024, assuming the company claims loss relief as soon as possible. **(4 marks)**

(f) Determine the date by which the loss relief claim must be made. **(1 mark)**

The sales director wants to retain a sales manager, Rachel, who has received a job offer from a competitor. The director wants to offer Rachel a company car as an incentive to stay but wants to know how much this will cost the company each year.

The car would be leased by Full Ltd and Rachel would use it solely for private journeys.

You are given the details of the car:

	£
List price	£45,000
Annual lease cost	£8,000
Fuel type	Petrol
CO_2 emissions	161 g/km
Annual running costs (note)	£2,000

Note: Full Ltd will not provide Rachel with fuel but will cover all other running costs.

(g) Calculate the annual Class 1A national insurance contributions payable by Full Ltd if the car is provided. **(2 marks)**

(h) Calculate the annual cost to the company of providing the car, taking account of any corporation tax savings. **(6 marks)**

Lynn did not work on payroll in her previous role. She wants information about the year-end PAYE forms that Full Ltd would have to complete relating to Rachel, assuming the car is provided for the year 2025/26.

(i) Prepare a schedule which records for each of Rachel's salary and car benefit:
- the PAYE form which is required after the year end
- whom the form is given to, and
- by what date the form must be completed. **(5 marks)**

(Total 34 marks)

3 You work for a small firm of accountants.

Alice is a new client. She needs your firm's help to get up to date with tax matters. Alice is a Scottish taxpayer.

Alice set up a new business on 1 February 2024. Before this, she had been caring for her daughter full-time. She has no other income. Alice told HMRC that she started a business but has not yet submitted any tax returns or paid any tax. She says she ignores any HMRC letters as she does not understand them.

Your colleague Sam has helped Alice prepare accounts for the 15-month period from 1 February 2024 to 30 April 2025. Sam has made the adjustments for tax, calculating taxable trading profits of £30,000 for the 15-month period.

Required

(a) State the date by which Alice must notify HMRC of her chargeability to income tax on her trading income. **(1 mark)**

(b) Calculate Alice's taxable trading profits for 2023/24 and 2024/25, clearly stating the basis periods. **(4 marks)**

(c) Calculate Alice's income tax payable for 2023/24 and 2024/25 as a Scottish taxpayer. **(3 marks)**

(d) Calculate Alice's Class 4 national insurance contributions for 2023/24 and 2024/25. **(2 marks)**

(e) Advise Alice of when the income tax liability and Class 4 national insurance contributions for 2024/25 must be paid. **(2 marks)**

You agree that you will complete Alice's tax returns for 2023/24 and 2024/25 and submit these electronically to HMRC by 31 December 2025.

(f) Advise Alice of the late filing penalty for the 2023/24 return if the returns are submitted on 31 December 2025. **(4 marks)**

Alice's turnover has been £4,000 per month to date and so she has not had to register for VAT.

Her sales would be standard rated supplies for VAT purposes.

However, Alice is currently bidding for a large contract. It is uncertain whether she will win this as she has many competitors. She will find out if she has won the contract on 1 January 2026. If she does win, she will make a sale of £100,000 under the contract on

20 January 2026. This will be in addition to her usual monthly turnover of £4,000. All figures are stated exclusive of VAT.

(g) Assuming Alice wins the contract, determine the date by which Alice must notify HMRC of her need to register for VAT, and the date from which she would be registered. **(2 marks)**

(Total 18 marks)

4   You work for a firm of tax advisers. Your firm has been engaged by Mila to deal with inheritance tax matters on the death of her uncle, Alex.

Alex was UK resident and UK domiciled. He died on 14 November 2024. Alex had never married and he had made no lifetime gifts. He left his entire estate to Mila in his will.

Mila has provided details of the assets Alex owned at his date of death.

These include share certificates showing Alex owned 50,000 shares in Court plc. This represented a 0.01% shareholding in this investment company. On 14 November 2024, the shares were quoted at 147p – 155p. There were bargains at 150p, 151p and 156p.

Required

(a) Calculate the market value of Alex's shareholding of the Court plc shares on 14 November 2024 for inheritance tax purposes. Work to the nearest pence (£0.00) for this part only

(2 marks)

Alex owned two properties: his main home in the UK worth £900,000 and a holiday home worth £125,000 in Stephy, an overseas country.

The country of Stephy charged overseas tax of the equivalent of £12,000 on the holiday home on Alex's death.

On 14 November 2024, Alex owned cash of £150,000 and chattels worth £4,000.

(b) Calculate the inheritance tax payable on Alex's death. **(8 marks)**

The inheritance tax will be paid, and an IHT account submitted, on 31 December 2025.

(c) Calculate the interest payable on the overdue inheritance tax if this is paid on 31 December 2025. **(2 marks)**

(Total 12 marks)

Past Exams: May 2023

1   You work in the Owner-Managed Business Department of a large accountancy firm, advising small businesses on tax.

Felix is a new client to the firm. He started trading on 1 October 2024 and registered for VAT from that date. He makes standard-rated supplies.

Felix has a business degree. Using this knowledge, he has prepared basic accounts for the six months ended 31 March 2025. He prepares and submits his own VAT returns.

However, Felix admits that he does not have up-to-date income tax knowledge. Your firm will complete his annual self-assessment tax returns.

Your manager Nikita has prepared the engagement letter and completed the necessary procedures to take on Felix as a client. However, Felix is still confused who is responsible for his tax returns, when your firm completes them. He also wants to understand the basis on which fees are charged.

Required

(a) Advise Felix of his responsibilities and the firm's role, under tax legislation, when his self-assessment tax returns are completed by your firm. **(2 marks)**

(b) Record two possible bases on which the fee for completing Felix's tax returns could be charged. **(2 marks)**

You review Felix's accounts that he has prepared for the six months ended 31 March 2025 and the extra information he has provided. Felix has used the cash basis to calculate his trade profits and he has correctly dealt with VAT on the amounts included in the accounts.

	£	£
Sales receipts		39,000
Expenses paid:		
Drawings by Felix for personal expenses	12,000	
Total running costs for car (note)	2,500	
Legal costs for preparing customer contracts	1,000	
Other allowable expenditure	5,500	
		(21,000)
Net profit		18,000

Note. In October 2024, Felix bought a car for £20,000 with CO2 emissions of 100 g/km and 40% business use. He has not charged depreciation in the accounts and he will claim capital allowances in relation to the cost of the car.

Additionally, Felix had incurred the following expenditure in September 2024, before he started to trade:

- a computer for £4,000, with 100% business use
- costs for advice on marketing of £500.

Felix has not taken any deductions in his accounts for the expenditure incurred in September 2024.

Amounts for the expenditure in September and October 2024 are stated exclusive of VAT. Felix paid VAT on each amount at the standard rate.

(c) Calculate the input VAT that Felix could claim on his first VAT return on the expenditure incurred in September 2024. **(2 marks)**

(d) Calculate Felix's capital allowances for the six months ended 31 March 2025. **(2 marks)**

(e) Calculate Felix's tax-adjusted trading profits for the six months ended 31 March 2025, demonstrating your treatment of each expense. **(7 marks)**

Felix contacts your manager Nikita about VAT matters. Felix admits that he is not as confident as he first thought when completing the VAT returns. Nikita agrees that your firm will advise Felix on various VAT matters. The engagement letter and fee are updated.

You find out that Felix was three weeks late submitting the first VAT return, for the quarter ended 31 December 2024, and paying the VAT due. Felix is worried that he will be charged a penalty for this.

From a review of Felix's VAT records, Nikita thinks that Felix has not claimed all the input VAT he could and so has overpaid VAT. Felix also needs advice on record-keeping.

(f) Prepare a summary for Felix of VAT matters in which you:

- explain whether a penalty arises on the late VAT return and payment
- advise on the time limit for reclaiming overpaid VAT
- advise for how long Felix must keep VAT records
- identify two records Felix must keep in relation to input VAT on his purchases.

(5 marks)

As Felix is struggling on VAT matters, Nikita suggests that Felix may not need to be VAT registered. Felix expects monthly sales of around £6,500 (exclusive of VAT) in future months.

(g) Advise whether Felix would be able to deregister for VAT. **(2 marks)**

(Total 22 marks)

2 You work in the Personal Tax Department of an accountancy firm. Gita is one of the firm's clients. She is UK resident and lives in England.

HMRC has carried out an enquiry (compliance check) into Gita's 2022/23 self-assessment tax return. On 20 May 2025, HMRC completed the enquiry, issuing a notice which details an amendment to the return to increase Gita's capital gains tax. The HMRC inspector says that this corrects a careless error, where Gita overstated costs in a calculation of gains.

Your manager agrees that there is a careless error but disagrees with the amount. She says that the amount of understated capital gains tax is £5,000, which is lower than the amount in the notice. She advises Gita to appeal the notice.

Required

(a) Advise Gita of the date by which she should appeal the notice. **(1 mark)**

(b) Assuming your manager is correct, calculate the maximum penalty due to the careless error. **(1 mark)**

In 2024/25 Gita received a salary of £170,000 from her employment at Bammbonet Ltd. She owned shares in Bammbonet Ltd and in December 2024 received a dividend of £8,000.

Gita also received bank interest of £20,000, of which £5,000 was from savings in a cash ISA (Individual Savings Account).

During 2024/25 Gita paid £10,000 into her personal pension scheme and Bammbonet Ltd paid a further £25,000 on her behalf. Bammbonet Ltd had made the same contribution for many years, but this was the first year that Gita made her own contribution.

Gita has never been a high-income individual for the purpose of the annual allowance for pensions.

(c) Calculate Gita's annual allowance for 2024/25, including any unused brought forward amounts. **(3 marks)**

(d) Calculate Gita's income tax liability for 2024/25. **(8 marks)**

Gita sold her house for £290,000 and bought a bigger one for £340,000. Both houses are in England and both transactions completed on 31 May 2024. Gita does not own any other properties.

(e) Calculate the stamp duty land tax payable on the purchase of the new house. **(2 marks)**

(f) Record the date by which Gita had to report the stamp duty land tax to HMRC. **(1 mark)**

Gita had bought her old house on 1 June 2004 for £165,000 including all costs. She lived in it until 31 May 2008 when she moved to live with a friend in that friend's apartment until 31 May 2013. Gita returned to live in her house after this, except for six months during 2018 when she travelled overseas.

(g) For Gita's period of ownership of the old house, prepare a schedule of the periods of occupation or deemed occupation, and of no occupation, stating the relevant dates.

(3 marks)

(h) Calculate Gita's chargeable gain on the sale of her old house. **(2 marks)**

Gita also owns a plot of agricultural land which she bought for £50,000. On 1 March 2025 Gita granted an option for £10,000 to Ricky, an unconnected individual. The option allows Ricky to buy the land for £100,000 within two years of the grant of the option. Ricky has not yet exercised the option.

On 29 March 2025 Gita sold shares in a company based in Erehw, an overseas country, for £35,000. She had bought the shares in March 2012 for £16,000 inclusive of all costs. No tax was charged in Erehw on the sale.

(i) Calculate Gita's capital gains tax for 2024/25. **(6 marks)**

Gita is worried about future HMRC enquiries. She wants to know how long HMRC has to enquire into her subsequent tax returns. She submitted the return for 2023/24 on 15 February 2025. Assume the return for 2024/25 will be submitted on 15 July 2025.

(j) Advise Gita of the latest dates that HMRC can open enquiries into her 2023/24 and 2024/25 returns. **(2 marks)**

(Total 29 marks)

3 You work for a firm of accountants in the Private Client department. Amara has engaged your firm to complete the inheritance tax calculations following the death of her mother Edna. Edna died on 29 January 2025. Edna had never been married. Edna was domiciled in the UK.

Amara had already attempted a draft inheritance tax computation for Edna's death estate, using information she had found online. The calculation contains errors but Amara has used the correct asset values. Amara has not calculated the inheritance tax due on Edna's only lifetime gift of cash to Edna's brother, Kris, of £800,000 made on 19 September 2020.

Required

(a) Calculate the inheritance tax payable on the lifetime gift on Edna's death. **(4 marks)**

You review the draft death estate calculation provided by Amara.

	£
Edna's house	490,000
Shares in Quirel Ltd (4% shareholding)	80,000
Cash	500,000
Chattels	20,000
Chargeable estate	1,090,000
Less nil rate band	(325,000)
	765,000
IHT @ 40%	306,000

You find out that Edna bought the shares in Quirel Ltd in September 2017. Edna did not work for this unquoted trading company.

In her will, Edna left £10,000 cash to a registered charity and the remainder of her estate to her daughter, Amara.

(b) Prepare a full, corrected computation of inheritance tax on Edna's death estate. **(6 marks)**

(c) Calculate the amount of cash that Amara receives on her mother's death. **(2 marks)**

(Total 12 marks)

4   You work for the internal finance department of a large manufacturing company, Facimus Ltd.

Facimus Ltd makes all tax payments electronically.

Ruby manages payroll. She will soon leave the company and has handed over work on various year-end payroll tasks for 2024/25 to you and your colleagues.

Facimus Ltd has a PAYE settlement agreement (PSA) with HMRC in respect of staff parties. The company held its annual staff party in December 2024, costing £240 per employee. Of the company's 130 employees at that date, 100 were basic rate taxpayers and 30 were higher rate taxpayers. There are no employees who are Scottish taxpayers.

Required

(a) Calculate the Class 1B payable by Facimus Ltd in respect of the staff party. **(4 marks)**

(b) Record the date when this is payable. **(1 mark)**

You and your colleagues work on the P11D forms for employees for 2024/25. Your colleagues calculate benefits that are similar each year. However, there were some different benefits provided in 2024/25 which Ruby has asked you to deal with.

A new sales director, Jamal, joined the company during 2024/25 and received benefits.

- Jamal had to move house to be near to Facimus Ltd's head office. The company paid for his moving costs of £10,000.

- The company gave flowers costing £60 to Jamal on his birthday.

- The company gave Jamal an interest-free loan of £5,000 which he used to improve the insulation in his home.

(c) For each of Jamal's benefits, record for income tax purposes whether it is fully exempt, fully taxable, or partially taxable. **(3 marks)**

The managing director Simon separated from his wife during 2024/25. From 6 July 2024, he has been allowed to live in a house owned by Facimus Ltd. Details of the house are:

Date bought by Facimus Ltd	1 April 2007
Cost in April 2009	£90,000
Extension cost in May 2021	£50,000
Market value at 6 July 2024	£275,000
Annual value	£12,000
Rent paid by Simon for use of house	£500 per month

(d) Calculate Simon's accommodation benefit for 2024/25. **(5 marks)**

You enter the accommodation benefit amount on Simon's P11D form. Ruby tells Simon if she had completed the form, she would not have included this as 'HMRC would be unlikely to find out about it'.

(e) Advise Simon why not recording the accommodation benefit on his form P11D would constitute tax evasion. Leah is an employee. She has left you a message asking for help in understanding her tax code for 2024/25. Before replying to Leah, you look up information about her. Leah is a Welsh, basic rate taxpayer. She receives an annual benefit of £500. PAYE on the benefit is collected by HMRC adjusting Leah's tax code. **(2 marks)**

(f) From the information given, determine Leah's tax code for 2024/25. **(3 marks)**

(Total 18 marks)

5   You work in the Corporation Tax department of a firm of accountants. Liz, one of your colleagues, has left the firm and you are finishing some of her work for a client, Redpar Ltd. Redpar Ltd is a trading company which prepares accounts to 31 December each year. Your VAT colleagues deal with VAT matters for the company so you can ignore VAT throughout.

On 1 December 2024 Redpar Ltd sold a factory building for £1,450,000. Redpar Ltd has used the building in its trade since buying it for £800,000 in December 2003.

Redpar Ltd bought a new office building for use in its trade on 18 January 2025. The cost was £1,370,000 inclusive of all fees and purchase costs.

Redpar Ltd claims all available reliefs.

Required

(a) Record and explain the date by which Redpar Ltd must claim any available relief on the sale of the factory building. **(2 marks)**

(b) Calculate Redpar Ltd's chargeable gain on sale of the factory building. **(4 marks)**

Your colleague Liz had already calculated Redpar Ltd's draft tax-adjusted trading profits of £25,800,000 for the year ended 31 December 2024. However, at that point Liz had no information about the research and development (R&D) expenditure incurred by the company.

The finance director of Redpar Ltd has now told you that no deductions have yet been made for the following R&D expenditure in the year:

	£
Staff costs	3,800,000
Consumables	500,000
Total	4,300,000

You have confirmed that these costs relate directly to qualifying R&D activities.

The company had no other income in the year ended 31 December 2024. It had a capital loss of £500,000 brought forward at 1 January 2024.

(c) Record the date by which Redpar Ltd must claim research and development expenditure credit (RDEC) for the year ended 31 December 2024. **(1 mark)**

(d) Calculate Redpar Ltd's corporation tax payable for the year ended 31 December 2024, demonstrating your use of the capital loss. **(8 marks)**

Redpar Ltd's profits continue to increase. As it is such a large client for your firm, you have been assigned a new trainee, Sanjeev, to work with you. Sanjeev has little tax knowledge so far. In May 2025, you inform him of upcoming actions in relation to Redpar Ltd's corporation tax.

(e) Record the next date by which a corporation tax payment must be made. **(1 mark)**

(f) Record the due date for submission of the corporation tax return for the year ended 31 December 2024, how this is submitted and the information which must be included with the return. **(3 marks)**

(Total 19 marks)

Past Exams: November 2023

1 You work in the internal finance department of Pandated Ltd. Pandated Ltd is a VAT-registered trading company which prepares accounts to 31 March each year. The company sells standard-rated goods and makes quarterly VAT returns.

In December 2024, the finance director became ill and suddenly left the company. The company took many months to recruit a new finance director, Anwar, who started work in October 2025.

Anwar has asked you to assist her with corporation tax and VAT matters.

The corporation tax return for the year ended 31 March 2024 was submitted on 31 October 2025. This is the first time that the company's corporation tax return has been submitted late. The corporation tax liability of £240,000 was paid on the same date.

Required

(a) Advise Anwar, with supporting calculations, of the late filing penalties for the corporation tax return for the year ended 31 March 2024. **(3 marks)**

Anwar is reviewing several transactions which took place during the year ended 31 March 2025.

Pandated Ltd sold a factory building, Greenlane, on 1 November 2024 for £1,900,000 because the company stopped selling the particular product being made there. The company had bought Greenlane new from a developer on 1 January 2023 and had immediately started making the product there.

On 1 November 2024, Pandated Ltd also sold the remaining stock (inventory) of the product for £200,000, with 40% sold to a company in the European Union (EU) and 60% sold to a UK company.

All these amounts are stated exclusive of VAT. No option to tax has been made. The previous finance director correctly treated the output VAT on these sales, retaining the appropriate documentation. Anwar wants the details for a file note.

(b) Calculate the output VAT charged on the sales of Greenlane and the stock in November 2024, recording the VAT percentage charged on each sale. **(3 marks)**

(c) Record on which VAT return the output VAT would have been entered and the date by which this return had to be submitted to HMRC. **(2 marks)**

You find purchase information about Greenlane from 2023. The VAT-exclusive purchase costs relating to the building itself were £1,400,000 and those relating to the land on which it stands were £100,000.

(d) Calculate the structures and buildings allowance (SBA) for the year ended 31 March 2025 and the total SBA claimed since Greenlane was purchased. **(3 marks)**

(e) Calculate the gain on the sale of Greenlane in November 2024. **(3 marks)**

Pandated Ltd also had transactions in Zooam Ltd shares during the year ended 31 March 2025.

On 1 March 2024 Pandated Ltd bought 1,000 Zooam Ltd shares for £50,632. The purchase was completed with a paper stock transfer form. Anwar is unsure of the company's obligations to HMRC in respect of the stamp duty payable and whether these were met. She commits to meeting any outstanding obligations by 31 December 2025.

(f) Calculate the stamp duty payable on the March 2025 purchase of Zooam Ltd shares. **(1 mark)**

(g) Advise Anwar of Pandated Ltd's obligations to HMRC in respect of this stamp duty and the consequences if these are not met until 31 December 2025.

You are not required to perform calculations when answering this part. **(4 marks)**

Pandated Ltd had originally purchased 2,000 Zooam Ltd shares on 15 January 2012. The total cost, including stamp duty, was £75,000.

Zooam Ltd made a 1 for 2 bonus issue of shares on 20 January 2020, immediately after which the shares were worth £40 per share.

The purchase on 1 March 2025 was Pandated Ltd's only other purchase of Zooam Ltd shares.

On 8 March 2025 Pandated Ltd sold 2,500 Zooam Ltd shares for £150,000.

Pandated Ltd's shareholding in Zooam Ltd was always less than 10%.

(h) Calculate the chargeable gain on sale of the shares on 8 March 2025. **(7 marks)**

The financial controller has already calculated the company's tax-adjusted trading profit as £980,000 for the year ended 31 March 2024. However, this figure is before deduction of the structures and buildings allowance and the following amounts of interest payable for the year:

	£
Interest on loan to purchase Greenlane	71,500
Interest on loan to purchase Zooam Ltd shares	1,000
Interest on late paid corporation tax	6,500

Pandated Ltd has no other income for the year ended 31 March 2025. The company makes claims to reduce the corporation tax payable as much as possible in the current year.

(i) Calculate Pandated Ltd's corporation tax payable for the year ended 31 March 2025, demonstrating your treatment of each amount of interest payable. **(6 marks)**

(j) Record the date by which any beneficial claims must be made. **(1 marks)**

(Total 33 marks)

2   You work for an accountancy firm which provides services to business clients.

One of your colleagues, Aliya, is on holiday. The tax partner has asked you to complete work that Aliya started for a client, Tremain, who is a sole trader. Tremain has always used the cash basis to calculate his trading profits.

Due to the loss of a major customer, Tremain has made a trading loss for the year ended 5 April 2025. You check Aliya's calculation of the tax-adjusted trading loss before taking account of expenditure on plant and machinery and capital allowances for the year and agree this to be £69,000.

Aliya has prepared the following computation of capital allowances but this contains some accidental errors:

Capital Allowances for the year ended 5 April 2025

Computation prepared by Aliya

	Main pool £	Special rate pool £	Total allowances £
TWDV brought forward	0	5,400	
Additions:			
Car		15,000	
Machine	9,000		
FYA @ 100%	(9,000)		9,000
		20,400	
WDA @ 6%		(1,224)	1,224
TWDV carried forward	0	19,176	
Total allowances			10,224

You confirm from your firm's files on Tremain that the brought forward tax written down values (TWDV) are correct. The balance on the special rate pool relates to a car used by one of Tremain's employees with 90% private use. Tremain tells you that he made no disposals during the year ended 5 April 2025.

You check the details of the purchases made of the car and the machine. Both were purchased new and the correct costs are shown in Aliya's computation. The car has CO2 emissions of 40g/km and is used by one of Tremain's employees with 80% private use.

Required

(a) Prepare a revised capital allowances computation, calculating Tremain's maximum capital allowances for the year ended 5 April 2025. **(4 marks)**

(b) Calculate Tremain's tax-adjusted trading loss, assuming he claims the maximum capital allowances. **(1 mark)**

The tax partner notices that you have changed the capital allowances calculation. She wants to address Aliya's performance at work and asks you to prepare for a meeting she will hold with Aliya on her return from holiday.

(c) Advise the tax partner of the main ethical fundamental principle that Aliya may be failing to meet, and of what the ethical guidelines require in respect of this principle. **(3 marks)**

From your firm's files for Tremain you find the following information:

Tax year 2023/24

Property income   £60,000

Trading profit   £5,000

You confirm that his property income for the tax year 2024/25 is also £60,000.

Tremain has already found new customers and expects his business to return to profit in the year ended 5 April 2026. He wants to claim loss relief against the earliest possible income.

(d) Calculate Tremain's net income for each of the tax years 2023/24 and 2024/25 assuming loss relief is used as early as possible. **(3 marks)**

(e) Advise Tremain of the date by which this loss relief must be claimed. **(1 mark)**

(Total 12 marks)

3   You work in the tax department of an accountancy firm. Your firm provides tax compliance services to the STP Partnership and its three partners. All three partners are UK resident and live in England.

Sue and Taz have been partners in STP for many years but Utu joined the partnership on 1 October 2024. Utu had been employed by an unconnected UK company, Ronsnook plc, until 30 September 2024.

Utu invested £50,000 in the STP partnership when he joined. He borrowed this money from a bank, paying loan interest of £2,000 in 2024/25.

Before Utu joined the partnership, Sue and Taz shared profits equally. After Utu joined, the partners Sue, Taz and Utu shared profits in the ratio 2:2:1.

The tax-adjusted trading profit for the STP partnership for the year ended 30 June 2025 is £360,000.

Required

(a) Calculate each partner's profit allocation for the year ended 30 June 2025. **(3 marks)**

(b) Calculate Utu's assessable trading profit for the tax year 2024/25. **(1 mark)**

Your manager Mitch has asked you to work on Utu's income tax return for 2024/25 and so you ask Utu about any other income he received in 2024/25.

Utu tells you he received overseas rental income of £9,000 after deduction of overseas tax of £1,000 and allowable costs of £2,500.

Utu also received a salary plus a bonus from Ronsnook plc, but he cannot remember the exact amounts. You remind him that Ronsnook plc will have given him a form when he left employment which will show this information.

(c) Advise Utu of the name of the form that Ronsnook plc would have given to Utu when he left employment. **(1 mark)**

You determine that in 2024/25 Utu received total gross salary of £80,000 and a bonus of £20,000. He contributed £3,000 to his employer's occupational pension scheme under net pay arrangements.

Ronsnook plc paid Utu at the end of each month. The company makes all payments electronically.

(d) Calculate Utu's income tax liability for 2024/25. **(8 marks)**

Before 2024/25, Utu's only income had been employment income from Ronsnook plc.

Your manager Mitch has received a message from Utu who is now confused about the different classes of national insurance contributions (NIC) he suffers in respect of 2024/25. Mitch asks you to prepare a schedule for Utu, covering Class 1 primary NIC and Class 4 NIC.

(e) Prepare a schedule for Utu which records, for 2024/25, for each class of NIC (Class 1 primary and Class 4) he suffers:

- the amount on which the NIC is charged
- the form or return on which this is first reported to HMRC
- who is responsible for paying the NIC to HMRC
- by when the NIC is payable to HMRC.

You are not required to perform calculations of the NIC payable. **(7 marks)**

Utu mentions that he inherited quoted shares in May 2025 and expects to receive dividends of £10,000 from these in 2025/26. He makes a comment that he will not want to include the dividend income on his tax return for 2025/26 given that HMRC will not know about it.

(f) Record the steps you and your firm would have to take to comply with anti-money laundering legislation if Utu were to refuse to include the dividend income on his 2025/26 tax return. **(4 marks)**

(Total 24 marks)

4 You work for a small firm of accountants. Your manager asks you to complete the inheritance tax calculations following the death of Marcia, whose family has engaged your firm for this work.

Marcia and her husband Bembe had both been UK domiciled and had not made any lifetime gifts.

Bembe had died on 31 December 2020. He left his entire estate worth £260,000 to his brother on his death.

Marcia died on 1 March 2025. She left her entire estate to her sister in her will.

Marcia owned the following assets on her death, with the market values shown:

	Market value £
Marcia's house	575,000
Agricultural land	80,000
Cash, of which £20,000 was held in an Individual Savings Account (ISA)	95,000
Chattels	72,000

The assets are all situated in the UK.

A valuer reports that the agricultural value of the land on 1 March 2025 was £55,000. Marcia had rented out the land to a farmer for 20 years prior to her death.

At 1 March 2025, Marcia owed income tax to HMRC of £8,000. Expenses for Marcia's funeral were £2,000.

Required

(a) Calculate the total nil rate band (NRB) available on Marcia's death, assuming all beneficial claims are made. **(3 marks)**

(b) Calculate the inheritance tax payable on Marcia's death, recording the amount of any reliefs. **(7 marks)**

(c) Record the date by which any beneficial claim must usually be made. **(1 mark)**

(Total 11 marks)

5 You work in the Private Client department of a firm of accountants. Matt and Simon, a married couple, are your clients. Your manager Delia wants your help preparing for a meeting with Matt and Simon.

Matt made disposals of capital assets during 2024/25. He is an additional rate taxpayer in 2024/25.

On 1 May 2024 Matt sold two hectares of land at an auction. The land did not have residential use. This had been part of a plot of five hectares that Matt had bought in January 2012. Matt has provided the following information:

	£
Total cost of five hectares in January 2012	100,000
Gross sales proceeds on sale of the two hectares	80,000
Auctioneer's fees on sale	8,000
Value of remaining three hectares in May 2024	150,000

Required

(a) Calculate the gain on disposal of the land. **(4 marks)**

On 25 December 2022 Matt gave Simon a painting worth £20,000. Matt had bought the painting for £13,000 in 2017.

On 18 February 2025 Matt sold his trading business for £2,000,000, which he had owned since 2007. Delia has already calculated the gain on the sale to be £1,500,000.

You confirm that Matt has not previously sold any assets. He claims all available reliefs.

(b) Calculate Matt's capital gains tax payable for 2024/25. **(6 marks)**

(c) Record the dates by which Matt must:

    (i) claim any relief available on the disposals **(1 mark)**

    (ii) pay the capital gains tax due. **(1 mark)**

On 30 March 2025, Matt used some of the proceeds from his disposals to buy a house in Wales for £230,000. Matt and Simon will use the house for holidays. Matt already owns the home where he and Simon live.

(d) Calculate the land transaction tax (LTT) payable on the house in Wales. **(2 marks)**

Matt wants to know how much money he will have left from the disposals he made in 2024/25 after buying the house in Wales, and after paying all taxes.

(e) Calculate the amount of cash remaining from the 2024/25 disposals after the purchase of the house and payment of all taxes. **(3 marks)**

Matt gives Simon half of this amount of cash remaining.

Matt will be a higher rate taxpayer in future years. Simon is a retired school music teacher. He receives pension income equal to his personal allowance each year.

Simon thinks he and Matt could generate more income. He wants to know the maximum income they could receive each year from each of the following proposals without having to pay more income tax:

- Matt rents out a room to a lodger, in the home where they live
- Simon gives weekly music lessons to the public, advertised online
- Simon earns interest by depositing the cash received from Matt in a high-interest savings account (not an ISA).

(f) Record the maximum amounts of income that could be received each year from each of the three proposals, without income tax arising. **(3 marks)**

(Total 20 marks)

Exam Answer Bank

Past Exams: November 2021

1 This question tests the ethical steps required, before work can begin on a new client. It requires the preparation of a calculation of capital gains tax, correcting errors of a client. Candidates must also determine the obligations for reporting the gains, including in the case of a disposal of a residential property. Penalties for late filing of returns reporting capital gains are tested. Use of the published tax tables is tested with these administrative elements.

Learning Outcomes
LO1, LO2, LO3, LO4

(a) Client take on procedures

The firm should:

- assess threats to the fundamental principles
- assess the money laundering risk of acting for Fara
- perform customer due diligence including verifying Fara's identity
- contact any existing advisers for matters to consider – professional clearance
- agree scope of work and fees, in a signed engagement letter.

> **Additional areas where credit might be given, note this is not an exhaustive list:**
>
> - A specific example of a fundamental principle which may be threatened would be awarded 1 mark. Examples would include professional competence and due care (the full scope of the work not being known) or objectivity. Similarly a specific example of a threat to fundamental principles would gain credit. There is the potential for the connection between the partner and the client's mutual contact to pose a familiarity threat or lead to a conflict of interest.

(b) Capital gains tax

	£
Sale of rental property	
Gross proceeds	250,000
Cost *(redecoration not allowed)*	(150,000)
	100,000
Less annual exempt amount	(3,000)
	97,000
Capital gains tax @ 24%	23,280
Sale of painting	
Gross proceeds	20,000
Less auctioneer fees	(200)
Less cost – husband's cost	(11,000)
	8,800
Capital gains tax @ 20%	1,760
Total capital gains tax	25,040

Tutorial note

The situation is typical in practice with a taxpayer performing a calculation of their own but making errors. One of the client errors is lack of deduction of the AEA, and the answer awards credit for both the deduction and for the use against the gain subject to the higher rate of tax. An incorrect rate has been used by the client for the residential property gain and cost deductions are incorrect including in relation to an asset received via a gift from a spouse. Candidates who are not led by what the client had done, but who apply the rules of CGT which they have learned, should find this question straightforward.

(c) Capital gains tax reporting obligations – returns

A return in respect of the property gain must be made within 60 days of completion of the sale (30 January 2025).

The total gains should be reported on her self-assessment tax return for 2024/25, due by 31 January 2026.

(d) Late filing penalties

Self-assessment tax return not late so no penalty in respect of the painting gain.

[Credit given without stating this, if penalties are stated as relating to the property gain]

Penalties for late return for the property disposal:
Immediate £100 penalty,

And after three months, possible daily penalty of £10 for 90 days
And after six months, penalty 5% of tax due (higher of this and £300)

Tutorial note

The requirement to report gains on residential property within 60 days is new and highly topical. In practice, the short time frame and lack of awareness of the new rule risks late filing and penalties. Candidates are expected to use the published tax tables when answering these administrative requirements but they must apply the information found there to the scenario, and not merely write out all the rules.

2 **This question tests aspects of corporation tax administrative obligations (payments, interest, records, claims) for which the published tax tables should be useful. It includes calculation of national insurance contributions payable by employers. It tests calculation of corporation tax including research and development relief, capital allowance and gains on disposals of shares including exemption under SSE. The question also tests the stamp taxes payable on the purchase of shares, and the inclusion of such taxes when determining gains.**

Learning Outcomes
LO1, LO2, LO32

(a) Quarterly instalment due dates

14 October 2025
14 January 2026
14 April 2026
14 July 2026

(b) Interest = 380,000 × 25% × 7.5% × 2/12 = £1,188

> **Tutorial note**
>
> Corporation tax instalment dates are easily missed in practice as some (all – in the case of very large companies) fall due during the accounting period itself. As detailed in the published tax tables, interest is charged at a special (lower) rate on overdue instalments, provided they are paid before the nine month and one day due date for other companies. This is the case here.
>
> This calculation uses the latest interest rate in the 2023 Finance Act edition of Whillans. Candidates using a more recent rate if this subsequently changes, would be given full credit.

(c) Six years from the end of the relevant accounting period/year end.

(d) Employer's NIC

	£
Class 1 secondary	
£(45,000 – 9,100) × 13.8%	4,954
Total for five employees	24,770

(e)

	£
Research scientists:	
Gross salaries (45,000 × 5)	225,000
Class 1 secondary NIC (part d)	24,770
Pension contributions 7% × 225,000	15,750
Consumables	66,000
Qualifying revenue expenditure	331,520
Rent payable on building	120,000
Allowable trading deduction	451,520
RDEC at 20% of qualifying expenditure	
20% x £331,520	66,304

(f) (i) Make the claim: 31 March 2026
    (ii) Notify HMRC of the claim: 30 September 2025

> **Additional areas where credit might be given, note this is not an exhaustive list:**
>
> - As the published tax tables highlight, HMRC may allow a later claim. This point is not required for full marks but ½ mark credit would be given if this is stated (and the candidate has not already scored full marks due to an incorrect claim date).

> **Tutorial note**
>
> There is valuable tax relief available for companies engaged in qualifying research and development. The relief takes the form of an R&D expenditure credit (RDEC) on qualifying expenditure. Additionally, costs which do not qualify for the RDEC may still be allowable trading deductions, as is the case for rent payable here. The claim deadline is given in the published tax tables.

(g) Capital allowances:

	Main pool £	Special rate pool £	Allowances £
TWDV b/f	58,000	16,000	
Van 18,500			
AIA (18,500)			18,500
Car addition		30,000	
	58,000	46,000	
WDA @ 18%	(10,440)		10,440
WDA @ 6%		(2,760)	2,760
	47,560	43,240	31,700

Tutorial note

There is never a private use adjustment for capital allowances of a company. The private use instead means that the director would have a taxable benefit charged to income tax, and the company would pay Class 1A NIC on the benefit. The question states that all adjustments have already been made, other than for the R&D project and capital allowances, and so no further adjustment is required in the next part for this NIC.

(h) Tax-adjusted trading profits

	£
Draft tax-adjusted trading profits	2,560,000
Less capital allowances (part g)	(31,700)
Less R&D (part e)	(451,520)
Trading profits	2,076,780

(i) Stamp taxes

Purchase of Lama plc shares – stamp duty reserve tax
Amount paid = 0.005 × £108,600 = £543

Purchase of Knightli Ltd shares – stamp duty
Amount paid = 0.005 × £310,400 = £1,552 rounded up to £1,555

Tutorial notes

The calculations of stamp taxes on shares are simple, but the rate of 0.5% can sometimes be incorrectly treated as 5%. Candidates are not usually penalised for arithmetic workings if their workings are correct, but an error here would instead indicate a lack of understanding of 0.5% and credit would not be given.

There is a distinction between stamp duty and stamp duty reserve tax which is tested here, and only the former is rounded up to the next multiple of £5 (this is stated in the published tax tables).

In this practical scenario, the stamp taxes are calculated because they are allowable costs in the calculation of gains in the next requirement.

(j) Chargeable gains

	£	£
Lama plc shares:		
Proceeds		250,000
Less cost	108,600	
Less SDRT (part i)	543	
		(109,143)
Gain on Lama plc shares		140,857
No gain re Knightli Ltd shares		-
Total gain		140,857

Tutorial note

The disposal of the Knightli Ltd shares only qualifies for the substantial shareholding exemption as a substantial shareholding (10% or more) in this trading company has been held for at least 12 months in the previous 6 years.

(k) Corporation tax liability

	£
Tax-adjusted trading profits	2,076,780
Dividends	-
Chargeable gains	140,857
RDEC	66,304
Taxable total profits	2,283,941
CT @ 25%	570,985
RDEC	(66,304)
Corporation tax liability	504,681

3   **This question tests income tax for an additional rate taxpayer with savings and dividend income. It covers the inheritance tax due on a death estate, taking into account the income tax outstanding on death, and including the transfer of a spouse's unused nil rate band and residential nil rate band. The taxation of property income is also examined, including in relation to a furnished holiday let. An ethical issue concerns giving investment advice.**

Learning Outcomes

LO1, LO2, LO3, LO4

(a) Income tax liability

	Savings £	Dividend £
Savings income	4,000	
Dividend		180,000
Personal allowance	-	-
Taxable income	4,000	180,000
Income tax liability		
£4,000 × 0% (savings starting rate)		0
£500 × 0% (dividend nil rate band)		0
£(47,700 (W) – 4,000 – 500) 43,200 × 8.75%		3,780
£(135,140 (W) – 47,700) 87,440 × 33.75%		29,511
£(180,000 – 87,440 – 43,200 – 500) 48,860 × 39.35%		19,226
Income tax liability		52,517

Workings

Extension of basic rate band = £37,700 + £8,000 × 100/80 = £47,700
Higher rate limit = £125,140 + £10,000 = £135,140

Tutorial note

The savings nil rate band is not available as the taxpayer's taxable income exceeds the higher rate limit (additional rate taxpayer) but the savings starting rate is available as she has no non-savings income. Her level of income means the personal allowance is clearly fully abated, even when the gift aid donation is taken into account.

(b) Income tax remaining payable at Anna's death = £52,517 - £23,000 = £29,517.

(c) Inheritance tax

	£	£
Chargeable estate:		
House	600,000	
Less mortgage	(80,000)	
		520,000
Cash deposits		200,000
Quoted shares in investment companies		700,000
		1,420,000
Less:		
Income tax remaining for 2024/25 (part b)		(29,517)
		1,390,483
Less		
RNRB Anna	175,000	
RNRB Stuart	175,000	
Anna's NRB	325,000	
Less lifetime gift £(157,000 – 6,000)	(151,000)	
Stuart's NRB	325,000	
		(849,000)
Estate chargeable at 40%		541,483
IHT at 40%		216,593

Tutorial note

The income tax outstanding at Anna's death is a debt owing and so reduces the value of the chargeable estate for inheritance tax purposes. Anna's nil rate band is restricted by the earlier gift, but her residential nil rate band is available as she has left her house to her son, a direct descendant. Anna's husband used none of his nil rate bands on death, as the transfer of his estate to Anna was exempt. Therefore, Anna's estate benefits from the transfer of both these nil rate bands.

(d) Property income

	Tulip Cottage £	Maple House £
Rental income		
30 × £1,000	30,000	
11 × £1,200		13,200
Less:		
Cleaning costs	(2,000)	
New bed	(800)	
Roof repairs		(700)
Washing machine £400 + £50		(450)
Mortgage interest	-	-
Total = £39,250	27,200	12,050

Tutorial note

Purchases of furniture for use in a furnished holiday letting are allowable deductions, so the cost of the new bed is allowable. In the case of other properties, relief is only available for the replacement of domestic items (here, the washing machine) to the extent the cost reflects the standard of the item being replaced (plus costs of disposal).

(e) Ethical issues re investment advice

The principle of professional competence and due care is threatened.
Such advice is not within the skill and qualification of a professional accountant.
The principle of professional behaviour is also threatened.
Giving such advice would be against the law and regulations.

Additional areas where credit might be given, note this is not an exhaustive list:

- Different points may be given credit for the reasoning (one mark per principle). For example, professional competence and due care would be breached as such service would be outside the terms of the engagement. Giving investment advice when not regulated may discredit the accountancy profession and so breach the principle of professional behaviour.

4 **This question involves a partnership and the taxation of a Scottish taxpayer's income. Calculations of national insurance contributions are also required for that partner. A calculation of net disposable income tests understanding of income tax and national insurance contributions as costs. The question tests land and buildings transaction tax, VAT and the PAYE obligations for new employees and on an ongoing basis. The published tax tables provide valuable information, including that necessary to determine the classes of NIC chargeable on particular payments for employees.**

Learning Outcomes
LO1, LO2, LO3

(a) Assessable trading profits for year ended 31 March 2025

	Total £	Agata £	Sunil £
Salary	30,000	30,000	
Profit sharing ratio 1:3			
£(130,000 – 30,000)	100,000	25,000	75,000
Total profits	130,000	55,000	75,000

> **Tutorial note**
>
> The tax year basis applies. Each partner is assessed on their share of profits arising in the tax year. For this purpose a 31 March year end is treated as a 5 April year end.

(b) Sunil's income tax liability

	£
Trading income (part a)	75,000
Less loss b/f	(1,000)
	74,000
Personal allowance	(12,750)
Taxable income	61,430
2,306 @ 19%	438
11,685 @ 20%	2,337
17,101 @ 21%	3,591
31,092	6,366
(61,430 – 31,092) 30,338 @ 42%	12,742
	19,108
Child benefit charge (W)	932
Income tax liability	20,040

Working

	£
Adjusted net income	74,000
Less threshold	(60,000)
Excess	14,000
÷ £200	70
Child benefit income tax charge: 1% × £1,331 × 70	932

> **Tutorial note**
>
> The tax tables show cumulative tax amounts, and credit is given for using figures directly from the tax tables up to the higher rate (ie for the figure of £6,366) without workings.
>
> Sunil's adjusted net income exceeds £60,000 but is less than £80,000 and so the full amount of child benefit received is charged on Sunil. The marriage allowance is not available as Sunil is not a basic rate taxpayer.

(c) National Insurance Contributions

	£
Class 4	
£(50,270 – 12,570) 37,700 @ 6%	2,262
£(74,000 – 50,270) 23,730 @ 2%	475
	2,737

(d) Net disposable income

	£
Income	75,000
Less annual living expenses	(30,000)
Less income tax	(20,040)
Less national insurance contributions	(2,737)
	22,223

(e) Land and buildings transaction tax:

	£
£(250,000 – 145,000) @ 2%	2,100
£(320,000 – 250,000) @ 5%	3,500
Land and buildings transaction tax	5,600

(f) P45

The P45 will contain that employee's:

- Tax code
- Employment income received in the tax year to date
- Income tax paid in the tax year to date

> **Additional areas where credit might be given, note this is not an exhaustive list:**
>
> - Credit would be given for the following details (not mentioned in the study material): NIC paid to date, national insurance number of employee, date of cessation of previous employment.

(g) Monthly PAYE reporting obligations.

The Agsu Partnership must report PAYE information electronically to HMRC using a monthly Full Payment Submission (FPS).

The FPS must be submitted on or before the date the employees are paid on 28th of each month (RTI system).

Agata can use HMRC's Basic PAYE Tools (BPT) software to submit this, as there are fewer than 10 employees.

The FPS includes the amount paid to each employee, the deductions made under PAYE for income tax and Class 1 primary national insurance contributions, and the Class 1 secondary contributions payable by the Agsu Partnership.

(h) National Insurance Contributions.

Payment of school fees – class 1A
Reimbursement of golf subscriptions – class 1 secondary
Mobile phone payments – no NIC

> **Tutorial note**
>
> This information can be found in Whillans Tax Tables, under Employer's contributions/ Common benefits subject to Class 1 and Class 1A NIC.

(i) VAT payable

	£
Output VAT:	
UK sales 36,000 @ 20%	7,200
Australian sales 5,000 @ 0%	
Input VAT:	
Business costs £(12,000 – 600) × 1/6	(1,900)
VAT payable	5,300

> **Tutorial note**
>
> Sales of goods to a country outside the UK are exports, so charged at 0%.

(j) The VAT return is due by 7 December 2025.

Past Exams: May 2022

1   This question tests the ethical threat relating to a fee issue. It requires the calculation of taxable benefits including the correction of calculations prepared by a client. It tests the calculation, reporting and payment of Class 1A NIC.

Learning Outcomes

LO1, LO2, LO3, LO4
Chapter References in AIA LPWB 4, 26

(a) Ethical issue

There is a self-interest threat to:
Either of:
objectivity
professional competence and due care.

> **Tutorial note**
>
> Candidates are required to apply ethical guidance here, but only need to identify (and not explain) one fundamental principle and the threat to this principle.
>
> There is a self-interest threat as the firm will want to retain the client and their fee income. Objectivity is always threatened by self-interest – the wish to retain overall fee income may influence Rebecca's judgement of what is an appropriate fee for this particular work. A lower fee may mean insufficient time and attention is spent by staff on the work, or there is insufficient supervision or review, and so threatens the principle professional competence and due care.
>
> Candidates are asked for one principle so stating more than one would not score more marks. If candidates were to list all the principles, they would not score any mark as they have failed to 'apply' to this scenario and 'identify' a relevant principle.

(b) Car and fuel benefits

Car benefit = (£38,750 − £3,000) × 12% = £4,290
Fuel benefit = £27,800 × 12% = £3,336

> **Tutorial note**
>
> The calculations of the car and fuel benefit should be straightforward but candidates need to pay attention to the type of fuel, to determine the correct percentage from the tax tables. They must also be confident to ignore the running costs and the specific detail on the costs of fuel for business and private mileage – the fact the company pays for any private mileage indicates that the fuel benefit arises in full.

(c) Taxable benefits

	£
Car benefit	4,290
Fuel benefit	3,336
Pension contribution	exempt
Private medical insurance	870
Loan benefit	exempt
Camera gift (working)	1,350
Total benefit	9,846

Working

Higher of:

MV at gift of £1,000
Less contribution by Sam of £250 = £750

Or

Original MV less use benefits to date = £2,000 - £2,000 × 20% = £1,600
Ie £1,600
Less contribution by Sam of £250 = £1,350

Tutorial note

A loan which does not exceed £10,000 at any point during the tax year does not give rise to a taxable benefit.

There are two calculations required in the case of an asset given to an employee where the employee previously had private use. The higher amount is taxable. Candidates who do not recognise this can still achieve marks for use of the market value, as reduced by the employee contribution.

(d) Class 1A = £862,000 × 13.8% = £118,956

(e) Class 1A payable by 22 July 2025 (for electronic payments) or 19 July 2025 if made by cheque.

Reported on form P11D(b) by 6 July 2025.

Additional areas where credit might be given, note this is not an exhaustive list:

- marks will be given for any relevant additional points

2   This question tests the calculation of trading profit for an unincorporated business, in this case an LLP. The published tax tables are useful to determine the allowances available on the purchase of capital assets. The question tests calculation of Welsh land transaction tax, the administrative obligations in respect of this tax and penalties if these are not met.

Learning Outcomes

LO1, LO2, LO3
Chapter References in AIA LPWB 5, 6, 25

(a) Tax-adjusted trading profits for the year ended 31 December 2024

	£
Accounting profit (before tax)	352,400
Add disallowable expenditure:	
Staff costs	0
Depreciation of office equipment	10,400
Lunches for clients	60,700
Parking fines incurred by partners visiting clients	500
Debt collection costs	0
Allowable office costs	0
Tax-adjusted trading profit before capital allowances	424,000
Less capital allowances £38,600 × 18%	(6,948)
Tax-adjusted trading profits	417,052

Tutorial note

Candidates are specifically asked to show expenses which do not require adjustment with a zero – failure to do so means easy marks are lost.

(b) Allowances for capital purchases

Car with CO_2 emissions of 66g/km = 6%
Equipment for charging electric cars = 100%
Office building purchased from developer = 3% × 7/12 = 1.75%

Tutorial note

The relevant percentages can be found in Whillans Tax Tables in the Capital Allowances/Rates section. The car emissions are such that it is a special rate pool asset. There is no adjustment for private use by an employee. The charging point qualifies for a first year allowance of 100%, and not for the super-deduction which only applies to a company. The office building cost, excluding any land cost, qualifies for the structures and buildings allowance but only from the date on which the building is brought into use.

(c) Land transaction tax

	£
(£250,000 – £225,000) × 1%	250
(£1,000,000 – £250,000) × 5%	37,500
(£1,320,000 – £1,000,000) × 6%	19,200
	56,950

Tutorial note

Land transaction tax is charged on the VAT-inclusive amount, regardless of the VAT being recovered by Advertz LLP.

(d) Both the payment and reporting of the land transaction tax is due by 9 April 2025 (30 days after the completion date). If this has not been done, there is a £100 penalty for late filing. There is a late payment penalty of 5% of the unpaid amount of £56,950 (£2,848).

> **Tutorial note**
>
> A late payment penalty for land transaction tax arises if payment is not made by the penalty date – 30 days after the filing date of the return (9 May 2025) which is the case here.

> **Additional areas where credit might be given, note this is not an exhaustive list:**
>
> - marks will be given for any relevant additional points

3   This question requires candidates to know when to amend a corporation tax return for an error, and the penalty which may arise for the error. An ethics element concerns a data breach. A corporation tax computation concentrates on property income (and the use of a loss), non-trade loan relationship income and overseas income, including double tax relief. A VAT element deals with tax points and prompt payment discounts, including the invoicing aspects of the latter.

Learning Outcomes LO1, LO2, LO3, LO4
Chapter References in AIA LPWB 14, 18, 20, 21, 22, 23, 26

(a) Amendment of corporation tax return

The latest date to amend the corporation tax return for the period ended 30 June 2023 is 30 June 2025.

(b) Penalty for incorrect return

Potential lost revenue (PLR) = (£210,670– £10,670) × 25% = £50,000
Maximum penalty = 30% × £50,000 = £15,000

> **Tutorial note**
>
> The error is likely to be at most careless rather than deliberate, as one figure has been omitted. The maximum error could be reduced to nil if unprompted disclosure is made.

(c) Data breach

The firm should report the breach to the Information Commissioner's Office (ICO) within 72 hours of the breach.

> **Additional areas where credit might be given, note this is not an exhaustive list:**
>
> - Credit would be given for noting that the tax trainee would inform the firm's data protection officer, who would then make the report to the ICO, or for noting that the client whose data has been breached should be informed.

(d) Corporation tax computation for the year ended 30 June 2024

	£
Trading profits (£680,000 - £45,000)	635,000
NTLR (W1)	9,000
Overseas interest income (£32,000 + £8,000)	40,000
Less property loss (W2)	(2,000)
Taxable total profits	682,000
Corporation tax liability @ 25%	170,500
Less DTR – lower of UK tax at 25% (£40,000 × 25% = £10,000) and overseas tax of £8,000	(8,000)
	162,500

Workings

1 Non-trade loan relationship income

	£
Bank interest receivable	20,000
Less interest payable on land loan	(11,000)
NTLR	9,000

2 Property income

	£
Rental income £5,000 × 2	10,000
Less resurfacing	(12,000)
Property loss	(2,000)

> **Tutorial note**
>
> The interest on the factory loan is an allowable trading deduction, as the factory is used in the company's trade.
>
> The interest on the loan relating to the land is a non-trade loan relationship debit and is not deducted from property income. However, the resurfacing costs are allowable repair costs meaning a property loss arises. This is deducted from the total profits of the current year – this is automatic and no claim is required.
>
> The gross amount of the overseas income (including overseas tax) is included in taxable total profits. However, double tax relief (DTR) is available, deducted from the UK corporation tax figure. The amount of DTR is the lower of the overseas tax and the UK tax on this income – candidates need to show their workings in respect of this.

(e) Output VAT for the quarter ended 30 June 2025

	£
Viollit Ltd:	
£60,000/6	10,000
Bluzonne plc:	
£20,000 × (100% - 7%)	18,600

> **Tutorial note**
>
> There are two tax points in relation to the Viollit Ltd order – for the deposit and for the remaining amount. The payment of the deposit means an earlier actual tax point arises on 15 April in respect of this, overriding the basic tax point (delivery date) which falls into a later VAT quarter. The VAT in relation to the deposit only must therefore be included in the VAT return for the quarter ended 30 June 2025.

(f) Invoicing obligation to Bluzonne plc after receiving payment

Greenby Ltd must issue a credit note for the amount of the discount.

Tutorial note

Where a prompt payment discount is offered, the supplier can either reflect this in the initial invoice (subject to various disclosure requirements) or issue an invoice for the undiscounted amount. Greenby Ltd has done the latter, and so must follow this with a credit note because the discount payment terms have been met by Bluzonne plc.

Additional areas where credit might be given, note this is not an exhaustive list:
- marks will be given for any relevant additional points

4 **This question tests capital gains tax, specifically chattels, gift relief and business asset disposal relief. Candidates are required to calculate stamp duty and recognise this as an allowable cost in the gains calculation. A calculation is also required – recognising tax as a cost – of the net proceeds after capital gains tax.**

Learning Outcomes LO1, LO2, LO3
Chapter References in AIA LPWB 10, 12, 13, 25

(a) Chargeable gain on disposal of painting

	£
Proceeds	9,000
Less commission	(900)
	8,100
Cost	(3,000)
	5,100
Restricted to:	
5/3 (£9,000 – £6,000)	5,000

(b) Stamp duty paid on purchase of shares
0.5% × £50,000 = £250

(c) Chargeable gain on disposal of shares

	£
Proceeds (market value)	300,000
Less cost (£50,000 + £250)	(50,250)
	249,750

Tutorial note

The calculation of stamp duty in the previous part should act as a prompt to candidates that this is part of the allowable cost on calculation of the gain. The proceeds are deemed to be market value, regardless of actual consideration received, because this is a disposal at undervalue to a connected person (the taxpayer's daughter).

(d) Claims

Gift relief claim made by 5 April 2029 by both Martin and Emma.
Business asset disposal relief claim by 31 January 2027 by Martin.

(e) Capital gains tax

	£	£
Painting (part a)	5,000	
Foodes Ltd:		
Gain before reliefs (part c)		249,750
Less gift relief		(120,000)
Gain chargeable (£180,000 – £50,250)		129,750
Less AEA	(3,000)	(0)
	2,000	129,750
CGT @ 20% and 10%	400	12,975
Total		13,375

Tutorial note

As the recipient made a payment for the shares, gift relief is restricted and a gain is chargeable to the extent that the actual proceeds exceed cost. A candidate who does not include stamp duty as a cost in part c) has already been penalised there. Full credit would be given for their chargeable gain of £130,000 resulting in CGT of £13,400.

As the question states, business asset disposal relief is claimed on the disposal of the shares, and so this gain is taxed at 10%. The annual exempt amount is used against the painting gain first, as this would otherwise be taxed at the higher rate of 20% due to Martin's level of taxable income.

(f) Net proceeds

	£
Proceeds from painting (£9,000 - £900)	8,100
Proceeds from shares	180,000
Less CGT (part e)	(13,375)
	174,725

Tutorial note

A client often wants to know how much money they have available to them after tax. This calculation of net proceeds should be straightforward but care should be taken. The amount received for the painting is the proceeds less the commission. The amount received for the shares is the amount Emma pays for them, not the deemed proceeds in the gains calculation, nor the gain itself. Candidates frequently confuse cash amounts (actual consideration), and taxable amounts (gains) in such calculations. Finally, the capital gains tax figure calculated in the previous part must be deducted.

Additional areas where credit might be given, note this is not an exhaustive list:
- marks will be given for any relevant additional points

5   This question tests inheritance tax payable on a gift to a trust, both when the gift is made and on death. It also considers the ethics of offering a tax avoidance scheme to clients.

Learning Outcomes LO1, LO2, LO3, LO4
Chapter References in AIA LPWB 15, 16, 17, 26

(a) Lifetime inheritance tax payable

	£
Value of the gift (W)	450,000
Less AE 2024/25 and 2023/24	(6,000)
	444,000
Less NRB	(325,000)
	119,000
IHT @ 25%	29,750

Working – value of gift

Greater of £300,000 (25% holding) and
2,500/(2,500 + 5,000) × £1,350,000 = £450,000

> **Tutorial note**
>
> Saul owns a 25% shareholding, but the related property rules mean he must value his shares as a proportion of the total holding of him and his wife (75% holding) as this is greater than the value of the 25% shareholding alone.
>
> The default position is that the donor pays the inheritance tax, hence the 25% charge, as his estate is reduced by the gift and the tax. The gross chargeable transfer (including the lifetime tax) is then chargeable on death.

(b) Payment of lifetime inheritance tax

The lifetime tax is payable by 31 August 2025.

(c) Inheritance tax payable on death

	£
Gross chargeable transfer (£444,000 + £29,750)	473,750
Less NRB	(325,000)
	148,750
IHT @ 40%	59,500
Less lifetime tax paid	(29,750)
	29,750

(d) Breach of Standards for Tax Planning

The product does not seem to be client specific – tax planning must be specific to the particular client's facts and circumstances.

As a member of AIA I must not encourage or promote tax planning arrangements that:

- set out to achieve results that are contrary to the clear intention of Parliament as this is and/or

- are highly artificial or highly contrived (the number of non-commercial steps suggests this)

- and seek to exploit shortcomings in the relevant legislation – the private bank indicates the legislation has been incorrectly written and the bank is exploiting this.

> **Additional areas where credit might be given, note this is not an exhaustive list:**
> - Credit may be given if the point is made (in relation to the 'client specific' standard), that clients must be alerted to wider risks and the implications of any course of action.

6 **This question tests income tax for a married couple, where the marriage allowance is claimed. Calculations of trading profits are required using the cash basis and fixed rate expenses. In addition to income tax calculations, calculations of national insurance contributions for a sole trader are required, as well as advice on payments on account and balancing payments.**

Learning Outcomes LO1, LO2, LO3
Chapter References in AIA LPWB 1, 5, 14

(a) Obligations to notify HMRC

Giovanni must inform HMRC of his new source of income by 5 October 2025.

He must complete a self-assessment tax return for 2024/25 by 31 January 2026 (if filed online).

> **Tutorial note**
>
> Giovanni has an obligation to notify HMRC that he is now in receipt of taxable income, and then, in his tax return, of the amount.

(b) Giovanni's income tax liability for 2024/25

	£
Dividend income (£20,000 - £3,000)	17,000
Less personal allowance (£12,570 - £1,260)	(11,310)
Taxable income	5,690
Income tax @ 0% on £500	-
Income tax @ 8.75% on £5,190 (£5,690 - £500)	454
Income tax liability	454

(c) Maria's trading profits for the year ended 31 March 2025

	£
Cash received for work done during the year	32,340
Deposit received in March 2025	400
Amount owed by a customer	-
Payments on materials	(6,400)
Fixed rate deduction for van: 7,500 × 45p	(3,375)
Running costs of van – no deduction as fixed deduction	-
Fixed rate deduction for use of home in business:	
8 hours/ week (25-50 hours per month) £10 × 12	(120)
Trading profits	22,845

> **Tutorial note**
>
> The cash basis is an easy way for many smaller traders to account for their taxable trading profits, but the calculations are different to those applying accrual accounting. Fixed rate deductions for the use of a vehicle and a home in the business should also offer simpler calculations for a sole trader. The published tax tables provide useful information on fixed rate deductions.

(d) Maria's income tax liability for 2024/25

	£
Trading profit	22,845
Less personal allowance	(12,570)
Taxable income	10,275

	£
Income tax @ 20%	2,055
Less tax reducer on marriage allowance 1,260 @ 20%	(252)
Income tax liability	1,803

Tutorial note

The marriage allowance claim means Giovanni transfers part of his personal allowance to Maria. However, Maria's personal allowance does not increase. Instead, she receives relief as a tax reducer at 20% of the transferred amount. The transferred amount is set by statute – it cannot be chosen.

The claim is available because both Giovanni and Maria are basic rate taxpayers. It saves tax as Giovanni only pays tax at 8.75% on his dividend income at this level, but Maria pays basic rate tax of 20% on her trading profits.

(e) National insurance contributions

	£
Class 4 (22,845 – 12,570) × 6%	616

(f) Payment of income tax and national insurance contributions

	£
31 July 2025	1,230
31 January 2026	
IT due	1,803
NIC due	616
	3,649
Less POAs £1,230 × 2	(2,460)
	1,189

Tutorial note

The payments on account (POA) for 2024/25 are based on the prior year liabilities, but the question states the correct amount of the first POA and so the amount of the second is the same. The balancing payment is calculated by deducting both POA from the total liability for 2024/25.

Additional areas where credit might be given, note this is not an exhaustive list:

- marks will be given for any relevant additional points

Past Exams: November 2022

1   This question requires correction of a property income computation, and calculation of income tax payable on this and dividend income. It includes the amendment of an earlier self-assessment tax return. The question also tests capital gains tax on the disposal of a residential property and a disposal of shares, for which the matching rules apply. It requires identification of stamp tax rates. A conflict of interest arises in an ethical scenario.

Learning Outcomes

LO1, LO2, LO3, LO4
Chapter References in AIA LPWB
1, 3, 10, 11, 14, 25, 26

(a) David's property income for 2024/25

	£
Income:	
Property 1 rent received	60,000
Property 2 rent received £18,000 – (£18,000 × 2/12)	15,000
Property 3 rent received during 2024/25	9,000
Rent received from Vikram – not taxable	0
Less expenses	
Plumbing repair costs for property 1	(800)
Replacement bed for property 2 (£1,000 - £100)	(900)
Insurance costs for all properties	(2,700)
Additional utility expenses – not deductible	(0)
Property income	79,600

> **Tutorial note**
>
> In practice, a client may attempt calculations, expecting that this may assist with the preparation of their tax return. A tax accountant must be able to identify and correct any errors made by the client.
>
> Property income here should be included on a cash basis, that is, as it is received, and not on the accruals basis. This reduces the income taxable in 2024/25 from property 2.
>
> The rental income from Vikram, for renting a room in the taxpayer's own house, does not exceed £7,500 and so the income is exempt under the rent-a-room relief rules. However, the additional expenses are then ignored.
>
> Expenditure on revenue items such as plumbing repairs and insurance costs are allowable. The cost of the bed is allowable as it replaces an existing bed, but the allowable cost is reduced by the proceeds from selling the existing bed.

(b) Amendment

David must correct this error with HMRC.

David should submit an amended tax return for 2023/24 prepared by our firm, as the deadline for making an amendment has not yet passed being 31 January 2026.

David will have to pay additional tax, interest and possibly penalties. However, penalties may be reduced to nil if the amendment (ie the disclosure) is promptly made.

> **Additional areas where credit might be given, note this is not an exhaustive list.**
> - Credit would be given for identifying that the additional tax due would include underpaid payments on account for 2024/25 (as well as the balancing payment for 2023/24).

(c) Income tax liability for 2024/25

	Non-savings income £	Dividend income £	Total £
Property income (a)	79,600		79,600
Dividend income (W)		84,800	84,800
	79,600	84,800	164,400

	£
IT on non-savings income	
37,700 @ 20%	7,540
41,900 @ 40%	16,760
79,600	
IT on dividend income	
500 @ 0%	0
45,040 @ 33.75%	15,201
125,140 to higher rate limit	
39,260 @ 39.35%	15,449
84,800 total dividend income	
Total income tax liability	54,950

Working: dividend income 2024/25

Dividends received 6 April 2024 to 5 April 2025 = £28,200 + 17,600 + 39,000 = 84,800

(d) Share gain

	Shares bought in next 30 days (13.2.2025) 2,000 shares £	Share pool 8,000 shares £
Proceeds £70,000 (2,000 : 8,000)	14,000	56,000
Cost (W)	(13,600)	(16,000)
Gains	400	40,000
Total gain (£400 + £40,000)		40,400

Working: share pool

Date of purchase	Number of shares	Cost £
1 May 2010	20,000	36,000
8 Oct 2015: 1 for 5 rights issue £3	4,000	12,000
	24,000	48,000
Less disposal from the share pool	(8,000)	(16,000)
	16,000	32,000

> **Tutorial note**
>
> Candidates must apply the matching rules here. The shares purchased after the disposal are treated as the first shares disposed of, because the purchase is within 30 days of the disposal.
>
> The rights issue shares are added to the original purchase in the share pool, and the remaining disposed shares are removed from the pool.

(e) Capital gains tax 2024/25

	Other gains £	Residential property gain £
Shares (from part d)	40,400	
Property:		
Proceeds		260,000
Cost		(170,000)
		90,000
Less annual exempt amount		(3,000)
Less capital loss brought forward		(12,800)
Taxable gains	40,400	74,200
40,400 @ 20%	8,080	
74,200 @ 24%		17,808
Total capital gains tax		25,888

> **Tutorial note**
>
> A taxpayer can use their annual exempt amount and capital losses against gains in the most beneficial way. Therefore, candidates are given credit for deducting both the annual exempt amount and loss brought forward from gains, but also for the deductions being made from their residential property gain to save the most tax.

(f) Rates of stamp taxes on investments

	Rate
Shares	0.5%
Residential property in England	3%
Commercial property in England	0%

> **Tutorial note**
>
> Stamp duty is payable on the purchase of shares where the transfer is effected with a stock transfer form. Stamp duty land tax is payable on the purchases of the English properties. As David owns other residential properties, the higher rate applies to this purchase of additional property. These percentages are all given in the published tax tables.

(g) Conflict of interest

It may be possible for the firm to advise David on this transaction if both he and Build LLP are notified of the conflict and both give their permission for your firm to continue to act.

To act, the conflict of interest must not pose too great a threat to the fundamental principles.

Safeguards [any 2 of the following]

- The use of separate engagement teams
- Procedures to prevent access to information (eg physical separation of the teams and secure data filing)
- Clear guidelines for team members regarding security and confidentiality
- The use of confidentiality agreements signed by team members and the firm's partners
- Regular review of the safeguards by a senior individual not directly involved with the engagements with David and Build LLP.

> **Additional areas where credit might be given, note this is not an exhaustive list.**
> - Credit would be given for identifying either objectivity or confidentiality as a specific fundamental principle under threat.

2 This question requires the computation of corporation tax, with an extensive capital allowances computation, adjustments for interest payable, and the calculation of non-trading loan relationship income. Loss relief is also covered. The question includes VAT recoverable on capital purchases and an ethical issue when HMRC overpays a refund of VAT. The question tests the concept of tax as a cost. It requires the calculation of the cost to the company of providing a car benefit, which involves NIC but also CT savings. Administrative requirements test year-end PAYE forms and the deadline for a loss claim.

Learning Outcomes

LO1, LO2, LO3, LO4
Chapter References in AIA LPWB
4, 5, 6, 18, 20, 21, 23, 24, 26

(a) VAT recoverable on plant and machinery purchases

	£
Processing machine £600,000 × 1/6	100,000
Zero emissions cars	0
Cutting machine £300,000 × 1/6	50,000
	150,000

> **Tutorial note**
>
> VAT on cars is not recoverable if the cars are to be used privately. The VAT-inclusive amounts have been given in the question and so the VAT recoverable on the other purchases is found by dividing by 6.

(b) Breach of fundamental principle

Either of:
integrity
professional behaviour

The company should contact HMRC about the error and repay the extra amount.

(c) Capital allowances for the year ended 31 December 2024

	FYA £	Main pool £	Special rate pool £	Allowances £
TWDV at 1.1.24		94,000	18,300	
Processing machine (£600,000 – £100,000)		500,000		
Cutting machine (300,000 – £50,000)			250,000	
AIA		(500,000)	(250,000)	750,000
Zero emissions cars	120,000			
FYA @ 100%	(120,000)			120,000
		94,000	18,300	
WDA @ 18%		(16,920)		16,920
WDA @ 6%			(1,098)	1,098
TWDV at 31.12.24		77,080	17,202	
Total allowances				888,018

Tutorial note

The cost figures to use for purchases are those after any recoverable VAT has been deducted. As seen in part a), VAT was recoverable on the machines so capital allowances are only available on the remaining cost to the company of these assets. The car cost inclusive of VAT is included in the computation as this VAT is part of the cost of the cars to the company.

On the processing machine, a main pool item, both the AIA and full expensing are available. The use of the AIA is preferred here so a balancing charge can be avoided on a future disposal of the machine.

We should exercise some care here. The cutting machine is a long life asset as it has an expected life of at least 25 years, and cost more than £100,000. Therefore, it is a special rate pool asset. A 50% first year allowance is available, but so too is the AIA which gives greater relief (100%). The AIA should be given to the special rate asset before the processing machine which is a main pool asset.

Cars do not qualify for the full expensing but zero emission cars qualify for a first year allowance at 100% in their own right. There is never an adjustment for private use when calculating capital allowances for a company.

(d) Trading profits for the year ended 31 December 2024

	£
Draft tax-adjusted trading profits	1,990,000
Less interest on machine loan	(31,000)
Less capital allowances	(888,018)
Tax-adjusted trading profits	1,070,982

(e) Corporation tax computation for the year ended 31 December 2024

	£
Trading profits	1,070,982
NTLR (W)	1,500
Total profits	1,072,482
Trading loss brought forward	(390,000)
Taxable total profits	682,482
Corporation tax @ 25%	170,621

Working: Non-trading loan relationship income

	£
Bank interest receivable	2,400
Interest received on overpaid CT	900
Less interest payable on share investment	(1,800)
NTLR	1,500

(f) Loss relief claim must be made by 31 December 2026

> **Additional areas where credit might be given, note this is not an exhaustive list:**
> - Partial credit would be given if candidates give an incorrect date but correctly note that HMRC may allow a longer time limit (this being stated in the published tax tables).

(g) Class 1A NIC on the car

Car benefit = £45,000 × 37% = £16,650
Class 1A = £16,650 × 13.8% = £2,298

(h) Cost of the car to the company

	£
Lease cost	8,000
Running costs	2,000
Class 1A	2,298
	12,298
CT saving @ 25% of £11,098 (W)	(2,775)
	9,523
Working deductible costs	
85% of lease cost = 85% × £8,000	6,800
Running costs	2,000
Class 1A	2,298
	11,098

> **Tutorial note**
>
> On the provision of a car benefit, the company incurs the costs it pays in respect of the car itself, and the Class 1A national insurance contribution payable on the benefit. However, the company's overall cost is reduced by the corporation tax saving on the costs incurred. Here, all costs are allowable except for the lease costs. The level of emissions means that only 85% of the lease costs contribute to the corporation tax saving.
>
> This question demonstrates that tax costs and savings must be taken into account when determining the overall cost to a business of an action.

(i) Schedule of PAYE year-end forms for Rachel 2025/26

	Salary	Car benefit
Form	P60	P11D
Recipient	Rachel only	Rachel and HMRC
Complete by	31 May 2026	6 July 2026

3. This question tests the basis periods on commencement of trade and the future test for VAT registration. It requires calculation of income tax liabilities for a Scottish taxpayer and of NIC for a sole trader. The question tests the payment dates of income tax and NIC under self-assessment and the penalties for late filing of the self-assessment tax return.

Learning Outcomes
LO1, LO2, LO3
Chapter References in AIA LPWB
1, 5, 14, 23

(a) Notify HMRC on or before 5 October 2024

(b) Taxable trading profits

			£
2023/24	1 February 2024 – 5 April 2024		
	2/15 × £30,000		4,000
2024/25	6 April 2024 – 5 April 2025		
	12/15 × £30,000		24,000

(c) Income tax for 2023/24

	£
Trading income	4,000
Personal allowance	(4,000)
	nil

Income tax for 2024/25

	£
Trading income	24,000
Personal allowance	(12,570)
Taxable income	11,430
2,306 @ 19%	438
9,124 @ 20%	1,825
11,430	2,263

Tutorial note

The personal allowance fully covers Alice's trading income in 2023/24 as she has no other income. A Scottish taxpayer pays income tax on non-savings income at different rates to other UK taxpayers.

(d) Class 4 National insurance contributions

	£
2023/24	0
2024/25	
(24,000 – 12,570) × 6%	686

Tutorial note

The class 4 contributions are nil in 2023/24 as the trading profits are less than the lower limit.

(e) Due date for payments

The income tax and class 4 NIC are both due by 31 January 2026.

(f) Late filing penalty

The return for 2023/24 should have been submitted by 31 January 2025.

There is an initial penalty of £100. HMRC may issue a notice for daily penalties of £10 for up to 90 days as the return is over three months late.

As the return is over six months late a further penalty of £300 arises.

> **Additional areas where credit might be given, not this is not an exhaustive list:**
> - Credit would be given if candidates correctly identify that the final penalty is usually based on the liability, but that this is nil here, hence the minimum penalty of £300 arises.

(g) VAT registration

If Alice wins the contract, she must notify HMRC by 30 January 2026.

She will be registered from 1 January 2026.

> **Tutorial note**
>
> The future test is relevant. If Alice wins the contract, on 1 January 2026 she will have reasonable grounds for believing that her supplies in the next 30 days alone will exceed £90,000, the VAT registration limit.

4   **This question tests inheritance tax, including the valuation of quoted shares and an overseas asset in the death estate. It includes double tax relief and an administrative element regarding interest on overdue tax.**

Learning Outcomes
LO1, LO2, LO3
Chapter References in AIA LPWB
16, 17

(a) Share value

The value of the shares is the lower of:
147 + ¼ × (155 − 147) = 149p
(150 + 156)/2 = 153p
Market value of 50,000 shares = 50,000 × £1.49 = £74,500

(b) Inheritance tax on Alex's death

	£
Quoted shares	74,500
UK home	900,000
Holiday home	125,000
Cash	150,000
Chattels	4,000
Chargeable estate	1,253,500
NRB	(325,000)
	928,500
IHT @ 40%	371,400
Less DTR	
Lower of:	
Overseas tax on holiday home £12,000	
UK tax on holiday home = £125,000 × 29.629% (W) = £37,036	
	(12,000)
Inheritance tax	359,400

Working: average rate of UK IHT = 371,400/1,253,500 = 29.629%

Tutorial note

Alex was UK domiciled and so inheritance tax is charged on his worldwide assets, including the holiday home in Stephy. However, double tax relief is available for the tax paid overseas.

(c) Interest on overdue IHT

Interest payable = £359,400 × 2.60% × 7/12 = £5,451

Tutorial note

Interest becomes chargeable if the tax is unpaid six months after the end of the month of death (ie after 31 May 2025).

As instructed at the start of the exam paper, candidates should assume that tax rules etc that apply for 2024/25 apply in all years. Candidates are expected to use the interest rate of 2.60% which is the latest shown in the published tax tables for 2021/22 for inheritance tax. They are not expected to take account of changes in interest rates, since the publication of the tax tables.

Additional areas where credit might be given, note this is not an exhaustive list:

- There are no anticipated additional areas for credit.

Past Exams: May 2023

1. This question tests income tax and VAT for a new trader. It covers ethical matters – who is responsible for the tax return and the basis on which fees should be charged for tax work. The question includes adjustments to profit including pre-trading expenditure and capital allowances (including the impact of VAT). VAT issues include pre-registration expenditure and administrative elements such as the default surcharge regime, overpaid VAT, VAT records and deregistration.

   Learning Outcomes LO1, LO2, LO3, LO4
   Chapter References in AIA LPWB 5, 6, 14, 23, 24, 26

   (a) Responsibilities for tax return

   Felix as the taxpayer is responsible under the tax legislation for submitting the return and for the information it contains

   The firm acts as his agent. Alternatively, the firm is not responsible under tax legislation.

   > **Tutorial note**
   >
   > Under tax legislation, the returns remain the responsibility of Felix. If the accountancy firm acted negligently, leading to a failure in the completion or submission of the return, Felix may be able to take action against the firm under other legislation, but the tax consequences would remain unchanged.

   (b) Fees charged for services

   > **Additional areas where credit might be given, note this is not an exhaustive list.**
   > - Credit would be given for identifying specific points given in the PCRT (Professional Conduct in Relation to Taxation) on this matter, where this relates to tax legislation.

   The fees could either be charged on a time and expense basis or as a fixed fee.

   > **Additional areas where credit might be given, note this is not an exhaustive list.**
   > - Other bases such as contingent fees would not score credit as these would not be suitable for compliance services.

   (c) Input VAT recoverable on pre-registration expenditure

	£
Computer: £4,000 × 20%	800
Marketing advice costs: £500 × 20%	100
Recoverable input VAT	900

   > **Tutorial note**
   >
   > Felix registered for VAT on 1 October 2024 and so the VAT is incurred on pre-registration expenditure.
   >
   > VAT is recoverable on goods which were purchased prior to registration if the goods were acquired for the purpose of the business to be carried on. The goods must still be held by the business on registration and the VAT must have been incurred in the four years prior to registration. The VAT on the computer is therefore recoverable.

> VAT is recoverable on pre-registration expenditure on services such as the advice on marketing as this was for the purpose of the business to be carried on. The services must also be supplied within the six months prior to the date of registration – these were supplied within one month.

(d) Capital allowances

	SR private use car £	PU adjustment	Allowances £
Car £20,000 × 120%	24,000		
WDA @ 6% × 6/12	(720)	× 40%	288
	23,280		288

Tutorial note

Traders who use the cash basis treat purchases of plant and machinery as a trading expense. However, capital allowances may be claimed on expenditure on cars. Alternatively fixed rate deductions can be claimed in relation to the car and its running costs.

The VAT on the car is not recoverable because there is private use and so the cost to the company – the VAT-inclusive amount – is given capital allowances. The car has emissions in excess of 50 g/km so WDA at 6% is given. The allowance is further restricted for the short period and for private use.

Additional areas where credit might be given, note this is not an exhaustive list.

- Candidates with incorrect VAT treatment in the previous part, can still get full credit for their treatment of the pre-trading expenditure for trading profit purposes (here and in the next part), provided the amounts are consistent with their VAT treatment.

(e) Tax-adjusted trading profits for the six months ended 31 March 2025

	£
Net profit	18,000
Add back disallowable expenditure:	
Drawings	12,000
Running costs for car 60% × £2,500	1,500
Legal costs re customer contracts	0
Other allowable expenditure	0
Less allowable pre-trading expenditure	
Computer	(4,000)
Marketing advice costs	(500)
	27,000
Less capital allowances (part d)	(288)
Tax-adjusted trading profits	26,712

(f) VAT matters summary

For late submission of a VAT return a penalty point is imposed on the trader. No penalty will apply until four penalty points have been imposed.

For late payments, there is no penalty as long as the VAT is paid within 15 days of its due date, however a penalty of 2% will be charged if it is paid within 16 to 30 days. Any unpaid amount outstanding on day 31 will be charged a 4% penalty, calculated on a daily basis.

You have four years to recover overpaid VAT.

You must keep VAT records for six years.

VAT records for input VAT on purchases include VAT invoices and the VAT account.

> **Additional areas where credit might be given, note this is not an exhaustive list.**
> - Credit is available for identifying different VAT records relating to input VAT but up to a maximum of two items.
> - The correct method to calculate trading profits is to take the net profit from the accounts and make appropriate adjustments such as adding back disallowable expenditure which has been deducted in the accounts. Candidates who use an unconventional approach such as deducting allowable costs from sales, are given credit if their tax treatment is correct. However, they must take care to show their treatment of each item (including where no adjustment is required). They are also more likely to confuse, and so mix, the two approaches.

(g) Deregister for VAT

Felix can deregister if his expected taxable supplies (exclusive of VAT and excluding capital items) in the next 12 months will not exceed £88,000 If monthly sales are £6,500, Felix can deregister as supplies in the next 12 months will be £78,000 (£6,500 × 12).

> **Additional areas where credit might be given, note this is not an exhaustive list.**
> - Credit is available for candidates who comment that the expected sales are close to the relevant limits such that Felix may have to re-register if sales exceed this.

2   **This question tests income tax and capital gains tax for an employed individual. Administrative elements include the closure of an enquiry with appeal and penalty for errors, and dates for future enquiries. Personal pension contributions including the annual allowance are tested with an extensive income tax computation. Capital gains tax is tested with private residence relief, the grant of an option and the disposal of overseas shares. The question also tests an SDLT calculation for residential property and SDLT reporting.**

Learning Outcomes   LO1, LO2, LO3
Chapter References in AIA LPWB 1, 2, 10, 13, 14, 25

(a) Appeal of enquiry closure notice

19 June 2025.

> **Tutorial note**
> A taxpayer can appeal a closure notice within 30 days of its issue by HMRC.

(b) Penalty for careless error

The maximum penalty = 30% × £5,000 = £1,500.

> **Tutorial note**
> The maximum penalty for a careless error is 30% of the potential lost revenue, ie the understated tax of £5,000.

(c) Annual allowance 2024/25

Unused annual allowance from each previous year = £60,000 − £25,000 = £35,000.

Unused allowance for three years b/f = £35,000 × 3 = £105,000.

Total allowance for 2024/25 = £40,000 + £105,000 = £145,000.

> **Tutorial note**
>
> Gita's annual allowance is £60,000 but this is increased by unused annual allowance brought forward from the last three years. The unused amount brought forward is the amount remaining after the employer contributions.
>
> Gita's own contribution plus that of her employer in 2024/25 is within this total amount, meaning there is no annual allowance charge in 2024/25.

(d) Income tax liability for 2024/25

	Non-savings income £	Savings income £	Dividend income £	Total £
Employment income - salary	170,000			170,000
Dividend income			8,000	8,000
Bank interest (£20,000 − £5,000)		15,000		15,000
No personal allowance	170,000	15,000	8,000	193,000

> **Tutorial note**
>
> The pension contribution made by Bammbonet Ltd is an exempt benefit and so is not part of Gita's employment income.

	£
IT on non-savings income	
£50,200 (W) @ 20%	10,040
£87,440 @ 40%	34,976
£137,640	
£32,360 @ 45%	12,944
£170,000	
IT on savings income	
£15,000 @ 45%	6,750
IT on dividend income	
£500 @ 0%	0
£7,500 @ 39.35%	2,951
£8,000	
Total income tax liability	67,661

Working: extension of basic rate band and increase of higher rate limit

Basic rate band = £37,700 + £10,000 × 100/80 = £50,200.
Higher rate limit = £125,140 + £12,500 = £137,640.

> **Tutorial note**
>
> Gita's personal pension contribution paid is grossed up to reflect the contribution of 20% that HMRC pays into Gita's pension scheme. The gross amount then extends the basic rate band and increases the higher rate limit with the effect that a further 25% income tax is saved on the contribution as more income is taxed at 20% instead of at 45%.

EXAM ANSWER BANK

> Gita's adjusted net income is reduced by her gross personal pension contribution, but still far exceeds £125,140, so no personal allowance is available.
>
> The dividend nil rate band is available, but not the savings nil rate band as Gita is an additional rate taxpayer.

(e) Stamp duty land tax

	£
(£250,000 – £125,000) × 2%	2,500
(£340,000 – £250,000) × 5%	4,500
	7,000

Tutorial note

The rates and bands are those for a residential property, as given in the published tax tables.

(f) Reporting the SDLT
14 June 2024.

(g) Occupation

	Occupation/deemed occupation (years)	Unoccupied (years)	Total (years)
1.6.2004 – 31.5.2008	4		4
1.6.2008 – 31.5.2013	3	2	5
1.6.2013 – 31.5.2024	10.5	0.5	11
	17.5	2.5	20

Tutorial note

Three years of absence are treated as deemed occupation provided that Gita occupies the house both before and after the period of absence. There is no further deemed occupation when Gita is overseas as she was not working there.

(h) Chargeable gain on sale of house

	£
Proceeds	290,000
Cost	(165,000)
	125,000
PRR (part g) 17.5/20 × £125,000	(109,375)
Chargeable gain	15,625

(i) Capital gains tax 2024/25

	Other gains £	Residential property gains £
Land – option (£10,000 – £0)	10,000	
Shares (£35,000 – £16,000)	19,000	
House (part h)		15,625
Gains	29,000	15,625
Annual exempt amount		(3,000)
	29,000	12,625
CGT @ 20% /24%	5,800	3,030
Total		8,830

> **Tutorial note**
>
> The grant of the option is a disposal with nil cost. The cost of the land is only deducted when the option is exercised.
>
> Gita is resident in the UK and so is charged to capital gains tax on her disposals, wherever the assets are situated.

(j) Enquiry dates

2023/24 return 30 April 2026.
2024/25 return 15 July 2026.

> **Tutorial note**
>
> The return for 2023/24 should have been submitted by 31 January 2025 but was late. This means HMRC have a year from the quarter end (30 April) after submission, to open an enquiry.
>
> The 2024/25 return will be submitted on time so the enquiry must be opened within a year of the actual submission date.

Additional areas where credit might be given, note this is not an exhaustive list.

- There are no envisaged areas of additional credit.

---

3   This question tests inheritance tax, including a lifetime gift, business property relief, exempt charitable donation and the residence nil rate band. It requires a correction of a draft inheritance tax computation. It also considers the cash received by a beneficiary, testing who bears the inheritance tax on gifts.

Learning Outcomes LO2, LO3
Chapter References in AIA LPWB 15, 16, 17

(a) Inheritance tax payable on lifetime gift

	£
Gift of cash	800,000
AE 2020/21 and 2019/20	(6,000)
	794,000
Less NRB 2024/25	(325,000)
	469,000
IHT @ 40%	187,600
Taper relief @ 40%	(75,040)
IHT payable	112,560

> **Tutorial note**
>
> The annual exemption of the year of gift and the previous year are available on this lifetime gift. The NRB at death is used first against this gift. Taper relief of 40% reduces the tax because the gift was made between four and five years before death.

(b) Inheritance tax on Edna's death estate

	£
Edna's house	490,000
Shares in Quirel Ltd – 100% BPR	0
Cash	500,000
Chattels	20,000
Less charitable donation	(10,000)
Chargeable estate	1,000,000
RNRB	(175,000)
NRB (£325,000 – £794,000)	0
	825,000
IHT @ 40%	330,000

Tutorial note

The shares qualify for business property relief (BPR) because they are in an unquoted trading company and have been owned by Edna for at least two years at the date of her death. There is no minimum shareholding to qualify for BPR if the shares are in an unquoted company. Edna did not need to work for the company to qualify for this relief.

The charitable donation is an exempt gift and so reduces the value of the chargeable estate.

As Edna has left her remaining estate, including her house, to her direct descendant (her daughter), the residence nil rate band is available. Edna's nil rate band has been used by the lifetime gift.

Additional areas where credit might be given, note this is not an exhaustive list.

- If candidates were to show only the differences from the inheritance tax amount given in the question, they would receive credit for the corrected differences. However, the question asks for a full inheritance tax computation so they would not be able to gain full credit for the unchanged amounts.

(c) Cash received by Amara on Edna's death

	£
Cash in the death estate	500,000
Less charitable donation	(10,000)
Less IHT payable on death estate only	(330,000)
	160,000

Tutorial note

As the residuary legatee, Amara suffers the tax on the death estate. However, the tax on the lifetime transfer is borne by the donee of the gift, that is, Kris and so the cash Amara receives is not reduced by this.

4   This question tests income tax and national insurance contributions in the context of payroll taxes. It tests employment benefits (including the use of the tax tables), Class 1B NIC, an ethical issue regarding an omission from the P11D form and the determination of a tax code for a Welsh taxpayer.

Learning Outcomes LO1, LO2, LO3, LO4
Chapter References in AIA LPWB 4, 26

(a) Class 1B calculation

	Basic rate £	Higher rate £	Total £
Gross cost per head			
£240 × 100/80: 100/60	300	400	
Total gross cost (× 100: × 30)	30,000	12,000	42,000
Class 1B @ 13.8%			5,796

> **Tutorial note**
>
> Under a PAYE settlement agreement, the employer pays the employees' income tax liabilities. The benefit on which national insurance contributions (NIC) is charged is therefore the cost of the party itself plus the income tax paid by the employer. This total is given by grossing up the party cost per employee at the respective income tax rates.

(b) Class 1B payment date
    22 October 2025.

> **Tutorial note**
>
> Class 1B is payable in October each year for the previous tax year, on 22nd of the month for electronic payments.

(c) Exempt and taxable benefits

Relocation costs – partially taxable
Birthday flowers – fully taxable
Beneficial loan – fully exempt

> **Tutorial note**
>
> Some benefits are exempt up to a certain limit. Here, there is no benefit on the interest-free loan as the loan does not exceed £10,000 at any point during the year. In some cases, once the limit for the exemption is exceeded, the whole amount is then taxable. This is the case with the flowers – as the cost exceeds £50, this is not a trivial benefit and the entire cost is taxable. With other benefits, such as the relocation cost here, only the excess above the exempt limit (£8,000) is taxable.
>
> The limit for each of the above benefits is given in the published tax tables but to answer successfully candidates need to understand the treatment if the limit is exceeded.

(d) Accommodation benefit

	£
Annual value	12,000
Additional benefit	
(£275,000 - £75,000) × 2.25%	4,500
Less rent contribution £500 × 12	(6,000)
	10,500
Available for 9 months	7,875

Tutorial note

An additional benefit arises as the house cost the employer more than £75,000 to buy. Usually, the additional benefit charge is based on interest on the excess of cost (plus the extension cost, as this was incurred before the start of the tax year) over £75,000. However, as the house was bought more than six years before first being provided to Simon, the market value when first provided has to be used instead. The amount of the benefit is reduced by the rent Simon pays – a contribution for use of the house.

Additional areas where credit might be given, note this is not an exhaustive list.

- Candidates may present their answers differently, taking into account the nine months of availability at each point in their calculation, rather than at the end.

(e) Tax evasion

Failing to include the benefit on Simon's P11D would constitute tax evasion because it deliberately misleads HMRC by suppressing information to which HMRC is entitled.

Tutorial note

Tax evasion is illegal and involves hiding information from HMRC or lying about that information.

Additional areas where credit might be given, note this is not an exhaustive list.

- Credit would be given if candidates explained evasion as providing HMRC with deliberately false information.

(f) Tax code

	£
Personal allowance	12,570
Less benefit	(500)
	12,070

Tax code   C1207L

Tutorial note

Leah is entitled to a personal allowance but to find the tax code amount this is reduced by the benefit. The last number in the resultant figure is removed. The letter L is added as she is entitled to the basic personal allowance. The letter C denotes that Leah pays Welsh income tax, although there is in fact no difference to that paid in other parts of the UK (except Scotland) in 2024/25.

5   This question tests corporation tax including rollover relief, the research and development expenditure credit for large companies, payment and filing.

Learning Outcomes LO1, LO2, LO3
Chapter References in AIA LPWB 18, 19, 20, 21

(a) Date to claim rollover relief

The claim must be made by 31 December 2029 as this is the later of four years from the end of the accounting periods of disposal of the old asset and purchase of the new asset.

> **Tutorial note**
>
> Rollover (reinvestment) relief is available because the company has disposed of and purchased qualifying assets which are used in its trade. The purchase is made within three years of the disposal.

> **Additional areas where credit might be given, note this is not an exhaustive list.**
>
> - The explained date of 31 December 2028 would be given only partial credit as this does not recognise the later of the two possible dates.

(b) Chargeable gain on sale of the factory building

	£
Proceeds	1,450,000
Cost	(800,000)
Gain before indexation	650,000
Indexation allowance £800,000 × 0.516	(412,800)
(278.1 – 183.5)/183.5 = 0.516	
Gain after indexation	237,200
Rollover relief (balance)	(157,200)
Chargeable gain (£1,450,000 – £1,370,000)	80,000

> **Tutorial note**
>
> The company makes a disposal of a chargeable asset bought before December 2017 and so indexation allowance reduces the amount of the gain. The indexation factor should be rounded to three decimal places and is applied to the cost.
>
> Rollover relief is restricted because not all of the proceeds of the disposal have been reinvested in the new asset. The gain chargeable is equal to the amount of the proceeds not reinvested. The rollover relief is the balancing figure between the chargeable amount and the gain after indexation.

(c) Date to claim RDEC
31 December 2025.

> **Tutorial note**
>
> The company must claim the tax credit within 12 months of the end of the accounting period.

(d) Corporation tax payable for the year ended 31 December 2024

	£
Draft tax-adjusted trading profits	25,800,000
Less allowable deductions for R&D	(4,300,000)
Add RDEC (W)	860,000
Trading profits	22,360,000
Chargeable gain £(80,000 – capital loss restricted to 80,000)	0
Taxable total profits	22,360,000
Corporation tax @ 25%	5,590,000
Less RDEC (W)	(860,000)
Corporation tax payable	4,730,000

Working: RDEC

	£
Staff costs	3,800,000
Consumables	500,000
Qualifying costs	4,300,000
RDEC 20% × £4,300,000	860,000

Tutorial note

The company is a large company for R&D purposes and so claims the RDEC. This is both a taxable receipt in the calculation of trading profits and a credit against the corporation tax liability. As no deductions have yet been made for the R&D expenditure, the full costs are allowable as trading deductions.

The capital loss brought forward may only be used against chargeable gains and must be used against these. The unrelieved amount is £420,000.

Additional areas where credit might be given, note this is not an exhaustive list.

- Credit would be given if candidates demonstrate their use of the capital loss by stating the correct amount carried forward.

(e) Date by which the next corporation tax payment must be made
14 June 2025.

Tutorial note

The taxable total profits (and so augmented profits) of the company exceed £20 million and so corporation tax payments are due by instalments, fully paid within the year to which they relate. Therefore, a payment is due by 14 June 2025 being the second quarterly instalment payment for the year ended 31 December 2025.

(f) Corporation tax return submission for year ended 31 December 2024
The due date for submission is 31 December 2025.

The return must be filed electronically and include a self assessment of the tax payable [½] along with supporting computations and accounts in iXBRL (inline extensible business reporting language).

Additional areas where credit might be given, note this is not an exhaustive list.

- The answer assumes the submission date given (12 months after the end of the period) is later than three months after the notice to deliver the corporation tax return was made (a reasonable assumption for an existing company with regular accounting dates). Credit would be given if candidates considered the notice as part of their answers. Credit would also be given if iXBRL is instead explained in terms of tagging, rather than the term used.

Past Exams: November 2023

1. **This question tests corporation tax, VAT and stamp duty. It includes late filing penalties, chargeable gains on disposals of a building and shares, the structures and buildings allowance, non-trade loan relationship deficits and the corporation tax liability. VAT aspects include the treatment of land and buildings and exports, and basic administration. The question tests the calculation of stamp duty and the administration obligations in relation to this tax.**

    Learning Outcomes LO1, LO2, LO3.
    Chapter References in AIA LPWB 6, 18, 19, 20, 21, 23, 24, 25.

    (a) Late filing penalties

    The return should have been submitted by 31 March 2025.

    There is an initial penalty of £100 due to the late return and this increases to £200 because the return is over three months late.

    As the return has been submitted over six months late, a penalty of 10% of the tax unpaid (£24,000) at that six-month date is payable.

    > **Tutorial note**
    >
    > The rules are stated in the published tax tables but must be applied to the specific facts of the scenario, from which it can be determined how late the return is and the amount of the tax-geared penalty.

    > **Additional areas where credit might be given, note this is not an exhaustive list.**
    >
    > - Strictly, the legislation, and so the published tax tables, refer to the 10% penalty arising if the return is not submitted within 18 months of the period end. In this case, this is the same as the return being six months late (given this return is due within 12 months), and so full credit is given whichever way this is expressed.

    (b) Output VAT charged on sales of building and stock

	£
Greenlane building: £1,900,000 × 20%	380,000
EU exports: £200,000 × 40% × 0%	0
UK stock sale: £200,000 × 60% × 20%	24,000
Output VAT	404,000

    > **Tutorial note**
    >
    > The sale of a commercial building is usually an exempt supply so no VAT is charged. However, as this is a commercial building less than three years old, VAT is chargeable at the standard rate.
    >
    > The company makes standard-rated supplies but exports to a company in an EU country are zero-rated provided the company has evidence of export. Supplies to UK customers are charged at the standard rate.

Additional areas where credit might be given, note this is not an exhaustive list.

- Candidates who do not understand the treatment of the EU exports can still gain credit for the sale of the UK stock if they charge standard-rated VAT on the entire sale of the stock.
- For full credit, the requirement demands that VAT of 0% is shown for the export (rather than merely no VAT charged).

(c) VAT return and filing date

The output VAT would have been included on the VAT return for the quarter ended 31 December 2024 due for submission by 7 February 2025.

(d) Structures and buildings allowance

SBA for the year ended 31 March 2025 = £1,400,000 × 3% × 7/12 = £24,500.

Total SBA from 1 January 2023 to 1 November 2024 = £1,400,000 × 3% × 22/12 = £77,000.

Tutorial note

The SBA is only available on building costs, not land costs. Unlike capital allowances for plant and machinery purchases, the SBA is only available for the period which the building is in use by the company. Therefore, only seven months of allowances are available in the year of sale, and three months in the year of purchase ie 22 months for the period of ownership in total.

(e) Gain on sale of Greenlane

	£
Proceeds	1,900,000
Plus total SBA claimed (part d)	77,000
Less costs:	
(£1,400,000 + £100,000)	(1,500,000)
Chargeable gain	477,000

Tutorial note

The structures and buildings allowances are clawed back, not by a balancing adjustment, but by increasing the consideration of the gain on sale. There is no indexation available as the building was acquired after December 2017 and a company does not qualify for the annual exempt amount so there are no further deductions than purchase cost.

(f) Stamp duty payable

Stamp duty = £50,632 × 0.5% = £253 rounded up to £255.

Additional areas where credit might be given, note this is not an exhaustive list.

- Calculations which apply 0.5% incorrectly (using say, 5% or 50%) will not be given credit, although it would still be possible to gain the credit for rounding the resultant figure up to the nearest £5.

(g) Stamp duty obligations

The stamp duty should have been paid when the stock transfer form was presented to HMRC for stamping. This should have been done within 30 days of the transaction (so by 31 March 2025).

If this presentation is late by up to 12 months which may be the case here, there is a penalty of 10% of the unpaid duty, capped at £300.

Interest is payable on unpaid stamp duty from when the 30-day period expires.

Tutorial note

It is unknown whether there has been a failure in compliance here, and this question should offer some easy marks for giving the obligations and possible consequences of non-compliance. The published tax tables should help with this, although care must be taken that answers address stamp duty, and not stamp duty reserve tax or stamp duty land tax, which have different rules.

However, the facts of the question should still be applied. Here the failure, if one exists, will not extend beyond 12 months and so answers should reflect this.

Additional areas where credit might be given, note this is not an exhaustive list.

- Candidates are instructed that calculations are not required for this part, but it may be obvious that the penalty could not be as great as £300 to candidates who have correctly calculated the stamp duty itself to be lower than this. Therefore, full credit is possible without mention of the £300 cap.

- Candidates may be given credit for referring to specific minima that apply in practice in relation to penalties and interest – HMRC do not charge amounts below £25 and £20 for interest and penalties respectively. However, as these relate to quantified amounts which are not asked for, they are not required for full marks.

(h) Gain on sale of shares

	Shares bought in previous 9 days (1.3.2025) 1,000 shares £	Share pool 1,500 shares £
Proceeds £150,000 (1,000 : 1,500)	60,000	90,000
Cost	(50,632)	
Stamp duty (part f)	(255)	
Cost (W)		(43,819)
Gains	9,113	46,181
Total gain		55,294

Working: share pool

Date of purchase	Number of shares	Cost £
15 January 2012	2,000	75,000
Indexation allowance:		
£75,000 × (278.1 – 238)/238		12,637
		87,637
20 January 2020: 1 for 2 bonus issue	1,000	0
	3,000	87,637
Less disposal from the share pool	(1,500)	(43,819)
	1,500	43,818

Tutorial note

The matching rules apply here so the first shares deemed to be sold are those purchased in the nine days before the disposal (1,000 shares). The remaining 1,500 shares are disposed of from the share pool, which includes the original purchased shares and the bonus shares.

Indexation allowance is calculated from the first purchase until December 2017. The bonus shares are added to the pool but for nil cost.

Additional areas where credit might be given, note this is not an exhaustive list.

- Candidates who appreciate the matching rules gain credit for correctly applying these and for allocating the proceeds between the two resulting gains. Those who do not, are still able to achieve many marks, for example, for recognising stamp duty is an allowable cost, for correct calculation of indexation, for appreciating that bonus shares are pooled but do not increase the cost of the pool, and for taking a proportion of the costs from the pool, even if that pool includes all the acquisitions.

(i) Corporation tax payable by Pandated Ltd

	£
Draft tax-adjusted trading profits	980,000
Less interest on loan to purchase Greenlane	(71,500)
Less SBA (part d, amount for this period)	(24,500)
Trading profits	884,000
Chargeable gains (£477,000 + £55,294) (parts e and h)	532,294
Less NTLR deficit (W)	(7,500)
Taxable total profits	1,408,794
Corporation tax @ 25%	352,199

Working: NTLR deficit

	£
Interest on loan to purchase Zooam Ltd shares	1,000
Interest on late paid corporation tax	6,500
Non-trading loan relationship deficit	7,500

(j) Claim for relief for the NTLR deficit

The claim must be made by 31 March 2027.

> **Tutorial note**
>
> Of the interest payable, that relating to the purchase of the building which has been used in the company's trade is an allowable trading deduction. The remaining interest payments are non-trading loan relationship (NTLR) debits. As the company has no NTLR credits, the total debits lead to a deficit which can be relieved against other profits in the year. A claim has to be made for this.
>
> Candidates must always separately calculate and label the different income sources and gains, which are then aggregated to give taxable total profits. For example, the SBA is a deduction when calculating trading profit and should be shown as such. Merely deducting all interest payments without clearly categorising these, will not gain credit – this is always the case but is emphasised in this requirement.

2 **This question tests income tax in the context of a sole trader who has made a trading loss. A pre-prepared computation of capital allowances contains errors and a revised computation must be produced. An ethical element tests the fundamental principle of professional competence and due care. The question tests loss relief including restrictions and the time limit for claims.**

Learning Outcomes LO1, LO2, LO3, LO4.
Chapter References in AIA LPWB 6, 7, 18, 26.

(a) Revised capital allowances computation

	Main pool £	Special rate pool £	Total allowances £
TWDV b/f forward	0	5,400	
Additions:			
Car	15,000		
Machine			
WDA @ 18%	(2,700)		2,700
WDA @ 6%		(324)	324
TWDV c/f	12,300	5,076	
Total allowances			3,024

> **Tutorial note**
>
> The car was originally placed in the wrong pool – its emissions (not exceeding 50g/km) mean it should be added to the main pool, as the UK tax system favours purchase of cars with lower emissions by giving higher tax relief. Credit is given for this in terms of the calculation of WDA at 18%. Further credit is for not adjusting for private use. Such adjustment would only be made for private use by the owner, Tremain.
>
> The machine does not qualify for full expensing (FYA @ 100%) because the purchase is not made by a company, but by an unincorporated business. As the client is a sole trader who uses the cash basis to calculate their trading profits, the purchase of the machine would be treated as a trading deduction.

Additional areas where credit might be given, note this is not an exhaustive list.

- Candidates are given credit for not adjusting for private use, regardless of whether they have placed the car in the correct pool. They are also rewarded for their calculation of writing down allowance in the special rate pool at 6%, provided this is calculated on their special rate pool balance (even if that erroneously includes the car).

- Candidates who realise that the super-deduction is not available on the machine purchase obtain partial credit if they instead add the machine cost to the main pool. For full credit for this aspect, a trading deduction must be given as the client uses the cash basis.

(b) Tax-adjusted trading loss

Trading loss = £69,000 + £3,024 + £9,000 = £81,024.

Tutorial note

Capital allowances and plant and machinery purchases increase the amount of the loss.

(c) Fundamental principle

The fundamental principle is professional competence and due care.

Under this principle, a professional accountant must:

- keep up to date with their professional knowledge and skill sufficient to provide competent professional service to clients.
- work diligently, conforming to technical and professional standards.

Tutorial note

The IESBA code of ethics requires professional competence and due care which means accountants must maintain the appropriate skill and knowledge level, and apply the relevant technical and professional standards in their work.

(d) Net income after loss relief

	2023/24 £	2024/25 £
Trading profit	5,000	0
Property income	60,000	60,000
Total income	65,000	60,000
Less c/b loss relief	(55,000)	
Less c/y loss relief		(26,024)
Net income	10,000	33,976

Tutorial note

Unlike for a company, a loss can be carried back for use in the previous year before a current year claim is made. This allows the loss to be used as early as possible, as the taxpayer here requires.

However, deductions against other income are limited to the greater of £50,000 and 25% of adjusted total income, clearly £50,000 here. Relief against trading income is not restricted and so the total loss relief in the prior year is £55,000. The remainder should be used against other income in the current year.

> **Additional areas where credit might be given, note this is not an exhaustive list.**
> - Candidates who restrict relief to 25% of adjusted total income receive partial credit.

(e) Loss claim

The loss relief must be claimed by 31 January 2027.

> **Tutorial note**
>
> The claim must be made within one year from 31 January next following the tax year of the loss. This rule is stated in the published tax tables but a date must be given to answer the requirement.

3 This question tests income tax and national insurance contributions for a taxpayer who was both employed and a partner during the tax year. It tests partnership profit allocation, opening year basis period, employment income, deductible interest and the taxation of overseas income, including DTR. The different classes of NIC and their administration are tested, as is the form P45. Ethics is tested in terms of the response to money laundering.

Learning Outcomes LO1, LO2, LO3, LO4.
Chapter References in AIA LPWB 1, 2, 4, 5, 8, 9, 14, 26.

(a) Profit allocation for the year ended 30 June 2025

	Total £	Sue £	Taz £	Utu £
Period:				
1.7.24 – 30.9.24				
£360,000 × 3/12*	90,000			
Split 1:1		45,000	45,000	
1.10.24 – 30.6.25				
£360,000 × 9/12*	270,000			
Split 2:2:1		108,000	108,000	54,000
		153,000	153,000	54,000

> **Tutorial note**
>
> The profit is first split between the period before Utu joins the partnership, and the period after. Then the profit sharing ratios for the two periods are applied.

(b) Utu's assessable trading profit for 2024/25

Utu's trading profit for 2024/25 = £54,000 × 6/9 = £36,000

> **Tutorial note**
>
> Utu started trading in the partnership in 2024/25 and so the opening year rules apply. Utu's basis period is from 1 October 2024 (when he joined the partnership) until 5 April 2025 (the end of the tax year). This is a period of six months of his nine-month profit allocation to 30 June 2025.

(c) Form given to Utu on leaving employment

The form is the P45.

Tutorial note

Utu is no longer in employment at the end of the tax year and so will not receive a form P60 but the P45 should detail his taxable pay up to the date of leaving.

(d) Income tax liability for 2024/25

	UK Non-savings income £	Overseas income £	Total £
Employment income:			
Salary	80,000		
Bonus	20,000		
Less pension contribution	(3,000)		
Employment income	97,000		97,000
Trading profit (part b)	36,000		36,000
Rental income (£9,000 + £1,000)		10,000	10,000
Less loan interest paid	(2,000)		(2,000)
Taxable income (no PA)	131,000	10,000	141,000

IT on non-savings income	£
37,700 @ 20%	7,540
87,440 @ 40%	34,976
5,860 @ 45%	2,637
131,000	
10,000 @ 45%	4,500
141,000	
Less DTR:	
Lower of	
UK tax on overseas income of £4,500	
Overseas tax of £1,000	(1,000)
Total income tax liability	48,653

Tutorial note

Utu took out a loan to invest in the partnership – the interest is deductible from Utu's total income.

Utu is UK resident meaning he is taxed on his worldwide income. The gross amount before deduction of overseas tax (but after deduction of allowable costs) is included in Utu's taxable income but double tax relief (DTR) is available, reducing the tax payable, for the overseas tax paid. The amount of DTR is the lower of the overseas tax and the UK tax on the overseas income. To determine the UK tax on the overseas income, the overseas income is deemed to be the top slice of the taxpayer's income.

(e) NIC schedule for Utu for 2024/25

	Class 1 primary	Class 4
Amount charged to NIC	£100,000 (salary and bonus) (no relief for pension contribution)	£36,000 (trading profits) (no NIC on rental income)
Reported on	Ronsnook plc's monthly Full Payment Submission (FPS)	Utu's self-assessment tax return

Payable by whom	Ronsnook plc	Utu
Payable by when	22nd of month following each salary/bonus payment	31 January 2026

> **Tutorial note**
>
> Utu suffers Class 1 primary NIC on his employment earnings but his employer is responsible for paying the NIC over to HMRC and reporting it each month. Both the salary and the bonus are chargeable to Class 1 primary NIC – there is no relief for the pension contribution paid.
>
> Once Utu joins the partnership he is self-employed and is responsible for paying Class 4 on his partnership profits. Utu will not have to make payments on account as in the previous year (2023/24) all of his income tax liability will have been collected at source as PAYE. Instead, a single balancing payment must be made.
>
> There is no NIC on rental income.

Additional areas where credit might be given, note this is not an exhaustive list.

- Candidates may present their answers differently and still achieve full marks, provided they address each aspect of the requirement, and it is clear to which class of NIC each point relates. As usual, they must apply the rules to the specific facts of the scenario, particularly in terms of amounts and dates – a general statement of rules will not score full credit.

(f) Steps to take in respect of money laundering

I would have to report this to my firm's money laundering reporting officer (MLRO).

The MLRO would then determine whether to make a suspicious activity report (SAR) to the National Crime Agency.

The firm may consider ceasing to act but should take care that this does not constitute 'tipping off' the client that such a report has been made.

> **Tutorial note**
>
> Failure to report suspicions of money laundering, and tipping off a client that a report has been made, are both offences under the money laundering regulations.
>
> At the current time, the client has not yet omitted the income and so has not yet committed tax evasion and money laundering. Before the return is submitted, the accountant would take steps to persuade the client that the disclosure of the taxable income must be made.

Additional areas where credit might be given, note this is not an exhaustive list.

- The requirement specifically asks for candidates to record the steps that should be taken in respect of anti-money laundering legislation so marks are not awarded for general points relating to tax evasion. However, it is appropriate that when recording the steps to take, an accountant records their conclusions why this action would fall under the anti-money laundering regulations. Therefore, limited credit is available for mentioning this written record, and for drawing the links between failure to declare income, tax evasion, the proceeds of crime and money laundering.
- Credit is awarded separately for considering whether to cease to act and for not tipping off – they do not need to be linked.

4   This question tests inheritance tax on a death estate, including agricultural property relief, debts and deductions, and the transfer of unused nil rate band from a deceased spouse.

Learning Outcomes LO2, LO3.
Chapter References in AIA LPWB 15, 16.

(a) Nil rate band

	£
RNRB – *credit given provided RNRB not used here or in part b*	0
NRB - Marcia	325,000
NRB - Bembe (£325,000 – £260,000)	65,000
Total nil rate band	390,000

Tutorial note

Marcia has not left her estate to a direct descendant and so the residence nil rate band is not available. However the nil rate band available is increased by her husband's unused nil rate band.

(b) Inheritance tax on Marcia's death estate

	£	£
Marcia's house		575,000
Agricultural land	80,000	
Less APR @ 100% of agricultural value	(55,000)	
		25,000
Cash including ISA amounts		95,000
Chattels		72,000
Less: Liabilities		
Income tax owing	8,000	
Funeral expenses	2,000	
		(10,000)
Chargeable estate		757,000
NRB (part a)		(390,000)
		367,000
IHT @ 40%		146,800

Tutorial note

The agricultural land is in the UK and has been let to a tenant farmer for over seven years, and so agricultural property relief (APR) is available. The relief is 100% of the agricultural value of the land.

Cash is an exempt asset for capital gains tax but not for inheritance tax. Despite the income tax exemption for interest generated on cash in an ISA, the cash is still chargeable to inheritance tax.

The income tax debt and reasonable funeral expenses both reduce the chargeable value of the death estate.

(c) Date of claim to transfer nil rate band

The claim must be made to transfer the unused NRB of Bembe by 31 March 2027.

> **Tutorial note**
>
> The claim must usually be made within two years **of the end of the month of death** of the surviving spouse. The information is not given in the published tax tables so must be learned.
>
> No claim is required to benefit from agricultural property relief.

Additional areas where credit might be given, note this is not an exhaustive list.
- There are no envisaged areas of extra credit.

5   This question tests capital gains tax, land transaction tax and income tax. The capital gains tax aspects include business asset disposal relief (BADR), part disposal, a spousal gift, and administration in terms of the BADR claim and payment of tax. The calculation of net funds (cash) available after disposals, a purchase, and payment of the relevant taxes, tests the concept of tax as a cost. A calculation of land transaction tax is required, in a scenario requiring higher rates. The small income tax requirement tests various allowances and nil rate bands which can be found in the published tax tables.

Learning Outcomes LO1, LO2, LO3.
Chapter References in AIA LPWB 1, 3, 5, 10, 12, 14, 25.

(a) Gain on disposal of land

	£
Proceeds	80,000
Less auctioneer's fees	(8,000)
Net proceeds	72,000
Less cost (W)	(34,783)
Chargeable gain	37,217

Working: Cost of two hectares
Cost = £100,000 × £80,000 /(£80,000 + £150,000) = £34,783.

> **Tutorial note**
>
> The cost of the portion of land sold is determined using the part disposal fraction, based on the values of the relative portions and not the respective sizes. While the auctioneer's fees are allowable costs of sale, the gross sale proceeds are used in the formula.

Additional areas where credit might be given, note this is not an exhaustive list.
- Limited credit is given in the marking scheme for any attempt at apportioning the cost of £100,000 across the five hectares.

(b) Matt's capital gains tax

	BADR £	Other gains £
Gain on disposal of land (part a)		37,217
Gift of painting *does not need to be shown*		0
Gain on sale of business – *BADR limited to £1m*	1,000,000	500,000
Chargeable gains	1,000,000	537,217

AEA		(3,000)
Taxable gains	1,000,000	534,217
CGT @ 10%/ 20%	100,000	106,843
Total CGT		206,843

> **Tutorial note**
>
> The gift of the painting is a disposal to a spouse at nil gain nil loss.
>
> The sale of the business qualifies for business asset disposal relief (BADR) as this is the disposal of an entire trading business which has been owned for more than two years. BADR allows a gain to be taxed at 10%. However, there is a lifetime limit of £1 million for the relief, and so £500,000 is taxed with other gains at 20%.
>
> The annual exempt amount is available to reduce chargeable gains and should be used against gains which otherwise are charged at the higher rate to save the most tax.

(c) (i) Date to claim relief

The claim for business asset disposal relief must be made by 31 January 2027.

(ii) Date by which to pay CGT

The capital gains tax is payable by 31 January 2026.

> **Tutorial note**
>
> Both date rules are stated in the published tax tables but must be applied to give specific dates. The nil gain nil loss treatment on the disposal to a spouse is automatic and no claim is required.

(d) Land transaction tax

	£
£180,000 × 4%	7,200
(£230,000 – £180,000) × 7.5%	3,750
	10,950

> **Tutorial note**
>
> The rates and bands are those for a residential property, as given in the published tax tables. The higher rate applies as Matt already owns a property.

Additional areas where credit might be given, note this is not an exhaustive list.

- Candidates who omit the higher rate lose the first mark, having no LTT charged on the first £180,000, but on follow-through are still able to access the other mark for the correct band using a rate of 3.5%.

(e) Remaining money/cash

	£
Proceeds from sale of the business	2,000,000
Net proceeds from sale of the land (£80,000 - £8,000)	72,000
No cash from gift of painting – *does not need to be stated*	0
Less purchase of house	(230,000)
Less LTT (part d)	(10,950)
Less CGT (part b)	(204,983)
	1,626,067

> **Tutorial note**
>
> The question asked for the cash remaining, therefore the disposal proceeds, and not the gains, should be included in the calculation. In the case of the sale of land, part of the proceeds were spent on the auctioneer's fee so these should be deducted. There is no cash arising on the gift of the painting.
>
> The question asked for the amount remaining after the purchase of the house in Wales and after paying all taxes – these include the land transaction tax and the capital gains tax.

Additional areas where credit might be given, note this is not an exhaustive list.

- Full credit is available where the candidates deduct their own calculated amounts for LTT and CGT.

(f) Limits before income tax payable

Matt could rent out a room for up to £7,500.

Simon could generate trading income of up to £1,000 from giving music lessons.

Simon could receive savings income of up to £6,000.

> **Tutorial note**
>
> The question tests various allowances/limits which are given in the published tax tables, if candidates can identify the particular allowance that applies.
>
> Rent a room relief, limited to £7,500 per annum, is available in respect of a room rented to a lodger in the taxpayer's own home.
>
> The trading allowance of £1,000 applies to Simon's trading income from giving music lessons.
>
> Simon's non-savings income is covered by the personal allowance. The first £5,000 of his savings income is taxed at the starting rate of 0%. Simon, as a basic rate taxpayer, then receives a savings nil rate band of £1,000 (again meaning 0% tax). Therefore, a total of £6,000 savings income can be received before Simon starts paying income tax.

EXAM ANSWER BANK

Mock exam questions and answers

TAXATION

Time allowed – 3 hours

Answer ALL questions

Time allowed – 3 hours

Answer ALL questions

You are allowed an additional 15 minutes reading time before the exam begins.

Assume that the tax rates, allowances and rules for Financial Year 2024 and tax year 2024/25 apply in all years.

Use your own hard copy of Whillans Tax Tables 2024/25 Finance Act Edition during the exam.

Unless instructed otherwise, work to the nearest £ and to the nearest month and show all your workings.

When answering a requirement, you may have to refer to information given earlier in the scenario or use your answers to earlier parts.

CREATING WORLD CLASS ACCOUNTANTS

Answer ALL questions

Question 1

You are a tax assistant in a medium-sized firm of accountants. You have been asked to help with the tax work for various clients.

Newcomer Ltd

Newcomer Ltd commenced trading on 1 October 2024. Its forecast sales are as follows:

		£
2024	October	18,500
	November	21,900
	December	23,400
2025	January	27,300
	February	22,700
	March	19,200

The company's sales are all standard-rated, and the above figures are exclusive of VAT.

Required

(a) Advise when Newcomer Ltd will be required to notify HMRC that it must compulsorily register for VAT, and from which date the registration will be effective. **(4 marks)**

Au Revoir Ltd

Au Revoir Ltd has been registered for VAT for many years and its sales are standard rated. The company has recently seen a downturn in its business activities, and sales for the years ended 31 October 2024 and 2025 are forecast to be £77,000 and £75,500 respectively. Both of these figures are exclusive of VAT.

Required

(b) State why Au Revoir Ltd will be permitted to voluntarily deregister for VAT, and from which date deregistration will be effective. **(3 marks)**

Ongoing Ltd

Ongoing Ltd is registered for VAT, and its sales and purchases are all standard rated. The following information relates to the company's VAT return for the quarter ended 30 April 2025:

(1) Standard-rated sales amounted to £120,000. Ongoing Ltd offers its customers a 5% discount for prompt payment, and this discount is taken by half of the customers. The discount is detailed on the sales invoice.

(2) Standard-rated purchases and expenses amounted to £35,640. This figure includes £480 for entertaining UK customers.

(3) On 15 April 2025, the company purchased a motor car at a cost of £16,450 for the use of a salesperson, and machinery at a cost of £21,150. Both these figures are inclusive of VAT. The motor car is used for both business and private mileage.

Unless stated otherwise, all of the above figures are exclusive of VAT.

Required

(c) Calculate the amount of VAT payable by Ongoing Ltd for the quarter ended 30 April 2025.

(5 marks)

MOCK EXAM QUESTIONS

Shaun Knight

Shaun bought new business premises in Aberdeen, Scotland, on 6 April 2024 and immediately started to trade. The premises was an office building constructed 12 years ago. It cost £230,000 (exclusive of VAT). The owner had exercised an option to tax the building.

Required

(d) Calculate the land and buildings transaction tax payable by Shaun on the purchase of his new business premises. **(3 marks)**

His tax-adjusted trading profits for the 15-month period ended 30 June 2025 were £645,000.

The profits figure of £645,000 has been adjusted for tax purposes. However, Shaun did not deduct any of the following either from his accounting profit or in his adjusted profit for the period ended 30 June 2025 because they were paid before the start of Shaun's trade on 6 April 2024.

		£
2023	Advertising, marketing and trade fairs (including £1,200 for client entertaining)	25,000
31 January 2024	Legal fees in connection with the new office building	8,500
6 February 2024	Plant and machinery bought before the commencement of Shaun's trade	200,000

In addition to the above Shaun also purchased a car for his staff to use for business travel (CO_2 emissions 45g/km) for £35,000 on 22 April 2024 and an air conditioning unit on 31 March 2025 for £15,000.

Required

(e) Calculate Shaun's assessable trading income for tax year 2024/25. Ignore VAT. **(8 marks)**

Partnership

Shaun is also a partner in a partnership with Melanie, a friend from university.

The partnership prepares accounts to 31 March each year and profit is split equally between Melanie and Shaun, after Shaun takes a salary of £50,000.

In the year ended 31 March 2025 the partnership had a tax-adjusted trading profit of £720,000.

Melanie already has property income of £162,000. This is without any deduction of her £24,000 of finance costs relating to loans used to acquire residential properties which are then let out.

Required

(f) Calculate Shaun and Melanie's share of the partnership trading profits in the year ended 31 March 2025. **(3 marks)**

(g) Calculate Melanie's national insurance costs in respect of her partnership income for a complete tax year. **(3 marks)**

(h) Calculate Melanie's income tax liability and post-tax income for 2024/25. **(6 marks)**

Frank

Frank is a long-standing client of the firm. He is married to Valerie and has asked for some tax advice around Valerie's tax affairs. Valerie is UK resident now but was born and brought up in France, and she has considerable assets and income from France. Valerie is not yet a client of the firm.

Required

(i) State the steps that should be taken by your firm before giving advice to Valerie. **(5 marks)**

(Total 40 marks)

MOCK EXAM QUESTIONS

Question 2

You work in the Finance Department of Katya plc, a UK trading company, which is a large company for all tax purposes. HM Revenue & Customs (HMRC) has raised an enquiry into the company's corporation tax return for the year ended 31 March 2025.

A taxable total profits figure of £9,560,000 was shown on the corporation tax return which had been completed and submitted on time by the previous finance director.

The HMRC inspector has queried the tax treatment of four transactions that took place during the year ended 31 March 2025:

Sale of loan stock

In July 2024, Katya plc sold loan stock to a third party for £3,000,000. Katya plc had bought the loan stock for £2,000,000 in July 2014. The finance director showed an indexed gain in respect of this disposal in the corporation tax return as follows:

	£
Proceeds	3,000,000
Cost	(2,000,000)
	1,000,000
Indexation allowance (£2,000,000 × 0.086)	(172,000)
Chargeable gain	828,000

The indexation factor of 0.086 is correct for a period from July 2014 to December 2017.

Sale of fixed plant

In July 2024, Katya plc sold an item of fixed plant to a third party for £860,000. The plant had been purchased for £730,000 in July 2014 when its cost was added to the main pool. When the plant was sold the capital allowances pool adjustment was made correctly.

A gain of £140,000 on the sale of a factory in June 2014 was fully deferred by a claim for reinvestment relief when the plant was purchased, and this deferred gain was not accounted for when the plant was sold in July 2024 and has not been included in the corporation tax return.

Dividends

A deduction from trading profits was made for dividends paid of £250,000.

Accrued director's bonus

A deduction from trading profits was made for an accrued director's bonus of £10,000, this bonus was not actually paid until 28th February 2026.

Required

(a) Calculate the revised taxable total profits and the corporation tax payable by Katya plc for the year ended 31 March 2025 after making any corrections to the transactions queried by HMRC.

(10 marks)

(b) Advise of the potential penalty in respect of these errors in the year ended 31 March 2025.

(3 marks)

(Total 13 marks)

Assume that the tax rates and rules for FY 2024 also applied in previous years.

Question 3

You work as a junior accountant in the Employment Taxes department of a large firm of accountants.

Dormers plc is one of your clients. Your firm performs all the payroll and employment taxes work for Dormers plc.

Dormers plc recruited a new logistics manager, Antonia, from 1 July 2024, but the company omitted to tell you about this. You have received an email providing you with the relevant information about Antonia's employment benefits.

(1) Salary of £6,360 per month, plus a bonus of £12,000 paid on 12 May 2025. She had become entitled to the bonus on 22 March 2025.

(2) Antonia contributes 6% of monthly gross salary into Dormers plc's registered occupational pension scheme.

(3) On 1 August 2024, Dormers plc provided Antonia with an interest-free loan of £120,000 so that she could purchase a holiday cottage. Antonia repaid £50,000 on 31 October 2024, but the balance remains outstanding.

(4) Antonia's two-year old daughter is provided with a place at Dormers plc's workplace nursery. The total cost to the company of providing this nursery place was £11,400 (190 days at £60 per day).

(5) From 1 January 2025, Dormers plc provided Antonia with living accommodation. The property has an annual value of £10,400 and is rented by Dormers plc at a cost of £2,250 per month. On 1 January 2025, Dormers plc also purchased furniture for the property at a cost of £16,320. The company pays for all the running costs relating to the property, and for the period to 5 April 2025 these amounted to £1,900.

(6) Dormers plc provided Antonia with a home entertainment system for her personal use costing £4,400 on 1 July 2024. The company then gifted the system to Antonia for free as a bonus in December 2024, when its market value at that time was £3,860.

Required

(a) Calculate Antonia's employment income for the year 2024/25. Clearly demonstrate your treatment of each item, showing a zero for any exempt benefits. **(12 marks)**

Dormers plc is thinking about offering assistance to Antonia with home to work travel. The company is considering two alternatives as follows:

Alternative 1 – provision of a motorcycle

- Dormers plc will provide Antonia with leased motorcycle for travelling from home to work.
- Provision of the motorcycle, including fuel will give rise to a taxable benefit of £3,160 for Antonia.
- Antonia will incur no additional travel or parking costs in respect of her work.

Alternative 2 – payment towards the cost of driving and provision of parking place

- Dormers plc will reimburse Antonia for the cost of driving her own car to work up to an amount of £2,240 per year.
- Antonia estimates that her annual cost for driving from home to work is £2,820.
- Additionally, Dormers plc will pay AB Parking Ltd £920 per year for a car parking space for Antonia near the head office.

You find out that Antonia only works at the head office and has no other sources of income.

Required

(b) Calculate the total cost to Antonia of the two alternatives for providing financial assistance for home to work travel. **(5 marks)**

(Total 17 marks)

Question 4

You work in the capital taxes department of a firm of accountants. Three unconnected clients need advice regarding capital gains tax.

Amanda

Amanda owns a plot of 10 acres of land as an investment which she acquired in June 2009 for a cost of £300,000. In June 2024 Amanda sells 4 acres of the land for £500,000 before selling costs of £1,250. The remaining 6 acres are valued at 750,000.

Amanda also has 100% shareholding in Whiskers and Cream Ltd, a trading company which operates as a cat café. Amanda is the sole shareholder and director of this company which she formed in January 2005 acquiring 1,000 shares for their nominal value of £1 per share. Amanda sold all the shares in August 2024 for sale proceeds of £1,300,000 and stopped working for the company on the same date.

Amanda is a higher-rate taxpayer and made no other capital disposals during 2024/25. She has not previously made any other gains which qualify for business asset disposal relief and has capital losses brought forward of £148,000.

Required

(a) Calculate Amanda's capital gains tax liability for 2024/25 and state the due date for payment.

(8 marks)

Jane

Jane is a higher-rate taxpayer who makes substantial capital disposals each year. She gifted a set of two matching antique chairs in May 2024.

The chairs originally cost her £15,000 twenty years ago. Individually the chairs are worth £20,000 each, but as a set they are worth £60,000 together.

Jane wanted to gift both chairs to her son but she decided instead to gift one chair to her son, Dave and gift Dave's wife the other chair, as she believed this would save her capital gains tax.

Required

(b) Calculate Jane's chargeable gains for 2024/25 on making the two gifts above. **(4 marks)**

Fred

Fred is an employee who has never completed a tax return. He sold a painting in November 2024 which he had inherited in January 2010. The sale gave rise to a gain of £23,000. Fred has not reported this gain to HM Revenue & Customs (HMRC).

Required

(c) Advise Fred of when he should have notified HMRC of the gain on the painting, and of the possible penalties for failure to notify chargeability assuming this is a careless error. **(3 marks)**

(Total 15 marks)

Question 5

You work in the inheritance tax team in a medium-sized firm of accountants. Your client, Nisar, was UK domiciled. He died on 31 December 2024.

Nisar had made two lifetime gifts.

Firstly, on 13 September 2021, he gave cash of £340,000 to a discretionary trust for the benefit of his nephew.

Required

(a) Calculate the gross chargeable transfer arising from this gift into a discretionary trust. **(2 marks)**

Secondly, on 25 November 2022, he gave land to his grandson, Dubin, on the occasion of Dubin's marriage. The value of the land, which had never been used for agricultural purposes was £483,000 on the date of the gift, and £490,000 on the date of Nisar's death.

On 13 July 2023, Nisar sold a painting to an art gallery for £50,000. Nisar believed this to be a fair price. The gallery sold the painting for £78,000 in August 2023.

Required

(b) Calculate the inheritance tax arising on all of Nisar's lifetime gifts as a result of his death.

(7 marks)

Nisar owned the following assets at the date of his death:

- House valued at £640,000
- Cash and other assets worth £170,000, including a car worth £13,000
- 10,000 shares (less than 1% shareholding) in Trimp plc, a quoted trading company, quoted at 200–224p, and with bargains at 202p, 208p and 216p on 31 December 2024.

Nisar owed income tax and capital gains tax totalling £12,000 at the date of his death.

In Nisar's will, he left the whole of his estate to his daughter Rehat. Nisar's wife had died in 2007, utilising the whole of her nil rate band.

Required

(c) Calculate the inheritance tax payable on Nisar's death estate. **(6 marks)**

(Total 15 marks)

(End of question paper)

[this page is blank]

MODEL ANSWERS

TAXATION

Question 1

This question tests a variety of issues. The first part of the question test various basic VAT rules.

The second part of the question looks at opening year rules for a long period of account and a capital allowances computation for the long period.

The third part of the question looks at forming a partnership and allocation of profits and salary, along with a calculation of income tax and NIC, and a calculation of post-tax income.

The final part of the question looks at ethics and a new client engagement.

Chapter references in the Workbook are chapters 4, 5, 6, 8, 23, 24 and 26.

(a) VAT threshold exceeded in January 2025:

		£
2024	October	18,500
	November	21,900
	December	23,400
2025	January	27,300
		91,100

Therefore, Newcomer Ltd must notify HMRC within 30 days of the end of the month the threshold is exceeded, ie by 1 March 2025.

The registration is effective from the end of the month following the month in which the registration threshold is exceeded, ie from 1 March 2025, or an earlier date agreed between the company and HMRC.

(b) Au Revoir Ltd is eligible for voluntary deregistration if HMRC are satisfied that the amount of taxable supplies (net of VAT) in the following one-year period will not exceed £88,000. As Au Revoir Ltd has taxable supplies below this deregistration threshold they can voluntarily deregister.

However, voluntary deregistration will not be allowed if the reason for the expected fall in value of taxable supplies is the cessation of taxable supplies or the suspension of taxable supplies for a period of 30 days or more in that following year.

HMRC will cancel a person's registration from the date the request is made or from an agreed later date.

(c)

	£	£
Output tax		
£[(£120,000 × 50% × 95%) + (£120,000 × 50%)] = 117,000 × 20%		23,400
Input tax		
£(35,640 − 480) = 35,160 × 20%	7,032	
£21,150 × 1/6	3,525	
		(10,557)
		12,843

> **Tutorial note**
>
> VAT is calculated after the deduction of the prompt payment discount taken up.
>
> UK entertaining is not an expense on which input tax can be recovered (overseas entertaining the input VAT can be recovered).
>
> Input tax on motor cars not used wholly for business purposes is irrecoverable.

(d) Land and buildings transaction tax (Scotland)

Consideration is the VAT inclusive price = 120% × £230,000 = £276,000.

	£
£150,000 × 0%	-
£100,000 × 1%	1,000
£26,000 × 5%	1,300
	2,300

(e) **Assessable trading income for 2024/25**

(W1) Taxable trading profits 15 M/E 30 June 2025

	£
Tax adjusted trading profits per question	645,000
Less:	
Advertising (£25,000 - £1,200)	(23,800)
Legal fees (capital)	-
Plant and machinery (trading deduction)	(200,000)
Air conditioning unit	(15,000)
Less capital allowances on car	
(£35,000 × 18% × 15/12)	(7,875)
Taxable trading profits	398,325

Assessable in 2025/26 = £398,325 × 12/15 = £318,660

(f)

Partnership	Total	Shaun	Melanie
	£	£	£
Salary	50,000	50,000	
PSR 1:1	670,000	335,000	335,000
Annual profits	720,000	385,000	335,000

(g)

Class 4 NIC	£
£(50,270 – 12,570) × 6%	2,262
£(335,000 – 50,270) × 2%	5,695
	7,957

(h) Post-tax partnership income for Melanie:

	Non-savings income £
Property income	162,000
Partnership profit	335,000
Personal allowance	(-)
Taxable income	497,000
£37,700 × 20%	7,540
(£125,140 – £37,700) × 40%	34,976
(£497,000 – £125,140) × 45%	167,337
	209,853
Relief for finance costs at 20% of the lowest of:	
Interest (£24,000), property income (£162,000) and ATI (£497,000)	
20% × £24,000	(4,800)
Total income	205,053
Less	497,000
Income tax	(205,053)
NIC contributions	(9,267)
Post-tax income	282,680

(i) File note: steps to take before giving advice to Valerie

Consider whether acceptance of Valerie as a client would create any threats to compliance with the fundamental principles.

Consider whether we have the professional competence to advise Valerie, particularly if she requires advice on French tax.

Consider the potential conflict of interest of advising both Frank and Valerie (husband and wife).

Verify Valerie's identity using passport or driving licence, and proof of address, for anti money laundering procedures.

Prepare and sign an engagement letter with Valerie. Valerie should also sign it.

Clearly define the scope of the engagement.

Additional areas where credit might be given, note this is not an exhaustive list:

- **Seek professional clearance from previous advisers or collate information on French tax.**

Tutorial note and commentary

The first part of this question deals with various aspects of VAT. In **part a(i)** even if the calculation of when the company exceeded the VAT threshold was miscalculated, follow through marks could be gained on the dates to notify HMRC and the date VAT will be charged from.

In **part a(ii)** of this question, candidates were asked to briefly explain about voluntary deregistration. Even if candidates did not mention why voluntary deregistration may not be allowed (ie if compulsory deregistration was instead applicable), most would have scored well on the sales being below the £88,000 threshold.

MOCK EXAM ANSWERS

Part a(iii) required a calculation of VAT payable for the VAT quarter, most candidates can score well here, picking up some easy marks. Calculations must be shown as marks are awarded for how a figure has been calculated.

Part b (i) dealt with the calculation of land and buildings transaction tax for a purchase of some business premises. The use of the tax tables would be useful here but it is important to remember that the stamp taxes use VAT-inclusive prices as the consideration.

Part b (ii) dealt with the adjusted profits for a sole trader with a couple of adjustments to trade profits, and capital allowances for a long period. Candidates often get the rules for sole traders and companies confused, especially with capital allowances. One long capital allowance computation can be prepared for a sole trader with a long period of account, whereas a company would have to prepare two capital allowance computations for a long period. Sole traders do not qualify for the temporary full expensing allowances.

Part c deals with partnership allocation of profits and salary with some easy marks available. The question then went on to ask candidates to calculate the NIC due for Melanie. Finally, a calculation of the income tax liability and post-tax income for Melanie was required, candidates often forget to deduct the NIC in this part of the question.

The final part of the question, part d was an admin question dealing with the steps that must be taken before a new client is taken on. Candidates can score well here if they think practically here about what they would want to know about a client before acting for them and whether they have the relevant expertise.

Marking scheme

		Marks	
(a)	*VAT Registration*		
	Date VAT threshold exceeded	1	
	Timeframe and actual date to notify HMRC	2	
	Date registration is effective from	1	
	Total marks part (a)		4
(b)	*Voluntary deregistration*		
	Deregistration limit and time scale	1	
	Limit VAT excl sales	0.5	
	Au Revoir Ltd under the threshold	0.5	
	When voluntary deregistation is not applicable	1	
	Date of cancellation	1	
	Total marks part (b)		3
(c)	*Calculation of VAT*		
	Output VAT on prompt payment discount sales	1.5	
	Output VAT on non-discounted sales	0.5	
	Input VAT expenses less entertaining	1	
	No input VAT recovery on car	1	
	Input VAT on machinery at 1/6	1	
	Total marks part (c)		5

MOCK EXAM ANSWERS

(d)	VAT inclusive price	1	
	LBTT at 0%/1%	1	
	LBTT at 5%	1	
			3
(e)	*Taxable trading profits:*		
	Advertising	1	
	Legal fees (nil deduction)	1	
	Plant qualifying for AIA	1	
	A/C unit qualifying for AIA	1	
	Calculation of AIA	1	
	Car main pool asset	2	
	Calculation of WDA	2	
	Assessment for 2024/25	1	
	Total marks part (e)		8
(f)	*Partnership income*		
	PSR after allocation of salary	1	
	Salary to Shaun	1	
	Split of profits between partners	1	
	Total marks part (f)		3
(g)	*Calculation of NIC and tax*		
	Class 4 NIC	2	
	Class 2 NIC	1	
	Total marks part (g)		3
(h)	*Calculation of income tax and post-tax income*		
	Taxable income	1.5	
	Income tax liability	1.5	
	Finance costs	1.5	
	Post-tax income	1.5	
	Total marks part (h)		6
(i)	Threats to compliance	1	
	Professional competence	1	
	Conflicts of interest	1	
	ID for money laundering	1	
	Scope of engagement	1	
	Total marks part (i)		5
	Total marks for Q1		40

Question 2

This question tests corporation tax in the context of an HMRC enquiry, where various errors have been made in a tax return. It covers the treatment of loan stock, and reinvestment relief involving a depreciating asset. An administrative element tests the penalties as a result of these errors.

Chapter references in the Workbook are chapters 18, 19 and 20.

(a) **Revised corporation tax liability**

	£
Taxable total profits figure per question	9,560,000
Add:	
Loan stock – removal of indexation (see tutorial note)	172,000
Gain on the fixed plant (W1)	67,220
Deferred gain back into charge (see tutorial note)	140,000
Dividends	250,000
Director's bonus not paid < 9 months of year end	10,000
Revised taxable total profits	10,199,220
CT @ 25%	2,549,805

(W1) Gain on the sale of plant

	£
Proceeds	860,000
Cost	(730,000)
	130,000
IA £730,000 × 0.086	(62,780)
Chargeable gain	67,220

> **Tutorial note**
>
> The loan stock is taxable as non-trade loan relationship credit, not a chargeable gain and so no indexation is deductible.
>
> The deferred gain of £140,000 was frozen upon the reinvestment in the depreciating asset (plant) and becomes chargeable on sale of the plant.

(b) **Penalty for error**

Assuming Katya plc did not deliberately make the errors to the corporation tax computation, the maximum penalty for careless error = 30% of potential lost revenue (PLR).

The PLR is the extra tax due as a result of correcting the errors.

The penalty can be reduced if the company tells HMRC about the errors ie makes disclosure.

However, as these errors were discovered as part of an enquiry, such disclosure is likely to be seen as prompted, and so the minimum penalty would be 15% of PLR. **(13 marks)**

> **Tutorial note and commentary**
>
> This corporation tax and administration question covers a correction to a corporation tax computation in the context of an enquiry by HM Revenue & Customs. The company has made various errors, which must be analysed and corrected in the main requirement.
>
> The first error concerns the treatment of the sale of loan stock by a company as a chargeable gain, rather than correctly showing the profit on sale as a non-trade loan relationship credit, and so indexation is not available. This is a common mistake by students. If candidates do not understand the error here, they should quickly move on to the next item.

MOCK EXAM ANSWERS

> The second area of error concerns the sale of an item of plant. There are two errors in its treatment. A reinvested gain comes back into charge. Candidates usually know the rules of rollover relief but are less confident when a depreciating asset is used. Candidates are often also more comfortable dealing with the original reinvestment, rather than what happens to the deferred gain in future. Additionally, the sale of the plant gives rise to a gain on disposal.
>
> The other two errors concerned a deduction for dividends and an accrued director's bonus which was not paid within nine months of the accounting year end of 31 March 2025. Both items must be added back into the computation. Candidates could easily miss the bonus by not reading the question correctly, it is the Y/E 31 March 2025 (not 31 March 2026) which is being enquired into by HMRC and so we are looking for accrued bonuses to be paid within nine months of this date.
>
> The small, follow-on, requirement considers the penalty because of these mistakes made. Candidates who have remained calm, should manage to score full marks on this administrative element.

Marking scheme

	Marks
Part (a)	
TTP per question	0.5
Loan stock removal of indexation	1.5
Gain on sale of plant	2.5
Deferred gain back into charge	2
Add back dividends	1
Add back entertaining	1
Revised TTP	0.5
Calculation of CT liability	1
Total marks part a	10
Part (b)	
Max penalty for careless	1
PLR	0.5
Reduction for disclosure	0.5
Min penalty in this case	1
Total marks part b	3
Total marks for Q2	13

Question 3

This question covers employment income. It involves a variety of taxable and exempt benefit calculations, and a cost comparison of two alternatives for home to work travel assistance.

The chapter reference in the Workbook is chapter 4.

(a) **Antonia – Employment income 2024/25**

	£
Salary (£6,360 × 9)	57,240
Pension contributions (£57,240 × 6%)	(3,434)
	53,806
Bonus (entitled during 2024/25)	12,000
Beneficial loan (W1)	1,331
Workplace nursery (exempt)	0
Living accommodation (W2)	6,750

MOCK EXAM ANSWERS

	£
Furniture (£16,320 × 20% × 3/12)	816
Running costs	1,900
Home entertainment system: use (W3)	440
acquisition (W3)	3,960
	81,003

Workings

1 *Beneficial loan*

Average method: (120,000 + 70,000)/2 = 95,000 at 2.25% × 8/12 = £1,425
Strict method: (120,000 × 2.25% × 3/12) + (70,000 × 2.25% × 5/12) = £1,331
Antonia will therefore elect to have the taxable benefit calculated using the strict method.

2 *Living accommodation*

Higher of annual value £2,600 (£10,400 × 3/12) and rent paid of £6,750 (£2,250 × 3).

3 *Home entertainment system*

Use: £4,400 × 20% × 6/12 = £440
Acquisition: higher of MV, £3,860 and cost minus benefit for use, £3,960 (£4,400 – 440)

(b) **Home to work travel**

Alternative 1 – provision of a motorcycle

	£
Income tax:	
Motorcycle and fuel benefit (£3,160 × 40%)	1,264
Class 1 NIC:	0
Total cost	1,264

Alternative 2 – payment towards driving costs and provision of parking

	£
Provision of a parking at/near an employee's normal place of work	0
Income tax:	
Reimbursement of driving costs (£2,240 × 40%)	896
Class 1 NIC:	
Reimbursement of driving costs (£2,240 × 2%)	45
Additional driving costs not reimbursed (£2,820 – £2,240)	580
Total cost	1521

Tutorial note and commentary

Part (a)

The first part of this question covered various employment benefits, providing candidates with an opportunity to pick up marks on each benefit they calculated, even if they didn't know how to deal with every single benefit.

Candidates often forget to pro-rate benefits and fall into the trap of not carefully reading the question, as some benefits are provided on different dates to other benefits. Candidates should show workings for any calculations needed as marks can still be picked up for the correct application of benefit calculations.

Any benefits which are exempt should be shown as a zero, so the candidate has demonstrated their knowledge that that particular benefit isn't taxable.

Part (b)

The second part of the question looked at alternatives for providing the employee with assistance for traveling to work. Candidates needed to calculate the income tax costs and any class 1 NIC. Candidates often get confused which amounts incur class 1 by the employee, and which amounts incur class 1A by the employer.

Antonia is a higher rate taxpayer, so will pay income tax at 40% on the annual taxable benefits

Motorcycle:

Antonia will have no national insurance liability in respect of this benefit as it is not cash or cash equivalent. Dormers Plc will instead pay class 1A NIC.

Payment towards driving costs:

The approved mileage rates are not relevant in this case as the driving costs are not related to journeys made in the course of Antonia carrying out her duties of employment.

Class 1 NIC is due by Antonia on the payment towards her driving costs as this is a cash payment.

Marking scheme

	Marks	
Part (a)		
Salary	0.5	
Deduction of occupational pension	1	
Bonus entitled 2024/25	1	
Beneficial loan (both methods)	3	
Workplace nursery exempt	1	
Living accommodation	1.5	
Furniture	1.5	
Running costs	0.5	
Home entertainment use	1.5	
Home entertainment acquisition	1.5	
Total marks part a = 13, max marks available		12
Part (b)		
Alternative 1:		
Income tax	1	
NIC	1	
Alternative 2:		
Parking	1	
Income tax	0.5	
NIC	1	
Additional costs	0.5	
Total marks part b		5
Total marks for Q3		17

Question 4

This capital gains tax and administration question covers gains on a part disposal of land, a share sale qualifying for BADR, and a series of linked transactions. The administration requirement considers the need to notify chargeability and the penalties for failure to do this.

Chapter references in the Workbook are chapters 10, 12, 13 and 14.

(a) **Capital gains tax**

	BADR Gains £	Non-BADR Gains £
(W1) Land		378,750
(W2) Shares	1,000,000	299,000
Less AEA		(3,000)
Less capital loss b/f		(148,000)
Taxable gains	1,000,000	526,750
CGT	10%	20%
CGT due	100,000	105,350

Total CGT due (£100,000 + £105,350) = £205,350 due on 31 January 2026.

(W1) Land

	£
Sale proceeds	500,000
Less selling costs	(1,250)
Net sale proceeds	498,750
Less cost:	
£300,000 × £500,000/(£500,000 + £750,000)	(120,000)
Chargeable gain	378,750

(W2) Shares

	£
Sale proceeds	1,300,000
Less cost	(1,000)
Chargeable gain	1,299,000

(b) **Linked transactions**

	£
Deemed proceeds (MV of set) ÷ 2	30,000
Less: cost (£15,000 ÷ 2)	(7,500)
Capital gain	22,500

Total gains = £22,500 for each chair = £45,000

> **Tutorial note**
>
> Jane gave the chairs separately so that the market value used as proceeds in the gains calculation is the lower £20,000 value in each case.
>
> However, making separate gifts of the chairs will not achieve this, because Jane is connected to her son Dave, and to Dave's wife, and the two transactions will take place within six years of each other.
>
> These would therefore be linked transactions, and so the disposal proceeds for each gain calculation will be a proportion of the value of the assets when taken together ie £60,000/2 = £30,000 each, ie the gains overall are the same as if Jane gave both chairs to Dave.

MOCK EXAM ANSWERS

(c) Fred should have notified HMRC of this new gain by 5 October 2025 (ie 5 October after the end of the tax year of the disposal).

The maximum penalty for failure to notify chargeability is 30% of the potential lost revenue (the capital gains tax due on the gain).

The penalty may be reduced for disclosure by Fred, to 0% if unprompted (10% if prompted), if Fred makes notification within 12 months of the notification date.

Tutorial note and commentary

This capital gains tax question includes a small administrative requirement. It involves three unconnected taxpayers.

In **part (a)** the first taxpayer has a part disposal of land, when calculating the A/A+B formula, A is always the gross sale proceeds. A sale of shares was also made, which is her personal trading company which she has owned for at least 2 years, and works in the company as the director, and so this gain qualifies for BADR at 10%. However, only the first £1m qualifies for the 10% rate and the balance of the gain is subject to normal CGT rates. Capital losses b/f and the AEA should be allocated against non-BADR gains first as those gains suffer a higher rate of CGT.

In **part (b)** candidates need to appreciate that this would be a series of linked transactions to connected persons, within six years of each other, and so the gain is effectively calculated using the combined value of the assets ie no tax is saved. This is a more technical requirement and only well-prepared candidates may spot this particular issue.

The final administrative requirement in **part (c)** concerns the notification requirements when a gain is realised and the penalties for failure to notify. Although this relates to a capital gains tax scenario, the penalties are part of the common penalty regime, detailed in Whillans tax tables, and so candidates should be familiar with them and be able to easily score marks.

Marking scheme

	Marks
Part (a)	
(W1) part disposal of land	1.5
(W2) share disposal	1
Allocation of capital losses against non-BADR gains	1
Allocation of AEA against non-BADR gains	0.5
BADR gains £1m lifetime limit	1
BADR gains 10%	1
Non-BADR gains 20%	1
Total CGT due and due date	1
Total marks part a	8
Part (b)	
MV sale proceeds used	2
Cost	1
Total gains	1
Total marks part b	4
Part (c)	
Date to notify HMRC	1
Max penalty	1
Reduced penalty	1
Total marks part c	3
Total marks for Q4	15

Question 5

This question tests some basic inheritance tax principles including lifetime gifts and the cumulation principle, and the death estate. It features the valuation of quoted company shares, the marriage and annual exemptions, deductions for debts owed at the date of death, and the transfer of unused residence nil rate band from a spouse who died before 6 April 2017.

Chapter references in the Workbook are Chapters 15, 16 and 17.

(a) **13 September 2021 CLT**

	£
Gift of cash to trust	340,000
AE 2021/22	(3,000)
AE 2020/21	(3,000)
	334,000
Less NRB 2021/22	(325,000)
	9,000
IHT @ 20/80	2,250
Gross chargeable transfer £(334,000 + 2,250)	336,250

(b) **13 September 2021 GCT**

	£	£
GCT (part a)		336,250
Less NRB at death 2024/25		(325,000)
		11,250
IHT @ 40%		4,500
Less taper relief @ 20% (survived 3-4 years)		(900)
		3,600
Less lifetime tax (part a)		(2,250)
Inheritance tax due on death		1,350

25 November 2022 PET

	£	£
Land		483,000
Marriage exemption		(2,500)
AE 2022/23		(3,000)
PET		477,500
Less NRB at death 2024/25	325,000	
Less gross chargeable transfers in prior seven years (Sept 2021 GCT)	(336,250)	–
Taxable PET		477,500
IHT @ 40%		191,000

There is no inheritance tax on the sale of the painting as Nisar did not have gratuitous intent when selling the painting at a value which appears to have been too low.

MOCK EXAM ANSWERS

(c) **Death estate**

	£	£
House		640,000
Cash and other assets (including car)		170,000
Shares in Trimp plc (W1) £2.06 × 10,000		20,600
Less income tax and capital gains tax		(12,000)
Chargeable estate		818,600
RNRB (£175,000 × 200%) (add wife's unused RNRB)		(350,000)
NRB 2024/25	325,000	
Less GCT in prior seven years (477,500 + 336,250)	(813,750)	–
Taxable estate		468,600
IHT @ 40%		187,440

(W1) Value of shares
Lower of:
200 + ¼ (224 – 200) = 206
(202 + 216)/2 = 209p
ie 206p

Tutorial note and commentary

This question tests some basic inheritance tax principles including lifetime gifts and the cumulation principle in **parts (a) and (b)**. Candidates often get confused with the NRB and the cumulation period, and so it is important to work in chronological when dealing with life gifts, and then life gifts that become chargeable upon death. Assets are always valued at the date the gift is made, so it is irrelevant that the land had increased in value at Nisar's death.

Candidates who have studied the syllabus very thoroughly, may be able to identify that the sale of the asset at an apparent undervalue (the painting in part (b)) is not a transfer of value for inheritance tax purposes. This is because there was no gratuitous intent when the sale was negotiated.

In **part (c)** there are standard elements such as valuation of quoted company shares, and deductions for debts owed at the date of death. Nisar's wife had fully utilised her NRB and so there was no transfer of NRB, but the transfer of the RNRB was available even though his wife died pre-April 2017. Nisar died after April 2017, and so a deemed transfer of the RNRB can be made.

Marking scheme

	Marks
Part (a)	
Deduction of 2 × A/E	0.5
Deduction of NRB	0.5
Calculation of lifetime tax	0.5
Calculation of GCT	0.5
Total marks part a	2
Part (b)	
Sept 2021 GCT:	
GCT from part a	0.5
NRB @ Death	0.5
IHT @ 40%	0.5
Taper relief	1
Relief for life tax paid	0.5

MOCK EXAM ANSWERS

Nov 2022 PET:

Marriage exemption	1
A/E 2022/23 only	0.5
NRB reduced by GCT Sept 2021	1.0
IHT @ 40%	0.5
No IHT on painting	1.0
Total marks part b	7

Part (c)

Death estate:

House	0.5
Cash and other assets	0.5
Value of shares (W1)	1.5
Deduction of taxes owed at death	0.5
Trf of RNRB plus own RNRB	1.0
NRB @ death	0.5
Life gifts <7 years deducted from NRB	1
IHT @40%	0.5
Total marks part c)	6
Total marks for Q5	15

MOCK EXAM ANSWERS